BECOMING CHINA

JEANNE-MARIE GESCHER

BECOMING CHINA

THE STORY BEHIND THE STATE

BLOOMSBURY CARAVEL

LONDON • OXFORD • NEW YORK • NEW DELHI • SYDNEY

Bloomsbury Caravel
An imprint of Bloomsbury Publishing Plc

50 Bedford Square   1385 Broadway
London   New York
WC1B 3DP   NY 10018
UK   USA

www.bloomsbury.com

BLOOMSBURY and the Diana logo are trademarks of Bloomsbury Publishing Plc

First published in Great Britain 2017

© Jeanne-Marie Gescher
Maps © Jamie Whyte

British Library Cataloguing-in-Publication Data
A catalogue record for this book is available from the British Library.

ISBN: HB: 978-1-4088-8723-3
         TPB: 978-1-4088-8724-0
         ePub: 978-1-4088-8725-7

Library of Congress Cataloguing-in-Publication data has been applied for

2 4 6 8 10 9 7 5 3 1

Typeset by Integra Software Services Pvt. Ltd.
Printed and bound in Great Britain by CPI Group (UK) Ltd, Croydon CR0 4YY

ACKNOWLEDGEMENTS

I am fortunate to have many friends, Chinese and not Chinese, who taught me with their questions, their answers and their stories. Far too numerous to mention, you know who you are, and this book exists because of you. I am also fortunate to have a Chinese 'family' without whom this book could not have been written.

I owe thanks to a number of people who helped me bring the book from the first rough pages to what you will read: Michelle Brown, who was with me through so much of the story, and then held up the sky and enabled me to write; Adam Williams, who read the very first draft and imagined what it could be; James Kynge, whose warning that writing the book would only be the beginning of the work kept me sane; Philip Chapnick who became my trusted librarian; Helen Wing, whose humour kept everything in perspective and whose poetic wisdom was a rock; Richard Spencer, who read every chapter and offered a journalist's eye and a philosopher's mind; David Kelly, Rod Wye and Jane Macartney, who read every chapter and applied lifetimes of China experience to their questions; Freda Murck who generously shared her remarkable expertise on the art of Chinese paintings. Lindsay Levin and Martin Gunnarsson, whose sharp eyes and deep humanity were much appreciated; Tristan Kenderdine whose perspective helped me tell the story through the maps and Jamie Whyte for the maps themselves; Vicky Barnsley, whose early encouragement was followed with invaluable practical advice; Richard Charkin for wonderful advice and encouragement, and Jayne Parsons who championed the idea of the book and gave it a name.

I would also like to thank my sons, Theo and Caspar, who lost their mother to a laptop, my parents who lost their daughter to the same (and my father who read every draft with wonderful encouragement), my first husband Valentin Gescher, who taught me never to give up, and my second husband, Sasi Kumar, who gave me the courage to let the book go.

All Under Heaven, tianxia, is the ancient Chinese idea that everything under heaven is in the charge of a single, responsible, Son of Heaven. Out of that idea came another idea: that if the single son could master the understanding of what heaven wanted, then everything under heaven would be at peace. And out of that idea came a dream: the dream of a heavenly empire on earth, modeled on nature, hierarchically ordered, and guided by principles designed to protect the common interests of a people. But what was heaven and *where* was it? Was it physical power or a moral force? Was heaven a single top-down mind that ordered everything across the four quarters of the earth? Or was it a reflection of the hearts and minds of the many different people,that lived within its lands?

Becoming China is the story of the *tianxia* dream of a heavenly order on earth, and of how that dream became the state of China today. It is also the story of what happened when the dream of the state and the dreams of its people went their different ways. Of course, it is the story of China and the Chinese. But it is also the story of some of the biggest questions known to man: what is a state, who are its people, and how do they live together? It may not be our story, but as the twenty-first century and its technologies challenge Western ideas of civilization and order, and as the same forces bring the very different people of the world together in common conversations, it is a story for us all.

If you try to possess it, you will destroy it:
If you try to hold on to it — you will lose it.
(wei zhe bai zhi, zhi zhe shi zhi)

from the surviving scrolls of the *Dao De Jing* (500 BCE)
composed by Laozi from texts written across the
previous 1,000 years

Only if one man rules all under heaven can all
under heaven uphold that one man.
(wei yi yiren zhi tianxia, qi wei tianxia feng yiren)

Emperor Yongzheng (1722 – 1735)
from a text hung in the Hall of Mental
Cultivation in the Forbidden City

CONTENTS

BOOK I

FROM THE BEGINNING

PART 1

A HEAVENLY EMPIRE

PART 2

DREAMS

PART 3

WHOSE HEAVEN?

BOOK II
TWENTIETH CENTURY IDEAS

BOOK III
WHAT CAME NEXT

CONCLUSION

LEADERS AND DYNASTIES

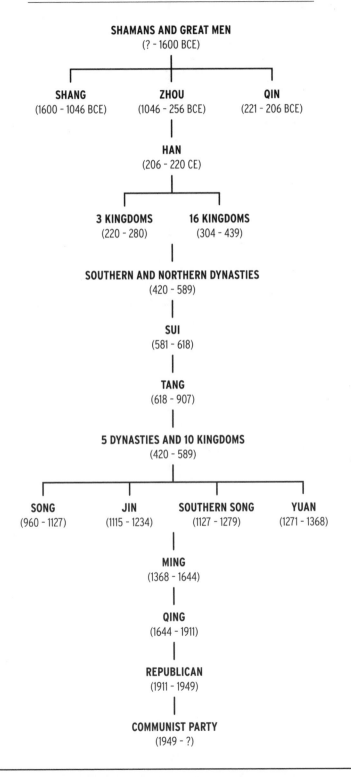

SHAMANS AND GREAT MEN
(? - 1600 BCE)

SHANG
(1600 - 1046 BCE)

ZHOU
(1046 - 256 BCE)

QIN
(221 - 206 BCE)

HAN
(206 - 220 CE)

3 KINGDOMS
(220 - 280)

16 KINGDOMS
(304 - 439)

SOUTHERN AND NORTHERN DYNASTIES
(420 - 589)

SUI
(581 - 618)

TANG
(618 - 907)

5 DYNASTIES AND 10 KINGDOMS
(420 - 589)

SONG
(960 - 1127)

JIN
(1115 - 1234)

SOUTHERN SONG
(1127 - 1279)

YUAN
(1271 - 1368)

MING
(1368 - 1644)

QING
(1644 - 1911)

REPUBLICAN
(1911 - 1949)

COMMUNIST PARTY
(1949 - ?)

THE PEOPLE'S REPUBLIC OF CHINA

R   U

KAZAKHSTAN

M   O   N   G

Altai Mountains

Ili River

Gulja
(Yining)

Urumqi

KYRGYZSTAN

Taklamakan

Desert

Lop Nur

XINJIANG

Kunlun Mountains

QINGHAI

Xining

G A N

Aksai
Chin

Ngawa
County

H I M A L A Y A

TIBET

K H A M   Chengdu

Lhasa

S I C H U A

M O U N T A I N S

N E P A L

ARUNACHAL PRADESH

BHUTAN

Y U N N A N

BANGLADESH

Kunming

I N D I A

M Y A N M A R

LAOS

Bay of

Bengal

THAILAN

PREFACE

On 1 September 2012, the man most likely to become the next leader of China disappeared. Of course, Xi Jinping might have disappeared a day or two before, but given that his life was lived behind the screen of the Chinese Communist Party, it was only when he failed to arrive at a meeting with Hillary Clinton that he appeared to be missing to the outside world. An empty chair at a later meeting of China's Central Military Commission (the highest military command of the country, of which Xi was vice-chairman) seemed to confirm that he was not only missing to the outside world, but missing in China too.

With only two months before the most important Congress of the Chinese Communist Party to be convened since the time of Deng Xiaoping – one at which a new leader of all would be appointed – foreign journalists went on a 'Xi hunt'. Clouds of speculation followed, while the world's internet found itself awash with questions not only about Xi Jinping's whereabouts (rumours included Xi lying in a hospital, battling Party tigers, or throwing a temper tantrum), but whether he might never return to public view at all (stranger things have happened in China). Meanwhile across the world, deeper spirits began to ask what his disappearance meant both for the succession of power in China and for the economic and political order of everyone whose fortunes were now sailing on the Chinese ship of state. At home, the Party and its presses remained silent.

On 15 September, Xi Jinping reappeared – quietly visiting a science exhibition at the China Agricultural University in Beijing. As soon-to-be leader of a Chinese Communist Party that never explained itself, no explanation was given. Far from heaving a sigh of relief, however, yet more clouds of internet speculation gathered. Was Xi Jinping fighting a bitter battle to remain the front-line candidate to lead China and the Party? Despite China having catapulted to the top of the world in terms of fortune, many even wondered whether its ancient history of dynastic rises and falls was about to repeat itself. Perhaps, just as

under the last years of Mao's leadership, the country was really in a
secret state of collapse.

Within China, the speculation was wide – and in highly political
Beijing, deep. But, as usual, it was all grounded in a story that everyone
knew had begun thousands of years ago, shaped by a cast of characters
and questions that were echoes of battles fought many times before.
The past had certainly thrown up stories far stranger than any fiction;
all, however eccentric, with implications for the economics that have
become the preoccupation of the present world. A world of shamans
who founded a civilisation on the footprinting patterns of birds. An
emperor who became so worried about the rising floods of the Yellow
River that he cut off all communications between his people and heaven.
Another emperor who was so concerned about the collapsing state of
imperial affairs that he created a celestial Jade counterpart with a heavenly court, which every earthly minister was directed to serve as well.
A foreign prince who was given the empire simply by turning up and
asking for it. And a farmer's son who founded a book club and went on
to become master of all. They were tales that seemed to confirm what
the Jade Emperor himself had once so wisely observed of the Chinese
lands: 'Made up of the essence of both heaven and earth, nothing that
goes on among these creatures in the world below should surprise us.'

Perplexed, Chinese speculators scoured the past for ideas as to what
might have happened. Heirs to an ancient tradition of burying secret
facts in the Chinese language, they pored over every official and unofficial Party sentence for the coded messages that might give them a
clue. (With thousands of Chinese characters and only a few hundred
syllable-sounds to match them, there is always a wide range of written characters, which, sounding the same as a word too dangerous to
write, can carry a hidden meaning). Guesses were everywhere, but no
real clues were found. The 'character code' was, however, very useful
to the many who, now convinced that China was on the brink of revolutionary change, used it to bury barbs of meaning in the internet
blogs with which they shared their more daring speculations. (They
also used the code to make some acerbic observations about life in a
land where the whereabouts of a leader is a matter for heaven alone.)

Outside China, the quality of the speculation was rather different.
Whereas Chinese minds had always understood the need to think
deeply, Western minds had been more concerned to find the shorter,

sharper, simpler answer. The observation of a fourth-century BCE shaman-scholar that 'he who perceives the oneness of everything does not know about the duality of it' had not been given much attention beyond China's Great Wall. Chinese with deep insights grounded in long study and experience were told to simplify their ideas for Western readers who could really only be expected to read a paragraph or two. Western minds themselves (many wise, but usually without the benefit of a China education or experience) made sweeping declarations on the basis of the fragments of facts, anecdotes and assumptions that had been gathered in the rush of China's rapid economic rise. Not surprisingly, everyone stayed confused.

The eighteenth of the five-yearly congresses of the Chinese Communist Party (the one at which the future leadership would be confirmed) was eventually convened on 8 November 2012 – a little later than originally expected, and on a date that was not announced until the very end of September. At the end of it all, Xi Jinping advanced to the centre of the stage, flanked by the highest echelon of his newly appointed Politburo. In his first speech to the public, Xi acknowledged the aspirations of the people for better material conditions in good and beautiful lives; he reminded everyone that every bit of happiness in this world has to be created through hard work and labour; and he noted the harmony of the *minzu* ethnic groups (the Tibetans, the Uighurs, the Hui Muslims, the Inner Mongolian Mongols, the Zhuang tribes, and all of the other fifty-two ethnic groups – including, of course, the greatest of all, the Han). Referring to the Party, Xi Jinping observed that metal would have to be turned into iron. Referring to the people, he pointed out that while the capability of any individual is limited, if everyone were united as a single heart and mind, there would be no difficulty that the Chinese people could not overcome. Looking at the challenges facing the country, he declared that the responsibility was weightier than Mount Tai, the way ahead was long and arduous, and the goal was to deliver a satisfactory answer sheet to history.

Every word had been carefully composed. Every Chinese could trace each of his statements about Party, people and country not only to a point in history but to a particular interpretation of China's ancient dreams of order. But few, if any, were clear about what he really meant. A few days later, Xi gave another speech, declaring that it was time for China to pursue its dream: the dream of the 'great rejuvenation of the Chinese nation'. No one was much clearer about the meaning of that either – although, latching on to the tantalising idea of a 'Chinese Dream', the internet, once again, ignited.

China's competing dreams are at the heart of this book: where and how they began, how they have shaped China's past and present and how they may well shape all of our futures.

One of the two most powerful states in the world, now seen as a competitor not only for territorial power but for the civilisational idea that will define the world, China continues to be seen as a mystery even after decades of an open door. How does China work, what does it want, why does it want it, and what does its rise to global power mean for the rest of the world? As the twenty-first century looks set to be the stage for a battle about competing ideas of order, these questions have acquired an urgency for everyone with an interest in what the future might bring. And the fact that the questions are still being asked after decades of a relatively open door to the West says as much about the West as it does about China.

Becoming China has a fairly simple structure: there are three main books corresponding to a beginning (The Ancient Past), a middle (Twentieth Century Ideas) and an end which, given that the story is still continuing, is really just as its title describes it (What Came Next). The conclusion (also entitled Becoming China) addresses the state as it is today: significantly redirected by Xi Jinping after nearly five years of dramatic change when compared to the last twenty years but less dramatic when seen in the context of its extraordinary history and perhaps more of a startling illustration of similar periods that many had thought would never return.

The Ancient Past opens at the beginning of Chinese time, where history blurs with myth, with a particular attention to the three thousand years from the last millennium BCE to the first of China's two twentieth century revolutions, in 1911.

Twentieth Century Ideas explores the journey from 1911 to the early years of the twenty-first century. Given the deep differences between China's cities and its villages, the stories of the cities and the countryside are told in two separate parts, with a third part covering the common experiences, of politics, policy and economics, of nature, and of the minority peoples (including the Tibetans and Xinjiang's Uighurs as well as a number of other less visible groups spread across China).

What Came Next tells the story of the early years of the twenty-first century, to 2014. A time of extraordinary energy but also great stress, capturing the very different perspectives of the Chinese Communist Party, the people and the intellectuals through three individual chapters: The Heavenly Party, Earth Below and Being Chinese (the story of the intellectuals, largely seen by the Party as anyone who has read a book and has an opinion, and including a number of individuals who are likely to be familiar to readers who follow China in the press). By the time you have finished reading this part of the story, while we may not know exactly where Xi Jinping disappeared to in 2012, we will see that the 'missing two weeks' have a lot to do with the remarkable power that Xi has gathered; we will also see that however fascinating the soap opera of his disappearance and reappearance might be, the most important part of the story is the fact that he could disappear and reappear without anyone outside the highest echelons of the Party knowing why.

Becoming China, the concluding chapter, tells the story of the last five years, from 2012 to Spring 2017. Much is likely to happen even between the Spring day when this book disappears to the publisher and the time it will reappear in a bookshop. Given that the Jade Emperor himself observed that '(m)ade up of the essence of heaven and earth, nothing that goes on among these creatures in the world below should surprise us', I expect that a lot will have happened between the final page and the day of publication. I hope, however, that this chapter, and the book as a whole, will have succeeded in sufficiently conveying the mechanics of the present era, and the landscape of the past, to provide a perspective through which we will be able to understand whatever unexpected events unfold, however extreme they might appear. For the Chinese, the past, both recent and ancient, is always seen as an essential part of the present. A humbling perspective, known as *shi*, potentiality, that reminds us that all of our futures are usually forged by what we have done before.

Becoming China, the book, is an account of China's past and present, written as a story. The reason for writing history as a story is simple: the truth, whether in China or anywhere else, is always more than facts. Indeed, it is my belief, after twenty-five years of living in China, that the principle reason why the West continues to find China so mystifying is that it looks at the country and its people through individual boxes and thus misses the fabric in which the explanations of almost any question are to be found. Think of it like the Indian fable of the six blind men who try to understand an elephant by feeling different parts of its anatomy: touching the trunk, one concludes that the object is a snake; touching an ear, another concludes that it is a fan. The moral of that fable is that the truth is not just more than a compilation of individual facts, but that compilations of facts are guaranteed to confuse. It is a moral that applies to everything, including the story of how China became the state that it is today. The focus on individual facts rather than the fabric of context is a Western weakness that the Chinese are very familiar with.

To this I would add that in writing *Becoming China* in the form of a story, I have as far as possible, told the story from the perspective of the people who lived it at the time in which they lived it. For the same reason that the truth is always more than facts, perspective is essential to our understanding of anything. China, like everywhere else in the world, is a place with a worldview of its own. That worldview is both distinctive when compared the West, and particularly pronounced in terms of its value to the people who hold it. Like all worldviews, it is based on how what has gone before – ideas and facts – are seen both by those who lived the past and those who inherited the stories told about the past. Destiny is forged at the point at which the soap opera of millions of small lives collide with grand events, whether those of great political powers or of nature. Given China's size and influence, this is a truth that is ignored by the West – Western states, Western businesses, Western individuals – at its peril.

Becoming China is also a book about a lot more than China. A world of its own, China is also in many ways both a microcosm and an amplification of questions and events in the wider world. In just the same way that it is often easier to see errors in someone else's garden, China's story offers us an opportunity to hold a mirror to ourselves:

to our own assumptions, to our values, and to our ideas about what it means to be human in the world of the state.

By size, China is one of the biggest masses of land in the world, with more terrestrial and sea borders than any other country. By population, it is so big that it accounts for nearly twenty percent of the people on earth, and so diverse that it includes almost all of the world's faiths and as many, if not more, minorities than any other part of the world. By production, it is the world's greatest manufacturer of almost everything; by consumption it now rivals the totality of the West. It has almost every climatic and topographical variation in the world – and almost the full spectrum of environmental risk. Notwithstanding its reductions in poverty, it is also a microcosm of much of the world's inequality: home to one of the world's biggest gaps between the rich and the poor, between the cities and the countryside. Perhaps most significantly of all, the technology that is changing everyone's world is advancing farthest and fastest in China. This is particularly, although not exclusively, the case with regard to the systems that order society, where the boundaries between the people and the state are being changed at such a speed and scale that it is not surprising that Chinese authors are becoming some of the world's most popular contemporary writers of science fiction. The change is not, however, limited to the relationship between the people and the state: it includes the relationship between the people and nature, and between the people themselves. It is a change that is happening everywhere but it is at its most striking, and thus easiest to see, in China.

Indeed, China reflects so many features of our world at large that it might be the closest example we have of what the world might look like if it were a single state. Or, to put it all another way, some of what seem to be the epic peculiarities and risks of the Chinese world are in fact concentrations of the peculiarities and risks of the world at large. China's story, with its powerful mirror to the order of the wider world, offers us some thought-provoking questions about the kind of order that our future world might expect.

Becoming China is not just the story of how a small group of people at the edges of the Yellow River evolved to become the state of China today; it is the story of the greatest questions known to man: What does it mean to be human? What does it mean to be human in a society of other people? And what does it mean to be human in a world where technology is not only changing how we live but how and what we think? While the West has typically divided these questions into 'morality', 'philosophy', and 'science', for the Chinese, they are part of the fabric of life.

There are, and always have been, significant differences between the answers given to these questions by the ruling state and the people. At the end of the day, the answers to both are heavily influenced by three perspectives. The first is the view that the world is in a state of constant change, driven by the interplay of opposites. The second, following from the first, is that the world is defined far more by contradictions than absolutes. The third, following from the first and the second, is that truth and reality are far more complicated commodities than anyone might prefer − and that 'heaven' is the moral working out, whether by a ruler or the people, of what to do. This might sound outrageously esoteric but the magic of China's story is that it is precisely at the collision between seemingly irreconcilable opposites that history has been made. Any history book can give you black and white. The fabric of the story of how China became the state that it is today provides a context which makes many things much clearer, including the questions of what it means to be human, what it means to be a state and how the two can coexist.

Over a hundred years ago, a Chinese intellectual wrote a book that changed the way the Chinese saw themselves and the state. Little known in the West, the name of the book was *Da Tong Shu, The Book of Great Unity*. In it, the author, Kang Youwei, imagined a world free of states, ruled by all of its people, with the people having qualified themselves to assume such rule. There would be no hierarchies, there would be no race. While the *yin* and *yang* changes would remain a fact of life imposed by the cosmos, the conquest of ignorance would diminish the contradictions, or at least their power to confuse. The only boundaries would be those imposed by the people themselves in their understanding of what it meant to be a human being living in the society of other humans. While *The Book of Great Unity* was seen by the state and many of the people as radical beyond belief, Kang Youwei drew on ideas that had been in the Chinese lands for thousands of years; ideas that periodically erupted into rebellions that were far more of a continuum than the individual incidents that they are typically portrayed as in conventional histories. Hopelessly idealistic, coloured in many ways by the assumptions of the time in which he lived, at the heart of Kang's book, however, was the ancient Chinese idea that the very quality of being human – what distinguishes us from animals or rocks – is our ability to learn to live in the society of other human beings, and in so doing, to cultivate ourselves. It is a stark contrast to a world in which systems are expected to relieve human beings of the burden of thinking for themselves.

Written at a time of dramatic change, not unlike the present, *The Book of Unity* has often been described as a book about universal democracy. It was certainly no description of Western democracy. It was not an argument that the fact of birth entitles one to a voice or a vote; it was an argument that it is our ability to apply our human qualities to the challenge of living in a society of others that qualifies us to govern ourselves. The idea of 'self-cultivation' is often seen in the West as either an unwelcome morality or code for state control. Few Chinese, however, would consider any state to be viable without the ability of a people to cultivate themselves so that they can live in a society of other human beings. However controversial Confucius may be, most Chinese would agree with the observation attributed to him that 'It cannot be that what is of great importance is slightly cared for': the art of being human can be hard work. Recent events in the West – not least a rise in populism that has led to the election of a real estate mogul as president of the United States and an uncertain balance of power in Europe – are leading many Westerners to think again about the idea of order, what it means and how, given so many competing claims, it is best achieved. Having separated morality from science long ago, and having taken political order for granted for so long, the West lacks a widespread understanding not only of the dimensions of order but of the knowledge tools, the philosophical and practical ideas and experience, required to think about change.

For as long as the West has been looking at China through its siloed boxes of spiritual morality and real life, it has asked itself two questions. The first is what the Chinese people believe in, and the second is why they seem to accept a top down idea of order so much more readily than the West. The answer to the first question is simple: while there are many different spiritual beliefs among the 1.4 billion individuals in China (including Christianity and Islam as well as Daoism and Buddhism), the most common belief is that it is in this world that we should look for our heaven, and it is through our cultivation of our greatest human qualities, including that of knowledge as well as those of integrity and virtue, that we should look for it. Hence a five thousand year pursuit of utopia, including the rebellions and dramatic dynastic changes, and including Kang Youwei's idea of a Da Tong world of Great Unity. Also including the dream with which Xi Jinping announced what has become yet another dramatic change in rule. The answer to the second question is that life on earth comes with a responsibility to be the best human being that you can be and that if individual human beings cannot work that out for themselves then a strong state is required. That this is believed does not make it always welcome: as many Chinese note themselves, whether one is cultivating oneself or being cultivated by the state, being Chinese is extremely hard work. The idea of a world where order could be delivered without such responsibility and hard work is a dream that has given the West a certain appeal to some Chinese, even as many others have wondered whether such a state of affairs could really be real.

As I write this preface, Stephen Hawking has just declared that human beings will need to colonise another planet within the next hundred years or face extinction. In his opinion, only a 'world government' will avert this risk. Hawking has not yet elaborated on the detail of that world government but the question of what form it should take, and most importantly, what dreams and what values it should be based upon, are already being debated in the rising importance attributed to state boundaries and spheres of influence and in the rising enunciation of state opinions in the increasingly important arena of geopolitics.

With more land and sea borders than any other country, and with a national determination to eradicate the humiliation of the century or more of Western conquests that began in the 19th century, China is naturally at the heart of many geopolitical questions. With a very different view of what it means to be a people and what it means to be a state, China's geopolitical importance goes beyond matters of territory to include the critical idea of order. Most obviously this is so because the belief of the Chinese state in a strong top-down order is significantly different to the Western ideal. Equally importantly, if a little less obvious to those unfamiliar with China's story, this is so because the very question of order – whether it is to be found under a single top down mind or with voices on the ground (and if the latter, what

quality of voices are required), has run like a faultline through most of
China's history. In the past, the West has seen that faultline in terms
of rebellions, of violent dynastic change and in the price paid by individual Chinese for telling the truth as they saw it. Today, we can see it
not only in the battle between a large number of China's intellectuals
and the state, but in very public protests emerging from the wider
world of people who share China's history and deeply disagree with
the conclusions drawn by the Chinese Communist Party, particularly
many of the people in Taiwan and Hong Kong. For those who can
separate the big life of politics from the small lives of human beings
it is a masterclass in the question of order. For those who cannot, it is
one of the most dramatic tales of our time. Whether or not the West
can see it, for all who have inherited the legacy of China's civilisation,
whether born in the mainland or not, that masterclass can only be fully
understood in the context of the five thousand year story of what has
gone before, both the facts and the ideas.

The Chinese people were not the first to have settled as a civilisation, but the fact that they can look back across a continuum of five
thousand years means that they have a five thousand year perspective
on what I expect to be the greatest question of our time: what does it
mean to be human in the world of the state? And the fact that, across
their five thousand year story, they have not only come together in an
ever greater territory but that many have also separated – including
those who have gone off in search of other lands with easier ideas of
order than those offered by a single-minded top down state – means
that we should not be surprised if some of the most important perspectives on that question come from the Chinese world. Indeed, I believe
that the question of what it means to be Chinese will become a metaphor for the question of what it means to be human in the world of the
state.

My hope, and the reason for writing this book, is that whether we
agree or disagree with China's ideas, we will be able to hear and understand them, as much for our own sake as theirs. Large numbers of
books have been written about China; almost all have written about
a particular part of the 'elephant'. Many have been written from a
Western perspective; a lot have focused on economics, with little
understanding that without the bigger picture no amount of economics will make sense; and many of the histories that have been written

have largely focused on facts over fabric. My hope is that *Becoming China* will enable Western readers to become as familiar with the Chinese story as many in China are familiar with that of the West. And with that familiarity, my hope is that we will all be able to explore the question of what it means to be human in a world of states, not as a West divided from an East, or even a people divided from a state, but as human beings on the verge of a technological future that will change all of our worlds. As Lu Xun, one of China's most thought-provoking authors wrote in the early twentieth century, 'Do we want to live in a counterfeit paradise or a good hell?' It is a serious question for all of us.

Obviously, this is not a small book. If you begin at the beginning and read to the end, you will see the full sweep of what has been an extraordinary journey. But if you don't have the time or the patience to read the whole book, jump in anywhere. Each chapter is certainly part of the chronology, and each reveals a particular feature of the journey to becoming China; if you read the whole, by the time that you get to the final chapters, you will not only understand how China came to be the state it is but you will also understand what it means to be Chinese. But, written as a story, each chapter can also be read on its own. So if you want to get started but you are worried about the commitment, start at the end, with the deeper story of what you can see in the daily news, and work your way backwards until the mysteries are fully explained.

Jeanne-Marie Gescher, 2017

AUTHOR'S NOTE

I make no claim to be a historian. While I hope that *Becoming China* presents some thought-provoking perspectives, it is a work that relies on a synthesis of a very wide spectrum of scholarship (from archaeology, anthropology and sociology, to history, philosophy and politics, and much more in between).

Many parts of China's history are highly contested – often because successive dynasties have reinterpreted past events to advance the goals of their time, with the reinterpretations forming part of the texts upon which education and cultural ideas have been built. Some of the most contested parts are to be found in the early to mid-twentieth century, many of which relate to the founding of the Communist Party and to the stories of key individuals, particularly Mao Zedong and the inner Party battles which have left a legacy that can be seen in contemporary politics and society today. Others relate to China's position in the wider world – where, with a rising interest in Asian geopolitics, once seemingly settled verdicts of history are now being re-opened.

Much of the contest today is between official Party history and relatively recent and more independent 'revisionist' accounts by individuals and historians – most benefiting from access to sources previously closed to scholars, and some, of necessity, published outside China. Many of the revisionist accounts – particularly those of the twentieth century story that draw on first-hand interviews with survivors – are compelling. Whether the revisions are to the recent or ancient past, however, I have set myself the task of writing it in such a way that it puts the reader in the shoes of the Chinese people as their story unfolds. Given that this book is the story of how the present Chinese state was forged from the dreams and experiences of its people, I have tried to balance truth with the reality that facts subsequently revised have been accepted as true by many people – whether within China or outside – and that in some cases the acceptance of such facts has gone on for so long that the 'untruth' has affected subsequent events.

Where the divergence is significant, for example on the nature of Mao's rule of the early Chinese Soviets, I took the decision to write the story as it appeared to the wider public at large at the time and as it has appeared in the most widely read Western and Chinese history books, and to describe the divergence in references to the 'revisionist' works in the Short Bibliographic Note. Given the complexity of China's history, and that *Becoming China* has as its goal the telling of the story as far as possible from the perspective of the time, the place, and the people who lived it, and given the fact that revised versions are well told by others whose works I have clearly referenced, this seemed to be the best practical approach for the reader. The serious China scholar will be familiar with all of the works (traditional and revisionist). The general reader will be able to see that there is a difference and to take a view as to whether he or she would like to dig a little deeper into the claimed facts of the Party's history.

For the period from 1989 to the end of the book, I was able to write from both contemporary and scholarly accounts – and I have taken my own experience, which was made in the company of others, both Chinese and foreign, as my truth. This does not necessarily make me right and on certain highly sensitive points (not least the story of June Fourth) it sets me, like many other authors, at odds not only with the official history but also the views of many younger Chinese.

The events of the last few years – particularly the renewed pursuit of the socialist dream since 2012 – have led to a sharpening in the contrast between official and independent accounts. This then leads us from a time when independent truths and official facts could – if one dug deeply enough – be seen side by side, to a time when independent truths have become 'rumours' whose repetition is discouraged if not dangerous.

As one of China's most famous novelists wrote in one of China's best-loved books (*A Dream of Red Mansions*): '*Shenme shi zhende, shenme shi jiade?*' – what is real and what is not real? This question haunts every history of China. And while the story of China's journey to becoming a state may test it to its limits, if we are honest, it is a question that haunts the history of many, if not all, states in the world, and indeed much of our human experience.

A NOTE ON THE CHINESE LANGUAGE AND VOICES

Chinese words used in this book are generally printed in italics –
followed immediately by the English language translation in the first
instance.

With minor exceptions, this book uses the *pinyin* system for translation of Chinese characters into pronounceable English. It works
reasonably well, but the following phonetic notes might help:

bo (as in Bo Xilai) is pronounced 'boar'

c (as in cang) is pronounced as 'ts', as in tsar

de (as in Deng Xiaoping) is pronounced 'der'

jiang (as in Jiang Zemin) is pronounced 'gee-ang', with a soft g

nü (as in Nüwa) is pronounced 'new'

q (as in Qin and Qing) is pronounced 'ch', as in chin

xi (as in Fuxi or Xi Jinping) is pronounced 'see'

xu (as in Xu Zhiyong) is pronounced 'sue'

zhou (as in the Zhou dynasty) is pronounced 'joe'

zhu (as in Zhu Yuanzhang) is pronounced 'jew', as in jewellery.

The exceptions include the use of Peking (for Beijing) in the case of
Beijing University, as it was known in the early twentieth century at the
time its story is told; also the use of Chiang Kai-shek as he is still largely
known in the West (rather than Jiang Jieshi as he is known in China).

Older texts referred to in the bibliography typically use a different
Romanisation system, known as 'Wade-Giles'. Typical examples are
the use of 'tao' for 'dao', 'ch'ing for Qing', 'ch' for 'zh', 'tzu' for 'zi'.

Having far more written characters than spoken sounds, the Chinese
language is rich in homophones. When translated into an alphabetical

language, individually different characters can appear to be the same. This is true, for example, of '*ren*', a spoken word that, depending on the written character, can mean either 'human being' or 'empathy', a quality that is seen as the essence of being truly civilised.

I have written *Becoming China* to reflect, to the greatest of my ability, the perspective of the people I am writing about. On this basis, I refer to the people who came to found the Qing dynasty (known in the West as the Manchu and referred to in *pinyin* as the Manzu) as the Manju, the Man people, as they referred to themselves.

I have also written it to capture, as far as possible, the humanity of the people whose stories are told, and of the times in which they lived. In doing, I regularly paraphrase rather than quote. This is for two reasons: first, to tame the formality of words that have come down to us in scholarly texts; second, to tame length. All paraphrased voices are marked with inverted commas.

LIST OF MAPS

LIST OF ILLUSTRATIONS

SECTION 1

Page 1 Top: *Fuxi and Nüwa*. Hanging scroll. Color on silk. Length 144.3 cm, Width 101.7 cm. Located at the Chinese History Museum. **Bottom**: Confucius and Laozi, fresco from a Western Han tomb of Dongping County, Shandong province, China. *ART Collection/Alamy Stock Photo.* **Page 2** *Confucius Sinarum Philosophus* (China's Philosopher Confucius), by Jesuit Prospero Intorcetta, 1687. **Page 3 Top:** Terracotta Army *China Photos/Getty Images.* **Bottom:** Tang Dynasty fresco of Zhang Qian going to the West found in Mogao Caves, Dunhuang, Gansu Province, China. *VCG via Getty Images.* **Page 4 Top:** Silk hanging scroll depicting Emperor Gaozu, founder of the Tang Dynasty. *Granger Historical Picture Archive/Alamy Stock Photo.* **Bottom:** Detail of a scroll called Going up the River at the Qingming Festival by Zhang Zeduan, Sung Dynasty c 1100. *Werner Forman/Universal Images Group/Getty Images.* **Page 5 Top:** Miniature from *Mongolian History in Verse* showing Chinggis Khan seated on his throne with his wife, Persia 15th Century. *DeAgostini/M. Seemuller/Getty Images.* **Page 6 Top:** Shaolin mural. *Paul Fearn / Alamy Stock Photo.* Bottom: Portrait depicting the Yongle Emperor of the Ming Dynasty. *Art Collection 3/Alamy Stock Photo.* **Page 7 Top** Scroll depicting the chief architects of the Forbidden City, painted during the mid-Ming Dynasty, c 1400s. Located at the National Museum of China. **Bottom:** Image of the Chinese poet Qu Yuan painted by Chen Hongshou during the Ming Dynasty. **Page 8 and 9 Top:** Artwork by Yosa Buson showing Liu Bei on a visit to Zhuge Liang. Now located at the Nomura Art Museum. *Art Collection 2/Alamy Stock Photo.* **Bottom:** Hanging scroll. Colour on silk. Features Bodhidharma atop an elephant. **Page 10 Top:** Acrobat in Nanjing portraying the Monkey King. *Dan Brinzac/NYP Holdings Ltd via Getty Images.* **Bottom:** Artwork featuring the armoured *Kangxi*, Qing emperor. *Paul Fearn / Alamy Stock Photo.* **Page 11 Top:** Manchu soldier wielding a bow and arrow, 1871. *Hulton Archive/Getty Images.* **Bottom:** Ink and colour on silk, showing the Qianlong emperor in ceremonial armour on horseback. *Universal History Archive/Getty Images.* **Page 12:** Prince Gong, photographed after the Chinese surrender at Peking, November 1860. *Felice A Beato/Getty Images.* **Page 13:** Western cartoon by artist Henri Meyer, depicting the division of Qing China by the imperial powers. *Heritage Images/Getty Images.* **Page 14 Top:** Junk passing through the Three Gorges, photographed towards the end of the 19th century. *Bettmann/Getty Images.* **Bottom:** Photograph depicting the 'self-strengthening' movement in China, taken by John Thomso, circa 1868. *Apic/Getty Images.* **Page 15 Top Left:** Kang Youwei, Chinese political and social reformer. *Library of Congress/Getty Images.* **Top Right:** Photograph of Liang Qichao. *Art Collection 3/Alamy Stock Images.* **Bottom:** The Dowager Empress Cixi in 1906. *ullstein bild/ullstein bild via Getty Images.* **Page 16 Top Left:** Chinese politician Sun Yatsen. *INTERFOTO / Alamy Stock Photo.* **Top Right:** Yuan Shikai, provisional president of the Chinese Republic. *Topical Press Agency/Getty Images.* **Bottom:** Temple of Heaven, Beijing 1932. *Bettmann/Getty Images.*

SECTION 2

Page 1 Top: Camels walking past the Beijing walls. *Photographer Hedda Morrison. The originals are held at the Harvard-Yenching Library of the Harvard College Library, Harvard University.* **Bottom:** Photograph from the 'May Fourth' movement, taken on 29 November. *Sidney D. Gamble Photographs, David M. Rubenstein Rare Book & Manuscript Library, Duke University.* **Page 2:** Chinese ambassador Hu *Shi*, who once taught Philosophy at Peking University. *Thomas D. McAvoy/The LIFE Picture Collection/Getty Images.* **Page 3 Top:** Group photograph taken in Shanghai in 1933, featuring Cai Yuanpei, George Bernard Shaw, Song Qingling, Lu Xun. *Sovfoto/UIG via Getty Images.* **Bottom Left:** Chen Duxiu, co-founder of the Chinese Communist Party. Bottom Right: Li Dazhao, co-founder of the Chinese Communist Party. *Sovfoto/Getty Images.* **Page 4 Top:** Chiang Kaishek, Chinese general and statesman, taken circa 1948. *Hulton Archive/Getty Images.* **Bottom:** Mao Zedong meeting with Joseph Stalin in Beijing, December 1949. *Visual China Group/Getty Images.* **Page 5 Top:** Chinese writer Ding Ling, author of propaganda works for the Chinese Communist Party, photographed in the 1930s. **Bottom:** Group photograph taken in 1942 at the Yan'an Forum on Literature and Art. **Page 6 Top:** James Yen and two colleagues, *Sidney D. Gamble Photographs, David M. Rubenstein Rare Book & Manuscript Library, Duke University.* **Bottom:** 'Great Leap Forward', *Universal History Archive/ Getty Images.* **Page 7 Top:** Tractors pictured arriving at Chung Hsing Hsiang in the Pai Chuan Province, dated 1 April 1958. *Keystone-France / Getty Images.* **Bottom:** A group of Red Guards, formed of high school and university students, photographed in Beijing on 1 June 1966. *JEAN VINCENT/AFP/Getty Images.* **Page 8 Top:** Soldiers of the People's Liberation Army reading from Mao's Little Red Book, circa 1970. *Keystone/Getty Images.* **Bottom:** The Democracy Wall in Beijing, 1978. *Orlando Henriques / Alamy Stock Photo.* **Page 9 Top:** Photograph of Chinese Astrophysicist Fang Lizhi. *Forrest Anderson/The LIFE Images Collection/Getty Images.* **Bottom:** Students in Tiananmen Square on 2 June 1989. *Forrest M. Anderson/Getty Images.* **Page 10 Top:** Deng Xiaoping during a visit from President Ford in Beijing on 1 December 1975. *David Hume Kennerly/ Getty Images.* **Bottom:** The special economic area of Shenzhen. *John van Hasselt - Corbis via Getty Images.* **Page 11 Top:** Jiang Zemin speaking to Hu Jintao, the Great Hall of the People, Beijing, 18 December 2008. *Frederic J. Brown/AFP/Getty Images.* **Bottom:** Dai Qing testifying in Washington on 19 July, 2000. *SHAWN THEW/AFP/Getty Images.* **Page 12 Top:** Potala Palace, once the home of the Dalai Lama, in Lhasa, China. *Yin Shichang/VCG via Getty Images.* **Bottom:** Uighur tourists from Xinjiang.. *MARK RALSTON/AFP/GettyImages.* **Page 13 Top:** Miao dancers performing at the 18th Shanghai Tourism Festival's opening ceremony, on 15 September 2007, *Shanghai. China Photos/Getty Images.* **Bottom:** Bo Xilai pictured at the NPC in 2012. *MARK RALSTON/AFP/Getty Images.* **Page 14 Top:** Villagers from Wukan in the Southern Province of Guangdong photographed during a protest on 19 December 2011. *STR/AFP/Getty Images.* **Bottom:** Taiwanese students protesting on 30 March, 2014 in Taipei, Taiwan. *Lam Yik Fei/Getty Images.* **Page 15 Top:** Police photographed facing protesters at Mongkok, Hong Kong, on 17 October 2014. *Lam Yik Fei/Getty Images.* **Bottom:** Chinese leaders taken at the Great Hall of the People, 15 November 2012. *Feng Li/ Getty Images.* **Page 16 Top:** Navy soldiers from the Chinese People's Liberation Army face Xi Jinping outside the Great Hall of the People, 16 September 2013. *Feng Li/Getty Images.* **Bottom:** 'Jia Jia' at University of Science and Technology of China 2016. *VCG/Getty Images.* Special thanks to Tristan Kenderdine for his work with the author on the formation of the maps, and to Jamie Whyte for cartography and illustration.

BOOK I
FROM THE BEGINNING

Things have their roots and branches. Affairs have their beginnings and ends.

To know what comes first and after is to be near the Dao

The Great Learning, Confucius (551-479 BCE)

PART 1

A HEAVENLY EMPIRE

That which was the beginning of all things under heaven.
The Yi Jing (1000 BCE; also known as the
I Ching or *The Book of Changes*)

CHAPTER 1

THE MISTS OF TIME

When Heaven and Earth were yet unformed,
All was ascending and flying, diving and delving.
The Huainanzi (139 BCE; early Han dynasty)

THE EARTH WAS COLD. The forests were wide. The sky was black. Far above the reach of man, a moon of white light stood firm, flanked by stars whose constellations surely held the secrets of everything.

Far above the reach of an ordinary man, but not above the reach of all. As the spirits of the dead found their way across the galaxies, watching from *mingtang*, halls of light, huts open to the skies, the most adventurous and curious of the earth-bound scoured the world to find the ways in which they could follow in the spirits' paths. Cloud-piercing mountains were found to offer natural bridges to the heavens for those prepared to climb; dragons, tigers and phoenixes provided willing carriages for those who dared to jump upon their backs; magic stems offered leaves whose juices could sweep a wise spirit to the skies.

Soaring above terrestrial boundaries, the shaman adventurers searched the spirit world for news of heaven's thoughts. Ancestors were consulted on the rains or questioned about the seasons. Those ancestors without the latest news were sent to search for other spirits who, having been longer in the skies, would be closer to the cosmic force that governed all. Answers secured, the exhausted shaman travellers would trace their path back to earth and whisper their reports to those on the ground. These were the shamans, the *wu*, diviners of the mind of heaven, spirit guides for the questions of men.

Time passed in its thousands of years. The land warmed and, question by question, the shaman *wu* continued to scour the skies for answers. Flights to the heavens were accompanied by peering

3

investigations into the constellations of the stars, supported by observations of the earth so intense that they were almost meditations.
And so, within a world that had once seemed consumed by chaos and
confusion, patterns of a more orderly change began to appear. From
a dark *yin* emerged a light *yang*, from which, in time, a dark *yin* would
once again appear. The promise of the 'wood' of spring gave life to an
early summer 'fire'. The energy of the early summer fire brought the
'earth' to a high summer's fecundity, whose harvests were gathered
by the 'metal' of autumn which yielded in turn to the winter still-
ness of 'water' in whose icy depths everything would rest before the
wood stirred again. Within these patterns of change, the land began
to reveal its secrets. Trees and plants opened their edible and medicinal strains, the ground revealed its treasures, and the ever-changing
seasons submitted their schedules – and those of all the animal creatures whose activities they governed – to enquiring human minds.

As the secrets of the earth were revealed, and man began to settle on
the land, forests that had stood like mountains were felled by axes made
of stone. Along a muddy 'yellow' river, which the ancestors had once
followed from westerly mountains in a broad meander to a far eastern sea, soft banks of yellow earth now offered themselves to receive
the selected seeds of foxtail millet and wild rice, which could feed a
man through winter. Cattle and sheep were tamed for human purpose.
Chattering monkeys were shooed away, preening peacocks lodged on
fragrant grasses, and elephants retreated before the greater order of
man. And as more of the people settled and the world continued with
its changes, the shamans, the *wu*, changed with it. Some would become
shaman kings: their knowledge of the skies bestowing an unquestionable authority upon a new world of rulers on earth below. Others
would become the shamans *of* kings: advisers to men who, with a natural authority over others, were determined to harness the celestial
secrets for the taming of nature and the ordering of all.

Yet others considered the idea of kings exercising authority over
nature and other men as a folly that could only bring heaven crashing
down on everyone's head. Keeping a quieter, meditating counsel these
others would leave the worldly battles to those who were determined
to subject heaven and earth to a human order. Taking their spirits to
the edges of the settled world, they would continue to insist on talking
directly to heaven, whenever earth or its people had a question to ask.

CHAPTER 2

A HEAVENLY PEOPLE

Bright, bright the heavens above, sparkling the serried stars; the radiance of the sun and the moon magnifies the chief of men.

The Book of Songs (1000–700 BCE)

A CROSS THE NORTHERN PLAINS, on the banks of the Yellow River, winter had begun its annual retreat. Ice had softened into water; bears and badgers had emerged from their long sleep. In fields cleared within the forests, black-haired men stretched every muscle to pull their ploughs; women, sowing seeds, followed behind. Spring gave way to early summer, just as it should. Rains fell, the skies were streaked with lightning and thunder rolled. Peach trees blossomed, goldfinches sang. Peewits, looking for worms spinning silken cocoons, found their way to the mulberry trees. Early summer rose to the heat of high summer, just as the flowering sow-thistles said it would. Millet ripened in the fields and grasshoppers threw themselves into their ritual chant of life. The backs of the black-haired people bent to gather weeds in aching arms. Then the high summer's blaze faded and autumn began to whisper in the wind.

Up in the skies, the swallows and geese gathered for journeys that would take them far away – and bring them back again when spring returned. Deep in the forests, tigers chased deer while crocodiles snapped in rivers and elephants kept their distance. In the fields, the heavy grain was ready for the sickles. Across days that began before dawn and ended long after the setting sun, the black-haired people, bones aching, gathered the heavy millet by the *gu* before winter's icy fingers crept back across the land.

5

In the city of Great Shang – the capital of the Shang dynasty who had long ruled the four known quarters of the world – conversations with heaven had clearly gone well. Across the fields of the second millennium BCE, the seasons had followed their promised schedule. As the rains watered the land, the Yellow River had remained within its banks, and even the locusts had stayed away. Threshed, the millet had been carried to the storehouses of the city – with plenty for those whose whips commanded the fields. This year there would even be food enough to carry a peasant family through the winter and punishment for none. Not starving, the peasants' lives in the villages at the edges of the fields could continue. Soon enough the winter frosts would bite into the earth. Dark nights would lengthen, the north wind would blow, water would retreat beneath the land, and the earth would send man and beast off to a dark rest. Huddling into caves, or sheltered by walls of mud and roofs of thatch, women's fingers would soon be weaving hempen plants and reeds into rough clothes, baskets and shoes. Meanwhile, the men would be completing the autumn tasks for their masters: walls built, ditches mended, goods called for from all directions. Unless, of course, heaven and the city had decided there were new lands to be discovered or a conquering battle to be fought. Then, cold or not, the labouring muscles would be raised and none could tell whether or when they might return.

The earth had not always been so. In the long winter nights, wise hearts talked of a time before the fields had spread and the cities had appeared. A golden age of *taiping*, great peace, when men had wandered wherever they wanted and eaten whatever they had hunted or found. Mountains had been crossed in freedom; rivers had been forded at will. Food had been plentiful and peace as natural as the air that everyone breathed. Some thought this was just a foolish dream. But others remembered the whispers of men who still lived beyond the four quarters of the settled lands, black hair flowing freely in the wind and food found a day at a time. Here was a deeper tale, going back to before the beginning of time. And when the sun spun to its nightly rest, willing ears would turn to hear that story of the past, told by tongues who whispered it, just as it had been whispered to them.

It was a story that no one ever tired of hearing. The story of a time and a space when heaven and earth had not yet been formed and separated, when everything was still twisting and turning, flying and diving: a *hun mang*, chaos, everywhere. From the chaos had emerged a *dao*, a way that anyone could feel, as long as they were willing to open not just their ears but every human instinct. A *dao* way that could be *felt*, but not described by the limited words of man. Indeed, the *dao* was a name that could not be named: a way that was known and knowable only to itself. It was a trace that was driven by the forces of a *qi*, energy, and by the constant changes between the dark *yin* and the light *yang* on which all the fortunes of life rise and fall and rise again. It was the power that governs everyone's destiny, at the heart of everything that is known. A way that, if carefully consulted, could reveal a natural order for heaven, earth and man.

From out of the *hun mang* chaos, so the wise hearts told, the *dao*, activated by the energetic force of *qi*, had revealed a natural order. Heaven and earth had separated; the one had become two, then three, then ten thousand things, all of them different. Heat and cold had settled into seasons. And where once there had been swirling mists there were now beasts, birds, trees, fish and men. It was a golden age of *taiping*, great peace – a time when harmony ruled like a symphony. Man and beast were friends. No one, neither man nor beast, had to be told what to do. And even though heaven and earth were now no longer one, those on earth could talk openly to heaven whenever they wanted, and say whatever they wanted to say.

Of course, sniffed the wise storytellers, it couldn't last. In the changing *yin-yang* world of the *dao*, everything had an opposite, which was neither more nor less than part of itself. Order and chaos are one and the same; difficult is nothing more than the completion of easy; nothing is high without a low; without a winter there can never be a summer. And indeed, blue skies eventually gave way to those opposites hidden within them: lightning flashed; rain poured in torrents, and a flood rose, so great that it swept almost everyone away.

Almost everyone, but not quite.

From the swirling waters emerged a man and a woman: Fuxi and Nüwa (some said a brother and sister). Acting swiftly against the torrential forces, Nüwa shored up heaven with the Buzhou range of mountains to keep the watery skies from falling again. And when she had secured the architecture of heaven and earth, she went on to mould a people out of clay, into whose cold shapes heaven itself breathed life. Nüwa having balanced heaven and earth, Fuxi studied the relationship between the two. Journeying to the skies and peering at the earth below, true to his shaman spirit, he tried to put himself in the shoes of the cosmos so that he could truly see and understand. Wondering at the majestic *ziran*, 'just as it is', nature, he stared at the stars above so hard that he almost became a part of them. And as he stared and thought, he began to perceive points at which the constellations correlated with the landscape of the earth: clearly these were special places from which man would be able to offer up sacrifices from earth to heaven, and so deliver order for all.

Fuxi went on to observe the land along the Yellow River: the constantly changing *ziran*, nature, and the patterns of the creatures that lived within it. Here, were footprints of birds in the damp ground and, there, on the back of a tortoise, was a magic square of nine smaller squares, a mathematical harmony that seemed to talk of the cosmos and its spheres. From the changes of nature, Fuxi concluded that the earth was engaged in a continuous conversation with the sky. And from the footprinting patterns of the birds and the magic square of numbers, he divined a series of symbols that man could use to communicate with heaven. With such an understanding of heaven and earth, Fuxi realised that the cosmos was governed by a secret code that man – unique among all the creatures on earth – could read, and thereby conduct the greater order of all.

Time turned, the wise storytellers told, and Fuxi was followed by others, who dug ever deeper into the mysterious codes of the natural world. Studying the seasons, testing the rocks, tasting the leaves of plants, flying to heaven for consultations with the spirits and ancestors, Fuxi's successors began to see a greater whole. At one point, the observations of a great man called Shennong revealed the secrets of the soil, from which food and minerals could be coaxed, and of the minds of animals, who could be tamed to become man's servants. Discovering the treasures of the earth, Shennong forged the tools that made planting, harvesting, even fishing, possible on a scale never known before. And seeing himself as just one man among others, he shared his knowledge with a black-haired people who were still sheltering in the trees with the birds. Before long, he was farming with them along the banks of the Yellow River. Everyone worked hard, but the 'great man' Shennong proved himself the hardest-working of them all.

More time turned, Shennong passed to another world, and those who had left the trees to the birds gathered themselves into a tribe and chose a leader. The first tribe grew and became many, and as each new tribe emerged, its members identified themselves with a common totem chosen from the storehouse of the natural world.

After an epic sweep of time, in the third millennium BCE another Great Man emerged from the people settling in the lands along the Yellow River – one with an idea so powerful that future generations would know him only as the 'Yellow Emperor'. Confident that man's duty was to deliver the order on which the cosmos depended, the Yellow Emperor brought together what had become myriad tribes scattered across the northern plains and settled them as a single people under an order which would be modelled on the patterns of heaven's stars and on the changes of the earth.

Drawing on Fuxi's observations, the Yellow Emperor created a harvesting wealth grounded in the wisdom of an annual calendar, which – based upon a constant and meticulous consultation of nature and the skies – set the seasons to a yearly order. Henceforth every ruler would be able to ensure that heaven and earth remained in an orderly harmony. Inspired by Fuxi's observations of the footprinting patterns of the birds, the Yellow Emperor captured the meaning of heavenly power in the characters of a written language and engraved them onto metal taken from the earth. Enthralled by Fuxi's observations of the chorusing songs of birds, he even tamed the notes of nature to order the human heart with music.

The Yellow Emperor: 'yellow' for the waters of the muddy river along which he had settled the people; 'yellow' for the colour of the watery dragons that carried him up to heaven whenever a conversation was required; 'yellow' for the rains he tamed. And 'yellow' as the colour that would forever be associated with the imperial centre of everything – the beating heartland of a people who would one day come to be known as the Chinese.

With such a clear cosmic authority, progress had been swift. Medicinal plants were ordered by purpose; fire was tamed to serve man; animals were set to useful tasks, nets were woven to catch fish; metal tools were cast to turn wild beasts into meat and to work the land; seeds were separated and sown. Altars, raised in locations that mirrored the heavenly coordinates, offered improved communications with heaven and the ancestors. As more forests were felled, villages were settled, and fields were laid in squares as far as the eye could see. Walls were raised from tamped earth – to keep at bay the jealous outsiders, 'barbarians' who had failed to understand the wise order of the settled world. And while some of the oldest shamans, those who considered the only true order to be that of the cosmos and the *ziran* nature, stubbornly continued to ask their questions directly of heaven, a people who had once been scattered now found themselves in an orderly Yellow River world.

For those leading the people of the Yellow River world, everything went well for a while. But, noted the wise storytelling hearts, by the time the Yellow Emperor's grandson, Zhuanxu, came to rule, the cosmos was getting a little out of control. A force from the watery underworld – a monster known as Gong Gong – rose up from below to capture the earth above. After a fierce battle, Zhuanxu emerged triumphant. Angry at his defeat, Gong Gong raged against Nüwa's mountain range, threatening to bring heaven tumbling down on everyone's heads. Nüwa (who, like all those who had once lived on earth, was now an ancestral spirit in the skies) did her best to limit the damage, but not before the pillars of the Buzhou mountains had been broken. Henceforth the sky would tilt upwards to the north and the west – while the earth would tilt downwards, the water sliding and settling to the south and the east.

Zhuanxu and his people adapted, but somehow problems in the form of rains, floods and droughts kept coming. Zhuanxu consulted his ancestor, the Yellow Emperor, and made a worrying discovery. From the time of Fuxi, heaven had received sacrifices with pleasure, and trust had been established between heaven, earth and man. Since then, however, the black-haired people had grown in number, and younger generations had forgotten the correct order of things: sacrifices were being made by anyone and everyone whenever they wanted, with no regard at all for the rhythms of the celestial world; spirits and ancestors were being called upon without a moment's notice and with little respect; gods, including those ancestors whose earthly glory had taken them closest to the power of heaven, were being constantly disturbed with thoughtless requests. Heavenly annoyance had turned to anger, and anger to rebuff. Sacrifices made were now being ignored; blessings were being withheld. And as the blessings stopped coming down from heaven, so the treasures of the earth were beginning to dry up. Zhuanxu and his people would soon be left with nothing to offer up, even through the most skilled of shamans.

Disaster looming, Zhuanxu asked the Yellow Emperor what he should do. The answer was clear: bring communications between heaven and earth under control, and quickly.

Zhuanxu summoned his two most trusted governors. One was commanded to take control of communications with heaven, the other to assume responsibility for ordering the proper conduct of the people. Both would answer to Zhuanxu. From that time on, communications between heaven and earth became a matter for the One, and only the One: the Son of Heaven and ruler of earth. Thus, order was returned to the relationship between man and heaven, and harmony was restored to the world. The responsibilities of the ruler, and of the ruled, were clear.

Heaven seemingly satisfied, the wise storytellers noted, all went well for a generation or two. Other 'Great Men' rose to lead the people, and the quality of earth's relationship with heaven continued to improve. The watery underworld, however, remained a challenge. While the Yellow Emperor had tamed its dragons, and while Nüwa had prevented another collapse of heaven, from time to time Gong Gong's fury would still erupt from underground, hurling the waters of the Yellow River far beyond its banks. To those responsible for guiding the harmony of all, the consequences were worrying. Under orderly conditions, the Yellow River looped in a leisurely manner across the land, brushing dry soils with moisture and nurturing fish that would spring into waiting nets. When Gong Gong raged, however, men, women and children were washed away from the banks and surrounding fields, carried off in the river's furious embrace. Dams were repaired and dykes were dug. But heaven inexplicably stood aside.

And then, towards the end of the third millennium BCE, another Great Man emerged, this one named Yao. Strengthening the dams and dykes, wealth spread across the earth, and an archer named Yi set about igniting the mountains and the valleys so that yet more land could be cleared for yet more order – more fields and fewer of the ravaging beasts who, once friends, were now stubbornly resisting the advance of man. And when, inexplicably, nine of what had until then been ten suns began to cavort so recklessly that their heat threatened the survival of earth and man, Archer Yi had shot them down.

Yao also laboured on communications with the spirit world. Shamans reported on their conversations with heaven and wherever there was a problem, sacrifices were offered to encourage the ancestors to intercede. Eventually, Yao discovered, like Zhuanxu before him, that the problem lay with the people, who were simply not behaving well enough. Arguments were breaking out in every direction. Children did as they pleased without consulting their elders. The calendar was disregarded, and planting took place at all times of the year, regardless of the celestial schedule.

Laws were introduced so that everyone knew how to distinguish good behaviour from bad, and punishments were polished to address the bad. It was not enough. By now, the waters of the river were surging over hills and rising high enough to even threaten heaven. Yao decided that the earth needed a man of such virtue that the people could be tamed by moral example. A long search eventually led to a man called Shun. Burdened with an obstinate father, a dishonest mother, and an arrogant brother, Shun was a man who had nonetheless honoured them all, creating a model of household harmony. Here was someone who clearly understood the importance of order. Yao abdicated in Shun's favour. Like Yao, Shun laboured night and day to deliver the ordering balance of the cosmos on earth. Humility became a compulsory virtue for all, as did the meticulous ordering of everything and everyone. Shaking their heads in disbelief, many of the descendants of the earliest shamans – those who had seen man-delivered order as a folly that would bring heaven tumbling down on earth – retreated to the natural order of the mountains and the forests.

For those fixed on the idea of a man-delivered order, matters seemed to improve. But the monstrous Gong Gong was still far from tamed. Realising that he had reached the limits of his abilities, Shun passed the watery challenge to a man of even greater promise: the son of the minister responsible for public works, whose name was Yu. Having watched his father struggle to control the waters of the Yellow River with dams and dykes, Yu was convinced that the answer lay in a greater understanding of the river and its banks. As clear as Yao and Shun about the all-important duty of keeping a cosmic balance, Yu ensured that communications with heaven were strictly maintained while dedicating his own attention to studying the challenging changes on earth. Through thirteen years of freezing winters, muddy springs, blistering summers and windy autumns, Yu summoned the spirits to help. Tracking the river, surveying every point on the land through which it passed, he even classified the surrounding soils.

At the end of his journey, his hands covered with callouses, and his children strangers to him, Yu drew a map and announced a plan. From henceforth, the land would be ordered into a grid of nine provinces, each identified by its specific geographic features, and each placed under the command of a local lord. Within each province, Yu gave instructions for the taming of all. The living would have their houses, their villages and their cities; the dead would have their temples; the animals would have their forests and grasslands, at least those that were not needed by the people themselves. Each to its own purpose and place: man and nature, heaven and earth, all would be at peace.

Province by province, the black-haired people were then diverted from the fields and tasked with restoring order to the waters. Rivers were dredged, marshes were drained, banks were raised, mountains were moved. Channels were laid so that the water could be delivered smoothly from what Yu had discovered to be the Yellow River's glacial mountain origins in the west to the welcoming arms of a sea to the east. Wherever possible, the waters were guided over level ground; and where the waters were too wild to be guided, they were divided into two, three, or even more channels. Up and down the land, over hills, across plains and in valleys, forests were felled to open yet more new lands for cultivation. The people were directed not to store the treasures of their land, but to exchange them with others so that each province could specialise in what it did best such that the whole would be in harmony. Once again, matching attention to celestial spirits with a diligent approach to understanding the earth, heaven's order was restored.

As Yu battled against the river, more men of greatness emerged to help him. Among them was a man called Xie, who, like many others who had been helpful to Yu, had been rewarded with a territory of his own. Xie named his land Shang. By now, the old worlds of Fuxi and Shennong were but distant memories. Where Fuxi had wandered among birds and animals, and where Shennong had farmed shoulder to shoulder with others, the one world of their descendants had separated into twos: a great and a small, a high and a low, a chosen few who were closest to the ruler in the great city, and a not-chosen many who were spread across the fields. The chosen and the great settled in high dwellings raised above the earth in places which, fixed by correlation with the stars, were surely grounded in the very thoughts of heaven. The not-chosen were settled below in dugouts carved into the soil, sheltered only by roofs of straw. While the chosen called themselves and their ancestors by family names, the not-chosen were called by their nature: 'the black-haired people'.

Across the next four hundred years, the wise storytellers continued, the ruling power of Yu (now 'Yu the Great') was passed down the line of his descendants – all possessed of an ever-increasing power. As each great ruler passed in turn from the living to the dead, across the Shang cities more altars were built from which yet more descendants could engage in the private 'family' conversations with the ancestors that offered privileged channels to heaven's thoughts. Harvests were offered up as taxes, and as the wealth of the fields flowed into expanding treasuries, so more of Yu the Great's descendants built more new cities, each greater than the last. Meanwhile, the nameless black-haired people, whose purpose was to clear forests, plough fields, reap harvests and battle the envious beasts and barbarian outsiders, stayed close to their fields, exposed, but for their dugout dwellings, to the elements at large. Their labours heavier with each new ruler, the whips applied to keep their earthly bodies in heavenly order eventually became more than some could bear.

In 1600 BCE, a man named Tang – a descendant of Xie and ruler of the lands that Xie had named Shang – announced that heaven had had enough. Gathering together the forces of his Shang army with those of other like-minded local lords, Tang confronted the latest descendant of Yu the Great in a battle which shook the earth. Outnumbered but determined to displace the brutal higher power, Tang, his warriors and their allies fought without fear. Miserable under an unbearable yoke, the peasant armies of Yu the Great's ruling clan looked up and saw a sympathetic sky – at the stars from which the Yellow Emperor, Shennong, Nüwa, Fuxi, Yao, Shun, and even Yu himself, seemed to gaze down in shock at how once-great ideas had turned to tyranny. Seeing hope in the opposing forces of Tang, the army raised by Yu's descendants dissolved. Heaven had spoken and the world had changed.

And so, the wise storytellers observed, the lords of the land of Shang came to occupy the cities, their leader now the Son of Heaven, ruler of all. Once again, cities became sparkling gems, glittering in a landscape of open fields, linked by the blood of the ruling family. Many in number, none of the cities was greater than Great Shang, a capital ordained by heaven and fixed by the constellations of the stars. Pivot of the four quarters of the earth, it was the central axis of the cosmos whose heavenly *qi*, energy, flowed through the city and out across the world beyond. A heaven on earth, some said, and so it almost was.

Rising up from the lands around, Great Shang was square, the shape that everyone knew the earth to be. Set within towering walls of earth, the city had been fixed by the heavenly compass of the Shang's master of works, the son of the son of the son of a shaman. With turrets soaring above its gates, no ordinary mortal could approach it without trembling at the sight. Temples and palaces had been built on the highest ground; pavilions had been painted; and pillars of pine held up gently curving roofs whose eaves tipped to the skies above. Proud horses and carriages coursed the streets, their passengers bedecked in silk and jade, with banners of heavenly power fluttering on the winds. Alongside them, ox and man pushed and pulled the luxuries of life from stores of plenty to the homes of the noble spirits whom heaven had blessed. Amid the clanging and carving, the chiselling and the forging, music seemed to float on the air. And at the great gates, soldiers and sentinels stood on guard. Heaven's order was everywhere.

The city of Great Shang became the heaven of earth, emulated by many smaller Shang cities, which spread like stars in the galaxy of the Shang lands. Surrounded by the nine known mountains, the lands reached to the four known seas in a world that worked in majestic alignment with the celestial seasons, delivering treasures of harvests for the Son of Heaven and his people. Sacrifices were made to ensure the continued goodwill of the ancestors; ox bones and turtle shells were treated as oracles, heated and cracked to divine the thoughts of heaven. The calendar was observed with humility.

At first, the labours of the people were measured with fairness. At peace with the representative Son of Heaven on earth, the black-haired people had grown in number and the wealth of the Shang seemed to know no end. But as time passed, the labour became harder, the rules tightened and the punishments increased. Confident in the heavenly mandate secured by their ancestors, new Shang rulers sent nobles to clear the way for more new cities to establish an even wider order – all forged by the labours of the black-haired people, and all supported by new fields of plenty, whose wealth of grains would shower like rain upon the Shang.

More forests were burned and, like the phoenix, more harvests rose from their ashes. More mountains were mined for the minerals and stones on which the Shang's earthly powers depended: iron for axes, hoes and weapons; copper and tin for the awe-inspiring bronze vessels which, used to smooth conversations with heaven, seemed to have captured living animals in their polished surfaces; jade for its power to conjure up the virtues of heaven on earth – the endurance of strength combined with the softness of beauty. Its spreading prosperity forged with the metal of its power, many of the barbarian tribes were persuaded to follow the people of the Yellow Emperor with their calendars and cultivated fields. Soon, like all the other treasures of the natural world, they, too, were submitting their tributes to a Son of Heaven who was clearly master of the harmonies of heaven and earth.

The story told, some thought that it made perfect sense: a heavenly order of the Shang settled through their cities on earth. Hard though life was, what fearful chaos might otherwise reign without it? But from time to time, a wilful heart would remember the whispers of the past and wonder.

As day had so inexorably turned to night, summer to winter, and winter to spring, it seemed to the wilful hearts that the early peace of the people had begun to change: more cities with ever-greater harvests to produce; more wars; and now seemingly endless battles against nature to be fought. There were fewer of the animals whose lives had once been so closely entwined with theirs. No more tigers lying down beside the people; no more monkeys chattering to their hearts' delight; no more of the elephants that had once wandered at will. All had retreated into the ever more distant forests and mountains that lay beyond the settled lands. With them had also gone so many of the shamans who had once read the footprints of the birds and who, in their reading, had been able to see the majestic order of the *ziran*, 'just as it is', nature.

Backs bent, arms aching, the wilful hearts reflected on days begun before dawn and ending long after sunset. In a good year, there would be food enough left to carry a family through the winter, and punishment for none. Not starving, life could carry on. But while the cities bathed in the warmth of ancestral blessings, the labouring bodies in the fields would huddle together for survival. And as winter turned the metal of autumn into ice, the calloused hands would labour on in the endless battle against nature and the envious barbarians. More, and more violent, punishments were applied whenever things went wrong. And more men were taken into the warring service of feudal lords – many never to return.

Thinking on these things, those wilful hearts remembered the golden age of *taiping*, great peace, when men had wandered at will and eaten whatever they had hunted or found. When mountains had been crossed in freedom and rivers forded at will. When shelter had never been further away than a nearby tree and no one, neither man nor beast, had ever needed to be told what to do or say. A time before communications between heaven and earth had been interrupted, when anyone could talk to heaven whenever they wanted, and say whatever they wanted to say.

Some thought it was just a foolish dream. A world without a single top-down order – how could that be real? Others wondered, remembering not only the stories of the past, but the whispers of men returning from the edges of the world to tell of a people whose black hair still blew freely in the wind.

And from time to time, captivated by the stories of old, one of the wilful hearts would make its escape in the dead of night, looking for the old world, the world of heaven before the time of the single mind and its punishments, a world of heaven without the order of the Shang.

CHAPTER 3
HEAVEN ON EARTH?

What can be said to be of heaven, what can be said to be of
human beings?

Zhuangzi (369–286 BCE)

E YES FIXED FORWARD, ears struck by sharp plucks of strings, the
audience held its breath in eager anticipation of the story to come.
A *pipa*, lute, thrummed, dragons snorting in the wind. Drums beat to
a soft rhythm and firm feet appeared; soldiers advancing to the front.
Suddenly a zither hummed and the marchers turned as if towards the
north. As the steps retreated, bamboo flutes whispered: *jiang jiang*,
a passing breeze. But not for long. *Cang cang*! Cymbals clashed and
strong bodies turned to face the audience, pushing themselves forward
as if fording the currents of the Yellow River. And then a single stroke
of bronze – *dong* – stopped the air. Two forests of flags fluttered into
view as if upon a field of battle: one white, as the fierce metal of the
Shang; the other red, as the cleansing fires of the rising Zhou. Slowly,
from the sound of silence came a drumroll; to which the drums was
added the sound of small chimes, tinkling like anxious spirits; and then
came the wooden clappers, beating the air faster than the watching
eyes could follow.

Axes struck, shields were raised and spears flew back and forth.
White on red, red on white, the flags battled for their lives, some
thrashing forwards, others falling back. Sharp strings plucked for
effect threw every heart into the air, only to be followed by deeper
notes that pulled them down. Then, just as it seemed that the scene
would explode, the fallen red flags gathered themselves up and,
leaving the white flags where they lay, stood to a proud attention.
Drums beating softly again, their triumphant feet advanced. Some
of the red flags stepped off to the left, east, others to the right,
west, and then the two flanks turned to join together. Finally, all

facing towards the audience and the propitious south, they knelt and touched their heads to the ground. Stone chimes struck. *'Wuhu!'* the red flags shouted: 'The iniquity of the Shang is destroyed!' And from the chorus at the sides came the oh-so-familiar refrain: 'It is heaven's mandate! A Zhou king across the Four Directions – may he be treated as a Son!'

Heaven had spoken and the orderly end had been revealed: the new dynasty of the Zhou had rightfully replaced the old dynasty of the Shang in a *tianxia*, all-under-heaven, order. Heaven and earth were, once again, at one. Henceforth, the world would be clear that the ruler of the earth owed his mandate to the approval of heaven alone.

It had been a long journey. Set on the western edge of the Shang lands, the early Zhou had first watched the Shang rise, then come to pay their rulers the tribute every barbarian tribe owed to the central axis of heaven and earth. Ever-watchful, it had not been long before the Zhou began to emulate the values of their Shang neighbours to the east. There was wealth to be found in a settled life, not to mention the greater blessings that seemed to flow when conversations with heaven were limited to the single voice of a ruling king. Altars aligned with the constellations of the stars, ancestors regularly consulted, and the power of animals magically captured in the burnished sides of sacrificing bronzes: all seemed to be the hallmarks of a greater mind. Watching, the Zhou had transformed their own rough lands into fields, guided by seasons that seemed as willing to submit their schedules to the responsible calendars of the Zhou as to those of the Shang. Fields settled, they had then mastered the heavenly art of raising cities to the skies.

Time passed: in the west, the fortunes of the Zhou rose; in the east, the Shang lost their way. In Shang, it seemed, the riches that had flooded from every quarter had been channelled only to the few, and even those few had found that treasures produced only the desire for more. Wealth-yielding fields were never enough, city walls always needed strengthening, once-bright palaces always faded: the need for labour was never-ending, all of it required in double-quick time. And for every barbarian brought to tribute-paying order, others seemed only too willing to test the edges of the settled Shang world, with battles demanding ever-greater sacrifices of the nameless black-haired peasants-in-arms. In the city of Great Shang, wine might flow at the snap of a finger, but across the Shang lands, hearts were silently chilling. Revelling in their glory, the mighty Shang missed the whispers that the smaller Zhou ruler had been so quick to catch: the Shang were losing heaven's trust.

Understanding that heaven would be looking for a new Son, Zhou generals had wondered how their fifty thousand spears could ever match the five hundred thousand of the Shang. But the Zhou ruler knew that other spears were prepared to rise up with them; he also knew that weapons would be only half the battle. Where spears loyal to the Zhou would be borne by hearts that beat with courage, those of the Shang had long ago lost their hearts.

Eventually, in 1046 BCE, on the fields of Muye, the fate of earth was decided. Bells chiming, drums beating, the spears had flown, blood had poured, and by the end of the day the Zhou had not just conquered the Shang but captured the mandate of heaven.

Over the years that followed their conquest of all-under-heaven, the Zhou discharged their *tianxia* ruling responsibilities with humility and awe. Dying shortly after the battle, the Zhou king, Son of Heaven, left a young son to the regency-care of his younger brother, the Duke of Zhou. Clear as to the heavy duty that he held on his nephew's behalf, the duke moved to ensure that the voice of heaven would never be ignored again. The power of the once-great Shang now defeated, the Zhou altars, complete with oracle bones and magical bronzes, were carefully polished so that the conversations with the ancestors could henceforth be conducted from the westerly Zhou capital of Feng. Shamed by their own descendants, the Shang ancestors were invited to adopt the living Zhou as their own. And in the Feng capital, the duke raised a new idea of the ancient shamans' *mingtang*, Hall of Light.

Calculated to carry the conversation between heaven and earth, the Zhou Hall of Light was raised on a square floor of earth, the shape of earth, and set under a domed roof, the shape of heaven, divided into nine chambers, mirroring the magic numbers of Fuxi's turtle square. From within its portals, assisted by descendants of the early shamans, the Zhou sent their sacrifices up; and from the observing terraces of the domed roof, open to the moon and stars, the blessings of heaven were welcomed down. The hall through which man would bring heaven and earth together, and from which man, with his sacrifices and oracle bones, would be able to divine the will of heaven and observe the changes of the earth; the pivot of heaven above, earth below, and the four quarters all around; the place where every Zhou decision would be taken and from which every command would be despatched from the centre to the edges; and the point to which every lower power living under the rays of the Zhou sun would travel to pay the tribute that linked it to the order of the heavenly world.

The foundations of communications clear, and with trusted members of the ruling Zhou family settled across the land, the Duke of Zhou turned his attention to ensuring the harmony of everything across what had become a much bigger earth. Now including not only the vast lands of Shang and Zhou, but the lands of others who, like the Zhou, had begun to emulate the Shang. Stretching from the Kunlun mountains, in the far west, to the coast of a great sea to the furthest east, it seemed to be a world of its own, wider and greater than anything the ancestors could have imagined. Reaching from the flat, fertile plains of the north to the undulating hills of the south, there was even a tip that touched the waters of another river almost as great as the Yellow River, one that raged through gorges of jagged mountains seemingly at the southern edge of everything. And scattered across the vast tracts of the land, spar-kling like gems, stood the walled cities – once-Shang cities, Zhou cities, and the cities of the tribute-payers who emulated the settled, city-ordered, world.

With so much earth to order, more cities would be required, and with the surviving Shang not to be trusted and the black-haired people able to muster only the rawest skills of the earth, the Duke of Zhou turned to the wider Zhou family for help. Uncles, nephews and cousins, each carrying a bond of blood across the new and greater Zhou world, and all beating to the single drum of a heavenly wisdom now spread out from the capital of Feng.

With trusted family settled across the four quarters of the world, the Duke of Zhou turned to the duty of heaven's appointed ruler to ensure the wider harmony of heaven and earth within a cosmos of constant change. Clear that the secrets of the natural order lay at the heart of success, he knew that understanding the changes of the seasons would enable him to do his duty best. The path of the moon revealed the first month of the year and unveiled the schedule of the seasons by which the annual calendar could be set. The trajectory of the stars foretold the rains. The warm winds whispered of new life. The high summer brought harvests, the cold winter a silent death. These were the most elemental features of a natural order so great that only a fool would see them as either good or bad – and so deep and intricate that only the most observant could hope to understand their course.

With the weight of heaven's expectations upon his shoulders, the Duke of Zhou then turned to the shamans' heirs, men to whom the ancient wisdom had been passed from father to son across the ages. Appointed to serve in his court, they were charged with searching their memories for the insights inherited from their forefathers, and to scour the ancient threaded bamboo texts which their fathers had bequeathed them. With the knowledge of the past accumulated, they were then to compile a book of wisdom upon which the heavenly empire could be made truly secure. Working night and day, thread by thread, the descendants of the shamans, henceforth to be known as 'scholars', traced meaning across cryptic characters until, eventually, they had gathered the learning into a text that held the wisdom of the changes on which heaven's order rested. The text was entitled *The Book of Changes*, the *Yi Jing*, a work that every Zhou ruler, and indeed the heads of all of the Zhou families, would be able to consult. With it, each ruler would be able to discharge his duty to heaven above and earth below. And in discharging that duty, each ruler would merit, and thus maintain, the mandate that heaven had bestowed.

At the heart of *The Book of Changes* was a simple proposition: the unified symphony of a constantly changing cosmos, 'conducted' by the wisdom of man. Solid though the principle of unity might be, it was essential to understand that the forces underpinning it were quite the opposite – a perpetual revolution between *yin* and *yang* opposites. *Yin*, dark and receptive, *yang*, light and creative; *yin*, female and passive, *yang*, male and active. And – like the undertow within a wave, the seed which becomes a fruit, or even the turning wheel of a carriage – within every yin, was a yang; within every yang, a yin. The mandate of heaven was not a gift of triumph over earth and all of its elements: it was a duty to observe the myriad features of cosmic change upon which the successful balance of the whole depended. With the knowledge acquired through such an intense meditating observation, the delicate path of the *dao* could be divined, the harmonies of heaven and earth could be perceived and order could be achieved for all.

The Book of Changes was no manual for a selfish individual. It was, rather, a call to the man who would so humbly devote himself to the task of observing the changes that he might be described as a master of change. The effort required would always be extreme. But to the dedicated sages who served the Son of Heaven, the prize would be the knowledge that with the discharging of the cosmic duty, heaven's mandate would be secure.

The Book of Changes compiled, the Duke of Zhou then raised a heavenly bureaucracy, charged with constant divination of the *dao* way. No more periodic 'ascending and descending' for consultations with the skies, but a permanent government of virtuous ministers. Each minister was given a specific responsibility, and all were supported by corps of scholars, descendants of the early shamans, dedicated to the meticulous observation of the changes, and producing regular reports on heavenly matters, with attendant adjustments of the affairs of earth. With every minister and scholar in his position and place, each would be aware that the correct performance of his duty was essential for the success of the whole. Equipped with such a virtuous government, not only would the correct policies be divined but they would be adjusted to the changes as and when required. Guided by the *dao*, order would appear as effortlessly as nature itself.

Following the model of nature, spring would be the time for repairs, when the east winds melted the ice and sleeping creatures began to stir; it would also be a time when no punishments would be permitted that might discourage the birth of new life. In summer, when the sow thistle flowered and the great heat loomed, peasant hands would be dedicated to encouraging the fruits of the land to grow. In autumn, when crickets chirped and the geese prepared for flight, walls would be strengthened, harvests gathered and granaries filled; it would also be the time when punishments were executed, and when wars would be fought. In winter, everyone would rest, like the animals, and everything would be stored away. With the actions of man so carefully correlated to the seasons of the cosmos, there could be no risk of the chaos that might ensue from an autumn arriving in the spring or snow falling in summer.

With spreading lands and orderly seasons, the Hall of Light blazed with heavenly communications and the lands of the Zhou bathed in blessings from the sky; the people were peaceful, and harmony spread across the spheres. So great was the symphony that even the uncles, nephews and cousins who ruled the cities seemed to conduct themselves like obedient stars in the constellation of the Son of Heaven's universe. Admiring tribes and smaller states found their way to the Feng capital to offer tribute, and, just as the Zhou had followed the Shang, they followed the Zhou's example of a settled path to heaven on earth. Indeed, so great were the blessings, and so great the tribute paid, that when the young Zhou prince came of age, many were astonished to see that the Duke of Zhou honoured his promise and passed the mandate of heaven to his brother's son. But others nodded knowingly: heaven's changes were essential to the order of the spheres, and nothing mattered more than a star that knew its place in the constellation of the whole.

Two hundred years passed and it seemed to most that heaven's blessings would truly be without end. Riches cascaded into Feng; and across the lands, the cities of the Zhou relatives grew into citadels of power; everyone was fed with the abundant grains of the vast surrounding fields. But over time, with blessings in all directions, and heaven seemingly satisfied, the dedicated example set by the Duke of Zhou began to wane. As the wealth and power of the Zhou relatives had grown, so their descendants had come to see the territories over which they had been given charge as fiefdoms of their own. What difference, many of them began to wonder, stood between themselves and the Zhou king? Little by little, the bonds that had once tied the Zhou world together weakened to an ever-expanding roll of titles and names. The sacrifices, now conducted from every city, multiplied with ever-diminishing meaning. And the music that had once commanded hearts and souls became a ritual without a heart.

Wonderings turned to murmurings, and murmurings to mutterings. Where once respect had flowed across the cities of the Zhou world, by 800 BCE even heaven seemed to be raising questions: the weather began to step out of its seasons, while earthquakes and comets added their own celestial concerns. Anxious to restore their centrifugal power, successive Zhou kings hoisted martial banners and ordered their forces to stretch heaven's earth and create a greater wealth with which the muttering relations might be pacified. To the north, the west and the south, barbarian lands had been seized and, briefly, the murmurings were quelled. But the city stars at home were not convinced for long. Blood had long since turned to water. While no one wanted to question the Son of Heaven directly, every relative with a city was raising his own Hall of Light: the cities began to turn away from the Feng capital and look towards fortunes of their own.

Heaven had waited – no doubt hoping that the Zhou would succeed in ordering the family house. But in 771 BCE, it finally shook. When the Zhou king led a vast army against one of the most stubborn of the westerly barbarian tribes, the Rong, the barbarians had replied with a force of troops unleashed not only on the field but in a march directly on the capital of Feng. The Zhou world held its breath.

Heaven, however, was not quite ready to withdraw its mandate. Help arrived in the form of a rescuing barbarian tribe that had modelled itself on the order of the Zhou world. In a heavenly lesson to a wayward Son, Feng was lost, but the barbarian rescuers escorted the Zhou king to a new capital in surviving Zhou lands to the east. The Zhou line had been saved. The heavenly reputation of the Zhou dynasty, though, had not. And while heaven might have saved the Zhou, it seemed undecided as to their future. With no obvious replacement, a weak Zhou king sat on the throne, and the conclusion reached across the Zhou cities was that bets should henceforth be hedged. As the Zhou king raised a new Hall of Light in a new eastern capital, the relative-rulers of the Zhou cities decided to keep their own Halls of Light as well.

Over the next two hundred years, with Halls of Light in every city-state, the Duke of Zhou's *Book of Changes* was consulted everywhere – although few now had the patience to look for its deeper meanings. The rituals were observed, but with minds increasingly narrowed to the possibilities of power, eyes lost their hearts, and everyone's local circumstance was now governed by mere pomp. The Duke of

Zhou's idea of everything in its place and with a purpose retreated to the mists of a 'golden' past, and once again the majestic order of the spheres began to fray, not only within the central Zhou court but within the now-myriad courts of the Zhou world. The rulers of the Zhou's cities began to look for ever-greater scholarly bureaucracies of their own, which, with their prized knowledge and power of writing, could help them keep an independent order. With scholars now less in demand at the declining central court of the Zhou, many were happy to wander.

Side by side with the scholarly bureaucracies, the rulers of the city-states also looked to their armies and generals: as the old order had begun to fray, power had become a competition. Highly prized were those generals who could snatch at a neighbouring state that might be ready to fall. In an increasingly uncertain world, covenants of peace, written in blood and copied to heaven, became the currency of rule. But with the stakes so high, ambition almost always proved more powerful: the drums of war rolled, the blood of covenants was regularly spilled and, more often than not, heaven was simply notified of a change.

Still under the heavenly umbrella of the Zhou, but with the Zhou rulers now in a celestial slumber, successful stately cities became individual city-states. Within the city-states however – without the higher 'golden' order of the Duke of Zhou – everyone began to question everything. Younger brothers questioned the right of older brothers to rule. Men whose place had been to provision the household of a noble began to look to their personal fortunes – trading their masters' wealth for causes of their own. Rulers of the city-states looked for greater wealth; in so doing, they offered peasants who had been bonded to the land the chance to replace their labouring duties of the past with taxes tied to the success of a harvest.

Everywhere, once simple lives were exchanged for a game played with the dice of uncertain change. Some won, others lost. The greatest of the losers lost their city-states, their positions or their homes. The poorest of them, peasant labourers who succombed to a failed harvest, not only risked the forfeit of their land to a tax-insisting city-state but, without land to farm, also lost the ability to exercise the only skill with which they could survive. Merchants became willing buyers of lands buried in the debts of unpaid taxes, and of desperate peasants and their children. And when children became the stuff of trade, few were surprised that theft became a valued talent and violence a price that everyone had to pay.

By 600 BCE, the old story of the Duke of Zhou had faded into a fairytale; unity was a dream of the past. Heaven and earth were parting company, and on earth each city looked to itself. Heartfelt reflections on the duty of a ruler to find and follow the *dao* way had long ago yielded to narrow calculations of territory and power. Battles and punishments were the order of the day. The past, and all of its principles, was gone; the future was clearly waiting for a map.

With the old order weakening, new minds expressed opinions. The loudest were to be found among the scholars, who had the advantage of special insights into heavenly thought. But they were not alone. As the fortunes of the city-states rose and fell, the roads of the old Zhou world were travelled by craftsmen and traders whose talents had built the pavilions of power. And as the peasants continued to deliver harvests far more reliably than any ruler kept his promises, even the fields developed ideas of their own. While the Duke of Zhou's *Book of Changes* might have been forgotten by many of those at the heavenly top, down on the ground, copied onto bamboo strips, it was memorised and shared by the many others who consulted it for their own enlightenment and in concern for the state of the collapsing Zhou world. From temple courtyards to marketplaces, along roads and at the edges of fields, the opinions flowed in all directions.

By 500 BCE, with the city-states now fat with ambition, with battles casting shadows across everyone's horizons, and with minds chattering at every junction, demand for the talents of the scholars rose. From the portents of the stars to the choreography of ritual, from the archiving of what had gone before to the stratagems of power, the scholars' skills were talents an anxious ruler could always use. Those who brought knowledge from afar were particularly prized.

———

One of the many scholarly officials who decided to travel along the roads of the fading Zhou empire was a man named Confucius. Born in the city-state of Lu, distant descendant of a shaman, tutored in *The Book of Changes* and in each great text that had followed, Confucius had mastered every skill that a scholar-official could acquire. But, like so many others, the state of Lu had fallen prey to men who grasped rank with money rather than acquiring it through virtue. Ruled more by intrigues and machinations than by its Hall of Light, supported more by punishments than shame, in the state of Lu, as elsewhere, the changes of the cosmos had become the least of anyone's concerns. Temples hosted rituals without meaning; pavilions were flooded with music that chimed regardless of the seasons.

Dreaming of the golden age of the Duke of Zhou, but without the independence of an inherited income, Confucius made no public comment, simply doing his best to model his own contributions on the discipline and diligence of the selfless, golden, past. But as he worked his way up the bureaucratic ladder, he wondered how the purity of that past might be recaptured and how, in an age of greed and division, the ruler of a state could become the force of harmony and unity through which peace and security could appear again.

Casting his mind across his own decades of thought and experience, Confucius contemplated the wisdom of ancient shamans. In so doing, he found himself continually returning to *The Book of Changes*, to the tenets that had guided the duke and the rituals that had underpinned his court. Eventually, Confucius discerned a set of ordering principles on which, he believed, the golden age of the past could be restored. Of course, he observed, no ruler should be worrying about life after death: if one had not yet understood life, what could be the point of speculating on matters after death? But, charged with co-ordinating the affairs of heaven on earth, there were, he felt, certain qualities and relationships which could ensure that a ruler would find the *dao* way, and that the people would conduct themselves in a manner conducive to the greater harmony of all.

The first and most fundamental of qualities was *ren*, the empathy, or benevolence, with which all men were born, and which, as the greatest of the ancient shamans had demonstrated, enabled man to identify with the cosmos and his fellow man. Key to all knowledge and understanding, and key to the harmony that such knowledge and understanding delivered, *ren* was the attribute that made possible the civilisation of society. It was the essence of humanity. It was what distinguished man from beast.

From *ren* sprang the qualities of *yi*: integrity, *li*: ritual, and *de*: virtue. *Yi* was a matter of clarity and truth, grounded in a meticulous correlation of the names of things and their purposes. *Li* was not a spectacle of vain glorification but a prompt which, grounded in stories and carried out in the rhythms of music, dance and sacrifices, would choreograph everybody's lives. Constantly practised, *li* would ensure that everyone remembered where he stood in the heavenly hierarchy. *De* not only ensured that the Son of Heaven would find the *dao* way of the state, but that the men within the all-under-heaven lands would cultivate themselves to such a degree that they would become *junzi*, gentlemen, and the *dao* would be found and followed by all.

To these, Confucius added the quality of *zhi*: the pursuit of knowledge that would ensure every decision taken was wise. To be complete and reliable, such knowledge would be grounded in a *ge wu*, investigation of things: a constant and enquiry into everything. Things present, that could be observed with one's own eyes and heart; and things past, that could be understood through a mastery of the wisdom contained in the ancient texts, such that none of the accumulated discoveries on which the Duke of Zhou's golden age had been founded (and the Yellow Emperor's lands originally raised) would ever be lost.

Each of the qualities described by Confucius was part of an inner life that every *tianxia*, all-under-heaven, citizen, from the Son of Heaven through the hierarchically ordered heads of families and down to the youngest sons of the land, should cultivate. The cultivation of these qualities was not to be sought through an abstract reflection on the civilising features which distinguished man from beasts, but as a practical pursuit of the greater order on which civilisation itself is based.

Alongside these qualities, Confucius added an ordering set of *jia*: family, relationships as a mirror of the cosmic hierarachy. Grounded on a fundamental principle of *xiao*, the filial piety upon which every individual household and the greater family of the state depended, fathers would be at the helm, older brothers would be above younger brothers, men above women. With the conduct of each family being as harmonious as the music of the spheres, the state, which was surely just a gathering of small families into one, would be a symphony, with the ruler above as the conductor of heaven and earth, the chorus of the people below, and the ministers, officials and scholars in between. Such a symphony, standing at the apex and heart of the heavenly civilisation, would stand as a sun whose rays of cultivated qualities would spread like a light across the lands of tribute-paying followers and on to the darker lands of the barbarian world beyond.

Applied by all, Confucius insisted, these qualities and relationships would deliver a new golden age of peace and unity, resurrecting the golden age of the Duke of Zhou, when the Son of Heaven governed with integrity and respect rather than rules and punishments. And with everyone's eyes on heaven, hearts would turn against the selfish pursuit of individual gain that could only ever result in everybody's ruin.

Looking for opportunities to apply his principles to the government of Lu, Confucius worked as hard as any of the Great Men of the ancient past. Eventually, he became a junior minister to the Duke of Lu. But the city-state of Lu was far too caught up in battling intrigues and machinations for its duke to take any interest in the dreams of a man who seemed to have lost touch with the real world. Eventually, at the age of fifty-four, Confucius concluded that Lu had irretrievably lost its way. Heaving a sigh of regret, he packed up his modest belongings and set off to find a ruler who would welcome the chance to build a more solid future by understanding the wisdom of the past.

The roads were long, and the city-states many. At every opportunity, Confucius presented his model of good government: pursue the *dao* way by being a master of change; embrace the quality of *ren* empathy by putting yourself in other people's shoes; hold on to the *yi* integrity which ensures that things are called by their correct names, and that names and purposes are always carefully correlated; observe the *li* ritual which ensures that no one forgets their place in the whole. Keep to the true *zhi* knowledge; hold to the *ge wu* investigation of things; strive for the *de* virtue of diligence and discipline. And never stray from the concept of the *jia* family as the pattern for all.

The wisdom was clear: be good and the people will follow; cultivate yourself and the order of heaven will naturally appear on earth. Indeed, as Confucius observed, if you cannot cultivate yourself, how could you try to cultivate anyone else? Many fellow travellers who met Confucius on his journeys were quick to see the wisdom of his words – more than words, some suggested, surely his ideas were a manifesto of civilisation itself. But within the gates of every city, Confucius found the same intrigues and machinations that had plagued the state of Lu, and the same fuzzy thinking and ambition: rulers wanted scholarly minds that could supply a quick solution to a problem: increasingly, they wanted military strategists who could prepare a battle plan at will. In a world where everyone wanted to command as much as they could, quick results were everything. True, not everywhere was quite as lost as the state of Lu, but no ruler seemed able to grasp the value of the treasures that Confucius was placing before them.

After fourteen years of travel, Confucius turned for home and applied himself to teaching smaller men the precepts he had prepared. In the disturbing chaos of the time, many came to his door to learn, but none had the power to apply his ideas to the grander scale of government. When Confucius died in 479 BCE, at the age of seventy-one, he had little hope that much would change. But at least, he thought, he had lived according to his principles, and taught others to follow in his modest steps. A small start, no doubt, but heaven had its reasons and he had done his best.

Those whom Confucius had taught taught others in their turn. But as they travelled, they found men with much older ideas of a different cosmic wisdom wandering across the troubled lands of the Zhou. Taught by masters of the ancient shamanic knowledge, they had no dreams of holding up the city-states or of conducting heaven and earth for the greater harmony of all. Seeing the idea of cities and states as an epic mistake, they insisted that the only force on earth was that of the natural order of the cosmos – an order within which man had neither responsibility nor power, but to which man could adapt, and in adapting become something greater than himself. Encountering such ideas on the road, Confucius' students found themselves confronted with questions that left them almost speechless. 'What on earth had any human being to do with the idea of order?' was one. 'How could anyone believe that the Duke of Zhou, let alone the Yellow Emperor or Yu the Great, had anything useful to say?' was another. '*Ren* empathy and *yi* integrity? Good principles if you can find them, but if you're looking for them in a city-state then you're wasting your time.'

'*De* virtue?' others queried. 'Nothing but the arrogance of city men who fail to understand that nothing they do can have a cosmic consequence any greater than the sneezing of a gnat.' And as for *li* ritual, their disdain was almost palpable: 'Self-distracting mumbo-jumbo. However much kings and emperors might wish it otherwise, the *dao* way of the shamans cannot be reduced to a handbook for anyone – least of all for a family or a state.'

Expounding on their beliefs, the cosmic thinkers explained to Confucius' followers that the ancient texts from which *The Book of Changes* had been written were not designed to put man under the order of a ruler but were the accumulated wisdom of those who, having humbled themselves before the greater order of nature, had understood that heaven and earth were far more powerful and complex than any human being could ever imagine. Forces that could scarcely be contemplated, no paltry human words could ever describe them – and man tinkered with them at everyone's peril. As for Confucius' *ge wu* idea of investigating things, their contempt was clear: the narrow human identification of what is useful and what is not, an idea beloved of every ruler since the Yellow Emperor, had been nothing but a recipe for the disasters with which everyone was now living. Surely any fool could see that, in the constantly changing *yin-yang* world, it was only those who knew the value of the useless who could understand the value of the useful.

As Confucius' students struggled to answer, the cosmic ideas were increasingly embraced by others strained by the troubles of the times. A few, struck by the force of the cosmic proposition, left the city-states for the greater meditational possibilities of mountains and forests where man was not at war with nature. Others stayed in the cities but kept the cosmic ideas warm in their hearts, consulting them in the quiet of night, thinking of them when the ups and downs of human life became too much for any man to bear. And many memorised the text of a work known to some by the name its readers had given to its self-effacing author – Laozi, 'old master' – and to others by its title: *Dao De Jing, The Classic of the Way.*

Composed before Confucius had lived, and in lines whose poetry echoed the mysteries of the cosmos itself, Laozi's work revealed that, in a world of changes, the wisdom of the shamans had been the discernment of a way of thinking and living that, if followed, would bring man into harmony with the natural order. Grasp this simple wisdom, Laozi had written, and the 'myriad things' would fall at your feet; lose it, he added, and sooner or later everything would evaporate from your grasp. Watching as the ancient knowledge fell on ears deafened with ambition, Laozi had reached the conclusion that the jostling lands of the Yellow Emperor would be unlikely ever to understand its meaning. With the city-states expanding, he walked to the farthest wall that divided the Yellow Emperor's lands from those of the barbarians to the west, and passed through the Jade Gate into a natural world where man was free to find his peace within the truer cosmic order that governed all.

Time passed, and the Zhou's dream of heavenly rule continued to crumble. As many embraced Laozi's ideas in their hearts, Confucius' principles also gained greater currency, particularly among scholars who saw a renaissance of the golden age of the Duke of Zhou as the only hope for the settled world. With so many scholars wandering between the city-states, the time would come to be known as that of the 'hundred schools of thought'. And then, another cosmic mind appeared. This one tried to put some of the oldest ideas of the *dao* into words and to set them against Confucius' misguided premise that a simple set of principles could deliver order for the settled world. The name of the man was Zhuang, and he and his work came to be known as (the) Zhuangzi. Taking up the argument against cities and states, Zhuangzi declared that 'good government' was a contradiction in terms: the only order was that of the cosmos, within which man was no more than a speck of dust. In Zhuangzi's opinion, the idea of heavenly appointed rulers was a gross deception, which had simply legitimised the arrogance of man. All that the Great Men of the past had achieved was a tyranny of obstacles that put brambles under everyone's feet and prevented the ordinary human from finding peace. And if anyone on earth truly wanted to look for order, they should stop moving mountains, give up the pursuit of straight paths and accept that the way of the cosmos is as crooked as a brook.

By 400 BCE, the city-states were flinging themselves into a warring race to replace the sleeping Zhou. Smaller states had fallen to larger neighbours; many had turned their troops against each other. Engineering talents honed in the taming of rivers were now applied to defence and attack: moats to defend one's own walls, and siege machines designed to collapse the walls of others. Peace became a disappearing dream. Covenants and ritual had long ago given way to generals and strategy. Fathers and elder brothers went off to one or other of the many fronts and were never seen again; younger brothers followed in their footsteps. For the peasants in the fields, the ravages of war were only a conscription away.

Loaded back and forth, the arguments between the city-states were never short of words. From time to time even heaven was brought into the equation. But it was the chariots, the battle-axes and the armies that won the day. And as the generals fought, the minds of their rulers turned inevitably to the knowledge that would bring victory in the battlefield. 'Know your enemy and know yourself,' urged one general, in his thoughts on war. To which, he added, 'If any soldier, hearing and understanding, fails to obey, he should be despatched to his death without a moment's hesitation.' The general's name was Sunzi, and one day his wisdom would come to be known as the *Bingfa* – the Rules, or 'Art', of War.

By 300 BCE, with every ruler's attention fixed on winning what had now become a war of all against all, criticisms of the present could only be safely expressed within a carefully constructed code – with all truths masked in observations softened for sensitive ruling ears. But scholarly minds continued to carry their critical questions up and down the roads of the collapsing Zhou world, each seeking new ideas of order that could restore peace to all. In private homes, or in the open chaos of the marketplace, the failings of the present and its rulers were constantly exposed to a searing criticism, with new ideas regularly rising to challenge the old.

One of the newer ideas of order came from a man known as Mozi. A carpenter and master of the 'cloud ladders' used to conquer the walls of enemy cities, Mozi saw the greatest challenge in establishing order as that of preserving the humanity of man. With a deep belief in the importance of man's love for his fellow human beings, Mozi was sympathetic to Laozi's idea that the cities were the enemy of human hearts. 'Bind the fingers of those who would keep building the city-states,' he argued, 'smash their arcs and plumb lines, throw away their compasses and squares.' The battling rulers, the busybody bureaucrats, the punishing officials and the warring generals were obstructing everyone's way. In a world where misfortune showered down like rain, and where good fortune was as light and evasive as a feather, everyone should stop and think about what it meant to be human. 'More has been forgotten by man', Mozi argued, 'than man has ever learnt; and more has been destroyed by man than man has ever created.'

Mozi then turned to Confucius, as Zhuangzi had before him, and observed that here was a man who, however good his intentions might have been, had rushed off down the wrong path. Looking at footprints rather than shoes, Confucius had misunderstood the ancient ideas brought together in *The Book of Changes*. Obsessed with his hero the Duke of Zhou, he had conspired with the Great Men of the past to create an illusion of human order based on a bureaucratic dabbling that could only make things worse. In reality, Mozi noted, these so-called 'Great Men' were no more than a succession of overactive busybodies who had worn themselves out in a bid to impose a human idea of order on heaven's earth. Forget cities and their states, Mozi argued, discard glory, step out of the yoke of the sacrificial ox and follow the old shamans to find your own simple way in your own simple life; consult the changes of the cosmos with the same natural instinct with which you take each breath.

Mozi was not the only man with another idea of order. Others looked back to one of the earliest of the Great Men: Shennong, the original farmer, whose star had faded beside the glittering triumphs of the Yellow Emperor and Yu the Great but who was surely a far better model for an orderly future. The shaman who had discovered the secrets of the soil and of the animals, it was Shennong who had turned the earth into a treasure-trove for humans. And, unlike those who had come after him, Shennong had not tamed rivers or built cities, but had put his back to the plough and worked among the people in a community where every man was an equal brother. Forget the grander visions of delivering a heavenly triumph on earth, these others argued. Forget the cities with their raised pavilions and armies of peasants, who laboured until their backs broke. Go back to the fields and to the very earliest idea of *de*, virtue. Put every hand to the plough; live within the treasures that nature offers and make every heart count.

The many sceptics of Mozi's ideas and the Shennong ideal countered that Shennong's dream had been given up as impractical a long time ago, not least by the Yellow Emperor, who had realised from the age of ten that a people needed a state and that a state needed a ruler with a plan.

Some, however, saw much to be recommended in the dreams of Mozi and Shennong. Guaranteeing human security through universal love, living through sharing, ruling by example rather than force: surely these ideas offered a better route to order than anything that the dreams of the Yellow Emperor, or Confucius, offered. Skip the rituals, cancel the music, and bridge the gap between the rich and the poor: what could be more orderly than that? Many, particularly the peasants and the artisans at the tightly ordered bottom of the city-state world, agreed that Mozi's ideas had much to recommend them.

Those at the increasingly precarious top, however, were unconvinced. The Shennong ideal seemed a little dour. It also seemed to miss the point. The Zhou king was clearly no longer ruling, and mysteriously, heaven appeared to have gone to sleep. But at some point soon, heaven would wake up to the fact that a new ruler was required. The only real question was who it would be. And the only way to find the answer was to keep going to war.

The arguments continued. Those who believed in the essential importance of a Great Man in conducting the harmonies of heaven and earth were convinced that unity, within each city-state and across the whole, was essential; but how to achieve such unity was as clear as mud. Punishments were meted out in all directions but everyone continued to hold their own opinion, even as the practicalities of order hurtled out of anyone's control.

Eventually, though, the great debates of the past began to narrow. Laozi, Zhuangzi, Mozi and Shennong were increasingly set aside: not only was it clear that men were not equal, but it was obvious that the men of the city-states were not going to take themselves back to small communities in the fields. And then there was the practical observation that Confucius had once made: 'Given that man is neither a bird nor a beast, what is the point in hankering after an ancient time in the wild?' The question of order began to turn to Confucius' preoccupation with the self-cultivating possibilities of man. And in focusing on the importance of self-cultivation, attention soon returned to the matter of man's nature: was man inherently good, in which case he could be trusted to cultivate himself; or was he inherently bad, in which case any idea of self-cultivation would be a fool's errand and the only solution would be to bend his nature to a greater will.

Those who argued that man was essentially good pointed to the innate ability of human beings to recognise and accommodate the needs of others, and to a natural sense of shame that responded far better to kind acts of correction than to brutal punishment. Those who argued that man was essentially bad pointed to a deep self-interest which meant that only the application of painful punishments could lead him to change his ways. The champions of 'man as good' retorted that even brutal punishments seemed to make no difference; the champions of 'man as bad' replied that the punishments were obviously not brutal enough. With death and destruction in every direction, the latter added that it was time to make it clear that the order of a city-state was essential for everyone's survival; that order required leadership; and that leadership required responsibility.

And heaven? Nobody was really very sure any more what heaven thought – or even if there was one. Some went so far as to argue that every 'fact' of the past was nothing but a mistake, if not a delusion, including the very idea of heaven itself. Others, hearing such words, caught their breath in shock.

With wars in every direction, little hope of peace, and with the minds of the scholars, and everyone else, hopelessly divided, a small number of men left the city-states of the collapsing Zhou world to seek their fortunes in a new state that was rising rapidly in the barbarian west. A rough, dry place where there was no room for contemplation or argument, it certainly had no time to wait for heaven to make up its mind. With the war of all wars to be won and the prize of the old Zhou world at stake, its successive rulers had begun to welcome men of talent from the old Zhou world, to join them in facing up to the responsibilities of the time in which they were living, rather than speculating about what a Yellow Emperor, or a Great Yu, or anyone else who had lived three thousand years ago, might do.

Leaving one of the Zhou city-states to start a new life in the new barbarian west, one scholar observed that while mothers might love their children twice as much as fathers, the orders of a father were ten times more effective; and while a state might not love its people, its orders were ten thousand times more effective than those of any father. The world had changed. As the rising power in the barbarian west had understood, it was time to be hard in the interests of doing good. Laws should be stated clearly and uniformly applied, without regard for either humanity or generosity. The good should be rewarded and the bad truly punished as a lesson to themselves and an example to all. And if anyone tried to muddy the waters by appealing to the past to condemn the present, they and all of their family should accept responsibility for the error of their ways – with the forfeit of their lives.

The name of the state was Qin.

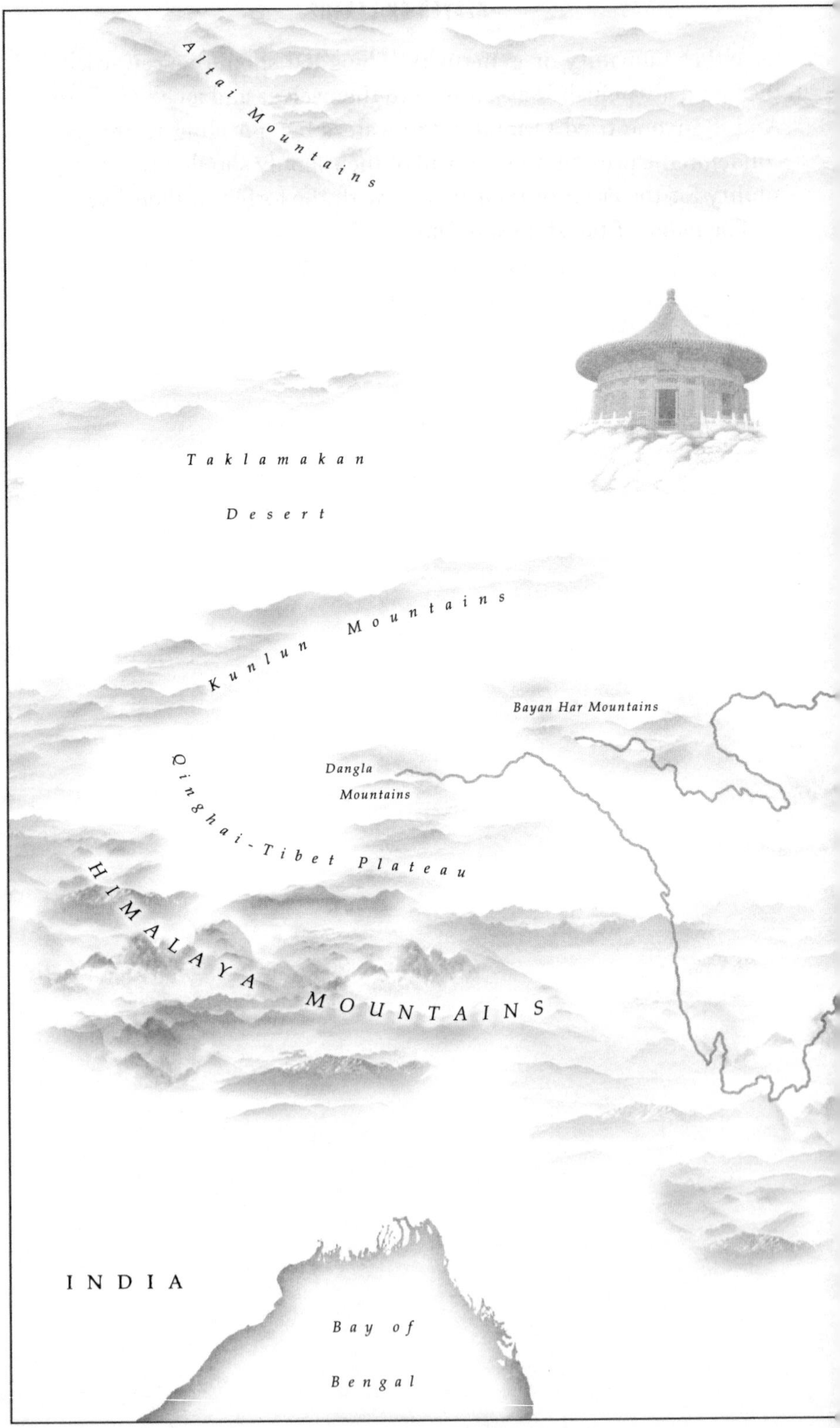
Altai Mountains
Taklamakan Desert
Kunlun Mountains
Bayan Har Mountains
Dangla Mountains
Qinghai-Tibet Plateau
HIMALAYA MOUNTAINS
INDIA
Bay of Bengal

THE HEAVENLY LANDSCAPE
3RD CENTURY BCE

XIONGNU

Gobi
esert

Ordos
Desert

ZHAO

YAN

Taihang
Mountains

QI

WEI

QIN

▲
Mount Tai

Lu

Luoyang

Feng / Xianyang
(Xi'an)

HAN

Ba
(fell
316 BCE)

Yangzi River

CHU

Yue

East Sea

Japanese Archipelago

Nanhai

CHAPTER 4

A SINGLE HEART

All under heaven are of a single heart's resolve, gripping a
single will.

First Qin Emperor, Qin Shi Huangdi
(inscription at Mount Tai, 219 BCE)

T
HE FORCE MOVED LIKE a dark cloud. The ground trembled.
Behind the fortress walls of the Shangdang garrison of the small
state of Han, no one in that year of 265 BCE was in any doubt about the
threat. Peering into the dust-filled distance, long-feared shapes began to
take their terrifying form. A thousand banners beat the air. Ten thousand
snorting horses hurled themselves forward in a storm of thundering
hoofs. Sharply drilled to order, five hundred thousand pairs of following
feet pounded at a heavy pace. Swords swinging at their sides, axes glinting on their backs, first ten thousand soldiers came into view, and then
ten thousand more. And still they came, like waves, ten thousand at a
roll. Suddenly, a bronze gong struck, the depths of its echo calling a halt.
Hoofs and feet obeyed. For a moment, silence hung like a thread in the
air. And then the drums began to beat, the thread was cut, and an army
of men rushed to the front. At a single piercing command, crossbows
were loaded and ten thousand arrows turned the sky to black.

Within the Shangdang garrison it was clear to all that the small state
of Han could not withstand the forces of the mighty Qin. The heavenly Zhou king was still sleeping in the east, languishing in a celestial
dream. Only Zhao to the north – once a brother within the great Zhou
family, now one of the many warring states – could push Qin back
behind the western mountains. But would Zhao come? Battles were
two-a-penny, the loss of a state was nothing new, and with the idea of
brotherhood now a relic of the past, what had Zhao to gain? Messages
were despatched with haste, and sealed with a promise: 'Shangdang is
Zhao's,' they offered, 'simply for the taking. Anything but a fall to Qin.'

Meanwhile, the arrows rained down upon Shangdang's garrison walls, and Qin roamed as the terror of the world.

———

More than five hundred years had passed since 771 BCE when the heavenly Zhou had fled from west to east. Challenged by the wild tribe known as the Rong, its barbarian rescuer had been a small state at the north-west edge of the Zhou world: Qin. A dry patch of rainless earth locked behind the western Taihang mountains, Qin had only narrow mountain passes to bring it into contact with the settled eastern world. More often described as a 'pack of wolves and tigers', founded by a horse-breeder with ambitions to join the settled world, Qin was rarely accorded recognition as a 'state'. But having granted himself the title of duke, as he rescued the Zhou from their attackers, the horse-breeder's descendant had not only secured respect but had also stretched his domain: forced to flee, the escaping Zhou had offered their abandoned western lands to Qin – if Qin could wrestle them from the Rong. Where the softening Zhou had failed, the tougher Qin succeeded.

The new Zhou capital had faded into a heavenly cloud, and the once-mighty noble families of the now 'Eastern Zhou' had begun the spiral of battles that would eventually lead to the war of all against all. Standing on the sidelines to the west, Qin had watched the unfolding events with interest: thousands of battling stately cities reduced to hundreds, and almost all simultaneously shattering under competing branches of the noble families who had built them. Ambitious sons conspiring to take kingdoms for themselves, jealous uncles seizing opportunities for gain, once-friendly advisers changing colour: the permutations of intrigue knew no end. By 400 BCE, the warring states were battling each other in mutual destruction – and the greatest of them all, Jin, had found itself torn into three: Zhao, Wei and Han.

While the Zhou family and its many stately cities had been crumbling from within, the Qin 'pack of wolves and tigers' had raised an army and, learning their lessons scrap by scrap, pushed their way through the rough western mountain passes out to the east and the fertile banks of the Yellow River. When the hundreds of surviving Zhou city-states had been reduced to seven major powers, to everyone's astonishment, those powers included the upstart state of Qin. Struggling to understand how a paltry place could have swelled to such a force, Zhou family minds paused to reflect.

Clearly, it must have been luck. While Qin had the usual barbarian pretensions to the heavenly virtues of civilisation, its rabid population of wolves and tigers could certainly have no place in heaven's order. Their banging pots and swaying bodies could not charm the spheres; their clumsy sacrifices would never achieve the magic of the *li* rituals; their brash brawls held no *yi* integrity; and the brutal animal code by which they lived certainly showed no *ren* humanity.

Somehow, though, Qin turned its barbarian fate to fortune. Even the Taihang mountains, which separated it from heaven's world, had been transformed from an obstructive wall to a defending shield; and the rough lands, lucky to see rain, no longer seemed to be a curse but a blessing: forcing the thirsty Qin to push outside and wrestle more fertile lands from those who were either too distracted or too weak to answer back. Reaching out to the north-east, Qin had snatched at the fertile banks of the Zhou's Yellow River. Turning to the south, nothing had been easier than to grasp great plains from tribal kingdoms that seemed to have no appetite for war.

Indeed, Qin feats on the battlefield were a marvel to behold – few of anyone else's generals hoped with any confidence to strike them down. But triumphs of war alone could not account for Qin's run of luck. Powerful alliances had regularly been forged among the other six warring states in bids to defeat the barbarian upstart. In every case, though, almost before the covenanting blood had dried, a whisper or a word crumbled their fragile trust to dust. A king would be persuaded that a brother's rediscovered love was a ruse; allying armies would find themselves led by generals who had no intention to unite; agreed battle plans would be changed at a moment's notice. Defeat seemed to stalk every attempt at unity, and, as often as not, it would be followed by war between those who had come closest to peace. With the oddest spirit behind it, Qin was gaining a foothold in heaven-on-earth. With every battle won, its might expanded. And when its troops had pounded into Shangdang, it had been clear that, unless Qin was checked, nothing short of heaven itself would satisfy its thirst.

When the appeal for help in saving the Han state's Shangdang garrison had reached the state of Zhao in 265 BCE, the calculation had seemed clear: save the Han garrison from Qin and take the opportunity to push the pack of wolves and tigers back behind their mountain passes. Qin's army was mighty but Zhao's was mightier still. The Zhao king had taken time to be convinced but eventually troops were rallied, drums rolled, and a Zhao army marched south under the greatest general of its time – an army so big that surely even Qin would quake at its approach. Arriving in Shangdang in 262 BCE, the Zhao general surveyed the field. Qin had calculated well: every natural vantage point had been exploited, with troop formations meticulously shaped to pitch Qin strength against Zhao weakness. But, as every general knew, few battles could be won with arrows alone. Far from home, Qin's supply lines would surely be quickly stretched, and even wolves and tigers get hungry. Drawing on nerves of steel and a lifetime of battling experience, the Zhao general busied himself with fortifications and settled his army down to wait.

One month became two, two became three; a year passed and then another. The Zhou world held its breath. At the court of the Zhao state, whispers rustled across the corridors of power, casting barbs of doubt about the general at the front while spreading rumours of martial expertise that had been overlooked. 'Wasting all this time,' some murmured, 'the stresses of war must have softened his courage.' 'Qin must have been delighted', muttered others, 'that we put such a coward at our helm.' One particular whisper went even further: 'Qin is secretly relieved that Zhao has not deployed its greatest living force: a well-born scholar whose mastery of the written texts of past battles has never been sullied by the doubts of any experience of the front; if sent to the field such a highly cultivated brush would surely have the Qin quivering in their boots.'

The whispers reached the ears of the king and led him to wonder if he had somehow missed a trick. It was not long before his doubts led to the recall of the great general from the field, and the advance of the well-born bookworm to the front. Within days, the new Zhao general had marched the army from its cowardly defences and opened up his forces for all to see.

The immediate result was indeed spectacular: the mighty Qin seemed to race away in fear; with the great Zhao army sweeping after them, victory had seemed all but assured. But as the Zhao rushed to what appeared to be the clear front lines of the Qin, a message flew from the back to the front: four hundred and fifty thousand soldiers deep, the back end of the Zhao army was coming under a storm of arrows from behind. Buried in his books, the new Zhao general had forgotten to look to his rear.

Within less than a day, three years of waiting patience had been lured into a trap. While Qin's supply lines were badly stretched, Zhao's had now been severed; the tide had turned. Qin waited. Cut off, Zhao's troops were forced to eat their dead. With the nerves of their scholarly general made of little more than paper, the bravest of the Zhao soldiers were commanded to follow him in a desperate bid to break out. Courage never wanting, they obeyed. Within an instant, the general was shot down and the four hundred thousand surviving Zhao soldiers were left without a leader. Within days, they surrendered.

As the news spread across the greater old Zhou world, heads nodded sadly: yet another battle lost in the wars that had scarred the past two hundred years; more defeated soldiers straggling home, shamed. When would it ever end? Surrendering its soldiers to Qin, however, the Zhao state had confidently expected the usual *de* virtues of heavenly war to apply. Shangdang would now be Qin, but surely the Qin ruler would return the vanquished troops with the same *ren* humanity that every heavenly ruler ritually observed.

Behind the mountain passes, though, Qin had taken a different view. The charge of heaven demanded leadership, which required responsibility, and responsibility required unswerving attention to the facts. The garrison of Shangdang was indeed a prize, but with such a force of fighting men returned to the ranks, Zhao could always fight again. Better to wipe the board clean and bury the beating hearts of the living in a settled field of death. Four hundred thousand Zhao souls were swiftly despatched to meet their ancestors. Across the old Zhou world, everyone's blood ran cold.

———

To the few who had taken the trouble to become familiar with the state of Qin, the brutal outcome had been a foregone conclusion. While the scholars of the old Zhou world had been debating the finer points of heavenly order, Qin had been strengthening its might. And just as new ideas had travelled across the warring states, they had also wandered

into Qin. Not the finest ideas, of course. A hardy people, Qin had little
to commend itself to a Confucius or a Laozi; this was a land that saw
nature more as a beast than a gentle path. But for some of the Zhou
world the rough ideas of Qin had a strong appeal. Qin might be barbarian, but within its tough exterior was a glittering metal with a value.
Unconcerned with *ren* empathy, for Qin, survival itself was the greatest virtue. Undisturbed by *yi* integrity, Qin minds were quick to grasp
any advantage that could twist itself into triumph. And untrammelled
by *li* ritual, Qin had no scruples about disguising its men to roam the
courts of its enemies, spreading rumours as they went.

One man who had seen Qin's breathtaking triumphs from afar was
a scholarly son of the distant sibling-state of Wei. A man who had
watched the fine ideas of the old Zhou world crumble into the dust
of war, and with it the lives of men he had called his friends: his name
was Shang Yang. Struck by what he had heard of the fresh energies
of the west, in 359 BCE Shang Yang had packed his bags, and, presenting himself to the court of Qin, had been enchanted by what he heard
and saw. Here was a land where the past was not even a memory, and
where any golden age that might once have existed had long ago been
buried along with any soft hearts that dreamt of such a thing. A heavenly family? Nothing but a luxury. Virtue above survival? Pure vanity.
Musical harmonies to temper human chaos? A wilful blindness that
deserved to fail. If man had ever been good, and it was unclear that he
ever had, those days were clearly over. Government by a family fixed
in heaven had obviously failed. There might well be a *dao* way; but if
there was, it was reserved for the ruler who had the courage to order a
state. That Zhou general, Sunzi with his *The Art of War*, who had tried
to teach the city-states the rules for winning wars, had hit the nail
right on the head: discipline was everything.

Delighted with the ideas he encountered, Shang Yang sought an
audience of the king of Qin. Listening to Shang Yang's praise of the
order of his state, the king of Qin had been equally delighted: finally a
mind from the refined world of the east that understood the wisdom
of the wilder west.

Sheltered behind the mountain passes, free from the chattering of
idle scholarly minds, and with the full trust of his new ruler, Shang
Yang dismissed the state's scholars and transformed Qin ideas into a
'reforming' manual for rule. Clear goals were set: agriculture for food,

war for survival, and the people as guarantors of both. The principles were clearly stated: *ding fa yi min*, fix the laws, order the people.
Convert all useful knowledge into laws; set down the laws in black and
white; achieve the correct standards of behaviour with painful punishments as reminders that every deviation has its price. With Shang
Yang's more detailed order, the Qin people were turned into a power
that could snatch victory in any war, and could even be trained to
order themselves.

For Shang Yang, turning a people into the force of a state was a
three-step matter of discipline conducted to a level of detail from which
none could escape. The first step was to control the land with registers and maps: registers to keep a record of every human head in the
country; maps to divide the land into county units of administration
and then to mark every village in the land upon them. The second step
was to use the registers and maps to order the population into groups
of households, which – each charged with paying its taxes from the
produce of its fields and the soldiering of its men – would be constantly
available for the service of the state. The third step was to transform
the people into instruments of their own command. Learning from the
successes of the battlefield, and with family affections seen as a foolish distraction that no successful state could afford, Qin households
were ordered together in groups of five, with each household bound
to guarantee the orderly obedience of all. Any failure, of any member
of any household, to comply with any law was to be reported to the
head of the group, who would report it to the officials above. Those
who made their reports would be rewarded with an exemption from
military duty; those who failed to do so would be put to instant death:
a swift stroke to the waist with a sword.

Seasons were set in stone, calendars were fixed as farming regulations; even seeds were subject to laws for sowing. Depending on their
gravity, derelictions of duty attracted anything from a stiff rebuke and
a fine, to a mutilation that would mark a man for life. Performance
was measured meticulously; production was tallied by the day; and
the results, good or bad, were despatched across the country and
reported to the ruler himself. Good harvests and productive weaving
could earn a holiday from tax. Poor harvests or failure to meet a quota
of cotton cloth attracted the white heat of a brand to the face. One
rat-hole discovered in a granary would bring the responsible family a

sharp rebuke, two would carry a fine, three the slicing off of a foot or a nose. As obvious enemies of efficiency, quarrels and complaints were banished; anyone unable to restrain their tongue would feel the sting of the lash, just as their own lack of discipline had stung the order of Qin itself. There were no exceptions. Out in the fields, heads ducked and bodies laboured. Everywhere, branded foreheads and lost limbs became a common sight. Trust vanished from the land.

But while Qin's fortunes often seemed to defy the natural principles that applied to everyone else, even wolves and tigers have their *yin* and *yang* changes. In 338 BCE, a new Qin ruler decided that Shang Yang's 'reforms' had gone too far. Tutored as a child in some of the romantic ideas of the Zhou, as a man, the new ruler saw the merits of *yi* integrity, and *ren* humanity. He also saw the brutality of ideas that had pushed Qin beyond the pale of proper rule, turning it into a state whose silenced scholars were too ashamed to lift their heads. Shang Yang was executed. But while a sigh of relief momentarily passed across the land, with Qin and the other six surviving warring states still battling to the death, little else actually changed. And with Qin constantly on the brink of war, the harvesting of food and the securing of survival could brook no luxuries of finer taste: the registers and the maps remained, the responsibilities of the households stayed fixed, and the people continued to guarantee the order of their own behaviour to the state.

With matters clarified at home, the new ruler felt free to settle the surrounding world. To the north, present-day Mongolia, long walls were raised where nomadic tribes from the steppes constantly worried at the Qin frontier. To the south, where wild forests and mountains beckoned, softer tribes were vanquished and brought under Qin command: from the lands of the people known as the Shu, the Ba and the Yue, emerged provinces that would become known as Sichuan, Jiangsu, Zhejiang and Anhui; on down to the Nanhai tip at the bottom that would one day come to be the province of Guangdong. Vast pantries of southern plenty: fields of rice, rivers of turtles and fish, mines of metal, iron ore and salt, and lacquer-bearing trees; vast scented forests of pine, cypress and bamboo; and herds of elephants and rhinoceroses, which had long since disappeared from the north.

As the new lands were conquered, triumphs of human engineering (the now-shared legacy of millennia of river-taming honed over centuries of war) began to turn Qin's rough pastures into expanding fields. Water being everything to men of the dry west, Qin turned its armies to the redirection of the rivers which splashed so unevenly across its rocky lands. Wherever a mountain was an obstacle, its rock was heated and cooled until it cracked enough to open new channels to the other side. Wherever rivers were prone to flood, levees, built from thousands of bundles of rock wrapped in bamboo, were raised like walls. Qin lands that had once been hostage to the vagaries of an unforgiving nature became watered valleys traversed by rivers as tame as the people themselves.

The rivers tamed, Qin's fields spread and, with its population growing, they filled with labour ready for any task. With war never more than a winter away, every seam of Qin possibility was mined. Across the fields, the growing army of peasant farmers, trained to fight to the last inch of their collectively responsible lives, become a battle-machine-in-waiting. Within the Qin court, minds constantly turned to the destabilising possibilities of whispering campaigns. And while many battles were fought and won, the Qin remained proudest of the intrigue that had put a bookworm at the head of the Zhao army and so had finally won the battle for the Han garrison at Shangdang.

As Qin counted its victories, by 250 BCE, the greatest minds of the old Zhou world were stumped. How could Qin's relentless conquests be brooked? And where on earth was heaven? Enquiring souls began to question everything, not least the thorny question of whether man was essentially good or bad. Looking at the success of Qin's brutality, some nonetheless held stubbornly to the view that man was essentially good and the only way forward was to align oneself with the changes of the *dao* and embrace the Confucian virtues that would, eventually, put everyone on a better path. After hundreds of years of war, though, others were less sure. The Confucian principles of r*en* humanity, *yi* integrity, *li* ritual and *de* virtue were all predicated on the premise that man was essentially good. But what if man was essentially bad? Then Shang Yang's *ding fa yi min* principle of fixing the laws and ordering the people into a single unity through punishment would be a much better idea.

As the warring states continued to battle, more searching souls set off from the crumbling Zhou east to the barbarian west, crossing the mountainous passes into Qin to take a look. Of those who went, many of the younger ones were persuaded by what they saw: fields neatly tended, granaries full, people in orderly awe of their officials, wars won, wealth rising, and not a bandit or robber to be seen. Older spirits, although impressed by the results, held to their stubborn questions about the means by which it had all been achieved. Certainly, they accepted, it was about time that one stopped leaving everything to heaven and began to recognise that heaven's mandate required a strong sense of human responsibility for the order of all. But violence could never be more than destruction, they argued, and coercion was a blind hammering of metal that could never win the love of the people. Qin's methods might seem to offer the promise of success, but if the order of a state set itself against the mandate of heaven, such a state would ultimately be tilting for a fall. Wars might be won, mountains might be moved, but a state unable to hold the hearts of its people could never hope to hold its peace.

One of the many men who travelled to Qin was a district clerk from the southern state of Chu. A scholar who had studied at the feet of one of the greatest Confucian minds, his name was Li Si. Having studied all of the heavenly virtues, like many others, he could not help thinking that while there was a certain scholarly logic to Confucius' ideas, they had clearly failed. Surely, he thought, it was time for the old Zhou world to accept that the future was Qin. As the surviving states of the Zhou world prevaricated, an opportunity to be part of that future beckoned to him – a chance of finding the kind of influencing success which would come only once in every ten thousand years.

As Li Si packed his bags to leave, his teacher gave him a parting lesson: 'True, the old Zhou world is failing. But its failures lie with its unwillingness to take the time to think. And, true, man is essentially weak and needs a responsible ruler to lead the way. But a responsible ruler is not immune from the order of the cosmos itself. Marvel all you like at the temporary triumphs. But do not forget to fear.' To which, the teacher added: 'When seasons are regulated without a sensitivity to nature, when calculations of loss and gain are limited to numbers, when fortunes are measured in deaths, and when men lose the trust that binds them not to life but to each other – those are the times when man should be on his guard. Grasp your chance at fortune if you will; ignore the abstract portents of heaven; but do not forget to keep a ready eye for the *human portents* that can overwhelm even the greatest of worldly triumphs.'

Arriving in the state of Qin in 246 BCE, Li Si seemed to have fallen on the best of times. The previous king had died before his time and, highly unusually, a wildly successful merchant had risen to the heights of advisory power and been appointed as regent to the king's young prince. A native of the state of Wei, the merchant-regent had aspired to add a touch of old Zhou heaven to the new Qin success, recruiting a corps of three thousand Zhou-world scholars to bring more of the older heavenly principles into the Qin court. Li Si was included in the corps, and before a year was out, his talents clear, the merchant-regent made him mentor and guide to the prince.

The years of youth passed; Li Si and the young prince grew ever closer. But by the time the prince came of age, the Qin world was beginning to experience a momentous change. Shocked and insulted by years of the outsider merchant's regent-rule, the nobles of the great Qin ruling family had looked for revenge and found it in a rumour. The young king, it was murmured, was a cuckoo, the bastard son of the old king's wife and a man who was none other than the merchant-regent himself. In 235 BCE, the merchant-regent was sent to his death, and the young king, his position precarious, turned to Li Si. The moment which came 'only once in ten thousand years' had arrived.

Observing the daggers of gossip floating around the court, Li Si's advice to the stunned young king was swift: put the family at arm's length and distract everyone's attention by taking up the unfinished business of the warring states. Whatever rumours might be on the tongues of the restless nobles across the rest of the crumbling Zhou world, Qin was still a force that everyone held in awe. Unlike the other states, Qin was well prepared: fields of willing soldiers stood ready to march. Victory over the six surviving states was only a command away; heaven's mandate would be as easy to win as sweeping dust from the top of a stove. And in the final winning of the war to end all wars, the young king would not only defy his doubters, but would unify the world.

Li Si's exhortations struck their target. Peasants set to martial training, the fields were turned to armies and the armies began to march. This time they would not return until heaven was Qin's. In 230 BCE they turned to the east and the state of Han. With its Shangdang garrison already under Qin control, the rest of Han fell with little effort.

In 225 BCE, Qin looked to the nearer state of Wei and consulted the terrain. Washed by the waters of the Yellow River, its lands were vulnerable to a flood. The Qin army was instructed to deploy the engineering skills used to master its own rivers, and divert the Yellow River from its natural course. Without the shooting of a single arrow, the Wei lands disappeared under muddy waters. Qin had won again.

In 223 BCE, turning to the south and east, Qin went on to conquer the mighty Chu – a state where warning voices had long ago been silenced by the whispering campaigns of Qin (and from where the spirit of a poet-prince who had been exiled for his warnings, would long outlive his time).

In 222 BCE, its path now clear, Qin advanced east and north to meet the state of Zhao. Thirty-two years after the slaughter of Shangdang, the Zhao troops had yet to recover their confidence; a Qin victory was assured. But, never leaving a hostage to fortune, Qin deployed its usual stroke of whispering campaigns. Smoothed with gold and silent daggers, they ensured that the fatal errors of Zhao command were repeated; Zhao was again defeated.

Qin then moved on to the more distant north-eastern state of Yan: a state whose ruler had once despatched his greatest swordsman to kill the king of Qin. The assassination had failed, and when the Qin troops arrived, the wrath of Qin swept like a tide of natural retaliation.

By the end of 222 BCE, all that remained of the six Zhou powers was the very distant state of Qi, settled on the shores of the eastern sea. Flanked until recently by stronger rivals, Qi had never seen Qin as much of a threat. But as Han, Zhao and Wei had fallen, every road into Qi seemed to invite destruction. Scrambling its army, the Qi ruler directed the defending sights of his generals to the most likely origin of a Qin attack – the west. But in 221 BCE, Qin's forces found their way to Qi through the newly conquered lands of Chu to the south and east. Taken by surprise, Qi, the last of the old Zhou states, fell to yet another triumph of Qin calculation.

Li Si's advice had won the day. In fact, it had won the world, as far as Qin knew it. From the deserts of the west to the sea of the east, from the frontiers of the settled north to the tip of the occupied south; all of the lands and all of their people were now Qin. It was a world wider than any the Shang or the Zhou had ever known, with a wealth far greater than even the greatest of anyone's ancestors could have imagined. With it came a unity that had been forged not from the old ideas of heaven and Confucius, but from the brutal back of a western beyond.

———

Reflecting on his conquests, the still-young king of Qin, now master of all, wondered how his victory should be styled. No known expression seemed sufficient to capture the scale of his triumph. The word 'king' hardly hinted at the power he had acquired. In fact, no single title seemed to convey the enormity of what had been achieved.

Ministerial heads were scratched; every annal of the past was consulted. *Huang* was one suggestion: 'yellow', the colour chosen by the emperor who had first united the people along the river of the same name, and a word which, across the intervening millennia had come to mean the great and central pivot of everything. Certainly, it was a step in the right direction. On its own, however, it was not quite evocative enough. *Di* was suggested as an addition – the suffix of a title given to the greatest of the ancestors whose wisdom and labours had raised the original heavenly lands from the mists of the past. Almost, but not quite, thought the king. Perhaps one could add *shi*: first. *Qin Shi Huangdi*, the first and greatest emperor. The highest title that any mortal mind could imagine, and one that suggested that 'the first' would unquestionably be followed by a second, a third and a fourth – and so on, across the ten thousand years over which the Qin dynasty would inevitably rule.

Title settled, the young king's attention, so carefully tutored in the old ideas of the Zhou, turned to the critical matter of finding the imperial alignment with the cosmos that could ensure eternal success. Every secret of the ancient texts was consulted to find the colour, the element and the season that would best express the power of his rule. Shang had been the white metal of autumn, Zhou had been the red fire of summer: conquering Qin would take the gripping black power of winter, with its terrifying ice. Black banners, black pennants, black clothes – black everywhere. And as for the essential magical number that would define the power of the Qin state, with the black ice of winter fixed, this was now easy to see: six, *liu*, a number whose written character when pronounced sounds the same as that for 'running water'. The hats of office were ordered to be six measures high, the carriages of state were to be six measures wide – and every carriage that bore the badge of empire was to be led by six horses. The message was clear: winter had arrived; power was complete; order would be everywhere.

The First Qin Emperor then looked at the vast lands that were now a true empire and considered the challenge of command. The old registers and maps, which had covered the original Qin domain, were stretched to cover the newly conquered lands; and every corner was placed under the power of a military governor. To improve the speed of control, highways were added, built the length and breadth of the new world and bringing everything and everyone within the imperial reach. Goods could now be traded in all directions; taxes could flow from the peripheral edges of order to the centre of power without interruption. Pockets of inconveniently placed people could be moved. Even prisoners could be despatched in an instant to provide labour wherever it was needed.

As the land settled to a greater productive order, a new capital city was raised to match the triumphal nature of the state: close to present-day Xi'an, its name was Xianyang. The central point of a single top-down order, it sat at the apex of all. With the geography of power now set, commands would pass from the centre to the edges as smoothly as grain, and the value of labour would flow swiftly from the edges to the centre. A single world with single standards for everyone to obey. No special circumstances to be bent by any wind; no exceptions to prove a rule. And to ensure that any competing idea could be swiftly extinguished, every noble family from every old corner of the new empire was wrapped in an icy embrace and escorted to a new palace home – in Xianyang.

Empire and capital ordered, the remaining differences of the old Zhou world were hammered to a single iron die. Weights and measures, long since fixed in Qin, were set as standards to be observed across the new imperial lands. Coins were carved to a single Qin image. Taxes were paid with a common currency. The ruts of roads followed the single width (six measures) of the Qin carriage. Language was unified: a single spoken tongue with a single script of commands, which no one, however far away, could argue they had not been able to read and understand.

Words put in their place, the occupations of the people followed suit. With the greatest human purposes being the tilling of fields and the fighting of battles, farmers and soldiers were ranked at the top. The ordering of trade being a matter for the state, and merchants being an untrustworthy distraction from imperial business, the purveyors of goods not useful to the First Emperor were despatched to the chilling edges of the empire. As was every other useless person who failed to deliver a value to the state – including any independent minds that had not already been excised from public life. The privileged few permitted to remain and trade within the Qin cities found themselves under constant watch. In the markets, prices were fixed, and towers were raised so that every transaction could be observed by official eyes; brands were kept ready for anyone who failed to obey.

As the grids of Qin were flung like a net across the rest of what must surely be a grateful world, the First Emperor decided that it was now time to observe the ancient rituals and present his credentials to heaven and the ancestors. In 219 BCE, following in the footsteps of the ancient Zhou (and indeed the the Shang before them), he proceeded north and east to the greatest mountain of all: Mount Tai. The peak which had been declared by ancient shamans to be the highest intermediary between heaven and earth; the point at which every great emperor marked the triumph of his rule.

Raising his sacrifices, the First Emperor duly announced the glory of Qin to the skies. And, lest heaven be tempted to forget the spectacular accomplishments of its newest emperor, he paused to inscribe his achievements upon a rock: order fixed with laws and measures, chaos quelled, peace and stability for the black-haired people; heaven established on earth. The messages clearly communicated, the First Emperor and new Son of Heaven journeyed on across his world, seeking out the other mountains his shamans had told him would connect a ruler directly with heaven above.

Returning back to earth (eventually) there was always something to do – even with an army for a population. There were roads, palaces and dams to be built, ditches to be dug, mountains to be moved and canals to be carved, like veins, into the land. Riding a tiger and flogging the sun, the First Emperor found that there were never enough days in a year to get everything done; from time to time, he even had to shout at the moon. And then, up at the northern edge of the world, a troublesome tribe of nomads appeared – seemingly unaware that the world was now under the order of an imperial winter. The emperor's most trusted general was despatched to bring the nomads up to date, with hundreds of thousands of men commanded to follow him and raise a single, long wall of four thousand kilometres from beaten earth and stones. Exposed to some of the world's greatest extremes of heat and cold, the bones of many fell by its side, never to leave. Meanwhile, in the south, it seemed that other tribes had also not yet understood that heaven had arrived. More generals were despatched to announce the news, each accompanied by an army, all charged with building occupying garrisons to make sure that everyone was clear.

Back in the capital of Xianyang, more palaces of splendour were being raised, many with terraces touching the clouds, and all designed to replicate heaven on earth. A little to the west, a vast park of palaces appeared: protected by two mountains serving as gates, and connected by a suspension bridge in the image of the Milky Way, to carry the emperor from one sparkling palace to the next. And to the northeast of the city, another Xianyang continued to expand, this one an underground masterpiece populated with soldiers, horses, and chariots, and designed to host the mortal remains of the emperor in the unlikely event that he should die.

As the First Emperor had been proclaiming the orderly end to any history other than that of the Qin, however, ill winds were gathering close to home. Earlier, clumsy, attempts at assassination had failed to kill, but they had, nonetheless, hit a mark: as far as the First Emperor could see, the world was full of conspiring minds and, quite possibly, some very malevolent spirits. Summoned to advise, tamed shamans could only agree – suggesting that it would be best if the emperor were not seen. Walkways were elevated, imperial pavilions and roads were walled: no expense was spared nor punishment for any breach. Anyone even suspected of revealing the movements of the emperor would be sliced in two without a question. And as the walls went up around the First Emperor, any walls that stood elsewhere in the city were ordered to be pulled down. Security depended upon the people's buildings being open for all to see, with secrecy reserved for the emperor alone.

The costs were enormous and the labour so great that even the punishments struggled to keep pace. Branded faces appeared everywhere; lost feet and missing noses took no one by surprise. Honest men found that they could not help but break laws that were impossible to keep: many became outlaws by default.

Conveyed along covered roads, carried across elevated walkways, the First Emperor seemed oblivious to the terror around him. Did he not know or did he not care? Few had the courage to ask. But in the privileged debates of his courtly scholars, a risky comment was occasionally advanced. And so it was that in 213 BCE, a scholarly Confucian from Qi, who had survived the conquest of his fallen state, stood up and suggested that if the emperor wanted to be secure in his empire both he and Li Si, now chief minister, might like to gaze back to the lessons of the past. Order was clearly desirable; hierarchies were obviously important. But while a world of single-minded commands blindly issued without regard to the qualities of *ren* humanity, *yi* integrity, *li* ritual, *de* virtue or even *zhi* knowledge might work for a time, it was evident to anyone with eyes to see that a protracted tyranny could only end in tears. There was also the matter of the greater imperial family to consider: a family which, in the opinion of the scholar, the emperor had foolishly set aside.

A master, like all Confucians, of the history books, the scholar had gone on to suggest that the First Emperor had only to consult the story of the ancient defeat of the Shang by the Zhou to realise that eventually the power of human hearts would out. Men might be bad, but Confucius had a point: virtues were of value. To which he added that families were a treasure too. With the empire at peace, perhaps the First Emperor might like to invite his own relations to return to serve the imperial state.

Responding on the First Emperor's behalf, Li Si was quick to snap: 'Study the past to guide the present? What kind of claptrap are you peddling?' To which he added that no ancestor had ever scaled the heights of human triumph by looking back to the past, and if the scholars had not understood that simple point, what on earth must be going on in the country at large? Announcing that it was time for a new communications policy, Li Si declared that anyone using the past to criticise the present should be put to death, along with their immediate relatives, the common blood obviously carrying a dangerous strain.

In addition, with the scholars daring to question the roots of risk, every home should be commanded to burn its books, with the exception of useful works on agriculture, medicine and divination, of which one copy of each could be kept. Confucian scholars were buried, the bamboo burned and Qin fell silent.

A year later, in 212 BCE, the emperor, now aged forty-seven, turned to a matter that had long troubled his heart: immortality and the importance of perpetuating his imperial life. Guided by his shamans, fortunes had been spent on journeys to find a paradise known as Penglai. Set in misty eastern islands, roughly in the region of present-day Japan, Penglai was thought to be the home of eight immortals who held the secret of eternal life. Exploring boats were stuffed with virgins – far more likely than soldiers to be able to tempt the secret of eternity from the immortals. But not a drop of the secret elixir ever made its way back to Xianyang. Meanwhile, every year, the First Emperor's tomb was getting bigger, even as the emperor himself advanced in age: if the shamans' journeys did not find the elixir soon, the emperor might have to occupy the magnificent underworld he had created. One shaman-captain, returning from a particularly promising (and expensive) mission without the promised secret, blamed his failure on a giant sea monster that had suddenly reared out of the sea. Given another ship and a company of crossbowmen, he was told to make sure that this time they reached their destination. Reading their own omens, however, and fearing for the worst, the fastest of the remaining shamans fled from Xianyang, and the shaman-captain set sail, never to return. Slower others, including hundreds of equally unreliable scholars who had failed to burn their books, found themselves buried alive. Only the First Emperor's son and heir dared to raise a question: 'It seems a little extreme', the young prince suggested: 'Surely even heaven should have a heart.' Despatching his oldest son and heir to the wintry northern frontier with an order to apply his energies to the building of the Long Wall, the First Emperor's rebuke was sharp and swift: 'The desert sands and the freezing steppes would be delighted to listen to your opinions.'

The punishment clear, the First Emperor returned to the matter of his own life and death. With the promised elixir of immortality still eluding his grasp, the sea monster that had thwarted the most promising of his missions was now occupying his dreams. Deciding to send his cold-blooded nemesis to a watery grave, in the summer of 210 BCE, crossbows assembled, the First Emperor led an imperial progress to the coast. No longer trusting his scholarly ministers, and with his eldest son and greatest general building the Long Wall far to the north, he was accompanied only by his palace guards, favourite eunuchs, a younger son and Li Si. When a giant fish was duly observed, it was executed. But in the days that followed, it seemed that the spirit of the fish had fixed upon revenge. A minor illness became a fever, and immortality began to slip beyond reach. An imperial letter was dictated to order the return of his oldest son and heir. Within a week, in the fire of a Zhou summer, the First Emperor fell victim to the winter of death, leaving the letter confirming that his eldest son should inherit the empire in the folds of his favourite eunuch's robe.

Secrecy being everything, Li Si, together with the First Emperor's favourite eunuch and the younger son, decided that it might be easier if no one knew that the First Emperor was dead. And much easier if the country's greatest general and the outspoken heir were kept out of the complicated picture. Letters were written in the name of the now-dead First Emperor commanding the general and the heir to take their own lives.

Trusting the soothing words of the eunuch and Li Si, confident that the punishments of the law would guard the throne against any inconvenient questions, the younger son, now 'Second Emperor', directed his thoughts to heaven-on-earth and redoubled the building of everything – with no expense spared. The next two years saw rising costs, accompanying taxes, a scarcity of food, an increase in punishments, and so many executions (as arbitrary as they were final) that they became a daily fact of life. Backs almost broken, those who could fled to the mountains and the forests. Those who could not struggled on until the laws became impossible to obey. Faced with a choice between death by execution for a duty failed, or flight to a rebellion that might succeed, many chose the latter. It was not long before the Qin's labouring peasants began to march to colours of their own.

Sheltered in the covered walkways of his father's cities, and with everyone who ventured a contrary opinion swiftly executed, the Second Emperor might not have known the risks he was taking. Young and new to power, he was easily persuaded by Li Si and the eunuch to preserve his dignity by avoiding any ministers who might be inclined to tell him the truth. Meanwhile, out in the open streets, rebels began to rise and blood to run. Li Si's thoughts belatedly turned to the parting advice of his teacher so many decades ago: 'Beware the human portents.' But it was already too late: a whispered word from the eunuch led the credulous Second Emperor to send Li Si first to prison and then to a public dismemberment of himself and all his family.

By 207 BCE, the rebels were so much at large that the state of Qin was struggling to defend the capital of Xianyang, let alone the empire. With the young Second Emperor now increasingly asking questions, the eunuch despatched him to a death disguised as suicide, and replaced him with a younger sibling – the 'Third Emperor'. Younger he might have been, but with the human portents now obviously at large, he was not entirely blind. In 206 BCE, with the wider empire lost, a battalion of rebels threatened the gates of Xianyang, and the last Qin ruler – no emperor now – acknowledged the limits of his father's wintry order. Placing a simple rope around his neck, seating himself in a plain white carriage, the young man rode out of the palace and delivered the imperial seal into the hands of the rebels' leader.

The single heart of the state had been broken – and with it, the single will had fallen, too. Where would heaven go next?

PART 2
DREAMS

Heaven does not have two suns; the people do not have two kings.

Mencius (372 – 289 BCE)

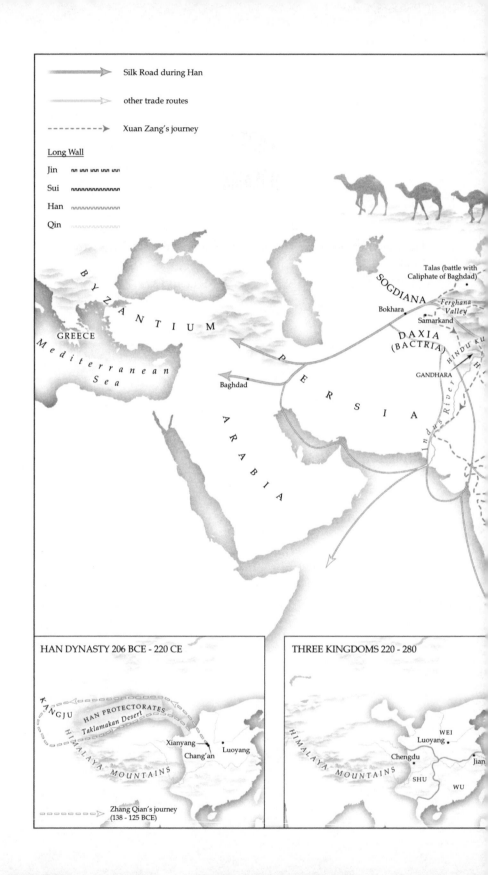

Silk Road during Han

other trade routes

Xuan Zang's journey

Long Wall

Jin

Sui

Han

Qin

BYZANTIUM

GREECE

Mediterranean Sea

ARABIA

PERSIA

Baghdad

SOGDIANA

Talas (battle with Caliphate of Baghdad)

Bokhara

Ferghana Valley

Samarkand

DAXIA (BACTRIA)

GANDHARA

HINDU KU

Indus River

HAN DYNASTY 206 BCE - 220 CE

KANGJU

HAN PROTECTORATES

Taklamakan Desert

HIMALAYA MOUNTAINS

Xianyang

Chang'an

Luoyang

Zhang Qian's journey
(138 - 125 BCE)

THREE KINGDOMS 220 - 280

HIMALAYA MOUNTAINS

WEI

Luoyang

Chengdu

Jian

SHU

WU

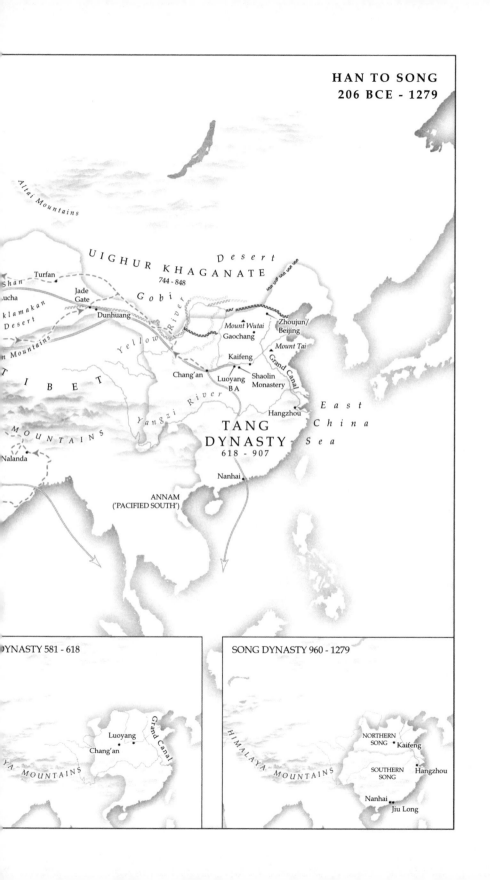

Altai Mountains

U I G H U R   K H A G A N A T E
744 - 848

Desert

Turfan

Jade
Gate

Gobi

Shan

ucha

Dunhuang

klamakan
Desert

Yellow River

n Mountains

T I B E T

Mount Wutai
Gaochang

Zhoujun/
Beijing

Mount Tai

Kaifeng

Grand Canal

Chang'an

Luoyang
BA

Shaolin
Monastery

Yangzi River

M O U N T A I N S

Hangzhou

E a s t

C h i n a

S e a

Nalanda

**TANG
DYNASTY**
618 - 907

Nanhai

ANNAM
('PACIFIED SOUTH')

)YNASTY 581 - 618

Luoyang

Chang'an

Grand Canal

YA MOUNTAINS

SONG DYNASTY 960 - 1279

HIMALAYA MOUNTAINS

NORTHERN
SONG

Kaifeng

SOUTHERN
SONG

Hangzhou

Nanhai

Jiu Long

CHAPTER 1

ONE HEAVEN, ONE EARTH

If one grasps the One and does not lose it, one can be lord of
the ten thousand things.

> *The Guanzi* (compilation of older texts, named
> after Guan Zong, 720 – 645 BCE)

A HINT OF TURKISH PASTRY touched the early afternoon air. Up
and down the wide streets, shops offered passers-by an array of
treasures while teahouses invited conversations. Camels wandered
with a lazy air. Falcons, perched on brocaded arms, flashed talons fit
for a hunt. Heavenly horses, fresh from the Ferghana valley of the far
north-west, were paraded for a price; rich with trade, many could afford
it. Last week's tiger had been sold, but rumour had it that another was
on its way. Wrapped jackets of white cotton, well-worn by the people
at large, rubbed past the robes of officials where red or green was
outranked by blue, with neat caps completing the greater attire. And
in everyone's midst flashed coats of many colours, swirling skirts and
leopard-skin hats, all marking out their wearers as men of a different
breed.

Narrow lanes beckoned with signs proclaiming special wares for
sale, thronged with Sogdians who knew the stuff of their trades.
A turn to the west and a lane of Byzantine threads would dull the
sounds of the market with damasks that tore at the heart. A few steps
further, and purple-robed monks offered a Buddhist fairyland: scrolls
of paradise illuminated with divine Himalayan creatures sitting on
spreading pink lotuses; bodhisattva saints carved from amber; and
the coral trees of utopian gardens bedecked with brilliant gems.
Another step, and stands of boxes from Arabia opened up a haze of
perfumes and powders: plumes of myrrh and puffs of frankincense. A
turn to the north, and on stall after stall, the wonders of the steppes
appeared: purple forest furs, red deerskin boots, wild horsehides, and

heavy saddles of scarlet felt; tucked in a corner, there were even leopard tails, charged with the power to ward off even the most stubborn spirits.

On and on, the market maze continued. Down a lane, the musical instruments of Kucha, conjuring up wild dances, were offered for sale by men with high noses and green eyes. Left, and lapis lazuli appeared from Khotan. Right, and gold sparkled from the princely kingdom of Tibet. Round a corner, books and maps appeared, stirring everyone's imagination with Sanskrit stories inked in Chinese characters, and routes to the west marked along a string of oasis states. On a little further, and heavenly jades from beyond the singing sands of the Taklamakan desert would come into view, followed by mountains of pearls from the shores of Persia, and phosphorescent gems from who knew where. Between it all, cardamom from Kashmir, peaches from Samarkand, and strings of cash counted by Turkish-speaking Uighur lenders whose blue eyes flashed like gems, and whose talents with money smoothed everyone's trade.

Streets stepped, lanes explored, treasures acquired from the corners of the earth: time passed like a flash of silver. Eventually, the sun began to dip and the drums of dusk began their tattoo. The market gates closing, merchants and customers wended their way into the evening and the city at large. Chang'an in the early Tang dynasty, seven hundred years after some of the foreigners had begun to count the years following their Christ: the city of eternal peace; the heart of China; the unifying centre of the world.

The concept of 'unifying everywhere' had all begun with horse-borne nomads worrying at the northern walls (although some would later wonder whether it was the building of the walls in the first place that had really caused the problem). A distraction for as long as anyone could remember, the barbarians had endlessly tried to thrust their wild ideas of a roaming trade into the settled Yellow River lands, with roving pillage their resort whenever the Yellow River people had refused to play their game. What to do with a people who refused the idea of a centrifugal civilising sun and rejected the tradition of tribute paid from the edges of order to the centre, threatening to unsettle everything? When battles had failed, walls had seemed the obvious answer.

Unifying the world under his black wintry watch, the First Qin Emperor had looked at the northern walls he had inherited with his conquests and decided that they must match the singular strength of his own iron will. Sending his most trusted general to push the barbarians back to the grassland steppes where they clearly belonged, he had directed the army to raise the greatest wall ever imagined. Strung with towers, punctuated with garrisons, constantly built and rebuilt, great though it might have been, the wall was named the *Chang Cheng*, the Long Wall, and remained a formidable barrier for as long as the First Emperor ruled the world. But when the emperor's wall-building general and his eldest son had been treacherously dismissed to their deaths, the army, like so much of the rest of Qin, had crumbled; the walls had followed suit.

Watching the collapse of Qin from the steppes above, it was not long before strikes of galloping nomads flashed into the northern lands, pillaging as they went. And it was not much longer before the wealth captured from the settled lands opened an opportunity for an ambitious horseman to sweep across the vast steppes and unite some of the myriad tribes into a mounted federation of horse-borne power. Three million strong, riding under the command of a man they called the 'Heavenly Wolf', they were known to the terrified Yellow River people as the Xiongnu. Looking down at the settled lands below them, the Xiongnu themselves saw one of many sparkling gems in a world which, seen from the spreading roof of everywhere, reached farther than anyone in the settled lands could ever have imagined: to the north and east as far as the ice-flocked seas, and to western places which other worlds would come to know as India, Persia, Greece, and Rome.

The Yellow River people, however, had little time for imagining. After the end of the First Qin Emperor, rebels had battled back and forth, not only sacking the once-iron state, but charging against each other too. Year after year, the rubble had risen until, in 202 BCE a rebel named Liu Bang emerged triumphant. A minor official in the twilight of Qin, he had been charged with the custody of a group of convicts when some escaped. Balancing the certainty that he would be executed for his carelessness against the possibility that, as a rebel, he might survive, Liu Bang chose survival. Founding his own band of men, he eventually defeated every other rebel contender and inherited the wreckage of Qin. Crops crushed underfoot, pavilions destroyed, one of the most pressing of his victory tasks was to return the peasants to the fields upon which everyone's fortunes had always depended.

Liu Bang set his star for a restoration of unity and gave his family the dynastic name 'Han', after the southern district of Hanzhong where he had built his strength. Styling himself 'Gaozu' (High Ancestor) to ground his rule in the golden past, he welcomed back the surviving Confucian scholars. Brutally silenced by Qin, they were happy to accept a renaissance of the romantic Zhou idea that the mandate to rule was issued from heaven. Having vanquished the black waters of Qin, Liu Bang then took the fire of summer as his element, with red the colour of all. Raising a new capital – not far from Qin's secretive city of Xianyang – he named it Chang'an, Eternal Peace.

Proclaiming a golden age and rebuilding a city were, however, the least of Liu Bang's challenges. Far harder were the questions of what kind of state he was going to rule, and what, given the fraying edges of the old Qin empire, he was going to do about the age-old problem of the northern barbarians.

Looking, as tradition ordered, to the lessons of the past, Liu Bang realised that they pointed, unhelpfully, in two different directions. The first, the model of the Zhou, offered a vision of a heavenly kingdom across the lands inherited from the Yellow Emperor, all governed by a Son of Heaven. Under this model, the Son of Heaven conducted the delicate balancing of a constantly changing cosmos, supported by a body of ministers, officials and scholars whose own spirits, and households, were guided by the Confucian qualities from which order naturally flowed. The second, the model of Qin, presented a vision of the same lands as the kingdom of a ruler who, although mindful of the heavenly power, discharged an earthly responsibility to deliver order through a set of laws applied with an iron hand. The contrast of the two was striking. The soft world of the Zhou had dreamt of harmony and lasted eight hundred years, although only the first two hundred had been truly 'golden', with the last six hundred spiralling through a chaos of human ambition into the catastrophic destruction of the warring states and their war of all against all. The iron world of Qin had seen a spectacular rise from dust to triumph, culminating in twenty years of unity grounded in terror, only to collapse from within. Each clearly had its advantages, but both had fallen. While the old Zhou idea of a heavenly order based on cosmic changes and human virtue had much to recommend it, it had failed to avert the rise of Qin. And while Qin had understood that to govern an empire man, like nature, must be tamed, it had failed to grasp the risk that when an iron will casts its people as prisoners, the people will eventually rebel.

Confronted with two seemingly irreconcilable alternatives, Liu Bang looked again. While the Duke of Zhou might have had the luxury of believing men to be good, everyone's experiences over the past six hundred years had shown that goodness was more a matter of potential that could be realised only if laws and punishments were in place. It was obvious that the people preferred the softer Zhou ideas; and it was clear that laws and punishments were essential to order. Accordingly, Liu Bang decided that the state of Han would be formally fashioned after the Zhou *and* that laws and punishments would continue; the laws and the punishments would be a little less extreme but they would be reinforced with an imperial interpretation of what Confucius had really meant. At the centre of the model would be the pursuit of the *dao* as the particular and exclusive task of the emperor, to which would be added an unquestioning acknowledgement that an effective Confucian rule should be touched with a flash of steel. *Ren*, humanity, would be dedicated to the single ideal of heaven as an order of all, rather than any individual ideas of good or bad. *Yi*, integrity, would be a formal correlation of names and purposes (let the ruler be the ruler, the subject the subject, the father the father, and the son the son), rather than any matter of personal judgement. *Li*, ritual, would ensure that actions taken would be appropriate within the wider context of the order of the state rather than by reference to any local ambition. The *jia* bonds of family, fixed with the *xiao* duties of filial piety, would ensure that everyone was bound to the imperial centre, with a hierarchy of of order flowing from the Son of Heaven at the top, through the fathers and their families below.

With the Confucian rule of the Han underpinned by the more practical principles of Qin, the Son of Heaven would be the greatest power on earth. And while Liu Bang's management of heaven and earth would be supported by a bureaucracy of scholars, the scholars would come not only from the ranks of the Confucians but from the ranks of the realists who had been schooled in the Qin's art of crafting effective laws. Confucian or Qin, every scholarly bureaucrat would keep to his particular name and place, with the full force of the law and its severe punishments applied to anyone who stepped out of their appointed line. Of course, the laws and punishments were not quite what Confucius had had in mind, but since the First Emperor had burned the books that told everyone what Confucius had actually said, what did it really matter? More importantly, who was there to make a fuss?

Liu Bang then turned to the northern edges of the once-Qin empire, badly battered by the end-of-Qin rebellions and now threatened, once again, by the nomadic barbarians. With the fields returned to their harvests and the mulberry trees again supporting the silk-producing worms, the Heavenly Wolf's nomadic horsemen had been raiding ever deeper into the resettling lands. Of course, the grain and the bolts of silk could have been offered for sale on open markets. But, keenly aware of the heavenly mandate on his shoulders, Liu Bang preferred to keep to the settled order: fixed farming for all, with any disorderly trade limited to the exchange of necessities across the land, all carefully controlled by the Son of Heaven, in the faithful discharge of his duty to balance the harmonies of everything.

Liu Bang's refusal to contemplate a wider trade left the fields vulnerable to the pillaging forces of the Heavenly Wolf. Harvests were seized, villages set alight, farmers and their families were carried off to the steppes as a warning to the rest. Battling against men whose horses, faster than the wind, seemed to have come from heaven itself, the Han armies struggled to hold their lines.

Reluctantly reviewing the position, Liu Bang eventually warmed to the idea of an 'ordered' trade. Han diplomats were sent north to conclude a treaty: silk, grain and wine were to flow up to the Xiongnu; horses, camels and sheep were to come down to the Han. Aware of his heavenly responsibilities, and thinking in the longer term, Liu Bang also suggested that Han princesses might be sent as gifts of brides for steppe warriors who, becoming mothers of steppe children, would raise a new generation of barbarians who would prefer the settled world.

Time passed and Xiongnu horses trickled south, accompanied by men accomplished in the extraordinary skill of shooting arrows from the saddle. As the Han delighted in their new treasures, successive Xiongnu leaders began to consolidate their steppe-wide power by emulating the settled glory of their southern neighbour. Modelled on Chinese cities, great camps of martial tents were raised, albeit with the Xiongnu warning their people against the seductive comforts of a settled life: comforts that no expanse of steppe would, ever be able to support and which would gradually eat away at the fighting skills of a force honed by the constant hunt of the wolf.

More time passed, memories faded, and with horses and archery skills now under their belts, the Han began to wonder if the bargain had been a mistake. Too much silk for too few horses; princesses going north but steppe-born children still behaving like wolves; and a treaty which had been interpreted by the barbarians as being between themselves as masters and the heavenly Han as Xiongnu vassals, even as the obligations of the treaty seemed to be written in dust. When signing the treaty, the Xiongnu had presented themselves as a confederation: as solid as the settled Han. But whenever any question arose about a detail of the terms, the 'solid' confederation scattered into disparate hordes of unruly tribes. Some of the emperor's advisers suggested that it was time to think again. Others, particularly the few Han diplomats and generals who had personal experience of the steppes, argued for caution. Across the entire roof of the world, they warned, no one dared brave the force of the Xiongnu's wrath.

For a time, caution prevailed. But as the decades and succeeding emperors passed, the influence of the generals and the diplomats began to float away, like clouds on a wind. Trade from the Han lands began to slow: fewer bolts of silk, lighter loads of grain, and soon even the princesses stayed at home. As the stream of treasure waned, Xiongnu tempers frayed. The raids returned and, pushing ever deeper into the Yellow River lands, harvests again began to vanish, while villages quaked with fear. By 140 BCE, the barbarian terrors to the north had forced the Han diplomats to return ten times to renegotiate the treaty. Each time, the 'renegotiation' had simply increased the pile of tribute (silk, grain and wine) moving from Han south to Xiongnu north, with new generations of Han princesses following in its wake. With every failed negotiation, the empire's scholarly officials directed the Han generals to consult their arts of war and find the martial strategy that would finally restore heaven's order on earth.

The most preferred of the strategies advanced was to divide the barbarians so that they attacked each other. This could most easily be achieved by chipping away at the Xiongnu's 'federation'. Individual treaties offered trade to the smaller tribes in return for a promise to ride against their barbarian brothers whenever the Xiongnu swept down on the fields of the Han. Some thought this an excellent idea. Others, including generals who had served at the front, were less sure. With Han soldiers constantly exposed to death, and the outcome of any battle never more than yet another renegotiation of the relationship between the settled and the barbarian worlds, the generals had long ago concluded that the real question was of the very nature of heaven and earth. Given the force of the barbarians, it was a question that needed far more careful consideration.

Certainly, the experiences of the last two thousand years had shown that the idea of settled fields and a ruling son who was constantly attentive to heaven's cosmic changes was better than anything else known on earth. It was equally clear, though, that each time the Han opened trade with the barbarians, the pillaging stopped and peace returned. Must a heavenly order turn its face against a wider trade from which everyone seemed to benefit? Confucius' cascading hierarchy of relationships seemed to say that there could be only one son at the top. But if one looked further back, cosmic minds had long argued that heaven's order lay not in a single top-down human will, but in a more accommodating meditation on the complicated order of nature. From the earliest shamans who had stepped away from glittering opportunities to advise kings, to the spirit of Laozi with his *Dao De Jing* and the arguments of Zhuangzi about crooked paths, the lands around the Yellow River had been full of men who insisted that order was much greater and more complex than forcing a ruling will upon everything in sight. Surely, the generals argued, the unity of heaven and earth lay in the power of an idea, not in the force of a fight.

The bureaucracy shocked at the heresy of the argument, Confucian scholars painted black memorials to the emperor, pointing to the cowardice of the generals as the true cause of all the trouble.

In 141 BCE, imperial patience snapped. A new emperor had come to the throne (one who would come to be known as 'Wudi', the 'Martial Emperor') and decided that the cost of the trade, including the raids and the battles, was now beyond all bearing. The Xiongnu barbarians were not only destroying fields but sitting in tight control of rising silk routes flowing west, across the roof of the world, to distant lands the Han could only dream of. Determined to end the barbarian challenge to heaven's authority, the Martial Emperor moved to restore the military architecture of Qin. Roads to the north were repaired; walls with their watchtowers were reinforced; and, thanks to the trade in Xiongnu horses, the empire's army was strengthened with a grand new cavalry. Declaring that the world would be turned to the order of the heavenly lands, in 134 BCE, the first of a series of martial campaigns was launched.

The terrain was tough, but the enemy was tougher. Thousands died, the imperial treasury was drained, and the Martial Emperor soon realised that pushing the Xiongnu back to their own wild world would be a long battle. Standing firm on his military position though, he decided to push forward with the strategy of dividing the barbarians by exploring the possibility of another front to the north and west, in a land rumoured to be home to a warrior tribe just as anxious as the Han to push the Xiongnu federation off their pedestal of the steppes. The name of the land was Kangju, and the Martial Emperor decided to send a trusted military man to discover whether there might indeed be such a distant ally to be found. The man he chose was Zhang Qian: a military officer whose battling career had taken him up to the steppes and brought him closer than any other to the Xiongnu foe.

Setting off in a camel caravan, Zhang Qian journeyed beyond the heavenly limits of the Kunlun Mountains to the west, driving deep into Xiongnu territory. A world of deserts as well as grassland steppes, it was not long before the caravan lost its way – and not much longer before Zhang Qian was captured by the Xiongnu. Ten years a captive, Zhang Qian eventually escaped and continued his search for the mysterious Kangju ally, who might turn the barbarian tide. Skirting the deadly Taklamakan desert, whose *kara buran*, black storms, buried men alive, and edging around formidable mountains, Zhang Qian finally reached Kucha, first in the line of oasis states known to thread across the roof of the world. From Kucha, he found his way to Ferghana, home of horses so sleek and strong that they could only be described as 'heavenly'. From Ferghana, he went on to Daxia, the Bactrian kingdom founded by the Greeks and awash with stories of a Sindhu land around an Indus river (present day Pakistan, once part of India) below.

From Daxia, on to Sogdiana, with its trading states of Bokhara and Samarkand, and the kingdom of Kangju. There, the Kangju ruler confirmed that the nomadic people who roamed his lands did indeed include the sought-after tribe. But, he added, the spark of the rebellion they had tried for years to ignite had long ago blown out: Zhang Qian was ten years too late.

Retracing his steps past the formidable deserts and the blockading mountains, Zhang returned to his emperor in 125 BCE and admitted defeat. Though disappointed, the Martial Emperor realised that, in his failure, Zhang Qian might have found the solution to the question of how to manage the wider world. True, he had failed in his goal; but he had opened up lands beyond the Kunlun Mountains and found the routes of trade. The Xiongnu were still a powerful threat, but heaven's reach had been significantly expanded. There was indeed a bigger earth, and it was high time that heaven's appointed son stretched his order across it.

Initially, it seemed like a good idea. But it soon became clear that stretching the heavenly lands opened up the cavernous 'Confucian-Qin' compromise on which Liu Bang had founded the Han idea of the state. For the Confucian scholars, the matter of order was a simple question of heavenly-imperial command and control. Technically, this was the prerogative of the emperor but, given the complexity of 'the changes' and the many 'things' that had to be 'investigated' in these times of complicated empires, it would be delegated to the Confucians. For the Qin scholars though, 'legalists' charged with crafting clear laws and strict punishments, the matter was anything but simple: how could unity be achieved with precision over deserts and mountains that stretched further than the eye could see?

With the emperor clear that he wanted to unify the world, any question of whether or not the Han armies should advance to the west had already been answered. But how was success to be achieved? Once again the past was consulted and, once again, a compromise seemed to offer the best solution. An empire that included the vast west would be too big for the Son of Heaven to manage singlehandedly, but the Son of Heaven had many relatives and trusted military advisers to whom, following the example of the Duke of Zhou, he could give fiefdoms. And where the empire was girded with clear laws, heaven's territory could surely be successfully stretched.

The matter of unifying the world now settled, one critical question remained: who would make the laws for the advance to the west and, indeed, everything else in the heavenly lands? Those closest to the Confucian tradition argued that they should be written by Confucian scholars, who understood the ever-changing mind of heaven best. Those of the Qin tradition of legalists, schooled in crafting clear laws and strict punishments with nothing left to anyone's discretion or imagination, argued that the laws should be set out by those scholars whose mastery of law-making gave them the greatest talent for fixing things in writing.

Certainly the legalist Qin tradition had the advantage of clear commands: highly appealing to any busy emperor. But, as it transpired, the Confucians had the advantage of every emperor's greatest fear: the wrath that followed a failure of heavenly duty. Every time the rains failed, an earthquake struck, the Yellow River changed its course, or a comet flashed across the sky, the Confucian scholars rushed to their brushes and inked a memorial to the emperor, advising him that heaven was unhappy. And if heaven was unhappy, it could only be because heaven's son had failed to apply the right policies. The duty to balance the cosmos was personal to the emperor: a constant and unwavering obligation to ensure that the actions of man and the changes of nature were properly aligned. A momentous task for one man, it was a duty that even the greatest emperor could only discharge with the loyal support of a bureaucracy of Confucian scholars. Looking fearfully up at the unpredictable skies, the Martial Emperor had little choice but to agree with the Confucians.

Charged with the emperor's confidence, the Confucian scholars recommended that a new Hall of Light be constructed to ensure the highest and brightest reflection of the cosmos possible on earth. Centred on the Pole Star, it would be the point at which heaven and earth came together in the person of the Son of Heaven, and the point from which the Son of Heaven would issue the commands that would bring all together in a unity of everything, everywhere. Modelled on the relationship between the sun and the earth, the mystical numbers of Fuxi's magic square were to be embedded in every rafter. And from terraces open to the stars, the emperor's advisers would scour the skies with their eyes and make their recommendations.

The Martial Emperor raised the new and greater Hall of Light without delay. No sooner had it had been constructed, though, than it became clear that a new kind of army would also be required. Not more of the cowardly generals who lobbied for trade, but an army of scholars who, in helping their emperor balance the weighty matters of heaven and earth, would 'investigate everything' through a careful consultation of the written word. For this, the scholars argued, a heavenly library would also be required, with a large and constantly expanding number of heavenly books – composed, of course, by the Confucians. Once again, the Martial Emperor could only agree.

Without a moment to lose, the new Confucian army picked up its brushes, and ink was splashed on bamboo. Soon, confident interpretations of everything Confucius had ever said (or might have said) appeared on the library's shelves. To these were added a surprising stream of 'original' texts, which seemed to have re-appeared from the past. Some were described as having miraculously survived the flames of Qin, hidden within the walls of scholarly households. Others were presented as faithful transcripts of conversations with Confucius, passed down from fathers to sons over a mere three hundred years. The texts of the 'recovered' works varied, but the ones most valued by the emperor were those that attached the greatest weight to laws and punishments – albeit appearing under a reassuringly Confucian title.

Under the spreading eaves of the new Hall of Light and its accompanying library, the Confucian ink spread and Confucian knowledge swelled. Then came the question of how a reliable supply of recruits might be found to guarantee the scholarly reserves necessary to maintain the strength of the new Confucian army. The answer was not long in coming. In 124 BCE, a scholar suggested that a Grand Academy might serve a valuable purpose, and a class of fifty was admitted for a course of study that would equip them to hold office in the heavenly bureaucracy. With every year that passed, the Confucian army expanded, within the Grand Academy and increasingly outside, as alumni took over the most powerful imperial positions. And as the Confucian army expanded, so did the number of interpretative Confucian texts – and with them, the Han's Confucian idea that the only topic worth pursuing was the unity of everything. And with the question of unity clearly being something which only Confucian-trained bureaucrats could master, the idea that the Son of Heaven could discharge his duties by waiting for wild tribes of horsemen to see the error of their ways was confirmed as being nothing but the product of a military cowardice. Far from the bureaucrats getting too big for their boots, as the generals had so foolishly argued, the bureaucratic boots were obviously not big enough.

With everyone's duties now Confucianly settled, the Martial Emperor turned to the ordering of heaven's earth. Fortunately, it looked as if heaven itself had understood that the northern barbarians were a problem, and the power of the Xiongnu seemed to be on the wane. The Han armies pushed forward, and the Long Wall, with its watchtowers, was stretched ever further towards the west. Corps of Han diplomats were then dispatched to follow in Zhang Qian's footsteps, offering treaties of tribute and trade to the oasis states across the roof of the world. The north at last seeming to bend to his will, the Martial Emperor turned his thoughts to the south.

Softer than the north, and already opened once by Qin, the southern lands spread below that of another great river, flowing parallel to the Yellow River through the lands of present-day Sichuan to coasts swept by far-off tropical seas – the Yangzi. Home to myriad southern tribes, as far down as present day northern Vietnam (Annam, the Pacified South), this was a world of hot and humid forests punctuated with peaks, dotted with marshes, and touched with strange fevers – not a place where the treasured heavenly horses and their archers could be of any help. Consulting the changes, the Martial Emperor turned to the Han dynasty's chosen element for a vanquishing solution: fire. When flames were thrown at forests, the tattooed men with flowing black hair who lived amid the trees were easily scattered: some to far-off mountains, others further south. Now reduced to a more manageable stubble, the forests were populated by Han armies of migrant peasants – and a number of stubborn minds who, asking inconvenient questions in the Han capital, had been dispatched to serve out punishments at the fever-drenched frontier.

Forests fired and fields sown, the Martial Emperor then commanded the peasant army to raise new cities. As the cities rose, yet more people were sent from a now-overpopulated north, to find new homes in the south. As hundreds of thousands of the Han's northern people flowed south, those southern barbarian tribes who had not managed to reach a rescuing mountain, were invited to tie up their hair, put on some shoes, and learn the arts of the heavenly settled order. Willing to learn or not, it didn't really matter, because the old three-step discipline of the Qin was ready to ensure that everyone was ordered by their name and place: registers and maps to capture everyone in a grid of administrative power; families settled as households, all charged with taxing duties for the state; and groups of households, bound together in fives, guaranteeing the obedience of all.

Heaven was stretching. By the time the Martial Emperor joined his ancestors in 87 CE, the territories of the Han spread far beyond even the wildest reaches of the preceding Qin. The cost of the conquests, though, had been great; and the cost of securing the lands thus conquered, even greater. Even with taxes, the expanded empire found that wealth flowed out of the imperial treasuries faster than it flowed in. The Martial Emperor's successor instructed the imperial officials, now spread across vast lands, to balance the books.

With no resources of their own, the officials turned to the smallest of the local households: those who, while they might have least to spare, would also be least able to make a fuss. As time passed, poorer households burdened by taxes lost their lands to richer landowning men with deeper pockets. For those struggling to keep up, moneylenders offered loans against rights to the land. While the rich flourished on solid ground, yet more of the poor lost their fields. With nothing to their name other than the muscle of their arms, and nowhere to sell their muscle other than in markets already stuffed with desperate labour, many struggled in seas of despair. As the Martial Emperor's successor continued to pursue unity across the four quarters of the earth, at home everything was separating.

At the turn of the millennium, heaven issued stern warnings. With forests felled, stripped soils had turned to dust, rains were failing, and even the seasons seemed to falter. Droughts were followed by floods, locusts chimed in, the Yellow River repeatedly changed its course, comets flew, and earthquakes added to the toll. The first century turned painfully to the second, and things got worse. Out in the fields, desperate men began to question whether heaven was indeed to be found in Han. Whisperings turned to mutterings, mutterings turned to bands of self-help – and in 184 CE, a peasant army rose. Wearing turbans in the cosmic colour of the Yellow Emperor, they claimed to be warriors for a new golden age – one of a *taiping* great peace, which went back to the most ancient of times when Shennong had farmed the fields, side by side with ordinary men. Named the Yellow Turbans, the rebels infected so many labouring men with the idea of revolutionary change that they were able to declare themselves the battling vanguard of an independent Kingdom of Taiping. In 189 CE they presented themselves for heavenly approval in the palaces of the last of the ancient Zhou capitals, one that had become a capital for the later Han: a city now known as Luoyang.

Then, just as it seemed nothing could get worse, the Xiongnu terrors of the steppes, who seemed to have been so effectively vanquished, were replaced by a new and even more ferocious confederated force: the Xianbei.

As the battling price of unity rose, more rebellions broke out and successively weakening and desperate emperors found themselves and their borders increasingly dependent on their generals. With the heavenly empire collapsing, the generals, keenly aware of their power, became warlords in their own right. By 195, the strongest of the generals controlled most of the northern plains of the Yellow River heartlands. Named Cao Cao, in 196, he swept the Son of Heaven off to his own military base. Leaving the emperor with his life and his title, Cao Cao proceeded to try to unify the world himself, albeit through commands issued from behind the heavenly façade. Four years later, his son flung off the pretence and declared a new heavenly dynasty, the Cao Wei, across the north. Before long, he was challenged by two other warlords, each claiming a heavenly dynasty of their own: one, to the south-west, including present-day Sichuan, leader of a new state of Shu-Han; the other, to the south-east, including provinces surrounding present-day Shanghai, the leader of a new state of Wu.

For the next forty-five years, the unity of the Han world was divided into three kingdoms, each with its own warlord waiting to become the single Son of Heaven. Three warring brothers, all inheritors of a common dream from a common past that included the golden age of Zhou, the iron grid of Qin, and the compromise of the Han, not to mention the Confucian scholars and the cosmic shamans before them. Each dug deep to find the defining understanding of order that would enable them to unify the broken world and claim the mandate of heaven. In the end, in 251, it was a general from within the Cao Wei who brought the Three Kingdoms to an end: snatching power from the Cao Wei ruler and laying the foundations of what would become the short-lived dynasty of the Jin.

Meanwhile, as Yellow River warlords had been battling, in the steppe lands above the Long Wall the Xianbei confederation seemed to mirror the disintegration that was taking place below. Steppe tribes threw themselves into wars against each other and, as each fought for supremacy, many concluded that the best way to win the roof of the world was by capturing the treasures of the settled Yellow River lands.

But no sooner had the Jin claimed the mandate of heaven, than hordes of other challengers – steppe warriors and former Han warlords alike – set out to capture as much as they could of the lands below the Long Wall. As battles raged back and forth in the north, displaced people flooded down to the fertile lands of Sichuan and the wider south. Eventually, sixteen kingdoms emerged above the Yangzi River, many led by steppe generals, each claiming a dynasty of its own, and all looking for advantage over the others. And as the north began to settle to a fragmented order of sorts, below the Yangzi, the southern lands erupted in a succession of short-lived and competing kingdoms all of their own.

As generals battled, north and south, scholars of both stripes, Confucian and legalist now better identified by the dynasty they served, continued to counsel the succession of conquering rulers on the weighty matters of heaven. In the northern kingdoms ruled by men from the steppes, their advice was secondary not only to the overriding power of the totem of the wolf but to a vanquishing power of Buddhism that had harnessed the sutras to the unstoppable force of the horse. With steppe people following new rulers across the wall, the tougher notes increasingly crept into northern Han hearts. In the south, while lands once home to other tribes with strong shaman traditions of their own had come to be ruled by men who followed the Confucian tradition of a scholarly bureaucracy, most of the people's hearts were governed by less rigid ideas, closer to the shaman spirits of the mountains and forests than to any wolf. Indeed, with rain in abundance, and the fruits of nature everywhere, many in the south found it hard to understand why heaven had to order everything.

Meanwhile, changes within the heavenly lands notwithstanding, to the world outside, the lands, the people and their language, unified by the Qin's First Emperor under a single spreading heavenly bureaucracy, had come to be known as Qin: Chinese.

———

Time passed and heaven, north and south, seemed to float, tantalisingly suspended somewhere above the earth. An order of sorts had been established by many dynasties, but the unity of everywhere, upon which a truly heavenly order must surely depend, was as elusive as ever.

Then, in 581, an official serving the latest of the conquering steppe kingdoms, a man claiming distant descent from a Han dynasty general, turned the trust of his rulers into an opportunity to re-establish the line of the Yellow Emperor's people. His name was Yang Jian. By 589, styling himself as a universal emperor whose wisdom enabled him to direct the wheels of his army in any direction he wished, Yang Jian had forged the sixteen northern kingdoms into one and established a dynasty of his own, the Sui. A navy was then raised to defeat the rulers of the south on the Yangzi River and within a decade the Sui had reunified the north and the south. Determined to seal the unity for all time, they then applied the old engineering feats of Qin to build a Grand Canal, stretching from the southern city of Hangzhou to the northern city of Zhoujun (which would, one day, become Beijing). With the heavenly lands now united, the Sui armies marched to the four quarters of the known world. To the west, they swept deep into the oasis states that Zhang Qian's journey had opened to trade – lands the Han had held and lost. To the east, they snatched at the lands of Goryeo, present-day northern and central Korea. To the south they chased the lost lands of Annam, present-day northern Vietnam. And across the north they strengthened the Long Wall as it had never been strengthened before.

For a while, all went well. The Grand Canal more than served its purpose – trade took to the water, and boats carried rice from southern terraces of plenty to northern plains that were now drying in a climate of change. But the wars of reunification, the building of the canal, and the strengthening of the Long Wall, had not only emptied the empire's pockets but bitten deep into the people and the land. Legions of young men had been torn away from their families, with many lost to an early death. Fields failing, once again, misery was everywhere. Just as in the ancient times of the Shang, the Zhou, the Qin and the Han, the weight of a single great empire was taking its familiar toll.

Once again, whisperers spread the idea that heaven was changing its mind. Rebels began to rise, and rumours rustled that a new Kingdom of Taiping, Great Peace, was on its way.

In 617, with Sui rule crumbling from within, the ambitious son of a general in charge of a garrison in the near-west persuaded his father to seize the reins of power and sweep the Sui into the dust. Named Li, both father and son had higher noses than most, with slightly darker skins. Claiming to be descendants of Liu Bang's Han family, like so many people now on the northern plains, the ancestral blood that flowed in their veins clearly included a touch of the steppes – Xianbei and even Turkic *Tujue*. In 618, from the old Han capital of Chang'an, Li the father declared a new dynasty, and named it Tang. By 626, Li the son had grasped the throne, under a title that anticipated a glorious reign: Emperor Taizong (the Supreme Ancestor).

Dedicating himself to restoring the vast wealth of the Sui, Taizong, like so many of his predecessors, looked for a stronger unity that would, this time, keep everything together. Consulting the steppes, he found that the world of the *Tujue* was dividing into an east and a west. As schooled in the idea of 'divide and rule' as any of his Yellow River ancestors, Taizong put all of his weight behind the Western Tujue, and within three years, the east was forced into a surrender. Taizong then looked at the surviving Western Tujue power that now controlled a string of states from the oasis edges of the Tang's west to far-off Persia. Twisting Western Tujue words into jealousies, Taizong sparked a storm within the Western Tujue ranks. By 642, he had pulled the rug of power out from under the feet of their rulers as well. Already the Son of Heaven Emperor of the Tang, Taizong now became a Heavenly Khan of Khans – a Turkic *qaghan* – and ruler of the steppes. Surely this was unity indeed.

But not everyone accepted that this was the kind of unity heaven had in mind. Remnants of the Tujue began to win back friends, and when, in 639, Taizong was forced to quash a rebellion in the oasis state of Gaochang, Confucian officials – who had now learnt the costs of war – began to repeat the old questions of the generals and ask whether Taizong's idea of heaven-everywhere was really wise. Quoting a line of Confucius to the effect that it is better to be master of what is close before rushing to seize control over things far away (a line presumably missed by the Confucian scholars of the Han), the officials pointed to the disasters that had eventually befallen the acquisitive Qin, Han and Sui and concurred with the view of the, now long-dead, Han generals that conquests waged beyond the edges of one's own lands were more likely than not to bring heaven tumbling down upon one's head.

Preferring the older Han-Confucian idea of 'unity everywhere', Taizong was unimpressed. If one is truly dedicated to pursuing the heavenly way of the *dao*, he observed, one has no choice but to chase it to all of the corners of the earth. The Confucian doubters were dismissed. But Taizong had underestimated the Tujue. Hearts burning at his betrayal of both East and West, they determined to displace the interloping 'Heavenly Qaghan'. Unleashing their fury across the roof of the world, they also rained down their rage upon the earth of the Tang.

In 649 Taizong passed the reins to a weaker Tang successor – unfortunately just as a new power was rising to the south-west, known as the *Tubuo*, Tibetans. Taizong had dismissed them as upstarts, even refusing the now-common request for a Tang princess. Expanding swiftly, however, the Tibetans had pushed north and west, biting into the oasis states, and threatening to push the Tang off their already-weakened perch. Looking at the rather difficult lie of the land, Taizong's successor had a change of heart: treaties were concluded and a Tang princess made her way to Tibet. But the battle for the earth had already stretched into realms beyond the charms of a princess. Far to the west, beyond even Persia, the future fortunes of the Tang were being mixed with those of yet another nomadic power. Having seized control of Baghdad, in present-day Iraq, it had risen as an empire of Islam, stretching east across the oasis states of the central Asian roof of the world. As the Islamic power marched east, the wider world seemed not only to be getting closer but also carrying a host of risks.

Meanwhile, as one Tang emperor was succeeded by another, imperial envoys struggled to keep abreast of the changes, and the western lands were clearly so complicated that it was as difficult as ever to follow the news. Battles in every direction were demanding bigger and bigger armies with the skills to fight across distant desert and mountain terrains. With peasants endlessly dispatched for uncertain distant victories, by 740, the Tang decided that their only hope was to invigorate their own fading battalions with tougher commanders drawn from the terrifying steppes. It was a brave decision, but it came a moment too late. In 750, the Caliphate of Baghdad marched into the central Asian lands of present day Kazakhstan and seized a victory over the Tang that turned the roof of the world into a new Islamic west. Soon afterwards, a new Muslim force rose from the Turkic Tujue. Calling themselves Uighurs, it was their leader who would capture the now coveted roof-of-the-world title: Khan of Khans, *Qaghan*.

With battles blazing, affairs in the Tang's sparkling capital, Chang'an, had become a little fiery too. Already in 685, under an earlier emperor, the Tang armies had been strengthened by wild steppe warriors chosen as officers to lead them into battle. It had not been long before one among their number, a particularly spirited and seasoned commander, caught the attention of the new emperor. Part Sogdian, part Tujue, known by the Chinese name of An Lushan, he had been given charge of one of the Tang's most important garrisons. Contemplating a devastating loss of ordering influence, the imperial officials convinced themselves that his swift upwards trajectory could only have been the result of a seduction of the emperor's wife. Determined to recover their positions, they launched themselves into a whispering campaign, rubbing away at the emperor's trust to such a degree that An Lushan concluded (much like Liu Bang, the Qin rebel who became the first Han emperor) that, with little chance of a fair hearing, he would be better off at the head of his own rebel army.

An able man with an easy command of confidence, An Lushan was quickly joined by other generals from across the northern plains, many, like him, with the blood of the steppes in their veins. Before long, the Tang generals had divided, and the country was launched into a brutal civil war.

In 756, An Lushan captured the now-secondary capital of Luoyang and proceeded to march upon the riches of Chang'an. As the imperial court fled, the emperor reached out to the only nearby powers that could overcome his treacherous rebel general: the Tibetan Empire and the Uighur Khaganate, who, as heavenly fortune would have it, were already allied. Prices were named in princesses, silk and almost everything else that a desperate Tang emperor could offer; and the secondary capital of Luoyang was recaptured. The civil war, however, raged on. But then the fragile friendship between the Uighurs and the Tibetans fractured and, while the Uighurs held firm, the Tibetans tore away. While the Tang dynasty would eventually restore its power, the price it would pay was more than even a Son of Heaven could have imagined: acutely aware of their own value, the generals who had stayed loyal to the Tang demanded fortunes of gold, while the Uighurs raised the price of the heavenly horses, whose western trade they now controlled, to that of a king's ransom. Meanwhile, the Tibetans hurled their forces against the empire. In 763, Chang'an itself was attacked. Over the next twenty years, it would be attacked again and again.

In 783, desperate for heavenly order to return, the Tang emperor eventually offered the Tibetans a treaty of equals in return for peace. It lasted just a year. The Tang then turned back to the Uighurs for yet more assistance. But the Tibetans defeated them both, and the Tang emperor found himself, like so many of his unity-pursuing predecessors, at the mercy of generals whose loyalty had been bought. Navigating a chaos of his own making, the emperor felt he had no choice but to pass on the costs of battle to the people at large. Taxes rose – particularly, as always, for the smallest households.

And then, predictably, heaven chimed in. Harvests failed, locusts flocked and, once again, the people – in tatters after so much war – became 'human portents'. Bandits roamed like dogs, and from the embers of a dying dynasty, a host of new rebels arose. Once again, chaos was everywhere.

In 907, the Tang reached the end of their empire and their dynasty. For the moment, the idea of unity seemed to lose its appeal.

———

Over the next fifty years, the heartlands of the northern plains fell to a myriad of competing claims, most led by warlord generals, some by yet more wolves from the steppes. Meanwhile, the southern lands, now the richest of all, fractured again into competing dynasties fuelled by disputes of their own. And then, from the north, a Song dynasty rose, founded by a general from the heavenly lands. Briefly uniting north and south, the Song went on to seal treaties with the barbarian wolves, buying a fragile security from the most amenable of the steppe tribes. Under a short-lived peace, and with a smaller idea of unity, the Song managed to conjure up splendours of heavenly treasure, restoring spirits that had been badly damaged by the fall of the Tang to such a degree that heights of art, ideas and innovation were not only reclaimed but exceeded.

As wealth rose at the top, however, it was not long before emperors returned to their usual denial of the desperate state of the peasants at the bottom. Many imperial scholars held their tongues. While many scholarly artists painted spectacular images of heavenly order, however, one or two brushes risked life and liberty to paint the truth plainly enough for an emperor to see. Others, more cautious, applied their artistic skills to bury carefully coded messages of warning in deceptively peaceful images of the natural world.

Meanwhile, on the steppes, the glittering wealth of the Song had caught the eye of another new tribe, the Jurchen, which had declared a dynasty – another Jin – and raised a terrifying army with which to chase its dreams.

In 1127, the Jurchen-Jin snatched the Song's northern capital, the splendid Kaifeng, and the Song court fled across the Yangzi River to the southern city of Hangzhou. Friends and relations with northern estates too big to abandon stayed behind, where they struggled under a steppe dynasty whose rule felt like an icy winter which would never end. Smaller people followed the Song court south.

The now 'Southern Song' settled in their new capital, with lands reaching to the south-eastern coast, from which they built a navy to protect themselves from the advancing hordes of the north. North and south, everyone whose heart had been attached to the once unified Song dreamt of a day when the steppe usurpers would return to the barbarian wilderness and leave the treasures of heaven-on-earth alone.

While the north lamented, those scholars who had migrated to the softer south looked again at the idea of order. Surrounded by the wealth of plentiful rains and terraced fields, riches rose, and new treasures flourished – from gunpowder, with its fireworks, to the printing of texts, and a delicate drinking of tea.

With a prosperity and leisure denied to their northern cousins, southern dreams returned to the golden age of the Duke of Zhou. Contemplating the memory of a ruler who had so carefully consulted the cosmos, their thoughts then naturally turned to the exhortations of Confucius to establish their order through heavenly qualities and relationships – and to the haunting words of the ancient shamans and their cosmic ideas. The words of Laozi's *Dao De Jing* echoed in their ears: 'If you try to possess it, you will destroy it: if you try to hold on to it, you will lose it.' Also echoing in their ears was the story of Zhuangzi's meditation on a dream about a butterfly, which had left him wondering whether it might have been a dream a butterfly was having about him. Indeed, the tale of the butterfly dream seemed to be a poignant reminder of the ephemerality of everything. In the north, the ancient homelands had once again been caught in the rough embrace of a steppe power. In the south, forests had been felled in every direction. And everywhere across lands where *qilin*, unicorns, had once wandered and where *feng*, phoenixes, had flown, new cities were rising to the skies, even as more and more migrating people were floating desperately on earth. What was true in this world? And how could one tell the difference between the true and the not true?

Scholarly hearts full of questions, the imperial court saw nothing but a challenge to its idea of order. Punishments following, the questioning scholars picked up their brushes and painted images of the natural world in which they buried their opinions for only the most trusted to see.

As questioning brushes painted coded communications, however, other scholars scoured the texts of the ancient past, searching for the still elusive key to order. Known as 'new', or newer, Confucians, they began to see a grand arc of wisdom that, this time, might really be able to unite the ideas of almost everything in a harmony of heaven and earth. One of the scholars, Zhu Xi, described the arc as more than just having a *ren*, humanity, embracing *yi*, integrity, and observing *li*, ritual. What was really important, Zhu Xi suggested, was the *zhi*, knowledge, that, founded in the meticulous *ge wu*, investigation of things, was essential to the harmonious order of all. To this he added that in investigating things one had to be careful not to be misled by any individual judgement or emotion and to remain constantly guided by the texts that set out what Confucius had thought. Not everyone agreed, but even among those who did, the question naturally arose as to what it was that Confucius had originally thought – and whether any of the texts truly reflected it. After the Qin's burning of so many books and the mysterious resurrection of so many texts, how could anyone know what Confucius had really thought?

For Zhu Xi, the answer was simple. There were, in his opinion, four books, rescued from the flames of Qin in the early years of the Han, which were the authoritative Confucian texts: *The Great Learning*, with lessons on the harmonious pursuit of the *dao* way; *The Doctrine of the Mean*, with ideas of moderation as essential to the balancing of all; *The Analects of Confucius*, with a description of the heavenly qualities and relationships, including the filial piety on which the strength of the family-state rested; and the work of the greatest interpreter of Confucius: *The Mencius*. Insisting that these texts were the key to any successful investigation of things, Zhu Xi declared that if the people who traced their origins back to the Yellow Emperor were ever going to find their order, they would need not *less* Confucius but *more*.

As the captured north tried to keep its spirits warm, the sheltered south, separated by the great Yangzi River, and now with a navy to keep it safe, wrapped itself in its dreams. But the steppe world of the wolves had not finished with them yet. In 1206, a new leader had risen up from the swirling northern tribes to gather together yet another federation. Raised at the harshest edges of the steppe world, he agreed with the settled lands that the key to rule was unity, but not the kind that put a single Son of Heaven in charge of everyone (look where that had got the settled people). Rather, it was a unity that took the form of many *different* hearts all beating to the common call of a Mongol wolf. Born in 1162, by 1206, his federation reached across the wild grasslands of the north. Known to his people as the Blue Wolf, he had come to be known across the steppes as Chinggis, Genghis, Khan.

Charging to the west, to the east, then down to the former Song lands already snatched by the Jurchen-Jin, Chinggis Khan treated every battle like a hunt. Seemingly blessed with the magical talents of his totem wolf, he scarcely blinked at the forces arrayed against him. Like every wolf in charge of a hunt, he gathered intelligence like gold, and harnessed the wild temperaments of his warriors with strict rules and punishments that seemed to mirror the ideas of the once-barbarian Qin – albeit directed to the mastery of the hunt. Men were organised into groups of ten, with a single deserter from a unit triggering the deaths of the remaining nine. For any unit that deserted *en masse*, a hundred would pay the price. Clear as to direction, bound together like a single heart, Chinggis' united warriors tore across the steppes and down into the settled lands below. Besieging Song cities that the Jurchen-Jin had captured before them, they deployed the lessons of siege warfare learnt from Chinese captives whose ancestors had invented them during the centuries of the warring states.

By the time Chinggis Khan died in 1227, the Mongol empire was bigger than anything that the Xiongnu, the Xianbei or the Sui had ever created. Bequeathing it to sons and grandsons, he had commanded them to spread the Mongol idea of unity across the world through four khanates. In the far west of Persia, present-day Iran, a grandson founded the Il-khanate state. In the lands of the Rus, present-day Ukraine and western Russia, another founded a khanate that would be known as the Golden Horde. Across the steppe lands of the Mongols, another ruled the khanate at home. And in the lands to the south, those of the northern Song, captured by Jurchen-Jin, yet another grandson, Kublai, proclaimed himself emperor of a new Great Yuan (long-lasting, far-reaching) dynasty. Moving his commanding camp to a once-Jurchen-Jin-conquered area around present-day Beijing, Kublai raised his own cosmic city: Khanbaliq, the great residence of the Khan, known to the Chinese as Dadu, the great capital. With Dadu in place, he turned to the further south and the softer Song.

Gathering the captive soldiers of the old Song north under the flag of the Mongol Yuan, and adding inventions discovered in his cousin's Persian world, Kublai led his forces swiftly south. Vast catapults set their sights on solid walls; exploding bombs thundered through the sky. Terror spread, and city after city fell.

In 1276, Hangzhou was laid to siege, the Song navy fell to the Mongols, and their young emperor, surrendered by a doting grandmother desperate to save his life, was marched away to the north. Taking whatever vessels they had snatched from the jaws of defeat, the Southern Song, including the lost emperor's younger brothers, set sail for present-day Guangzhou. But having conquered Hangzhou and captured the Southern Song's navy, the Mongols simply set their own sails and followed them south.

In 1279, the southern coast close to present-day Hong Kong erupted into the greatest sea-battle that the Yellow Emperor's people had ever fought. More exploding bombs crashed in every direction. Flames soared to the sky. One young emperor already lost to the Mongols, his succeeding brother then fell to a fever. As the sea-battle raged, the Southern Song clutched the only surviving imperial son, now an eight-year-old emperor, close to their hearts. Dreams sinking to the depths, they watched in disbelief as Song vessels fell to ships manned by northern cousins – all commanded by men of the horse who seemed to have taken to the water like ducks.

The battle won, Kublai Khan returned to his new capital in the north and proclaimed a bigger heaven with a new Son. Meanwhile, the last Song general carried the young emperor to the top of a range of eight 'dragon' mountains on the southernmost peninsula, and jumped with him into the sea. Holding him tight, as man and child flew through the air, the general whispered to the boy that he should not be frightened: when they reached the water below them, the eight dragons would become nine and he would join his father in the heavenly sky. In the language of the Song, the nine dragons were known as *jiu long*. One day they would find themselves tied to a rock called Hong Kong, and known by the name of 'Kowloon'.

Shocked and exhausted, the people who traced their origins across the Song, the Tang, the Han, the Qin, the Zhou, the Shang, and all the way back, through the Yellow Emperor, to Fuxi and his sister Nüwa, looked up at the sky and asked themselves who and what they were. Children of the shamans and the *dao*, inheritors of the soft wisdom of Confucius, the dreams of Zhuangzi and the iron will of Qin, they seemed to have ended up in a watery mess. A people whom heaven itself had breathed into life and who, in their turn, had painstakingly studied the cosmos and measured their every step by reference to heaven's will. But along the way, they had lost their path.

Once upon a time, it had all seemed so crystal clear: a heavenly people singled out by their *ren*, humanity, and their *yi*, integrity, by their *li*, ritual, their *de*, virtue, their *zhi*, knowledge and their *ge wu* investigation of things; united by their *jia* families. Under the Han, it had seemed even clearer: inheritors of a Yellow River heartland whose very earth held the traces of their story, they had gone on to unite the world under a heavenly order. But then everything had got mixed up – not just the places, but the people too. And eventually, the virtues of a hundred million Chinese had fallen prey to a wolf, who now claimed to be some kind of heaven's son.

What did it mean to be Chinese? And did heaven really care?

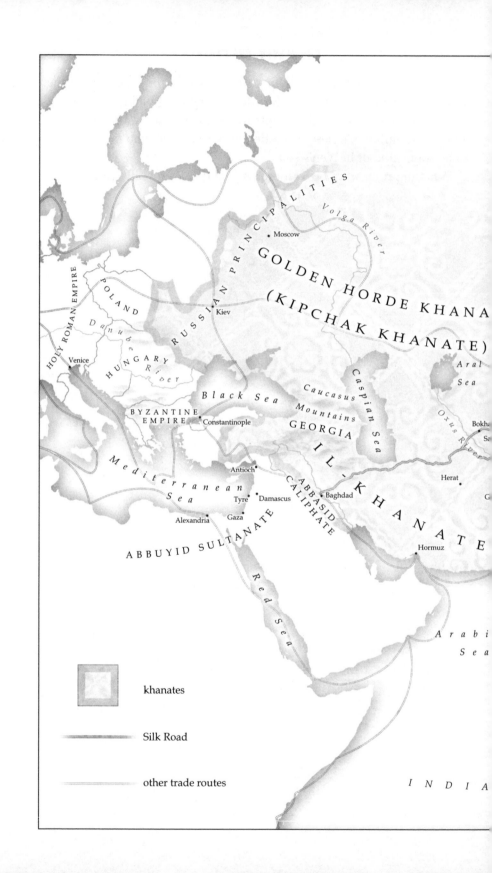

MONGOL EMPIRE
1206 - 1368

Lake Baikal

Amur River

Altai Mountains

KHANATE

CHAGATAI

Ili River

Tian Shan

Urumqi

Kucha

Turfan

KHANATE

Dunhuang

gar

Khotan

TIBET

HIMALAYA
MOUNTAINS

Lhasa

Karakorum

Gobi Desert

River

Yellow River

Yangzi River

invasions of Annam

ANNAM

Bay
of
Bengal

CEAN

invasions of Goryeo
and Japan

Khanbaliq
(Beijing)

YUAN

Xianyang

Chang'an   Luoyang   Kaifeng

Grand Canal

GORYEO

East
China
Sea

Hangzhou

South
China
Sea

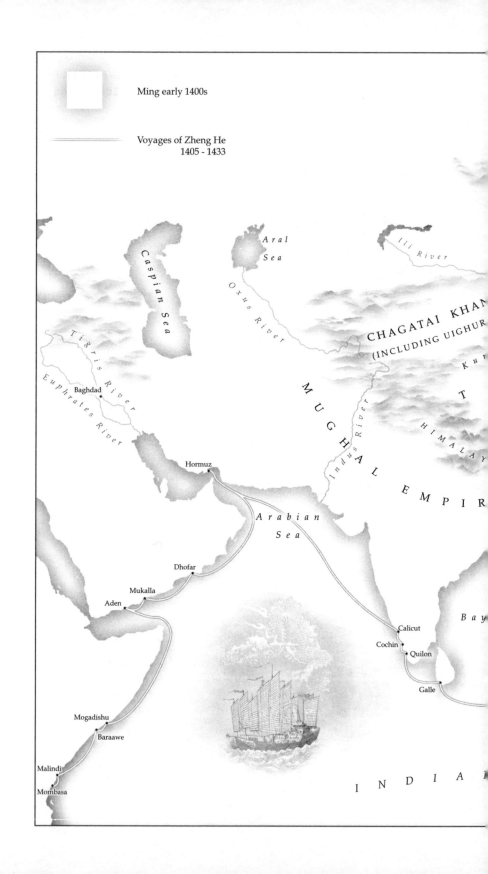

Ming early 1400s

Voyages of Zheng He
1405 - 1433

*Aral
Sea*

Ili River

*Caspian
Sea*

Oxus River

CHAGATAI KHAN
(INCLUDING UIGHUR

Tigris River

Euphrates River

Baghdad

M
U
G
H
A
L

Indus River

Kur

T

H
I
M
A
L
A
Y

E   M   P   I   R

Hormuz

*Arabian
Sea*

Dhofar

Mukalla

Aden

Calicut

B a y

Cochin

Quilon

Galle

Mogadishu

Baraawe

Malindi

Mombasa

I   N   D   I   A

MING DYNASTY LAND AND SEA, EARLY 1400s

CHAPTER 2
A BRIGHT IDEA

Displaying its splendour, the cosmos is filled; hiding away, nothing is revealed.

> Zhu Yuanzhang, the Hongwu Emperor (first emperor
> of the Ming dynasty, fourteenth-century)

To a casual dragon sweeping overhead, everything seemed to be moving towards its perfect position and place. From the dark of a cold night sky above, with the Pole Star at their heart, the stars of the *ziwei*, purple enclosure were scattering their energies down like blessings. Under the flickering lamps of a forbidden square of a city set within a city, all hidden behind purple walls, earth in the form of a host of scholarly officials was preparing to talk to heaven. Rising before dawn, red lanterns held aloft, the officials had gathered like a soft wind at the Meridian Gate, the southern gate which guarded the innermost walls of the 'Purple City', marking the point at which the emperor's 'forbidden' enclosure met the wider imperial city, the point at which heaven came to meet earth through its Son. Passing from south to north through its lofty portals, they then made their way swiftly on through the Gate of Supreme Harmony, and into the stone expanse of a courtyard that spread beyond.

Accompanied by the gentle chimes of heavenly bells, every scurrying scholar searched for the small bronze marker that, set in stone below their feet, ensured that the official rank of each was not only matched with badges embroidered on their silken fronts and backs, but also with the precise position at which they should stand. Those whose embroidered badges showed two stately cranes soaring above heavenly clouds knew they would be at the top and front; those whose badges displayed a pair of earthbound quails pecking at the grass knew they would be at the bottom and behind; and those whose badges were composed of pheasants, peacocks, geese, egrets and ducks knew they would be somewhere in between. Shuffling almost done, a whip cracked, official bodies stiffened, and the imperial censors proceeded to step along the ranks – the power of their own particular office proclaimed by the badge of the legendary *qilin*, unicorn, who could smell good from bad at a thousand paces. A peacock feather out of place here, a sleeve askew there, a whisper off to the left: each misdemeanour was sharply noted and quickly corrected.

As disciplined hearts contemplated heavy prices that would later have to be paid, an altogether different procession began a more sedate advance from north to south. Yellow silk fluttering in every direction, the Son of Heaven was carried as softly as a cloud from his forbidden enclosure towards the Meridian Gate point at which heaven met earth. Floating on, across small and silent courtyards, the imperial sedan advanced through the Gate of Heavenly Purity and up the marble steps to the heights of Mount Sumeru, the spreading terrace on which the Dragon Throne awaited. Set under the eaves of the Hall of Supreme Harmony, placed directly under the central Pole Star point of the *ziwei* enclosure, the emperor was now at the centre of the cosmos. Facing south, he was ready to address his officials at an hour so early that the sun had not yet risen to declare the new day. Gathered in the courtyard before him, and facing north, his officials were ready to receive the commands of the day.

'*Xia gui!*' came the command to kneel, and the stiff joints of older age disregarded, hundreds of bodies rippled to the ground. '*Ke tou!*' followed the command to place all foreheads upon the ground, with kneeling bodies dipping their heads to such a position that not even the greatest of them could fail to feel respect. '*Ping shen!*' came the command to rise. All heads now facing into the full force of the wind, eyes fixed expectantly forward, heaven's representative on earth then issued the edicts of the day. As his orders echoed across the ocean of stone, the leopard tails of guarding soldiers stood stiffly to attention, while gilded dragons, tamed from the deep, curled obediently around the pillars of red which flanked his sides.

Suddenly, even the wind seemed to stand still. The imperial edicts announced, the heavenly cloud then swept back to the forbidden enclosures of the emperor's purple city within a city – and the hundreds of cranes, quails and lesser ranks of office stepped off to carry out their duties. On this morning of no particular significance in the year 1500, under the dynasty of the Great Ming, heaven and earth had met. The orders had been given. The day could begin.

The power of Kublai Khan's dynasty had not even lasted a hundred years. Fewer than a million Mongols governing a hundred million Chinese, the Great Yuan had been quick to appreciate the sparkling treasures of the settled world and the ordering value of a disciplined Confucian bureaucracy. But they had been slow to understand the will of heaven, and even slower to understand that the disciplined appearance of an order accepted could always mask a hidden, and very different, point of view.

Early errors seemed to have been easily ironed out. Arriving on the northern plains, one Mongol suggestion had been that the flat fields might be better used for grazing horses, rather than wasted on crops. Fortunately, wiser Confucian minds had prevailed, gently pointing out that taxes from the fields far outweighed the value of even the most heavenly horse. Of course, such a big and populated expanse of land would take a lot of ordering. But so great had been the prescience of earlier dynasties that the necessary layers of bureaucracy were already to hand. True, after a hundred of years of brutal battle, trust and loyalty could not be assumed – particularly given the fact that, although valiant on horseback, few if any Mongols had acquired the skill of writing, let alone the art of administration. But the Mongols had strict laws and punishments of their own, and the Yuan were part of a much bigger empire, which stretched across the vast roof of the world into European and Middle Eastern lands, with many, particularly Muslim, men of blue and green 'coloured eyes' who were just as good as the Chinese at mastering the power of the pen and would be perfectly capable of overseeing the Chinese bureaucracy. It was not long before the scholarly minds of the old Song officials seemed to settle down to a new prosperity under the riches of a greater 'Pax Mongolica' trade that had surely soothed any temporarily broken hearts.

Once again, cities sparkled, the Grand Canal was extended to the Dadu northern capital, and the routes of the vast Mongol empire were opened up to anyone who wanted to travel to the west. For those in the cities, opportunity seemed to beckon; for those in the fields, it might have seemed that little had really changed. True, there were many scholars whose spirits refused to embrace the new Mongol order, but their dissent, mostly missed by the Mongols, seemed to be limited to the delicate strokes of ink with which their brushes painted visions of rocks, bamboo and plum blossom: secret declarations of endurance, perseverance and a resolute insistence on the ultimate triumph of scholarly civilisation over any brutal conquest of force, all seemed unlikely to overturn the totem of the wolf.

But heaven, as usual, had a different idea. Cooling over the last few centuries, the winters of the northern lands had begun to turn into a longer, deeper age of ice – and the fragile waters on which the plains depended had evaporated into drought. By 1320, the finely predictable details of the seasons had begun to unravel. First locusts, then famines, and then, sweeping like a scythe, a black death, which cast a pall across everyone's skies. Farms abandoned, any harvests were left to rot in the fields. Canals without keepers, boats lay empty. Rivers without regulators, floods were two-a-penny. Once-piling taxes crumbled like dust. And out of the dust rose armies of desperate men with nothing left to lose, and clouds of orphaned children, for whom chaos had become the stuff of life.

Finding themselves adrift in settled lands that seemed to have closed around them like a trap, the Mongols struggled to master the costs and complexities of ordering a once-flourishing world now stopped in its tracks. By the middle of the fourteenth century many of the Mongols were muttering that it might be time to go: leave the chaos to heaven, and the coloured-eyed Muslims, to sort out. When a rebel Chinese leader stormed out of a childhood lived at the edges of hell, they jumped on their horses and raced back to the steppes.

Zhu Yuanzhang was born to a family of peasants in the south, and raised an orphan on the charity of a Buddhist monastery. The man who would snap the old lands of the Song back to a heavenly order, he was nothing if not clear about the responsibility of a ruler to rule. Once a member of a brotherhood of bandits, the White Lotus Society, followers of the Maitreya Future Buddha devoted to the enlightenment of all, Zhu swept away the Mongols in 1368. Settling his capital in the southern city of Nanjing, he titled his dynasty Da Ming (Great Brightness).

Styling himself Hongwu (the *Vastly* Martial Emperor), Zhu Yuanzhang set about repairing a country that had been shocked to its core. As emperor, his ideas about order were as simple and clear as those of any rebel peasant: scholars might have an important imperial function but their soft hands would never coax a harvest from the land. And after nearly a hundred years of Mongol misery (not to mention the periodic crises that had punctuated the millennium before) it seemed rather unrealistic to expect that scholarly minds would be able to offer much in the way of practical suggestions to anyone. The road to order did not lie in a book or a brush but out in the villages and the fields. In this simple world, if everybody kept to their proper position and place, taking no more than required for moderate needs, the order of a once-golden past would surely return.

Acting on his convictions, Zhu proceeded to give land to any hand willing to farm it, and to set everyone under the old bureaucratic grid of Qin. The registers and maps would be updated; households would be ordered in groups of mutual guarantee; villages would be set under the supervision of village heads who, in their turn, would be commanded by imperial officials above; taxes would be fixed and quotas for harvesting production would be allocated, for each village, county and prefecture to meet. The occupations of the people would also be recorded, and fixed, in a hierarchy of purpose according to their value to the heavenly lands. In the first and second places there were the scholarly *shi* officials, the brushes of imperial order, and the productive *nong* farmers; in the third and fourth places there were the *gong* artisans and the *shang* merchants, both men who lived on nothing but the hard work of others, with profits always gained at someone else's expense. And given that in any orderly society, the scholars and farmers were the bedrock of everything, Zhu Yuanzhang also declared that every son should follow the same occupation as his father so that the number of less useful artisans and merchants should not increase.

To these rules, Zhu Yuanzhang further added that, from the Nanjing capital down, imperial commands would be relayed to local magistrates set in county towns, whose *yamen*, official compounds, would become the frontline of the emperor in the fields. Empowered to deal with anything and everything on the ground, their work would include the collection of imperial taxes and the settling of neighbourly disputes. And in order to ensure that everyone was clear about the heavenly nature of the empire, every month, and within every village, the Confucian texts would be read aloud for everyone to hear, with the heads of every village responsible for ensuring that everyone understood. Places fixed and purpose clear, as in the state of Qin, only those whose job was to carry goods from one place to another would need to travel. Canals were cleared and roads were mended, but if anyone wanted to go beyond the distance required to reach a locally approved market, official permits would be required. With simple self-sufficiency the order of the day, the coasts were also closed, and outsiders dreaming of trade with the lands of the Great Ming were told that their offerings were no longer required.

Foundations set, the yields were remarkably swift. Farmers returned to their fields, the fields returned to plenty, roads and rivers carried whatever officially needed to be circulated, and Zhu Yuanzhang was able to address the higher forces of order. There was an empire to regain and an army ready for the task.

But the lands were vast and, in Zhu Yuanzhang's opinion, the soldiers were also in need of some stiff lessons in discipline. As were the ministries of scholars whose failure to rebel against the Mongol Yuan had clearly proven their lack of any practical skills required for reliable rule. Leading from the front, Zhu Yuanzhang rose before the cock crowed, and did not sleep until long after everyone else had found their beds. Military men in the field found themselves led in person by their emperor; those who failed to obey an order were executed on the spot. And from the chief minister, who was closest to the emperor, across the six boards of ministries, which managed every aspect of the realm, ministers and their officials were subjected to the same kind of discipline that the emperor imposed upon himself. Called before the sun rose, they were charged with presenting painstakingly detailed reports, all stuffed with information gathered from every point of the imperial grid and carried to the centre by horse-borne couriers for whom any delay was a punishment and a half. Every official body, high or low, was expected to work for a modest Confucian return. No decision of any weight whatsoever could be taken without the emperor's personal seal. Meanwhile, useful lessons learnt from the Mongols were brutally applied: a secret service, responsible for intelligence at home and abroad, was created; a special corps of censors was established and empowered to investigate anyone at any time (except, of course, the emperor); and all derelictions of duty were met with a Mongol-style public beating which, depending on the severity of the infraction, might easily result in death.

The first decade of the Vastly Martial Emperor's reign passed and, with such meticulous attention to detail, the paperwork of the bureaucracy grew so large that new archives had to be built to hold it. For Zhu Yuanzhang, however, the size of the bureaucracy was hardly a reason to trust it. Indeed, the very cleverness of the scholars made it difficult for the emperor to trust them not to take decisions on his behalf. In 1380, alerted to the fact that his chief minister had abandoned imperial discipline and met with a foreign envoy without his approval, Zhu Yuanzhang turned the full force of his martial attention to the misdemeanour. Arrested on the spot, within a week the chief minister and all of his family were executed. In the weeks that followed fifteen thousand others – anyone who had ever had anything to do with the chief minister – were similarly condemned to death. The emperor's fragile trust broken, the very position of chief minister was itself dismissed. Never again, for as long as the Ming ruled, would such an office be able to stand between the emperor and his imperial affairs. Neither, the emperor decided, would there be any central secretariat trying to weave its own web of power across the six ministerial boards. Henceforth it would be the emperor, and the emperor alone, who would govern the ministries. The only people permitted to help him would be a small number of lowly clerks: too lowly ever to dare to presume, but just educated enough to serve as document-drafting scribes. As the emperor worked across the heavenly day and night, the fields prospered, the empire strengthened, and every suspicion of official obstruction or failure was unfailingly followed with beatings and blood.

In 1394, at the age of seventy, Zhu Yuanzhang died, bequeathing the empire of his making not to the eldest of his surviving sons – a military man – but to the teenage son of his first-born but predeceased favourite son. Raised in the courtyards of the imperial palace in Nanjing, the grandson had been trained by the brush, schooled in the classics, and taught the language of Confucian texts which was so scholarly that only the similarly schooled could speak it. Not exposed to fields of battles or back-breaking ploughs, the boy had never quite understood why his grandfather beat and executed so many of the finely educated minds that his own tutors had held in such high regard. While many were surprised that Zhu Yuanzhang had chosen a scholar over a soldier, no one was very surprised when, on his accession to the dragon throne, the grandson styled himself the Jianwen (Establishing Civility) Emperor, placing himself firmly on the side of the Confucian brush.

For Zhu Yuanzhang's eldest surviving son, Zhu Di, the appointment of his nephew as emperor was a shock. Sent to guard the northern Dadu city (now replaced as the principal capital by the southern Nanjing) against any return of the Mongols, Zhu Di had not only served his father faithfully but, trained on the battlefield and exposed to the harsh reality of peasant life, he had fully embraced and shared his father's suspicion of scholarly skirts. Watching as a faint-hearted nephew raised Confucian scholars to the highest pedestals of the imperial court, Zhu Di gathered his army around him and stormed the seven hundred miles from Dadu to Nanjing, setting light to the empire as he went. City after city fell to his fury and in 1402, he and his troops appeared before the gates of Nanjing, commanding that they be opened so that they could rescue the nephew-emperor from the pot of scholarly brushes that had obviously put him under a spell. The gates were opened, Zhu Di entered, and the imperial palace, with the nephew-emperor inside, suddenly shot up in flames. With the 'so-called emperor' (surely his father had made a mistake) apparently nowhere to be found, Zhu Di ascended to the dragon throne: not a usurping third emperor, he insisted, but a rightful second, who would style himself Yongle, the Emperor of Perpetual Happiness.

Having raised himself to his rightful saddle, the Yongle Emperor set about establishing the legitimacy of his rule and repairing the empire from the ravages of his own destruction. The establishment of his own legitimacy would require another battle. Having raged against his father's will and 'lost' the appointed heir, the scholarly brushes struggled to accept him as their emperor – while Zhu Di blamed them and their influence for causing the upset in the first place. Imperial edicts were confronted with official intransigence. The son of his father, Yongle responded with purges of blood – and a redirection of his trust towards his personal household of eunuchs: men without sons to make them ancestors seemed far more trustworthy servants of the present moment than Confucian scholars whose obsession with family and ancestral ritual meant they were constantly contemplating the riches of their own posterity.

With the eunuch-household now in charge, and his father's great wealth at his feet, Yongle began to dream of a vast unified empire that would far exceed the reaches of the Mongol Empire, all led by a grand new imperial capital to be commissioned for the north. On land, troops were marched in almost all directions: north to push the Mongols further back on the steppes; north-west to wrench them out of the oasis gems; and south-west to reclaim the lands of Annam, present-day northern Vietnam, once part of the Han and the Tang but which had then been lost to the more local power of the tribal state of the Yue. Adventures on land, however, were just the beginning. Turning his sights to the coast, which his father had so firmly closed for business, Yongle decided that he would outshine Chinggis Khan and his vast land empire with a tribute-receiving embrace of the oceans as well.

With scholarly minds still out of favour, Yongle chose his most trusted eunuch to carry the heavenly glory of the Great Ming out to sea. A tiger of a man-who-was-not-a-man, Zheng He had been born a Muslim. Captured in Yunnan when Zhu Yuanzhang seized the south-west from an outpost of Mongol forces, he had been castrated and sent to serve in Zhu Di's household. Over two metres tall, he became a soldier who fought alongside his master with a courage and skill that few others matched. When Zhu Di as the Yongle Emperor set his sights on the sea, Zheng He was charged with raising the ships to realise his master's dream. From 1403, the shipyards at Nanjing were stretched beyond anything ever known. Three hundred new 'star-guided' vessels, including sixty-two 'treasure ships', were built within two years. Once completed, they were loaded with the treasures of the heavenly empire, and launched on the first of what would become seven great voyages across the western seas. Calling first on the southern coasts of *Yindu*, India, the new Ming navy went on to *Hu-Lu-Mo-Ssu*, Hormuz, southern coast of present-day Iran, *A-tan*, Aden, present-day Yemen, and *Mu-ku-tu-shu*, Mogadishu, present-day Somalia. Treading the waves as they might advance along a highway at home, Zheng He and his crew distributed gifts and titles at each port of call. In return, they received the tribute of the world: lions and leopards, ostriches and unicorn giraffes. There seemed no end to the treasures that the four quarters of the world (once they were clear about the heavenly order of things) were ready to bestow. As Zheng He's ships sailed like clouds across the waves, even dragons appeared to pay a thundering tribute of their own. And when, on a few occasions, a suitable recognition of heavenly authority was not accorded, local kings were taken as captives and carried back to the lands of the Ming for a clarifying audience with the Yongle Emperor, before being returned to the patch of earth that heaven and its Son permitted them to rule.

On 2 February 1421, with the Mongol empire if not quite matched at least imaginatively emulated, the Yongle Emperor unveiled the centrepiece of his dream – a new imperial city on the site of the old Dadu, now 'Beijing', the northern capital. Paid for with a fortune of peasant taxes delivered in the form of grain, it was a spectacle whose construction knew no bounds. Timbers of forests had been floated along tamed rivers and up the newly restored Grand Canal. Craftsmen and artisans had travelled from across the empire, including the now-secondary city of Nanjing and the southern city of Hangzhou to deliver the exquisite products of ancient talents and skills. Even the Confucian scholars, who by now had adjusted to the imperial will, joined in the endeavour of conjuring up a city greater than anything man had ever known before (albeit required to work alongside the still far more trusted eunuchs).

Declaring the heavenly mandate for all the world to see, Yongle invited envoys from the four quarters of the world to an audience with the Son of Heaven that no one on earth would want to miss. Carried like a cloud towards the Hall of Supreme Harmony, where he would receive the tribute of earth, Yongle had cause for a confident celebration. Watched by statues of wise tortoises, his heavenly sedan passed through pavilions whose very foundations contained the mysteries of Fuxi's magic square, ascending and descending stairways of loyal dragons that had consented to fix themselves in stone. With everyone's paths perfumed with mists of incense, the watching envoys found themselves floating in a dream of their own, all noting that the mandate of heaven was surely one that would last for ever.

The celebrations over, Yongle returned his attention to the matter of the bureaucracy. Experience had shown him that however much he might doubt the loyalty of his officials, an empire as vast and glorious as the Ming would require something more than a single hand on the tiller of the state. While his father might have been a powerhouse of self-disciplined labour, no ordinary son could be expected to follow that feat. Unable to appoint a chief minister, Yongle decided to work with what he had inherited. The lowly body of clerks created by his father was transformed into a Grand Secretariat, which, headed by three grand secretaries, was charged with guiding and coordinating the six ministerial boards on which the ship of state depended. In keeping with the Confucian tradition of humility, and his own father's emphasis on modesty, pay remained low. But as Yongle delegated greater levels of power to the scholarly officials, experience soon showed that an official life could offer considerable, if less visible, rewards. As humble in their formal appearance as they appeared to be in their imperial remuneration, over time the piles of the officials' personal riches rose so high that they soon began to look like treasure ships of their own.

Unsurprisingly, interest in an official career grew – and with it an interest in the scholarly books on which such a career was founded. As long as everyone was clear that official positions did not include the right to abrogate any of the imperial powers he might choose to delegate, Yongle was happy to encourage them. Indeed, kept to their proper places, he could see that schools of scholars might be rather helpful. Certainly that had been the opinion of the Song dynasty mind, Zhu Xi, who had insisted that the order of everything depended upon an emperor who could bring heaven and earth into harmony through a dedicated investigation of things, grounded in the mastery of the four Confucian books. One just had to be sure that the minds who were doing the investigating had been perfectly trained.

Seeing the logic of the emperor being at the pinnacle of everything, Yongle put Zhu Xi's wisdom into the heart of the Great Ming, declaring that his ideas should be taught to a new age of imperial officials whose qualifications for investigating things would be tested by the passing of imperial exams. The four Confucian books, which Zhu Xi had explained were the only authoritative statements of what Confucius had actually meant, were set as texts. To these were added five interpretative classics, which could be relied upon as guides. With these texts, and no others, the imperial curriculum was fixed and a system of examinations was set. Each student would master every

Confucian word and every would-be official mind would be bent to the Confucian way of thinking: no essay could be tainted by any other influencing thought or personal opinion. Supervised by the Board of Rites, the rigour of the exams was such that years (often decades) of dedicated study were required before a candidate could hope to craft the kind of literary scripts that would ensure a successful result. And a successful result was essential if a candidate was to unlock the lucrative offices of power: whether in a position at the imperial heights of the Grand Secretariat and the ministerial boards in Beijing, or at the lesser levels of administering provinces and prefectures, right down to the magistrates in charge of affairs at the lowest (county) level of imperial authority.

With the Grand Secretariat and the imperial examinations in place, Yongle set out an architecture of administration grounded on Zhu Xi's insistence on the critical importance of investigating things under what had become the iron will of the classical Confucian texts. A hierarchy of bureaucratic minds was established, which put the most successful of the scholars closest to the emperor, with everyone else spread across the country at large. Within the imperial city, the investigation of things became an intellectual battle of minds for the greatest mastery of the classical texts upon which any and every argument would have to be won. Across the lands, the investigation of things became a responsibility for local officials to manage affairs so tightly on the Confucian precepts that there would never be a ripple of a problem to disturb the harmonies of the heavenly emperor's rule – or, at least, not one that the emperor or a superior official could ever hear about.

As Yongle advanced heaven on earth, lesser minds were once again left to count the cost. Lands reclaimed, waterways restored, battles fought, voyages raised, and with a new imperial capital to crown it all, the treasury was struggling to make ends meet. Taxes of grain had been collected – but judging by the number of wandering beggars, peasant backs had borne the brunt of their payment. And while the empire seemed to have far more people than in his father's time, the amount of taxes collected did not appear to have risen. The boards of imperial government in Beijing were asked to explain the gap. But simple facts on the ground were hard to find. Ten-year censuses ordered by Zhu Yuanzhang seemed to have run out of local steam: the tax registers appeared to insist that there had been hardly any increase in the population, even as many of the households clearly fixed in the registers seemed to have disappeared. Suspicious minds had their doubts: local officials looking to supplement their own incomes were very likely burying the bigger population numbers so that tax quotas remained unchanged and, in exchange for the gratitude of the local rich, spreading the collections of harvested grains more thinly across a wider base – with the greatest taxes, as ever, collected from those who had the least ability to complain, and the least ability to pay.

But the problems in the treasury were not limited to the taxes; and the causes lay as much with Yongle's new Beijing, as with any self-interested local officials. Under the original edicts of Zhu Yuanzhang, the vast majority of the population was expected to be tilling the fields – with trade limited to the essential needs of the empire. When Yongle raised the city of Beijing, though, the demand for materials and crafts had been so great that the studios of the artisans had expanded to become factories of kilns and looms, while the waterways of trade had been opened up like floodgates. With the city completed, the artisans and the traders had found that hosts of now-wealthy scholarly families with country-estates wanted to emulate the elegance of the capital's splendours with purchases of their own. The kilns and the looms had expanded their production, and the imperial waterways had found themselves carrying ever-greater volumes of splendid objects. With everyone piling into the boats of trade, there were fewer hands to till the fields and deliver the taxes of harvests that the empire required. Peasants unable to pay their taxes turned to the moneylending arms of ever-richer landlords, often losing both their lands and their livelihoods. As Yongle's treasury struggled with its income, across the land peasants took to the roads – peddling whatever they could in a pale imitation of the grander trades, and wandering ever-greater distances in an increasingly desperate forage for food. The rich had got richer, and their relentless pursuit of wealth was sinking the straw boats of the poor. Far from the order that Zhu Yuanzhang had dreamt of – where everyone stayed at home in self-sufficient villages – the Great Ming's people were moving all over the place. Some, of course, were merrily moving goods and profits. Others were moving body and soul to wherever a mouthful of food might be found. No wonder the registers did not tally and the taxes did not add up.

Clear as the problem and its causes were to those on the ground, and in the whispered recesses of the court, it was equally clear that any investigation of things should not be allowed to disturb the harmony of the emperor's heavenly rule. Fortunately, heaven was high, and the emperor was usually too far away to see the inconvenient facts. Certainly, while the scholarly officials responsible for the treasury were fretting, the eunuchs who ran the imperial household did not seem at all concerned about the costs. From time to time, of course, the problems became a little too obvious for even the emperor not to notice that the official order of things was dangerously slipping. But the upper echelons of the bureaucracy could always be relied upon to issue reassuring edicts to the officials below: commanding the bottom to do its job and fix whatever was wrong.

And so it was that while the empire was set to the pivot of the Pole Star, the bright idea of the Ming's first emperor was unravelling at the seams. Rather than being bound together in comforting Confucian villages, the people were separating. And even as Confucian lessons about the fabric of the family continued to be regularly read aloud to the people at large, everyone was off in a cloud of their own. Some were busily stashing private balances in their sleeves and calculating profits in rising piles of money. Others were descending to the edges of despair.

―――――

When Yongle died in 1424, sharper imperial eyes – those of his son and, rather swiftly thereafter, his grandson – inherited the throne. Zheng He's voyages were quickly cancelled, and the great treasure ships were relegated to yards where they would gradually turn to dust. Other grand construction projects were slowed to a more appropriate pace, many to a stop. Steps were taken to liberate the farming peasants from a little of their taxing burdens. When Yongle's grandson Xuande (Spreading Virtue) followed his father Hongxi (Great Brilliance) to an early death in 1435, the throne passed to Yongle's seven-year-old great-grandson. A regency of three grand secretaries was created, and the boy was given the reassuring imperial name of Zhengtong (Upright Continuation). While the highly educated grand secretaries held the tiller of the state, in the inner residential recesses of the

Forbidden City, the child-emperor was ruled by a world of eunuchs. Men with no complicating dreams of becoming ancestors, they had even acquired a school of their own through which they could master the practical skills of household administration. Banking on a lifetime of future influence, they indulged the young emperor's every whim.

When Zhengtong came of age, he chose to recognise the devotion of his eunuchs with a promotion. Once a household, they would henceforth also be a bureaucracy, combining the intimacy of daily personal care with powers of administration applied to wider matters of ordering heaven on earth. For the scholarly officials, the unfair competition of a bureaucracy of eunuchs was shock enough, but there was worse to come. Encouraged throughout his childhood to explore every tantalising possibility of his power, the Zhengtong Emperor decided to emulate the conquering glories of his great-grandfather Yongle and set his sights on creating an even bigger empire. A new wall at the northern frontier was surely required; and military campaigns against the now-resurgent Mongols were long overdue. Naturally, the only way to pay for it all would be to raise the taxes.

The grand secretaries looked at the skies, consulted their texts, and wondered what on earth to do. Whenever they were offered an opportunity (which was not often), they tried patiently but firmly to point out that things in the treasury were not quite as glittering as they might appear from the residential recesses of the heavenly city. While the empire might seem to be floating on pavilions and silk, below the imperial capital, there was a world of invisible souls struggling to survive. Seeing that the young emperor was uninterested in such earthly matters, the scholars added that there was another problem to be considered: the weather was taking a turn for the worse and it seemed that heaven might be unimpressed.

Bored with their fussing and preferring to dream of a bigger empire, the Zhengtong Emperor left the important planning to his eunuchs and the messier details to the scholars. And so it was that when the Yellow River again burst its banks, it was the (surviving) poor whose backs were put to fixing it. Here and there, mutterings of discontent turned to local rebellions. But charged as they were with maintaining heavenly harmony, local officials applied every lesson from the Confucian book to make sure that news of the rebellions stayed buried in the fields.

In 1449, encouraged by the eunuchs, galvanised by a recent Mongol insult, and tired of listening to scholarly warnings of woe, the Zhengtong Emperor set off on a northern campaign of his own. Poorly provisioned, the emperor and his troops wandered around the edges of the steppes looking for a fight. It was only a matter of weeks before they were sighted by Mongol scouts. Once sighted, it was only a matter of moments before the emperor was captured: a prize for the Mongols to wage against a future bargain. Official minds aghast, it was obvious that Zhu Xi's recommended Confucian texts were not going to be of much help in resolving the situation. It was equally obvious that the 'household academy' of the eunuchs would struggle to offer advice. The emperor was captured, not dead. Yet without a heavenly son on the throne, there could be no heavenly bureaucracy – and therefore no heavenly empire. Zhengtong's younger brother was swiftly pushed into place and proclaimed as the Jingtai (Exalted View) Emperor. Having doted on the older son, and disregarded the younger one, the eunuchs struggled to absorb the shock. Heaven, however, has its mysteries. In 1450 the Mongols suddenly returned the Zhengtong Emperor to Beijing. Having already replaced him with his brother, the grand secretaries did their best to keep their preferred younger emperor on the throne and Zhengtong off the stage. But a strange illness kept the Jingtai Emperor confined to his courtyard, and after a host of tempestuous weather conditions rattled everyone's nerves, the imperial guards were summoned for a change. Zhengtong (now restyled 'Tianshun' – Obedient to Heaven) was carried to the Hall of Supreme Harmony, and under the cosmic light of the Pole Star, pronounced the Son of Heaven – for a second time.

Obedient to Heaven ruled for another seven, rather angry, years. Determined to settle accounts with those who had kept him off his throne, punishments were thrown like missiles in every direction, and only those who learnt to polish their tongues could find any fortune in the change. Most were relieved when the Zhengtong-Tianshun Emperor died in 1464, and was followed by his oldest son, the Chenghua (Accomplished Change) Emperor. By that time, though, the world outside the Forbidden City had clearly parted company with the original Ming dream. As the scholars buried themselves in the classical Confucian texts, so essential to the winning of any argument at court, yet more peasants were floating across the countryside.

Conversely, those lower down the occupational hierarchy – the artisans and the merchants – were struggling to keep up with demand for their goods. Fuelled by the rising wealth of the gentrified officials, demand for practical and precious objects was going through the roof. Indeed, the trading of everything had become such a popular occupation that it was difficult to remember that the artisans and the merchants belonged at the bottom of the social pile. Imperial disapproval notwithstanding, barges of goods sailed up and down the waterways in such force that some wondered whether there would be any space left for the water, let alone the imperial vessels whose transports of taxes-in-grain delivered the revenues on which the empire depended. And along the Grand Canal, within the walls of every city and town, and at the points at which two roads met (or where local rivers met with the canal), markets sprang up like harvests – or weeds, depending on one's point of view.

As the goods moved, so did the money. Not the clumsy copper coins of empire, but new private paper, flying back and forth across the imperial highways. Not at all the currency of an emperor, these were personal promises to pay created by families and even whole villages who could not, even if they wanted, dream the farming dream. Born into parts of the country where grain simply refused to grow – typically southern parts, such as the hilly lands and mountains of the south-east, around present-day Wenzhou – the families and villages who created the new paper were led by men who had come to see trade as a necessary alternative to farming, and the profits of trade as just another kind of harvest. Sons had been sent across the vast Ming lands to sow the seeds of supply and demand, matching them in complex webs of exchange covered by the paper money that their families printed, and with harvests in the form of profits on the trade.

While many considered that the first Ming emperor's dream of a simple society was being rightly updated, to the scholarly officials responsible for the treasury, and to the magistrates responsible for collecting taxes in the imperial currency of copper coins and grain, it was beginning to look like a nightmare.

In 1487, a new emperor came to the throne, at the age of seventeen. Titled Hongzhi (Great Good Order), he worked hard to live up to his name. The officials were set to strict Confucian standards, and Hongzhi himself did his best to follow the shining example of his greatest ancestor, the first Ming emperor, Zhu Yuanzhang – not least in applying himself daily and directly to the matter of governing the lands. At the same time, after nearly a hundred years of grand and reckless imperial expenditure – and with the idea of a land of farmers having failed to capture the imaginations of so many of his ancestors – Hongzhi did his best to steady the ship of state. One scholarly suggestion, an idea from the past, was for the empire to take over production and trade. In this way, prices could be reliably fixed for the benefit of the people, and private exchanges could be prohibited, thus ensuring a tidy profit for the treasury. Various attempts at such an order were made, with particular attention paid to the most essential of commodities. But no sooner was an edict passed than quick local wits opened up new seams of profiting possibility. Officials applying the new imperial rules regularly found themselves blinded by sleights of hand on the ground, and those who managed to retain their sight were soon persuaded, for the usual gratuity, to believe that whatever it was they thought they saw, their eyes must have been deceiving them.

Looking at the tangled web of intrigue, one brave, or reckless, scholar who had reached the heights of the imperial court in Beijing suggested that the best way to protect the people might be to look less to the state as trader and more to the state as a guarantor of rules that were fair to all. The Hongzhi Emperor noted the suggestion with approval. But the Grand Secretariat and the Board of Revenue, both of which had profiting interests in the trades, were unimpressed. Imperial astronomers anxiously reported an azure comet plummeting to the south, and noted that the moon was wandering off its usual course, even as a heavenly earthquake shook the north-west: with which, imperial attention was successfully redirected to more pressing matters of ritual and morality. Aware, however, that something needed to be done to head off any human portents of rebellion, punishments were eased and, in extreme crises, grain was redistributed. Far too difficult to solve without disturbing official incomes, the troublesome matter of trade was pushed to one side.

Hongzhi's 'Great Good Order' came to an early end with his death in 1505. Following his father, a thirteen-year-old son ascended to the dragon throne, styled the Zhengde (Upright and Virtuous) Emperor.

By now, the rich had become very much richer, and the poor had almost fallen out of sight. At the narrow top, every thread of profit was carefully calculated. At the broad bottom, the peasants found themselves under the despotic rule of a god of copper, whose taxing greed could never be sated. For those with money, the acquisition of things became a consuming passion, even as the delivery of an honest day's work came to be seen as a fool's paradise. Lanterns lit up every market. Objects of beauty spread in every direction: paintings and porcelain, silks and scents, jade and jewellery, and everywhere, the exquisite furniture of a grand new life. Indeed for the rich, the question of how to spend their accumulating fortunes had become a far more pressing question than whether or not they should have been accumulated in the first place. Old-fashioned ideas of virtue and humanity had long ago been swapped for handy books to teach the new man with money how to spot true value, and how to avoid a fake. Meanwhile, more and more peasants were getting lost in an underworld from which there seemed little chance of escape. Muttered observations that heaven had receded into the distance seemed to have more than an ounce of truth.

Surrounded by a heavenly bureaucracy revolving around a throne meticulously placed under the Pole Star, the young Zhengde Emperor himself quickly concluded that it mattered little what he did. The bureaucrats and their books were in a galaxy of their own, which clearly had nothing to do with him. Mesmerised by *The Art of War* and Yongle's adventures – but, after Zhengtong's unfortunate kidnapping by the Mongols, not even allowed to think about going into battle – he decided to create his own palace army and conduct field exercises within the imperial city. Soldiers on active service at the northern front were recalled for a more heavenly duty, and soon, the imperial days – and the imperial city – were occupied with military manoeuvres. Intoxicated by stories of the front told by returning soldiers, Zhengde decided to liberate himself from the stuffy closed quarters of the Forbidden City. A Leopard House was raised in the wider imperial city, where he would be far freer to mix with his men and where it would be very difficult for the scholarly sleeves to pester him with the daily questions of order that any fool could tell had nothing to do with real life. Having deftly removed himself from the cloying presence of the officials, he then suggested that any important questions which might require imperial attention could be given to the eunuchs: they not only understood his need for independence but could also be relied upon, if any further opinion were ever needed, to consult the more experienced soldiers under his own personal command. Shocked Confucian officials could do little more than resort to volleys of stately memorials and petitions – so many of them that the emperor eventually decided to limit his replies to brutal and public beatings.

With such an emperor, few of the scholars were surprised when the weather took a sudden turn for the worse. Dragons (now seen as messengers of heavenly displeasure) rolled into clouds of thunder, pulling every inch of water from the earth, and then showering it back as red rain. Even fewer of the people were surprised when the human portents began to rise. When the Zhengde Emperor eventually died in 1521 – from complications after falling out of a fishing boat on yet another adventure – the heavenly bureaucracy heaved a sigh of relief. Unfortunately, he departed without leaving an heir.

With Zhengde's sudden, unregretted, departure, the officials moved quickly to rescue the Confucian integrity of the heavenly empire from the eunuchs. Consulting the classics and the family, they tried to find, and justify the appointment of, an imperial candidate who would see things from the scholarly point of view. A fourteen-year-old cousin was found whose rectitude seemed to offer the greatest promise. With Confucius rather rigid about the importance of family lines, the gene-alogies were meticulously consulted. Unfortunately, once consulted, they seemed to support a number of less attractive candidates instead. The greatest of the scholars stretched every possible interpretation of the texts until they found a solution: the now-dead Zhengde Emperor could posthumously adopt the young cousin and thus transform him into a son and heir. The boy was placed upon the throne, and confi-dent in their selection, the officials styled him the Jiajing (Admirable Tranquillity) Emperor.

Within a month it was clear that any idea of tranquillity was noth-ing but an illusion. Confucianly educated and thus filially pious, when informed of the plan, the new emperor refused to be adopted, explain-ing that if he cut himself off from his own dead father, he would be unable to make the necessary ancestral sacrifices. And if he was unable to make the ancestral sacrifices, then he could not possibly satisfy the greatest ritual responsibility that Confucius had given to man. Scholarly heads were scratched. The young man, now emperor, suggested that if one were going to get into the business of a posthumous reordering of family relations, it would be far better, and more acceptable to him, if it were his father, rather than himself, whom Zhengde adopted. In Confucian terms, the new emperor's logic was unassailable. But as the officials scoured the classical texts and the genealogies, they realised that if the father were adopted rather than the son, the dragon throne might be opened to a flood of competing family claims. The scholarly officials politely suggested that the new Son of Heaven might like to think again. He would not.

Once again, a battle of the brushes ensued – but Jiajing stood firm. After three years of heavenly distraction, one day in 1524 the several hundred officials who kow-towed before the emperor at every morning audience assembled as they always did. But this time they refused to disperse. Remaining prostrate before the Hall of Supreme Harmony, they pressed their position in a masterful display of *li*, ritual, as an instrument of imperial shame. 184 were arrested; brutal beatings followed. Still the officials stood their courtyard ground. In the stand-off, however, one senior minister by the name of Wang Yangming looked beyond the black ink of the classical texts and saw a much more fundamental problem: one that was certainly at the heart of the present crisis, but if the truth be told, had haunted the Ming for over a century. It was a problem that had nothing to do with Jiajing and everything to do with the question of what Confucius had really meant when he talked about 'investigating things'.

In the Song dynasty, the scholar Zhu Xi had made it clear that any investigation of things should be exclusively conducted through the officially approved classical texts. With Zhu Xi's opinion having been adopted by the second Ming (Yongle) Emperor, the fabric of the Ming dynasty's reign – from the imperial examinations to the arguing of every point of policy – had been predicated on the supremacy of the written word. But had Zhu Xi really been right to limit the investigation of things to a fixed set of classical books? Senior minister that he was, Wang Yangming dared to suggest that he had not. Surely, he argued, in asking everyone to 'investigate things', Confucius could not possibly have been referring to four books and five interpretations that had not been written until after his own death. If Confucius had been concerned with investigating things, he must have been referring to an investigation of the things in the real world during the time of his life. In which case, insisted Wang Yangming, he must have been telling everyone to exercise their own innate human judgement as to whether an idea was good or bad. Concluding that no intelligent mind worth its salt should need an ancient textbook, however much of a classic it might be, to tell it what was right and what was wrong, Wang Yangming suggested that the officials should stop pestering the new emperor and let him investigate the matter of his ancestry himself.

For an imperial court schooled in the four books and the five classics, the senior minister's ideas were nothing short of treason. But listening to the senior minister, those officials who had managed to retain the power of independent thought agreed that he had a point: the texts were indeed a tyranny that had been burying schools of fine minds not only for the last hundred years but across the last millennium and a half, since the time of the early Han. As one of Wang Yangming's bravest followers observed: 'Confucius never instructed anyone to learn Confucius.' It was, the follower argued, the tyranny of an imperially constructed Confucianism, rather than what Confucius had actually thought, that had buried schools of talented minds − a tyranny that had also deprived every imperial scholar of the simple human power to look at any plain set of facts and draw his own conclusions. No wonder the empire was in such a mess.

Jiajing eventually triumphed in his battle of conscience-over-Confucianism, and was permitted, at least in the matter of the ancestors, to do what he himself thought right. Tranquillity, however, was not to be won. As the oldest son of his father's princely household, Jiajing had been raised to be the summit and centre of everyone else's world. It was this quality that had enabled him to stand up to the scholars with the intransigence required to win. Unfortunately, it was also a quality that made him cruel: so cruel to those around him that at one point his concubines attempted to strangle him. The concubines failed and were brutally executed. But by then Jiajing had become convinced that the Forbidden City was a nest of hostile vipers. Following the example of Zhengde and his Leopard House, he took himself outside the purple walls of the Forbidden City and set himself up in a palace in the wider imperial city beyond. From there, like Zhengtong, he directed the affairs of the empire through a small group of trusted advisers, mostly eunuchs, from without. In any event, like Zhengde, imperial power was of limited interest to him beyond the possibilities of pursuing his own pleasure – and the important matter of extending the span of his own life. Jiajing went on to dedicate most of his energies to exploring the power of mercury in acquiring the immortality that had eluded everyone's ancestors. Devoting himself to the mysteries of alchemy, he left the reins of state in the hands of the eunuchs. Corruption soon stalked the land: even the passing of examinations or the acquisition of an imperial office could be purchased. And with a cruel heart now representing heaven, violence began to spread out from the imperial city like a plague.

Over the next forty years, the Ming lands spiralled ever further out of heavenly order, even as wealth continued to soar to the skies. Those in the cities and towns pursued precious objects and spectacular clothing; those languishing in country estates did everything possible to follow their example. Honest officials disappeared, replaced by men who, as like as not, had purchased their positions in the new market for official situations. Even those who had not purchased their positions were usually willing to sell their decisions to someone who offered a high enough price. With the local magistrates as much a part of the corrupted fabric as anyone else, disputes between rich and poor could have only one outcome, even as resolving disputes between the rich had become a matter of finding the highest price. Trust between the people became as elusive as the elixir of eternal life. With all eyes fixed on using any means to get to the top, and everything and everyone seemingly up for sale, ambition seemed to become a virtue – and whenever ambition was thwarted, rage was quick to follow. Oddly enough, although it was the poor who had everything to rage against, it was those with the greatest wealth who were most likely to fly into an incandescent anger – venting even the tiniest of thwarted whims with tempers that left the objects of their rage in terror for their lands and lives. For those who could afford it, order was everywhere.

When Jiajing finally died in 1567, the throne passed momentarily to his thirty-year-old son who took the title of Longqing (Great Celebration). Dead before the end of his thirty-fifth year, in the short time that he ruled, Longqing nonetheless managed to appoint a grand secretary who was ready and able to confront the chaos of the country. His name was Zhang Juzheng. One of the leading scholars of his time, Zhang was a man who believed that if one knew what was right, one had a moral obligation to do it. Corruption was placed at the top of his host of issues: a plague that had been allowed to spread as if carried by a pack of rats greedily gobbling up every inch of heaven. Costs were cut and taxes were reduced for the poor. Zhang even tried to tackle the age-old riddle of there being more people everywhere except in the registers upon which the imperial taxes were raised, and a country-wide survey of land and people was launched. The fortunes of the imperial treasury revived. But few of the gains would survive Zhang Juzheng's death in 1582. A posthumous assassination of his character not only left his family in ruins but prompted a purge of official positions, which removed almost everyone who had ever agreed with any of his reckless ideas.

Longqing was succeeded in 1572 by a nine-year-old son who would rule under the title of Wanli (Ten Thousand Ages) for nearly fifty years. Few of those years were easy. As a boy, the son had been advised by the sternly moral Zhang Juzheng, and by the time Zhang died, the still-young emperor had decided that things in the Forbidden City were being taken a little too seriously. Once again, the scholarly officials were left to settle their battles on their own. And, looking fondly at the eunuchs who had raised him from childhood, Wanli followed those of his predecessors who had concluded that they would probably make a better job of everything, with a lot less fuss. The scholars kept their official positions but with their influence reduced to dust, most of their highly educated hearts divided into factions. Before long they were at each other's throats. The few scholars who tried to step aside, foolishly thinking that the whole point of office was sacrifice of the self for the greater purpose of a Confucian order, were viciously attacked by peers who wanted to keep things simple and get rich quick. The same few were also exposed to the searing judgements of their families: fathers and relatives who had made heavy investments in securing a son's examination success, and who had no intention of sacrificing their own returns.

The best and most fortunate men took the opportunity to retire from official life to pursue a more meditative existence, far from the reaches of Beijing. As they retired, the eunuchs were offered their positions. Some of the eunuchs were appointed as tax collectors, others as heads of imperial enterprises responsible for essential imperial commodities. With more opportunity than time or dedication, they quickly delegated as many of their responsibilities as possible to local thugs and mercenary officers, who were more than willing to step into the breach.

In 1586, yet another ritual dispute arose. This time, the problem was the Wanli Emperor's desire to leave the empire to his preferred third son, rather than to his eldest, as Confucian tradition required. The most senior officials decided to make a stand and stick to it, withholding their co-operation until the emperor changed his mind. Exasperated at the lock in which the bureaucracy held his powers, from 1601 Wanli refused to make any kind of heavenly appearance at all. Every day for the next twenty years, the heavenly officials gathered before dawn and, scuttling to the Hall of Supreme Harmony, prostrated themselves before the terraced summit of Mount Sumeru and an empty dragon throne.

As the older officials battled on their knees, a number of younger scholars, sharply schooled in the classical texts and newer to the heavenly game, decided it was time for a change. In 1604, the bravest of them founded a society that many saw as a faction. Naming themselves the *Donglin*, East Forest, Academy, after a Buddhist temple at which a respected Song dynasty scholar had once taught, they gathered in the same Wuxi city as the temple, in a southern world that seemed safer than Beijing. Applying a moral compass to the state of heaven on earth, the young members of the academy argued that things could never have come to such a pass if the senior officials had been men of integrity. Nor, they added, could it have happened if the eunuchs had been kept in their place and the Grand Secretariat had not risen across the generations to acquire a power close to that of the emperor himself.

Confucianly trained, and seeing filial piety, rather than personal advancement, as a virtue, the Donglin scholars declined to form an institution that might be seen as questioning Heaven's Son. Their activities were limited to intellectual discussions across literary clubs. But for all of their learning and studious care, they underestimated the depths to which both the senior officials and the eunuchs would go to retain the order of the day. They also underestimated the power of two devilish institutions which had been established in the past. The first was the imperial censorate, created by the first Ming emperor within the scholarly bureaucracy. Able to inspect anyone at any time without rhyme or reason, the imperial censorate pursued the individual members of the Donglin without a measure of heavenly humanity.

The Donglin scholars suffered, but when the Wanli Emperor died in 1620, they were still alive. At that point, however, the leader of the eunuchs, Wei Zhongxian – one of the most calculating and tyrannical imperial servants of all time – decided to take matters into the hands of the eunuchs' own secret service: the *Dong Chang*, Eastern Depot. Originally created for the personal protection of the first Ming emperor, its greatest power was torture. The Donglin Academy was brutally destroyed – and all of those whose lives had touched its members found themselves in the grip of the most terrifying of the Ming dynasty's secret powers.

For the next seven years, a pack of wolves in the shape of a household of eunuchs controlled every inch of the corridors of power. Once again, the weather howled at the injustice of it all. Heaven pretended to rule: first through a young emperor (Taicheng, Great Goodness), who came to power in 1620 but was mysteriously ill for most of his year-long reign; and then through a teenage emperor who took the name of Tianqi (Heavenly Opening). In 1627 both Tianqi and Wei Zhongxian, the tyrannical eunuch, died. The imperial city heaved a momentary sigh of relief at Wei Zhongxian's departure, and a new emperor (Chongzhen, Honourable and Auspicious) ascended to the dragon throne. The empire dared to hope.

The new emperor tried his level best to live up to his name. But as a boy of sixteen who had never been expected to rule, he struggled to do more than hold his place. Unresolved, the problems of the past prowled at large. The tyrannical eunuch was gone, but so was much of the flower of the Ming's intellectual youth. The lands at large were now governed by the lord of silver, with demons riding at his side. Nine out of every ten people were drowning in the mud of poverty, and one in every hundred was floating without a home. As the people were being washed away, official papers rose within the imperial city like mountains while the treasury lay bare. Proclaiming a restoration of the ideas of integrity, humanity and the conscience of the individual, Chongzhen cut every possible cost in sight. Desperate to please – and desperately aware of the chaos into which the heavenly lands had fallen – he even issued an edict commanding each head in the land to purge every evil thought, so that heaven might forgive them all.

Proclaim as he might, good and bad, Chongzhen's officials were exhausted. Cut as he might, the imperial revenues had dried up. Up and down the highways, the times resembled those dangerous days at the end of the Mongol Yuan. Orphans and refugees floundered amid throngs of men whose misfortunes had turned them into bandits. Unpaid soldiers stood ready to serve anyone offering a coin. Cities, towns and villages found themselves hostages to bands of blood brothers who, exhausted by the tyranny of local powers, raised their flags and, lighting torches of flame, looted at will. The hungry, having exhausted the bark of the trees, turned first to clods of earth, and then to the rotting corpses of their fellow men. Perhaps in protest, a freezing shock of weather locked the Yellow River into the metallic grip of ice. Floods and droughts, famines and locusts, earthquakes and epidemics: heaven unleashed them all.

Many no longer had the energy to hope. But, as in the past, there were some who, spurred by rage and driven by a desire to free the people from a dynasty that had so clearly lost its way, found a spirit of rebellion.

As the heavenly lands began to rock, above the Long Wall, up on the steppes, the old Mongols were being challenged by yet another rising tribal power, this one calling itself Manju, the Brave. Settling at the north-eastern edges of the Ming lands, on a peninsula that curved around the eastern sea, the Manju had been one of the tribes offered preferential trade as part of the age-old strategy of dividing the barbarians. Situated at such close proximity to the Ming, they had had ample opportunity to observe the treasures of heaven-on-earth; they had also been quick to note the fading of the Ming dream. When, predictably, the trade turned to border battles, the Manju had invited any Ming official who wanted a better life to join them as they raised a new kingdom: one patterned on the greater ideas of heavenly order, that the Ming themselves had obviously forgotten. As the Manju rose and the Ming crumbled, the border became a constant battleground, even as heaven's treasury struggled to cover the cost. Decorated generals wept at the sight of troops sent to battle with neither weapons, food nor dress. Victims of the final economies of desperation, those soldiers who stayed with their battalions offered their lives, again and again. Seeing brothers sacrificed to a Ming dream that had lost its mandate to rule, many deserted, abandoning the tattered forces of the empire to join the new armies of rebels now pushing towards Beijing.

Among the deserters was a man called Li Zicheng. Born a shepherd, he had long ago lost his sheep, floating from one itinerant job to another until he became first a soldier, and then a rebel in command of his own small band of men. His band became a conquering army and in 1644, having captured Chang'an, present-day Xi'an, he looked east and saw Beijing standing almost defenceless on the plains.

On 24 April 1644, Li Zicheng advanced into the city, quickly laying any objecting Ming forces to rest. Within the innermost recesses of the Forbidden City, the Chongzhen Emperor was in no doubt that heaven wanted a change. Walking out of the now-unguarded Gate of the Black Tortoise at the north end of the Forbidden City, he marched up a hill that had once been raised to provide a *feng shui* shield for the back of the heavenly household. Unable to face his ancestors for shame, the Chongzhen Emperor humbly tore a strip of yellow silk from his imperial gown, tied it in a noose and hanged himself from a tree.

The 'bright' idea of the first Ming emperor had come to a very bad end indeed.

CHAPTER 3

THIS WORLD AND BEYOND

When I watch this benighted world's devices I despair; but
where else can I go?

Li Sao, from *The Songs of Chu* (Qu Yuan,
Warring States period)

SHUFFLING THROUGH LEAVES touched with early-morning dew,
the old master pushed softly on. Appearing and disappearing, the
hint of an upward trail stretched through a mountain landscape of
shadow and light: the omnipresent *yin* and *yang*. Soft bends in the path
presented bamboo groves where leaves brushed the master's passing
shoulders with respect; stalks yielded with grace to the gentle steps
of a thoughtful mind. Every now and then, a sudden turn took his feet
to the brink of a precipice along which he calmly placed one precarious step above another, even as his hands felt their way forward, inch
by inch. Eventually, a clearing was reached: soft earth below, and a
midday sun casting its beams, like blessings, on rocks that towered
above. Flat and firm enough to provide a simple perch for a human life,
the clearing was also sufficiently far away from the dusty flatlands of
the settled plains that few from the settled world below would care to
follow in his wake.

Nearby was a wood: space enough for a simple hut, with trees
providing the necessary timber for a home, and branches ready to
supply a roof. Underfoot, roots tethered in the ground would ensure
a simple sustenance, and in the near distance, the sound of a gurgling
stream promised water for drinking and all necessary reflections. As
as the seasons turned, flowering chrysanthemums would offer tea and
beauty, while bushes of varying shapes and sizes would offer up the
wilder infusions of leaves that could carry a questioning mind on journeys to the mysteries of the world beyond. In the heat of summer, a
cool coppice of low spreading pines would offer an ancient shelter. In

the cold of winter, twigs and branches would fuel a warming fire. By day, the sun would offer a natural warmth. By night, the moon would spread the land with light enough to read. Night and day, clouds would come and go, offering the eternal wisdom that their mists described so well: 'Try to possess your desire and you will lose it. Let it go and it will be yours for ever.' Up before dawn, dancing late into the night with the moon, quietly watching, gently meditating, the master had found a place where the secrets of the ever-changing cosmos could be explored in all their splendour.

Down in the cities below, rushing here and there, frantic minds would, of course, still be raising and demolishing their earthly empires, oblivious to all but the most pressing of ambitions. Their air full of words, their eyes flitting from one glinting prospect to another, their hearts would be lost even to themselves. But that was a world away. From this simple perch above, looking out across the beckoning ridges of a thousand misty mountains, one could see clear to the Kunlun west where heaven truly meets the earth. Breathing in the silence, one could never forget that any deeper meaning was always well beyond words. Nothing false, nothing real: only a treasure beyond compare.

Of course, every now and then an intrepid spirit would try to pay a visit, imagining that heaven was a place, and clumsily clamber up stone steps that some had carved into the sides of rocks to take them to it. The most observant might even detect the hints of a human life – the smoke of a fire not long extinguished, a trail of dust swept with recently fallen leaves, a patch of glowing chrysanthemums by a hint of a hut. But the master would never be there to be seen. Off to heaven or just wandering amid the forest's pines – who could ever know? Seeing the shadows fade like the early-morning mist, even the most persistent would eventually heave a sigh of regret and turn their steps reluc- tantly back towards the plains.

But as they made their way down to the boundaries of this world, their hearts would yet be tugged by the dream of what might lie beyond.

—————

It had all begun so long ago, in that *hun mang* chaos out of which the idea of a *dao* way had beckoned like a siren, eventually revealing a natural order sustained by the energetic force of the *qi*. As heaven and earth had separated and the seasons had formed, out of those swirling mists of everything and nothing had come beasts, birds, trees, fish and eventually, with Nüwa's help, man. In that most ancient *taiping* great peace, the original 'golden age' where man and beast had lived in sympathy with one another under a heaven that seemed to spread as far as the mind could wander, children had lain down with tigers, everyone had chattered to the birds, and carefully contemplating eyes had pierced the secrets of the stars. Fuxi had observed the symphony of numbers from the magic square on a tortoise's back, while other revelations had leapt out of the mysterious natural world. And while more and more men had foolishly concentrated on gathering ever-greater piles of grain, deeper minds, putting their faith in the natural world, had never stopped peering at the treasures of ideas hidden within the physical terrain. Some had plumbed the depths of the inner cosmos, meditating until their spirits stepped into another world. Drinking the offerings of plants, they had climbed onto the backs of willing beasts and soared to the sky for a conversation with heaven above. Feet back on the ground, they had stared at the footprints of the birds and found yet more heavenly messages. And with every day, they had danced in the changing rhythms of the seasons and found themselves in the presence of an order that caused them to catch their breath with awe.

Time, of course, had turned, and the soft creative *yang* had become a harder *yin*. Lesser hearts had captured the magic and cast it into bronze vessels of power, ensnaring gullible human minds with illusions of a natural authority. Meanwhile, the myriad sounds of the skies had been ordered into melodies of music, with every note becoming a prisoner of somebody's composing power. So much attention-catching music that it was hardly surprising that everyone lost their senses. Bundling the people into obedient tribes and settling them along the banks of a yellow river, the most narrow-minded of men had taken the mysteries of the earth and turned them into nothing but the cluttered facts of clouded minds. Yet it was these narrow-minded men who had come to be seen by a foolish world as 'great'. The one had become two: those who wanted to understand the mysteries of the cosmos, and those who simply wanted to order the earth. Even the people of the earth had been divided into a high and a low. While the humble Shennong had tilled the fields shoulder to shoulder with his fellow man, it had not been long before cities had risen and the fields had fallen to the command of the high. Advised by once-shaman spirits who had abandoned the skies for a more profitable pursuit of the order of man, the high had then taken the crests of birds and turned them into hats, whiskers had been transformed into fringes, and furs had been replaced with the silken produce of worms in mulberry trees for clothes.

Then Yu the Great had divided the land into nine ordering provinces. Forests had been tamed with flames, mountains had been opened with gunpowder, rivers had been twisted and turned until none of them, least of all the Yellow River, knew what they should call their beds. Ordered by the high, the low had found themselves as farming hands, set to fields of labour that seemed never to end. The shapes of the provinces had been engraved on a map: the order of the spheres had become the order of man, and the infinite promise of the cosmos had shrunk to the power of a glittering city at the helm of a state.

The Duke of Zhou had tried to recover the most ancient of the golden ages. Gathering together whatever lost wisdom he could find in the bamboo strips and the memories of the surviving shamans, he had put it all into his *Book of Changes*. But setting a book as a guide, it was hardly surprising that later generations had lost the point. While *The Book of Changes* was a masterpiece, once its mysteries had been written down in words, narrower minds had lost the light and seized upon the illusion that the cosmos was a chaos that could and should be ordered into something more convenient for man. Trying to recover the Duke of Zhou's dream five hundred years later, Confucius had doubtless been well intentioned, but what a fool. Caught up in the ropes of the settled city world, he had not been able to see the powers that truly were. Mixing up the order of the cosmos with a set of rules for man, he had done more damage than many of a lesser mind. It was said that he had once encountered Laozi and quickly understood that he had missed something. But if that was the case, the meeting had come far too late: fixed on saving the city-states, Confucius had already lost the plot.

Laozi had tried to help, leaving the legacy of the *Dao De Jing*. Opening with a warning to the reader not to be mesmerised by the written words of any text, if any spirit could have conveyed the mysteries of cosmic order, it was surely this. As the city-states grew in arrogance and power, it was hardly surprising that Laozi himself had chosen to escape the settled world. This world or something else? It was a choice that every spirit of heart and mind was forced to make. Stay, and lose any possibility of discovering the *dao*; or leave, and look for a mountain or a forest where you would be free to find your way.

The plain-speaking Zhuangzi had seen the false promise of the cities for what it was; in his dream of a butterfly (was he dreaming of the butterfly or was the butterfly dreaming of him?), he had not only put his finger on a cosmic question but had sown the seeds of an understanding that the cities, with their promises of paradise, simply made it harder to distinguish between the real and the not real.

As the Zhou world had spiralled into the Warring States, some stubborn minds had tried to have their mooncake and eat it. Confusing the simple life of humanly ordered villages with the mysteries of the cosmos which only an inner meditation could reveal, they tried to recreate the old world of Shennong – the one in which a ruler picked up his own hoe and ploughed his furrows in a community of equal men; they had failed. Later, when Liu Bang as first Han emperor had rewritten the past, it was not only Confucius' works that had been recast. Some even tried to stitch together Laozi's ideas about the *dao* with the Great Man triumphs of the Yellow Emperor, stuffing them both into Shennong's egalitarian seams. But that 'big idea' had only turned the *dao* into an 'ism', offered up for the benefit of those who simply wanted to use heaven as a means of ordering the earth. And then, all sorts of mumbo-jumbo had appeared, including an idea that the Yellow Emperor and Laozi were at the head of a pantheon of heavenly gods, with the *yin* and the *yang*, the five elements of wood, earth, fire, metal and water, not to mention the elemental energy of the *qi*, all wrapped up in a hocus-pocus that would eventually deliver not just equality on earth but immortality for everyone: a whole new idea of a *taiping*, great peace.

Of course, by that point, the waters of the earth had been well and truly muddied by the 'unity' the Han held so dear. Sent off to embrace the rest of the world in the heavenly dream, the Han generals had, however, come upon something rather unexpected. Encountering caravans of trade, they had found golden figures of a meditating man folded in the robes of merchants and accompanying western monks. It soon became clear that the precious treasures of the near-west included a jewel of an idea, which, rather like the *dao*, had been narrowed into an article of faith. Unaware of the existence of Gautama Siddhartha, the Himalayan prince who became the Buddha, many assumed that the meditating statues were of Laozi, who, having made it to *Yindu*, India, was now bringing his ideas back to the heavenly lands. On closer inspection, though, and with a little conversation and reflection, most realised that the man represented by the statue was someone rather different: a prince with a dream of justice and human compassion, offering a promise that there was a place for everyone in a land called Nirvana. This was obviously something very different from Laozi's ideas, although, translated through the many trading languages of the steppe world, it was hard to be clear about what exactly it was. Rather confusingly, everyone who mentioned the place called Nirvana also talked about a 'Buddha nature', which released man from human suffering by melting him into the ocean of a single cosmic consciousness. And somewhere in the baffling descriptions there were strange ideas about *maya*, illusions, that had to be lost, and *sunyata*, an emptiness in which there was no individual self. Mesmerisingly beautiful, it was all a little bit strange.

The simple words of trade failing to convey the truth, travelling imaginations had been stretched and everyone had got confused. And so it was that with a dearth of good translators, the basic elements of the foreign and the familiar wove themselves together. *Dharma*, cosmic duty, became the *dao*, way; *sila*, self-restraint, became *xiao*, filial piety. Nirvana became *tian*, heaven, a world floating somewhere above the earth where the ancestors conferred with the gods. 'Buddha nature' became the Confucian virtues; and the Confucian virtues – *ren*, humanity, *li*, ritual, and yi, integrity – were paired with the Buddhist precepts of non-violence, truth and celibacy. None of these ideas were really diametrically opposed, just sufficiently out of focus for nothing to be clear. One idea, though, stood out on its own, even as it seemed impossible to believe. Apparently, there was a real Buddhist kingdom on earth. Far away in the mountainous west, it was a place where every horizon was lit with glittering temples, the lands were swept with monasteries, and a king sat down among his people and, offering them food of his own, bowed his head to a monk.

A heavenly kingdom that put compassion before considerations of order: now that was a truly novel idea.

As the Han had set off in pursuit of unity, the Yellow Emperor's people received lesson after lesson about the costs of the settled world. Every triumph, and even the losses, had to be paid for in taxes on grains that came from harvests reaped by working hands. And as the triumphs and the losses had piled higher and higher, the peasants had been pushed first into seas of despair and then into storms of bandits. To which, the weather had then added its own flooding judgements, with epidemics of famine and disease following in their wake.

Pushing the barbarian tribes back beyond the Long Wall in the north, and pulling the distant oasis states under the single heaven on earth, the glittering carriages of wealth had retreated behind their own city walls. Struggling to survive in the fields outside, the peasants began to appear like shrunken monsters: faces black, skin as rough as mulberry bark, feet twisted in strange directions. For the people at large, survival had become a matter of chance, with any hope of charity being far more likely to come from the poor than the rich. In such a world, was it any wonder that the minds in the fields wandered to the stories of the most ancient of the golden ages – not the golden age of the Duke of Zhou, but the earlier time of *taiping* great peace, when men had wandered wherever they wanted, and eaten whatever they had hunted or found, when the weather had cast its blessings on all of heaven's people, and when anyone could talk to heaven whenever they wanted, and say whatever they wanted to say. And while some chided them for their foolish dreams, foolish or not, the dreamers were many.

While the fields dreamt of that ancient time of *taiping* great peace, many of those who had come across the Buddhist idea of a heavenly nirvana began to think again. The pursuit of the elusive *dao* seemed to require a meditating human order. Even Confucius had observed that the golden age of the past could be rediscovered only if men would set their hearts straight. Perhaps those Buddha followers had hit upon something important: if an understanding and practice of the Buddha ideas merited the organised faith of a 'Buddh*ism*', supported by temples and monks, then surely the ideas of the *dao* should be given the respect of 'Dao*ism*' as well. Thinking back to Zhuangzi, not everyone agreed:

surely, they argued, the very essence of the *dao* was that it was independent of human machinations.

It was not long, though, before a new text emerged, known as *The Taiping Jing (The Classic of Great Peace)*. Dedicated to the resurrection of an earthly order of Taiping, Great Peace, it included all the roots and branches of the shamanic past: the *yin* and the yang, the five elements of spring wood, summer fire, higher summer earth, autumn metal and winter water, and, of course, the wider wisdom collected in *The Book of Changes*. To these were added the shamanic ideas of meditation and the teaching of a style of breathing that would guide the heavenly *qi* towards earthly harmony and could even prolong the life of man. Under the guidance of the Yellow Emperor and Laozi, and led by an earthly representative in the form of a Celestial Master, the people could be guided back to the purity of the past. Thoughts would be cleansed of disharmony, individual paths would be corrected, and as the proper practices of breathing and eating were taught, the people would be protected from any diseases in this world and be able to find their way to an immortality which would mean they never had to worry about the hidden terrors of any world beyond. Individual hearts and minds corrected, heaven would be happy, and peace would be secured: the peace of the people, and of the seasons and the weather upon which everyone's lives depended.

In 142 CE, a scholar stood up and declared a dream. Born in the northeast but serving as a magistrate in the Jiangzhou commandery, part of present-day Chongqing, his name was Zhang Daoling. Describing his dream to the Jiangzhou people, Zhang said that he had been visited by Laozi, who had commanded him to purify the Han of its destroying decadence by seeding a vanguard of penitent people. A kingdom was to be declared in which the purity of each individual's life would be so great that peace would be guaranteed and immortality would be as natural as the air. Listening, the people of Jiangzhou thought about their own dreams, and the stories of their many different pasts. Some were descendants of families that had been sent south by the First Qin Emperor in the wake of the early southern conquests. Others were later-arriving migrants, who had floated in on the recolonising waves of the Han. But many were the descendants of an earlier Ba people whose Ba state had, like so many others, been conquered twice, first by the Qin and then again by the Han. Looking at his motley flock,

Zhang Daoling invited everyone, Han Chinese and Ba alike, to join him in a movement to raise a new order of Taiping Great Peace, led by himself as Celestial Master, and supported by a celestial bureaucracy. Everyone would confess the sins of their past and find their illnesses cured. Inhaling and exhaling in harmony with the cosmos, they would be a community of brothers and sisters, united as the single breath of the people's peace. Lost by the decadent dynasties of the past, the blessings of heaven would return. All that was required to join was a contribution of five pecks of rice to a common pot from which everyone would eat.

For a people labouring under the taxes of the unifying Han, the vision was intoxicating. Backs breaking, many of the Han migrants joined the new community, as did the Ba: dreaming of regaining their lost independence, they saw the possibility of a greater freedom from the iron fist of imperial rule.

Time passed, the Han dynasty weakened from within, and in 156 CE Zhang Daoling passed away. But his son and grandson followed as Celestial Masters in his footsteps. The taiping dream spread across Sichuan and beyond: envoys of the Celestial Masters not only went up to the Zhang family's north-east heartland, but even reached into the souls of imperial officials, who, like the people, were now struggling with the turmoil of a crumbling power. By the beginning of 184, seeing itself as the 'breath of the people's peace', the movement had acquired the colour of a rebellion and a name after a cloth: 'Yellow Turban'. Yellow, the colour that had come to mean the centre of everything; turbans after the scarves the peasant rebels wrapped around their heads. Led by spirit troops and generals, the peasant rebels swept across the land like a purifying wind. And as the rebels fanned to the east, west, north and south, in a mountain-wrapped valley in deepest Sichuan, an independent 'Daoist' kingdom was proclaimed: the Kingdom of Taiping, Great Peace.

Across the year of 184, the Yellow Turbans inflicted shocking defeats upon the imperial Han army. Startled by the speed with which these 'human portents' had spread, the Han Emperor promised everything to the warlord-generals of his garrisons if only they could remove the blight of the peasant rebels. The sweeping body of the Yellow Turbans was defeated within a year. But the Kingdom of Taiping, Great Peace survived in its Sichuan valley for another thirty years of celestial self-rule. When it finally collapsed, its many limbs scattered rather than disappeared, continuing to break into rebellions for decades, if not centuries, to come.

The defeat of the Yellow Turbans had come at a high price. It was not long before Cao Cao, the great general, took advantage of the weakness that the rebels had created, and kidnapped the emperor. The emperor lost to a warlord, it was not much longer before the whole of the once-unified Han lands splintered into three, more temporal, kingdoms, each led by a warlord in pursuit of the heavenly mandate that would bring everywhere back under the order of a single heavenly son. Each warlord was armed with the same ideas of the *dao* and the same Confucian texts; all were guided by Sunzi's *Art of War*.

With such a common past, each of the competing rulers looked for the great idea that would give them a defining advantage in the present. One, the ruler of the Kingdom of Shu-Han, whose lands included part of present-day Sichuan, was directed to a hermit, whose thoughts were said to be as sharp as crystal and whose talents apparently included an ability to call down cascades of rain. So great and so mysterious were the man's powers that, although his name was Zhuge Liang, he was widely known as the 'Crouching Dragon'. When the Shu-Han ruler suggested that the Crouching Dragon call upon him for an audience, he was informed that this was a man who did not call upon anybody, and rarely allowed anyone to call upon him. The ruler swallowed his pride and made the journey – several times – to persuade the Crouching Dragon to give up his lair for the Shu-Han cause. Refusing all distractions from a meditating life, and without the least interest in who might be running the settled world, Zhuge Liang remained intransigent – until the ruler hit upon the argument that a meditating mastery of the cosmos would be worth nothing if the physical world collapsed.

Entering Shu-Han service, Zhuge Liang brought with him treasures of uncluttered concentration: a deep knowledge of astronomy, a cosmic mastery of the changing principles of *yin* and *yang*, and flights of shamanic imagination which left other minds far behind. It was not long before the Shu-Han scored a string of victories, almost all from situations that had appeared to be certain jaws of defeat. Stories of the Crouching Dragon's powers flew across all of the Three Kingdoms, becoming a force of their own. A favourite was the story of how, trapped by a general of the opposing Kingdom of Wu, Zhuge Liang played a leisurely game of chess on the walls of a city, in full view of the encircling Wu troops. So brazen was the game, and so great was Zhuge Liang's reputation, that the Wu general assumed it must be an ambush and withdrew his men.

The best of the Zhuge Liang stories, though, the one that shot itself into everyone's heart, was the Battle of the Borrowed Arrows. Set on the banks of the misty Yangzi River, it unfolded when the Shu-Han were about to face the other of their two opponent kingdoms: the Cao Wei. Arriving at the appointed place of battle after a long and exhausting march, the Shu-Han found that their troops had run out of arrows. Spirits already tired and fear now beginning to rustle through the ranks, Zhuge Liang stood calmly on the bank of the river and looked for the *dao*. Consulting the elements around him, he listened to the wind, watched the clouds, observed the bend of the river and its currents, and reflected on what he knew of the enemy warlord, and on the likely state of mind of the Cao Wei troops assembled on the opposite bank. Everything considered, Zhuge Liang told the Shu-Han ruler that they should 'borrow' some arrows from their Cao Wei enemy. Eyebrows were raised, but a squadron of Shu-Han ships was summoned up for a sail, and a crew was created not from standing soldiers but out of bales of straw, clothed to look like men. The evening mists fell, and silent feet were commanded to lead the ships up the river towards the Cao Wei camp, pulling them by ropes from the Shu-Han bank. As expected, sharp Cao Wei scouts were quick to spot the shadowy movements in the mist and instantly informed their general of an impending stealth attack. Congratulating them on their powers of observation, the Cao Wei general roused his archers from their rest and ordered them to shoot a hail of arrows towards the Shu-Han ships. As the arrows settled obligingly into the straw, the Shu-Han troops shouted out in jubilation. That night, the Cao Wei troops tossed and turned, wondering what kind of trick had been played at their expense, while the Shu-Han slept soundly in the knowledge that the Crouching Dragon had fooled their enemy before the battle had even begun. The story of the borrowed arrows spread like wildfire, over a thousand years later becoming one of the most loved stories in the *Romance of the Three Kingdoms*, a people's classic that told the tale of the times. For every ear that heard it, then and thereafter, the wisdom of the *dao* became the promise of a secret inner power that could snatch a saving miracle from the trembling terror of any threat.

The death of Zhuge Liang, in 234, would weaken the power of the Shu-Han, eventually opening the gates of all three kingdoms to a battling succession of dynasties founded by warlord-rebels and steppe conquerors alike. By 304, the northern lands were shattering into what would become sixteen kingdoms in the north, and a succession of short-lived dynasties in the south. Many of the new northern states had been founded by horse-borne conquerors who had already embraced the travelling ideas of the Buddha and now carried them into the settled world. As Daoist Celestial Masters were gathering souls both north and south, in the northern plains of nomadic conquests Buddhist temples began to rise on the horizon. Offered a choice, many stayed true to the dream of a Laozi-led Taiping, Great Peace. But others began to float towards the Buddha, whose soft face seemed to promise a much simpler compassion and an even more tantalising dream: a world free of an all-controlling heaven, one where even a king might sit down among his people, and bow his head to a monk. A dream where the people would be free talk to heaven whenever they wanted, and say whatever they wanted to say. As the heavenly lands had separated, so, once again, had their hearts.

As the temporal kingdoms battled, within the Daoist world, two new celestial kingdoms were founded. One, naming itself the Kingdom of Great Perfection, was raised in 306 in the old Ba lands of central Sichuan. Claiming a direct descent from Zhang Daoling's old Kingdom of Taiping, Great Peace, its Celestial Master took the name of Li. Although it lasted for less than fifty years, just like the old Kingdom of Taiping, Great Peace, its followers scattered to all corners of the country, bringing with them a belief in a coming apocalypse, which only those who sought the grace of the *dao* could escape – and also the idea that their salvation would eventually be delivered by man called Li.

The second of the celestial kingdoms attached itself to a temporal power for greater success. Rising in 424 in northern lands recently conquered by one of the Buddhism-embracing steppe tribes ruling as the dynasty of the Northern Wei, it was founded by a Daoist priest who also claimed a link to the old Kingdom of Taiping, Great Peace. Declaring, like Zhang Daoling, that he had been visited by Laozi, the priest told the Northern Wei Emperor that, while he might be labouring under a delusion of Buddhism, he was in fact a reincarnation of the Perfect Lord of the Daoist Taiping, Great Peace. The revelation led the ruler to convert to Daoism, and a large part of northern China became a Daoist state. The Daoist priest was rewarded with an imperial title; and as the Taiping Kingdom of the Northern Wei stretched, Buddhism was purged like a plague. Buddhist images and texts were set to flames; Buddhist monks were dispatched to whatever world awaited them beyond. And as each Buddhist pagoda was smashed to the ground, it was replaced with a temple dedicated to the new Daoist idea.

Like the earlier Kingdoms of Taiping, Great Peace, however, the Daoist hold on the north did not last long – no longer than the death of the steppe emperor who had been converted by the dream. Bloodied, but by no means defeated – and never really wrenched from the hopeful hearts of its followers on the ground – Buddhism returned to the northern plains. While the old Daoist temples were left to stand, new temples raised the Buddhist idea to even greater golden heights, with vast images of the Buddha carved into the towering cliffs of the north-eastern landscape.

But the Taiping, Great Peace did not suffer its fall from northern grace in silence. While the idea of a Daoist kingdom might have been suspended, whispers of a coming apocalyptic reckoning were spreading and becoming louder by the year: Laozi would return in the shape of an avenging saviour called Li, and under the purifying sword of that saviour, the Daoist good would once and for all be freed from everything Buddhist and bad. As the northern Daoists waited for their avenging Li, the earthly representatives of both persuasions energetically competed for the people's souls. Buddhist and Daoist alike, monks began to call upon every charm they could muster, borrowing the best of them from each other. Miracles were declared from all directions. And the stage was set for a tussling dance of celestial ideas that would last for centuries to come.

As the north battled for souls, down in the south, a softer style of Buddhism had been arriving on the trading winds of the southern sea. In the early years of the sixth century, an entirely new Buddhist idea arrived in the southern garrison of Guangzhou – in the form of a south Indian monk wandering under the name of Bodhidharma: *bodhi* being the name of the tree under which Gautama Siddhartha had become the

Buddha; *dharma* the Sanskrit word for actions that correspond with the cosmic order. The monk had come out of present-day Kerala, walking through south-western lands that had been home to individual states before conquest by the Han, and were now, again, a host of independent southern kingdoms. Teaching as he travelled, and broadly following in the steps of earlier Indians who had gone before him, Bodhidharma eventually found his way to a monastery that had been established by earlier Indian monks. Set on Mount *Shaoshi*, in the thick of *lin*, woods, its name was *Shaolin*.

Offering to teach for his keep, the monk shared the secrets of a martial art he had learnt in the Indian south: a skill of hand-to-hand combat known as *kalaripayattu*. Shaolin's monks were trained to fly like lightning, strike like thunder, and appear silently behind an opponent whenever least expected. Lessons taught, Bodhidharma then turned his body to face a wall and spent the next nine years sitting in a waking silence. When he left the Shaolin monastery, he bequeathed an art that, combined with Daoist ideas about the cosmic energies of the *qi* and the constant movement of *yin* and *yang* change, would come to be known as *tai qi*. He also left the inspiration for a new method of meditation so powerful that, developed under later Chinese monks, it would come to be described as 'the sound of one hand clapping'. Named *chan*, a transliteration of the Sanskrit word *channa* for meditation, it would eventually travel from China across the sea to Japan – where the character for *chan* would be pronounced as 'zen'.

In 589, when the many battling kingdoms in the north were united under the single dynasty of the Sui, the Buddhist idea that had arrived on horseback from the steppes stayed with them. And when Yang Jian, the first Sui emperor, reunified the north and the south he not only availed himself of the valuable administrative services of the Confucian scholars, but strengthened the force of his army with an appeal to the common attachment to a Buddhism that had now, albeit by very different routes, found its way into both the north and the south. Under the Sui, the heavenly lands were touched with glittering Buddhist temples, all stroked with graceful groves of bamboo and sheltered by lofty pines, and all intoning the charms of golden sutras. To these, Yang Jian added a string of pagoda-like stupas, each holding a relic of the Buddha as a talisman of his ideas. Yang Jian did not ignore the fact that the north had been swept with Daoism – or that Daoism had become a faith with many following hearts. Acknowledging the equality of the Daoist idea, he permitted the Daoist temples to continue their dreams. But taking note of their rather stormy history of rebellion – and clear that any other worlds, whether Daoist or Buddhist, would naturally compete with the temporal order of an empire – he also created an imperial bureaucracy devoted to the management of both the Buddhist *and* the Daoist realms. Temples and monks of both persuasions were ordered to register with the state; and anyone wishing to leave the productive purpose of the lay life for the meditations of a monastery was required to secure an official certificate of ordination.

Firm foundations laid, Yang Jian then followed his own heart. Climbing to the tops of mountain peaks from which earlier emperors had proclaimed the successful fulfilment of their duty to heaven above, he described a universal empire touched with Buddhist bodhisattvas floating on clouds. Noting the ancient proclamations engraved on mountain rock – not least, those of the First Qin Emperor – he acknowledged them as little more than the footnotes of a foggy past. Instead, on sacred places that had once been seen as fit only for the single conversation conducted by a Son of Heaven, Yang Jian raised a host of Buddhist temples and monasteries designed to lift everyone's hearts and conversations closer to the skies. Gifted Chinese hands, inspired by the wider vision of the Buddhist world, and trembling at the thought of the endless wheel of an unenlightened life, then picked up their brushes and painted images of elaborate layers of reincarnating Buddhist heavens and hells. Touched with golden sutras and protected by the precious relics of the Buddha, gems of temples conjured up dreaming visions of other lives. And the lands of the north became increasingly devoted to the pursuit of Nirvana by a people whose past had left them in desperate search for the justice, compassion and truth of another world.

As the Sui offered a Buddhist route to paradise, however, Daoist hearts began to grumble. Daoist dragons muttered in dark caves; Daoist tigers growled in their lairs; Daoist tortoises drew in their heads in disbelief at the parlous state of affairs; and Laozi, the greatest Daoist of them all, was said to be sighing to himself like the wind. As the Sui praised the Buddha for his blessings, Daoist priests reminded everyone of cosmic warnings of apocalypses that had not been heeded. By the early 600s, while Buddhist souls meditated on mesmerising sutras, a

new generation of Heavenly Masters and followers were not only raising their eyes to their own Daoist heaven but were anxiously watching
for the second coming of Laozi – in the form of a man called Li.

Confidently expected since 512, Li's arrival had obviously been
delayed. Heavenly calculations had been made again, and although no
one was prepared to set another date, hopes had risen that it would
not be long before the saviour arrived and led his people back to the
promised Kingdom of Taiping, Great Peace. Buddhism might be rising
to the rafters, but every time there was a flood, nodding Daoist heads
muttered about the punishments of heaven, and pointed to visions of
Laozi appearing across the skies. Added to which, dragons were now
regularly seen blowing flames in the clouds above, with mysterious
verses appearing on the air chanting magic numbers and pointing out
meaningful colours for everyone's attention. With every flood, every
vision and every floating dragon, more and more rumours spread of an
imminent reckoning that was about to sweep the Sui away.

Deaf and blind to the Daoist dreams, the Sui continued to build
their world, adding the flourishing triumph of the new Grand Canal,
the digging of which tore hundreds of thousands of men from their
fields and families. The higher the Sui glory rose, the more deeply the
labouring people suffered. And the more deeply the people suffered,
the faster rebellions began to rise up all over the place. By the early
600s, the latest descendants of the Celestial Masters had decided that
the time must surely now be nigh. In 617, the warlord in charge of a
Sui garrison in the near-west was persuaded by his son to seize the
reins of power and sweep the Sui into the dust. No one was surprised
when his name turned out to be Li. As visions of a jubilant Laozi were
widely reported to have been seen in the skies, bigger than ever before,
Li father and son presented their celestial credentials for all to hear
and see, and announced the founding of a new dynasty of the Tang.
True, they had obviously useful military talents, but their fitness to
rule was grounded on the fact that they were surely none other than
the descendants of Laozi himself.

―――――――

Once the dust of rebellion had settled, the new Tang dynasty
declared a return of the age of *taiping*, great peace. As filially pious

descendants, Li father and son raised Laozi and the Daoist idea from what had been the margins of the Sui's Buddhist world to the highest peaks of imperial faith. Daoist scholars were invited to join a new bureaucracy, which would serve a now Daoist imperial court – albeit one that would continue to be grounded, like all preceding dynasties, on the practical principles of Confucianism. When Li, the son, proclaimed himself the Taizong (Supreme Ancestor) Emperor, Laozi was given the even loftier title of Taishang Xuanyuan Huangdi (Supreme, Mysterious and Primordial Emperor). As Daoist temples, and the calendars of Daoist festivals, spread across the land, imperial ears were also opened with a greater sympathy to the warnings of officials who, both Daoist and Confucian, reported their collectively deep concerns about the dangers of the Buddhist faith. Millions of misguided souls had stepped out of the settled life, they argued, abandoning their filial duties and now wandering about in the meditating emptiness of monasteries dedicated to a devilishly foreign idea. Burying themselves in clouds of sutras, they had left their loyal brothers to carry the burdens of farming and to provide the labour for imperial construction and war. While others toiled, these turncoats were worshipping gilded figures of mud in rituals that were nothing if not barbaric. Having taken vows of celibacy, they were also a threat to the most fundamental of all of the Confucian beliefs: the duty of sons to revere their fathers. And if celibate Buddhists no longer had sons who could revere any fathers, then it would not be long before everyone started to question the value of the family, and with it the essential and unquestioning submission of every human heart to heaven's imperial Son.

Increasingly urged to 'do something' about the people who had been seduced into the Buddhist world, the Taizong Emperor searched for a solution. As the reincarnation of Laozi, he was sympathetic to their concerns. As the Son of Heaven with an empire to run, he fully appreciated the importance of having obedient heavenly offspring. But having reached the pinnacle of temporal power, he was also anxious not to offend the millions who had stubbornly attached themselves to the Buddhist call. Neither was he quite ready to sack the Buddha who, judging by the miracles that the Buddhist monks proclaimed, was still a power to be reckoned with. Assuring the Celestial Masters that they were closest to his heart, he declared that he would protect the

Daoist faith, and vest full imperial trust and confidence in the Daoist priests. With Laozi now the greatest of the imperial ancestors, it was the Daoist priests alone who were qualified to supervise the appropriate ritual offerings. But as aware as the Sui of the dangerous power of the 'other world', the Taizong Emperor was careful to set limits on the numbers of temples and monks, and to apply them to Daoists and Buddhists alike.

Out of imperial favour but still known for its deep compassion, Buddhism continued to attract a mass of faith. It also inspired a lot of searching questions about the Indian lands from which it had originally come. With translators still in short supply, these included a number of questions about what the Buddhist texts really meant. From time to time, frustrated with the twisted tongues, brave Buddha-following hearts had set off from the heavenly lands to try to find the truth for themselves. Following in the footsteps of Zhang Qian, one intrepid monk set off to India in 399, risking his life across the Taklamakan desert and the *kara buran*, black sandstorms, that were the terror of man and beast. Returning safely, much to the surprise of everyone, not least himself, he brought back astonishing tales of another world where tribute really *was* offered by kings to monks. He also brought back stories of a remarkably happy people, who, unlike those in the heavenly lands, were free to roam wherever they wanted and even free to farm any open piece of land at will. In 629, another monk decided to go and dig a little deeper: his name was Xuanzang.

The times were challenging. Rebellions in the Tang world had unsettled imperial spirits, even as a new confederation of Turkic tribes was gathering up a storm at the northern frontier. Imperial permissions for travel abroad, never easy to secure, had been suspended, and Xuanzang's application for a pass was denied. But Xuanzang was not only curious, he was also driven by a dream in which he had seen the sacred Buddhist mountain Sumeru, standing at the centre of the cosmos. Surrounded by sea and seemingly impossible to reach, in his dream a sudden wind had carried him to the top and shown him a view that surpassed all others. After such a revelation, the mere matter of an imperial prohibition was not enough to stop him. Xuanzang set off for the Jade Gate at the west of the settled world, the same Jade Gate through which Laozi had departed over a thousand years before.

Arriving, he waited for the cover of night, and slipped silently out of the heavenly kingdom.

Travelling west, the young monk passed across deserts whose perils were almost too numerous and terrifying to recall: the black sandstorms that buried men alive, and singing sands that turned to flames. Eventually, he found his way to the bustling Turfan oasis, then on to glittering Samarkand and from there to Bactria, present-day Afghanistan, once battled over by Alexander the Great. Eager to learn, Xuanzang listened to everything that the inhabitants of the oasis states could tell him, then pushed on across the mountains of the Hindu Kush, struggling over trails deep in snow, and even deeper in bandits. Finally, he hit upon a path that carried him down into the valleys of the northern Sindhu lands. Over the next sixteen years, Xuanzang travelled across a wider India and observed a living – although if truth be told, a now slightly fading – Buddhist world. Starting at Gandhara, where Bactrian Kushan kings had carved huge images of the Buddha into towering cliffs, he went on to Nalanda, which thousands of Buddhist teachers and even greater numbers of students had transformed into the greatest centre of knowledge the world had ever known. From Nalanda, Xuanzang wandered on, further west and far to the south, touching every Buddhist temple and mind that he could find. On his way back to the east, travelling through northern India, he was even invited to attend a grand Buddhist Council – attended by no less than two Buddhist kings.

By the time that Xuanzang returned to Chang'an, in 645, he had acquired hundreds of Buddhist texts and a new understanding of the Buddhist idea, which would sharpen everyone's translations. Although he had crept out in the dead of a 629 night, he was welcomed back as an exploring hero: the man who had gone further than any descendant of the Yellow Emperor before him, pushing knowledge of the western world of India to unimagined heights. Opening his imperial arms wide, the Taizong Emperor invited him to exchange his monastic vows for any one of a host of imperial positions. Humbly declining, wary of the risks, Xuanzang suggested instead that he write an account of his journey to satisfy the imperial curiosity. Retiring into the safety of his own Buddhist heart, he then set about translating the treasures he had so painstakingly carried home.

In 649, the Taizong Emperor passed on to another world. Daoist or Buddhist? So deep had been his conversations with the returning Xuanzang that no one could be entirely sure. On earth, however, the still-Daoist throne passed to his son, the Gaozong (High Ancestor) Emperor, who seemed to have no interest in Buddhism at all. More temples were raised to Laozi; more heavenly titles were added to Laozi's name. Once again, the old sacrifices were made to heaven, raised from mountains that, once blemished with Buddhist colours and names, had now been firmly reclaimed for the Daoist glory of heaven and its son.

The Gaozong Emperor ruled for thirty-four years. When he eventually joined the ancestors, he passed the throne to a young son under the regency care of his second wife, the boy's mother, Wu Mei. An earthly force to be reckoned with, after seven years as regent, in 690, Wu Mei raised herself to become First Empress in her own right; she would later be known by the imperial name of Wu Zetian (Flourishing Heaven). Across the imperial bureaucracy, Confucian brushes unleashed storms of outraged opinion. Wu Zetian stood firm. Dismissed from Confucian favour, she decided that, while the Confucian bureaucracy had its uses, it was time to turn everyone's hearts back to the Buddhist faith. Within the blink of a year the shocked spirits of the court – Daoist and Confucian alike – saw their positions of influence disappear. To emphasise her point, the imperial court was then transported from what had become the Daoist trenches of Chang'an to a Buddhist reinterpretation of the old Zhou capital of Luoyang. Once installed in Luoyang, declaring the foundation of a new Zhou dynasty, Wu Zetian raised her own Hall of Light, constructed according to all of the heavenly principles inherited from the ancient shamans and gathered together by the Duke of Zhou – with a grand statue of herself, as a Buddhist Bodhisattva, set in the middle of Fuxi's old magic square.

Contemplating her heavenly position, Wu Zetian then turned her attention to the imperial titles that adorned her name. Keeping all those she had inherited from the Daoist-Confucian heaven, she added a Buddhist flourish: 'Maitreya the Peerless' – a reference to herself as the reincarnation of a famous 'future Buddha' who, having found enlightenment, declined to take up his rightful place in Nirvana and instead returned to earth, determined to save the world. Now the Maitreya

Buddha in an imperial heaven, Wu Zetian opened the lands of her empire to Buddhism, like a pool of shimmering lotuses. Mountains recently returned to the Daoists recovered their Buddhist names. Buddhist temples were bestowed with imperial fortunes. And the treasures of the Tang's unified riches, with their spreading conquered lands and sparkling trades, were turned towards those monasteries that put the Buddha at their heart.

Wu Zetian eventually floated away from the earth in 705. On her death, the flower of Buddhism was swept aside and imperial attention was redirected to the Dao. Daoist hearts leapt in relief, and the Celestial Masters were returned to their heavenly positions at the old court of Chang'an, restored to its position as the capital. Within ten years of her death, her grandson, the Xuanzong (Mysterious Ancestor) Emperor was setting the Buddhist monasteries alight and redirecting charitable donations of gold and jewels to other causes. Monks were firmly reminded of their filial duty to place parents and the emperor above any distracting Buddhist dreams. And anyone unable to provide an official certificate of ordination was returned to the farming fields. Meanwhile, Laozi's *Dao De Jing* was declared the most important of all heavenly works (required reading for all), and Laozi himself acquired yet another heavenly title: Tianbao (Heavenly Treasure). But Tianbao notwithstanding, the Buddhist spirit did not disappear. While the bigger temples struggled to survive the redirection of imperial donations, smaller temples remained. And the Buddhist sutras, learnt by heart, were secretly sheltered by loyal souls hoping for a future change.

Over much of the next century and a half, the lotus floated out of imperial favour. A symbol of enlightenment for its power to grow in splendour out of the muddiest of water, the flower of Buddhism was nothing, however, if not resilient. From time to time, depending on the nature of the emperor, purging flames were unleashed just to make sure that everybody knew which celestial kingdom was in power. But after each and every outburst, the stubborn lotus would open its petals once again, blossoming ever more brightly than before. Each time, Daoist and Confucian officials would mutter darkly that foreign ancestors were not to be welcomed in heaven's lands. But as the years passed, up and down the wider streets of Chang'an and out across the empire, it was increasingly the Buddha's temple bells that chimed most clearly, the images of Buddhist bodhisattvas that gazed down with the greatest compassion, and the soft Buddhist sutras, murmured on chanting Buddhist processions, that coloured the best days of earthly life. And while charity was provided by Daoists and Buddhists alike, Daoist alms were distributed on strict family lines, whereas those of the Buddhist monasteries provided for all of the poor, even those without a family.

Eventually, in 860, after 150 years of celestial ups and downs, the imperial tide turned again. A new emperor, the son of a father who had secretly found much to be recommended in the Buddhist idea, returned the Buddha to the highest peaks of imperial favour. Once again, Tang riches poured into Buddhist temples and Tang hearts followed the lotus: stupas and pagodas sparkled with gold; the Buddha's birthday became a festival for all; and, lighting the streets of every new spring year, a lantern festival shone the brightest of Tang lights on departed Buddhist souls. So great was the emperor's devotion, that even the relics of the Buddha's bones were worshipped.

A hundred years later, in 960, after another set of battles had given way to the new dynasty of the Song, the Confucians finally decided that it was time to take a look at their own articles of faith. Always sharply focused on the temporal order, under the Tang they had experienced something of a battering from the competitive spirits of the Daoist and the Buddhist worlds. Slowly, however, they had learnt the lesson that, great though the heavenly classics might be, the people of the earth needed something more than books. Pondering the possibilities, new Confucian thinkers stretched the Han interpretation of the Confucian idea to embrace the cosmological elements of the Daoist Great Peace. Just to be on the safe side, they added a golden stroke of Buddhist compassion. While everything remained firmly within the old trinity of heaven, earth, and the emperor as a Son of Heaven in between, the newest version of Confucianism had a stronger emphasis on the idea of charity as a quality of human life.

The Confucians were not the only ones to revisit their beliefs. In the eleventh century, a Song dynasty emperor found himself facing the typical challenges of the north: bad weather, failing harvests, and a peasant people who were losing their way. One night, he had a dream in which a Jade Emperor appeared from the mists and promised him a triumph over all. Waking up to an earth that delivered nothing but trouble, he was reassured when a favour-seeking scholar-artist presented him with a painting of harmony in the form of a majestic mountain where men and women wandered in a land of plenty; it was entitled *Early Spring*. Aghast at the lie, a braver scholarly artist decided to tell the truth with a darker set of brushes. Painting a picture of desperate men, women and children, blown by buffeting winds, stung by storms of sand, and wandering through a chilling landscape, dotted with stumps where trees had once stood and dashed with ponds so dry that anyone could pick up a rotting fish, he called it: *Floating People of the Earth*, and delivered it to the emperor. Staring at the shocking images of the 'floating people', the emperor had a quiver of human conscience. But not for long: official spirits ensuring that the reckless brush was despatched to the feverish south and, looking to the skies for blessings, the Jade Emperor was raised to some of the highest imperial honours that a desperate Son of Heaven could confer: 'Highest Author of Heaven, of the Whole Universe, of Human Destinies, of Property, of Rites and the Way; Most August One; and Grand Sovereign of Heaven'.

One hundred years later, another Song dynasty emperor would confer yet more honours on the Jade Emperor, adding an entire celestial bureaucracy to be served by the imperial court. Replicating every imperial position on earth, every official was commanded, henceforth, to serve their celestial counterparts as a natural extension of their earthly duties. To ensure that the punishing possibilities of such an extension were fully exploited, the terrifying powers of the Buddhist deities who presided over the lower levels of hell were also incorporated into the heavenly pantheon.

But the Jade Emperor and his new bureaucracy seemed to be as vulnerable as any of their mortal counterparts to the events of this world. In 1276, when the Song finally fell to the Mongol Yuan, it was a shaman spirit, Tengr, who took pride of place, touched by strokes of Buddhism from the western steppes.

Settling themselves into the saddle of a greater power, keen to maintain heavenly efficiency, the Mongols were happy to let the Confucian officials keep their new-found faith in a Jade Emperor, and the celestial bureaucracy was retained. Confucian hearts were not, however, pacified. Although not every official felt able to make the dissenting journey up to remote mountains of retreat, many retired into their studies and conjured up other worlds with brushes of poetry and painting. Carefully coded to avoid Mongol detection, these were just as clear a protest as anything that might have been said out loud. The Mongols found themselves serenaded with soft images of the natural world – delicate scenes of rocks, bamboo and plum blossom, all of which seemed, to their untrained eyes, to be evidence of nothing but a foolish Chinese love of natural beauty. To the trained Chinese, though, the painted images were piercing daggers of defiance. Bamboos swaying in the wind might look to the invading Mongols like pictures of a rural idyll, but to Song dynasty hearts they were declarations of a Chinese endurance that would outlive any steppe usurpers. Plum blossom flowering in winter was nothing less than a silent statement that the heavenly idea would ultimately triumph over the brutality of even the greatest northern force.

As heaven would have it, the force that ultimately swept the northerners back to the steppes did not come from scholarly brushes but from the peasants who, as usual, had borne the greatest of the burdens. More than half of them had died in the catastrophes of icy drought, famine, locusts, and a Black Death that haunted the last decades of the Great Mongol Yuan. Many of those who survived owed their lives to the undiscriminating charity of Buddhist monasteries. Open to all, beyond offering a rescuing bowl of soup, these spreading refuges offered lessons in writing characters so that even a peasant could learn to chant the sutras. And the chanting sutras held the promise of a future world in which men could free themselves from material chains.

When Zhu Yuanzhang, the rebel who became the first Ming emperor, swept into the Mongols' northern Dadu capital, he and his followers rode under the military colours of a secret society that called itself the White Lotus. Buddhist in inspiration, it was dedicated to watching for the reincarnation of the Maitreya Future Buddha – the very same Maitreya Future Buddha adopted by Wu Zetian, representing the idea of a spirit who would save hearts struggling in the present world. The White Lotus Society was also dedicated to the restoration of a world in which men would live simple lives with no personal possessions, free from the torments of desire. While the first Ming emperor would later lose his trust in everything (from Buddhists to chief ministers), the dream of another world on the present earth, a simple land populated by people with simple wants, would become the foundation of his empire. Buddhist in inspiration, it was not so different from the older dream of resurrecting a Taiping Great Peace. Ultimately, the dream would be betrayed by a wealth his own great order had paradoxically created – swept away by the reign of a son whose pursuit of pomp and glory would unleash a tide of trading greed in which the worst of hearts would flourish and take root. But it was a dream that would long outlive the Ming.

For the Ming emperors, and for those officials who could afford to emulate them, the greatest interest was not in reaching another world but avoiding death in this one. Buddhist or Daoist, it did not really matter which persuasion a priest followed, as long as he offered immortality. In the event, it was Daoism's inner alchemy, with exotic concoctions of gold and mercury inherited from the desperate dreams of the First Qin Emperor, that proved the most seductive: not only to emperors but to officials as well. Outside the Forbidden City, though, the vast majority of the population was more immediately concerned with understanding whether and how 'another world' might help them navigate the challenges of this one.

Both Buddhism and Daoism offered the promise of salvation. Indeed, after a thousand years of competing for Chinese souls, their boundaries had become rather blurred. Popular Buddhist bodhisattvas had been 'borrowed' regularly by the Daoists' ever-expanding pantheon of gods; and the Song dynasty's Celestial Bureaucracy had come to include so many Buddhist layers of heavens and hells that even Laozi would probably have got lost.

By the middle of the Ming dynasty, the two faiths were no longer life-and death-defining choices, but alternative guides with which to navigate the tempests of the present world – while doing one's best to optimise one's chances in whatever might come next. Daoists continued to offer ancient wisdom: breathing techniques for instant help in the face of malicious influences; dragon slips of paper on which requests for celestial assistance could be written, then swiftly swept up to heaven in a puff of ethereal smoke. Buddhists, now also amenable to the idea of earthly rewards, offered their own particular forms of magic. These included drawing on the mystic arts of India's ancient Tantra and the promise that, since every human being represented a union of all universal energy, everyone always had everything that they could ever need. As many a Buddhist monk advised, just repeat a bodhisattva's name over and over in a deep state of meditation, and enlightenment, with its freedom from the painful wheel of life, would suddenly dawn.

To all of this, of course, everyone added the ancestors. These were not to be confused with the terrifying hungry ghosts – those men, women and children who had departed from this world in violence or misery and who should be carefully kept at bay. The true ancestors were the spirits of the departed who had floated peacefully up to heaven to join the others who had graced the earth – and whose descendants maintained the requisite filial sacrifices. Naturally there was a hierarchy, with the greatest of the departed (the Yellow Emperor, for example, or Laozi) obviously becoming gods. But while other ancestors might not have made it to the status of a god, a deceased relative who had reached the dizzy heights of ministerial office could clearly catch the attention of the highest heavenly powers more easily than someone who had simply swept the floors. Trusted as guides to the favours of the spirit world, sacrifices to such ancestors were readily and regularly made, with Confucian exhortations about the importance of ritual duly observed.

Consulting all of the available pantheons, those pursuing practical professions then added men whose fabulous talents must surely have catapulted them to the status of gods. Carpenters put their faith in Lu Ban, a god of a man who had constructed magnificent city buildings in Confucius' state of Lu, and even set a wooden falcon to flight. Goldsmiths favoured the laughing face of the Maitreya Buddha, whose popular depiction with a big belly (not quite the same image as Wu Zetian had chosen) was a reassuring promise of material success. Candidates for the imperial exams dedicated their sacrifices to the god of literature, Wendi, and his two assistants: one giving out the grades, and the other offering special protection for those who had not properly prepared.

Meanwhile, the Confucian scholars realised that, without the power of magic, Confucianism had become little more than a hat. It was high time, they decided, that Confucius became a god. (Covering their bets like everyone else, they also decided that he should become a Buddha as well.) Encouraged with a direct stake in the court of the Jade Emperor, the Confucians created a pantheon of their own – with a host of scholars to keep the Great Man company. Meanwhile, growing as fast as it could, and borrowing from everywhere, the court of the Jade Emperor became as big and as complicated as the imperial bureaucracy on earth, and just as demanding. Every minister was charged with submitting an annual report to the Jade Emperor, with all earthly promotions and demotions contingent upon the success with which it was received. Noting the value of such reports in improving order, the idea was expanded to include everybody's households, with a 'Kitchen God' despatched to take up residence in each one. Charged with constant surveillance, the Kitchen God would be summoned to deliver his report to heaven at the spring festival of every New Year.

One way or another, by the end of the Ming dynasty, paperwork was everywhere – with mountains of imperial paper on earth easily matched by the smoke of written petitions addressed to the relevant celestial authorities and burnt to ensure that they reached their heavenly destination.

While the rich and scholarly conjured up ever more elaborate visions of other-worldly support, the peasants took their usual, far more practical, view, worshipping the gods of local rivers and woods. But with the arrival of the celestial bureaucracy, their troubles had spread beyond the greed of earthly landlords. With an empire of imperial gods and heavenly assistants now reaching directly into the most private corners of a human life, even heaven itself seemed to have become a foe. Who could withstand the pressure of a local official who had teamed up with a god? And with Daoist temples typically beholden to the highest family on the local land, even the power of the rich now reached to the skies. Fortunately, though, those gods who had been co-opted into imperial service were often open to a deal – and not all of the gods had joined forces with the rich. The Kitchen God offered the most obvious opportunities for persuasion. A resident spy in everyone's hearth, when he flew up to heaven to deliver his annual reports, there was not a family on earth who did not try to smooth his lips with honey before he left. And there was always Cai Shen, the god of wealth, who rode on the back of a tiger: stealing from the rich to give to the poor, he satisfyingly shot everyone's enemies with pearls that exploded like bombs.

At the top of almost everyone's heart, peasant and gentry alike, was the Bodhisattva of Compassion: Guan Yin. Originally the Buddhist bodhisattva Avalokitesvara, who hears the cries of the world, he had been translated into a female form whose essence was compassion. Part of every pantheon, Guan Yin was clutched with particular fervour to the poorest of hearts. Close beside her was Guan Yu, a bear-like general who had fought alongside the Crouching Dragon, Zhuge Liang, in the service of the Shu-Han. Never leaving his master's side unguarded, Guan Yu had also made it his business to ensure that the weak on any side of a battle were always protected. After his death, he had become a god of war with a very special characteristic: for those who could not look after themselves, even the mention of his name could be counted on to scatter any demon, even one in official clothing. And while Guan Yin and Guan Yu towered above all the others, they were only the vanguard of a world of divine rescuers who could be called upon by the poor, the downtrodden and the betrayed. Even Zhuge Liang himself became a god – a man whose mastery of the *dao* gave everyone the confidence to challenge their fate.

Other much-loved gods included an outlaw called Song Jiang. An honest man pushed into banditry by lost battles with local tyrants, his Robin Hood escapades terrorised the early decades of the Song dynasty. They would later become immortalised in a popular novel known to those who read it (and to the many more who heard it read aloud) as the *Outlaws of the Marsh*. Hidden in mountain lairs, so the story told, Song Jiang and a band of outlaws who had suffered similar fates used their blood to turn themselves into brothers, then mastered the art of turning cliffs, rocks and trees into natural weapons and defences. Over time, the outlaws succeeded in creating a kingdom of their own under the nose of the emperor. No one was surprised that, in death, Song Jiang became a god.

Then, of course, there was Sun Wukong: the 'Monkey King'. Bouncing into heaven on a bag of tricks, his was the spirit which showed everyone that even the lowest of the low could twist the celestial bureaucracy into knots that not even the greatest official spirit could unpick. The figment of a writer's imagination, his tale told in a novel entitled *Journey to the West*, the monkey became as real as any other god who had started as a mortal hero. Despatched to accompany the Tang dynasty monk Xuanzang on his journey to the Indian west, the monkey acquires a magic stick of such power that, with a simple *bian!* (change!), dragons could be tamed, oceans moved, and even the Jade Emperor taught a lesson or two. Flashing like lightning, whirling in circles, swooshing over thousands of miles in single cloud-somersaulting leaps, the monkey wreaks havoc in heaven and protects his monk with all the skill of a Shaolin warrior. Refusing to be dazzled by the heights of others' learning – and insisting that any conversations be conducted in the common Chinese of the ordinary people, rather than the rarefied language of the Confucian scholar-officials and the gentry – he defeats even the most scholarly of minds. By the time the monkey brings Xuanzang safely back to Chang'an, he has managed to show heaven, earth and even hell that courage and a good dose of plain speaking can triumph over any demon, and all officials. Printed by the presses that powered earth's greatest literary bureaucracy, immortalised by the travelling troupes of actors and puppets who trod the highways and waterways of the empire, the story of the Monkey King would become far more famous than many an emperor – and much better loved.

As the Ming dynasty cycled towards collapse, many dreamt of leaving the dusty and often terrifying flatlands to find a retreat at the top of a mountain. Few were able to make the journey. For those who stayed behind, though, it was always possible to find another world – a place full of gods with hidden sympathies, populated by bands of heroic hearts who would join with you to fight for justice, whatever the imperial odds. Concealed in deep cracks so secret that terrestrial celestials could not reach them, these heroes were a world of brothers who shared their plans only with those who were willing to mix their blood in a common cause. Schooled in all of the arts of celestial wars (Buddhist, Daoist and Confucian alike) they relied on nature to provide their weapons, and fought with bare fists so skilled that they could outwit any sword. Driven by causes so heartbreaking that heaven itself would weep, if only it could hear them, their battles were fought with the unshakeable conviction that Guan Yu, the god of war who so loved the people, would never fail to stand guard at their side.

This world might be fraught with danger and distrust, but there was always something else.

PART 3
WHOSE HEAVEN?

The Lord of Heaven is Heaven itself.

The Yongzheng Emperor (1722–35)

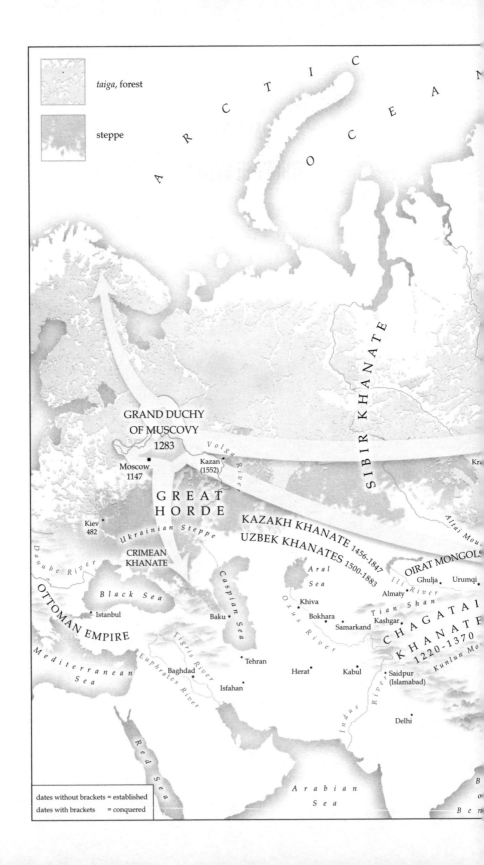

taiga, forest

steppe

A R C T I C   O C E A N

SIBIR KHANATE

GRAND DUCHY
OF MUSCOVY
1283

Moscow
1147

Kazan
(1552)

Volga River

GREAT
HORDE

Kiev
482

Ukrainian Steppe

KAZAKH KHANATE 1456-1847
UZBEK KHANATES 1500-1883

CRIMEAN
KHANATE

Danube River

*Aral
Sea*

OIRAT MONGOLS

Altai Mou

OTTOMAN EMPIRE

Black Sea

Istanbul

Caspian Sea

Baku

Khiva

Oxus River

Bokhara

Samarkand

Ghulja

Almaty

Ili River

Urumqi

Tian Shan

Kashgar

CHAGATAI
KHANATE
1220-1370

*Mediterranean
Sea*

Tigris River

Euphrates River

Baghdad

Tehran

Herat

Kabul

Isfahan

Indus River

Saidpur
(Islamabad)

Kunlun Mo

Delhi

Red Sea

*Arabian
Sea*

dates without brackets = established
dates with brackets = conquered

B
o
B e n

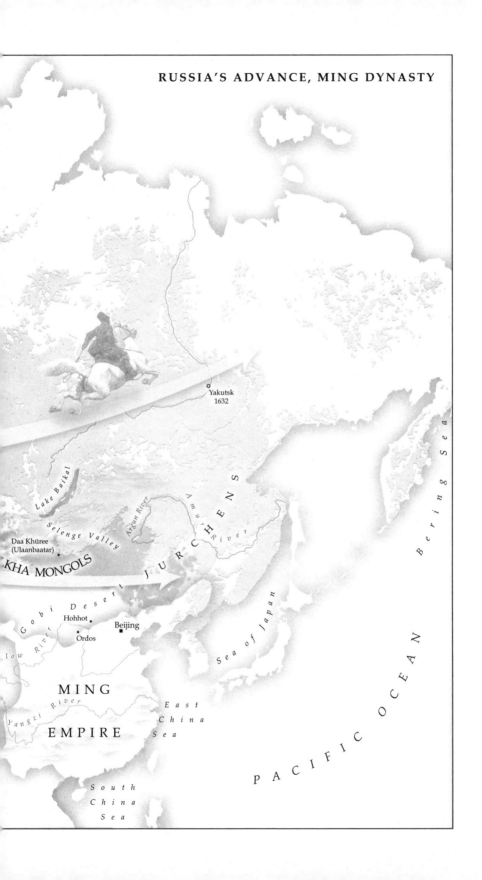

Yakutsk
1632

Bering Sea

Bering Sea

Lake Baikal

Argun River

Amur River

J U R C H E N S

Selenge Valley

Daa Khüree
(Ulaanbaatar)

KHA MONGOLS

Gobi Desert

Sea of Japan

Hohhot

Beijing

Ordos

low River

MING

Yangzi River

EMPIRE

East
China
Sea

South
China
Sea

PACIFIC OCEAN

taiga, forest

A R C T I C   O C E A N

R U S S I A

Trans-Siberian Railway
(1891 - 1916)

Trans-Manchurian Railway
(1891 - 1902)

dates without brackets = established
dates with brackets   = conquered

Moscow
Kazan
Yekaterinburg
1723
Omsk
1716
Kr
Kiev
Orenburg
1743

Volga River

Ukrainian Steppe

Danube River

OTTOMAN EMPIRE

Black Sea

Istanbul

Baku

Caspian Sea

Tigris River

Euphrates River

Mediterranean Sea

Red Sea

Aral Sea

Khiva
Tashkent
(1865)
Bokhara
(1866)
Samarkand
(1868)

Almaty
(1854)
Kashgar

Herat
Kabul

ZUNGAR KHANATE
1634 - 1758

Ghulja

Ili River

Tian Shan

Taklamakan D

Kunlun Mo

Qinghai

Altai Mou

Indus River

Arabian Sea

B
o

B n

THE QING EMPIRE AND BEYOND
1644 – 1911

G O B I
D E S E R T

Liao River

Chang Cheng (Long Wall)

Ordos
Desert

Beijing

Tianjin

Mukden
(Shenyang)

Yalu River

Shanhai Guan
(Mountain and Sea Pass)

Vladivostok

S e a

o f

J a p a n

J O S E O N

J A P A N

Yellow River 1853 - present

Weihaiwei

Liugong
Island

Xi'an
(Chang'an)

Kaifeng

Yellow River 1324 -1853

Mount Tai

Qingdao

Y e l l o w

S e a

Yakutsk

Okhotsk
1647

S e a   o f

O k h o t s k

B e r i n g   S e a

Lake Baikal

Chita
1851

Irkutsk
1652

Amur River

Khiatka
1727

Nerchinsk
1659

Argun River

Khabarovsk
1858

Kuril Islands

Daa Khüree
(Ulaanbaatar)

Selenge Valley

E R   M O N G O L

I N N E R   M O N G O L

Harbin
1898

Q I N G

Hohhot

Vladivostok
1860

S e a   o f   J a p a n

P A C I F I C   O C E A N

Ordos

Beijing

Xi'an
(Chang'an)

Kaifeng

M P I R E

Chengdu

Yangzi River

Hangkou

Donting
Lake

Xiang River

Changsha

Shanghai

Hangzhou

E a s t

C h i n a

S e a

Kunming

Xiamen
(Amoy)

TAIWAN

Pearl River

Dali

Guangzhou
(Canton)

Hong Kong

S o u t h

C h i n a

S e a

CHAPTER 1

SOMEONE ELSE'S SKY

He who wears the great circle of heaven as his hat will take
the great square of earth as his shoes.

The King of Huainan (139 BCE; early Han dynasty)

SNOW WAS STILL ON the top of the mountains when the message
arrived. Lapping softly against the walls of the Shanhai Guan,
Mountain and Sea Pass, the waters of the Eastern Sea still had their
winter chill. The Manju north had been rather quiet in recent months,
but home reports from Beijing had brought nothing but tears and
alarm. Decades of droughts and famines, locusts and bandits had
finally given way, as everyone knew they would, to a rage of rebellions, which had swept across the land. Unpaid and hungry, the
generals of the Ming army had been forced to choose between the
heavenly honour of their emperor and the earthly growls of their
soldiers' stomachs.

Even so, little had prepared General Wu Sangui, the commander
in charge of the Shanhai Guan garrison, for the devastating strokes
of black ink that were delivered into his hands on 24 April 1644. Li
Zicheng's rebel force had arrived in Beijing and was sacking everything in sight; overwhelmed with shame, the Chongzhen emperor
had taken himself to another world; distraught at a chaos they were
powerless to control, the city's greatest officials were following
the emperor's suicidal suit; it could not be long before the rebels
would advance on Shanhai Guan, now the last bastion of the north.
One of the greatest and last surviving of the martial talents of the
Ming, General Wu Sangui drew in his breath and looked up to the
skies. Despatched to defend the eastern end of the Long Wall and
protect the Ming from the latest horde of barbarians in the north,
the Manju, he found himself in charge of perhaps the only pocket
of peaceful heaven left on earth. It would be only a matter of time

before Li Zicheng and his rebels would storm the 150 separating miles to find him. Suddenly the barbarians seemed more like friends than foes.

Saddling his horses, Wu Sangui turned them north to Mukden, the capital of the Manju, with an offer that surely no barbarian could ever refuse: join us in defending the Ming against the rebels, and the trading gifts of heaven will know no bounds. Seeing an unexpected opportunity, the Manju's regent leader, Dorgon, had quickly agreed. Within a month, Li Zicheng's rebel troops appeared at the Mountain and Sea Pass. Dorgon and Wu Sangui were ready. Dorgon's barbarians were easy to spot: heads shaven at the front, long hair plaited at the back; masters of the horse, demons of the bow and arrow. But it was Wu Sangui's troops who were to lead the charge. After months of no pay and wearing uniforms that had seen far better days, they would have been difficult to distinguish from their rebel brothers had they not sewn patches of white cloth onto their backs. By noon, both sides of the Ming, soldiers and rebels, were close to exhaustion. And then, suddenly, heaven seemed to intervene: a whistling wind appeared as if from nowhere and, gathering up the sand of the shore, cloaked the battlefield in a yellow haze. Men and horses scattered blindly. The time for the barbarians' horse-borne talents had come. The Manju cavalry in their element in storms of dust, Dorgon unleashed them into the fray. Arrows firing with perfect precision from the back of every horse, the Ming rebels turned and fled.

In the days that followed, Wu Sangui's exhausted Ming army struggled to recover its breath. Dorgon's exhilarated forces rode on, pushing the Ming rebels back towards Beijing. On 5 June 1644, holding the line in Beijing, Li Zicheng saw the storm advancing and raced a retreat to the far south. In the echoing silence of the following day, rumours whispered that a real crown prince was about to arrive from the north. Perplexed, but determined to be prepared for every possible heavenly eventuality, a few surviving scholars found an imperial carriage and ventured out to meet him, whoever he might be. Scanning the horizon in vain for an appropriately imperial procession, a dusty horseman suddenly appeared. A dagger at his waist, and the front of his head sharply shaven, this was clearly no Ming prince. Dismounting from his horse in a single swift jump, the figure introduced himself politely to the small gathering in a passable Chinese: 'I am the Prince Regent

Dorgon,' he said. 'The young crown prince will arrive in a while. Will you allow me to be your ruler?'

With the imperial city in ruins behind them, and no other crown prince in sight, the only sensible answer seemed to be 'Yes.'

Over the following days and months, those whose horizons had been limited to the skirmishing courtyards of Beijing had to catch up with decades of news and events from the north – and quite a bit of older history and geography as well. Still shocked at the dramatic turn of events, they found that the story was a little long, but at the end of it things were a lot clearer.

It appeared that for most of the last 150 years, while emperors, scholars and eunuchs had been battling with each other in the imperial city, yet another group of barbarian tribes had been rising in the lands to the north-east of the wall. Horse-borne hunters, they had emerged from a world of heavy forests stuffed with hides, feathers and furs, washed with sparkling streams, and full of leaping fish and treasures of pearls. Each tribe had a different name and story to tell. Some traced themselves back to Chinggis Khan and the Mongol Yuan, others to waves of steppe barbarians who had been storming in and out of northern China for a thousand years and more. As time had turned, twists of weather and clashes of ambition had regularly scattered them to the four directions, pushing each of them out against unexpected others. Those pushed to the south had traded with, or raided, the Chinese lands. Those pushed to the north had found themselves in a wide steppe world that rolled into the northern tundra of Siberia, before opening on to the shores of an Arctic Sea. Those pushed to the west had found themselves pressing against the Mongols, the Uighurs and the Tibetans. And those pushed to the coastal east had found themselves in the company of Ming migrants who, looking for new lands and a better life, had settled around an inner, Yellow, sea above the Long Wall, in an area known as Liaodong: just above the secretive and now united peninsula of Goryeo, Korea, which dropped down into the even bigger East China Sea. From time to time, marriages and pacts had pulled the various tribes together, supported by the common threads of Chinggis Khan and Buddhism: Chingghis Khan, whose confederated empire had conquered almost all the world; and a Buddhism that had long ago transformed the Mongols into a land of lamas closely linked to brothers in Tibet whose spirits exercised a powerful force over all steppe hearts, whether Mongol or not.

Charged with guarding the wall, Ming generals had become meticulous observers of the rise and fall of the various steppe alliances. Responsible for keeping the northern tribes at bay, they had also regularly deployed the old Han strategy of offering the rewards of trade to one tribe on condition that it would help them to defeat the others. At one point, the Jianzhou, a branch of the once-mighty Jurchen who had defeated the northern Song in the twelfth century and gone on to establish a Jin Dynasty, was selected for advantage. With the borders guarded by the Ming army, the trade had been tightly controlled, but richly rewarding. The Ming were in constant need of powerful horses, ginseng, pearls and furs, while the Jianzhou had an insatiable demand for the tea, silk and weapons of iron which could be traded across the wider steppes. Trading fortunes rose, and as time passed, the Jianzhou, like so many barbarians before them, came to appreciate the finer values of a settled life.

At one point, and with an eye to an improving education, the chief of the Jianzhou's Aisin Gioro clan sent his son into the service of a Ming general, who had settled his household not far from the Jianzhou Jurchen lands. As expected, the young boy, Nurhaci, added the Chinese language to his tongue and, watching and learning, observed the Chinese ways with interest. Nurhaci also buried himself in the tales of their heroes. The story of Zhuge Liang and the 'borrowed' arrows gripped him with excitement; the adventures of Song Jiang and his band of brothers on their outlaw marshes kept him awake deep into the night. And although, like all steppe boys, the triumphs of Chinggis Khan held the greatest power over his imagination, he could not help but be captivated by the stories of the men of the settled lands. By the time his father died – during one of the Ming-incited battles of the tribes – Nurhaci had become a young man of twenty-three. Left with little but a few family suits of armour, he decided that the time had come to create a new force on the steppes.

Over the next thirty years, Nurhaci rose to the top of his Aisin Gioro clan, and the Aisin Gioro clan rose to the top of the Jianzhou Jurchen tree. Galvanising the Jianzhou Jurchen with a dream of recreating

Chinggis Khan's empire, Nurhaci campaigned across the lands to the east and west above the Chinese wall. Befriending, trading, marrying, capturing, threatening – and where threats failed, attacking – he forged the path in every possible way. With each step gained, the strands of many different nomadic people were gradually woven together, not into a single way of thinking but into a unity of many ideas. One of the Mongol tribes directly descended from Chinggis Khan became such an ally that even brothers could not have been closer. Tibetan warriors brought hearts of steel; Tibetan lamas added the deeper spirits of the Buddhist world. Chinese and Koreans – many captured as the spoils of war – brought the reading and writing power of the brush as well as Confucian thoughts on the hierarchical order of a heavenly family, which seemed to make a lot of sense. And everyone brought their languages: Mongolian, Tibetan, Turkic, Korean and Chinese to name but a few.

Riding, hunting, archery, falconry and fishing remained the essential skills for Nurhaci's people. But as their wealth spread, more and more of the Liaodong lands were put under the plough – to be farmed by peasant soldiers captured from the Ming. Villages multiplied. Some became so big that they were almost like cities, and it seemed only right to put walls around them. In 1587, Nurhaci raised a capital, Fe Ala, on top of a hill. Meanwhile, Jurchen men were organised under fighting 'banners' and ordered under a military command. Their hearts, however, were free to wander wherever they wanted: Buddhist bodhisattvas, gods of mountains and rivers, the old Mongol Tengr god of the sky (who, as the Mongol brothers had explained, was really just another way of thinking about heaven): all were worshipped at will.

As Nurhaci's power rose, he became khan of the steppes, and as khan of the steppes, he also applied the Chinese lessons learnt in his youth to his own people, ensuring that they were consistently reinforced with the firm Manju discipline of the hunt. Villagers were ordered into military units and charged with hunting for animals or men, as well as tilling the fields. The spoken sounds of Jurchen were translated into a written script, which used the Mongol alphabet, itself taken from Persian, for its form. With a written language in place, Nurhaci then commissioned a written story of his people. Tracing their ancestry across the tribes of the vast and varied lands, it was a chronicle that counted among its heroes not only the Jin dynasty of earlier Jurchens, but also Chinggis Khan's empire, and Kublai Khan's triumphant conquest of the Southern Song, from had been raised the Mongol dynasty of the Yuan. Tales of glorious deeds were gathered from all over the steppes, and dreams of heroic hunters, with vanquishing bows and arrows, promised to grip every reader's heart. As the history neared completion, Nurhaci decided to give his new and great collection of people a name: Manju – the brave.

Across the steppes, the Manju had become a force that every other tribe had learnt to respect. To those in the settled lands below the Long Wall, they were just another confederation of barbarians. But in 1616, Nurhaci caused something of a stir. Issuing a list of grievances against the Ming, he accused their generals of inciting the tribes to fight against each other, and their officials of abusing his trading people. To his list, Nurhaci added the claim that his own father's death had been the result of the Ming's meddling interference in tribal affairs. Reparations were demanded, which, if not forthcoming, would be met with Manju measures. Occupied with its own concerns, and supremely confident in its heavenly position, the Ming ignored Nurhaci's demands. The threats became attacks. Over the next seven years, piece by piece, starting with Liaodong on which the Chinese had settled above the Long Wall, land was successively captured, culminating in the prize of Liaodong's provincial capital, Shenyang. Nurhaci renamed it Mukden, Rising Power.

When Nurhaci died in 1626, his son, Hong Taiji, took on the Manju cause. Turning the conquered lands into a granary for his own people, he invited the Chinese scholar-officials of Shenyang-now-Mukden to remain in their places and create a mirror of the Ming bureaucracy for the Manju. 'A healthy animal', he explained, 'finds a tree and climbs it; the wise minister finds a ruler who serves him; the southern dynasty has come to the end of its natural life; its time and course have been exhausted.' Watching the collapsing catastrophes of the late Ming, a number of Ming officials in Shenyang could only agree. Convinced that heaven was about to inflict yet another violent change in its mandate, they accepted the Manju invitation.

Hong Taiji turned his sights to the Mongol west. Dreaming of Chinggis Khan and of the Mongol conquest of the Song, he reached out to the nearest tribes of Mongols, who had been slow to join the Manju idea, and wrapped them into his swelling ranks. At one point, rewarded with the gift of the long-held and much-treasured imperial seal of the Mongol Yuan, he decided that it was time to proclaim a new, Manju, dynasty. Observing the now crumbling corruption of the once-bright Ming below the wall, it was not difficult to strike upon the name that would put them on notice of his unifying intent: after the disaster of the 'bright', Ming, Chinese idea, he would call it Qing: the dynasty of the pure.

By 1644, when Wu Sangui appeared with his offer of a trading reward for help in defeating the Ming rebels, Hong Taiji had died, leaving Dorgon, his half-brother, as regent for his very young son. With the Ming dismissing the idea of a purifying Qing dynasty as the foolish dream of an upstart barbarian, Wu Sangui's offer had given Dorgon quite a surprise. But while Wu Sangui might not have appreciated the force of the Manju ambition, for the Manju the idea that they might one day acquire the mantle of the once-heavenly Ming was far from a fantasy.

The crown prince was only six years old when Dorgon led him to the Hall of Supreme Harmony and placed him on the throne – styled as the Shunzhi (Humble Rule) Emperor. The throne itself had been an unexpected gift, but it would take all the years of Shunzhi's short reign (he died at the age of twenty-three) and twenty years of the rule of his valiant son thereafter, to bring all of China under the purity of Manju Qing rule.

The battles on land were initially led by Wu Sangui. With Dorgon installed as regent before he had fought his own way back to Beijing, Wu Sangui had found the tables turned: it was Dorgon who offered Wu Sangui 'a reward' if he would help the Qing to push their conquest to a successful conclusion in the south. Wu Sangui had little choice but to accept – although, having read, like Nurhaci, the same stories of the Crouching Dragon, Zhuge Liang, and the outlaw, Song Jiang, he almost certainly decided that his co-operation would last only until he was able to turn the tables once again. Flanked by horse-borne Manju bannermen, and supported by Portuguese gifts of cannons (the Portuguese as keen as the northern barbarians to get permission to trade), Wu Sangui advanced to the south and south-west, sweeping away waves of rebel armies, all led by men claiming dynastic Ming descent. With Chinese fighting Chinese, it must have seemed as if heaven had truly washed its hands of its people. By 1670, however, the battling south was finally subdued. Wu Sangui's promised reward was delivered: a princely title and governorship of the remote south-western provinces of Yunnan and Guizhou, which he had done so much to pacify.

No sooner had his efforts been imperially recognised than Wu Sangui declared his own colours. Proclaiming Yunnan as the heart of a new and ambitious state, optimistically called the 'Great Zhou', Wu Sangui marched east and north. Announcing alliances with other loyalist Ming generals, he served 'Manju' Beijing with notice of his intentions to reclaim the entirety of the lost Ming lands. Indeed, Wu suggested, having completed their temporary heaven-sent task, perhaps the Manju might like to retire to their old Liaodong – naturally, with the grateful thanks of the Chinese people.

With Wu Sangui and his rebel generals armed against them, it took the Manju Qing another ten years of battles before the lands of the south and south-west were truly pacified. Eventually, though, and largely because the Chinese people saw Wu Sangui as a traitor at-heart, his rebels were defeated.

But as the mist of war on land lifted, off the coast of Fujian, another force of resistance appeared to have risen, this time out of the sea. Anchored on the coast, it was led by the son of a sea-faring family called Zheng.

The Zheng were merchants who, as a result of Ming prohibitions on coastal trade, had become 'smugglers'. Combining a natural trading talent with a prodigious mastery of maritime maps, they had woven a watery empire of their own, sailing up and down the island-fringed coast of the country and trading with ships visiting from further afield. When the Spanish conquest of Mexico had washed everyone's coasts with silver, the Zheng family found itself drawn into an explosion of Iberian trades around the Asian seas. But in 1644, the arrival of the Manju Qing had split the family. Father and uncles had pragmatically transferred allegiance to the new Qing, but a son, Zheng Chenggong, had declared eternal loyalty to the Ming. Sharp of mind and keen of heart, he set about creating a loyal Ming navy, with a fortress in Xiamen (Amoy), the sea as his battlefield, and his family's network of smugglers as his crew. By 1651, he controlled a force of more than two thousand ships, becoming the most powerful ruler of the southern waves. By 1655, he had matched his navy with a land army, which then attacked cities across the now-Manju Qing lands of Zhejiang and Jiangsu, including the first Ming capital, Nanjing.

No longer smugglers but loyalists with a heavenly cause on land and at sea, Zheng's troops were trained to win the hearts of the people – just as the fictional heroes of the *Outlaws of the Marsh* had done hundreds of years before. By the time that the Qing, hitherto preoccupied with Wu Sangui, were able to fling their forces at them, it looked as if it was all too late: local hearts and minds had been won across vast swathes of land, and the terrain seemed almost impossible to capture. The Qing decided that the best thing would be to clear the coast, banishing the local population from within twenty miles of the sea. Not even a plank of wood was permitted to set out on the waves. The coast secured, the Qing forces then battered the Zheng fortress in Xiamen. Rich in the wealth of its vast trades, Xiamen was able to hold out. But by 1661, Zheng Chenggong decided to find a fortress a little further away. Looking out across a stormy southern sea, his eyes fell on a beautiful island: named 'Formosa' by trading Portuguese, it would come to be known as Taiwan.

With an indigenous people of its own, the beautiful island had already become home to a steady trail of Chinese, who had been sailing out of the tumultuous and regularly trade-banishing mainland for centuries. From the 1620s, it had begun to attract the ambitions of the Spanish and the Portuguese, both keen to find a foothold in a world of rising Asian trade; they were soon followed by the Dutch. Zheng's trading army dislodged them all, and the Manju Qing suddenly found themselves facing a Ming power on an island that few of them had ever heard of. Zheng Chenggong died of malaria shortly after his arrival, but his son, Zheng Jing, took up the family empire. Transforming Taiwan into the hub of what would become a great Ming-pretending maritime empire, the Zheng family's trades confidently reached across South East Asia, all grounded on an 'imperial' order that included both Confucian academies and Ming-style taxes. For twenty years, Taiwan flourished as an independent power, while claiming the right of Ming loyalists to rule over the lands now held by the alien Manju Qing. But eventually, in 1683, Shunzhi's 'valiant son' was able to turn the full force of the Qing's attention to the Taiwan straits. In the ensuing war, the Zheng were defeated and offered an honourable return to the mainland. Taiwan, including its own indigenous population as well as the harbouring Ming loyalists, was wrapped into the bureaucratic embrace of Fujian province; and the fishermen, who had been banned from the coasts, were allowed to return home.

Challenging though they were, however, the Wu Sangui rebels and the sea-trading Zheng had been only the most obvious of a number of rebellions seeking a restoration of the Ming. Most had been dealt with on battlefields, but some could only be addressed with a brush. Following the moral example of the last Ming emperor, in the months after the fall of the Ming, and in successive waves afterwards, many Confucian officials committed suicide, paralysing not only the capital but almost everywhere else as well. Others chose to register their protest by wandering into Daoist retreats: climbing to the tops of mountains for a hermit's life or retiring into silent studies in the country estates of family homes. Battle as hard as they might on land and at sea, with less than two million people to China's (albeit exhausted) hundred million, the Manju knew that a successful conquest of the heavenly lands would depend on their ability to return the fields to farming. For that, they would need the bureaucratic talents of the Confucian scholars.

Commanders of the archives, masters of the refined art of managing the imperial bureaucracy, diviners of heavenly virtue, interpreters of earthly changes, the scholars were a resource that no emperor could live without. The tax-delivering foundations of any heavenly rule, they were essential not only in the capital of Beijing and the cities of the empire but also across the fields. This was the world of the Confucian fabric: one that went beyond magistrates appointed by the empire to include a wider 'gentry' of scholarly officials who, while retired, continued to busy themselves with the local order of things; they were joined by their sons who, embarked on the decades of learning required to achieve success in the imperial exams, hoped to inherit everything. Dedicated from birth to the idea of filial piety, the gentry's support of local magistrates was typically rewarded with blind eyes turned to taxes: even heaven could not have afforded the true cost of their unpaid services.

The early capture of Liaodong and its Shenyang-now-Mukden capital had given the Manju important insights into how the Chinese imperial order worked. It had even given them a starter-corps of officials, who were quickly catapulted to bureaucratic prominence in the newly Qing capital of Beijing. But with waves of suicides and hermit-like retreats, it was not enough: more scholarly bureaucrats were urgently required. With Dorgon ruling as regent, the young Shunzhi Emperor had been set to a Confucian education, which, it was hoped, would win some scholarly approval and stem the suicides. To further reassure the scholarly class, the imperial examinations were resurrected. Candidates, however, were few, with many of the country's greatest scholars refusing to attend. Matters had not been helped by the fact that one of the earliest edicts, issued by Dorgon as regent, had insisted that the scholars, like everyone else, display their commitment to the new and greater Manju 'family' by following the practice of wearing their hair in the style of the Manju 'queue'. Foreheads were to be sharply shaven, with hair plaited neatly in a single long tail at the back; punishments were applied to anyone who failed to obey, including those who argued that the queue should not apply to the Chinese, who were obviously of a very different 'family'.

More suicides followed, and more scholarly minds retired to the mountains or into their studies. The edict of the queue was not rescinded. The Chinese part of the greater Manju sky was going to have to fall into the pure Qing line. But the vacuum of scholars was a worry. The regents and their all too few Chinese advisers scratched their heads. Special attention had already been given to mastering the Confucian knowledge in a bid to recommend the dynasty to scholarly minds: trained to be a model Son of Heaven, the Shunzhi Emperor was steeped in the classical Confucian texts. Sacrifices were raised at every possible opportunity; every imaginable ritual was meticulously observed. So desperate were the Manju Qing to please, that the Bureau of Astronomy, under the all-important Ministry of Rites, retained the services of a German Jesuit to help them predict not only the detailed changes of the seasons on which the agricultural calendar depended, but the eclipses through which heaven so often chose to speak. The Jesuit, one of a number in the Qing lands of the time, seemed happy to offer his talents for the privilege of touching heaven's skirts; indeed, Jesuit hopes were high that his meteorological calculations would bring the Confucian world around to a Holy Roman way of thinking. But while the accuracy of the Jesuit's predictions was noted, scholarly hearts remained unmoved.

Shunzhi's 'valiant son' had been eight when his father died in 1661. Named Aisin Gioro hala i Hiowan Yei in Manju, the boy also took the imperial name of the Kangxi Emperor (from the Confucian ideal of *kang*: peaceful prosperity). Already well on his way to the classical Confucian education that would surely, this time, win the war of minds, with the country under the rule of a council of regents, the young Kangxi had been settled in a quiet corner of the Forbidden City, with the Hall of Mental Cultivation as his own personal Manju camp. As he grew older, it became clear that the boy would match prodigious scholarly talents with the kind of fighting spirit that might one day turn the Qing into a truly great power. At the age of thirteen, in 1667, Kangxi threw off his regents. At fifteen, he issued a 'Sacred Edict,' setting out sixteen Confucian maxims for the guidance of all of his Chinese subjects. At twenty-three, he took the hitherto unheard-of step of permitting a group of young scholars to set up a society of their own, and to do so in a corner of the Forbidden City. At twenty-five, with the assistance of the young scholars, he set a special Grand Examination, for which candidates could only be nominated, and thus, which only the stubbornest of vain minds could resist. A few years later, he added another temptation: an imperial literary project that would tell the history of the Ming: with many scholars already penning histories of their own, the idea that their words would acquire the official seal of an imperial history had a powerful appeal. Confucian minds beginning to bend, no one had been surprised when, in 1683, Kangxi had finally brought the island of Taiwan into the lands of the Manju Qing.

By 1685, Kangxi had become a thirty-year-old emperor who was both clear about his own will, and thoughtful about the practical dreams of his Chinese people. Rebels tamed on land and at sea, scholars charmed, the Ming lands, devastated by decades of war, had been restored under the greater order of the Qing. Farms abandoned by landlords had been returned to harvests; peasants had been offered lands of their own with which to start anew. Rivers and canals had been reclaimed from the clogging silt of neglect. With the continued assistance of the Jesuits, calendars were being successfully set; and with the seasons returned to order, the cash of crops and the following trade rose higher with every year that passed. Taiwan secure, fishermen and traders had been allowed to go back to sea and the pirate watchtowers of the dark Zheng family past had been redirected to the collection of imperial taxes on trade. Judging by the gentler weather, even heaven seemed happy. Trained for perfection, however, Kangxi looked out across the once-Ming lands and reminded himelf that they were only part of the much bigger Manju dream. With the heavenly lands in order, he looked to the north and the wider world above the long Chinese wall.

Some, like the Manju, thought it was about time the empire expanded. Others, with more painful memories of conquests lost – and everyone with a sense of history – wondered where on earth it would all end. Certainly, in the forty years that had passed since the Manju had taken the dragon throne, much had happened in the steppe world. All of it was complicated, and while it included other powers as well, it almost always involved the Mongols.

Returning to the steppes after losing their Yuan dynasty, the Mongol heirs of the unifying Chinggis Khan had first descended into a tumult of battling clans and fluctuating federations, and then split into a northerly west and a southerly east. It was the Mongols of the southerly east that Nurhaci's son had swept into the rising Manju world – a people who had taken the Manju name and whose lands, falling under Manju control, had come to be called 'Inner Mongol'. The Mongols of the northerly west had been a different matter. Not directly controlled by the Manju, their wilder lands were known as 'Outer Mongol'. Rising and falling in successions of battling federations, the Outer Mongol lands seemed to switch between war and peace as quickly as the seasons, and their history was so full of twists and turns that it could reduce even the greatest scholar to tears. Unfortunately, it was a history with a direct bearing on Kangxi's dreams for the expanded future fortunes of the Qing.

When Chingghis Khan had divided his empire, he had left the lands at the far western end of the steppes – then known as Rus, now present-day Russia – in the hands of a grandson who controlled what would come to be known as the Khanate of the Golden Horde. Trade had been encouraged, and city-states had emerged, each with princes of their own. Time had passed, and eventually a line of princes had risen from present-day Moscow, who, having learnt the art of war from the Mongols, eventually chased the Golden Horde out of their lands. Pushing the Mongols back east across the steppes, and noting the treasures of timber, gold, feathers and furs in the eastern lands, the Moscow princes, by now titling themselves 'tsars', also battled every oasis khan they met along the way. By the time that Nurhaci had been born in 1559, with the help of Cossack 'pirates' (men who traced their own roots back to the nomadic hordes that had roamed the early forests of Europe, with traces of steppe blood added over time) they had swept from west to east. Finally conquering the tundra lands of present-day Siberia, the descendants of the Rus had become Russian neighbours of the steppe tribes, including the Manju.

With a new power suddenly at their side, the Outer Mongol tribes struggled to maintain their own unity. Battling against each other, they had turned to the still formidable powers of Tibet for spiritual support. Inhabitants of a vast land of mountains and grasslands to the south and west, once valued allies of the Tang and then terrifying foes, the Tibetans had once been a formidable military force. By the middle of the Ming dynasty, while their temporal powers had diminished, they had embraced Buddhism with such intensity that their lama teachers had become the spiritual leaders of the steppe world. With many different Buddhist schools within Tibet, the Mongols, like most of the other Buddhist steppe powers, including the Manju, had come to be spiritually led by the teacher who, as the recurring reincarnation of the Bodhisattva of Compassion, was known as the 'Ocean of Wisdom': the Dalai Lama. With both Mongol and Manju sons regularly trained under the Dalai Lama's supervision, in 1651 the Shunzhi Emperor, Kangxi's father, had naturally submitted the Manju Qing dynasty to the Dalai's eternal spiritual authority. Whatever other heaven or sky they might look up to, every ancient power across the steppe world understood that the influence of the Dalai Lama was far greater than that of any temporal king.

It was in 1677 that Kangxi first sensed that the affairs of the north-west would eventually need Manju military attention. At that point, Wu Sangui's rebels and the Zheng maritime empire had still been at large, but Kangxi found time to receive the usual tributes of the northern and westerly world. One of those who delivered the tribute on behalf of the ruler of a small Outer Mongolian tribe was the young lama-trained son of its ruler: the tribe was the Zungar, and the son was called Galdan. Galdan had gone on to build a federation of Outer Mongolian tribes. And as Galdan's territory and ambition had risen, Kangxi had received messages from the old oasis states asking for Manju Qing assistance in repulsing his attacks. Kangxi admired Galdan's ambition but the idea that a young upstart might be trying to resurrect Chinggis Khan's great steppe confederation was a nagging cause of concern. True, Galdan's campaigns were small and far away, but the rapid advance of what had become a vast Russian empire had shown that even a small problem could quickly become a bigger one. There was also, as always, the great uncertainty of what the all-important opinion of the Dalai Lama of the time might be.

As soon as Kangxi had rid the Manju empire of the Ming restorationists, he picked up his imperial brush and wrote to all of the Mongol khans, informing them that the time had come to talk. Setting a date, he added that the spiritually all-powerful Dalai Lama would, of course, be invited. The talks were convened in 1686, with the question of Galdan's oasis state conquests at the top of everyone's list of concerns. With opinions raised against him, and unhappy at the way the winds were blowing, Galdan mounted his horse and left. Before the year was out, the Inner Mongols, who had stood with the Manju, found themselves under a Galdan attack.

Guided by maps helpfully drawn by the Jesuits, when Kangxi heard about the attack on the Inner Mongols, he was convinced that, while Galdan was a worry, the real problem – and probably the destabilising cause of everyone's problems – was the advance of the Russians into the steppe lands. The vast distance between Moscow and Beijing made imperial communications difficult at the best of times, to which was added the further complication that neither side could speak the language of the other. But Russian ambition had made them neighbours, even though no one, neither Manju, nor Russian, nor even Jesuit, was clear about where exactly the borders were. Matching Jesuit maps with what the Manju Qing knew of their own tribute-payers, Kangxi laid claim to the territory south and east of an expanse of water that the Ming had once called 'the Northern Sea' and was known on the steppes as 'Lake Baikal'.

Kangxi's position was communicated to the Russians, through the Jesuits, in Latin. The Russians responded by pointing to a host of trading posts established well to the east of Lake Baikal and deep into the earliest Manju heartlands. Kangxi's answer was simple and clear: a string of battles was fought. On each of the occasions on which he emerged victorious, however, Kangxi was perplexed to find that as soon as his troops left in any serious number the Russians returned and behaved as if nothing had changed. Strong of will, under normal conditions Kangxi would never have given an inch. But in the back of his mind he saw the worrying prospect of another battle, one in which Galdan and the Russians were united and, blessed by the Dalai Lama, swept the Manju Qing entirely off the map.

In 1689, a treaty was struck at Nerchinsk, which gave neither side exactly what they wanted but offered enough for them to come to terms. In exchange for permitting the Russians to trade with the heavenly lands – and subject to a corresponding Russian duty to pay tribute – Kangxi secured a clear border at the western end of the steppes. This left Galdan's Mongols, and indeed everyone else on the steppes other than the Russians and the Manju Qing, without a land to call their own. Galdan, having impressed Kangxi with his bravery, was offered an amnesty. But his heart was set on independence; the Zungars and the Manju Qing went to war. By 1696, Galdan's Zungar forces had been defeated, and within a year Galdan was dead – but not before he had reached out to sympathetic spirits in Tibet, and not before his Zungar tribe had gained a foothold on the Tibetan plateau.

Over the following years, the Zungars regrouped under the leadership of Galdan's nephew, with Lhasa as their base. Fortified, they then launched themselves across the old Outer Mongolian lands, which the Manju Qing had ceded to the Russians. The old northern 'Mongol' problem had suddenly become a 'Tibetan' problem as well. By 1720, older now and tiring of the endless to-ing and fro-ing, Kangxi determined to settle the matter once and for all. Strapping cannons to the backs of camels, and throwing every soldiering force he had at the coldest and highest terrain his troops had ever had to master, he eventually forced the Zungars out. Order was restored to Lhasa under the watchful gaze of a Qing *amban*, a resident adviser, and Kangxi proclaimed himself saviour of the Buddhist faith. Ruler of heaven, earth and everybody's sky, he was now also brother-at-heart of an endlessly reincarnating Dalai Lama, who was henceforth to acknowledge the universal power of the Manju.

When Kangxi died in 1722, he left a Manju world wider and richer than Nurhaci's wildest dreams. Forced to grapple with both the rebel forces of an unsettled Chinese world and the endlessly swirling dust of nomadic warriors, nothing had been easy. Seated as confidently on the back of a horse as in the Hall of Mental Cultivation, however, Kangxi had achieved great prizes. A vast territory had been won, now spanning the once Ming and Mongol worlds; tribute flowed from all respectful directions, including the upstart Russian tsars; all of it was blessed by the Dalai Lama; and the Chinese lands that had been so very hard to win were not only now lying tame at Kangxi's Manju feet but eclipsing even the greatest productive heights of the Ming.

Kangxi's prizes clear, the imperial scholars had also come to see that heaven had no favourites, Ming or Qing, as long as an emperor could rule. Where once the Ming had struggled against the idea of making money, the Manju Qing (with their own early fortunes grounded in the trading of ginseng and fur) were demonstrating the value of the typical steppe opinion that the people could work out their money affairs far better than any emperor. Coasts that had once been cleared were now full of people; fishing villages were on their way to becoming bigger ports of call. Peasants had flocked back to the land, multiplying in such great numbers that they were now spreading everywhere: flattening surviving forests, draining marshes, raising dykes, digging ditches, and creating villages at every possible point. Grain and rice were sweeping across the fields, silk was tumbling from mulberry trees, cotton was spreading, tea was flourishing like a terraced treasure. And whenever the peasants had a moment to spare, they took their cotton and wove it into anything that could be sold to make an extra copper coin. On the spreading back of the rising prosperity, merchants returned to the roads and the waterways, rebuilding fortunes and threading together new and ever-wider routes of exchange. Markets appeared at almost every crossing, whether of roads or rivers, many growing into towns: struck up by trade and unconstricted by imperial city walls, the towns were open to all-comers and free to expand. With such a peaceful prosperity in place, Kangxi was able to fill the imperial treasuries with taxes on trade, even as he kept a promise to his father that taxes would never again strangle the peasants in their fields.

The lands of the Manju Qing basked in a new glow. But not everyone was impressed. In a far-off place that nobody other than the Jesuits seemed to have been to (its name sounded like 'Rum') there was a somebody who called himself the Pope. Claiming to be a heavenly power on earth, it seemed that he had no understanding at all of the achievements of the Qing. Described by the Jesuits as 'father' and 'the greatest ruler on earth', he had distinctly fuzzy ideas about heaven, and no Confucian manners at all. Apparently, he talked to someone called God, a man in the sky with a long beard who sounded a bit like the Jade Emperor and whom the Jesuits saw as the greatest of the heavenly powers, even though he didn't seem to know anything about the Son of Heaven at the centre of everything. Certainly, whatever the Pope was, he had become far too big for his boots. And given that the Jesuits seemed to be so devoted to Kangxi and his conquests, it was all a bit confusing: scanning the stars, offering mathematical equations, translating barbarian languages, fixing the clocks of heavenly time, scurrying around the roof of the world with their maps and dictionaries; some of them had even learnt to read the classics of Confucius and openly acknowledged that they had a lot to learn.

Not everyone in China, though, had appreciated the Jesuits' worth. Even Kangxi himself had some serious reservations when he was told they were intent on resurrecting the old heavenly taiping, great peace, idea, albeit marching to the call of a man named Jesus, rather than Laozi. But in 1692, the Jesuits' scientific ideas cured Kangxi of malaria and, balancing up the good and the bad, he decided to let them stay – although, it seemed prudent to redirect their obviously prodigious talents to some less sensitive areas of the Manju world: the design of an exotic *Yuanming Yuan*, garden of perfect brightness, for example, as the setting for an imperial summer palace.

It had all been rather a shock, therefore, when, rather than expressing any gratitude, and pointedly not congratulating Kangxi on any of his territorial triumphs, the Pope from 'Rum' had insisted on an extraordinary principle with which no one in their right minds could possibly have agreed. According to 'Rum', heaven was that man in the sky with the long beard, who, they insisted, had created the world in six days and then (obviously exhausted) had needed to take a rest. From such a flimsy intellectual foundation, the Pope had then had the temerity to proclaim that any Chinese who accepted these ludicrous ideas was directly under the imperial power of Roman Christendom, rather than that of the Qing. More specifically, the Pope had then insisted that, as his subjects, they should immediately stop making sacrifices to the ancestors. In Kangxi's opinion, anyone who could believe that the world had been made once and for all in six days must be completely mad. And if the Pope could not learn better manners – or appreciate the power of a constantly changing heaven, which obviously went far beyond a man in the sky – then, however long a beard he might have, the empire would be better off if no one was allowed to make any mention of the so-called 'Christian' idea. Henceforth, the Jesuits, and their Pope, were to be banned from fishing for Chinese souls.

———

When Kangxi died in 1722, after a reign of sixty-one long and rather extraordinary years, he was followed by a forty-four-year-old son who had had quite a lot of time to think about the empire he was going to inherit. Taking the imperial title of Yongzheng (Righteous Justice) the new emperor sent a clear message that he would be consolidating what his father had achieved. Steeped, like his father and grandfather, in the Chinese classics, and most at home in the Hall of Mental Cultivation, Yongzheng was a highly accomplished scholar. He was also, like his father, extremely proud of what he considered to be his far more important Manju roots. While the classical texts might have given him a deep understanding of the fine details of Confucianism, in Yongzheng's unwavering opinion it was his Manju family's qualities as highly disciplined horsemen, hunters and archers that gave them their right to rule. '*Manjusai fe doro,*' he was often heard to remark in approving tones: 'the old Manju ways'. With which, edicts were regularly sent to his bannermen, exhorting them to remember their inheritance: 'Stick to the saddle and be brave!' Not words, of course, that the settled Chinese, sheep as they seemed, would ever be able to understand.

From the earliest days of the Manju, the ruling Aisin Gioro clan had been aware of the risks that the settled world posed. Riding, hunting and archery had remained firm features of life even when the Manju had settled as the Qing, and every Manju, man, woman and child, continued to be organised into banners of military units. And whenever they were not engaged in active battle, every fighting bannerman's energies were directed to the highly ordered hunt of game. Indeed, from the moment of their conquest of Beijing, everything in the Chinese lands and in their own Manju homelands had been organised to reflect the importance of the hunt. Just as the bannermen's tents surrounded the central tent of their emperor on any military or hunting expedition, the old palaces of the imperial city had been rearranged so that the camps of the military banners surrounded the 'inner city' of the court. (As part of the rearrangement, the scholarly Chinese officials had been removed entirely: placed outside and to the south, with day passes for any bureaucratic business that required their presence within.) As soon as Kangxi's conquests had tamed the battles at the borders, he created a number of vast and carefully cultivated 'imperial hunting grounds', devoted to the regular training of every bannerman in the highly skilled art of the hunt.

Thickly forested, full of lakes and streams, the imperial hunting grounds were painstakingly managed to ensure that the large beasts, on which the success of the hunt depended, were given everything they needed to thrive. Stocked with game, and spread with valleys and glens, the hunting grounds were also carefully punctuated with clearings into which the abundant prey could be skilfully driven. Divided into military units trained to think and act like disciplined packs of wolves, the Manju bannermen were then sent in their thousands to practise their hunting skills for months at a time. Rules were strict; discipline was sharp. Each unit was put in charge of a large forested area of its own and, fanning out to encircle their designated territory, each bannerman was given a precise position to hold. Once in their places, all were required to work together: each advancing in concert with the rest of their unit, everyone concentrated on drawing the circle gradually tighter. Successfully executed, large, increasingly frightened and highly dangerous beasts would be corralled into a centre within which they could be expertly held for the kill. Only the greatest intelligence, the most acute alertness and the most vigilant observation of their prey – with the highest co-ordination of physical movement and mental skill between each man and his horse and across the pack as a whole – could deliver success. The bannermen were expected to be nothing less than masterly wolves on horseback: failure was met with punishment, brave success with rewards.

Observing their rulers' dedication to the hunt, a number of Chinese whispered that the Qing were nothing other than barbarians. One, rather recklessly, published his opinion, citing the texts of ancient Zhou dynasty officials as authorities on the barbarian nature of the northern tribes. The whispers did not last long: many were arrested and some not seen again. And the man who had published his point of view was swept up by the new emperor, Yongzheng, who sat him down and gave him a lengthy lecture on how barbarians were nothing other than civilised men waiting in the wings.

Immaculately trained, and with a sharp military attention to the detail of everything, Yongzheng was always keen to set an example. He was also aware of the paralysing (not to mention mischievous) potential of an imperial bureaucracy. Leaving the scholars to carry on with their daily business, he set up his own Office of Military Intelligence, conveniently located to the immediate south of the Hall of Mental Cultivation in which he spent so much of his own, studious, time. Trusted correspondents were invited to deliver secret memorials in individual caskets to which only the emperor and the memorialist had a key; replies were sent by the same secret means. It was not long before the Office of Military Intelligence became the heart of the empire. The formal mechanics of Confucian order continued but the real power of the dragon throne narrowed to a secret box, a shadow, and the fierce eye of an emperor who was determined to personally tackle every sign of disobedience he could find.

Seeing the welfare of the people at large in much the same terms as that of the beasts in the hunting grounds (both needing to be nurtured), Yongzheng was careful to pay attention to their material needs. Martial eyes were directed to tackling the famines of wayward weather, as well as the floods of any rivers that might decide to slip their leash. Imperial budgets (inflated not only by his father's wars, but also by an expanding population) were personally examined down to the smallest coin – and slashed. Quick to see the costs of corruption and the value of eradicating it, Yongzheng announced a moratorium on punishments for those who told the truth; and, with the help of the secret memorials, chased those suspected of taking a bribe down every possible corridor. On closer inspection, however, it was often discovered that some of the reported corruption was a matter of local officials taking the initiative to raise levies for essential local projects overlooked by the central imperial budget. Yongzheng suggested that all local levies be put on a more formal footing, with magistrates co-ordinating local gentry fund-raising on behalf of a benevolent Beijing, and with any and all local funds first delivered to the provincial treasuries, from which more senior imperial officials could then spend them back. In that way, reasoned Yongzheng, the local people would be clear that, whatever the details, the real source of support was the emperor's concern for the welfare of all.

Even the most honest of expenses were put on notice: garrisons at the outposts of the empire were directed to take up local farming in order to earn their own keep. And as spending was scrutinised, so new revenues were explored. Long recovered from the devastating Ming rebellions, by 1720, breaking all previous bounds, the Qing's Chinese population was now approaching 250 million. However much money might be saved, more would need to be raised: more wealth-creating income would need to be generated for the people; more taxes would need to be raised for the state; and somehow more of something would be needed to help replenish a soil that had become so overworked that it was beginning to give up its ghost. One obvious way to help everyone get richer, and to relieve the pressure on the earth, would be to tease new fields from hitherto unused, and therefore 'wasted', land. Another would be to help the peasants grow more food, and faster. Loans were provided for sickles, hoes and cows; and everyone was introduced to the new seeds of potato and maize, discovered in the recently settled American world.

Yet another way to help everyone get richer was to improve the returns from the remote south and south-western lands. Many of these areas, including the provinces of Yunnan and Guizhou, were occupied by the descendants of tribes. Some had been there as long as anyone could remember; others were the descendants of northern tribes who had been pushed south by successive conquering expansions. Looking at their lower levels of productivity, Yongzheng declared that the tribal people should get a better education from the settled world. Confucius seemed to offer the best place to start, followed by a more heavenly approach to local affairs than any of their own chiefs had been able to achieve. Once the essentials of bureaucratic order were set in place, forests were felled, surviving marshes dredged, rivers diverted, dams raised and dykes dug. And when a stretched production on the mainland was still not enough to feed the burgeoning people, imperial eyes turned to the possibilities of Taiwan. Now administratively embraced within the province of Fujian, and with its original inhabitants clearly too barbarian to be able to make best use of its natural advantages, the island was opened up to as many mainland settlers as might choose to go.

Yongzheng's rule was far shorter than his father's: thirteen years in all. But his hard work left its mark. The Chinese lands had been firmly placed on the footing of the Manju hunt, silent whispers had been encouraged to flush out disobedience, all game had been nurtured for a greater wealth, and the net of the empire had been tightened so that few could escape. No one was very surprised when, in 1735, Yongzheng died, at the age of fifty-seven.

In the year of his father's death, the imperially titled Qianlong (Enduring Glory), Yongzheng's fourth son, inherited a vast Manju empire. Adorned by a host of tribute-paying neighbours, it also included a China that was richer in people, land and trade than ever before: all achieved through the discipline of the hunt and the intelligence of the wolf.

Fiercely proud of the towering achievements of his father and grandfather, Qianlong determined to be even clearer about the ruling qualities of the Manju. Books with even a hint of Confucian disapproval were burnt in their thousands; any voices that had openly used the word 'barbarian' were summoned back to court so that their misunderstandings could be straightened out. It was not, the misguided opinions were told, because the Manju had learnt to become Chinese that they were no longer barbarians – anyone could do that. It was because the 'barbarian' Manju were a superior race: true wolves on horseback who had not only learnt to corral the useful ordering talents of the settled Chinese man, but had even managed to tame the dangerous excesses of the scholarly brushes. Unsolicited opinions, endless preoccupations with what Confucius thought or didn't think, not to mention an inexplicable pride in the fact that their complicated language had so many layers of meaning that no one could actually tell the truth – how on earth could anyone have thought that the Chinese could govern themselves? As far as Qianlong could see, it was the so-called 'barbarians' – the Manju, and the Mongols before them – who had created the truly great empires, while the Chinese had achieved little more than two thousand years of bickering, with any attempts at a greater unity usually ending in tears. While Confucianism certainly had its values for ordering the settled world, opined Qianlong, for the true potential of the heavenly lands to be realised, a wolf on horseback was required.

With Qianlong keen to prove his point, his father's spartan cost-cutting was set to one side and the splendours of the Manju mind were displayed for all to see. The imperial hunting grounds were stretched beyond anyone's imagination, literary projects were raised to the skies, and the Forbidden City was converted into a veritable museum – with sumptuous palaces, sparkling porcelains and spectacular paintings as far as the eye could see. With the most obvious way to demonstrate the greater quality of the Manju Qing being through the size of the empire itself, it was not long before Qing bannermen were back in the saddle.

At first, Qianlong sent his bannermen and their accompanying Chinese troops to the south-west, around present-day Yunnan: commanded to pacify a Miao tribe whose people had not quite understood that being conquered meant doing what you were told. Judging by the huge numbers of Miao willing to sacrifice their lives for a lost idea of freedom, it seemed a difficult lesson to learn. Not long after that, Qianlong found that the lesson needed to be repeated in the wider west as well, largely as an unfortunate result of what Yongzheng, his father, had done in Tibet.

Troubled by the same Mongol problems in Lhasa that had worried his own father, Kangxi, Yongzheng had wrapped the eastern parts of Tibet – an area known as Kham – into the settled Chinese province of Sichuan. True, the result had been a bigger Sichuan, but with a Sichuan west that was now full of a Kham Tibetan people, who were anything but settled. By 1747 the Kham were foolishly flinging themselves against a tightening circle of Qing control. In a tug of wills that had looked as if it would never end, Qianlong was forced to send his troops to fight a war on mountainous precipices at the western edges of Sichuan. It would take thirty years to win. In 1750, however, he was also obliged to race his troops up to the western north. The old Zungar Mongols, who had so terrorised his grandfather Kangxi's reign, had once again risen up and unsettled the fragile Tibetan peace. Qianlong's troops managed to restore a certain order. But it was now patently clear that any permanent solution to the Mongol problem was going to require control of a much bigger piece of the western sky. Instead of returning his troops to Beijing, Qianlong pushed further north and west, into lands across which the Zungars regularly roamed. Advancing through the old deserts, and into the oasis states, Qianlong instructed his generals to conquer everything in their way.

As the old oasis states were conquered by the Qing, in a bid for peace, Qianlong offered to soften their losses by conferring Qing titles on their leaders – all followers of Islam. Meanwhile, Tibetan lamas were pacified with warm invitations to spread their spiritual blessings in an imperial Beijing, which, after a hundred years of Manju rule, was beginning to glitter with Buddhist temples. Steeped in the painful lessons of the ancient past, Confucian officials not only frowned at the temples but looked aghast at the vast and unfamiliar deserts that were now being brought back into the empire. There would be consequences, they warned.

Some pointed back to the Han dynasty and the expeditions that had followed Zhang Qian's journey to the west – campaigns which had opened up such a tinderbox of northern trouble that one might easily argue they were the sparks which eventually led to the disastrous thirteenth-century sea battle when everything had been lost to the ships of a Mongol navy. Others pointed to the later travails of the Ming against the Mongol north – lands where the Long Wall had proven to be nothing but an expensive frontier, with costs so high that in the end everything had crumbled, including the wall itself.

Qianlong was unconvinced. Tracing his own Manju inheritance to the power of the steppes, he saw the failures of earlier Chinese expeditions to the west in simple terms: they had just not understood the ordering discipline of the hunt. And as far as the Long Wall was concerned, any bannerman worth his saddle could have told them that the idea of raising a pile of bricks to keep out horsemen was nothing but a foolish fantasy. Ignoring the squawks of his scholarly officials, in 1768 Qianlong rolled his western conquests into a Qing province, calling it the 'new frontier': Xinjiang.

For the next thirty years, Qianlong would march his Manju banner-men and his now much larger force of Chinese troops, up and down, left and right, conquering the world as he went. In so doing he would, like his father and his grandfather before him, bring to bear the full authority of the hunt, including a careful attention to the welfare of the settled people whose fate, like that of every captive creature, he held in the palm of his hand. By the end of his life, he was able to congrat-ulate himself on leaving the legacy of a moderately well-off people to his son and heir: an example of the *xiaokang* ideal of modest pros-perity that Confucius had once declared to be the hallmark of a good ruler – and which had been the inspiration for the *kang* character of his grandfather's name. Qianlong also, however, quietly noted that the future might be a little different. Counting off the costs of his trium-phal conquests, the pacification of tribal rebellions, and the feeding of a large and growing population that regularly broke out in plagues of brotherly bandits, not to mention the costs of the hunting grounds, the literary projects and the palaces, he suggested that unless everyone tightened their belts, disaster might be looming.

While the discipline of the hunt had guided his every campaign, abroad and at home, Qianlong had always set his sights on something much, much greater. Wearing the circle of China's heaven as his hat, and carrying the totem of the wolf, which Chinggis Khan had known as the power of the Tengr sky, Qianlong had not measured his own achieve-ment by the Chinese ideal of a Son of Heaven. Dreaming of himself as Manjusri, the Buddhist bodhisattva of wisdom, he had pursued the very different dream of being a *chakravartin*, a conquering wheel. First imagined in the plains of India, where it had been immortalised by the towering achievements of the ancient Indian emperor Ashoka, then whispered for nearly two thousand years across the steppes, before finding its way into the Buddhist realm, his was the ideal of a wise and universal ruler whose carriage wheels were so great that they could roll in whichever direction he wished, without any obstruction at all.

When Qianlong died in 1799, it was in the confident belief that he and the Manju Qing were not rulers of this piece of sky or that: they were emperors of emperors, universal rulers not only under heaven but across all the earth, before whom everyone should tremble and obey.

CHAPTER 2
RIVERS OF FORTUNE

A hundred thousand households of one determination – how
else can one run a business?

Hankou, seventeenth-century poem by Jia Shenxing

As a brisk breeze blew among the masts, choppy waters
bumped hundreds of brightly coloured hulls against each other,
all packed as tightly as the scales of a fish. Even then, more fan-tailed
sails hauled in for anchor, rising with sudden swells of fortune, only
to drop into a following slough; all jostling for an inch of advantage.
Not that many in the bustling early 1800s were paying them much
attention. Stretched out along the shores as far as the eye could see,
the junks were a permanently floating warehouse with the riches
of everywhere pouring daily from their decks, all unloaded by an
army of porters whose swift movements seemed to beat to an eternal drum.

The biggest of the junks had fought their way up or down the
oceanic Yangzi. Fighting the current up from the sea-mouth of
Shanghai, their hardened crews rowed and pulled treasures of silk
and lacquerware gathered from across the south, up the mighty river;
and when the rowing became impossible, men accustomed to breaking
backs descended from their cargo-laden boats and hauled them up the
river from the land. Floating down from the mountainous tropics of
Yunnan, braving rapids and hairpin bends, their flat-bottomed hulls
carried precious minerals and timbers, stopping to collect harvests
of rice and wheat along their Sichuan way. Smaller junks, built for
narrower waters, sailed in on the converging waters of the river Han,
carrying northern cloth and salt, all hoping for a higher southern
price. And then there were the sampans. Poled in from thin streams
of rivers which threaded all around, they were the simple carriers of
everything a village might want to sell in the market of markets, the

city where the great Yangzi crossed the mighty river Han and everyone met for a trade: Hankou.

All sterns, large and small, set to the shore, bare feet and narrow shoulders picked up the slack without dropping a beat. Headmen commanding
from the quay, sacks and cases were hauled ashore by the hundredweight
and despatched, either to waiting shoremen or to another junk or a
sampan, which would carry them along lesser rivers to their contracted
destination. Hempen sacks slung on to bent backs, heavy cases suspended
from both ends of bamboo poles slung across shoulders, the porters ran
to orders so heavy that only the bitterest, *kuli*, strength could serve. And
as they ran, the porters, 'coolies', chanted mantras of bitterness-eating endurance on tongues that spoke in the languages of far-off fields.
Turbaned heads bent to the ground, above them, the red rafters and
glittering gold of Hankou's splendour passed them by: mighty pavilions,
raised by men on whose calculating minds the biggest trades depended;
men who had, themselves, come from many different places to find the
spot where river met river and fortunes could be made.

Standing on their piers of plenty, as the coolies pulled below, these
new Great Men peered out across the floating warehouses: scanning the
horizon of waiting masts, counting the junks that were angling for a bay
beyond, and considering the tally of profit and loss which the trading day
would bring. For the coolies, all that really mattered was the crowded path
around their feet: the clattering hoofs of donkeys, whose tails swished in
their faces; the running feet of sedan chairs bearing someone to a temple
or a teahouse; wheelbarrows zigzagging to a market; hawkers casting
around for a customer; and the myriad hurried Hankou souls – all pushing hard, this way and that, to reach whatever particular dream their
personal heart was pursuing. Counting off the bitter paces to the end of
a hard day, each of the coolies' thoughts was fixed on the slivers of metal
with which he would be rewarded, and the bowl of noodles he would buy.

Meanwhile, on the piers of plenty, the higher souls of the Great Men
regularly fired off triumphant shots of fire-powder that crackled like
guns. For those able to lift their eyes above the ground, flurries of red
paper dust could be seen exploding like a bountiful cloud. Fortunes for
the truly fortunate, from the market of markets, which was everyone's
home.

Set in the centre of China, at the confluence of two of its mightiest rivers, over the past thousand years Hankou, the 'mouth of the Han', had gradually become the beating heart of the Manju Qing. A market that had become a city, it was a cauldron of trade into which, one way or another, all of China's waterways eventually poured their wealth: the Yangzi, the Han and all of their tributaries; the tributaries of the tributaries; and here and there, connecting canals, dug by ancestral engineers for circulating purpose, with the greatest of all being the Grand Canal constructed so long ago by the unifying Sui. From the time of the Tang, mountains of rice, grain and salt had been travelling up, down and across the many rivers of the land. By the time of the Song – with the land divided north and south along the Yangzi's line – the great river had become the lifeline of a smaller but richer southern empire: one in which the god of wealth had an increasing pride of place. Even under the 'bright idea' of the first Ming emperor, simple goods had continued to flow, including grain gathered as heavy taxes and passing through Hankou. And by the end of the Ming's first century, the idea of a land where everyone would stay at home had vanished like a puff of smoke, replaced with an empire of trade.

The trade had exploded with Yongle's fifteenth-century building of the city of Beijing. As the new northern capital had risen, rafts of pavilion-raising timbers had been floated up to its hungry gates, with copper and iron following suit. Precious porcelains, heavenly silks and lustrous lacquers had been added to their train: all necessary adornments, gathered from the finer southern cities for the Son of Heaven. As the scholars and the gentry sought to emulate the imperial splendour, flotillas of junks and sampans had found themselves carrying returning trades of cloth, salt and grain from north to south, and increasingly being asked to strike out in other directions: wherever anyone was eager to acquire the splendours of a consuming life. Stuffed in sacks and packed in cases, goods of every description sailed north, south, east and west – so many sacks and cases that as the Ming advanced in years, the imperial barges had often had to push for a place on their own overcrowded waterways. The first Ming emperor's dream of a simple life had faded: but who was there to question the change? If ever someone in Beijing raised a querying eyebrow, palms could always be crossed with silver; and if that didn't work, the goods could always be concealed below the decks of seemingly honest junks or, even better, hidden under the planks of the very smallest sampans, which could pass under anyone's nose. At the height of the Ming, while the dreaming imperial city had little idea about the detailed ways and means, the empire was floating on a rising triumph of trade, much of which was passing through Hankou.

When Hankou first flourished as a market, few could have imagined the heights it would reach. Trading ever more ably on the differences across the empire, the once simple market had soon become a town. Food and all of the daily necessities of life arrived by water, and goods flowed out with the tide. Individual fortunes began to rise, firmer foundations had been settled, and it had not been long before the usual pavilions of splendour had started rising. As the market-town spread, its fortunes were built on the principle of being open to everyone. No official magistrate had had a hand in its design, its builders had never subscribed to the heavenly idea that a city must have walls, and those who raised its riches had never been the kind of scholarly gentry who saw themselves as having a responsibility for any surrounding fields. Well before the end of the Ming, Hankou had grown to challenge the size of a city, without receiving a single stroke of approving official ink. By the time of Qianlong's death, it had become, outside the imperial capital, the richest city of the Manju Qing's world. And while the ancestral spirit of the first Ming emperor must have watched from heaven in horror, for the Manju Qing its prosperity was simply an illustration of the most fundamental principle of the hunt, applied to the population at large: 'Store wealth among the people.'

The greatest beneficiaries of the Manju's hunting principles were, as under the imperial dynasties before, those families whose fathers had been well enough placed to understand and navigate the currents of change. Confucianly trained, imperially examined, and with large heavenly families to please, the fathers were scholarly officials who had seen nothing wrong in applying the powers of heavenly office to recoup the great investments made in their own prodigious education. Imperial compensation rarely sufficient to keep food on an official table, let alone a banquet, silver had been found by mining the seams of imperial opportunity. For those charged with raising taxes, it was a simple matter of adding a supplementary fee – call it the cost of carriage. For those charged with running the emperor's factories of silk or porcelain, it had been the addition of a personal interest into the

trading equation. And for those responsible for applying the regulat-
ing edicts of the empire, all that was required was the turning a blind
eye – while delicately indicating that a gift was required.

Whichever direction the profiting opportunity came from, the silver
had piled up. And the higher it got, the quicker attention had turned to
the possibilities of how to spend it. Most expensive, but most rewarding, was the purchase of one of the empire's many trading monopolies
with which the empire vainly tried to control its prices. Salt, that staple
of everyone's life, was one of the most highly prized, iron was another:
anyone able to secure a position in either of those trades instantly
acquired a licence to print money. More affordable, and very popular, was a patient and ongoing acquisition of land. With the peasants
carrying the burden of almost everyone else's taxes – and borrowing
from money-lending landowners to keep themselves afloat – the small
patches of land that the first Ming emperor had intended every man
to own had, over time, been transformed into a currency of desperation. Unable to pay their taxes and repay their loans, once the bullock,
the plough, next year's harvest and any surviving daughters had been
sold, the only remaining way to settle the mounting debts was to sell
the land itself. Patch by patch, small men reduced to penury had sold
their fields to silver-rich officials and their related gentry. Land sold,
shoulders that had once pulled their own ploughs, pulled the ploughs
of landed masters instead. The emperor had his treasury; and across
the imperial world, the scholarly officials reaped the harvests of their
heavenly credentials with an inheritance of the land.

That, at least, was the dream. But with big families, and the offices
of empire limited to the lifespan of a successful examination candidate,
the vast estates were difficult to hold beyond a few generations. Not
every son could master the exacting literary skills required to follow
in a father's official footsteps – and without a well-placed scholar in
the family, land would almost certainly be lost. Fortunes were spent
on tutors, books and decades of learning. But few fathers managed to
repeat their own success through their sons; and even fewer managed
to repeat it through a grandson. Constantly aware of the risk of losing
everything, by the time the Qianlong emperor jumped into his father's
saddle in 1735, China's landed gentry was beginning to hedge its bets.
Confucian study for everyone, and nothing but Confucian study for
the eldest upon whose shoulders all family hopes depended. But with

the tragic lessons of human failure scattered across the fields for all to see, as time passed, younger sons were also trained in the trading equations of profit and loss.

The mastery of arithmetic was essential – protecting the family silver required a scrupulous accounting for every copper penny spent; that, and an understanding that the protection and expansion of wealth required a close relationship with the officials charged with the empire's affairs. And just to make sure that no son ever forgot his place, founding fathers wanting to preserve their families' fortunes applied their literary talents to creating genealogies which not only reminded everybody of the descending order of who was related to whom, but also included detailed sets of rules about what could be spent and when. Written and read like edicts, the genealogies were compendia of rules intended to govern the conduct of every following son. They were, however, only good as far as they went: they could try to slow down the rate at which a fortune was spent, but in a world of rising prices, but they certainly could not raise a new fortune from the ground. With this in mind, whenever a son or grandson failed to pass the imperial exams, fathers and grandfathers did their utmost to ensure that they made themselves indispensable to more successful candidates, who would be in a position to share their wealth. Imperial officials, charged with raising money for an emperor's dreams, were to be given every possible assistance. And given that local magistrates were never attached to their own home districts – too great a risk of corruption – they were always in need of helpful guidance on perplexing local decisions. Grounded in the local lands, familiar with the up and down fortunes of the local people, who else could be better placed to advise on general matters of judgement, or offer an opinion on which groups of households might most easily yield the taxes the emperor required. And if anyone in the higher orders of the imperial office wanted a wife – first, second or third – dutiful daughters were always in ready supply.

For quite a while, some of the gentry even dreamt that the peasant households could become traders, albeit in small ways: already weaving everything they needed, their households produced clothes, hats, shoes and baskets from the meagre land they farmed. Indeed, almost every field of grain had been edged with patches of cotton plants so that when the ploughing, sowing and reaping had been done, hands idled by winter could turn to making the cloth that, rolled into a bundle, could be taken to the nearest market to sell. With little hope of affording a textbook, let alone passing an imperial exam, peasant hands, particularly those in the harder north, had needed little encouragement to apply every spare moment to turning the bare harvest of a patch of land – their own or someone else's – to a spinning trade. As times had toughened, weaving goods for sale had become as much of a necessity as the harvest itself. It had not been long before men from the trading towns, alerted to the possibility of a profit, had come in search of industrious households, offering 'putting out' commissions for the peasants to weave at home. And it had not been much longer before the fruit of those peasant looms was washing into Hankou. The peasants certainly became sellers, but the profitable position of trading in the middle passed to those who ran the markets. Lands lost, peasants in penury, by the time Qianlong left his *chakravartin* wheel, bequeathing the legacy of a much bigger population and a much hungrier treasury, the cloth that went to Hankou was increasingly being followed by its makers: newly landless peasants desperate to find a foothold in which to survive.

When Qianlong's son, the Jiaqing (Great Celebration) Emperor, assumed his father's seat, the imperial costs of the last hundred years were well on their way to becoming a nightmare. Empire-stretching conquests had exacted a painful price, as had misfit tribes battling against the conquerors, and hungry peasants rampaging as brotherhoods of blood. When the imperial books were opened after Qianlong's death, the worst of everyone's fears was confirmed. Having fallen victim to a friendship with a Manju bannerman who bore an uncanny resemblance to a departed and much-loved concubine, Qianlong had opened up the imperial treasury to satisfy his beloved's every desire. The bannerman had seen no reason to contain his greed: family, friends and wider relatives had been woven into every imaginable budget – as had the 'special expenses' that the bannerman himself had claimed. One way or another, under Qianlong's reign half of the imperial revenues had found their way into other people's pockets. By the end of his life, the imperial treasuries, so full of cash at the beginning, had been emptied and the dream of imperial frugality, so dear to his father Yongzheng, inspired nothing more than a sneer.

The problems inherited by Qianlong's son were not limited to silver. While 'storing wealth among the people' had repaired the fortunes of many, by 1799 the population had reached three hundred million, and even after Kangxi's reclamations, the land upon which everyone's fortunes depended was struggling from the relentless demand for ever-greater harvests. With so many forests felled, any surviving stand of trees had been axed for the increasingly profitable returns it could yield; and with so little land for so many people, every foot of earth was supporting a family of many mouths. It was hardly surprising that the weaving of cotton cloth had gone back to being a necessity for survival. But still the population kept growing.

As if that was not enough, Qianlong's ideas for reclaiming land from surviving forests and marshes seemed to have created some devastating, if unintended, consequences. Where northern farmlands, long cool and dry, had once been protected by canopies of green, they now found themselves threatened by dusty deserts. Similarly, rain-swept southern slopes, once held together by the roots of trees, turned into muddy landslides, sweeping away crops and burying the peasants in their wake. Wherever a marsh had been reclaimed for a paddy field, it seemed that a flood was sure to follow – on the paddy field itself, and up and down the rivers all around. It was one thing to flatten the forests and fill in the marshes in the expectation that new land taxes would more than cover the costs, but now that many of the lands were beginning to fail, who would cover the costs of fixing nature?

The problem was a knotty one. While it was the Son of Heaven who had the responsibility for managing the wellbeing of the imperial lands, it was Hankou that was reaping the fortunes of trade. Carrying everybody's food and taxes up and down the country, and receiving ever-greater tides of bitterness-eating labour, as sea-borne trade expanded, Hankou was also carrying a rising quantity of Chinese treasures destined for foreign shores: cotton, silk, tea, porcelain, lacquer and lanterns, all gathered from across the Chinese lands, and almost all of them passing through Hankou's watery markets before journeying across the seas.

The old Ming solution of raising taxes was a tempting one. Since wealth had been 'stored among the people', it was surely time for the people, at least the richer ones, to share it back with the empire. But Jiaqing's great-grandfather Kangxi had promised that imperial taxes on land would never rise and, indeed, had it not been for Qianlong's devotion to the bannerman, the books might well have balanced. It would be a brave great-grandson who was prepared to face a towering ancestor with such an act of filial disobedience. With barely enough money to keep the imperial household going, let alone the burgeoning empire, other solutions would have to found. The imperial cloth would have to be cut to the size of its purse. And more of the costs of empire would need to be transferred to the private accounts of the gentry, whose fortunes had been built on the scholar-official titles of fathers and sons.

In terms of cutting the imperial cloth, the obvious place to start was with the officials. Compensation should, of course, remain Confucian and frugal – certainly the officials seemed to have managed well enough across the centuries. From the courtyards of imperial Beijing, where self-important scholars always seemed to have too much time for their own learned opinions, it also seemed sensible to put a stop to the creation of any new bureaucratic positions. It would be hard on the tens of thousands who were studying themselves blind in the confident expectation that, once passed, the imperial examinations would naturally deliver a rewarding situation; but they were young, and needs must. It would be particularly hard on the magistrates. Charged with tax-collecting, peace-keeping, dispute-resolving, water-taming and morality, they were generally responsible for keeping the harmonies of heaven in place in every local county – in an era when some county populations were now edging past a million. But, having passed the imperial examinations, their wits should be more than quick enough to cope with the changes.

In terms of meeting the wider costs of the empire, it was time to look a little more closely at the gentry. A lot of officials had retired to country estates, and all had sons and grandsons who, with fewer prospects in the imperial bureaucracy, were now lounging longer in the wings. The heart of the gentry, they had always been more than willing to share the imperial burden: surely, they could be relied upon to help a little more. Sitting on personal fortunes accumulated over the years, they could afford to fund any necessary heavenly projects a local county might require. True, no one ever liked to spend their own money, but confused though the ancient empire might have been in many ways, it had always been crystal clear about the filial piety on which everyone's heaven – from the emperor down to landlording fathers and their tenanted estates – depended. As Confucius had observed so astutely: 'Family is everything.'

Hankou certainly had more than its fair share of wealth. As the tides of trade had washed up in its waters, so its shores had become a popular home for anyone with a bargaining turn of mind, whichever part of the empire they might have been born in. Truth be told, the greatest of them usually seemed to have come from a handful of provinces in which they had first monopolised fortunes from salt, tea, timber and other natural treasures, and then bet the profits on financing trade up and down the empire's rivers. The mountainous Shanxi, with its natural wealth at the northern end of the Han River, was one; the fertile land of Anhui to the southern-east was another. From wherever they came, in Hankou the greatest of them had gathered together under the pavilions of their individual provinces and ordered their trades and themselves with the tried and tested principles of the Confucian family and its values. *Dao, ren, yi, li, zhi* and *de* – the emphasis and the meanings had changed a little over the past two thousand years but the principles were the same: *dao*, the mastery of change; *ren*, putting yourself in other's shoes (these days, particularly a brother's); *yi*, the integrity which ensured that names and purposes were constantly correlated; *li*, the observance of ritual obedience, so that no one forgot their place; *zhi*, the knowledge that enabled every profitable opportunity to be exploited; and *de*, applying yourself to whatever the task at hand with such discipline that the energies of heaven would constantly keep you afloat.

With mountains of silver at their disposal, the migrant merchants had spared no expense in raising the guilds which would order the interests of provinces or trades, complete with portals of piers and palaces of halls from which the changes that affected everyone's fortunes could be mastered. From the piers, each guild managed the boats of its members. From the palaces, temples were dedicated to the spirit of the god of wealth, while inner halls set out the rules and regulations that every member would observe. By the time the Jiaqing Emperor was looking for families to share the burdens of empire, it was not only to fathers and sons that he looked, but to the guilds as well. And remembering the early trade in pelts and pearls on which the fortunes of his own Aisin Gioro clan had been grounded, Jiaqing noted with pleasure how happy it was that the Manju idea of using trade to store wealth among the people should fit so easily with the Confucian idea of the family; and how strange it was that the Confucian Ming had failed to see its virtue.

———

Piers of fortune rising for Hankou's merchants, for a while even the lowest tides seemed to be touched with silver. But by the time Jiaqing passed the heavenly lands to his son the Daoguang (Bright Way) Emperor in 1820, for those at the bottom of the pile, the idea of wealth being stored among the people had become nothing but a dream. With the surrounding land too exhausted to support the peasants, and cotton cloth no longer a source of relief but an essential labour, the poorest families were clutching any available wooden plank and floating to Hankou. Under Qianlong, the city had already become a babel of migrant dialects and accents that few could understand. The well-placed corners in which someone with a few pennies could hang a trading hat of their own had long ago become firmly occupied. And as more people came, even the bare-handed positions, from barbers and bakers to tailors and fortune-tellers, even the more skilled boatmakers, were also filled. For those floating in at the later time of his grand-son, Daoguang, it looked as if every inch of opportunity had already been covered. But although all of the obvious trades were more than adequately represented, it always seemed that if one squeezed hard enough there would somehow be room for yet another sturdy pair of shoulders, or yet another basket of something more to sell. More barbers, more tailors, more singers of stories, more tellers of fortunes, more hawkers, more beggars than anyone could ever imagine. And swarming along all of its shores, more would-be boatmen and coolie porters ready to sweat even harder than the men before them. Indeed, Hankou seemed to have discovered a new trade in the labour of desper-ate men with nothing to sell but their ability to endure: *chi ku*, as the peasants called it – eating bitterness. If you could take enough of that desperate fruit, you might just survive.

With everyone, from top to bottom, regularly contemplating either triumph or destitution, there was, naturally, a heavy interest in respite. From the calculating top (where every trade was a risk) to the bitterness-chewing bottom (where every morning of life-extinguishing endurance might be one's last), at some point or another in the working day everyone wanted to find a soft cloud they could call their own. And, like so many other things in Hankou, the cloud that everyone dreamt of arrived up the Yangzi, on a boat.

The magical powers of opium had long been understood by Daoist alchemists: shaman successors who had been exploring other worlds since the beginning of time, not to mention helping anxious emperors in their search for the elixir of eternal life. For many centuries, opium had even been grown to imperial order in the easy tropical climate of the south: full of masculinely creative *yang* properties, Ming emperors had spent fortunes procuring its powers. Soon the scholarly officials were following suit, with exquisite pipes finely crafted for wider imperial appeal. And then the families of the scholarly officials began to pick up the habit: wealthy wives shut behind protecting walls and languishing in boredom; stressed sons who thought they might explode if they had to read another studying book. Eventually everyone with a headache or a twinge was turning to the poppy for relief, as were the labouring backs and shoulders that needed bitter strength. With simpler sticks of wood for pipes and the magic sold in tinier pinches – and cut with cheaper properties – it became a universal fixer, far better than a meal. Observing the relief acquired, Hankou's merchants had been quick to see how opium could also be a treasure, certainly valuable for its profits, but also offering a dose of personal comfort when negotiating the often-stormy seas of trade.

By the beginning of the 1700s, opium had already become a dangerously captivating power. One of Qianlong's brothers had been an addict, and their horrified father, Yongzheng, had banned its use by anyone for anything other than medicinal purposes. But time had passed, the stresses of wealth had risen and the power of the poppy had grown. Before long, southern fields were struggling to satisfy the volume of demand, and with many growers favouring a faster production, quality began to be a challenge. By the time the Daoguang Emperor came to the throne, in 1820, cases of opium were not only arriving in Hankou from the southern fields but from the southern seas as well. Handled initially by Portuguese mariners keen to insinuate themselves into the currents of South East Asian trade, they were later delivered by

British traders who had fields of Indian poppies to sell, and a lot of silver to make.

Confucian values notwithstanding – or perhaps because it was just so hard to live up to them – taels of family silver were smoked away. Entire estates then followed in their wake, all puffed into clouds by otherwise dutiful fathers and sons. Even the attentions of the imperial troops were captured by the pipe. Shocked by the news that the empire had failed to vanquish a tribal rebellion because its soldiers had been floating on a cloud of opium, Jiaqing tried, in vain, to banish it completely. But the cost was not limited to the gentry's estates and the security of the realm. With Indian opium increasingly flooding in on British ships, taels of silver were rolling out; and as the taels of silver rolled out, the price of silver at home soared to the skies. What had begun as a problem of an imperial addiction was ending up as a crisis in the balancing of the books. Imperial displeasure notwithstanding, across the failing estates and in dark city dens, the charms of opium seemed to conquer all. Hankou traded on.

In the early 1830s, a string of poppy tales began to float in on Hankou's rivers: apparently the imperial officials had once again been commanded to flatten the opium fields, and once again the coasts were being cleared. Hankou paid them little heed: it was not the first time, it would certainly not be the last, and it usually didn't last for long. Following whispers confirmed that there was little to fear: with Guangdong's port of Guangzhou ('Canton' to the tongues of the West) exclusively appointed by the emperor to handle all trade across the southern seas, the local merchants had been quick to realise that the sea-faring barbarians had mountains of opium to sell. And although there was an imperial ban on the selling or buying of opium in China, the southern coast was fringed with thousands of tiny islands: all one had to do was send a smaller junk or a sampan to meet the foreign ships off the mainland's shore. Silver handed over, the forbidden treasure then swapped ships and the smaller vessels – craftier at navigating the narrowest rivers of the empire and always in need of a cargo – carried it off across the watery highways and byways until they reached Hankou. Heaven being high and, usually, far away, it seemed as if the problem was solved.

By 1835, with Hankou now supplier of clouds of pain-relieving pleasure to a grateful empire, its fortunes were riding higher than ever before. There was a bit of a squall in 1839, when heaven rather unexpectedly decided to investigate Guangzhou's 'port affairs' in the person of a highly Confucian official named Lin Zexu. Known as a stickler for smugglers, it was obvious to all that he would need careful handling. As expected, the Guangzhou merchant brothers were given a serious telling-off, with promises of future perfectly heavenly behaviour insisted upon, accompanied by hellish pictures of punishment for anyone in need of persuasion. As the exclusively appointed imperial traders of everything, the Guangzhou merchants were also ordered to ensure, on pain of death, that the barbarian traders dumped every ounce of opium in their holds. Apparently, it wasn't easy to get the barbarians to understand the need for this, but eventually, after a year of fussing, three million pounds of poppy dust were finally handed over and Lin Zexu poured them into the sea. 'The risks of trade,' Guangzhou's merchant brothers sighed, 'but once the waves have washed this particular harvest of opium away, it shouldn't be long before the stickler for smugglers is called back to more important imperial duties, and everyone can get on with the business of trade.'

Up in the centre of the country, Hankou had not been consulted by the Guangzhou brothers, but it couldn't have agreed more. Floating in a world of its own, the empire's emporium had found a silver lining to the cloud of poured-away losses: when the southern opium was thrown into the water, Hankou merchants made fortunes from the opium in their stores. True, there were quite a few sons and fathers who, smoking away their estates, were now losing their fortunes even more quickly than before. But fools were everywhere, and one man's loss was another's gain. Firmly anchored at the heart of the merchant world, Hankou's trades were bobbing up and down very nicely, thank you; and if one kept one's Confucian wits about one, the rafters of fortune could still reach to the skies.

Of course, there were always killjoys. Some said the exodus of silver was a problem – but as far as Hankou's teahouse conversations could tell, it was nothing that the clever merchant-bankers from Shanxi hadn't been able to fix. Paper notes might not be popular with an emperor who preferred to receive his taxes in silver, but for the merchants they were an obvious means of smoothing trade, with the added advantage of creating a whole new industry of exchanging money. Then, of course, there were the usual old Confucians, muttering in their studies about the shame of Hankou's splendour. Mutter they might: every day brought another junk of eager peasant hands clinging to Hankou's shores for dear life. But while the burred accents of the migrants might be impossible to understand, they were willing to eat any amount of bitterness to get their toes into the city's waters. Pickpockets, however, were certainly a problem: with so much of the countryside washing up, penniless, in Hankou, they were becoming a natural pest. They, and perhaps even the bitterness-eating coolies themselves. With the price of opium so high that many of the coolies were having to eat their bitterness raw, some in the trading terraces suggested that things might start to get a little bit bumpy on the streets.

In 1841, Hankou's self-satisfied merchants began to hear some stranger stories. Having lost their opium, and clearly untrained in the Confucian ways, the barbarian foreigners had apparently thrown down their anchors in a temper and insisted on compensation. When they (obviously) had not got it, they had gone one step further and demanded the right to sell whatever they wanted, to whomever they wanted, up and down China's shores. Although Lin Zexu – still in charge of port affairs – had been very clear about the heavenly principles, the barbarians had loaded their arguments with gunpowder, and were now training their sights up and down the coast. No one was quite sure what to make of it all. But as the southern merchant brothers got themselves snarled up in the spat, Hankou's trades continued even more buoyantly than before.

At one point, one of the foreign ships had the temerity to sail up the Yangzi, and Hankou jaws dropped in disbelief. But once its strange curiosity had apparently been satisfied, the ship seemed to understand that no barbarian could ever hope to match the trading powers of the Hankou merchants, and turned back down the Yangzi to the mud-flats of Shanghai. That being the case, it was quite a shock to hear, less than a year later, that the emperor had suddenly given the Western barbarians an imperial licence to trade not only in Guangdong province's port city of Guangzhou but in a clutch of other ports up the coast, as far as and including Shanghai. 'Treaty ports', they called them. To which were to be added millions of taels of silver, which the foreigners had demanded as 'reparations', for heaven's sake.

What could one expect from the Manju Qing? As everyone knew, barbarians themselves, they clearly could not be depended on to understand the heavenly lands, let alone be relied upon to keep them safe. Having squandered their early fortune on conquests and the corrupting charms of that greedy bannerman, was it any wonder they didn't have the necessary forces for a fight? How on earth the emperor was going to find the money for the reparations was anybody's guess. But as far as Hankou was concerned, heaven really was high and, whatever his troubles, the emperor was far away. Guangzhou and those coastal 'treaty ports' might be experiencing a few problems, and a lot of cheap foreign cotton was probably going to be working its way up the Yangzi, but Guangzhou's loss was probably Hankou's fortune, and cotton, after all, was just another trade.

For the next few years, Hankou's teahouses settled back to their usual roaring business. Even the opium dens were going great guns. Whether as paper, silver or even the odd old-style copper coin, the cash was flowing. Most of the merchants were so busy calculating the constant rise of their accounts that the wider world of human beings seemed not to exist. From time to time, some visiting curmudgeonly Confucian would start lecturing on the idea that the rich were vying with each other for splendour while the poor were being squeezed to death. There were even madmen (when had there ever not been?) who had started muttering about ominous vapours rising and a darkness beginning to spread across the earth. No one paid them much notice.

But then, even stranger tales began to arrive from Guangzhou. Particularly the one about a failed imperial scholar who was talking about a new Taiping, Great Peace. As if all of the Taiping Great Peaces of the past had not taught everyone more than enough about how dangerous they could be. Special breathing, confessions of sins, brothers and sisters dreaming of a pure land where everyone could be equal *and* immortal: one way or another, every one of them had been swept away – as often as not betrayed by the very idiots who had dreamt them up in the first place. Usually, some northern barbarian had then ridden down to take advantage of the chaos.

Those close to the south explained that this particular scholar had failed his exams so many times that he had not only lost his head to visions, but had started to mix them up with one of those foreign ideas: the one about the man with a long beard in the clouds. Of course, the idea of a man in the clouds was nothing new, but this one wasn't

Laozi: it was a foreigner with a bigger nose and a beard: the character the Jesuits had chattered about until Kangxi had told them to keep their delusions to themselves – the one called 'God'. And as if that was not enough, the scholar was now declaring that he himself was none other than the brother of the old man's more famous 'Jesus' son. Well, what could you expect if you opened up your ports? The madman's name was 'Hong something' and apparently he was not just railing against the Manju Qing (well, who wouldn't rail against that barbarian shower?) but against Confucius as well. Of course, it wouldn't be the first time that someone had had a bone to pick with Confucius, but it was very rare that anyone dared to stand up and speak their mind. For the settled Hankou merchants, it was all a bit confusing. But while the stories about the deranged scholar kept floating in from the south, Hankou, nestled in the beating heart of China, and with all the seasons turning as usual, continued to trade.

In 1847 and 1848, however, it began to look as if there might indeed be a few problems. A drought in neighbouring Henan, then a famine in southern Guangxi were both a bit too close for comfort. Calculating hearts duly noted that the cost of grain would go up – and duly proceeded to buy as much as they could. But even those most absorbed in their abacuses began to wonder if heaven was about to turn. Boatmen shipping in to Hankou had been muttering about hard times in the north for a few years now – along with tales of yet more of the rebellions that always blew up when heaven was unhappy. Apparently, the peasants were anxious about cheap foreign cotton flooding across the country: for the northern lands, which had so few other crafts to offer, this was obviously going to cost them dear. That and the fact that, with not much money in the imperial treasury, the Grand Canal was not being dredged and had become too silted for many to use. Inland traders were now shifting their cargoes to the coast, and it looked as if the boatmen were about to lose their jobs.

Was any of this really any different from the past? More people, less land and less land that could be farmed; empty coffers in the imperial treasury and a gentry who would rather buy a city palace than dig their hands into their pockets for a peasant in need. There had always been poor peasants, and they had regularly raised local rebellions – so much so that the idea of *human portents* seemed to have become a bit of a mantra. Someone had written an essay about the origins of the present problem during the time of the Jiaqing Emperor (and been banished for his pains): twenty times more people than there had been a hundred years before; not enough land or food to go around; and a lot of the rich eating so much and buying so many things that they were swallowing the food of future generations. What to do? As even the smallest schoolboy was taught, the times were constantly changing and the cultivated man simply had to find a way to adjust. And as every trader knew, fixed as it was at the heart of the empire, the source of Hankou's fortunes might change but the direction of trade was almost always up.

In 1850, the problems of the empire suddenly rolled a lot closer when the Yangzi River burst its banks not far from Hankou. Oceans of fields were swallowed under water and floods of washed-away families suddenly floated into Hankou. Then, in 1851, the news went from bad to worse. In the company of twenty thousand men, the deranged scholar, now well known as Hong Xiuquan, had proclaimed a Kingdom of Taiping, Great Peace, and raised a 'Heavenly Army' that was now marching north up the Xiang River valley, with the riches of Hankou clearly in its sights. Word was that its numbers were swelling with every village they passed. Of course, everyone had known Hong Xiuquan was on the move. But rebels were always moving somewhere, and no one had thought it would come to this. True, rumours had been washing up since the previous year that ten thousand men had gathered under the Taiping banner on a mountain in Guangxi, with hundreds more joining every day. But Guangxi was such a long way away.

It had been a little more worrying to hear that, in addition to converts to Hong Xiuquan's mad visions, the Heavenly Army's numbers included members of other, much older, brotherhoods of men. The old White Lotus Society was one – the brotherhood with which the first Ming emperor had swept himself to power and which had been erupting periodically into northern rebellions ever since. The Heaven and Earth Society was another: a well-known brotherhood, dedicated to ousting the Manju Qing, its ranks had long ago been swollen by a host of Shaolin monks, after their loyalist monastery had been destroyed by that other rebel, Li Zicheng, the shepherd who had marched against the Ming. There was even a society called the Three Harmonies – although heaven knew what could be harmonious about a rebellious brotherhood. Who could have known that these brotherhoods talked to each other, and that their members could reach such a mass? Now it seemed that, although many were primarily dedicated to the overthrow of the Manju Qing, the brotherhoods were also committed to the rise of every peasant, with the idea of joining everyone together in one great harmonious family of brothers, which any peasant willing to share his blood was welcome to join. Nor was it just the peasants. As the Grand Canal had clogged up and the watery trade had shifted to the coast, the crews of the once-canal-plying boats had pledged their blood to a heavenly order of their own – and now they had decided to throw in their lot with the Kingdom of Taiping, Great Peace.

Breath held, Hankou watched and waited, quizzing every boat and sampan that arrived. Then, in the early December of 1852, news arrived that the Heavenly Army, one million strong and rising, had arrived just south of Hankou, at Dongting Lake. Awash with thousands of empty boats, the banks of the lake also happened to be piled with guns and ammunition abandoned from the rebellions of Wu Sangui, two hundred years before. Trading minds quickly made their calculations: it would be only a matter of days before the peasant hordes sailed into the Yangzi and climbed aboard the floating emporium of the empire. Everyone who could rushed to the piers in a bid to escape; only the very richest made it. By the end of the year, Hong Xiuquan's Great Peace lovers had sailed into Hankou's fortunes. Silver and food had been redistributed for all. And the beating heart of trade had stopped.

Slow to understand the threat, and almost as slow as the Hankou traders to catch up, the imperial troops were nearly as far away as the emperor when the city fell. With Hankou under its control, and hundreds of new recruits joining every day, Hong Xiuquan's Heavenly Army moved on. Three months later, the once-capital of Nanjing was captured and declared the capital of a new Taiping 'Southern Empire'. As the Qing imperial troops mustered to confront the Heavenly Army in the south-east, pent-up anger began to explode in almost every other quarter of the country as well. Tribal people who wanted their own worlds back, brotherhoods of men who wanted justice: north, south, east and west, there was not a corner that could keep its peace. At one point, it even seemed as if the Heavenly Army would capture the new treaty port of Shanghai – but then suddenly a Small Sword Society popped up out of nowhere and occupied it before they could get there. Some said the Small Swords were cousins of the Heaven and Earth Society, others insisted that they were just another branch of the Taiping, Great Peace lovers. Most, however, realised that, when a man has nothing left to lose, it doesn't really matter what he joins as long as it promises help.

In 1854 Hankou would be saved, only to fall again. In 1855, it would be saved once more. Meanwhile, the rest of the Yangzi world descended into a battling hell that would last until 1864.

In the end, their saviour, and the saviour of the Manju Qing, was a Confucian scholar who had never fought in a battle, let alone led a battalion of troops. His name was Zeng Guofan. Ordered by a desperate emperor to raise an army from his home province of Hunan (just south of the Yangzi and home to Dongting Lake), he succeeded by appealing to everyone's sense of Confucian values. Painstakingly searching for the *dao* way, he consistently expressed the *ren* humanity, which put himself and his men in the shoes of the people. Insisting on an *yi* integrity, which matched people up with their places, he did nothing without a dedication to the pursuit of *zhi* knowledge, which went well beyond the learning of books. Applying a *li* ritual to the order of the ranks, he never departed from the *de* principle of a disciplined virtue. Indeed, Zeng Guofan seemed to be the incarnation of everything that Confucius had ever taught. As the Qing's imperial army foundered (bereft of funding and now famous for scattering at the sound of a gun), Zeng Guofan raised an army from a ragtag bunch of Yangzi peasants, and created a host of local 'fund-raising' bureaus to persuade the gentry-merchants of central China to pay for it all.

Raised from the home villages of its soldiers – and with each recruit properly paid, reliably fed and organised under the strict Confucian bonds of father to son and older brother to younger brother – by 1855 Zeng Guofan's army was a force to be reckoned with. Known as the 'Xiang Army' (after a river in Hunan province of such importance to its people that the name was often used for the province itself as well), across the next ten years it would battle the Great Peace lovers up and down the Yangzi while tackling every other upstart rebellion that was cashing in on the chaos.

By 1864, when the ancient, and more recently Taiping, capital of Nanjing had been restored to the Qing, its saviours would be seen as an army of Confucian heroes standing stark against a mismanaged Yangzi landscape that was now in shreds. The battles had been followed by famines and plague, once-fertile fields had turned to tangles of weed and dust, with the bones of thirty million dead scattered across the landscape. Stunned survivors could only look on in shock. Heaven had certainly winnowed out its people. Many more would be lost in the years it would take for the shattered earth to find its feet.

Well before the end of the rebellion – a rebellion so big that many would whisperingly describe it as a civil war – Hankou's surviving merchants returned to the remains of their once-gilded city. Threading their way through the rubble of their rafters, they began to resurrect the floating emporium from its watery grave. As they worked, they applied every Confucian virtue in their books. Heaven may have taken its toll but the Qing's remaining people would need their rivers of fortune if they were to rebuild the past. Fathers gathered themselves and their sons together; guilds reached out to their members. Surviving souls without a patch of land to stand on sailed in on every possible sampan and offered their shoulders for the task. The order of trade painstakingly restored, everyone then set about rebuilding the glittering palaces and piers. Back in business long before the final triumph of Zeng Guofan's Xiang Army, more stories floated in of how the Western barbarians were redirecting their own fire against the rebels lest heaven completely collapse.

Then, in 1861, news had arrived that the emperor had given the British barbarians yet another imperial licence to trade – this one for Hankou itself. Good luck to them, the merchants thought. After everything Hankou had endured, there was little that a volley of foreigners could teach it. And in case the foreigners hadn't noticed, the rise of Zeng Guofan's Xiang Army had proved, beyond the shadow of a doubt, that their Confucian spirits were more than equal to any barbarian trade which might be thrown at them.

Looking out at the waters, though, and listening to the tales of the washed-up people who were floated in, some of Hankou's number did begin to wonder about the peasants in the lands around: rags and bones, clutching at the straws of an exhausted earth. Rumour had it that tides of them were not only flooding back into Hankou, but into the bonds of the brotherhoods as well. A world of secret societies where a family of blood brothers was all. If the past had been a problem, what on earth would the future bring?

CHAPTER 3
IMAGINE A PEOPLE

Heaven sees as the people see; heaven hears as the people hear.
The Great Declaration (from now lost pages of the
Book of Documents, second millennium BCE,
referred to by Mencius)

THE BLACK ICE OF winter had bitten deep into the northern
peninsula that curled around the inner gulf of the Yellow Sea.
Outmanoeuvred in a chilling sea-battle in late 1894, the ironclad
dreadnoughts of the Beiyang northern navy had slipped back behind
a sheltering island base, which sat just off the coast in the bay of
Weihaiwei. By all rights, they should not have lost the Battle of the
Yalu River. With bigger ships, and more of them – all fitted with the
latest Krupp German guns – they should have won not just the battle
but the war as well. But, as was so often the case, sighed Admiral
Ding, imperial meddling, wanton corruption and cowardice all seemed
to have got in the way. Gunners had been deployed before they had
received any training. Shells once fired turned out to have been stuffed
with porcelain and cement. Then the captain of the fleet's much-prized
armoured turret ship had preferred to duck out of the line of fire rather
than take a hit that would have saved the day. A damaging exercise
with painful lessons for all to learn.

Now sheltered by the generous length and convenient hills of their
base on nearby Liugong Island – and protected by newly armoured
fortresses along the shoreside bay of Weihaiwei – the fleet would at
least have time to get its positions clear before venturing back for
a more successful kill. Somewhere out there on the Yellow Sea was
the navy of the Greater Japanese Empire: a smaller fleet but with
fleeter ships; a chain of command that seemed to run like a clock; and
a cunning grasp of strategy that always seemed to find the weakest
flank. For now, however, the Beiyang fleet was at home, tucked under

the protection of artillery designed by the best of naval minds. On either side of the island, booms had been spread to keep out any Japanese opportunists who might try to get past – each spiked with mines, and all guarded by submarine torpedoes lying in watchful wait. And just to make sure that nothing had been left to chance, the Krupp cannons on the shoreside were fully armed, with the sight of each one facing firmly out to sea. They wouldn't, of course, be needed: the Beiyang navy had no immediate plans to move. But this time no one was leaving any fortune to fate – not where the clearly crafty Japanese were concerned.

As the old, lunar, year entered its last January month, temperatures plunged to 26 degrees below freezing and snow stormed across the skies. Admiral Ding turned his attention to his sailors and set about reminding them how to fight. At one point, there was a bit of a distraction: the Japanese attempted a clumsy landing, foolishly trying to take a heavily armoured fort to the west. Finally, something the Qing forces could easily rebuff. A week later, as the old Year of the Horse prepared to depart, the Liugong Island base relaxed its guard a little, cracking an armoury of fireworks to scare away the hungry spirits and welcome in a new Year of the Sheep.

Then, just when all seemed so quiet both at land and at sea, the Beiyang fleet exploded. Pummelled with shot and with black clouds of destruction in every direction, Admiral Ding peered towards the shore and saw the Krupp guns of the landside fortresses firing towards his harbouring ships with a faultless military precision. Jumping to clear orders, gunners were loading and firing the cannons like clocks. Newly hoisted on their turrets was the flag of the Rising Sun.

The Manju Qing had needed to learn a lot in the decades after Zeng Guofan raised his Xiang Army to stand against the Taiping rebels. Much of it was simply catching up on what had been happening in the rest of the world across the previous hundred years. But a lot of the learning had had to be grasped at the height of the Taiping rebellion – with the added obstacle of a new emperor, Xianfeng (Great Prosperity), who rarely managed to face up to challenges of the present, let alone the future.

It seemed that two hundred years ago, something called the 'sovereignty of nations' had been dreamt up at the barbarian edge of the world. Not surprisingly, given the barbarians' limited education, the idea of a *dao*, way, was completely unfamiliar to them – as were the Confucian principles of *ren*, humanity, *yi*, integrity, *li*, ritual, *zhi*, knowledge, and *de*, virtue. Apparently, when it was first conjured up as an idea, the sovereignty of nations did three things. First, it divided the world into individual countries, each defined by physical borders and populated by people who were 'citizens' of the state. Second, it seemed to agree that the merchants of every state could trade with each other, and even put their silver to work in each other's countries. Third, it declared that anyone within those sovereign states could practise whatever version of that barbarian Christian faith they liked (there seemed to be a lot of them). And then on top of it all (hardly surprisingly, given the poor foundations of these barbarian thinkers) someone called *A-da-mu Si-mi-te*, Adam Smith, from that very barbarian island of 'Great Britain' had magicked up a truly shocking idea of an 'invisible hand': a notion of self-interested greed, which he managed to convince everyone was far more natural than any *ren* benevolence. Arguing that this 'invisible hand' was such a positive force of nature that everyone should kowtow before it, *Si-mi-te* had gone on to insist that the idea did not just apply to individual 'citizens' but to the 'sovereign states' as well. Even the youngest of the Qing scholars could see that it was wrong – and any scholar worth his salt could easily point to its patent errors of morality. But the barbarians had raised a rather fat god, by the name of John Bull, who seemed to have told them not to bother with a discussion, and just repeat themselves, again and again – always louder, and, wherever possible, over the barrel of a gun.

Unfortunately for Confucius and the Manju Qing, John Bull's guns first arrived at just the point when the costs of the Qianlong emperor's conquests were taking their toll. Lin Zexu, the diligent official despatched to sort out the opium 'port affairs' in Guangzhou, had made the obvious Confucian arguments against the *Si-mi-te* idea. But the barbarians had simply fired their guns, and in 1842, it had seemed best to give them what they wanted (five southern coastal ports for trade and a rocky island with a *xiang gang*, fragrant harbour, that the foreigners called Hong Kong) and hope it would be enough. Of course it had not. Within a year, the British barbarians had come back, with an addendum insisting that no Briton visiting China should ever be subject to the vagaries of heavenly justice again. A year later, they had been followed by others from the West: French and American frigates demanding, and receiving, much of the same. Even that had not been enough. Sixteen years later, in 1856, pointing to the small print of the treaty text, the British had returned in the company not only of the French and the Americans, but the Russians as well. Their demands constantly rising, across the next two years, they had sailed their guns up and down the coast, forcing the Qing to split their forces even as they struggled to defeat the inner threat of the Taiping rebellion as well.

In 1858, and again in 1860, the Qing acceded to the outrageous demands: in all, another eleven treaty ports, leases on other lands, and all the lands of north of the Amur River, including Lake Baikal, to be ceded to Russia, as well as a bay on the Sea of Japan upon which the Russians raised a port city with the name of 'Vladivostok', Ruler of the East. As the Manju Qing lost some of their most important heartlands, Russia acquired a berth from which it could sweep through the Japanese archipelago and into the Pacific Ocean. To this blow was added shipping freedom up and down the Yangzi River, travel anywhere in China for any of their barbarian people, and more 'reparations', for the now-additional battles they claimed they had had to fight just to get the Qing to give in. On top of all this, the barbarians insisted on a right to post official representatives to the imperial capital of Beijing. (There had also been a punishing assault on the splendid *Yuanming Yuan*, the exotic garden of a Summer Palace that the Jesuits had designed for Kangxi).

With everyone's ancestors turning in their graves, the Xianfeng Emperor had died an early death. Under the heavenly title of Tongzhi (Restoring Order), his five-year-old son had been raised to the throne. This was naturally under a regency – one that began as a council of many and ended up as a partnership of two: the boy's mother, Yehenara Cixi (Xianfeng's unusually forthright concubine who henceforth styled herself the Dowager Empress), and a talented half-brother of the Xianfeng Emperor, Prince Gong.

While imperial minds had found it hard to concentrate on the barbarians during the years of the Taiping rebellion, in the twenty years that followed, the Manju Qing (Prince Gong in particular) worked hard to understand the new Western barbarian world. Not that anyone wanted to accept it, but since it seemed to have so many guns, there must be something to learn – and clearly it was not going to disappear. Somehow Confucian talents were going to have to find a way around the madness, but it was hard to know where to begin.

Even the question of names was a problem. This was hardly surprising given the fact that the Western barbarians had no idea of the intimate relationship required between the name of a thing and its purpose. Under the Manju, the heavenly lands were now called Da Qing Guo, the Great Qing Empire, although the people themselves were still referred to as the *laobaixing*, the old 100 names. But the uneducated foreigners kept talking about something called 'China', and referring to 'citizens', who seemed to be some kind of people who had a voice and an individual importance of their own: nothing that made much sense to anyone in the heavenly lands.

Behind the vexing problem of names was (as Confucius would have understood) the far more difficult question of how any of these new ideas could possibly work within the heavenly hierarchy of everything. Every emperor knew how to order a world in which barbarian rulers diligently studied the Confucian ways in the hope that they might become, if not part of the lands of the Son of Heaven (a privilege reserved for only the most diligent of the barbarians), at least acknowledged as tribute-paying states entitled to exchanges of treasures and, when required, protection. But what worked under a heaven where those not born to the Confucian wisdom were simply waiting to join it, seemed to have no place at all in a world of independent 'sovereign states'. Instead there were strange ideas with even stranger names: 'comity of nations', 'extraterritoriality', 'most favoured nation'. They all tripped off the tongues of the foreigners with the smoothness of silk. But whenever a foreigner was pressed to explain them, it seemed to come down to a wolf-like competition for raw wealth and power. True, the foreigners seemed to have a little bit of an idea about *ren* humanity and the putting of oneself in others' shoes – one of their favourite principles, on paper at least, was about the mutual and equal sovereignty of states. But they seemed to have no idea about the *dao* way with its changes – let alone *yi*, integrity, *li*, ritual, *zhi*, knowledge, or *de*, virtue. And they certainly didn't seem to understand the importance of unity under a single heavenly mind. Indeed, they seemed to have no understanding at all of the deep morality that underpinned everybody's cosmos – or any interest in it.

Shocked at the new ideas they were being asked to learn, the imperial officials muttered against the madness of the barbarian ideas. But Prince Gong, who had a wonderful grasp of the Confucian classics, suggested that one could hate the evil that a barbarian in his ignorance might do, but one should not hate the barbarian himself. Reminding everyone of Confucius' exhortation to 'be kind to men from afar', he suggested that, with a little patience, even these Western barbarians could surely be tranquillised over time. To which he added, that with enough self-cultivation and discipline, the *de* virtue of heaven would find its feet again. 'One must remember, however,' he counselled, 'not to call them barbarians – off in their own dark cloud at the edge of the world, and never educated in the Confucian classics, they cannot see themselves for what they are, and they do not like to be reminded that they are not at the centre of everything.'

In 1861, a new office was created to try to deal with the problem of the foreigners as the unnatural phenomenon they clearly were. Charged with exercising a single central responsibility for what would obviously be the highly specialist task of dealing with the foreign 'sovereign states', it was simply named the *zongli yamen*, general management office. A whole new corps of scholarly officials was recruited; all were instructed to apply their Confucian spirits to 'investigating the things' of the foreign world, and understanding as much about the barbarians as they possibly could. Obviously the four classical texts would not be enough: a translation bureau was created so that the *zongli yamen* scholars could read the same books as the foreigners. Every possible tome on international law was read, and then subjected to the same dissecting scrutiny the scholars applied to their own Confucian texts. Foreign newspapers were also discovered – and found to be particularly helpful. It seemed that in their inability to comprehend the towering importance of unity under a single heaven, the foreigners were perfectly happy to publish all sides of every argument. This was extremely useful in providing the scholars of the new *zongli yamen* not only with invaluable tuition, but rather effective ammunition as well. Indeed, after a while, the new foreign texts did not seem to be so difficult at all – it turned out that the literary mastery of the Confucian canon could be a powerful skill: once one had learnt the basic barbarian principles, how could three thousand years of bureaucratic experience not be useful? There was a little bit of a problem with the fact that the foreigners did not always keep their word – but once one understood that this was the case, adjustments could easily be made on one's own side as well.

Years passed, and as the *zongli yamen* grew in confidence, special academies were created to teach the geography and customs of the foreign world. In 1871, a group of young scholars was sent abroad to study the mathematics and the engineering that seemed to have made the foreigners so strong. In this, they had been advised by a man called Yong Wing who, in his youth, had found his way from Guangdong to America and Yale University, from which he had graduated in 1854. But nothing to do with barbarians was ever easy. Now settled in the treaty ports and protected by their 'treaty rights', the Westerners had created cities within cities, more like fiefdoms, particularly in the bigger ports of Tianjin and Shanghai. Barbarian boats were now trading up and down the Yangzi, stopping off wherever they wanted. And from the boats had descended legions of their own fanatical followers of the skies, who were wreaking havoc wherever they went. Men, and even women, called 'missionaries', now insisted on pushing themselves into the most extraordinary corners, all in the name of that man with the white beard who they said was everyone's 'king'. It was hardly surprising that a position in the *zongli yamen* was one of the most stressful posts any scholar could get. But there was an art to managing these foreign devils and, over time, a number of scholar-officials liked to think that it was one they were becoming increasingly adept at mastering.

As Beijing's bureaucrats tried to work out how to adapt the mechanics of the imperial bureaucracy to the demands of 'state sovereignty' – and, wherever possible, to adapt 'state sovereignty' to the more familiar mechanics of the imperial bureaucracy – the wider gentry and merchants began to explore new ventures of their own. Nowhere was this done with greater energy and imagination than in the province of Hunan.

Home of the Confucian general and genius Zeng Guofan, sitting to the south of Hankou and the neighbouring province of Hubei, host to a number of towns and cities of its own, Hunan's capital city was Changsha. The lands of Hunan had also once been home to one of the greatest of the Warring States – a splendid state by the name of Chu. Eventually falling to the unity of Qin, the people of Chu had, however, never lost their stubborn sense of having an independent mind. Not surprisingly, over the next two thousand years, few of Hunan's scholars had ever succeeded in entering the senior ranks of the imperial bureaucracy, which had made the rise of the Xiang army-raising Zeng Guofan to the heights of imperial office all the more remarkable; a veritable vindication of what it meant to be Hunanese. Successful in entering the scholarly courtyards of the empire, Zeng's subsequent triumph in raising the wildly successful Xiang Army had so touched his fellow Hunanese that they saw in his example the inspiration for a broader 'self-strengthening' of the Hunan world.

Triumphant, Zeng had certainly been. In 1852, when the Qing empire had needed an inland freshwater navy to launch against the Taiping Heavenly Army, Zeng Guofan had not hesitated to search out the necessary ship-building talent required. As far as he could tell, what was really needed was gunboats, but neither he nor anyone else in land-locked Hunan had ever seen one. Undeterred, he called upon the Confucian feelings of the merchant brothers in the south for advice. Three shipyards were suggested, and each was invited to send the best of their hands to help build the basic boats. Somehow working out how those foreigners had managed to attach brass guns to the sides of a boat without sinking everyone on board, Zeng had the new 'model navy' ready within two years.

In need of a bigger army, Zeng Guofan had then sent his most trusted aide back to his home province, neighbouring Anhui, and told him to repeat the recruiting successes of Hunan.

When, in 1862, the empire had needed an even bigger navy, Zeng hit upon the idea of asking the scholar Yong Wing, then just recently returned from Yale, to take himself back to America to buy whatever was needed to build an arsenal at the Shanghai mouth of the Yangzi River, in the region of Jiangnan. Unperturbed by the inconvenient fact of an American civil war, Yong Wing had gone back to America and, within a year, returned with everything required. And as far as technical skills for maintenance were concerned, Zeng noted that there were now, rather conveniently, a lot of foreigners sailing up and down the

4280 Kingston Upon Thames
Tel: 020 8549 7631 VAT: 238 5548 36

| Aud Irtc BKS | 3.00 |
| MCDONALDS VOUCHER | 0.00 |

| Total | £3.00 |
| Cash | 3.00 |

Thank you. Please retain your receipt
as proof of purchase.

14/06/19 13:01:38 04280 0005 684146 2659

0 4280 0 05 684146 140619

Yangzi. No doubt some of them would be available for hire to explain whatever his army and its friends could not work out for themselves.

By the time the Taiping rebellion ended in 1864 – with a battle in the heavenly capital of Nanjing that had destroyed thirty thousand lives – it was clear to everyone in Hunan, and, indeed, across the wider world of the Yangzi, that the answer to the problems of the day would not be found in the imperial city of Beijing. Hijacked by the Qing more than two hundred years before, the capital was in the grip of the barbarian Manju spirits; now burdened by foreign reparations, their empire was broke. The true answer lay in the self-strengthening powers of scholarly men like Zeng Guofan. Not just scholars in office, but a wider body of gentry, merchants and even retired generals whose *fu*, wealth, and *qiang*, power, had saved the day: 'self-strengtheners' all. With fields decimated by rebellion needing to be restored for everyone's food, it was also obvious that everyone's future would increasingly depend upon the city and its ability to gather together the new *fu qiang*, wealth and power of the gentry, merchants and retired generals on which Zeng Guofan had so successfully drawn. Hankou had been rebuilt by its ordering families of guilds; Hunan's Changsha, also attacked by the Taiping rebels, had likewise been rebuilt. Other cities had followed suit. All of them had been guided – and bound together – by the Confucian virtues. Where the empire and its emperors had failed, it was Confucius, at least the most up-to-date idea of what Confucius had meant, and the Confucian self-strengtheners who had really won the day.

In the decades that followed, self-strengtheners – from Hunan, from senior official posts in Beijing, and from across other provinces – set about building the basic blocks of a new Confucian world. Following Zeng Guofan's example of the Jiangnan arsenal in Shanghai, arms and defence came first. Then came the taming of nature and the resurrection of harvests, with the building of factories to produce the necessary articles of life for the *laobaixing*, people at large. Cotton and bamboo were particularly favoured commodities – with the industrial production process starting with the old 'putting out' system, which the merchants had introduced into the village households of the desperate fields. To these foundations were then added schools, academies, and societies, through which the new, mostly technical, knowledge could be spread.

Wherever required, the local fund-raising bureaus that Zeng had established for his army were replicated – now dedicated to the task of raising funds for whatever local construction might be needed. And whether from city pavilions or rural estates, the gentry organised battalions of local labour to take on a more formal responsibility for the rivers, dams, ditches and everything else that successful harvests required.

As the fund-raising bureaus were replicated and the rural militias were raised, the gentry wrapped themselves up in the fabric of the greatest common experience and network they had: the imperial examinations. As brutally difficult as ever, few candidates passed without several attempts; indeed many sat and resat them several times without ever passing. Travelling to Beijing for the highest of the tests, over the final weeks of anxious preparation, friends were made from across the country, with many forging bonds that would endure through the thick and thin of their lives. With such a fabric of relationships in place, it was not only funds and rural battalions that could be raised by the gentry but any good idea for a family sort of a society, for any kind of a task: patrolling streets against brigands, flattening roads, raising lamps to light streets, not to mention a host of other new scientific possibilities introduced by the foreigners. Even the foreigners' novel idea of a newspaper was adopted. Initially launched out of the foreign settlement within the Shanghai treaty port, these remarkable printed pages charged themselves with picking up any and all good ideas, then distributing them across the country for everyone to read.

Up and down the land, the new 'Confucian army' set itself to transforming the chaos left by the Taiping rebels into a new order. The strongest roots of the new order were in the capital cities of the provinces, where indeed the strongest roots of the Chinese world had been since the time of the ancient Zhou. The branches of the new order were scattered across the country: wherever there were gentry, merchants and retired generals to be found. Its communications ran across the world of examination candidates, whether successful or failed, now strengthened by a growing printed press. The founders and leaders of it all were men whose scholarly talents had made them powerful officials, and whose merchant money had made them not just traders on an industrial scale but owners of vast wealth. For the first time in two and a half thousand years of being at the bottom of the ancient hierarchy of human productivity, the merchants had found a pride of place in the new Confucian world. Heartened by a rising *fu qiang* wealth and power, the Confucian army was a new model for an old empire, which simply grew and grew.

———

While the new Confucians were going from self-strengthening strength to strength, however, the seas of the Manju Qing's new world were anything but calm. In fact, from 1870 onwards, the waters had become distinctly choppy. The *zongli yamen* might have been congratulating itself on a number of lessons well learnt, and the self-strengthening 'new Confucians' might have been rebuilding Da Qing China from citadels in cities and the countryside alike, but, near and far, the barbarians seemed to be intent on raising havoc with a host of selfish and unreasonable ideas.

The biggest trouble-makers were always going to be the Western foreigners who had arrived by sea – particularly those who had decided to push their 'God' into every possible corner of Confucian life. By 1870, they had set up missions in all sorts of directions, with some of them deciding to 'rescue' Chinese children into orphanages. Anyone could have told them that the local populations would struggle to understand where the children were going. And so it was that, before long, someone started rumours that the missionaries were in fact merchants – trading in Chinese children. Naturally, riots erupted.

In June 1870, a particularly messy misunderstanding resulted in the death of a Chinese official in Tianjin from the barrel of the French consul's gun. This was swiftly followed by the murder of the French consul, and then by a riot that nearly burnt the whole of Tianjin to the ground. As always in such situations, the foreigners loaded their gunboats, and the now-ageing Zeng Guofan was pulled out of retirement. But this time, even Zeng could not really help. Buoyed by their successes up and down the coasts, the foreigners insisted on something ludicrous to 'repair their losses': the foreign missionaries who had caused all of the trouble in the first place were not only to be allowed to go wherever they wanted and do whatever they wanted, but wherever they were, and whatever they were doing, the Great Da Qing Empire was to be held responsible for the safety of their lives.

Everybody – at least everybody Chinese – knew that such a state of affairs would only bring down more trouble on everybody's heads. But, as was usually the case, the foreigners simply shouted ever louder until they got their way.

As if all of that was not enough, the various conquests made by Kangxi and Qianlong began to collapse. In 1871, an indigenous tribe on the once-renegade island of Taiwan killed fifty-four shipwrecked Japanese sailors. Arguing that the Qing had no idea what was going on in that or any of the other southern islands that sat between their two countries, the Japanese proceeded to occupy the nearby thread of the Ryuku islands. With everything else that was going on with the sea-barbarians from the West, no one in the imperial bureaucracy had the heart for a fight. Then in the same year, up in the north-west, a stubborn Muslim, who had pronounced himself the King of Kashgaria – even exploring treaties with the Russians and the British – decided to launch an anti-Qing rebellion in the bare lands of the Ili Valley, part of present-day Xinjiang. Embarked on building an empire of their own, the Russians used the rebellion as an excuse to occupy the lands themselves. Only the spending of an imperial fortune managed to save the wider north-west, and even then the Qing ended up losing the Ili Valley to the Russian tsars.

The only bright light on the horizon was down in the Yunnan south-west, where, after decades of disaster, things had seen a rare but marked improvement. There had been the final end to a twenty-year rebellion of Muslims, who somehow felt they had not been treated as well as everyone else in the heavenly lands. It had taken a while, but eventually their 'southern sultanate' was finally brought back under heaven's powers, and its so-called leader, Sulayman ibn Abd ar-Rah-man (better known by the easier-to-pronounce Chinese name of Du Wenxiu) had fallen. And then there had been the hopefully final paci-fication of a stubborn misfit tribe in Yunnan's neighbouring province of Guizhou, who seemed to think that the land they lived on was their own. Some patches of blue in an otherwise distinctly cloudy sky.

But these small gains notwithstanding, as far as the Manju Qing were concerned, the decade just got worse and worse. In 1876, a British official surveying the border with neighbouring British-Indian Burma managed to get himself killed by one or other of the Yunnan tribes (there were so many that no one quite knew which). That had ended up with a letter of apology to Queen Victoria (something the *zongli yamen* was becoming rather good at), and another four treaty ports. Then, in 1882, a group of Chinese bandits, who had settled on the border with the tribute-state of Vietnam, got themselves into a fight with French explorers looking for trade. France lashed out at Vietnam and Vietnam naturally called upon its protectors, the Qing, for help. Sensing that things could easily get dangerously out of control, the *zongli yamen* did its best to negotiate for a quick peace. But in the end the Qing found themselves in a one-day war with France. In fact, it didn't even last a day: in just a single hour on 23 August 1884, the French navy destroyed the Nanyang, southern fleet. The peace that finally followed put Vietnam under French dominion – and reduced to an illusion the idea that the Qing empire could protect its tribute states.

It was only a matter of time before the other wolves circled. Russia continued to snatch at the remaining Manju homelands in the northeast, looking for any excuse to start a war. Japan, watching from its archipelago of easterly islands, began to sense that the weakness of the Qing might not only lose the Da Qing empire to the Western barbarians but the rest of Asia, including Japan. Having been 'encouraged' to strengthen themselves by an American ultimatum in the 1850s – and with the worrying example of the Qing's battles with Western powers so close to its shores – the old Tokugawa shogunate had opened to the outside world and built its own new 'sovereign state', forged with samurai steel. An enlightened 'Meiji' rule had followed, complete with the first constitution and parliament outside the West as well as an enthusiastic embrace of industry, which took everyone by surprise. Within the space of twenty years, the scattering of islands once seen by the Qin emperor as the misty Penglai home of the immortals had become a rising power.

With a Japanese empire rising, it had not been long before the Korean peninsula found its way into everyone's sights. Another state that had long paid tribute to the heavenly lands, when a rebellion erupted there in 1884, both the Manju Qing and Meiji Japan raced to the Korean court. In that encounter the Beiyang army came out on the winning side. But within ten years, the Qing found themselves at war with Japan over the terms of a broken treaty. It was at this point that the redoubtable Admiral Ding had found himself on the Yellow Sea battling the navy of the Greater Japanese Empire – and eventually losing the fleet. On 25 January 1895, two weeks before the final attack, Admiral Ito Sukeyuki, commander of the Japanese forces, had written a letter to Admiral Ding – once a friend with whom he had discussed the common question of how to adapt to the new Western barbarian world. Urging him to surrender, and offering him refuge in Japan until the Qing empire eventually, and inevitably, fell, Admiral Sukeyuki wrote: 'It is not the fault of one man that has brought the Qing dynasty to this position. The blame rests with the errors of the Government that has long administered her affairs.' Admiral Ding chose a loyal opium death. But by 1895 Admiral Ito was not the only mind in the East who thought there was something badly wrong with the Qing.

By the 1890s, back in Zeng Guofan's province of Hunan (the ancient state of Chu, and from where, more recently, the new Confucian army, with its ideas of self-strengthening, had emerged), younger minds had been watching everything. Like most others in the heavenly lands, they concluded that the Qing had had their time. But looking at the situation from the perspective of Hunan, the young Hunanese had a more distinctive point of view. After thirty years of self-strengthening, *fuqiang*, wealth and power, had certainly defeated the Taiping rebels and rebuilt much of the country. But had anything really changed? In Beijing, another infant emperor had come to the throne in 1875, adopted by the Dowager Empress and titled Guangxu (Glorious Succession). Imperial rule, for all of the good it was doing anyone, seemed to have been reduced to a strange Manju family affair. Of course, one couldn't expect much from conquerors who had run out of steam. But were the Chinese self-strengtheners any different? *Fuqiang* was all very well for a while, but the heavenly lands had seen it all before. Sooner or later, wealth and power would always fix itself at the top, and nothing but ignorance, poverty and blind dependence would settle again across the always much bigger bottom. While the latest Confucian fabric of order might bring a sparkle of pride to the eyes of the wealthy, underneath, the vast spreading foundations were composed of nothing more than the creaking shoulders of men who, across the imperial ages, had been taught to serve and never question.

In the Changsha capital of Hunan, highly educated young minds began to stretch their thoughts back to the ancient independence of the state of Chu. Thinking on the past, they saw in their mind's eye a happier world governed by men who had been free to talk to heaven whenever they wanted, and allowed to pursue their own destiny whatever it might be. They also recalled how the Chu state had first been eaten away by conspiracies of Qin whispers, and then destroyed by the First Qin Emperor, vanishing as if it had been a dream. But had it really disappeared?

As Hunanese hearts dreamt of a long-lost past, someone pointed to a secret classic that been written during the tumultuous times of the Ming. Presenting a rather different perspective from that of the single heavenly mind, it was not a text that had ever made it into the imperial curriculum; in fact, it had been hidden in fear. But its words had been rediscovered and quietly published in 1829 under a tempting title: *The Treasures of Chu*. And what a treasure it was: a compendium of secret writings from the oldest Chu minds, prepared by a brave Hunanese scholar in the Ming dynasty, who had patched surviving fragments together and pulled them into a single secret text. Hidden for so long, it was these newly rediscovered words that had led Zeng Guofan's Hunanese friends to encourage him to take up the idea of raising his Xiang Army in Hunan.

The Treasures of Chu might have inspired their fathers to raise a new Confucian army to save the empire. But as far as younger minds in 1890s Hunan were concerned, those fathers had completely missed the point. The magic of Chu had nothing to do with restoring a colonising empire, or even Confucius – and everything to do with the idea of an independent state led by independent minds.

If one wanted to understand the wonder of the state of Chu, the young Hunanese argued, one had simply to look at the story of the heroic poet-prince, Qu Yuan. Born in 340 BCE, he became a selfless and patriotic minister who, quick to perceive the rising threat of the iron state of Qin, urged his king to confront the rising power a hundred years before the final devastating battle. But the king's heart had been turned by those in Chu whose palms were already being crossed with soft Qin gold. Qu Yuan had been sent into a heart-breaking exile. And from beyond the borders of his much-loved home, he had watched the early battles of Qin against Chu with the anguish of a man whose warning cries had been cut to silence. Despairing at the treachery and corruption, when the Chu capital fell to Qin Qu Yuan cast himself into the Miluo River, hoping to find his way to another world where human beings could still talk to heaven. Before he departed, however, he crafted an epic description of his own battles with the greed and betrayals of this world and of his subsequent journey to heaven in search of something better. Entitled *Li Sao – Encountering Sorrow* – it was a poem that had been memorised by scholars across the ages, giving two millennia of despairing hearts the hope that another world might be possible.

To the younger scholarly minds of Hunan, the greatest treasure of Chu was Qu Yuan himself. A poet prince who had given his home and all he loved to protect the greatness of Chu, he stood for the idea that every scholar had a duty to his inner heart and the greater good of being human. Betrayed by lesser men, he had left his Hunanese descendants with a lesson: heaven was nothing to do with an empire that flattened everything in its advance, and nothing at all to do with a 'unity' that destroyed the human qualities of the people. Quite the contrary: heaven was the power of an individual mind to talk directly to a ruler whenever one wanted, and to separate truth from lies. At the height of its power, the state of Chu had been a land where good ideas had been shared by men who could think for themselves – even the ideas of Laozi and Confucius had been read – and where bad ideas had been seen for what they were. Looking at the state of the present, the young minds decided that nearly two thousand years after Qin's treachery, it was time for Qu Yuan's Hunanese descendants to stand up for the truth.

What did the young Hunanese think was the truth? Taking the ancient belief in the importance of *ren*, empathy, as a human quality, in 1896 a young intellectual by the name of Tan Sitong began to set out the answer in a book called *Ren, On Humanity*. Resisting all pressure to prepare for the stifling imperial exams, Tan Sitong read widely, thought deeply and wrote his mind with little care for the consequences. On the Manju Qing's troubles with the foreign world, he observed that the only really bad thing the foreigners had brought was opium – and the Qing should have been strong enough to deal with that themselves. And as far as the last thirty years of the *zongli yamen* were concerned, the 'general management office' seemed to have achieved a triumph of literary twists, now presented as the high art of 'diplomatic discourse', without solving anything at all. On the self-strengtheners, Tan Sitong's thoughts were even sharper: the only power worth having was the power of the people – and they had lost that long ago when the Yellow Emperor had become the Son of Heaven, when Zhuanxu had cut communications between heaven and earth for everyone except himself and his appointed governors, and when the First Qin Emperor had forced the idea of a single top-down mind on everyone, including the people of Chu. Since then, it had been nothing but a line of power-hungry emperors whose greatest achievement had been the deadening of everyone's minds.

In Tan Sitong's opinion, while the Taiping rebel leader Hong Xiuquan had been madly muttering about Jesus Christ being his brother, his millions of followers had been desperate people simply looking for change. And although Zeng Guofan had indeed been a remarkable man, he had stuck his colours to the wrong mast: shoring up the Qing when what was really needed was for the Manju to go home, and for the very idea of an empire to end. Misguidedly attaching themselves to Hong Xiuquan, the Taiping rebels had not, in their hearts, been wrong. The problem was that, after millennia of not thinking for themselves, the people had lost the ability to work out how to create and run a new world of their own. Having, long before, lost the ability to speak for themselves, the only thing left to them had been the wild rebellions in which the peasants had been regularly erupting over the previous two thousand years. For anyone with any surviving intellectual power whatsoever, the rebellions were an irrefutable confirmation that the very idea of a *tianxia*, all-under-heaven, order was a problem: without the power to talk to anyone above them, death and destruction had been the people's only possible voice. Self-strengthening was nothing but a deluding and dangerous distraction – with the only real 'strengthening' being that of the snare in which the people had been held for so long. The *fuqiang*, wealth and power, at the top was simply masking a *mangliu*, blindly floating misery, across the vast bottom: all in the pursuit of a great state that would eventually destroy not only man, but nature too.

For Tan Sitong, the time had come for China's youth to dig deep into the past and come up with something new: to go back to the most ancient of the golden ages, when human beings had minds of their own, and think. Awoken by the thinking experience, they could then forge a new future in which, having rediscovered the power of independent human thought, they could share that power with a state they felt they could call their own. The essence of it all was the ancient shamanic idea of *ren* humanity, or empathy, that Confucius had used in his principles: put yourself in other people's shoes and in so doing understand that the future is a fabric composed of *everybody*'s dreams – not just a commanding plan imposed from the top. In fact, *ren* was neither more nor less than the art of 'being human'. And if, as seemed quite likely, all of this was too difficult to be achieved across the vast spread of the Da Qing empire, Tan suggested that the province of Hunan should just return to being an independent state of its own, from which position of independence it would then be able to inspire a wider revival of the old Chu way. And while it might take a revolution to secure Hunan's independence, once secured, other provinces would be able to follow. Newspapers might be able to light torches to touch thousands of minds, but the time for idle words alone was over. The world had changed and those who knew the truth about the past now had a duty to act. If there was to be a state, it should be able to think for itself. For a state to be able to think for itself, it needed a people who could think for themselves as well. And in thinking for themselves, the people would need to ask themselves the question of what it means to be human.

The self-strengtheners could not have been more shocked. After everything that the last fifty years had thrown at the Qing lands, finally *fuqiang*, wealth and power, were firmly in their grasp. Yes, of course, if one went back to the time of the Duke of Zhou and the Confucian classics, some of the greatest scholars had recognised that the people should be esteemed by their ruler – but no one, in any of those texts, had ever suggested that the people should 'esteem themselves'. Counting off all the challenges that the Da Qing empire faced (a formidable list), one of the leading self-strengtheners dismissed Tan's ideas as the 'delight of foolish people', based, he argued, on a fundamental misunderstanding of the heavenly fact that, like any phenomenon of nature, the only purpose of the people was to explain their feelings so that the ruler could set the right path. Any idea that there should be more than one ruler, or more than one opinion, was nothing less than treachery; and anyone who thought in such a way was clearly not Chinese.

Tan Sitong was not the only one thinking about a state populated by a people with independent minds. Nor was Hunan alone in thinking that it had once all been very different, and could yet be different again. Down in Guangdong province there were other scholars, who, while seeing the need for change, had not yet given up on the imperial exams, and had also not yet given up on the possibility of a more peaceful evolution.

One was a thirty-seven-year-old man renowned for his mastery of the classics, even though his independent ideas had delivered a string of failures in the imperial exams; his name was Kang Youwei. Turning his vast classical expertise to a searing reconsideration of the Confucian texts, Kang had produced scholarly proof that the great literary edifice on which the heavenly empire had been built, was based on nothing but deceptions and lies. It had, indeed, all gone wrong when Zhuanxu cut communications between heaven and the people of the earth. But it was under the great deception of the Han dynasty that the rot had really set in. Bent on advancing the martial Wu Emperor's desire for a single heaven across the four directions, Han scholars had used the flames of the First Qin Emperor's earlier book burning as an excuse to rewrite the past. With this, the imperial scholars had excised an older idea of heaven as a reflection of the people – a heaven that hears and sees as the people hear and see – and replaced it with the idea, based on books of their own which claimed to be an authoritative Confucian canon, that heaven was whatever the Son of Heaven said it was. The imperial interpretation of 'what Confucius meant' had become a tyranny over everybody's minds. Pale imitations of past wisdom had been passed off as 'rediscovered' lost works, even as they had buried older debates about what it meant to be a state, what it meant to be a people, and what it meant to be human. Their own scholarly heads filled with the blind, and blinding, arrogance of the self-appointed wise, they had piled the people onto a raft of nonsense that had been compounded by the state-building ambition and vanity of every successive dynasty over the past two thousand years. The early questions about a state and its people had not been solved – they had simply been buried under two millennia of imperial, and imperious, rule. And as for the even earlier question of what it meant to be a human being, that had simply been swept under the carpet of the state.

With the courage and conviction of a mind that questioned everything, Kang Youwei then advanced the greatest heresy to have been heard for two millennia or more: there was no duty to a mythical Son of Heaven, only the duty of a ruler to the people who were heaven's ears and eyes. And, had it not been for the Han dynasty, the people, being essentially sensible, would have been perfectly capable of working out an order of their own. All they had needed was the freedom to take responsibility for themselves and for each other. With such a freedom, there would have been no need for a Qing empire at all, let alone the dynasties of the past, just a world in which local communities governed themselves in one *Da Tong*, Great Unity. Not the self-interested unity pursued by ambitious emperors keen to grab as much earth and sky as they could, but a truly great unity of all the people to rule themselves – one that would eventually include everyone across the wider earth as well.

As Kang Youwei inked letters of his ideas for others to read, he acknowledged that the achievement of a *Da Tong* Great Unity might take a while and that it would only be achievable by progressing through stages. But in the end, he argued, a truly 'harmonious society' would appear. On the journey to this future utopia, the first and most important step was to get the people themselves to stop behaving like sheep. Somehow, tired hearts had to be transformed from the old fatalism – the result of millennia of being silenced – into a belief that destiny was something the people could build for themselves. Such a future, built by such a people, could not help but be glorious.

As to how to get from here to there, Kang Youwei was convinced that it should be achieved as peacefully as possible. Given where they were, Kang reasoned, the safest course would be to persuade the young Guangxu emperor that the time had come for the people to be released from the Confucian bonds of 'the family' (family as imperial state as well as family as household), and for self-cultivated individuals – whichever positions they occupied in either of the state or household hierarchies – to be able, respectfully, to speak their minds. But heaven was high and the emperor was far away: how could a simple imperial examination candidate catch the emperor's ear? Kang decided to start with a book of his own. He called it *Da Tong Shu – The Book of Great Unity*.

One of the oldest and most scholarly of the imperial examination candidates, Kang Youwei held the respect of many of his peers and juniors. Of his respectful juniors, one was a younger neighbor and fellow scholar by the name of Liang Qichao. Studying for the imperial exams, but struggling, Kang Youwei became his tutor, and then a very close friend. While Kang worked on his *Book of Great Unity*, however, Liang thought less about the grand scheme of things and more about how to take the next practical steps. It seemed to him that the most immediate problem was that, after thousands of years of believing in a Son of Heaven, no one in Qing China had any idea about what a state of people – a 'nation' as the foreigners seemed to call it – really was. Certainly, since the Western barbarians' arrival had so forcefully demonstrated that the Qing lands were not the centrifugal middle of a flat world but, rather, a single point on a round globe, a lot of ink had been spilt in trying to understand what it meant to be a sovereign state. It had not taken the *zongli yamen* long to understand that it was something more than the ruling dynasty of the time, and that it also required a clear idea of territory. Yet it seemed to be a lot harder for them to get their heads around the idea that for a territory to be a nation it also had to have a people.

The Manju idea of *Da Qing Guo*, the state of the Great Qing Empire, was little more than an insulting description of the fact that the Manju had conquered China. Certainly, it could not be seen in any meaningful way as a description of the people who lived there. The foreign idea of 'China' was not much better – just the result of an ancient tangled twisting of the name of the upstart Qin state that had not only unified the Warring States but had also 'unified' the people into nothing more than the arms of a central imperial power. But the *tianxia*, all-under-heaven, idea had now been proven by Kang Youwei to be a tyrannical myth that had swept away thousands of years of human minds. And the idea that the rest of the world should eventually be embraced within a perpetual expansion of an all-under-heaven dream that had been shown to be a lie, could surely now be seen to be ludicrous. If the foreigners had done nothing else good for China, at least they had surely made that madness a little more unlikely.

Even the new word for 'country' – *guojia*, state family – which the *zongli yamen* had cobbled together like so many translations of foreign things, was a complete misunderstanding of what was required to be a nation. A *guo*, state, was nothing more or less than the old city-states from the time of the Zhou; and a *jia*, family, was simply the old idea of everyone being in their hierarchically-ordered place, with the emperor at the top, fathers next, sons in order of birth below, and women at everybody's beck and call. Where was there any mention of the people at large – the peasants – who, although highly esteemed by the Confucian hierarchy of occupations, never seemed to count?

For Liang Qichao, the solution was obvious, but it was clearly going to take a lot of hard work. The people were going to have to change the way that they saw themselves. Where to start? Tempting though it might be to think that the scholarly gentry might lead the way, judging by the last few thousand years, being literate – even magnificently literate – did not necessarily give one a sense of being human. In fact, it often seemed to do quite the opposite: a point that was obvious to anyone whose mind hadn't been twisted by an imperially Confucian education. Meanwhile, Liang noted, after thousands of years of being scattered like sheep, the now 450 million peasant people had become a sea of ignorance and superstition. And after an eternity of imperial divide and rule, the only thread between the scholars and the people was the Confucian idea that everyone's order depended on the peasants at the bottom doing whatever they were told. If the men and women now held captive under the Manju Qing were going to become a nation, and if the nation was going to have a people, everyone, scholars and peasants alike, was going to have to think again. The scholars would need to understand that they were but one part of a greater unity. And the peasants would need to understand that they were not just a hapless collection of arms and legs but had minds and a reason of their own. Obviously this was not going to be easy for anyone, and after so many millennia of imperial deception, there would be very few independent minds available to help. But if the so-called heavenly lands were going to move beyond the pattern of repeated rebellion, there was no other way. Looking at the state of the empire's affairs, there didn't seem to be a moment to lose.

Considering the past and the present, Liang Qichao concluded that the obvious first step would be to create small communities of people, with each community learning to apply their minds to local questions. Being local, and using all the faculties of being human, it was reasonable to suppose that they would care enough about the results that everyone, not just the gentry, would voluntarily roll up their sleeves and put their hearts and souls into the tasks at hand. Not at all to be confused with Zeng's self-strengtheners (who had simply become little emperors in disguise), this would be a true 'people', who would include both the top and the bottom, working together side by side. Eventually, argued Liang Qichao, it was obvious that the empire would have to become a republic, and that a constitution would be required to ensure that no ruler could ever cut off communications with heaven again. In the meantime, Liang Qichao decided, it was time to take up the idea of a society of people who were committed to changing minds.

Where better to start than by splashing it across a printed press?

In 1897, Liang Qichao was invited to put his thoughts to the test. A group of young Hunanese had persuaded the reforming governor of Hunan to open a new kind of school in the provincial capital of Changsha. The group included Tan Sitong, the author of *On Humanity* – who had by now gone on to found Hunan's first newspaper. Within the classrooms of the new school, Chinese and Western studies were to be mixed, and a curriculum was to be taught that had nothing to do with the classical Confucian texts of the imperial exams and everything to do with the practical tasks of building a nation. Offered the position of lecturer-in-chief, Liang Qichao leapt at the chance and soon found himself swimming in the company of fellow minds. Conversations between Liang and Tan Sitong went on long into the night. Indeed, with so much to talk about, the pair rarely remembered to eat; and if one of them ever travelled, the letters they sent each other were enough to fill more than whatever suitcases they had taken along for the trip.

There was, indeed, a lot to talk about. As 1897 turned to 1898, things in Qing China could hardly have been worse. After the Beiyang fleet had been lost in the disastrous sea battle of early 1895, the Japanese victors had extracted a treaty of Shimonosekei, which, apart from the usual punishing reparations, put neighbouring Korea under the 'protective' wing of Japan, and rolled the island of Taiwan into the Japanese state. The Japanese were also allowed to establish industrial factories wherever they wanted on the mainland of the Qing. Given that all of the foreign powers had acquired a 'most favoured nation' right to enjoy any additional privileges that any one of them might somehow acquire, this meant that all of the foreigners could do the same. Looking at the new map of Qing China (seemingly now a blank page as far as the rest of the world was concerned), the other foreigners had then decided that they needed a little more territory if things were going to remain in any kind of a balance. Russia demanded ports on the Yellow Sea coast of Liaodong. Britain decided that, in that case, it would need Weihaiwei, in the province of Shandong, on the opposite side of the Yellow Sea. Then, of course, Germany (who had turned up in 1861 to insist on the same privileges as everyone else), needed something on the Shandong coast as well: it chose Jiaozhou Bay, present-day Qingdao. And then, to the shock of almost everyone in China, and to the extreme consternation of Japan, Russian engineers, protected by a Russian army, began to lay a Trans-Siberian Railway right up to the Pacific and its inner Sea of Japan, ending at Russia's Siberian city of Vladivostok, Ruler of the East, directly facing Japan's northern island of Hokkaido.

Around the rest of the world, newspapers carried cartoons of a gigantic China feast where the 'Great Powers' gorged at the respective corners of the Qing state, and the remaining Chinese land became smaller by the day. Meanwhile, at home, newspapers began to carry stories about an idea that had come out of Britain and had apparently swept across the rest of the Western world. The theory of a man named Charles Darwin, it described an evolutionary earth within which the fittest species were 'naturally selected' to survive. To this, a man called Herbert Spencer had added the observation that it was not just species of plants and animals who were engaged in the process of 'natural selection' but the species of man as well. Indeed, according to Spencer, the world of man was engaged in a great battle for the 'survival of the fittest'. Putting the two ideas together, the foreign powers seemed to have concluded that only those who possessed the necessary military and human strength to win would survive. Many thought that it all sounded remarkably like the battles of the Warring States in the fading centuries of the ancient Zhou dynasty. And it certainly explained why the foreigners were competing so hard with each other to eat China up. Some wondered whether the foreigners knew that what had followed the Warring States was the iron state of Qin.

Reading the articles, however, and pondering over the new ideas, many began to think that, while questions about nations and citizens were obviously important, a far more urgent question was now looming: if the foreigners kept battling over Chinese soil, how much longer could Qing China survive? And if there were not a Qing or a China, what would happen to the people who lived on these lands?

Gripped by the sense that time was running out not just for what the rest of the world called 'China', but for the Chinese people as well, Liang Qichao, Tan Sitong, Kang Youwei and other like-minded friends travelled to Beijing in January 1898. Another round of imperial examinations was due to be held, and with many Chinese now fearing the risk of extinction, even the more imperially minded scholarly officials were beginning to appreciate the urgency of the situation. One, a high-ranking official and friend of Kang Youwei, promised to ensure that even though the empire only received memorials penned by senior officials, any suggestions that Kang and his colleagues might make would find their way to the personal attention of the Guangxu Emperor.

The friends prepared a series of memorials, modelled on the highly successful reforms of Meiji Japan, and each with a recommending strike of thunder designed to bring Qing China back from the brink. The first of the recommendations was that the Guangxu Emperor should throw off the dead hand of the Manju court, including the power of his imperially adoptive mother, the Dowager Empress, and make it clear that he was committed to reform. The second was that a new 'office of ideas' should be set up at the gate to the imperial city, with the purpose of discovering new talent and ideas – and making sure those ideas got past the bulwarks of bureaucracy to the emperor. The third was that a new 'bureau of government reorganisation' should be established to create a blueprint for a host of institutional changes, which, complete with a 'government of all the talents', would be committed to the eventual achievement of a National Assembly, with rule through the law of a constitution that would sit above the ruler, rather than by the unbridled power of a single imperial mind.

Reading the memorials, the Guangxu Emperor decided to take advantage of a temporary absence of the Dowager Empress – on holiday at a new Summer Palace built in the outskirts of Beijing – and act. In June 1898, an imperial edict announced that Qing China would henceforth pursue a policy of root and branch reform. In the following days, Kang Youwei was summoned to the Forbidden City to meet and talk with the emperor; in the following weeks, a cascade of reforming edicts was announced. A number of them were accompanied by appointments that leap-frogged Kang, Liang Qichao and other scholarly youths into senior positions of power. Rafts of imperial rot were addressed. The imperial examinations were to be rescued from the cloying classics by a new attention to 'substantial studies': subjects such as current affairs, which might help in the governing of a country. New schools, and new curricula for all schools, were to be created, all teaching the mathematics and science on which the foreign barbarians had built their sovereign states. Wasteful and obstructive ministries were to be abolished, with self-interested self-strengtheners to be removed from their helms. All ministries were to submit any proposals to the rigour of a national budget. Last, but by no means least, the Beiyang navy was to be replaced with a new fleet, this time supplied with proper ordnance and equipped with men who were trained in how to use it. The bigger ideas of a National Assembly and a constitution were not immediately accepted but, looking at all of the other edicts, few doubted that they would eventually find their time.

For those who liked to peer into the shadows, it was obvious that the emperor had entered uncharted and dangerous waters. But over the summer of 1898, hope rose like a spring. Quite apart from the youthful ideas that began to populate the dusty Qing bureaucracy, from across the land paper messages flooded into the new 'office of ideas'. Some of the messages were exquisitely brushed by the most educated of hands. Others, inked in big, clumsy characters, had obviously been painted by the working fists of farmers and fishermen. Hands or fists, all had been written from the heart.

For a hundred magical days, Beijing and the towns and fields of the great Qing empire sparkled like the stars. And then, on 19 September 1898, the Dowager Empress appeared in the Forbidden City cloaked in a cloud of rage. Alerted by a senior group of self-strengtheners, who saw their new Confucian world about to be reformed away, she had broken off her holiday and raced the imperial carriages back to the Pole Star of the empire.

The imperial city held its breath, waiting for the storm to break. Within two days, another edict appeared in the name of the Guangxu Emperor: no sparkling dream but a kowtow confession that, although nominally the Son of Heaven, he was clearly not fit to rule. The edict concluded with the announcement that, after repeated supplications, the Dowager Empress had graciously agreed to resume the regency of his youth. The edict issued, the Guangxu Emperor was then confined to the Forbidden City, from which he would never again be permitted to have a conversation with an outside mind. The heady edicts of the hundred-day summer were cancelled; and imperial orders were issued for the arrest and execution of the memorialists, as well as any other scholars who, having been in Beijing for the imperial examinations, might have been party to the plot.

Most of the memorialists and scholars, including Kang Youwei and Liang Qichao, managed to escape, fleeing to Japan where the Meiji reforms had created a number of schools and colleges ready and willing to share their new ideas with brave new Chinese minds.

Most, but not all. Tan Sitong had stayed behind, determined to stand his independent ground. On 24 September, he was arrested. Three days later, his mind was swept from its body with the swift stroke of an imperial sword.

In exile, the memorialists travelled along similar but different paths. Kang Youwei scoured the seas, looking for men who might be able to help him rescue the emperor from his palace prison and, in so doing, throw China and its people a lifeline. In 1900, he attempted to raise rebellions in the city of Hankou and the province of Anhui. But lines of communication got tangled up with distance, and yet another group of martyrs fell to the imperial sword. The losses were painful but Kang did not give up.

Meanwhile, Liang Qichao, now in the more open schools of Japan, set about exploring what the rest of the world had to say about how to be a citizen. Many of the other memorialists followed him, increasingly joined by a rising tide of youth looking for ideas that might save the independence of their country and their own minds. In 1902, Liang launched a new journal with the title: *Xin Min, New Citizen*. Full of articles on every imaginable independent idea, it was regularly posted back to China for those at home to read. Safe in exile, Liang wrote prodigiously and questioned even more: what was it that made a nation, and how did a people fit in?

In 1903, keen to understand the land of freedom in which President Lincoln had made the now-famous 1863 Gettysburg Address, Liang

Qichao travelled to America. 'Government of the people, by the people, for the people': a fistful of words that had not only changed America but had also deeply touched Chinese hearts who, across the separating Pacific Ocean, had heard it as a whisper. But once in America, and observing powerful men engaged in what seemed to be their own form of self-strengthening, Liang Qichao had been unconvinced. America's freedom from an imperial ruler seemed to have resulted in rule by its own self-strengthened rich. And looking at the streets of New York, it seemed to him that freedom had come at such a cost to equality that it did not appear to be at all the kind of freedom that the Chinese people needed.

While Liang Qichao retained his respect for the American ideal, he noted carefully that if even America, with all of its great regard for the people, could not manage to create both freedom *and* equality, then China had better beware.

———

Back in Qing China, as the shock of the palace coup of 1898 gave way to an anxious 1899, it was as clear as ever that it was not only a library of scholars who would have to understand the need for change if the Chinese lands and the Chinese people were to survive. Black and white newspapers, launched from the extraterritorial safety of Shanghai but read up and down the country, were now spreading the fears of thousands, for everyone to read.

The newspapers were also carrying reports of a new army of patriotic rebels, who had decided that enough was enough. Rising in a rage from the north-east (now home to British Weihaiwei and German Qingdao, not to mention a host of missionaries off on frolics of their own), the rebels declared that it was time the foreigners left – and if the Manju Qing could not get rid of them, they would do it themselves with their 'boxing' fists. To those who looked carefully, the usual sparks of human portents had been present for a while: a flood, a drought, a famine – all on lands where local cotton had lost its market to foreign imports of cheaper factory cloth, and where families who had once had a spinning wheel to cling to now had nothing but dust. To the 'Boxers', however, the greatest culprits were the foreign missionary devils. Free to go wherever they wanted, and say whatever they wanted to say, protected by the talisman of an 'extraterritoriality' that gave them immunity from the local justice of a magistrate, they had dug themselves into villages across the north, insisting that the kitchen gods be ousted, that the temple festivals be closed, and that anyone who converted to Christianity should be subject only to the order of their God.

With the missionaries waving their treaty-given rights in everyone's faces, feuds had followed. In missionary-occupied villages, the rules of the land had been replaced by the 'laws of God', applied by men who could not speak Chinese and who had no idea about the relationship between a name and a purpose, let alone the Chinese principles of the family.

Hardly surprisingly, heaven had become extremely upset and, naturally, the rains had failed. Hunger began to prowl, swiftly followed by a swelling of the ranks of the blood brotherhoods. Spirits were called upon, and a school of 'plum flower' boxing had been founded to give even the poorest man a transforming confidence in his ability to fight. Rooted in millennia of mixed-up Daoist and Buddhist beliefs, the brotherhoods of men also discovered magical talismans and 'invulnerability charms' guaranteed to protect their simple boxing fists against foreign guns.

Armed with the combined powers of Laozi, Buddha and Guan Yu, the god of war who never failed to protect the weakest, the leaders of 'the Boxers' urged them to fling the foreigners out of the land: rip up the railway lines that Russia was laying across the north-east; smash the telegraph poles with which the foreigners seemed to be communicating with each other at the speed of light; and wherever and however they could, apply their fists to throw the foreign devils out. A forgotten people on forgotten fields of misery, most − peasants and small landlords alike − saw the Boxers as heroes from the stuff of the old stories like the *Outlaws of the Marsh*. Propelled by the energies of so many nightmares, the various brotherhoods swept across the north-east, like a surging ocean.

In June 1900, the tide of the Boxers began to lap at the edges of Beijing. From the seclusion of a new Summer Palace, and with not much else left for the weakened empire to rely upon, the Dowager Empress decided that they must be a gift from heaven. Declaring that they should be allowed to try their magic in defence of the Qing, she offered the services of the surviving imperial army to help. Aghast that the Qing were prepared to unleash a killing tide of boxing rebels on foreign souls, the foreign powers turned their embassies into fortresses and prepared for a vanquishing war.

Over the next two months, forty-five thousand foreign troops were poured into the treaty-port of Tianjin, commanded to fight their rescuing way to Beijing and, as they advanced, to defeat Boxer rebels and imperial troops alike. Eventually, Beijing was reached and the embassies were liberated. But by the time the foreign troops had command of the city, hundreds of foreigners and thousands of Chinese Christians, not to mention tens of thousands of Boxers and others caught up in the fray, had been killed. In a chilling confirmation, if ever one were needed, that the foreigners were truly nothing more than barbarians, the foreign troops then sacked Beijing. As the city burnt with flames of rage, the foreign powers composedly sat down to compile their more formal demands: nine hundred million taels of silver, including interest, to be paid over thirty-nine years, with customs duties and taxes as guarantees; executions of Boxer rebels and of senior officials who had supported them; a moratorium on imports of arms; and twelve more cities to be opened up for foreign occupation.

From his exile, Kang Youwei noted that, amid the great foreign insistence that desperate peasants be executed, not one of the foreign powers had taken the opportunity to request the release of the imprisoned Guangxu Emperor. For Liang Qichao, it was just another example of what happened when a territory was seen as nothing other than a conquest, and when a people had no voice.

In the months and years that followed, China's youth flooded out of the country. Having given up on the empire and its examinations, many of the voyagers were now 'independent scholars': students looking for anything to help them save their country. Most found their way to Japan: geographically close, grounded in similar Confucian ideas, and with a written language that had been heavily influenced by the characters of Chinese. So many students went to Tokyo that the headmaster of the city's Higher Normal School opened a special academy for them, with a curriculum designed to 'strengthen China'. Deeply thoughtful about what the Chinese might need, the curriculum included not only instruction in the Japanese language necessary to enable them to read the large libraries of Western texts, which

At the beginning of time, a sister and a brother emerged from the hunmang chaos: Nüwa shored up heaven with the Buzhou Mountain and created a people of clay; her brother Fuxi investigated the wonders of nature.

Laozi's Daodejing captured an idea of being human that was very different to the Confucian ideal. This fresco depicts a meeting between Laozi and Confucius.

Early Chinese ideas included those of Confucius (pictured here) and Laozi; over two thousand years later, late 17th century Jesuits would translate them into texts read by some of the leading minds of the European Enlightenment.

Failing to achieve immortality, the First Qin Emperor was laid to rest in a tomb city modelled on the Xianyang capital of Qin and guarded by ten thousand terracotta warriors.

The Han Dynasty's Martial Emperor sent Zhang Qian off to find allies in the fight against the Xiongnu; Zhang Qian failed to find the allies but explored the fabled lands to the Central Asian west.

The founder of the Tang dynasty, Emperor Gaozu, was a man named Li (Li Yuan). Claiming descent from Liu Bang, the founder of the Han Dynasty, his darker skin pointed to ancestors from the steppes.

Capital of the Song Dynasty, the splendid Kaifeng had been sacked by Jurchen-Jin before being taken by the advancing Mongols, who would eventually defeat the Southern Song in a sea battle.

Chinggis Khan forged a Mongol empire that conquered the Song Dynasty; establishing a Yuan Dynasty, the Mongols connected China to Persia and beyond, including a Central Asia which would become inextricably linked with China.

The Mongol Yuan were displaced by rebels united under a White Lotus Society which traced its origins to warrior monks trained at the Shaolin monastery.

The Yongle Emperor, son of the founder of the Ming Dynasty, raised a new Beijing with a dream of outshining the Mongol empire.

The Forbidden City was a world where heaven met earth through the person of the Emperor as the Son of Heaven, and where the dream of a Confucian order reigned.

Qu Yuan, the prince whose poem, Li Sao, dreamt of a world where ordinary people could talk to heaven; casting himself into the Miluo River, he became a symbol of a deeper idea of being Chinese.

Persuaded to leave his retreat by the personal
entreaties of the Shu-Han ruler, Zhuge Liang,
the Crouching Dragon, would become one of the
greatest heroes of the Chinese world.

Bodhidharma brought an idea of
Buddhist meditation from southern
India; it would become known as
'Chan' in China ('Zen' in Japan).

The Monkey King, with his magic stick and his cloud somersaults, would become more famous than many an emperor – and much better loved.

The Qing emperor, Kangxi, reclaimed and expanded the lands of the Ming for the greater Manju dream.

Manju bannermen were at the heart of the discipline of the hunt, which was itself at the heart of 'manjusai fe doro', the way of the Manju.

Following in the saddle of his grandfather, Kangxi, Qianlong launched Ten Great Campaigns to stretch the empire of the Manju Qing.

Prince Gong reminded the Confucian bureaucrats to be kind to Western barbarians, who could not help but see themselves as the centre of everything.

Western cartoons caricatured the 'Great Game' competition of imperial powers –Britain, Germany, Russia, France and Japan – as they carved up Qing China.

Junks fought their way up and down the Yangzi, carrying cargo between Hankou and the sea mouth of Shanghai; this one, pictured at the end of the 19th century, is passing through the Three Gorges.

The success of Zeng Guofan's Xiang Army in defeating the Taiping rebels led to a 'self-strengthening' movement that looked everywhere for ideas about how to strengthen China, including Civil War America and its arsenals.

Kang Youwei smashed the illusion of an imperial heaven, argued for a National Assembly with a constitution, and dreamt of a more human Da Tong, Great Unity, for the people of the world.

Liang Qichao searched at home and abroad for the ideas and institutions that could transform the 450 million people of the Qing Dynasty into citizens of what would be a 'New China'.

The Dowager Empress Cixi ordered the Guangxu Emperor to cancel Kang Youwei's reforms; effectively placing the emperor under palace arrest, she would later embrace the Boxer Rebels in a bid to oust the Western powers.

Born in Guangdong, educated in Hong Kong and Hawaii, Sun Yatsen provided a bridge between anti-Qing rebels at home and cash-rich Chinese abroad; outmanouevred by Yuan Shikai, his dreams of a Constitutional Republic gave way to a militarised Guomindang.

The self-strengthener who hijacked the 1911 revolution; as president of the Republic, Yuan Shikai declared the National Assembly a mistake: 'Too many arguments, not enough results'; he then proclaimed himself Emperor of a new Chinese Empire.

Pictured here in 1932, Beijing's Ming Dynasty Temple of Heaven was built as a *Mingtang*, Hall of Light: a bridge between heaven and earth, raised by man.

Meiji Japan had translated (much easier than learning to read them in English), but a host of Western subjects designed to strengthen the students for the journey ahead: science for the mind, morality for the heart, and physical education for the body.

Not all of the voyagers went to Japan. Britain and France were popular destinations, as was the American power whose forceful example had so deeply influenced Japan. And not all of the voyagers, wherever they went, were travelling under their own steam. After the dust of the Boxer rebellion had settled, America converted some of the Boxer reparations it received into scholarships for Chinese 'Boxer scholars' to study the new and transforming sciences of America. And the Qing empire sent a number of students to learn the special skills of Western self-strengthening: the kind of skills that had won Japan the Battle of Weihaiwei and destroyed the Beiyang navy, while putting Western boats and railways on Chinese rivers and land. Whatever the origins of the students, by 1906, eight thousand of them – independent scholars, Boxer scholars, imperial students – had not only floated to Japan but on to bigger beacons of the wider world.

Encountering the outside world, the students read and learnt beyond the imagination of their fathers. More importantly, whether independent or imperially sponsored, they found a common conversation among themselves as well. With Qing China seemingly about to sink, they stretched their minds as far as they possible could in the desperate hope of saving their Qing-conquered land. And as they were learning, they set about creating societies that would share the new knowledge, and hopefully also begin the process of change upon which the survival of their homeland would depend.

Works read in foreign languages were translated into Chinese and posted home: for friends and relations to read, and for newspapers to print. There was a wealth of ideas to be found among the great mind-changing foreign texts. One had been penned by a man called Ma-ke-si, Marx, whose utopian idea for a new world seemed to have a lot in common not only with Kang Youwei's *Da Tong*, Great Unity, but also with the ancient dreams of a golden age of *taiping*, great peace, where all men would be equals. In 1905, a wave of Marx-inspired strikes and rebellions washed across Russia and a political party following Marx's thinking almost achieved a revolution. In 1906, a Marxist 'Communist' Party was founded in Tokyo – and Marx's *Communist*

Manifesto was translated into Chinese. In the same year, in Paris, a group of Chinese students established an anarchist society, which they called 'New World'.

To the students, it seemed that it was not only China that was changing, but everywhere. And while Qing China seemed to be at particular risk of drowning, the idea of a people rising up to save their country and themselves seemed to have spread well beyond the Chinese lands to include all four of the directions of the world.

———

By the early 1900s, while Chinese students were learning about revolution abroad, young minds at home were thinking about raising a revolution of their own. Their numbers were being strengthened by returning students from Japan and the West. But many were beneficiaries of a modernisation of schools and academies that the Dowager Empress and the imperial self-strengtheners had decided to create in a desperate attempt to shore up the flagging fortunes of the Qing; a belated recognition that, while change was challenging, a continuation of the past was perilous.

Many of the most questioning minds were to be found in Hunan's capital, Changsha, where the idea of education for independence rather than exams had already taken root. Inspired by both the ancient poet-prince Qu Yuan and the more recent Tan Sitong and his work *On Humanity*, the goal of Hunan's youth was first to prise Hunan's lands out of the grasping and incompetent hands of the Qing and then, province by province, to rescue the rest of China as well. Dreaming of an independent nation that would be led from the bottom instead of the top, Qu Yuan was to be vindicated and Tan Sitong's dream was to come true: two thousand years of imperial top-down bureaucracy were to give way to a republic that, founded by and for its people, would be able to stand as strong as the greatest mountain. From village to county to province, each ascending level of human community would have its own self-governing order. And at the root of it all would be a people who would be given the first and greatest quality of a 'citizen': the ability to govern themselves. In 1903, drawing on a Japanese-translated American work, *On Civil Liberty and Self-Government* which featured a preface by none less than the president of Yale University, they set out a plan for the self-government of Hunan – and decided to found a revolutionary society to bring their dream to life.

Recognising that any 'revival' of Hunan (let alone the whole of China) would require a fight, and taking a leaf out of the now-numerous revolutionary Russian texts, the young Hunanese also founded a Citizens' Military Education Society. Dedicated to teaching the art of assassination, it set the Dowager Empress Cixi firmly in its sights.

Over the first years of the new century, the young Hunanese reached out to anyone who might be able to help, including patriotic Hunanese merchant-gentry with funds to spare, and ancient brotherhoods of men committed to getting rid of the Qing. Successful assassinations turned out to be more difficult than they had imagined. But while they did not succeed in blasting the Qing out of China, or even assassinating Cixi, they did bump into a man who thought he might be able to help. A Chinese, born in Guangdong, his name was Sun Yatsen.

Educated in Hong Kong and in the then still independent island of Hawaii, Sun Yatsen had had an eclectic childhood, one that had given him an enviable eloquence in the English language, and roots in communities of overseas Chinese in the Pacific West. Seeming to be a magical bridge to the wider world, through his Pacific links, he had become closely acquainted with a 'lost' diaspora of Chinese: men and women whose ancestors had been sailing away from the lands of China ever since the times of the Tang, the Song, the Ming. Long the stuff of fantasy, it turned out that while many of them had gone on to make fortunes across Asia, a number had also found their way to wealth across the Pacific. Sun was also acquainted with the more successful of the recent departees: those large numbers who had left in the last fifty years, travelling as labourers, indentured to the mines and plantations of foreign empires, some of whom, applying both the same *chi ku* ability to eat bitterness that had sustained Hankou's labourers, and the same Confucian principles that Zeng Guofan had used to raise his Xiang Army, had become wealthy traders, and even industrialists. While many of those crossing the Pacific had found their fortunes in America, a number, including many of the most successful, had stopped in Hawaii, keeping their links with the wider diaspora, East and West.

Shocked by the rising chaos of the Qing, Sun Yatsen, like many other Chinese overseas, had watched events in Qing China with as much concern as the students. In 1891, supported by the funds of wealthy Hawaiian Chinese, he had founded a Revive China Society. Then, in 1896, calling on the Chinese embassy during a visit to London, he had been whisked off the street by secret forces loyal to the Qing. Eventually, Sun had been released and, writing a book about his kidnapping, he had become a Chinese hero, instantly recognisable around the world. Having held his breath in hope across the hundred days of the Guangxu Emperor's short-lived reforms, like Kang Youwei, Sun had then tried to instigate a revolution. Without schools of willing students to hand, he had reached out to one of the strongest of China's secretive brotherhoods: the Heaven and Earth Society. While Sun's uprisings were no more successful than Kang Youwei's, his powers of overseas funding – incalculably heightened by the fame of his kidnapping – were far greater than those of any students at home.

Plotting his revolution, Sun Yatsen was as aware as Liang Qichao that if China was to change, it would need to find its people. But while Liang Qichao tried to understand the mechanics of *building* a people, Sun, more familiar with the West, turned to America and the ideas of Abraham Lincoln: ideas that were much more concerned with the question of the government of a people who already had a sense of themselves as citizens, rather than waking up a peasantry who had long ago given up. Touching only lightly on the vast difference between the nameless bitterness-eating bodies spread across the fields, and those migrant hands that had already managed to get themselves to America, Sun repeated Lincoln's mantra: 'Governance of the people, by the people, for the people'. Rephrasing it as three breath-catching principles for a new China, he declared that it was time for the country to raise up a *minzu*, people who would be conscious of being a nation, a *minquan*, republican government that would be guided by a constitution, and a *minsheng*, people's state to provide for the wellbeing of everyone. Rich in foreign connections, but poor in links to the youthful energies of mainland China, when Sun Yatsen heard of the Hunan students and their dreams of revolution, he saw an obvious opportunity to build a more united force.

The Hunanese students were less enthusiastic. While Sun was looking for a new China, the students were looking for a Hunanese independence, out of which might *later* come the independence of the greater Chinese people, not only from the Manju Qing, but also from the ancient imperial deceptions that had so dulled everyone's minds.

With little access to money, they were certainly struggling to get their dreams off the ground. But when Sun suggested that they join forces, many thought it a distinctly bad idea. Divided, other students argued that while Sun might not have a clear enough understanding of the situation on the ground, he obviously had the power of a patter and a world of wealthy connections, both of which could help Hunan succeed. The rest of China might not yet be ready, but if Sun could trigger a revolution, then Hunan could snatch its independence, whatever happened to the wider Chinese lands.

To many of the students, however, Sun's vision was not only vague, but dangerous. A state of all the Chinese people when no one seemed to know who the 'Chinese people' were, and a number did not seem to care? Notwithstanding a lot of complaining, and with allowances made for a few exceptions, the wider scholarly class did not seem to be all that anxious to throw off the tyranny that had bound them to emperor and empire for the last two thousand years. True, the Hunanese did not have much beyond their hearts, but in those hearts, they held a strong sense of who they were and what they wanted. Where the myriad Chinese people were often described as a scattered tray of sand, Hunan was a firm foundation. And where many Chinese, scholars and peasants alike, often seemed to be a flock of sheep-in-bondage, always looking for a Great Man ruler who could come to their rescue, the young Hunanese were nothing if not clear about their dream of Hunan as an independent state, grounded on the idea of individuals whose independent minds were both a value in themselves and a value for the state as well.

In the end, the collapse of yet another Hunan rebellion in 1905 tipped the scales in Sun's favour and the two forces combined to create a *Tongmenghui*, United Alliance Society, to defeat the Qing. But the divisions remained and few, at least in Hunan, were in any doubt that Sun's dream was dangerously underdeveloped. Nor were they in any doubt that the United Alliance Society was united for one thing and one thing only: the violence necessary to bring a final end to the rule of the Manju Qing.

While the revolutionaries had been searching for success, the self-strengtheners had eventually come to realise that the Manju Qing were running out of ideas. In the aftermath of the Boxer rebellion and the foreign invasion that had followed in its wake, there had been no army left to speak of. And with foreigners having forcibly secured the right to pour their own capital and equipment into China to create their own fortunes, some of the self-strengtheners began to see that, while Kang Youwei's ideas of a popular *Da Tong*, Great Unity, were clearly extreme, he had been right in his insistence that reform was urgently required. A few had even gone so far as to suggest that some of his more practical ideas might have a grain of sense. Obviously the one about local self-governance was out of the question: no one was going to contemplate the chaos of 450 million Chinese specks of sand deciding what to do for themselves. But some of his more practical suggestions about technology, for example, and knowledge, might make for a stronger empire – one better able to stand firm against the foreigners, as well as against any Chinese who had got the wrong end of the stick.

From 1901, under the influence of the self-strengtheners, a series of 'new policies' had already begun to appear, reintroducing many of the changes Kang Youwei had originally suggested, and for which the Guangxu Emperor remained under palace arrest. Obviously, the most important place to start had been with the money. With China's fortunes now mortgaged to the foreign powers seemingly until king-dom come, it had been clearer than ever that only the gentry merchants would be able to finance any of the necessary changes – and that, as usual, all of the work would need to be done by the bitterness-eat-ing peasants. This time, however, the self-strengtheners were to apply their talents less to the promotion of their own individual interests and more to strengthening the empire.

The old guilds, of Hankou and everywhere else, were to be organ-ised into 'chambers of commerce'; and, given the importance of trade and new industries in the strengthening of China, the chambers of commerce would be closely bound to the state. A new and better army was also to be raised; and considering the travails of recent years, police forces were to be introduced as well. These had been obvious improvements. But Kang Youwei and the memorialists had also been right about the importance of ideas, and the need for a new bureaucracy with a more open mind. A new Bureau of Government Affairs was to be established to receive ideas from anyone and everyone, and to think, in a truer Confucian spirit, about which ones might work. Alongside it, a host of new ministries were to be created: with good practical ideas once identified, the grand bureaucracy could demonstrate a new-found ability to think beyond the classics and start getting on top of everything. The imperial examinations, already modified, would be abolished altogether, replaced with modern schools designed to teach the best of what was Chinese and foreign, with a firm focus on the science and engineering skills that had clearly carried the foreign powers to such conquering heights. And, given that the central imperial state was the most important ship of all, the provinces were told to dig deeply into their pockets, and start to pay off the imperial debt. Where more money was needed, taxes would have to rise – and if the taxes were not enough, then more money would simply have to be printed.

To the astonishment of all, even the memorialists' idea of representative public assemblies was floated: places where locally elected people could gather together and express their views. Of course, Kang Youwei had not got that quite right. Naturally, all of those 'elected' would have to come from a pool of people who had been carefully selected before anyone could choose to vote for them. And any decisions that the voters might make would have to be sent up to Beijing for the careful consideration of the imperial bureaucracy before any confirmation could be made. Heaven, obviously, would always know best.

From within the courtyards of the Forbidden City, it had all seemed like an excellent idea. And it had certainly seemed to be an improvement to many of the old self-strengtheners outside. But, seemingly oblivious to the revolutionary plots around them, as the years of the first decade passed, some of its wider enthusiasts began to have second thoughts. Taxes seemed to be rising by the month and, with new presses printing money, the value of the Qing's currency seemed to be falling through the floor. Pockets shrinking, a new selfishness began to rise. In the countryside, gentry-merchant owners of estates, anxious to shore up their family fortunes, set their fields to producing whatever cash crops the outside world wanted to buy, leaving peasant mouths to find their own food.

Meanwhile, in the expanding towns and cities, a new generation of the rich was taking root: country gentry who had left the land to find new fortunes, merchants whose wealth continued to soar on an empire of trade, and industrialists – who were mainly traders who had decided to invest their profits in factory futures. Even literary talents, once restricted to the imperial exams, were now turning their attention to the making of money.

Factories began to rise, more private hands began to bank, new steaming ventures of the boat variety shipped goods across the land and abroad. Peasants who had failed in the fields flooded into the towns and cities in a desperate pursuit of work. Many, cheap, and long trained in eating bitterness, there seemed to be no end to the hours they were willing to labour. And then there were the foreigners – now trading and founding factories of their own. Although, as the Hankou minds had presciently predicted, most of them had turned out to be just another opportunity. Hardly seeming to know up from down when they ventured out of their coastal enclaves, the foreigners usually left the running of their businesses to the locals, and it was naturally the locals who decided how much of the profits to share.

Some thought that the only real problem was the self-strengtheners who, notwithstanding the new imperial edicts, were once again weaving personal empires of selfish wealth within the reforms. Self-strengthening for the state was once again turning into self-strengthening for the officials of the state. Had it ever been otherwise? With millennia of experience behind them, and little understanding of the present, the gentry and the officials were picking up the tried and tested measures that had yielded imperial scales of riches across the millennia of the past.

Others saw a new and more worrying version of an older problem. As new industrial wealth had risen along with the city rafters, a growing tide of peasant hands had become city labourers; squeezed together within the city walls, they were now grumbling for better conditions. Calls for days off and better wages had become a mantra, and every now and then a rabble-rousing strike would break out, auguring much bigger and darker clouds. While the ship of the imperial state was congratulating itself on its self-strengthening wisdom, and while the gentry-merchants were working on managing the ambitions of the self-strengthening officials, a small but rising number of voices was beginning to wonder if the ship could possibly withstand a storm. The answer, whispered at first, then inked a little louder in the newspapers, was that any ship was only as worthy as its captain and its crew.

With the Dowager Empress Cixi as captain, and with the crew a host of self-strengtheners who were completely cut off from the scattered specks of the people, unless someone found a way to turn the people into citizens, and soon, it would be only a matter of time before everything ended up in a wreck.

In 1908 the Dowager Empress died, departing from this world only a day after the death of the still-captive Guangxu Emperor. Many quietly noted the coincidence of timing, which only she would have been able to explain. A two-year-old Manju prince, Pu Yi, was gently placed upon the dragon throne as the Xuantong (Declaring Unity) Emperor. Yet another regency began, this one under the cautious reins of the young boy's father, Prince Chun. Eyebrows were raised and hearts sighed.

Later that year, however, just as imperially reforming edicts had promised, the first steps were taken towards establishing a National Assembly in Beijing, with a written constitution promised by 1917. Before the end of the year, twenty-two provinces held elections to see which voices would be chosen to represent them. Anyone was able to stand – as long as they had been pre-selected by the imperial bureaucracy. And anyone over twenty-five was able to vote – as long as they had a serious education or a pile of silver. Once elected to provincial assemblies, in the following year, the assemblies would meet to elect from among their own number those who would then go on to be representatives in the promised National Assembly. No one, however, was quite clear how any of this was expected to work – the constitution would not appear for another nine years. A few inconvenient student voices argued that, given the delays, everyone should take control of everything and organise it themselves. This was not at all what the imperial state wanted to hear; nor did many conservative others think it sounded like a good idea.

Meanwhile, more serious critics had decided that, interesting though the imperial reforms might be, they were too little, too late, and obviously the work of an empire that had not yet understood the root cause of its problems. With Sun Yatsen establishing secret branches of the United Alliance Society abroad, chests of silver were flooding in to fund the revolutionary attempts of brothers at home. As more secret branches of the society had been established within China, uprisings were being shaken into action, guns had been stashed in corners, assassins had been trained and bombs had been prepared. The ranks of the members were flooded not only with revolutionary students, but with older others who had lost their imperial illusions – including a number of military men. They were also flooded with brotherhoods of blood, which had long been preparing for war against the Qing: the Heaven and Earth Society and the White Lotus among many others, all promoting one version or another of the three ancient harmonies of heaven, earth and man. So many were these brotherhoods that the missionaries who came across them had given them all the old Greek name for 'three', calling them the Triads. Whatever name they marched under, the swelling number of revolutionaries was increasingly being wrapped up into the secret heavenly families, led by men who were turning everyone's desperation into a power of their own.

———

In the event, the revolution was an accident. On 9 October 1911, just across the river from Hankou, in the Wuchang capital of Hubei (right next door to the province of Hunan), a revolutionary bomb-in-the-making exploded in an unlucky pair of hands. As injured underground revolutionaries were rushed to hospital, imperial troops swarmed to what had until then been a secret headquarters. Arriving at the premises, they executed three of the surviving revolutionaries summarily on the spot. Registers containing the names of other members (closed books that included the names of many imperial soldiers and their officers) were then swept off for inspection. Those who managed to escape – and particularly those revolutionaries in the ranks of the army – realised that even though the bomb had jumped the revolutionary gun, if they did not rise to the occasion now, everyone whose name was in the registers would be damned.

Before the light of 11 October found its dawn, the 8th Battalion of Wuchang Engineers mutinied, with transport and artillery units rushing to join them. By the end of the day, the chambers of commerce had pledged their support, and much of their silver, and Wuchang became China's first revolutionary city. The neighbouring province of Hubei then declared itself an independent republic, led by a rather reluctant general who, under the circumstances, felt he had little choice. Within two weeks, Hunan's own revolutionaries rose up and declared an independent state of their own. Across the following months, revolution by revolution, many of the other provinces followed suit. In America, raising money for the revolutionary cause, Sun Yatsen read about the explosions in the *Denver News*.

For a revolution, it was all remarkably peaceful – more so than many of the failed attempts that had gone before. Little blood was shed, and the overwhelming support of the army meant that order was largely maintained. Largely but not completely: after nearly three hundred years of conquest and the near-loss of the country, the massacres of Manju, which broke out by popular accord, could not be helped.

The only real problem was that since the revolution had taken even the revolutionaries by surprise it did not have a leader. And since the revolution did not have a leader, there was no one to talk to the new child-emperor; although it was reasonably clear to all that, even if consulted, neither the child-emperor nor his regent-father would have any idea of what to do. There was, however, an accomplished self-strengthener waiting darkly in the wings. The old commander of the Beiyang army, a meddler whose past machinations had included the betrayal of the Guangxu Emperor's dangerous dreams to the Dowager Empress Cixi, he was a man whose ambition for power had few if any limits: his name was Yuan Shikai.

Pretending to be an honest broker, Yuan convened a meeting of the imperial government and the revolutionaries, at the end of which the young emperor issued the last of his imperial decrees. The lands of Qing China, including the lands of those provinces that had jumped the gun and declared an earlier independence, would become a republic, and Yuan Shikai would lead them until elections could be held at the end of the coming year.

On 12 February 1912, the emperor formally abdicated. Over the course of the remaining year, the National Assembly was returned to try to be of whatever service it could. Given that it had been intentionally created without the power to do anything, this was a feat that few, even in the assembly itself, had any confidence it would be able to achieve. And with a written constitution, with its promise of a rule of law, still five years away, it was obvious that it was not going to be of any immediate help. With the members of the assembly unclear, the population at large was even more in the dark. 'What is a republic?' was one popular question. Others included: 'Where has the emperor gone?' and 'When is he coming back?'

Sun Yatsen had recently returned from America, and many assumed that Yuan Shikai would yield in the face of his greater popular appeal. But the Beiyang army was now firmly in Yuan's hands, the 'independent provinces' were being ushered back into the fold, and no one who had read their history really imagined that Yuan would stand down without a fight.

Facing a constitutional crisis without a constitution, in the National Assembly, Sun called on the elected representatives to organise themselves into groups of ideas ('political parties') and raise the assembly arguments on which national political decisions could be forged. To start the ball rolling, he changed the name of the United Revolutionary Alliance to a *Guomindang*, National People's Party, opening up its membership to anyone in the National Assembly who wanted to join.

Before long, everyone was launching parties – with banners of them fluttering in all directions. Many of the representatives did their best. But with so little experience, and representing so many different grains of sand, within the year almost everyone in the Assembly was hurling arrows at everyone else, regardless of which party they might technically have joined. Outside the National Assembly, puzzled observers looked on in dismay. And outside the heartlands of the Chinese people, those on the edges of what had been the mainstay of a Manju empire, and was now the Republic of China, decided to take their chance at an independence of their own. A republican flag had been raised in the unifying colours of all of the five peoples whose lands had been embraced by the Manju (the Han descendants of the Yellow Emperor, the Mongols, the Tibetans, the Uighurs and even the Manju themselves). But the Mongols and the Tibetans had stood up to say that they would rather find their futures on their own. (The Uighurs would have done the same if a warlord had not put them in their place.)

In the last months of the Chinese lunar year (across December 1912 and January 1913), elections were finally held. For all of the battling, or perhaps because of it, the *Guomindang* National People's Party won a clear majority. Sun Yatsen stood to be a popular president, and a rising revolutionary star within the young ranks of the *Guomindang* was confidently expected to become prime minister: his name was Song Jiaoren. But on 20 March 1913, while waiting for a train to take him from Shanghai to Beijing, Song fell to the bullet of an assassin's gun. Yuan Shikai's hand had not been on the trigger but whispers attached his name to the death.

By the end of the year, elections notwithstanding, and after a brief battle in which the young Guomindang had tried to overthrow Yuan Shikai's inherited 'New Army', Sun Yatsen was in exile in Japan, Yuan Shikai was still president – and, as president, he ordered the expulsion of the *Guomingdang* from the National Assembly. It did not really matter, because the following year, Yuan Shikai dissolved the Assembly altogether, declaring that the whole idea had been a terrible mistake: 'Too many arguments,' he observed, 'not enough results.' According to Yuan, the Chinese people were confused – even heaven was confused. It was time to go back to the old single top-down order of the past.

Critics of every colour were silenced, opinions were discouraged, newspapers were prohibited from publishing anything that might be detrimental to the 'republic's peace'. Across the country, military governors were appointed to each and every province, all reporting directly to the president. In 1914, as a war of the world broke out in Europe, Japan, allying itself with the British and the French, occupied German-held lands in the Chinese north. Less than a year later, it would follow up its occupation with a list of 'Twenty-One Demands' for wider power in the Chinese lands; demands which Yuan Shikai struggled to contain. And then, in November 1915, a 'special' representative assembly was convened exclusively for the purpose of unanimously appointing Yuan Shikai as emperor of a new 'Chinese Empire'. 'A collection of persons makes a family,' the new emperor observed, 'and a collection of families makes a state.' But, in Yuan's imperial opinion, a republic would achieve nothing other than the destruction of all.

In early 1916, wrapped in the protection of an armoured car, and with imperial robes on order, Yuan Shikai travelled to the Temple of Heaven – the blue-domed altar with which his Ming predecessors had reinterpreted the ancient Hall of Light. Following in the footsteps of every ancestor who had gone before him, Yuan obediently presented the sacrifices of earth to a waiting heaven above. With as little sense of irony as the emperors of the past, he then announced his imperial title: Hong Xian, Constitutional Abundance.

BOOK II
TWENTIETH CENTURY IDEAS

Speak in the language of the time in which you live.

Hu Shi (1891 – 1962)

PART 4
UP IN THE CITY

Our million hearts beating as one.
March of the Volunteers (written by the playwright,
Tian Han in 1937; now the anthem of
the People's Republic of China)

CHAPTER 1

MIDNIGHT

One by one, the white clouds set off to leave, Vanishing into
the distant oasis.

The Weak Flame of a Star Xu Zhimo (1922)

SOFT AUTUMN WINDS blowing from the west, the train sped
across the flat northern plains. Above, a bright blue rainless sky;
all around, the vast expanse of a dry earth fending off the advances of
a hungry desert. As steam billowed into temporary clouds, a whistle
pierced the silence of the land. Passing camels loaded with coal lifted
their heads and, from the windows of the train, excited eyes peered
towards the horizon. There, at the edge of everything and nothing,
was a vision like no other: the walls of a city appearing like a mirage.
Destination in sight, the engine picked up its paces and soon guarding towers appeared, lapped with an ocean of yellow and green tiles,
dashed with blue, all sparkling in the sun of a rising day. Within an
instant, or so it seemed, the thick walls of the *Zhengyang*, Gate of the
Zenith South, stood before them: terraces above floating towards the
heavens, portals of power open for the day.

Carriage doors eagerly opened, boxes and baskets clutched to anxious
chests, feet of many descriptions touched the ground: some leathered in
shoes, others wrapped in soft cotton slippers, the smallest ones tipped
with playful tigers. Silken robes rubbed shoulders with tailored trousers; bowler hats jostled with bare heads; military uniforms surged to
the front; all were swept into the arriving tide and carried towards a
waiting chaos outside. Once into the sparkling light of the 1918 day,
chaos pushed and shoved. With passengers pouring on to the street,
mules, carts and rickshaws edged ever closer in search of a fare.

And then a gathering of engines scattered everyone to the side.
Shining in their metallic glory, a pair of Dodges and what seemed to
be a Citroën purred into waiting place: ready to float a sturdy warlord,

a rising official or a 'money devil banker' smoothly off to a conversation or a club.

The Zhengyang Gate of the Zenith South had once been the foremost guardian of the imperial dragon, the boundary between the *nei cheng*, Inner City, heaven, and the *wai cheng*, Outer City, of the people's earth. The towering point at which every passing Chinese spirit had paused to observe the force of heaven, only the fewest of the few had ever entered through its portals. Whispers of the wonders of the Inner City had, however, long flooded the crowded lanes of the Outer City of Beijing: a world of walls behind which sat the glittering pavilions of the greater family of the emperor – each arranged as courtyards of low buildings with tiled roofs of yellow or green, all sitting like squares on a chequerboard, and the whole partitioned by narrow streets so straight that the eye could see from one end to the other.

Those few who had passed through the Zhengyang Gate into the Inner City had found themselves at the Gate of the Great Qing from which a Thousand Step Way – a dragonly avenue, guarded by Manju bannermen and long enough to humble even the proudest heart – led to the Tiananmen Gate of Heavenly Peace. Flanked by lions fixed in heavenly stone, across the top of the pillars of the gate hung a set of characters that every Chinese scholar knew by heart: *jieshou yutian, anbu zhiguo*, receive the mandate of heaven, and peace will reign. Passing through the gate from the Inner City, trembling visitors next entered the Imperial City within: a world of spreading gardens and contemplative courtyards. And then, ahead, the Meridian Gate: entrance to the *ziwei*, purple, Forbidden City. Set below the Pole Star and its surrounding *ziwei* enclosure, the Forbidden City was a pearl clasped within a city within a city: the secret beating heart of the heavenly empire.

But that was before, when Beijing had a dragon emperor, and heaven was a power before which everyone trembled, and most obeyed. By 1912, however, the six year-old Manju prince, Pu Yi, who had once pretended to be the Son of Heaven, had lost his imperial voice and been silenced with the childish pleasures of a now largely empty and echoing Forbidden City. The scholarly officials had gone to serve the new Republic. Even the guarding Manju bannermen, now surplus to reduced requirements, had found themselves cast into the Outer City, joined by Manju princes and princesses for whom the imperial world had become nothing but a dream. Reduced to the status of a barbarian pretender who had lost even his own original Manju lands, floating on the fortunes of an uncertain world, the young emperor was protected only by an army of eunuchs, all bent on strengthening themselves with the treasures of five hundred years of imperial silk, jade and gold. With the walls of the Inner City already breached by a railway, followed by roads, the wider Imperial City had soon been opened up to a public view: once-hidden courtyards and gardens were swept out of their dreams, and the Tiananmen Gate of Heavenly Peace was exposed to the city at large.

The winds had changed. Indeed, they had changed so much and so often that many wondered whether the idea of a heavenly order would ever return. And if it did return, whether the hope of a *ren* humanity (the ancient idea that Confucius had turned into a principle and the Hunanese Tan Sitong had turned into a revolutionary dream) would still be alive. Yuan Shikai's imperial reign had lasted less than a year: within days of its announcement in late 1915, newspapers reported that the military governor of south-westerly Yunnan had declared the province's independence; over the coming months, other southern provinces below the Yangzi followed suit, and continued to do so even after Yuan Shikai offered to cancel the imperial idea. With the south separating, and the idea of a single new empire on its way to an illusion, by June 1916, Yuan himself was dead. Beijing, now a Republican pearl, momentarily dropped into the hands of the same reluctant general who had been pressed to take the helm of the independent Hubei Republic after the 'accidental revolution' in 1911.

By the summer of 1917, the reluctant general had been ousted by a more ambitious peer who declared the restoration of the Qing, and of the young emperor. Having established a revolutionary party in exile, Sun Yatsen returned to the south, supported by guns of his own. Many members of the National Assembly followed, convening themselves in an 'extraordinary session'. Within two months, a stronger northern general, now warlord, Duan Qirui, stormed Beijing, declaring the restoration of the Republic, ordering the young emperor to abdicate once again and initiating a new National Assembly. With little time to call elections, and with a number of provinces refusing to participate, the new assembly was largely populated by men who bought their votes for cash or favours; the office of the Premier was assumed by the warlord Duan. Over the coming decade, just as in the distant past, warlords would split the country again and again, returning the provinces and cities to individual fiefdoms, each area ruled by a warlord who dreamt of unifying everything, with himself on top. In the messy mosaic of competing cannons, north and south would again divide.

When Duan Qirui's National Assembly proclaimed a continuation of the Republic from Beijing, the people were not convinced. With China once again a world of fiefdoms and warlords, what on earth could it possibly be a 'republic' of? Certainly nothing that seemed to have anything to do with the *ren* humanity of the people. The lands of the north had become a particular question mark: Japan and Russia were still staring warily at each other over the barrel of China's vulnerable expanse. Russia insisted on a Far East of its own, across lands that stretched to the lapping edges of the Pacific Ocean. Japan, which sided with the British in the First World War (obviously so named by barbarians who had never heard of the ancient time of the Warring States) insisted that the security of its island archipelago depended upon putting a stop to the relentless spread of the Western powers across the lands of the Chinese north. Meanwhile, representatives of the wider European powers were still quartered in the capital, not to mention being firmly anchored in the country's treaty ports. Chinese self-strengtheners had raised new industries in central and southern cities, but it was still Western banks that owned the foreign tracks of trains and telegraph lines that spread across the fields, and Western science that seemed to own so much of the wider Chinese world.

So desperate were the times that even the land itself seemed to be for sale, and certainly its people. In 1916, with the republican treasury in a parlous state – and doubtless a Republican pocket needing some cash – someone at the precarious top had had the bright idea of trading China's bitterness-eating labour for a victory deal: trenches were to be dug in France in exchange for a return of the northern Chinese lands that the Germans had taken in the event that the Allies won the war. The deal struck, nearly a hundred thousand peasants had set sail from nearby British-controlled Weihaiwei. At the end of the First World War, with the British and French victorious over the Germans, popular Chinese hopes anticipated a rare reversal of Western territorial fortunes.

On the evening of 2 May 1919, Beijing waited with bated breath for the decision of a European conference that was to decide the fate of the northern lands. Hearing the news on the ground, Chinese journalists in Paris tapped out a telegram that would be everyone's despair: the Treaty of Versailles had decided that the German lands in China would be given to Japan. The people of Beijing first gasped in disbelief – then realised that the betrayal had come from within. With everyone out for themselves, Duan Qirui, the northern general who had become both a warlord and premier, had secretly struck a different trade: in return for a Japanese advance of the softest of loans, not to mention a few personal arrangements, the once-German lands had been promised to Japan by a warlord purporting to be the Republic.

Two days later, on 4 May, Beijing exploded in protests, led by a student youth that had come of age only to find its future had been traded across the sea. Less than a decade had passed since a revolution had been won (admittedly accidentally). But the gap between heaven and the people was as wide as ever, with the new heaven populated by battles of self-strengthening warlord emperors who were as keen as any of their imperial ancestors to grab as much earth and sky as they could, even as they sold the heavenly lands from under the people's feet. Had China learnt nothing from its past?

Equipping themselves with banners, the students boldly proclaimed what they believed to be the greatest words of liberating wisdom discovered in their studies abroad: 'Mr *Sai* Science', and 'Mr *De* Democracy'. Mr Science to ensure that the ideas of both the state and its people would be grounded in objectivity, rather than distorted by personal self-interest and ignorance. Mr Democracy to ensure that an independently minded people would be able to guarantee an independent state. Armed with outrage, they carried themselves on a throbbing tide to the edifice that seemed to make their point: the Tiananmen Gate of Heavenly Peace and its *jieshou yutian, anbu zhiguo* proclamation, receive the mandate of heaven and peace will reign. Once there, they were joined by multitudes: pressing hearts who had been pushing and pulling at everything just to make ends meet; teachers who shared the students' anger; and exploding souls whose enterprises had brought them riches, but whose country could not hold an honest peace.

By the end of 4 May, the home of the government minister most conspicuously responsible for the loss of the lands had been burnt to a cinder; and many of the students had been marched to jail. Before long, neighbouring northern warlords arrived to stamp a stronger authority across Beijing's rebellious streets.

In the months and years of chaos that followed, any surviving belief in a Republic vanished into a cauldron of battles as warlords fought for a once-imperial capital that had become part of a greater northern prize. At the end of 1924, after yet another warlord had taken Beijing, the last Manju emperor was finally expelled from the Forbidden City, and the National Assembly was dissolved. Largely convened in the shadow of the warlords' guns, after eleven years of ups and downs it was widely considered to have been a catalogue of corruption, fraught with factionalism and notable for its endlessly futile debate.

As warlords continued to battle for the north, the flood of Beijing's once-heavenly wealth trickled to a stream, even as a tide of desperate refugees flocked to a city that was losing its walls. The palaces with all their imperial families and courtiers were turning to dust. The streams of heavenly retainers that had once kept everyone in silk had been cut asunder with the end of the empire. Across the wider city, everyone's diminishing savings had become the city's principal float. Scholars had been replaced by a new corps of 'Republican' officials. And as once-orderly streets were transformed into a chaos of competing claims, soldiers and beggars had captured the roads. Tan Sitong's old dream of a *ren*, humanity, let alone the newer lodestars of science and democracy, seemed a long way away.

Dedicated to the service of the Son of Heaven, Beijing had always been a city unlike any other. Far away from the industrious citadels of Hankou and Changsha, never a bustling treaty port like Tianjin, Shanghai or Guangzhou, the production of the practical had never thrived in this capital set on a dry northern plain. While emperors had risen and fallen within the Forbidden City and its wider Imperial and Inner City worlds, across the Outer City at large, it had been the crafting and consumption of luxury that had kept everyone afloat. Set behind grey walls, brushed by willow trees and passed by unwitting camels, the magnificent residences of once-scholarly officials had been a world of pavilions and courtyards, each with a name, a meaning and a delicate purpose, and all needing just the right furniture of a civilised life. With an ideal of 'five generations under a single roof', heads of households had commanded, and servants had procured: officials' hats and tailored gowns for the master of the house; silk slippers, feathered fans, embroidered skirts and jackets for wives; carved lacquer boxes and cloisonné vases for beauty; lanterns for light; paper and ink for painting; books for young and scholarly minds. Chattering in the streets as they went, maids had fluttered from their gates to secure the necessities of the scholarly courtyards: silk thread, reed mats, pig bristles, soap and candles for daily life; mountains of duck, rice, pork and wines to keep the banquets flowing. And as the great households reached out for their requirements, in the *hutong*, alleyways, all around, the purveyors and makers of everything that the courtyards needed had crafted simple lives of their own.

By 1925, however, with the last emperor gone and his scholarly officials long stood down, many of the purveyors of imperial dreams had melted into the tides of pedlars, vegetable vendors and prostitutes, all looking for a living. Who could now be in need of an official's hat? And with their husbands' minds surplus to requirements, which scholarly wives could still afford silk slippers and embroidered skirts? Many, declaring Beijing an unlucky place, had floated south, particularly to the foreign emporium of Shanghai – where the promise of wealth rose on waves of industry and trade, protected by treaties and gunships which had become far more reliable anchors than those of the shifting Chinese state. Meanwhile, the old skills, passed from fathers to sons from the beginning of Beijing time, and rarely written down, were fading like memories.

As the past became a dream, though, the new was arriving everywhere – relentlessly. With the once-separate Inner and Outer cities now open to all, in the modern spirit of the times every ordering mind, whether Republican official or newly successful warlord, had a wild idea for transforming Beijing into a Paris, London or Berlin. As the Imperial and Inner cities were exposed to everyone's gaze, once-secluded avenues opened up for everybody's progress. The temples, from which a long succession of Sons of Heaven had dedicated the seasonal rituals and sacrifices, became, for a small entrance fee, public parks. Walls were breached, or dismantled entirely. Gates that had guarded for hundreds of years were stood down to make way for the new. Free from the constraints of the walls and gates, the tracks of trains were matched with widened, asphalted roads; the trains themselves were soon followed by trams. Courtyards that had stood for generations found themselves swept away for the passage of a general's car. A telephone company brought distant voices into privileged homes, as often as not, with the conversation carrying sons and daughters off into dreams of new lives either in Shanghai or abroad. And as troops of warlords increasingly marched across the streets, the Forbidden City, relieved of its heavenly duties, became a museum.

Once governed by their own scholarly gentry, the people of Beijing found themselves not only under the corrupted orders of a Republican government, but under the barrels of warlords' guns. They also found themselves under the scrutiny of a novel phenomenon – a local 'Beijing government' which, working both with and around the warlords, seemed to think that its purpose was to tell everybody what to do. As the new government tried to re-imagine the city with an architecture fit for the new, even as spaces and vistas opened up, distances were shrunk by the new means of transport and communications. From within what had once been small pockets of Confucianly ordered people, everyone now emerged, blinking, into the new order of a single, and very earthly, city. In the new 'public interest', which only the government's officials or its police could define, the old Outer City and its people were pushed this way and that.

Shops that had served neighbouring imperial and official customers for two hundred years or more found themselves ousted by the trams. Some sank with the fortunes of their once affluent clients; others moved to new avenues of consumption built in new streets with new names, separated from old and now lost worlds. Wangfujing, named after the place where a 'Prince's Well' had once been, was one; Xidan, so-called after an elaborate 'West Gate' that had once stood in its place, was another. Suddenly, the brazen advertising of one's wares that flouted every Confucian principle, seemed essential for survival. Billboards appeared, full of the Western ABC alphabet that foreigners seemed to prefer. Electric lights were switched on to dazzle passing eyes. And anniversaries of establishment were regularly celebrated with a firecracking bang. Old stock was replaced with new – and the new was usually either foreign or produced in a part of China so far away that it might just as well have come from abroad. With everyone selling everything at any time of the day, night or year, even the order of the seasons was forgotten.

But as the shops called for greater custom, the market upon which they depended was following its people, and fading by the day. The old meaning, once threaded into the heart of Beijing, and into the very essence of what it meant to be a *Beijing ren*, Beijinger, had been cast to the wind. With so many sons and daughters departing for Shanghai or even further shores, fewer and fewer families could claim 'five generations under a single roof'. And the names of the pavilions and the courtyards of the magnificent residences of once scholarly officials no longer corresponded to any kind of purpose.

Purposes lost, meanings, identities and even names struggled to survive. Temples found themselves converted into factories, or left to the birds: who was interested in talking to ancestors when the past had been revealed to be a lie? Lanes that had once carried so much chatter lost the crafts after which they had been named, and then fell silent. A number of the *hutong*, alleyways, found that what had once been unique about them was scarcely even distinctive anymore: fourteen *jing'er*, wells; seven *tangzi*, ancestral temples; and sixteen *biandan*, carrying-pole, alleys. Many were obliged to change their names. Others found that the names of the past were no longer considered respectable enough for the new order of the 'public' world: *gou yiba*, Dog Tail Alley, was changed to *gao yibo*, Old Man with High Morality; *ji zhua*, Chicken Feet Lane, became *cui hu wan*, Emerald Flower Creed; even the *lu shi*, Donkey Market, was changed to *li shi*, Respect the Scholars Bazaar. As the changes were painted onto the streets, though, Beijing's people kept the old names firmly in their hearts and on their lips – in the stubborn belief that clinging on to the human fabric of their past was the only way they could save the future.

The new Republican world even ate into the filial hearth of the family home. *Li* rituals with which sons had dedicated themselves to fathers, and a *zhi* knowledge devoted to studying the Confucian classics, had obviously lost their purpose. With the Son of Heaven a receding memory, which son was going to sacrifice himself for the greater family? And with imperial examinations long gone, what was the point in learning any classics? Indeed, with the classics revealed as nothing but a grand deception, who would want to read the words that had kept everyone in chains for two thousand years? The employment of classical tutors trickled to a stream, and the great *Xiao Jing, Classic of Filial Piety*, which had once governed everyone's position in the family like a rod of iron, gathered dust unopened, its lessons for children on what it meant to be Chinese cast aside, along with the past. For those who could afford the expense, the teachings of the *Xiao Jing* were replaced with new and different classes. Lessons on the English language that seemed to be everybody's future, were particularly popular, usually followed up with a place at one of the many new colleges that had been opened in Beijing. For those who could not afford the expense, libraries and lectures were offered by the government on a host of subjects, to which were added the chattering meetings of new societies, dedicated to the creation of a new Beijing by and for a people who were, themselves, becoming new.

Sons, and even daughters, now looked outside the family to the possibilities of a more individual and modern success. Sons looked to new industrial or professional opportunities; daughters stepped out of their Confucian bonds to see themselves with opinions and futures of their own. Without an imperial treasury on which to depend, everyone in Beijing, other than a general, was looking for an income. It was not easy. The Republican government had few positions to offer in the city, and although some adventurous spirits had bravely opened factories, capital for industry was in short supply. Added to which, every line of production was exposed to the ravages of a much wider national market where competition was everything. No longer required within the courtyard households, the *xiao min*, little people, looked for possibilities as shop assistants, or as clerks in the small offices that were beginning to appear under any available roof. Out on the street, in the world of the smallest people (the rickshaw drivers and the travelling sellers of anything that could possibly be sold), survival had become a strategy that was crafted one day at a time. With cash much thinner at the top, and with troops of warlords now in occupation, little of value trickled into the lives of these lower orders; whatever did was often commandeered by regularly rampaging soldiers who were rarely paid.

As Beijing struggled with the shock of the new, further south, Shanghai rose and rose. Carried high on the wealth of its foreign treaty status, cycling cash in the freewheeling uncertainty of the times, the smoke of its ever-expanding factories billowed into the air, even as the waters of its mighty river groaned under the weight of the biggest trading ships on earth. Flush with foreigners congratulating themselves on having found the freedom of an international fiefdom, known as 'Shanghailand', the treaty-given 'foreign concessions' had become a magnet for everyone. New factories with foreign capital and tools, fresh presses printing newspapers and magazines for thousands, money to pay for the new city skills of doctors and lawyers, and modern enough minds to want it all. Unlike Beijing, this was a city that seemed to turn to the, very different, order of trade. And while the presence of the foreigners was a historical affront, their ruling powers seemed to have taken to the task of local government with an inspiring efficiency – even though they made a shocking distinction between the 'purity' of the city's Western residents and the yellow skins of any 'visiting' Chinese.

But behind the face of Shanghai, as every Chinese knew, sat the same local forces that ruled the rest of the land: warlords, who saw the city as part of their own fiefdoms from which they dreamt of eventually 'uniting' the broken Chinese world; and the leaders of the secret brotherhood societies, whose 'families' owned almost every labouring man. Meanwhile, stuffed into factories, labouring hands were struggling more than ever. From time to time, erupting into protesting strikes, they were met with the barrels of guns.

With the whole country gripped by warlords of one stripe or another, a slavish poverty was gnawing at hundreds of millions of feet. Even as a glittering train was carrying those at the top to some of the greatest riches on earth, ever-greater tides of human misery were descending upon cities seen by every peasant as citadels of desperate hope. New Shanghai, old Beijing, those who could make a living within their streets were feasting on the crumbling heaven, even as those who could not were descending into the furnaces of hell. The past had gone. The new seemed foreign in every respect. Survival was becoming harder by the day, and the *ren* idea of being human was becoming ever more difficult to sustain. What China would become was anybody's guess – and everybody's question.

As the old struggled with the new, the young were grasping the future with an energy denied to their ancestors. Those who had studied abroad in the last tumultuous decades of the Qing, whether as exiles or voluntary voyagers, had finished their foreign courses and many had returned. Slightly older and wiser, they had not, though, lost the conviction of the earlier rebels that a new order was required. Kang Youwei's *Da Tong* dream of a great unity to free the people from the deadening chains of a deceiving empire had changed forever the way in which they saw their futures; the dreams of Tan Sitong, Kang Youwei and Liang Qichao – of a people as human beings who could think and act for themselves – had become a beacon for almost everyone. Back in the changed, and still changing, fortunes of the new Republic, however, the returned students encountered the rubble of a revolution that had clearly been hijacked and was now struggling to survive. Some turned around and sailed back to the foreign world; others anchored themselves in Shanghai. Both were places where the future seemed a little more secure. But many, looking at the warlording chaos all around, decided it was time for an educated Chinese mind to set itself the task of finally addressing the errors of the past in the hope that, this time, the future might be different. And, as the early revolutionaries had so clearly explained, if that was to happen, the people were going to have to find a voice.

Of the thousands who had come back and stayed, some of the most questioning minds found themselves swept into the vast imagination of a once-revolutionary by the name of Cai Yuanpei. After studying in Germany and France, Cai had returned to Beijing and in 1917 had taken up the presidency of Peking University. Known, after its red brick walls and its four storeys, as the *hong lou*, red building, it sat on a busy thoroughfare just a short walk from the Tiananmen Gate of Heavenly Peace. Sunlit trees sparkling on a small front lawn, from within its gates the outside chaos of Beijing was clear for all to see. Trams clattered past, rickshaws vied with mules and bicycles, bean-curd sellers plied their trade, swaggering soldiers shouted raucous jokes; and the thin hands of wretched beggars reached out for any possible passing coin.

Within the *hong lou*'s sturdy brick walls, however, life was quite another story. Corridors home to the energies of youth, eager voices chattered on their way to class. Lecture rooms regularly erupting in debating shouts, silence would suddenly fall to the mesmerising observations of some of Republican China's greatest masters of words and new ideas. One of the most loved of its teachers was a mind who had returned from America in 1917: a philosopher by the name of Hu Shi whose thoughtful brush, stroked across an intellectual page, had crafted an early call to think. As warlords were loading their cannons back and forth, and as the battles of the past seemed to be rewriting themselves by the day, Hu Shi's compelling characters had painted a thundering storm. 'Write with substance', he had argued, in one of the most authoritative of the new journals, 'don't imitate the ancients, eliminate old clichés, speak only when you have something to say and, above all, speak only what is in your heart – and only in the language of the time in which you live.' In short: tell the truth, as you see it.

Under Cai Yuanpei, Peking University became the energetic eye of the storm of new ideas that had been sweeping across China since the early 1900s. Carried back on the wings of students returning from abroad, written in letters sent to parents and friends, copied into pamphlets and newspapers for wider distribution, idea upon idea – now increasingly translated directly into Chinese – tumbled into the university's classrooms. After Liang Qichao had founded his *Xin Min, New Citizen*, journal from Tokyo in 1902, magazines and journals had spread like wildfire, introducing new and foreign ideas. In 1914, from a small group of Chinese students at Cornell University, a *Ke Xue, Science*, journal had appeared. Mailed, like *Xin Min*, direct to China, *Ke Xue* translated a whole new world of science for a country whose ideas had, until so recently, been firmly fixed on heaven. The following year, from within the foreign fortress of Shanghai, something even newer had been launched: a journal entitled *Xin Qingnian, New Youth*.

Founded by a philosophical revolutionary whose intoxicating thoughts had led thousands of hopeful hearts to imagine the toppling of the Qing, from its very first edition in 1915 *New Youth* was a call to the energies of a student youth. Opening with an article written by its founder, its pages described the power of the young to renew the old, and the responsibility of youth for shaking off the bonds of other people's ideas. In so doing, and for the first time ever in the all-under-heaven lands, it conjured up the idea of a student spirit: students at university; students at school; students from every walk of China's new life, high and low, including many of its new rich; students as ordinary people who just wanted to learn, as well as students who wanted to understand what a new world might be and where in that world they might find themselves. The philosophical revolutionary who founded *New Youth* was a man called Chen Duxiu. In 1917, Cai Yuanpei invited him to join Peking University as dean.

Ideas about the order of man were everywhere: what it was, what it wasn't, whether it could ever truly be found, how it might be built, and what the individual could do. Order and society, society and science, science and people, people and order: ideas from everywhere, and seemingly all at once. From the translations of earlier students who had gone abroad at the end of the nineteenth century, many returning as revolutionaries and then becoming teachers, the thoughts of distant foreign minds were once again conjured up for examination: Jean-Jacques Rousseau whose Social Contract paved the way for the French revolution; John Stuart Mill on liberty (the quintessential importance of the individual and the tyranny of the majority); Charles Darwin and natural selection (the 'tooth and claw' of survival in the natural world); Herbert Spencer on the 'survival of the fittest' (natural selection applied to the society of man, including both people and states); Thomas Huxley on evolution and ethics (why good is better than bad); Tolstoy's searing portraits of people whose lives had been changed by their times; Ibsen's heroes and heroines who challenged destiny, and sometimes won; Nietzsche on the nihilistic idea that the only truth was that of the scientific force of human will. Not to mention the man who had come up with the idea that had triggered the changes on which so many of the foreign ideas had been predicated: Adam Smith and his *Wealth of Nations* (why self-interest can be a positive good). And, of course, Karl Marx, whose idea of class struggle as the engine of social evolution had triggered the revolution that had turned Russia red.

Older ideas from abroad were quickly followed by new ones: Bertrand Russell's logical revolt against abstract ideals, and his passionate belief in the forging power of experience for human transformation; Einstein's insistence that science was a human endeavour – with human beings like the atoms on which everything depends, and human morality an essential part of any equation; James Joyce's *Ulysses*, which turned a country into a character of epic proportions; Shaw's transformation of theatre into moral debate; and John Dewey's ideas of education and the psychology of man (why the mind and voice of each individual human being is important, and why real change is never a sudden fact but always the slow result of an evolutionary sequence).

To all of these were added the great works of Chinese who had sacrificed so much for the dream of being human: Tan Sitong (the human conscience of individuals as the essential foundation of any truly independent state); Kang Youwei (a unity of people, rather than the deceiving and dividing powers of a single top-down mind); and Liang Qichao (a new people, informed by a responsible press, and supported by societies that the people, as human beings, would create themselves).

Across all of the ideas – the foreign and the Chinese alike – three common strands seemed to stand out as key to everyone's future: the empathetic conscience of man as a *ren*, human being; the 'science' of actual facts; and the essential importance of some form of 'democracy' as a means of ensuring that the voices of the people were able to keep a truly independent state on track. Tumbled together, the treasury of works – scientific, philosophical, political, literary, foreign and Chinese – came to be known as a 'New Culture'. Not 'culture' as a frivolous excursion to the opera, but culture as the crucible of ideas that made one both human and Chinese. New Culture as an essential component of what would be required to finally 'imagine a people.'

For Cai Yuanpei, as president of Peking University, the ideas translated into practical questions: what to teach, how to teach, and where? It seemed that one only had to open a magazine to find new knowledge splashed across a page – accompanied by the energetic debates of a quickly growing forest of Chinese minds. Highly educated, hungry for answers, impatient for change, all of the voices insisted that whatever new order arose, and however much it might be inspired by the myriad of ideas around the world, it would be nothing if it was not Chinese. The chaos of ideas was a garden of delights. But even knowledge needed an order of sorts – particularly one that had its sights set upon securing the independence of hundreds of millions of minds. Cai began with a university senate, grounding the pillars of thought in the principles, and responsibilities, of organisation that his liberated students would need to learn as their own societies grew.

To answer the question of what to teach, Cai opened up the doors of the *hong lou* and invited a pantheon of Chinese spirits to raise a powerhouse of ideas. Hu Shi had been beckoned to teach philosophy, with a department populated by thinkers drawn from worlds away. Liang Qichao was asked to make an occasional contribution of his thoughts on journalism and the building of a people. Back from Vassar, a female academic, Chen Hengzhe, was invited to teach the history of the West – the first woman to be given a lecturing voice. To these were added visiting Chinese authors who brought some of China's most powerful stories to life. By far the most electrifying, though, was a man who had taken the name of Lu Xun. A writer of novels and poetry, he was also the man whose creation of the 'critical essay' had inspired a generation to write with searing questions rather than quotes, and whose *Diary of a Madman* – a short story with a haunting image of China's imperial past as a cannibalistic deception that had eaten the country's youth – had filled everyone with a sense of the urgent need for change.

Cai then searched for a mind that could bring order to the clutter of journals, magazines, newspapers, books, and scripts that were now piling up in every direction. For this, a chief librarian was uncovered in a political economist with a deep interest in what it meant to be Chinese; his name was Li Dazhao. Freshly returned from Japan, with a talent for bringing the chaos of paper under filing rule, Li was an enthusiast of the Russian Revolution – indeed, he was famous for sending a congratulatory message to Moscow on the success of the recent Bolshevik triumph.

Faculty and library established, Cai Yuanpei looked at how to teach and where. Cai's ideas of learning went well beyond the narrow classroom and the library. In the gaps between lectures and the twilight evenings that followed, he seeded a sea of societies. Launched for everyone and anyone, student of Peking University or not, they gathered in a borrowed study here, on an open spread of grass there, or in a teahouse: wherever a conversation could be had. A Confucian society was created to pick at the fragments of the old ideas and see if the ancient principles held any surviving value for the new. A society for the cultivation of morality was launched to explore what might be possible in a world where every heavenly principle, and many human ones, seemed to have collapsed. A university press committee was founded; a society for painting and art appeared; a patriotic comrades' society for women took root; and a *hu zhu*, mutual aid, society opened new doors. The central point in a galaxy of new ideas, hub of the new magazines, journals and books that were turning thousands into students, Peking University became the place where everyone flocked to – even if it was only to touch the edges of its dreams.

Given the deep relationship between the university and the wave of ideas for a new Chinese future, the students and teachers of Peking University had watched with enormous interest when Liang Qichao had travelled thousands of miles to Paris to observe the Peace Conference the foreign powers had convened in Versailles in 1919. Committed to the dream of a Chinese state grounded in the dreams of its people, Liang wanted the foreigners to understand that, while the Republican government was too corrupt to speak for the people, the people were discovering a voice of their own. Letters written home soon showed the depths of the challenge. The foreign powers were squabbling among themselves, and it was clear that Europe and America had no understanding at all of what had been happening on the Chinese lands. Even more importantly, though, Liang described a Western abandonment of the very philosophies and values that had inspired the young Chinese: morality, it seemed, had been on a collision course with science; mechanistic thinking and materialism were leading many to fear the annihilation of the human spirit, and while individual authors painted high ideals, at the end of the First World War the weak were still the fodder of the rich.

Liang had spoken as loudly and clearly as he could. But when the 'great Western powers' had decided that Germany's Chinese 'possessions' were be transferred not to China but to a preferred Japan, it was clear that neither he nor the Chinese people had been able to speak loudly enough in a world that was obviously governed by the 'surviving fittest'. Back in Beijing, when the voices of rage rose in the burning protests of 4 May, many of Cai Yuanpei's most promising students had been among those swept off to jail; within months, Chen Duxiu would be arrested for his role in the protests, and forced to stand down as dean.

By the end of 4 May though, and for the first time in thousands of years, scholarly Chinese minds had found a public voice. Over the coming weeks, the voice would fly, first as letters to friends telling the tale of a spirit found, and then as a throbbing tide crashing against the biggest cities and the smallest towns, both north and south. The spirit was the old Hunanese idea of independence: an independent state, guaranteed by the independent minds of its people. And it was now firmly tied to the idea of a strong and unified nation, as free of meddling foreign powers as of its own corrupt officials. The throbbing tide was the old 'scattered tray of sand', which now included the voices of labourers and the minds of scholars who had become students, both raising the banners of *'Mr Science'* and *'Mr Democracy'* aloft with every wave. 'Science', as the empiricism that would ensure that no imperial scholars could bury truth in sleeves of silk. 'Democracy', as the voice of the people that would ensure that the human truth would always be told.

The great wave of protest on the late spring day did not bring down the government of the Republic. But in carrying intellectuals and labourers onto the streets of a common cause, it would become the tide of a May Fourth movement that would eventually sweep away every inch of the order of the old Chinese world.

In the heady aftermath of the 4 May protests, more students and would-be students flocked to Beijing. With its Peking University and its questioning minds, it was a once-imperial city that had become a citadel of ideas and a beacon of hope. Visitors also arrived from afar: intellectuals from all over the world, as eager to learn as to teach. Many were scholars, some were authors; a few were revolutionaries. And so it was that on a summer's day in 1920, a man from Moscow called upon the university's chief librarian, Li Dazhao. Representing Russia's newly established Communist International organisation (a 'Comintern', founded to forge a brotherhood of independent non-imperial states), the visitor had read Li Dazhao's congratulatory letter on the success of the Bolshevik revolution and wondered whether China might like a Communist Party of its own. Minds meeting, Li leapt at the suggestion, and Chen Duxiu (no longer dean of Peking University and now living in the relative freedom of Shanghai) was invited to lead the new Party organisation – and to spread the conversation to other Chinese cities selected for the launch of small Communist groups. Within months, the Party was established, with Li Dazhao and Chen Duxiu formally recorded as the Party's founders, and Chen Duxiu, the man with the most obviously revolutionary credentials, elected general secretary.

The first of what would become the Party's many 'Congresses' was planned for July, 1921. The sentinels of nervous and trigger-happy northern warlords across Beijing made the European-controlled Shanghai a safer city for the meeting; although even in Shanghai, secrecy seemed to be the best order of the day. In all, fifteen men came together on 23 July. Thirteen of the men were Chinese, representing the fifty-three individuals who had so far signed up to join the Chinese Communist Party; two were representatives of the Russian mothership, Comintern. Also attending, although rather on the sidelines, was Li's toweringly tall assistant librarian. Invited more for his enthusiasm than any Communist credentials, he was an odd fish. From Hunan, born in 1893 to a family of richer peasants rather than scholars, he seemed to have taken his education into his own hands, leaving the foothills of local schools for further studies in the provincial capital of Changsha. There, he had attached himself to a highly regarded scholar, the brother of one of the founders of the Citizen's Military Education Society (created in 1903 to train revolutionaries to kill), and a friend of Chen Duxiu. One thing had led to another: the highly-regarded scholar had gone to Beijing and in 1918 his pupil had followed, finding his way to the library shelves of Peking University. His name was Mao Zedong.

Permitted to sit at the margins of the university's Marxist Study Group, Mao found that his comments were invariably disregarded. Having been a student in Changsha in the spring of 1911, it was true that he had observed the violence of the first – accidental – revolution, but he had few if any Communist credentials. And although he seemed to have read a lot of the relevant literature, from Kang Youwei and Liang Qichao to the foreign ideas of Rousseau and Marx, and the all-important social Darwinian theories on the survival of the fittest in the battle of the human races, he seemed to have given little thought to much beyond his own education. Rather confusingly, he was also a devotee of the First Qin Emperor and of the destructive force with which the Qin people had been transformed into a brutal state – a devotion that was rather oddly combined with a passion for the stories of the Crouching Dragon, Zhuge Liang, the Monkey King, and the bandit *Outlaws of the Marsh*. Not surprisingly, his contributions always seemed to be a little offbeat. But as a native of Hunan, and with a useful pair of hands, in 1920, he had been given the chance to open a bookshop in Changsha to sell the Party's literature. By the time of the Party's first Congress in 1921, the bookshop had found its feet. A

Hunanese twang, a clumsy education and an admiration of the wilder ways notwithstanding, perhaps this was a man who could get a few things done.

———

Back in Peking University, at the time of Comintern's initiation of the Communist Party, the order of everything had still been a matter for debate. In the avalanche of ideas that had arrived from across the world, many of the big things seemed certain and were fairly easily agreed upon by almost everyone: nationalists, Communists, reformers, intellectuals, and even the few remaining Confucians. A stable government that did not suppress, arrest or kill its youth was obviously required. A written constitution that protected the people from the risk of any imperialist ruler putting themselves above the law, was key. Also essential was an objective and empirical science with which a modern nation would be able to raise the industries that could employ the people and strengthen the state – and with which, after nearly two thousand years, 'things' could finally be truly 'investigated'. At the heart of the investigation would be, as it had been at the accidental revolution, the question of how to create a people who accepted a responsibility both for their own personal actions and for the security of the state, including the welfare of all the other people who lived in it.

Other things, however, were neither quite so clear nor so easily agreed. How, in the grip of warlords and in the face of an ambitiously rising Japan, could China navigate its way back to statehood – let alone create a constitution that could both proclaim rights *and* protect them? How, with its broken and starving people, could the country's human hearts be lifted above their misery, and their minds be freed to build a new and better world? And, most importantly of all, how, after millennia of a seemingly inevitable cycle of all-under-heaven rises and falls, could the dream of heaven be finally fixed to the Pole Star of the people's will? United on many of the fundamentals, to these more difficult questions, nationalism and Communism offered very different answers, not to mention the wider competing claims of a now-humbled Confucianism, as well as an early anarchism that continued to attract.

As the competing claims were bandied back and forth, Peking University's department of philosophy proposed two interesting but quite different ideas. The first idea was offered by Hu Shi, who brushed another article with a self-explanatory name: *Study More Problems, Talk Less of 'Isms'*. Noting that progress is not achieved in an evening, Hu urged his friends and peers to see civilisation as a patient study in solving problems: 'Bit by bit, drop by drop, one by one'. China and her people would need to find their own way and, like the crossing of any great river, there was not a map or an 'ism' to guide them: everyone would need to feel their best way forward, using whatever stones they could find.

The second idea was offered by one of the rare surviving Confucianists, a man called Liang Shuming. Having spoken to many visiting foreigners, and having read the reports of Liang Qichao (no relation) on his journeys across the wastelands of post-war Europe, Liang Shuming said that he had been struck by the European idea of science as separate from human morality – and urged his fellow minds to think twice before following the West on a course that might carry everyone over a cliff. Reflecting on the warnings carried in Liang Qichao's letters from Europe to home, Liang Shuming cast his thoughts back across the history of great civilisations, and to the 'human will' that had shaped them.

There were, Liang Shuming said, three great wills in the history of mankind – expressed by three great but very different people. The first was the will of the West: a world where man saw himself as having a duty to tackle nature. The second was the will of Oriental China: a world where man felt an obligation to bend to nature. The third was Asian India: a world where man set aside his will, and recognised that his only true nature was the inner, and also greater, cosmic self. For Liang Shuming, these were not so much competing perspectives, but rather an evolutionary sequence that would unfold, rather like a novel, across the future span of human time. The Western beginning was man's engagement in a righteous battle of nature-taming reason. The Chinese middle was where man bent his own desires to a greater natural order grounded in the harmony of all. And the Indian end was the understanding that the physical world, of both man and nature, was an illusion.

Seen as an apologist for the Confucianism that had been used to justify thousands of years of a single top-down imperial rule, Liang's ideas were swiftly dismissed by the students. As were India's illusions, presented by the mesmerising figure of Rabindranath Tagore but considered to offer nothing but a distraction from the important task of revolutionising the order of man. And while Liang Qichao and Liang Shuming had both urged caution in pursuing Western science without considering the importance of a human morality, it seemed to many of the Beijing minds that only the impartial objectivity of science could prevent a return to the arbitrariness of imperial power.

Debates about order and civilisation followed, and in 1923, a powerful mind at Beijing's other great university, Tsinghua, stepped forward with an observation of his own on the question of science and morality. His name was Zhang Junmai. Agreeing with Liang Qichao and Liang Shuming on the importance of the question of science and humanity, Zhang noted that, while the objective powers of empirical science had a value, science without the subjective moral compass of human feelings would be a dangerous thing. Within days, a geologist-biologist by the name of Ding Wenjiang swept off a searing reply. Science, Ding retorted, was nothing if not absolute, and to think otherwise was to open the door to a return of the imperialism of the past. Liang Shuming was mistaken: there was only one world to be considered, and that was the material one which could be objectively measured. And as far as risks to the ordering civilisation of man were concerned, the greatest risk was a failure to understand that subjective human feelings and beliefs, irreconcilable with the objective facts of a material life, were a danger.

With both positions published in *New Youth*, the arguments of Zhang Junmai and Ding Wenjiang were marshalled for everyone to consider. Few were in any doubt as to the importance of the question: was order dependent on the quality of morality and the human heart, or was it simply an empirical challenge to be met by the scientific talents of the mind? At stake was everyone's future: which of these two competing ideas would be most likely to ensure that the single top-down mind of the imperial past would never be able to return?

Backwards and forwards the characters raged, with *New Youth* and its pages the battleground and not an end in sight. Eventually, Liang Qichao stepped in. Trying to bring peace to the bitterly divided factions, he insisted that he had never said that science had no value, only that human feelings and science needed to be looked at together. Ding Wenjiang's fury was not assuaged. Flourishing an inky full stop, he proclaimed that human feelings had no place in science. At which point, Hu Shi added some ink of his own. Worried that a world which accepted subjectivity could toss China back to the heavenly superstitions of its imperial, Confucian and even Daoist past, he reluctantly decided to agree with Ding Wenjiang.

As the battle of man and science raged in the corridors of the universities, out on the streets, the cannons of military power were getting louder by the year, with the cleansing energies of military censors increasingly following suit. After the 4 May arrests, the tightened security led to a constant student fear that any mind seeming to question the fragile authority of the guns could be snatched off the street at will. Those at greatest risk were students with an interest in the new Communist Party: clearly contemplating a second revolution, and obviously training young bodies for the cause, the Party was seen as the shadow behind an increasing number of uprisings and strikes. But even with the risk of an arrest, and the likelihood that an arrest would result in a brutal punishment, the Party's ranks of student members were growing. Chilled by the changes in the political air, in 1922 Cai Yuanpei had returned to the foreign world to think about what might come next. Peking University's students and faculty carried on, but Beijing's clouds continued to darken, and judging by the news reaching the capital, events in the increasingly militarised south were threatening an even greater risk.

Having resurrected the Guomindang in 1919, and headquartered it as a southern government in the Guangdong capital of Guangzhou, Sun Yatsen now presided over a dream that had become an army. With competing warlords in control of many parts of the country, Sun had then looked for outside support and found it in a friendship with the new Communist Russia, a country with a Party that had demonstrated an ability both to launch a revolution and to keep the revolutionary victors in power. Sun had been as keen to learn from Moscow as Chen Duxiu had been happy to accept Comintern's invitation to found a Chinese Communist Party. And, concerned that such a large and important neighbour as China should not fall victim to the guns or the charms of either the still-imperial West, or the rising Japan,

Moscow was happy to hedge its bets and support more than one party for success. That said, looking at the military force of the Guomindang and the youthful idealism of the new Chinese Communist Party, a rising Stalin concluded that the chances of a successful second revolution would be stronger if the Guomindang and the Chinese Communist Party were to join together.

Members of both parties, Guomindang and Communist, had their doubts, to say the least. Those within the Guomindang responsible for raising funds from Chinese industrialists were shocked at the idea of an alliance with a reckless group of Communists who wanted to bring down the very factory foundations of *fuqiang*, wealth and power, on which any strong Chinese state would depend. Almost everyone within the Communist Party was equally shocked at the idea of an alliance with a militaristic group of capitalists, who were nothing but bourgeois self-strengtheners. Some within the Communist Party even ventured to suggest that Russia's experience of a Moscow-led rebellion was, in any event, hardly relevant: after the failure of the accidental 1911 revolution launched from the city of Wuchang, surely the ultimate Chinese uprising was far more likely to come from the countryside.

Within the Guomindang, Sun Yatsen dismissed his doubters with a reminder that Russian help would be essential in evicting the foreign imperial powers from China's lands. He had also noted that, wherever the Russian revolution might have come from, it was the force of Lenin's organising skills that had transformed the energies of an uprising into the iron power of a solid state.

Within the Communist Party, Chen Duxiu addressed his own doubters with a lecture on Marx, a personal observation and a fact. Marx, Chen noted, had not only been clear that revolutions always came out of cities, but in describing the stages necessary for every society to pass through on its way to a Communist utopia, he had expressly stated that it was essential that the old feudalism be replaced with an industrial capitalism that would trigger the laboring classes to rebel. To this, Chen added his view (shared by many in a young Communist Party whose founders and members had been drawn from among China's most highly educated minds) that, whatever Marx might have said, any future China would need to include not only the laboring classes but also the intellectuals who had become the new conscience of China, as they were the driving force of the new Party. Given that finding solutions in difficult times required education and the luxury of time to work out what to do, they would also naturally need support from the self-strengthening bourgeois classes that were the bedrock of the Guomindang. To all of this, Chen added a final practical argument: although the selfish capitalists of the Guomindang would eventually be ground into the dust in the eventually successful revolution, their skills and experience in the art of war, not to mention their guns, would be essential if the Communists were ever to defeat the warlords.

In 1923, Moscow brought the Guomindang and the Communist Party together in a 'United Front'. Cash, and an education in the Leninist mechanics that kept revolutionary parties in power, were offered to both. Meanwhile, the Guomindang was instructed to invite the younger Communist brothers to join their Whampoa Military Academy in Guangzhou, and the young Communists were instructed to turn up. Sun Yatsen then despatched the most trusted of his own younger men to Moscow to learn both the art of winning wars and that of securing enduring political power. So close became the co-operation with the Chinese Communist Party, and so promising were some of the young Communists, that the Guomindang even welcomed some of their most talented members into its own official ranks.

It was not long, however, before the differences in the dreams had begun to tell. When Sun Yatsen's most favoured student returned from Moscow to lead the Whampoa Academy, he declared that the combination of proletarian Marxism and iron-will Leninism with which the Russian Communist Party ruled its state, was not for China. While Confucianism might have failed in many ways, the ideals of personal virtue and family harmony were far too deeply rooted for such a brutal discipline to prevail; the only way that China would be able to tame her warlords *and* defeat the foreign imperial powers would be to learn from the lessons of the nineteenth-century self-strengtheners, and build the *fuqiang*, wealth and power, that would eventually conquer all. Born Jiang Jieshi in the province of Zhejiang, to the West that learnt his name through the Cantonese tongue, he would come to be known as Chiang Kai-shek.

Chiang's pronouncement split the Guomindang. Some continued to support Sun's pragmatic alliance with Moscow and its Chinese

Communist Party. Others, particularly the industrialists on whose support the Guomindang depended heavily, sided with Chiang, insisting that the Russian Communists were barbarians, and that the Chinese Communists were nothing but wolves in their midst.

Before the dust could settle, though, in 1925 Sun Yatsen died from his own longer battle with cancer. And while a lefter leaning rival succeeded him as chairman of the Guomindang's southern National Government, it was Chiang, as commander-in-chief of the Guomindang's National Revolutionary Army, who had the power to change the lie of the land.

In 1926, with warlords still at large, and the Guomindang and the Communist Party bound together in their United Front, Chiang Kai-shek announced a 'Northern Expedition' to storm the north from the south. Nearing warlord-controlled Shanghai in March 1927, the Communist brothers were asked to raise workers' militias in diversionary strikes. As the strikes were unleashed, the righter wing of the Guomindang argued that there was little point in success if it brought down the very industrial pillars that were supporting them. With his sights firmly set on a self-strengthened China that would be able to tame the warlords, get the foreigners out of China's lands, and ensure that she was 'fit to survive', Chiang decided that the time had come to cleanse the country of the Communist dream.

So it was that on 12 April, 1927, as the forces of the United Front arrived at the outskirts of the Chinese quarters of Shanghai, Chiang Kai-shek commanded the Communist flanks under his command to lead the advance, in concert with the organised militia of the city's workers. With secret orders already delivered to the Triad brotherhoods, and with the silent support of the foreign powers, he then ordered his own Guomindang battalions to swoop down upon the Communists and the workers' militias alike. Launching what would come to be known as a 'White Terror', across the following days, the Triads and the Guomindang purged the city of its Communists, union members, brothers-in-arms and anyone else known for their left-leaning sympathies. Three hundred were executed; a thousand died. Over the weeks and months that followed, convinced that Communism would tear up the material foundations of a future industrial Chinese state, Chiang turned his sights to tracking down every other heart that looked as if it might be Communist, across the land and within the

Guomindang – and executing it. Within a year, hundreds of thousands had been pursued to their deaths.

Shattered by the betrayal, surviving Communists did their best to find each other and regroup. But by the end of 1927, the Party was in tatters. Li Dazhao had been captured by a warlord and executed; Chen Duxiu had been forced to resign for the fatal error of recommending the Party's collaboration with the Guomindang. Meanwhile, a still minor Mao Zedong, increasingly captivated by the scientific possibilities of revolutionary destruction – and always keen on country guerrilla ways – suggested that he be given an army of peasants to raise an autumn harvest uprising in Hunan. The uprising struggled to take off and then fell, but Mao was able to secure the all-important charge of a troop of men. Advancing further south and up to the protecting mountains that sat between the provinces of Jiangxi and Fujian, Mao led them to a safer haven in a desolate place known as Jinggangshan, the Jinggang Mountains.

With the heavenly order once again divided, Chiang Kai-shek marched on.

When the Guomindang arrived in Beijing in 1928, they did not bring quite the kind of order the city had hoped for. The incumbent warlord was defeated, but it was clear to Chiang Kai-shek that other warlords were simply waiting in the wings. With the Guomindang's forces now severely stretched, it was hard to see how they could be kept at bay. A series of reluctant alliances with the most amenable of the warlords seemed the best bet of all bad options, and with these settled, Chiang, now elevated to top of the Guomindang, moved what little remained of the Republican government south, to the old Ming capital of Nanjing. As the government's offices moved, so did its remaining officials. With Beijing's fortunes already fragile, many wondered how the city would survive.

Then, in 1931, the Japanese declared a new land in the Chinese north. Already occupying the old Manju capital of Mukden, Shenyang, together with the wider once-Manju lands of Liaodong, including the eastern part of Inner Mongolia, Tokyo declared a new Manjuguo state, Manchuria; the discarded Manju Prince and last Qing emperor, Puyi, was invited to be its monarch. By 1933, the lands around Beijing were not only home to fluctuating corps of Guomindang-allied warlords, but were also under the sights of nearby Japanese guns.

Northern fields trampled to dust and any dreams of a heavenly peace buried in fear, yet more refugees began to flood into the once-imperial capital for a future that could surely be no worse than their past. Many of the incomers turned to pulling the rickshaws that had once roved the streets and lanes: so many, that a trade which had once provided a living wage now struggled to offer even survival. Others found their way to factories that flickered in the half-life of sixteen-hour days, seven-day weeks, at wages that could scarcely clothe and feed. With every hand hungry, even children queued for work. Rag-picking became a jealously guarded profession; many survived on the bones of someone else's meal; soup kitchens became a fixture. And from time to time, misery would break out in bands of brotherly feeling, complete with uprisings and strikes.

Meanwhile, across the country, Chiang Kai-shek was reinforcing his guns with a combination of the social Darwinian idea of the survival of the fittest on the one hand, and the princples of Confucius on the other, into a new mantra for a Guomindang Nationalist state: a 'New Life' movement for a return to the ancient morality that had always been grounded in the self-cultivation of both rulers and the ruled. Telegraphing extracts from Confucius' *Analects* to government officials, city industrialists and the supporting gentry across the countryside, he exhorted them all to follow four key virtues in daily life for the wellbeing of the individual and society and for the survival of the state: *li*, the ritual of proper rites; *yi*, integrity as righteousness and justice; *lian*, honesty and cleanliness; and *chi*, a sense of right and wrong. Urged to to rediscover Zeng Guofan's self-strengthening spirit, everyone was also reminded that, in the words of Confucius, 'When the wind moves, the grass bends'. Responsibility and discipline were all. However new anyone might think they were, officials and people alike were instructed to strengthen the state with the self-cultivating power morality, and to apply themselves to the established hierarchies of order. Once again, however, as the self-strengtheners' wealth and power rose, so crept corruption, and so spread the desperation that forced others to sell their children on the street.

What to do? Over the next four years, the question echoed around the now fading teahouses, batted back and forth across tables that had seen better times. A Chinese world without a Son of Heaven had been shock enough. A Chinese world without a heavenly family had seemed a recipe for chaos. But a nation of individuals all selfishly fending for themselves? And a city where everyone might technically be a citizen but where the very fabric of life that made them human had disappeared? Beijing's orderly past was gone. Memories had already been lost, along with the imperial gates and the walls that had carried them. Crafting skills were disappearing without a trace of ink to hold their light. And while Sun Yatsen's last-century dream of a nation of people, guided by a constitution which provided for the wellbeing of all, had once captured the popular imagination, with a million people in Beijing, four hundred million in the rest of the country, and guns everywhere, it was difficult to see how it could possibly come true.

There were, however, some cheerier spirits. Looking at the relics of Beijing's imperial beauty, these wondered if the city's treasures might be able to create a future not just for the city but for its human beings as well. If Beijing could not find the industries that seemed to keep other cities afloat, why not trade in the past and all of its memories? Itinerant carts with *dagu*, drums, were already soliciting the unwanted past, turning it into second-hand items and antiques to pay for the present. Surely, abandoned palaces and temples could be reopened for visiting souls? Thinking about the value of the old, the mayor of Beijing had an idea: why not offer the city and its imperial dreams as a story to sell? Turn the old crafts to the tune of new customers: outsiders, whether foreigners or even other Chinese, who might not have that special Beijing ability to see the meaning in every detail but who would surely love the tales that had been woven into the hearts of every *Beijing ren.*

The tapestry was certainly rich. The kitchen god, who made an annual new year report to the celestial Jade Emperor (and the honey that everyone applied to his lips to make sure the family fortunes would be safe for the year to come). Cai Shen, the god of wealth, who stole from the rich and gave to the poor, riding in on a black tiger and shooting his enemies with pearls that burst like bombs on impact. There were even stories in the dust that annually stormed the city, straight from the sands of the stretching deserts beyond. Then there was everything else that Beijing had to sell: gliding swallows with whistles tied to their backs, turning blue skies into song; pomegranate trees with goldfish bowls guaranteeing families of sons; red everywhere for luck. Twelve ways to cook a fish; sixteen ways to eat a chicken; sweet and sour plum sauce; noodles with a special heavenly flavour; candied fruits skewered on a stick; not to mention the special spring pancakes rolled in sesame oil. All treasures that only Beijing knew how to make. Operas with swishing sleeves, rolling eyes and clanging gongs; the market at Tianqiao with its puppets and stilts in eye-commanding colours; astrologers who could see the fortunes of the future; story-tellers with clappers to catch the ear; songs that told the tales of centuries; mechanical mice which jumped at the tickle of a hair; bird-shaped lanterns that flapped their wings – Beijing had it all. Surely somebody would want to buy? But try as hard as the dreamers might, it soon became clear that midnight could not be postponed.

In July 1937, a Japanese wind swept past the Long Wall and made its way down to Beijing. Circling the city, just like the yellow sands that dusted Beijing's streets with their storms, the wind choked off food and supplies. It was only a matter of time before the city would fall to the Japanese idea of order.

Some chose to stay, accepting the future with a Daoist resignation. Others wanted to leave, but where to go? To the new Guomindang capital of Nanjing? To a Shanghai that seemed to have become an imperialist New York? For the hardiest youth, the choices even included a new Communist city, founded in the caves of a far-off place called Yan'an.

Back at the Zhengyang Gate of the Zenith South, the railway station heaved with uncertainty and confusion. Willow and pigskin suitcases battled with baskets, bedding and pots. Fathers and sons, wives and daughters, surviving maids and servants: all tumbled on to the trains. The heavenly order was long gone. The city and its people were moving – but no one was quite sure where.

CHAPTER 2
A BRAVE NEW WORLD

The Golden Monkey wrathfully swung his massive cudgel,
And the jade-like firmament was cleared of dust.

Mao Zedong (1961)

A S THE RED CURTAIN parted, five thousand pairs of wondering eyes looked up from the near-dark of the war god's temple.
With little room to breathe, let alone move, bodies were locked in
concentration and hearts were spellbound by the sights before them.
Singing the *Rice-planting Song*, and stepping the *Defeat Japan Dance*,
the energies unleashed on the stage before them seemed to know no
bounds. Somewhere on the makeshift boards there was supposed to
be a famous face, someone called Ding Ling – a writer *and* a woman.
But it was hard to tell in the blaze of so many brightly performing faces. As the bombs pounded outside, the sights and sounds
of the stage were enough to help everyone set aside their troubles
for an evening's delight: brothers and sisters gone to heaven could
be momentarily forgotten, and tomorrow's food was a problem for
another day.

For the performing troupe of the Front Service Corps of the 8th
Route Army it was a night like many others, only bigger and the culmi-
nation of a journey that had begun months before. Donkeys loaded
to the limit, they had left the caves of Yan'an in August, following
the waters of the Yan to its Yellow River master. Passing through the
seasons, red banners had first flapped in soft breezes, then whipped
into autumn winds. Crossing rivers by stones, advancing to the front
line of the province of Shanxi, they had worked their way across a
fragment of China's vast north-eastern lands: *Heijiapu*, black family
store; *Yancheng*, salt city; *Zhangjiatan*, family rapids; *Heishanguan*, black
mountain pass. Wherever they had gone, men, women and children,
dressed in the tattered straw and the handwoven cotton of the land,

had flocked to their path, eyes filled with hunger but hearts brimming with hope.

The Front Service Corps had not been the first to pass along the way. Red volunteers had come before them: unbinding women's feet, tracing characters on sandy ground, teaching skills that would stretch the land to feed its people, and standing up to landlords who had once ruled all under their own particular spot of heaven but were now being sent to the bottom of the peasant pile. By the October night when the performing troops arrived at the war god temple in the city of Linfen (a major stopping point on the prized railway that was attracting so much of Japan's exploding military might), they had seen the Communist countryside and it was good. As their voices strained to reach the furthest listening rafters of the full-to-bursting temple, and as their feet jumped to the beat of a revolutionary song, victory seemed only a leap away.

Arriving in the Jinggang Mountains in late 1927, Mao Zedong had set his company of followers to the task of creating a Communist stronghold of their own. Battered by competing instructions from the surviving upper echelons of the Party's Central Committee, he applied a set of his own ideas: grounded on the historical example of the First Qin Emperor, touched with his own observations of the rough violence of the 1911 revolution and its following years, and shaped by his own thoughts on Marx and Moscow. Keen to make his mark, the results included local rallies to celebrate the arrival of his forces with public executions of landlords.

The Party had been a little uncertain about the maverick that had sprung from their midst, but with Communists constantly at risk of arrest and execution in the wider Chinese world, news of Mao's stronghold spread and new recruits began to arrive. When one of the largest units of the newly formed 'Red Army' came looking for refuge, his wild outpost acquired a certain standing, and even Moscow, still banker to the Party and the Guomindang, took note. Soon the Jinggang Mountain base was struggling to hold the rising tide of refugees and Mao's revolutionary ambition. In 1929, Mao moved the base to join up with another of the Red Army's units, further south and deeper into the mountainous province of Jiangxi.

As competing ideas of the Communist dream collided, battles arose about whose Party it was. Sheltered by the mountain mists, Mao applied his own revolutionary principles, touched with a hint of Qin: whispers were spread, red blood ran, traitors were hunted out and destroyed, dissenting voices were silenced and eventually Mao's idea of local unity prevailed (although it would take over a decade and a half of intrigues and campaigns to truly vanquish the other Communist ideas). With Moscow's treasury watching, greater Party powers began to find their way to Mao's red enclosure. In November 1931, Mao proclaimed Jiangxi as a 'Chinese Soviet Republic', with the county town of Ruijin as its capital. Within a month, the highly educated and much admired political commissar of the Party, Zhou Enlai, arrived to assume command. Soon, the earth below was ringing to rumours of a Communist state hidden in the mountains. And as the Soviet Republic of Jiangxi swelled, Chiang Kai-shek turned the sights of his forces to encircling a Communist stronghold that seemed to have appeared out of nowhere.

By 1933, with nearly a hundred thousand men, women and children in the Jiangxi Soviet, more of the Party's leaders were beginning to arrive. Looking at the skies of Guomindang planes, they soon realised it would be only a matter of time before Chiang Kai-shek destroyed them. Snatching at Mao's maps, they decided to move: not only eighty-six thousand of the people who were deemed fit to march but the pots and pans, the files and field phones that made up the daily necessities of life and the furniture of the Party's order. Thanked for his efforts, but with his voice now diminished by a Party suspicion of his Hunanese twang and his country-guerrilla ways, Mao and his then, third, wife were attached to the tail of a march that some suspected might be very long indeed. Departing in October 1934, over the next 370 days and more, navigating some of China's harshest nature, encountering tribes that no one had ever heard of, pushed to the edge of their own existence and humanity, the first of the walked six thousand circling miles from south to west and north. A year later, in October 1935, the first of the surviving fittest arrived on the northern plains of China, in a once-proud and ancient city that had shrunk to a remote and isolated market town. Surrounded by soft loess mountains where almost everyone lived in caves, its name was Yan'an.

Between leaving and arriving on what would come to be known as the 'Long March', seventy-eight thousand fell by one wayside or another. Traipsing in and out of some of China's remotest provinces, the marchers had passed through the hunger of lands where food was nothing but a dream, under burning sun, through piercing hail, freezing snow, and with almost constant clouds of senior squabbles about direction, tactics, and survival.

As they marched, Mao Zedong worked his way up from the tail to the front, seemingly propelled by a superior grasp of strategy in the unpredictable terrain of the wild, although those closest to him were less convinced. With lectures offered to everyone who followed him, he seemed to have a deep appreciation of the harsh lessons that needed to be learnt from the past, including a high regard for the calculating ruses that had led to the triumphs of the ancient Qin. The costs to the Long Marchers were high, but the Moscow treasury, which was funding all, seemed pleased with progress. Victory seemingly snatched from the jaws of defeat, and a number of messy internal battles resolved, upon arriving in Yan'an, the Communist Party acquired a new Soviet Republic in the north-east, led by its new chairman: Mao Zedong. The greatest prize, however, was a story to end all stories: the triumph of red hearts over almost every adversity that man and nature could contrive. As the survivors, now joined by rivers of new recruits, began to carve themselves into the caves of the new Soviet-city, Mao was wondering who might be able to tell it.

When, in 1927, Chiang Kai-shek had launched the anti-Communist pogrom across the country's cities, not everyone had fled. One of those who had stayed in Beijing was an impecunious young poet by the name of Hu Yepin. An ardent Communist, he was also the lover of a young writer, Ding Ling, who, having captured the newly independent female spirit in the pages of one of China's most popular novels, found herself clasped to the heart of China's youth. Travelling to a Shanghai which was now twitching with guns of its own, despite keeping to his own shadows, Hu Yepin fell to the greater forces of the dark. Arrested on the orders of the Guomindang, on the night of 7 February 1931, he was executed with a shot.

Within a year, Ding Ling had penned his story. And having pitched the first of many young stars into the constellation of the Communist

Party's heroes, she found herself seen as an inspiration by thousands of young Communist hearts, and marked as a threat by the warlords and the Guomindang. Two years later, she was placed under a house arrest that would last for three years until, in 1936, a band of Communist brothers arrived to help her escape. Disguised as a Guomindang soldier, accompanied by some of her rescuers, Ding Ling, the heroine of so many dreams, carried her pen to the sanctuary of the new Communist city in Yan'an. Pushing her way on mule and by foot across the gruelling miles to her destination, wondering not only whether she would ever get there but whether, even if she did, the Communist dream could possibly survive, she constantly remembered the final characters with which she had brushed her tribute to Hu Yepin: 'When will it be light?'

When Ding Ling eventually arrived in Yan'an, the now-chairman Mao was clear about the nature of the treasure that had appeared from the dark. Famous for her works and her dazzling circle of literary friends, Ding Ling had the power to tell a story and make it real. By 1938, two years after Moscow had once again pushed the troops of the Guomindang and the Communist Party to unite in order to defeat what it considered to be the greater Japanese foe, hers was a talent that had become one of the greatest prizes in a Communist armoury now fixed on a propaganda battle against the Guomindang idea. Looking out across the vast expanses of the old Chinese world which had yet to be touched by the Communist dream, Mao decided to despatch Ding Ling to the performing boards of the front line in the company of the Front Service Corps of the 8th Route Army. Arriving back in Yan'an in late 1938, her mission accomplished, Ding Ling's literary senses had been sharpened by a first-hand understanding of the lie of China's land. Like every other new arrival, she was then sent to the Party's Revolutionary Central School to train her mind.

Taught by brothers returned from Moscow, Ding Ling found that she was listening to the lectures of new Yan'an friends who were also rising Party stars. One was the powerful Party secretary for all of northern China, Liu Shaoqi, who delivered a directive text entitled *How to be a Good Communist*. The lesson was apparently simple: at all times and on all matters, take account of the Party's interests as a whole, and put them above any possible personal considerations or ideas. Beyond the formal lessons and across the many quiet evenings,

Mao Zedong added personal thoughts of his own, largely delivered over the dinner table in the cave that he shared with his new, fourth, wife, Jiang Qing, a young actress recently arrived from Shanghai.

Away from the front, Ding Ling found that time in Yan'an passed slowly, particularly for the thousands of highly educated young intellectuals who had arrived. Students of all ages, artists, authors, historians, poets, scientists, doctors, lawyers, economists, linguists and every other mind that could be imagined: many had fled the 1937 advances of Japan, particularly its bombardment of Shanghai; all had come to build a new and stronger China. Ding Ling noticed that not all of those who arrived were permitted to stay; some minds, apparently too rooted in bad old ways of thought, were discarded or returned. Those who stayed were given a Communist education, and set to their appointed tasks. Some were despatched to carry out peasant education and land reform. Many of the men marched to wherever the northern front had most recently moved. Left behind, their wives – women who were only following battle-commanding husbands – found themselves, like so many others sitting behind the lines, with little to do.

From the multitudes who successfully passed through the revolutionary education, Ding Ling found herself among the chosen few who were offered a cave, a clackety typewriter, and a chance to describe the new world. Looking at those around her, she watched as the organisations of the new Party city grew from within the caves. There was a central committee to craft the decisions of the day, and a Party school that would make sure that intellectual minds understood the rules of Mao's order, while forging more detailed socialist principles for the future. There was also a *Liberation Daily*, a newspaper to tell Yan'an what was going on at home and abroad, a journal to tell the tales of a Communist life, and a Propaganda Department, whose job was to tell the story of the Party and its Yan'an caves, to teach the new young Communists the Party line, and to tap out the Communist promise of a brave new world across the wires of the land. The dream was for a revolutionary order delivered not by a single man or even by a top-down government, but by a unity of the mass of the people at large. A challenge indeed.

With so many beings, all in such a remote location, and with those behind the lines not always having enough to do, Ding Ling found that authors and editors were everywhere in demand: a policy here, a story there, a poster to catch an eye, not to mention essays to teach the new Communist lessons. And everywhere, writers were required to make sure that '*i*'s were dotted, '*t*'s crossed, and that intellectual logic kept up with the Communist page. But with the Party's institutions telling everybody not only what to do but what to think, Ding Ling also noticed that questions were beginning to play like fountains, particularly for the authors and artists who, like herself, had been trained to look for the truth on which any human order surely depended.

As far as Ding Ling could see, contradictions were everywhere. While almost everyone had risked life and limb to get to Yan'an, the Party spirit whose word she was supposed to be spreading seemed to be floundering on many fronts. As an overzealous top seemed to be trying to reorder everyone's ideas, loose-ended minds were making an industry out of idle chatter, with those offended being quick to rally troops in their support. Meanwhile, leaders of the front (and the rear) appeared to find a ready supply of new wives, pushing first choices far from inconvenient sight. Food and pay gravitated to the top. Democracy appeared to have twisted into a funny turn where only some votes seemed to count. And equality seemed to have been upended, with some people very clearly at the top, and a lot of others focused only on how to climb up after them. Blind bureaucracy was everywhere; and some people (particularly Mao) just talked and talked. While it wasn't always obvious what they meant, there seemed to be a rule that everyone had to listen to them. Where in this new city of caves, Ding Ling wondered, was the dream of being human?

Finding their feet in a confusing new world, the authors and artists began to ask their questions out loud. What exactly was the Party's position on science and democracy? And why was it that the Party was constantly telling everybody not just what to do but what to think? Mao, the one-time assistant librarian, now chairman of the Communist Party and in charge of achieving a revolution, listened. And as he so often did with everything, he gave a series of lecturing lessons in reply. Starting with science and democracy, he explained that the two were really one and the same thing. To which he added that, in the new scientific world, the goal was not the messy 'old democracy' of the National Assembly on which the Republic had clearly floundered but a New Democracy on which a successful revolution could be built. New Democracy was apparently as simple as a scientific equation: in the new Communist world, there was only one truth, which was the truth of facts. The facts of such a new world could either be made by evolution or by revolution. Communism was committed to the path of revolution. And the primary fact on which the new Communist world would be built was the will of the mass of the people (the working and peasant classes) to rule – as a result of which, the state would eventually wither away. The Communist Party being the vanguard of the people, the will of the people was of course the mind of the Party. Any other mind was an enemy. As Nietszche had pointed out, the only real truth was the scientific force of the people's will.

As far as telling everybody what to think was concerned, the answer to that, Mao noted, must surely be self-evident. It was, once again, a matter of science – with objectivity being everything, and subjectivity being the greatest danger of all. Obviously the only true revolutionary thought was the objectively scientific one that reflected the real will of the mass of the people. Liberalism, with all of its bourgeois ideas about the importance of the individual, was nothing but a subjectivity that had to be combated as the enemy of the people's will. The greatest risk of subjectivity was that the scholarly minds always used twisting ideas to trick the masses into settling for a past in which they were endlessly trodden underfoot. But the revolution had declared war on the past with its highly educated minds winning wars of words with claptrap. Naturally, therefore, the Party would need to teach those intellectuals who wanted to serve the revolution what to think.

Drawing his lectures to a close, Mao suggested that those who wasted their time on questioning and complaining should take a look at the wars: the war of the classes, the war with the Guomindang and the war with the Japanese, with Chinese men, women and children dying real Chinese deaths. Freedom was nothing more than the understanding of historical necessity, and the use of that understanding to change the world. Darwin and Spencer had understood it, with their ideas of the survival of the fittest; and the First Qin Emperor had understood it long before them, bringing an end to the era of the Warring States and unifying the lands that had become the Republic of China. Of course, Mao concluded, the Party and Yan'an could always improve. But the real battle was bigger than most understood: it was not just a battle between the classes of the workers and the peasants on the one hand, and bourgeois landlords and intellectuals on the other, it was a battle between the old individual self and a new revolutionary being who understood that the triumph of the masses was the prize.

Ding Ling took her notes. But like many of the authors and the cleverer minds, she found them a little hard to understand. The revolution was being conducted to deliver the will of the people, but the only voice of the people was that of the Party. As sole producer of the opinions that could be classified as scientifically objective, it sounded as if the Party could not be questioned – in which case, surely everyone in Yan'an was becoming little more than a 'scientific' cog in a greater machine. Where was the art of being human? And if the idea was that there weren't supposed to be any human beings, who on earth would tell the truth? Mao seemed to be saying that truth was a matter of science, reserved for the objectivity of the Party. But hadn't it been precisely that way of thinking which had delivered the tyranny of thousands of years of emperors, a tyranny that had only just been thrown off? Surely, thought Ding Ling, and many others, they must have missed something in one of the lectures. While it might make sense on complicated matters of Communist theory, Mao's ideas on scientific objectivism couldn't possibly be meant to apply to the daily ups and downs of human life. Somewhere, there was obviously a mistake.

In 1941, one of the authors asked Mao if the Party had a policy on literature and art. Observing that, with a war to fight and millet to bring in from the fields, there hadn't been much time, Mao suggested that the authors might like to work on it themselves: 'Base it on my thoughts on New Democracy,' he added.

Gathering together, Ding Ling and the authors struggled to see how art and literature could be reconciled with Mao's mechanistic ideas of science and truth. But the more time they spent trying to understand what seemed to be a conflict, the more the editors began to press for copy – anything to fill the hungry pages of the *Liberation Daily* with something other than what had become the boring back and forth of a slow war. Eventually, mindful of a duty to deliver something, and still convinced she must have failed to understand the detail of Mao's lectures, Ding Ling obliged with a paper recalling the 'critical essay' that Lu Xun, the great revolutionary author whose works were so much admired that they had become classical Party texts, had created: a revolutionary form of an essay that was not designed to meet the artificial standards of the old imperial examinations but to shoot piercing arrows of criticism into the institutions and ideas that stood in the way of revolutionary change.

Within weeks, it was clear that Ding Ling's 'bourgeois' mind had wandered off the Communist path. Standing to open a new Party school in Yan'an, Mao squarely addressed the problems of the Party as he saw them; and his observations had nothing to do with any 'critical essay'. Repeating his view that the subjectivism of individual opinions was a muddled currency, he addressed his words to intellectuals who gave themselves airs, and sharpened his sights on individuals who wanted to put themselves in the limelight. A sickness had emerged, he warned, hindering everybody's revolutionary progress: it would have to be cured. In the weeks that followed, once again, the cleverest minds seemed to be very slow in getting the point.

Ding Ling (among the slowest) proceeded to pen another paper, this time suggesting that it would be better if there were less empty theorising, more talk about real problems and, in light of the growing number of leaders discarding old wives in favour of younger models, a little more attention to the moral conduct of males. Ding Ling was not the only one to write or speak. Another who picked up his pen was a young journalist and writer with a fierce dedication to the integrity of truth – a truth that, in his subjective opinion, was the only possible foundation for any human order. His name was Wang Shiwei. In early 1942, Wang spoke his mind through the same critical essay that Lu Xun had used to tear apart the feudal past. 'Wild lilies,' he wrote, using nature as a masking metaphor for inconvenient human voices, 'are the most beautiful of the flowers in the hills around Yan'an and, slightly bitter to the taste, they have the greatest medicinal value.' With the free and open skies of nature behind him, Wang Shiwei then launched his thoughts on the troubles in the Yan'an world: crawling obsequiousness, inhuman arrogance, a sense of criticism as a crime, special wifely interests who hid their own petty privileges behind a shield of anti-bourgeois principle. A place of light but also a place of dark, where great minds seemed to occupy themselves with petty passions. And, like a shadow at the edge of sight, a place from which emanated the constant threat that the expression of any different idea would bring down not only heaven but the Party on your head.

As Mao himself had once observed – and Wang Shiwei had seemingly not heard – a single spark can start a prairie fire. And so it was that on 2 May 1942, as soft breezes heralded a north China summer, a Yan'an Forum on 'Literature and Art' was convened with a group of seventy or eighty participants from among the intellectuals in the caves. As had become the Party custom, Mao Zedong was invited to provide the opening and closing address. '*Tongzhimen!*', Comrades!, he shouted in his usual emphatic tone. 'Literature and art for who?' he demanded. 'And literature and art for what?' 'Authors,' he advanced, 'might think that it was literature and art for intellectuals, but they would be wrong: literature and art were for the workers, the peasants and the soldiers. And authors,' Mao continued, 'might tell us that literature and art were all for the love of man and nature, but they would clearly be wrong. The only story worthy of being written and painted is the story of man's power to change the world through a revolutionary force of will with which each heart struggles to conquer its treacherous individualism and all combine together to triumph over the chaotic forces of nature, including the chaotic forces of men who have failed to understand the need for change.' 'Literature and art may have some practical value in advancing man towards his socialist destination,' Mao went on, for the benefit of intellectuals who were clearly struggling to keep up, 'but not without a literary and artistic criticism which remembers that nobody's ideas or thoughts should put themselves above the Party.' To which he added that a new order would require not only a military army of its own but a *cultural* army too. Closing with the ominous observation that a Rectification Movement had already been established to 'rectify the rectifiers', Mao expressed his confidence that the literary and artistic comrades would understand the need to 'move in the direction indicated'. More darkly, he noted that those 'still lacking in knowledge and understanding' would find themselves in difficulty: subjective minds that had so far failed to grasp the revolutionary force of literature and art would have to change.

No one had long to wait. Ding Ling was one of the first encouraged to criticise herself, instructed to do so in the new objective language of the time. And then on 27 May, Mao Zedong chaired a special committee to consider the case of Wang Shiwei. In a process that was as personal as it was official, Mao's deputy was his trusted and feared head of security, Kang Sheng, while the interrogators included a representative of the maligned chattering classes: Kang Sheng's wife. Questions were fired, silence was not permitted; and to every one of Wang's muffled answers, a volley of 'Nonsense!' was shot off in reply. Behind the scenes, deprived of sleep and food, Wang Shiwei was taken across a seemingly endless day-and-night process of thought reform, whose violent criticisms were designed to twist the muscle of his humanity, and break every thread of his mind.

On 8 June, a thousand 'cultural troops', drawn from schools and organisations across the Party city, were gathered in the open air for an all-out attack. Reminded of their revolutionary duty to turn against even the most loved of one's family and friends if they held on to ideas that were wrong, literary peers were invited to add their criticism to the guns.

Nearly a year later, in April 1943, after months of crippling detention, Wang Shiwei was formally arrested, and the rectification spread like wildfire, paralysing the caves with its purge. Advising Yan'an's 'specialists in literature' to pay attention to the wall posters that the Propaganda Department had now plastered across the Party city, thousands were questioned and criticised until they dropped with exhaustion. Once-sparkling minds struggled to tell the difference between black and white. Anyone who could, left. For many, it was clear that they were no longer free to leave. Not least, Wang Shiwei himself. Derided as a 'Trotskyite' (after the Russian revolutionist whose 'errors of thought' had been seen by Stalin as a threat to the survival of Communist Russia), and denounced as a bourgeois mind, Wang was condemned as an enemy of the people. Incarcerated in the bowels of Yan'an, from time to time, he was invited up to the sunshine: presented to visiting foreign journalists, as an example of open Party minds.

Meanwhile, as the 'cultural' battle for everyone's thoughts was being fought within the caved fortress of Yan'an, Mao spread his troops across the wider northern countryside, apparently fighting for national unity, although those closest to him noticed that maintaining Moscow's positive attention, and its purse, seemed to be commanding a lot of his attention – as had been the case for some time.

Years before, in 1936, with Japan's forces growing and China's defences undermined by a civil war, a desperate warlord had kidnapped Chiang Kai-shek in a bid to force the Guomindang to rebuild its links with the Communist Party. Ever fearful of Japan's imperialist advance,

Moscow had stood behind the warlord and, long armed with Chiang's son as a 'friendly hostage', forced Chiang to accept a second United Front with Mao Zedong. Once united, and as the Japanese proceeded to advance on China's cities, both had been instructed to concentrate their attention on defeating the Japanese. It was not easy. In 1937, as Mao penned important Party pieces on the importance of guerilla warfare, on discovering truth through practice, and on contradictions as the basic law of material dialectics, large parts of northern China, including Beijing, fell to Japanese control. Shanghai was bombarded and occupied; the Guomindang's capital of Nanjing was besieged and Chiang Kai-shek led his people up the Yangzi to Wuhan (a trinity of Hankou and its sister cities of Wuchang and Hanyang created by the Republic). By 1938, as Mao wrote further on dialectical materialism, Wuhan was also lost. In 1940, with Mao writing on New Democracy, the Guomindang retreated further up the Yangzi, to a new capital in the inland Sichuan city of Chongqing, and the world had gone to a wider war in which Republican China and Communist Russia would join the 'allied' West. With Stalin and Chiang Kai-shek appearing on the same side, and Chiang Kai-shek continuing both the already-long fight against Japan ('a disease of the skin') and against the Chinese Communist Party ('a disease of the heart'), and with other Party members still promoting competing Communist ideas, Mao's greatest battle was to hold on to Moscow's support.

Mao's pursuit of Moscow's favour would continue throughout the war and beyond it – as Chiang and Stalin found themselves on the same winning side in 1945, and as Stalin, declaring a late war against Japan, proceeded to occupy large parts of northern China surrendered by the Japanese. In 1947, however, drawing closer to America, Chiang declared a constitution and a new National Assembly for the Republic of China. Mao decided that the time for his own final push for power had come. With Japan now defeated, Chiang Kai-shek moving ever-closer to America, and Mao having clearly established control of the Chinese Communist Party, Moscow finally agreed. Stripped of any useful assets, the northern lands were handed to Mao.

There would be two more years of battles with the Guomindang before Mao could finally announce a revolutionary victory over the majority of the lands of China. But on 1 October 1949, flanked by his central committee, he ascended to a viewing terrace constructed at the top of the Tiananmen Gate of Heavenly Peace. As an autumn wind blew, he announced the 'liberation of the masses', the founding of the People's Republic of China, and the Communist Party's fulfillment of the dream of a People's Democratic Dictatorship. Waving to what would be described as a sea of radiant faces, the revolutionary notes of the *March of the Volunteers* were played: 'One million hearts beating as one: march on!'

Just over a month later, down in the last Sichuan stronghold of the Guomindang, Chiang Kai-shek led his defeated troops on to the boats and planes that would carry them to the once-renegade (and for most of the last fifty years, Japanese) island of Taiwan. Remembering Sun Yatsen, their broken hearts sang the anthem of an older dream: *Sanmin Zhuyi*, the Three Principles of the People. Singing of a government of the people, by the people, for the people, they chorused: 'one heart, one soul; one mind, one goal'.

Once again, the single dream had divided and the old question returned – what did it mean to be Chinese? For Wang Shiwei, it was a question that had long since floated away: when the Party city of Yan'an had set off towards its liberation of the Chinese lands, he had been taken to the silence of a remote valley and, with the swing of an axe, his head had been severed from his heart.

As early as January 1949, when the renamed People's Liberation Army captured the once-imperial capital, Mao and the senior ranks of the Party explored future new offices in the *Zhongnanhai*, Central and Southern Sea, garden corner of the Forbidden City. It had quickly become clear to the Party and its generals that decades of uncertainty had created chaos. Mountains of rubbish lay all around, food was in dangerously short supply, money had no value, and even the trains had lost their tracks. The People's Liberation Army was ordered to step in and clean up the rubbish, a duty which, to the considerable surprise of Beijing's people, it discharged with revolutionary efficiency.

Looking at the wider problems, the Party realised that the city had also been deeply damaged by refugees. The most visible damage had been inflicted by those flooding in: tens of thousands of incomers, who had washed up, like a river, from the countryside, in search of shelter from the guns, carrying hunger and disease in their wake. On closer reflection, though, it was clear that the loss of those who had followed the Guomindang, would also have a cost: the many who had left included a number of the city's greatest talents.

The choice to stay or leave had not been easy. In the chaos of two decades of warlords and war, and the uncertainty of any outcome, many of the students who had raised the roof of Peking University had not known which way to turn. Everyone had heard whispering stories of Yan'an and its strange ideas, not to mention its hidden prisons; some had even heard whispers of a tyranny that had started in the earliest of Mao's mountain years. Given, however, that the caved city was already home to many friends from the past, some decided that the whispers must have been the propaganda weapons of a Guomindang desperate to win the war. Certainly, everyone had seen the lengths to which the Guomindang were prepared to go for victory: guns in everyone's faces, arrests at every turn, and the Yellow River unleashed as a weapon against the advancing Japanese – a desperate attempt to save Wuhan, with the unfortunate consequence that hundreds of thousands of Chinese peasants had been swept off to watery graves. Not to mention the fact that the corruption of the Guomindang's selfish self-strengtheners was so vast and deeply rooted that it seemed to have been directly inherited from the dying embers of the Qing. Those who left had decided that the known world of the Guomindang would be safer than the mysterious caves of the Communists. Those who had stayed had decided that 'red' or 'white', Beijing was a city like no other.

Looking at the efficiency of Mao's cleaning up, many of those who had stayed behind began to think they had probably made the right choice. Clear about the importance of discipline, the generals of the People's Liberation Army had trained their troops in three revolutionary 'musts': 'modesty and prudence without arrogance', 'plain living' and 'hard struggle'. Armed with these mantras, from the earliest days of their entry into the capital, the troops of the People's Liberation Army had introduced themselves politely to the people and set themselves up as examples. Unlike the cold guns and the barked commands of the Guomindang and their warlords, the rules for the cleaning-up operation had even been thoughtfully announced to the public in the press: 'three main rules of discipline', 'eight points for attention'. Rather than the nightmare everyone expected, the entire process seemed to be

a masterclass in revolutionary order. Roads were cleared to the tune
of cheerful songs, damaged property was restored to rightful owners;
and the human misery that flooded the streets was either gathered up
and encouraged to go home, returned to healthier feet or sent respectfully on to a better life beyond.

By the 1950s, the wider order of the city was being systematically
restored. Trains and trams were returned to their tracks, radios broadcast programmes, newspapers reported events, markets set out their
wares for sale, shops reopened their doors to trade, and the poorest were
presented with work and food. After so many years of destruction, even
more of the early doubters dared to dream that the 'liberation' would be
exactly what it promised: a change of past misfortune into hope.

Curious about the changes around them, many of Beijing's people
turned to their much-loved bookshops, consulting the works of Marx
and Mao to get a clearer idea about what they could expect from the
new order of the Chinese world. Opening crisp new volumes, they
learnt that man is determined by his society, and that if man studied
society scientifically, he would be able to change his fate and usher
in a golden age of socialism where everyone would have what they
needed. That seemed to make sense. Reading further they noted that
when the scientific force of human will (objective thinking) is applied
to serve the people, a new abundance can be achieved, rubbing out
the differences between manual and mental labour, erasing the gaps
between the cities and the countryside, and evening out the inequal-
ities between rich and poor. Reading the conclusion of one of Mao's
own works, they saw that a New Democracy had been established, one
that was dedicated to guaranteeing the Democratic Dictatorship of the
People, with the Communist Party as the revolutionary guarantor, and
with the eventual 'withering away' of the state as the goal.

Thinking on the chaos and destruction of the past two decades, it all
seemed perfectly reasonable. Indeed, to those who were familiar with
the past, it sounded rather like Kang Youwei's late nineteenth-century
idea of a *Da Tong*, Great Unity. Looking at the trains, the telegraphs
and the telephones, even the cars and the very polite tanks, many
began to whisper in admiration that there seemed to be no end to what
this new science could achieve. Apparently, all it required was a more
objective perspective on how to make things work for the better order
of all. Well, that and a sharper attention to the idea of class.

According to Mao, and Marx before him, class was everything. Digging deeper into the books, Beijing's people read that idle land-lords and imperialist compradors had no place in the new world. Well, that had been obvious for a long time and most of them had already left, following Chiang Kai-shek to Taiwan or some other part of the capitalist world. Those who had been friends and neighbours would be missed, but if things went well, perhaps they would come to real-ise that they had underestimated Mao's dedication to the people and, chastened, would return with new and redder hearts. As for those land-lords and compradors who had failed to flee in time, they would, just like everyone else, have to learn to adapt. Then there were the 'right-ist' bourgeoisie. According to Mao, these were people who claimed to be all for a change, but didn't want any kind of a revolution that threatened to put their own personal limbs to labour. Fair enough: it was obvious that everyone was going to have to learn some lessons, but hopefully a better, more selfless, people would come out of it all. Within the broad ranks of the bourgeoisie, though, apparently there was a higher and a lower. The higher bourgeoisie were people who just wanted to live off capital rather than turning their minds to any kind of labour: they were apparently scarcely any better than the landlords and the compradors. But almost anyone with that kind of capital had picked up their belongings and gone, and if they had stayed behind they would just have to take their lessons. As for the lower, petty, bour-geoisie, these were students, teachers, clerks, and shop-keepers: the people who had kept the capitalist ship afloat. That seemed to cover quite a few of those left in Beijing. There was apparently an argument in the Party that they were, in fact, a higher-bourgeoisie-in-waiting, but before writing them off as a socialist risk, Mao was apparently willing to let them prove themselves with an offer of service to the people at large.

And then there were the people at large, the proletariat who had been propelled to the top, which had obviously been the whole point of the revolution. The most advanced of these were the factory and railway workers who had laboured hardest for the strikes of the past. Also included were the craftsmen, shop-workers, rickshawmen, street cleaners and pedlars: men and women who had been a little slower to understand the call of change but who, while they might not have read their Marx or their Mao, were really at the heart of everything. That seemed to account for most of the rest of Beijing. The greatest number of people across the country at large, and now the dictatorship of all, it was this proletariat which was to dedicate itself to the elimination of the oppressive classes, including the treachery of tricky minds. Where once the peasants and workers had pinned their hopes on secret brotherhoods of men, they now appreciated that stronger measures were called for: an elimination, once and for all, of the classes who had stood against them, with a root and branch re-education of bourgeois minds so that they could never again use their clever tongues to climb back on top. To do this, of course, having been so oppressed by the upper classes for so long, the people would need ongoing revolutionary help. And after twenty-eight years of battling, it was precisely that help which the Communist Party, vanguard of a revolution that would take some time to achieve, would provide.

Reading the Communist texts, it all seemed very ambitious. As Mao himself had pointed out, it might take twenty years before the golden age of socialism finally arrived. But if everyone played their part, it seemed as if victory would deliver a bright new future where the state and all of its powers would gradually be eliminated, and everyone's needs would be met: the people would be equal and free.

As the people familiarised themselves with the principles of the new revolutionary world, the Communist Party's bureaucrats got down to the business of recreating the administering machinery of Yan'an in the much grander city of Beijing. Party leaders having replaced their caves with spreading courtyard homes in Zhongnanhai, attention turned to the maze of new ministries that would now be required. Meanwhile, with the Party stretching its wings in the freedom of the old capital, and with mountains of work to be done, new recruits to the Party were welcomed on a daily basis.

For those who had experienced the greatest bitterness of the past, the changes were intoxicating. More questioning minds held their judgement. Some thought on the millennia of Taiping Great Peace dreams, which had risen and failed so often before. Others, understanding that this new society was clearly going to promote the cause of the common man at others' expense, wondered whether there would be a place for everybody – and what would happen if you didn't want to join in. Eventually, however, encouraged by what they began to see and read, a number of the sceptics decided to get on board. Passers-by seemed to find a new spring to their step, people smiled in greeting, and the harrowing memories of the recent past became distant ghosts. Revolutionary songs were taken to heart; children sang in the streets. Inspired by the Communist victory, students were moved to join the new youthful organisations for singing and drama; and everyone was encouraged to join the collective physical exercise on which the health and strength of the revolution depended. Beggars who had been taught new working ways reappeared as street performers of revolutionary dances, celebrating their own reform. Handcarts selling snacks at the roadside were emblazoned with exhortations to join the spirit of the times: *Gong he!*, Work together!, *Gong he!* And after a while, those who insisted on holding on to their questions began to seem a little bit selfish, with increasing numbers of newly converted minds observing that perhaps they had something to learn.

Of course, nothing was going to be easy. After decades of war and destruction, how could it be? The essentials of life were in short supply, and the means of producing any kind of wealth had been blasted out of existence. Newspapers printed under the Communist star explained to Beijingers that living in a city was a privilege to be earned. Editorials urged them not only to reform their thoughts but to embrace frugality and equality with enthusiasm. Consume less electricity and water; offer to take a reduction in your pay. And if you were one of those lucky enough to have a courtyard or a business, think about what might be possible if you opened your profits to the workers, and your rooms to people in need.

Schools were asked to cut their courses to a more efficient cloth: fewer hours, fewer subjects, fewer years; less attention to academic tricks; more attention to the discipline that trains a young body to endure, and strengthens the revolutionary resolve to build a better world for the common good of man. Families were told to think twice about how they fed themselves and raised their children: in the pursuit of a glorious future, a big consuming city was an extravagance no one could afford. Along the streets and alleys, once-idle housewives were encouraged to step out of working in the home to find a purpose in a life outside: set up a committee and become a revolutionary, sweep the neighbourhood, look after the sick, sort out arguments. Barbers, pedlars, noodle-sellers and owners of small corner shops were all pushed into groups that would be collectively owned by all of their members (although how, on earth, that was going to work, nobody knew). And the newspapers, in addition to carrying everyone's daily reminders, were asked to match their stories to the new revolutionary goals: irresponsible rumours were to be swept to the past; revolutionary heroism was to be printed on the front page.

As Beijing's residents were set to a new order, some were surprised when they were required to register at local police stations, and then told to help the police in keeping track of everyone. But apparently, the Guomindang had their spies everywhere, just waiting to tip the city back to the chaos of the past. Residents were to live in their registered homes; visitors were to present themselves to local police stations for checks; strangers were to be reported whenever and wherever they might appear. And everyone received a *hukou* passbook that confirmed a right to live in the city – as long as you didn't do anything so terrible that it might be withdrawn.

Attention then turned to work. Not just the earning of an individual living, but the dedication of everyone to the Communist goal of achieving the productive abundance that would deliver equality for all: work was to become everybody's purpose. In 1953, a Five Year Plan was drawn up to set out what the country needed and how it would be achieved. State-funded industrial production was to put China onto a solid socialist track, creating a footing firm enough to enable the country to catch up with the obvious benchmark of the imperial and capitalist West. With inputs and outputs fixed by the Plan, the state went on to raise or acquire factories to get production on the road. Workers were told that they would need to live closer to their place of work and that, once at work, they would need to dedicate themselves to revolutionary heights of production. How to achieve this? Part of the answer was the creation of the *danwei*, work unit, to unite the people with their workplaces, all under the leadership of a new corps of 'Party cadres'. And where would the Party cadres come from? Taking volunteers with the correct class credentials, the Party school was training them as fast as it could.

Before long, loudspeakers were calling everyone to the early morning exercises that would prepare them for a day of work. Committees were created to carry out whatever non-productive work – from cleaning to security – needed to be done. Meetings to hear government announcements were helpfully convened on site. Welfare groups were established to make sure that everyone had the bare essentials. And with everyone still needing to learn the art of objective thinking, study groups were raised to teach Marxist purpose and responsibility, together with the fervour that every successful revolution required. To all of this was added a system of *dang'an*, personal files, to make sure that everyone stayed on track. And for those who lost their way, groups of peers were gathered to voice the criticisms that could clarify right from wrong – guided, of course, by the Party cadre in charge.

Businesses acquired by the state took the new working ideas to heart and reorganised themselves accordingly. The collective groups of sundry spirits – the barbers, peddlars, noodle-sellers, corner-shop owners and any other local community service providers who had cared to join – did their best to follow suit. Everyone was clear that productivity was key: the industrial kind of productivity which would deliver China into self-sufficiency, and for which cities with their large collections of people were so ideally made.

The order of work settled, it was also clear that a high degree of organisational efficiency would be required if the city was to afford to run itself. Municipal district administrations had little value to offer and came at a high cost; they were more consumers than producers. Conversely, the people themselves were a revolutionary force; an ocean of labour that could be applied not just to industrial production but to the business of running the city itself. Costs could be further reduced through the institution of the new 'mass organisation': whole troupes of people organised under 'All China' banners. Dedicated to everything from women to work, from youth to the disabled, they would be an essential part of a Democratic Dictatorship of the People in which everyone would have a voice, as long as the voice was at one with the Party's revolutionary stand. No more need for unions in the factories, or for anyone to argue individually for whatever they thought they wanted: the mass organisations would take care of it all.

The people, the newspapers and productivity all set firmly on the tracks of the brave new world, everyone dug deep to display the revolutionary courage that would make the dream come true.

Contemplating the new model of scientific man he was creating, Mao turned his attention to the architecture of the city in which it was all taking place. Standing on the terrace of the Tiananmen Gate of Heavenly Peace, he was asked by the mayor of Beijing what kind of view he would like to see. Looking down the ancient Thousand Step Way, and observing the still-remaining flanks of tiled roofs, glittering yellow and green below, Mao paused for a moment, and then replied: 'A forest of chimneys'. Quickly concurring, the mayor, Peng Zhen, declared it 'an excellent idea'. City officials were commanded to commission a plan from Beijing's most famous architect: a Princeton-educated scholar who had developed an encyclopaedic knowledge of the imperial buildings of Beijing, and who, braving the revolutionary changes, had offered his experience and skills to the service of the People's Republic. The son of Liang Qichao, the early revolutionary who had gone on to launch a school of journalism at Peking University, his name was Liang Sicheng.

So familiar was Liang Sicheng with the structure of the city to which he had dedicated his life that he had no need to stand and look at anything. Without being asked, he knew that the Inner and Imperial cities – with the Forbidden City at their heart, and with their heavenly chequerboard of princely courtyards and dividing lanes – were not fit for the industrial purposes that Mao had in mind. The courtyards were treasure troves of an ancient beauty and painstaking skill that were testaments to the great art of Lu Ban (the god of carpentry to an ancient city built of wood) and, indeed, to the old idea of what it meant to be Chinese rather than efficiency. The dividing lanes were so narrow that they could scarcely carry a car, let alone a truck. Unable to imagine the transforming scale of Mao's dream, Liang thought he saw an obvious solution: keep the heart of China's government in the centre of the city, but locate the critical functions of bureaucracy, industry and knowledge outside the remaining walls. 'Imagine the People's Republic as a paradise for all,' he suggested. Outlining his idea to Beijing's Party bureaucrats, he went on to explain that the walls and their surrounding moats could be turned into a people's park, with tunnels underneath to carry any vehicles that needed to pass. Originally constructed to be wide enough to carry ten horses abreast, the walls could easily accommodate gracious walkways for the workers. Curving all around the old Imperial City, the moats could offer boating and fishing to ease the spirits of the masses at the end of a hard-working week. But Liang's ideas could not have been further from Mao's material mind. The imperial city of the past was nothing but an enemy of the revolutionary future. The walls came down.

The architect's subjective thinking noted, Liang Sicheng was then invited to self-criticise the opinions that had led him to disagree with the will of the people at large. But Liang was not the only one to shed a tear at the idea of the old walls falling. And while the walls were monumental, they were not the only problem to have struck those minds that wanted to hold on to their own powers of thought. Mao's views on the scientific force of human will were clear, but the single-minded ordering from the top was becoming rather hard to distinguish from the imperial edicts of the past.

After two revolutions in fifty years, both of them fought so that the people could have independent minds and independent voices with which to express them, many had begun to mutter that the promises of the past were not being kept. Looking at the *danwei* work units, with their study groups and their insistence on the leadership of Party cadres, university professors argued they were an assault on the academic spirit. Finding themselves wrapped into a mass All China Federation of Trade Unions, workers pointed to an even deeper contradiction: just because 'the people' were in charge of the Republic, didn't mean that the Republic's factories were always in the right. The All China Federation of Trade Unions would need to decide whether it was on the side of the factories or the workers – and if it wasn't on the side of the workers then new trade unions should be created to make sure that everyone was represented. And then lawyers, doubtless trained in the West, chimed in, arguing that even in socialism one needed to be clear about duties and rights – including the duties of the new People's Republic, and the rights of the people at large.

'Quite right,' replied Mao in 1956, 'We should all be clear about our responsibilities. Why not let me hear your individual suggestions and we can let a hundred flowers bloom and a hundred schools of thought contend?'

Eager minds inked their subjective thoughts onto enthusiastic pages and pasted them up on walls for everyone to see: 'too much top-down decision making', 'too many bureaucratic rules' and 'a stifling of individual energies and ideas' seemed to be the gist of it all. But everyone had their own particular point to make. Across the city, on almost every *danwei* work-unit door and wall, posters appeared, detailing complaints about things that were not working, with well-intended ideas for solutions, including the suggestion that it was all perhaps a bit too much for the state to do on its own. Perhaps, suggested the posters, the people (the real ones on the ground, rather than the abstract ones who were theoretically in charge of everything) ought to lend the state a hand. Even the old landlords and compradors (those who had survived and obviously forgotten the lessons of peers who hadn't made it) ventured to add a splash of their own: after eight years of socialism, wasn't it about time they were allowed into the people's fold?

At Peking University, a wall was dedicated to 'democracy' and quickly plastered with hundreds of big character posters arguing that socialism had been distorted by the dangerous idea that the Party was always right. As reports of the postering treachery reached Mao, it seemed that the voice of Wang Shiwei (dead but apparently not buried) was everywhere. Even Ding Ling seemed to have forgotten her newly learnt lessons: gathering together with groups of authors, arguing that taboos on subject matters and styles would inhibit human creativity and jeopardise the country's reconstruction, she was once again spreading her dangerously subjective ideas.

The brutal rectifications of Yan'an having cost more than a fair number of Party lives, many of the Party's leading spirits (not least Zhou Enlai, once Mao's superior, now vice-chairman of the Party and Mao's premier) thought that the questioners – the doctors, lawyers, scientists, historians, authors, and artists – had a point. If the country was going to be reliably rebuilt, surely every qualified mind needed to be able to tell the truth as they saw it. As the ink splashed across the posters, and as Party minds joined in, it was clear to Mao that these subjective opinions were just the kind of revolutionary risk he had been warning about, and an early essay that he had written 'On the Correct Handling of Contradictions Among the People' was fine-tuned.

Mao told himself that he should have seen it coming back in 1953, when Stalin had died of his stroke, and Krushchev and the other Russian brothers had started pawing over the legacy of Stalin's 'personality politics', even as they had begun to bite each other's backs. Not surprisingly, three years later, unreliable Hungary had erupted with a bunch of intellectuals who wanted a more subjective life, and the Russians had nearly lost it.

As Stalin's personality had fallen out of favour in Moscow, Russian winds of change began to blow towards Beijing. While his own, Mao Zedong, thought was now the most popular of all the national Party pieces, those bureaucratic men in skirts in the Party quarters of Zhongnanhai had already taken to wondering whether Mao's personality had become too much of a cult. 'Perhaps it might be time,' they suggested, 'for Mao and the Party to adjust to more dignified positions, with Mao formally a little higher but in reality more towards the rear. *Honorary* chairman perhaps?' Oblivious to the foolishness of their bureaucratic preoccupations, they even took to suggesting that the adoring public should be encouraged to sing the hugely popular *'The East Is Red'* (with its vision of Mao as a great sun without whom there would be no China) a little bit less.

True to his guerrilla spirit, and following his own essays on guerilla warfare, Mao bided his time and conceded gracefully. As he bit his tongue, though, his mind had already begun to turn to the intellectuals who were plainly at the root of a confusion of bureaucratic preoccupations better suited to the time of the Ming. True, the bureaucrats and their specialist skills had their uses. But, chronically unable to rid themselves of their subjective bourgeois thoughts, they had failed to understand the bigger revolutionary picture and were now leading everyone up the wrong path – at what cost? Time and again, he had submitted grand schemes for revolutionary change to Party committees; almost all of them had been buried by men who lacked the courage to live the dream. A bunch of chickens who seemed to be more like women with bound feet, their petty cowardice was threatening to bring the soaring triumph of the revolution down to earth with a thud.

Contemplating both the revolutionary risks of the subjective intellectual minds outside the Party, and the treachery of his own foot-dragging bureaucrats within, Mao chose to reply with the now much-longer lecture On the Correct Handling of Contradictions Among the People – that tricky law of opposites, which meant that it took the objectivity of a truly revolutionary mind to be able to work out what was what. Not sure that his words had conveyed his message clearly, Mao followed it up with another sharp lecture on class. 'There are good class elements,' he explained, 'who understand the importance of being on the left of everything. And there are bad class elements,' he continued, 'who, after all this time, still do not appreciate that the left is where they need to be.' The gist of it was that anyone who criticised the Party was obviously one of the latter – bad class and a bourgeois 'rightist' to boot.

The lecture delivered, but to little obvious effect, Mao decided that it was time for everyone to get the point. That old Beijing bourgeoisie of intellectuals, who could have bent to the revolutionary wind but had clearly failed to learn their lessons, were not to be trusted. Just as bad were the city's workers with their ideas of unions to champion petty personal interests: a would-be bourgeoisie, if ever there was one.

The message as clear as he could make it, across the early months of 1957, Mao flooded the Party School and its cadres with his own preferred opinions. Looking to the population at large to support him, he turned to the danweis and suggested that they raise a cultural army of popular opinion which, consisting of everyone's work colleagues, including friends and relations, would report those whose hearts were not in the revolution, and, in so doing, demonstrate that they them-selves had overcome their own subjectivity and banished any and all emotional loyalties to the back of beyond.

By the end of the year, three hundred thousand intellectuals had been declared 'rightist' enemies of the people. The worst offenders were charged with counter-revolution, and despatched to another world. Others were marched off with their arms in the twisting heli-copter position, and expelled from the city: clearly undeserving of its revolutionary riches, and obviously in need of the kind of re-educa-tion that only the peasants in the countryside could provide. For those lucky enough to stay in Beijing, the working day would acquire a little more discipline and a sharper attention to the *dang'an* personal files that daily recorded the colour of everyone's hearts.

For those expelled from the city's ideological purity – the ones who had not been sent to jail, or to labour camps, or committed suicide during the harrowing struggle sessions launched against them – the fields were waiting. Among the exiles, was Ding Ling.

———

As the city was emptied of its questioning minds, a cloud of silence settled. The streets lost a bit of their shine, and many faces looked a little heavier. But socialism seemed to have a boundless energy, and Mao marched bravely on.

Having thought about the challenge of beating the imperial and capitalist West, to say nothing of withering away the state, Mao had concluded that, on its own, the danwei was too small to guarantee the industrial scale of success required. Something bigger and more ambitious was needed: obviously not a city, with all of the consuming distractions and clutter that the Party had struggled so hard to tame, but something dedicated to realising the essential productive purpose of the city. Mulling over the possibilities, Mao contemplated the factory. Not just one factory, but many factories. And not just factories producing goods for sale, but satellite factories and workshops, conveniently delivering whatever materials the leading factories needed – and equally conveniently, relieving the leading factories of the discarded materials and waste which were left behind. Indeed, not just factories, but every other kind of entity that would enable the workers to concentrate their time and attention on the productive tasks in hand: tailors, barbers, schools, post offices and essential shops for basic needs. Simple dormitories and housing, tightly packed to fit everybody in, so that everyone and their families could live close by and concentrate their efforts on their work. Industrial productivity would shoot to the stars, and whenever the Party had anything to announce or teach the masses, everyone could be easily gathered together for the kind of meeting that would improve the efficiency of everyone's thoughts.

Seeming to search for an idea, though, Mao had, in fact, long ago found his answer: what was bigger than a danwei but more tightly organised than a city? A commune. A tremendous step towards the withering away of the state – even as it got rid of all the layers of meddling bureaucrats who might otherwise get in his greater visionary way.

Hearing of Mao's dream, the bureaucrats scratched their heads in consternation. Of course, Russia had its farming collectives in the countryside, but no one, beyond the few who had read their French history, had ever heard of a commune in a city before. Neither did anyone have much of an idea of what it should look like. Being bureaucrats, those responsible for running city administrations wondered how the new 'communes' could possibly be fitted into the geographic districts into which the city had always been divided. Given that the state was supposed to disappear, they also wondered how the communes would deliver any kind of order. Meanwhile, bureaucrats in the Party struggled to understand how the communes would fit with the Five Year Plans.

Explaining that the whole point of a commune was to get rid of the wasteful city bureaucracy – not to mention simplifying planning by pushing as much production as possible through communes, rather than lots of smaller danweis – Mao redirected the local city bureaucrats to new jobs, and set the central Party bureaucracy to redesigning the Plan. Minds confused, but revolutionary spirits anxious to please, the bureacracy set off to try to work it out.

For the businesses of the state – the army and the essential industries, like iron and steel, which had been acquired or set up from scratch – the proposition seemed relatively easy. For work and workers already anchored in the Plan, the Party cadres simply had to identify empty adjacent spaces, and invite related producers to join them in the new higher efficiency. The collectives, however, were more of a challenge. Building a motley collection of individuals into a danwei had been difficult enough, but how could one conjure up something the size and complexity of a commune out of a bunch of collected livelihoods on the streets? And, not included in the Plan (and thus not supported by any budget) where would the collectives get the cash? Inspired by Mao's challenge to revolutionise society with discipline, energetic Party cadres soon came up with an answer. In the absence of any money from the state, the members of the small collectives would just need to do their own self-strengthening, and provide according to their means. Collective members who still had private businesses would have staff and buildings they could contribute; surviving small landlords would have courtyards that could easily double up as workshops and even dormitories for the night; workers could contribute their wages; and everyone with a pair of hands could offer their labour or skills.

Some were enthusiastic, others more sceptical. But with the disappearance of so many of the flowering minds who had dared to ask their questions, most were quick to read the writing on the wall. There were, however, a few stragglers who seemed slow to get the point. Some wondered if they could hire others to do their work for them; others asked how much profit each individual would be able to take.

Hadn't they bothered to read the books? Quiet chats – as many as required and as late into the night as necessary – soon set them to rights. With little or no money to rub between them, paper-makers remembered their skills, shoe-menders offered their tools, housewives delivered their sewing machines, and the unemployed offered their time. Courtyards were soon commandeered for production, managers with Party cadre credentials emerged, and the larger factories of the state were approached, either in search of an invitation to fill an empty space or for some sort of productive order that could squeeze the collective misfits into the circularity of the Plan.

With the danweis of the state enterprises now marching into communes, and smaller collectives somehow finding a niche within the Plan, newspapers began to report industrial miracles by the day. Party confidence rising, in early 1958 a second Five-Year Plan was introduced to usher in a Great Leap Forward. Industry would rocket, and the precocious steel production of imperialist-capitalist Britain would be overtaken in fifteen years: that should show the Russian brothers that China was a serious contender in the expanding Communist world. With similar innovations to be introduced in the countryside, the fields would be able to support everyone with bumper harvests that would fuel the cities' industrial success.

Looking at the details of the paper projections, bureaucratic minds that had successfully survived the treacherous straits of the Hundred Flowers campaign and its following Anti-Rightist campaign, began to feel a little queasy. Accordingly, even in the highest corners of Zhongnanhai, very few flowers bloomed. Daily models of productivity appeared in the pages of the newspapers. It was even said that a city had risen from the middle of nowhere in which industry and agriculture had been combined, and where everyone did everything with almost nothing – and all without a single human cost. Factory workers were divided into teams, with competitive targets set for all. The people were invited to imagine a new China: one where, once the ground of hard work had been laid, everyone's needs would not only be met but they would all have more time to do whatever they wanted. Once achieved, such a country would become the envy of the once-so-vainglorious outside world.

Inspired by Mao's supreme confidence, on the ground, and undisturbed by the paper details, many hearts began to beat a little faster.

Perhaps 'the great sun rising from the East' had a point about those questioning rightists: maybe they really had been slackers who had not been able to understand the greater revolutionary purpose. Inspired by the cause of the common good, workers set aside personal families and their problems, turning their energies to the 'big family' of the commune and the even 'bigger family' of the state. Practical problems of making meals and the daily care of infants were solved with communal dining halls and industrial nurseries. And with the countryside now producing just the kind of bumper harvests Mao had said they would, even the weather seemed to be showing some revolutionary fervour: the sun shone on the fields, and food seemed to pour straight on to open tables. Hope began to soar. Housewives who had never worked before got so excited that they forgot to eat, sleep, or even go home. Students, inspired by stories of superhuman men who had defied the odds to achieve the impossible, saw themselves as revolutionary pioneers, readily accepting assignments to work in whatever factory needed them. And with everyone keeping an eye on the ambitious targets for iron and steel, backyard furnaces were built wherever there was a space, with pots, pans and pipes contributed for the good of the nation. In awe of their achievements, Mao penned poems as paeans to the wonders of the mass human will.

But while many hearts rose, some remained heavy, intent on counting the cost of it all. Working hours had stayed the same but under the Democratic Dictatorship of the People, endless meetings had been piled on top. Dormitories were opened up to constant inspections. Thoughts, and the personal files that recorded them, were subject to constant scrutiny. Permissions were required for everything. Without the approval of a Party cadre, nothing could be done. Bonuses for extra hours ('to each according to his work'), marriages and travel, all needed a stamp; and the job of stamping appeared to have acquired a spirit of its own, with a strong preference for the reddest hearts of Party members. While good class backgrounds seemed to have no trouble in getting whatever approving ink they needed, those whose backgrounds had any sort of a question found that the ink had usually run out. The heavy hearts bit their tongues: Mao's poems were clearly not for them.

Mao's own heart set on ever-greater revolutionary heights, he had left the details of the communes to the bureaucrats and the Party cadres, addressing his own thoughts to a jubilant celebration of the more constructive possibilities of socialism. By mid-1958, it was clear to him that a new China would require a new capital. The old capital, built for a ritual consumption of China's people and things, should not only give way to new productive purpose, but also to monuments that would recognise the triumphant will of the masses. Across the 1950s, palaces and walls had already yielded to the productive future, and factories had risen for the glory of all. Now it was time to create a Communist cityscape for the nation.

Casting his eyes across the remaining imperial indulgences, Mao's sights fell on the Tiananmen Gate of Heavenly Peace. Where the avenue of the Thousand Step Way had once conveyed humble subjects to its gate, Mao imagined a vast square, big enough to hold 'a million' people: a parade ground for everyone, including the army, and a taming of the past to serve the present. Of course, a lot of the clutter of the surrounding imperial buildings would need to be removed. And if the square was to serve the practical purpose of marching people and military parades, there would need to be some sort of a boulevard running east to west and wide enough to accommodate the peoples' army.

Once imagined, it was only a matter of applying revolutionary hands to make the dream come true. With the tenth anniversary of the October 1949 declaration of the People's Republic advancing, what better than ten monumental edifices as revolutionary testaments to the triumph of socialism in Chinese hands? In early 1959, newspapers announced a contest for designs, and a thousand architects were invited to liberate their imaginations. Within a few revolutionary weeks, plans for ten vast buildings were completed and approved: a Workers' Stadium to host mass games; the biggest railway station in China, from which revolutionary trains could set off to the remotest of the country's corners; a Military Museum to celebrate the triumphs that had won the peace; hotels to welcome foreign guests and visiting 'overseas Chinese'; a Diaoyutai State Guest House to display the socialist power of China to the visiting world; a Cultural Palace for all the different tribal 'nationalities' who were part of the great Chinese people. And at the centre of the city, commanding the two corners of the new Tiananmen Square closest to Zhongnanhai and the wider

Forbidden City, a Great Hall of the People, and a Museum of the People's History.

Inspired by socialism, each of the great new buildings was designed to put the purpose of production into the heart of the city. Utility and efficiency were evident; beauty would take a little familiarity to see. With brash positions on vast new avenues, all of the new monuments would oblige passing eyes to look in their direction. Concrete columns would push their way to the skies. Cavernous façades would summon up the sense of a revolutionary Great Man. Heavy roofs would draw sharp lines between this world and any misguided ideas of the next. Each edifice would be bigger than anything that China had ever seen; all would be a capital reminder of the power of the people's scientific will.

Plans having been produced at lightning speed, work soon followed. Ground was broken in April – less than six months before the sun would rise on 1 October 1959. Clearly, a triumph of man would be required. Mao was confident. Hearts still thudding after the shock of the Hundred Flowers and Anti-Rightist campaigns, few of even the greatest Party stars dared to urge the caution that many of them felt would be wise. Of those who did, Zhou Enlai was the only one to remain standing, although not without a lecture. Across the country-side, tons of solid materials were torn from the earth, while tens of thousands of peasants were invited to leave their fields and raise the revolutionary capital. Military principles were applied to annihilate all obstacles; revolutionary songs were sung to raise the spirits; feats of human endurance became matters of daily fact. As Mao had so confi-dently predicted, in the world where the will of man created history, success was to be theirs.

As the sun rose on the morning of 1 October 1959, the ten monu-mental edifices were ready for inspection, and Tiananmen Square opened its arms to receive an anniversary parade. Trucks pressed past in carefully geared formation; cannons and howitzers followed. Silver F5 fighter jets streaked across the skies. Green battalions of soldiers marched in the tightest of blocks; the navy followed in shipshape squares. Advancing eyes swept up and to the right, to the greatest revolutionary spirits standing on the terrace of the Gate of Heavenly Peace, beaming with pride: eleven thousand military men on a march-ing display, with not a single step out of place; all followed by seven hundred thousand representatives of the people, advancing a hundred and fifty abreast. Trumpets trumpeting, pipes piping, drums beating, cymbals clashing, the notes of the *March of the Volunteers* conducted them all.

Up in the clouds, red lanterns swaying in a gentle breeze, Mao Zedong, the sun of the East, waved to the masses, with Zhou Enlai and the galaxy of Party stars standing loyally at his side. Down below, the slogans of the times flooded everyone's hearts and minds: 'The East Wind overwhelms the West Wind!' 'Work hard, struggle upstream, build more, better and more efficient socialism, faster!' '*Renmin gonghe guo wansui!* Long live the People's Republic of China!'.

It was a ten-year triumph; a revolution that had overturned a revolution; a battle that had swept aside every occupying foreign power; and a victory that had delivered a People's Republic into the heart of once-imperial Beijing. And with the temples of socialism now successfully raised to the skies, the peasants were invited to return to their fields: the city was not for everyone.

As 1959 passed into 1960, the winds began to change. In the dining halls of the communes, food began to lose its flavour and there was a lot less of it than before. No one was quite sure what was happening but rumour had it that the harvests, which had seemed to romp to abundance in 1958 and 1959, were beginning to fail. The Great Leap Forward seemed to have foundered.

From the commanding heights of the capital, 'pests' were blamed – certainly insects, but possibly even pests of the foreign human kind as well. Whatever the cause, food was thin, and the workers were getting thinner. Suddenly the sun seemed to have dimmed a little. Factories that had conjured up storms of orders found that demand was slimming down. The state managed to keep its enterprises going, together with their iron bowls of rice; but many in the collectives began to feel more than a pinch of struggle. With too little food coming in from the countryside to feed everybody, any remaining recent migrants were returned to their village homes. Still the hunger growled. In the quiet gardens of Zhongnanhai, Mao forgot about razing imperial palaces and raising chimneys, and set a model example by digging up the mulberry trees that graced his courtyard, replacing them with chillis and corn.

Ever-present in the posters splashed across the communes, a radiant Mao continued to spread his blessings. But out across the city, as the pangs of hunger were followed by a loss of steam, the purpose of production lost its power to command and inspire. Hearts stumbled; hands began to slow. Anxious to raise the people's spirits, the leading lights of the Party looked for uplifting images and words. A rising Party star conjured up a model soldier by the name of Lei Feng, who, having braved the bitterest of winds to keep the Chinese people safe, had lost his life in the course of his productive duties; images of the hero appeared on posters everywhere, as a beacon for all. And another selected volume of Mao's prolific works appeared on the spartan shelves of bookshops; recommended reading for all, it flew off them just as quickly. A new campaign was launched through the danweis, this one supposed to be all about 'cleaning up': apparently not only had the fields collapsed, but someone at the top had noticed that some of the Party cadres in the canteens had been feeding themselves and their families first. As with all such campaigns, though, it started out as one thing and ended up as quite another. Before anyone knew it, it was all about class struggle and criticism: of oneself and everyone else. Few doubted the warmth of Mao's personal sun, or the integrity of the people at large, but red hearts were beginning to think that something in the city was not quite right.

By the spring of 1961, while Mao's personal sun continued to glow, the nightmare of the Great Leap Forward's failure was seeping through the upper echelons of the Party. No one in Beijing, or anywhere else, could be sure of the exact numbers of the dead, but many in Zhongnanhai were aware that millions of Chinese had disappeared; others, less close to Party policy, were beginning to guess. Natural disasters and foreign conspiracies were invoked. But most at the top of the Party knew that the dead were victims of a mass campaign whose revolutionary fervour had created an 'objective' fabric of lies so scientifically unassailable that they had stamped out human truth.

Mao, aware of the human costs but refusing to sacrifice the scientific force of the revolution for the sake of a few mistakes, threatened to remove his colossal personal appeal from the Party altogether. And the Party – aware that it was Mao's great personal sun that kept them all afloat – was anxious not to step any further on his toes. Skirting around the chairman's sensitivities, some of the Party's bravest leaders

– Zhou Enlai, the premier, Liu Shaoqi, the Yan'an author of *How to be a Good Communist*, who had become president of the People's Republic, and Deng Xiaoping, vice-premier and increasingly Zhou Enlai's right-hand man – tried to bring the calamity under control, suggesting an easing of the scientific principle that had eliminated the corrective powers of subjectively human judgement from the decision-making equations. It was not easy.

From time to time, however, encouraged by anxious Party minds hiding behind Mao's public posters, one or two small weeds had begun to push their heads above the grass. One was a Party writer and accomplished historian, by the name of Deng Tuo. Having tapped out an anonymous suggestion in 1957 that the 'politics of simpletons' should be discarded, he had been swiftly sacked from his position as editor of the *People's Daily*, the Party paper. But Deng Tuo's brave words had earned him a number of clandestine friends, not least some in the upper echelons of the leadership who saw the idea of constructing a country without a drop of human truth as a disaster in the making. When it had become clear to anyone with eyes to see and a stomach to growl that something had gone very wrong with the Great Leap Forward, Deng Tuo bravely returned to his typewriter.

As far away from the countryside as anyone else in a city, Deng Tuo decided to consult the pages of history to see what lessons might be found. There, he came across a host of stories that seemed to tell a similar miserable tale: someone at the top blindly telling everyone what to do at the bottom, and everyone at the bottom too scared for their skins to have the courage to speak up. Moving on to consult the more recent past, Deng Tuo found a series of Mao's old speeches: those from the very early days, when his thoughts had seemed to urge a mastery of facts and to embody an earthy common sense. Heir to the same literary codes with which earlier imperial scholars had tried to protect their lives, Deng produced a series of articles that seemed to shower Mao with praise, while leaving careful readers in no doubt about the real, and very critical, nature of his ink.

By the late summer of 1961, Deng Tuo was regularly contributing a column to the *Beijing Evening News*. Entitled *'Evening Chats at Yanshan'*, it was a series of coded essays and observations, with the 'evening chats' easily recognisable as the endless lectures Mao had been delivering since Yan'an; and *'Yanshan'*, Swallow Hill, not only sounded like Yan'an, but also instantly recognisable as another ancient name for Beijing: *Yanjing*, Swallow City, the capital of the Yan state that had been one of the last of the Warring States to be conquered by Mao's greatest hero, the First Qin Emperor. Character by character, Deng Tuo shot arrows of derision deep into his typewritten text. 'Some people have the gift of the gab,' he tapped, 'they can talk endlessly on any occasion, like water flowing from an undammed river. After listening to them, however, when you try to recall what they have said, you can remember nothing.' Secretly, subjective hearts smiled as they read the words. With Mao seemingly not a reader of the *Beijing Evening News*, Deng Tuo continued to type.

Though close to his seventieth year, Mao was not yet a spent force. Withdrawn from a Party whose other leaders seemed determined to thwart the perpetual revolution which would change the destiny of man, Mao quietly set his sights on the still-adoring masses, and waited for an opening. In 1965, it came in the form of a play staged in Beijing.

Entitled *Hai Rui Removed from Office*, the play told the story of an upright Ming dynasty official who had lost his job after attempting to protect peasants from a calamitous imperial decision. Quite possibly guided by Mao's wife, Jiang Qing (the one-time Shanghai actress who had now risen to become China's cultural tsar), a literary critic with Party ambitions read up on his history and, in the wake of the catastrophic Great Leap Forward, informed the head of Shanghai's Propaganda Department that the play was clearly a disguised attack on Mao. Mao was delicately alerted, the author of the play disappeared from view, and a critique of the play's 'subjective errors' was published to set the masses straight.

With Mao already clear about the need to replace his closest lieutenants with new men who better understood the importance of 'objective thinking', some of the most powerful Party members began to disappear into the bowels of the Party's investigating offices, invited to the kind of thought reform and struggle sessions from which even the strongest minds would dream of suicide. And as the subjective minds disappeared, a *Little Red Book* began to circulate across the country. Spread by Mao's newest rising star – a senior military man by the name of Lin Biao – it was composed entirely of quotations of Mao's words. For the innocent city youth who still saw Mao's red heart as the greatest treasure of the revolution, a copy quickly became the most treasured of possessions.

And then, in the early months of 1966, it became clear that Deng Tuo's columns had been read far more widely than he had appreciated. Opening the newspapers, he found that he had become the leading headline in a mass press campaign, with Jiang Qing accusing him of 'using cultural sophistication as a mask for bourgeois restorationism'. Branded an enemy of the people, before the inevitable struggle sessions could begin, Deng Tuo jumped to his death.

The winds of yet another revolution were now gathering pace. Judging from their own personal experiences, it seemed to Beijing's youth that the problem must be the petty minds of lecturers and danwei leaders. Whether in the universities or communes, it was all the same: endless bureaucratic meetings telling them what to think and do; study groups to check their inner thoughts; cleanliness drives; dormitory inspections. Orders here, there and everywhere: none of this could possibly have come from their hero, Mao. The glittering dream of a revolution had faded to a mechanical power and, given Mao's grand vision, it must be the Party's officials who were to blame: the sparkling socialist future had been hijacked by a bureaucracy. As 1966 arrived at the dangerous date of May Fourth – with all of its 1919 memories of a people betrayed – university students and young workers alike clutched their *Little Red Books* and hurled themselves against those who seemed to be trying to derail Mao's dreams.

In the early summer, finding himself subjected to a rising pile of Party complaints about an unruly youth, Mao followed his own principles of guerilla warfare as a means of getting things done. First establishing a 'small leading group' for a cultural revolution, with members including his wife, Jiang Qing, and Kang Sheng, once-head of security now personal-ally at large, Mao then let it be known that his heart was with the students and the workers. In July, keen to demonstrate his fighting fitness, he swam for two hours in the Yangzi River. Then, turning directly to his own corps of busybody bureaucrats, he observed that anger was actually a form of revolutionary spirit. On the campuses of the universities and in the rooms of middle schools, an ocean of students, struggling under the commands of teachers, and facing the prospect of more of the same in commune life beyond, saw that Mao had, as ever, understood the matter completely. When Mao went on to suggest that the students *fa fen du qiang*, draw strength from anger, few needed much encouragement. Taking him at his word, they flung off the shackles of the teachers and the danwei leaders and decided to create a revolution of their own.

On 5 August 1966, Mao inked a big character poster claiming that 'leading comrades' had taken a bourgeois stand against the revolutionaries, and exhorting his followers to 'bombard the headquarters'. On 8 August, the newspapers carried a Party piece announcing a new stage in the perpetual revolution, one in which the stubbornly subjective minds of the past would finally be brought under the revolutionary will of the people.

On 18 August, tides of students from across the country swept into the newly created Square of Tiananmen for a promised audience with Mao. Fearing that the bureaucrats were going to try to bury their hero, they had wrapped red bands around their arms, and appointed themselves as a personal protective cordon: the *hong weibing*, Red Guards. Orderly in anticipation of Mao's arrival, and clutching precious copies of the *Little Red Book*, they chanted his quotations like mantras. And then, like the great red sun they knew him to be, Mao appeared on the terrace of the Tiananmen Gate of Heavenly Peace, offering a revolutionary blessing to the will of the people, whatever that might be. 'Throw off the Four Olds,' Mao exhorted: old customs, old culture, old habits and old ideas. 'Make way for the Four News,' he shouted: 'new customs, new culture, new habits and new ideas'. To which he added: 'Without destruction there is no construction.'

Once a vastly popular hero, Mao suddenly became everybody's god. As more mass rallies followed over the coming days and weeks, the students looked up to the commanding heights of his big character poster and its exhortation to 'bombard the headquarters'. Which headquarters? For the young Red Guards, it was the schools and universities, sources of the greatest tyrannies against youth, which seemed to be the most obvious. The students' rage unleashed, lessons were suspended, exams were postponed, and suddenly teachers and professors found themselves in the midst of the rightist ranks, and in the line of the revolution's fire.

Still battling against his own demons within the Party – petty minds that had been unable to see the Great Leap Forward in the historical glory of its revolutionary purpose and were still bent on obstructing his dream – within a few months, Mao generously expanded the ranks of the 'Cultural' Revolution to include anyone and everyone who had a grievance against someone sitting on top: 'Why shouldn't a revolutionary democracy embrace all of the oppressed, including the children of the old bad class elements as well? Ink,' he declared, 'should flow freely for all, and posters should be everyone's prerogative.' To this he added that, while violence was to be avoided, if the energies of youth discovered the means to produce their own rockets and artillery, who was he to stand in their way?

Every authority was instructed to give the students all necessary support for their revolutionary battles, not least providing the names, addresses and *dang'an* personal files with which they could launch the struggles that, one way or another, would rid the Party of its foes. It was not long before the remains of some of China's greatest minds and hearts were being pulled from fish-ponds, or picked up in pieces after precipitous flights down stairs. Everywhere, the old made way for the new and, quickly becoming old itself, the new found itself the target of the next revolutionary idea.

By the end of 1966, Beijing's communes and their factories had joined the universities as permanent pitches of battle. Production for purpose slowed and regularly came to a halt, save for the rockets and artillery that the Red Guards were now producing from workshops they had commandeered. As some suggested that the city's traffic lights might be better off flashing red as the colour for 'go', the palaces, temples and shops that had so far survived Mao's vision of a forest of chimneys, fell to the wrath of youth; many of their owners followed suit. Poems and paintings, family photographs, relics of the ancient past, surviving figures of the gods and heroes of this and any other world: all were fed to the flames of an anger that was directed to rid the present of the past. And as the past went up in smoke, many of the capital's greatest hearts gave up their ghosts, including an architect with a foolishly unscientific love of Beijing: Liang Sicheng.

Over the following two years, proclaimed by Mao as the 'soldiers of a new democracy', the revolutionary youth determined to ensure that no busybodies at the top could destroy Mao's dream that the people should have their 'will'. Youthful sights expanded to include everyone and everything that anyone could argue was a counter-revolutionary tyranny.

Among the targets were the surviving students of Cai Yuanpei's Peking University. Now in their middle age, their May Fourth dreams of science, democracy and the art of being human had become the great crime of a subjective thinking that dared to question a leader who was clearly heaven's sun. Teachers and danwei leaders having already been dismissed, parents came next. But as every battle won seemed to result in some busybody or other rising to the top and telling everyone else what to do, after a while there were so many targets that it was hard to keep count. Factions fought factions; counter-factions fought back.

Meanwhile, Mao retired to his personal train, and the surviving Party leaders (those who were still alive and not in the avenging clutches of the Red Guards), trembled behind the gates of Zhongnanhai. Outside, the students' 'objective' army battled, released from any subjective ideas of being human. As fear stalked the nation and millions jumped or were jumped to their deaths, the subjectivity of emotions became nothing but ammunition in the hands of those who could rise above history and human nature. Darwinian evolution had followed the teachings of Nietzsche and Marx; nature had been submitted to the revolutionary will of the people at large. Order had come from a cave and the material world had triumphed, but there could be no construction without destruction. If it didn't quite make sense, not to worry: fight every subjective thought ferociously and obey the masses, whether you understood it all or not.

After two years of rage, with even the city now at war with itself, Mao conceded that it might be time to invite the army to restore the peace and rid Beijing of a youth that had gone too far: 'Send them up to the mountains and down to the countryside'.

CHAPTER 3

THINKING AGAIN

What is right the previous day,
Could be wrong today.

> *Great Chant on Observing Weiqi*, Shao Yong
> (poet-philosopher, eleventh century,
> on the Chinese game of 'Go')

SIMPLE CHAIRS LOW to the ground, shoulders hunched forwards, the players pondered their positions. A rising moon had tempered the fiery heat of the sun, the whisper of a wind had tugged away the cobwebs of the day; willows wept as they soughed in the warm evening breeze. Chests stripped to their vests, teeth sucked in deepest concentration, life and death was on the board. Every now and then a fan was waved to attention, and friends leant forward to murmur grave observations. Not even the simplest of them would make the mistake of thinking that this was just a game of chance. In the struggle for territory, every move would bring a change, and only the most prepared of players would be able to scan the terrain and grasp the guerilla possibilities. As the black and white stones struggled to encircle each other in the *weiqi* game of 'Go', one would win, the other would lose. And while the coins and notes of the people's money, *renminbi*, were nowhere to be seen, the assembled company would be keeping a silent tally of the ups and downs of the evening in their heads, with a certain reckoning to come.

In the late 1960s, after the rages of the Red Guards had been redirected to the countryside, Beijing's people found themselves in a very grey world indeed. With the collapse of the Great Leap Forward, and the chaos of the Cultural Revolution, Mao's star had definitely dimmed. It had then been further eclipsed by a decline in his health and a marked retreat from public view. Across the *danwei* work units of the capital, the state-owned factories were now running at close to empty; the collective workshops had almost given up the ghost. Iron rice bowls had thinned; ration books, long a fact of life, were stretched beyond their limits. The population having grown, small rooms struggled to squeeze everyone in. The idea of simple, self-less housing for productivity had lost its revolutionary appeal: with shared kitchens, queues for bathrooms, and paper-thin walls that left no one with any peace, privacy had become a dream, and sleep not much easier to find.

Outside on the streets, there was little relief. Roads were empty, buses were scarce, and any destinations on offer were unlikely to be any different from the place where one was already standing. Most of Beijing's shops had shut their shutters long ago; those that were still open offered little to tempt the eye. Electric lights and waving red banners had faded. Thoughts of anything other than necessity had become little more than a hallucination. Toothpaste and toiletries, light-bulbs and glue were the fabric of Beijing's existence, with cigarettes and peanuts for a treat. Once in a while, a rich red blanket or a small television might make an appearance in an otherwise dull shop, but they would be set so high above the reach of the spartan counters that everyone knew they were destined for an official purse, well beyond the possibilities of an ordinary man. Anyone brave enough to ask for the impossible was likely to be met with a quick '*mei you*', 'not available', snap (or, rather, 'not to the likes of you').

Those who asked were few. The last ten years had taught everyone that serving the people was a principle reserved for speeches. Amid the winds of every campaign, the masses had watched factory heads and cadre officials pay far more attention to advancing their own careers than pursuing any truly socialist construction. It was obvious to all that the Democratic Dictatorship of the People had become not just the dictatorship of the Party, but the dictatorship of every Party official who stood above your head. But after scouring the four directions for the bare essentials of daily life, hardly anyone had the time or the energy to argue. Fridges were a fantasy, and queues were the stuff of conversation: so long that every meal was like a military campaign. Beyond the queuing and the endless danwei meetings, life in Beijing seemed to have little to offer, particularly to its youth. Even work was a matter of bureaucratic allocation. And apartments were in such short supply that marriage was a matter of camping in the corner of an already-crowded parental home, with brothers and sisters just more of the clutter that made it hard to breathe.

Grey walls, grey factories; after twenty years of industrial energy, even the sky itself was beginning to look pale. Firecracking spring festivals had long ago lost their colour, temples had been lost to dormitories, fortune tellers had been redirected to futures in socialist reality, and the motley pedlars who had once sold jumping toys and sticky sweets in hutong lanes had become the stuff of fairy-tales. Even the huge poster-faces of the revolutionary heroes were fading. And whenever a study group was convened to hear about a new speech or an announcement, the hours were spent in yawning, with eyelids struggling not to close.

Minds tried to wander to a more colourful future, but few managed to conjure up the dream of a life beyond. The socialist spirit had narrowed to swapping for the essentials of everything. The only hope of a better future seemed to lie in the calculated pursuit of personal advantage, with eyes sharply fixed on climbing up the iron rungs of Party power. Marx was long dead, Mao was fading and, as both of them had been at such pains to point out, any idea of heaven above them was nothing more than an illusion. '*Leng leng, qing qing*', a cold and dreary world.

Behind the closely guarded entrance to Zhongnanhai, life also had its challenges. Over the course of the previous ten years, as the dream of the Great Leap Forward had collapsed and the avenging Cultural Revolution had first raged and then whimpered, Mao had turned his remaining revolutionary sights on the Party people immediately around him, in a deeper 'cultural' backlash that had carried off a number of those who had once been the Party's brightest lights. Deng Xiaoping had been revealed to be a 'capitalist roader', as had Liu Shaoqi, Mao's erstwhile successor-in-waiting and the man who had once tutored everyone on *How to be a Good Communist*. Both had been guilty of recklessly suggesting that the Great Leap Forward had been a step too far

– to which Deng had added the heresy of agreeing with a suggestion, originally offered by Zhou Enlai, that Four Modernisations (of agriculture, industry, national defence, and science and technology) would get the Party get out of its economic doldrums – adding that black cats could be as good as white ones, as long as they caught the mice. Deng was sentenced to time in a southern tractor factory; Liu Shaoqi was beaten to a brutal death. Then the man Mao had brought in as a replacement successor, Lin Biao, had turned out to be a clandestine counter-revolutionary as well; heaven's punishment was a plane crash. Judging by the loudspeakers, the greatest stars of the day now seemed to be Jiang Qing, Mao's wife, and a gaggle of men who clung to the hems of her revolutionary trousers. In fact, so strong had the pull of these new stars become that many in the Party began to wonder if Mao's ageing sun had any energy left.

Of course, the treacherous ups and downs of what went on within Zhongnanhai were, as they had always been, mysteries to everyone outside. But if the gusts of wind coming out of its gates were any indication, by 1973 heaven was struggling. Mao's health failing even further, China limping from one grey day to the next, even Zhou Enlai was now looking haggard. The only man to have survived his own opinions, having escaped the terrors of the last fifteen years, he found himself the unspoken victim of a new campaign that, mysteriously to most, linked him to Confucius. Apparently, the two shared a slavish attention to human values, a preoccupation with questions, and a lack of conviction about the historical triumph of the iron-willed ideas that had made the First Qin Emperor ruler of all. Confucius' principles – considered to be both subjective and imperial – had made him an 'enemy of the people'; Zhou Enlai's sympathies with the people were deemed an 'unfortunate mistake'. Zhou was able to survive with his position relatively intact, but not his health: few were surprised when rumours of a ravaging cancer floated out.

In 1974, though, spring brought a change. At Zhou Enlai's request, Mao reluctantly agreed to return Deng Xiaoping from the countryside, and resurrect him as a vice-premier, albeit on a very tight leash. Once restored to Zhongnanhai, Deng realised why Zhou had risked Mao's wrath to bring him back. What had been clear in the tractor factory was even clearer from the capital of the country: over the years of struggle and across the land, far from rising, proletarian production had almost come to a halt. Indeed, if one factored in the disasters, it was probably in retreat. Abandoned to fluctuating revolutionary committees, planning had become a piece of paper fluttering in the wind. Thrown to the mercy of the fates, food and every other item of daily human and industrial necessity had become a matter of a Marxist wing and a Maoist prayer. There was not a moment to lose.

While the gates of Zhongnanhai remained just as closed as they had always been, out on the streets those who had the time and inclination to listen to the loud-speaking broadcasts that assaulted everyone's eardrums daily began to hear strains that made them wonder if Deng's return might be a hint of a thaw. But Deng, as trained as Mao in the shaman-guerrilla ways of the ancestors, bided his time; life in the city continued in its Communist routine; and the stars who had stayed closest to Mao continued to sing the praises of the communes and every other revolutionary hymn Mao liked to hear. In 1975, however, Deng began to speak his mind. Emphasising that the past was, of course, a revolutionary triumph to be proud of, he observed that it might now be time for some self-strengthening – of the kind that had enabled Zeng Guofan to rescue China from the rubble of the Taiping rebellion. Gathering up his courage, Deng repeated Zhou Enlai's earlier idea of Four Modernisations, suggesting that, in addition to applying the best of their own abilities to catching up with the times, the Party should energise the country with some capital imports from the West.

Weak though Mao was, the idea did not last much longer than the Guangxu Emperor's hundred-day reforms. Rising from their Zhongnanhai courtyards, a loyal gathering of left-leaning East Winds gathered into a gale: 'launch ourselves into the Western capitalist breach once again', they gusted, 'have you learnt nothing from the past?' Battered by anti-bourgeois sentiment, Deng was invited to criticise himself.

In January 1976, with the East Winds still in a rage, Zhou Enlai passed to another world. To many across Beijing, the loss of the Party's most human heart was both a sadness and a shock. Gusting hard, the East Winds scarcely seemed to notice. Three months later, though, on the 4 April eve of the ancient *qing ming*, grave-sweeping, festival – a day when everyone visited the graves of the most beloved of the ancestors – Beijing's people decided that it was time for Zhou Enlai to receive some respect. Advancing, in their hundreds and thousands, to the Tiananmen Gate of Heavenly Peace which had now become Tiananmen Square, they made their way to a monument the Party had erected to the memory of its revolutionary martyrs. Bearing poems and banners as well as wreaths and flowers, they poured out their tributes to the ghost of the departed Zhou.

Returning the following morning, however, the crowds found that the square had been swept clean and the open spaces of yesterday had been cordoned off. Spirits already high, a hundred thousand Beijingers rose up and swept the barriers away. Sacrificing the vehicles of the police patrols to the attention of a higher god, they then raised their voices in a mighty protest against Jiang Qing – Mao's wife, and the woman who had unleashed the flights of propaganda with which the Cultural Revolution had been turned into a war of all against all – and the three others who, as members of her 'Gang of Four', were being whisperingly presented as the demons who had betrayed everything.

In the midst of the protesting chaos, two new banners flew high. The first proclaimed an end to the seemingly eternal rule of the First Qin Emperor. The second demanded the return of the original spirit of Marx that had, once upon a time, promised a new golden age of equality in which the people would be freed from the imperial conditions that enslaved man. The forces of the People's Liberation Army were summoned and by dusk the hundred thousand had disappeared. Some had been arrested, others molested, but in the pointed silence of the next day, it was difficult to say whether or not they had been defeated. Blamed for the chaos, and still not forgiven by the East Winds of the Party for his resurrection of Zhou Enlai's Four Modernisations, Deng was set aside again.

Three months later, in the July heat of summer, nature joined the general rebellion and Beijing rocked. A hundred miles to the east, an earthquake shattered the steel city of Tangshan; factories and dormitories in Beijing shuddered. The People's Liberation Army rushed to demonstrate its constructive credentials. But some of Beijing's older people suspected that they might all be missing the deeper lesson of nature's rage. And then, on 9 September, as if to make the point, Mao Zedong passed into the darkness of an eternal night.

Less than a month later, on 6 October, Jiang Qing and the other members of the Gang of Four were arrested. Over the following weeks and months, a stream of official broadcasts began to report the nature of their crimes to the people at large. Colourful detail was released across the newspapers and on the rare black and white televisions; deeper digests were delivered in the danwei work units. The reports described a treachery so cunning and evil that even the reddest hearts were shocked. The Cultural Revolution, it appeared, had been nothing but a game played by the Gang of Four: a choreography of chaos, in which the Chinese people had been played as puppets on a stage of breath-taking ambition. The pitched battles, the lost youth, the hounded, the wounded, and the dead; all had been for naught. While the Gang of Four's guilt was assured by their arrest, it would be five years before they were brought to a very public trial in Beijing. (When the trial eventually took place, the benches stuffed with a host of journalists waiting to observe her fall, Jiang Qing would declare that she had only done what Mao had instructed her to do, and that she, as a victim, had simply done her best to return an eye for an eye: *chi shenme, huan shenme*, give as good as you get).

As the people digested the extraordinary news that the Cultural Revolution had been nothing more than a soap opera, old hearts sighed. Not even a hundred years had passed since the Boxer Rebellion, with two revolutions and sacrifices beyond imagination, yet the petty spirits of emperors and empresses had managed to enslave the people once again. Younger hearts, those who had spent years of their youth adoring Mao's revolutionary sun only to find themselves transported to the desolation of the countryside, felt as if the very earth had been pulled out from underneath their feet. Winter passed to spring, and in the stunned silence of the city, those youths who had managed to smuggle themselves back from the countryside began to reach for their ink, penning secret poems and critical essays so black that even the strongest Party hearts would have fainted.

By the summer of 1977, with factories now going so slow that they were hardly moving, Deng was back. Clear that the communes had been a mistake, and with the factories now even deeper in the red, he repeated his call for the Four Modernisations, with science and technology at the helm. While the Party was still stuffed with a number of

East Winds to whom his ideas were heresy, in December of 1978 it was Deng who rose to command the pulpit at the Party's annual, 'plenum', meeting. And when Beijing woke up the following morning, the news was everywhere: 'Emancipate your minds, seek truth from facts, come together in unity. And if you have something on your chest, don't be afraid to say it'. To the Party's cadres, Deng added another note: 'Class struggle is over; get ready for change.'

The single-minded Five Year Plans, which had controlled every branch of production and consumption for so many years, had sapped the life from everything. The time had come for a triumph of man over his landscape – a *jingji fazhan*, which the West might blandly translate as 'economic development', but which every Chinese would recognise as nothing less than a repeat of the ancient taming triumphs of Great Man over nature. While Mao Zedong Thought would remain the guiding star for everyone, the idea of perpetual revolution was to be quietly set aside. From now on, the Chinese world would march to the more practical tune of the Four Modernisations. And although everyone knew that the Chinese people were made of such mettle that one year of their efforts would equal twenty of anyone else's, Deng suggested that even the mighty Chinese might need to take a rest from time to time. The hard work having been done, perhaps it was time to allow the foreign barbarians to contribute some of their own science and technology to the sparkling socialist future that was still beckoning to all.

The East Winds rose in yet another gale of anti-bourgeois rage, but Deng once again declared that one should not confuse the colour of one's cats with the matter of catching mice. Science, he stated, (as opposed to the messier 'literature') was a force of production, just like any other. And scientists could be patriotic members of the proletarian working class, just like their labouring peers. That did not, of course, mean that the heaven of the Democratic Dictatorship of the People would change; and it certainly did not mean that scientists could go about expressing reckless intellectual opinions whenever they felt like it. Indeed, just to make sure that they didn't, Deng declared that he would set the Four Modernisations under the clarity of 'Four Cardinal Principles': keep to the order of the socialist road, uphold the dictatorship of the proletariat, uphold the guidance of Marxism-Leninism and Mao Zedong Thought, and uphold the leadership of the Communist

Party. Think of them as four guarantees, he suggested, to ensure that the Four Modernisations don't jump off their tracks.

As Deng was battling with Zhongnanhai's East Winds in the late 1970s, 550 miles to the south, a group of students was hungrily scribbling equations on to the flimsy pages of their books in the dusty Hefei capital of what had become one of China's poorest provinces, Anhui. Enrolled in the University of Science and Technology, newly reopened after the tumult of the Cultural Revolution, they were listening to a lecturer whose classes were unlocking the secrets of the cosmos, and whose ideas, while obviously advancing the Four Modernisations, were on a clear collision course with the Four Cardinal Principles. The lecturer's name was Fang Lizhi. Wrists taut, minds clutching at every scientific stroke, each of the students was aware that they were sitting in the presence of China's greatest scientific mind. By the end of the class, Einstein's ideas about relativity had been explained. And then the questions had really begun: questions about Newton's older 'truth' that time and space were fixed and absolute, and about Einstein's challenging proposition that the cosmos, while finite, was a still-exploding fireball in which time was speed and space continued to expand.

The science was hard enough, but for the students in that dusty lecture hall the wider 'cultural' questions were even harder. Across the ups and downs of the last thirty years, astrophysics, and science in general, had taken a beating. After 1949, the science societies, journals and research faculties that had proliferated in Republican Beijing had been 'liberated'. Research institutes had been released into a single Chinese Academy of Science; journals and societies had been rolled into the All-China Confederation of Special Societies; and the scientists of the past had been ordered to serve the masses. Every institute had been instructed to free itself from its 'subjectivism', and all had been introduced to a new world of Party science, grounded in the 'single scientific truths' of Marxism-Leninism and Mao Zedong Thought. It had not been long, though, before the scientists had been seduced by Mao's invitation to let a hundred questioning flowers of thought bloom. Revealing their true bourgeois colours, in 1957 China's scientists had become some of the most important catches in the following Anti-Rightist campaign.

With the industrial challenges of a Great Leap Forward to deliver, however, the more useful scientists had been returned to the city and offered a chance to redeem themselves under a Twelve Year Science Plan whose goals included a satellite, two bombs and propelling China to the top of the world in the mastery of quantum physics (the science of sub-atomic particles, which fascinated Mao, and were the 'solid-state' building block on which China's new industrial future was being planned). In the event, the reprieve had been short-lived. Having successfully tested a nuclear bomb in 1964, and confronted with a Party of foot-draggers who seemed so easily seduced by the twists of subjective minds, Mao had reappraised his priorities: scientists might have a productive value, but the cost of the intellectuals' subjective opinions was always far too high.

Never had the problem of subjective minds been clearer than in the case of Einstein. A man whose ideas about relativity had ignited young Chinese minds in the 1920s, upon closer Party inspection he had failed the most basic political tests. The posthumous personality cult that had grown up around him was an obvious problem – as were his later literary works. Writing a book under the outrageously subjective title of *The World As I See It*, Einstein had argued that the state was made to be the servant of man, and that man was on no account to become the slave of the state. The really fatal flaw, however, was the fact that Einstein's theory of relativity was wholly incompatible with the unassailable science of the far greater Marx and Engels. Einstein's logic posited an expanding but ultimately finite universe. But as everyone who had read their Marx and Engels knew, the universe was infinite, expanding by the constant energies of change. It was what Marx and Engels had described as *dialectical materialism*, and what Mao (aware of the yin and yang changes) described as the law of contradictions: a universal unity of opposites which was also the propeller of the constant revolutionary struggle through which the Chinese masses would ultimately overcome the feudal imperialist past and achieve their Communist dream. Einstein had got it wrong.

Abstract though the matter of relativity might seem to many, for Mao the importance of an infinitely expanding universe was both practical and critical. In practical terms, it was a matter of the power of man to triumph over circumstance – a perpetual revolution in which a new world of scientific humans would learn to put the interests of the masses above those of the individual. Objective minds over subjective opinions: wasn't that what science was all about? In critical terms, it was nothing less than the ability of the Chinese people to triumph in the battle for the survival of the fittest and reach their goal, not by a random wave of happenstance, but by the determination of scientific man to establish new facts on the ground.

Putting the practical and the critical together, the question of the nature of the universe was not an idle philosophy to be debated over dinner tables, but a fundamental truth on which every action should be predicated, and from which no individual spirit should be permitted to deviate. To see the world otherwise, as Einstein so obviously and erroneously had, was to infer the existence of a divine creator and to accept the idea that every subjective individual should be able to talk to him – a reckless chaos that the Yellow Emperor's grandson Zhuanxu had, rightly, banished from the settled lands. As every Marxist scientist knew, not just in China but in Russia as well, the only creator of anything was the objective will of man, more helpfully described as 'the will of the people'. Of course, Mao acknowledged, one should not be surprised to get such subjective sophistry from scientists who, like all intellectuals, were captives of their own personally subjective minds and not to be trusted with any collective, let alone revolutionary, cause. Indeed, he continued, a true revolutionary leader should steel himself to fight against them, tooth and claw. Just as with the other intellectuals, the battlefield would be the printed page – and the mind would be the prize.

By the time the Cultural Revolution had been launched in 1966, denunciations of Einstein had become common fare in the *People's Daily*. Then in February 1968, a middle-aged schoolteacher from the provinces had advanced to deliver the final blow to Einstein's treachery. Clutching a carefully crafted paper, he had climbed aboard a train and traveled to Beijing, at the invitation of the Revolutionary Committee of the Institute of Physics at the Chinese Academy of Sciences. Delivering his thoughts, he had hit the nail on Einstein's error-filled head with a new scientific theory fit for a revolution: Einstein's theories were nothing but a mischievous attempt to assert the supremacy of the bourgeois capitalist classes over the heroic working classes; they were also a failure to understand that there could be only one principle for the cosmos, scientific or otherwise, and that Marx, or more particularly Engels, had already found it, with the idea of dialectical material-ism. The preposterous, limelight-catching idea that the universe was guided by a constant speed of light was nothing but a devious trick: an attempt to present Western science as the centre of everything. But the Chinese masses, asserted the schoolteacher, were not to be fooled. Grounded on the breath-taking clarity of Mao Zedong Thought, and ignited from the East, a proletarian scientific revolution was on its way. The West, as usual, had got it wrong: Einstein was not a scientific hero: he was the greatest of all of the reactionary bourgeois minds to tread the intellectual boards of the twentieth century.

Thinking again, it had become clear to the powers of the Cultural Revolution that the errors could not be limited to Einstein: it was not only relativity that was wrong, but much of the rest of Western science too. All it took was a clear standpoint to see the truth, and that was easily supplied: a Mao Zedong Thought Study Class for 'Criticising Reactionary Bourgeois Standpoints in Theories of Natural Sciences'. Blessed into existence by Mao, it added a critical mass to the science of the people and put the surviving scientists firmly in their place. Those still unable to appreciate the errors of their ways were strug-gled to their deaths, or reassigned to the countryside to learn new and different thoughts. With each research institute experiencing a revolu-tionary nightmare of its own, China's surviving scientists entered into a seemingly endless struggle against the dark.

Mao having concluded that the cost of the scientists' risky subjectiv-ity was far too high, the attention of the Red Guards had been directed to the University of Science and Technology, laboratory home to some of the most hopeful projects in China's science world. Fearing for its safety, Mao's bureaucrats had put it out of sight in the far-off province of Anhui. It was not, however, far enough. No sooner had it arrived in 1969 than the Red Guards were alerted to a group of its rightist scientists who had escaped the revolutionary net. Fang Lizhi was one of them. It mattered little that he was the greatest scientific graduate of his era, or that he was the brightest star in the pantheon of living Chinese scientific minds. It mattered even less that he had been tasked with conjuring up the solid-state physics whose equations were to form the building blocks of China's new industrial future. Initially confined to a cowshed, Fang would eventually be banished to the reforming labours of a mine.

Finding himself in the bowels of China's yellowest and dustiest earth, Fang had not been entirely without company. Before he left his library, he had managed to snatch up a forbidden book with his belongings; its title was *The Classical Theory of Fields*. It was not the solid-state physics on which his mind had been told to concentrate but a detailed analysis of the various physical fields of the cosmos and what happens when particles collide. It also included a description of Einstein's theory of relativity. With nothing else to occupy his thoughts, Fang turned its pages over and over in the dead of every night, until he knew the text inside out. By the time the storm of the Cultural Revolution had died down and the scientists (those who had survived) had been recalled from purgatory, Fang Lizhi had fallen in love with Einstein and made a quantum leap into the astrophysics of the cosmos, far ahead of anyone else in the Chinese field.

In 1971, as the Cultural Revolution's gales began to blow themselves out, Fang was returned to Hefei, this time to a brick factory that was under orders to produce a constant supply of building blocks for the soon to be resurrected University of Science and Technology. Carrying the cosmos in his head, Fang's hands made bricks while his counter-revolutionary thoughts secretly leapt across the equations of a higher truth. And then, in 1972, he was released from the brickworks and returned to the classroom with instructions to stick to Mao's facts. But the call of the cosmos was too great. Defying Mao's 'immutable principles' of dialectical materialism and an infinite universe, Fang Lizhi set about exploring the unfinished depths of Einstein's equations.

Within months, supported by new advances in radio-telescopes which probed the cosmos and proved with the power of the eye that the galaxies were moving away from each other, Fang published an article in China's *Physica* that rocked the Party. He called it 'A solution of the cosmological equations in scalar-tensor theory, with mass and blackbody radiation'. He could simply have called it 'Big Bang', for that is what it was. Where steady state theory postulated that matter was static (constantly created and recreated within a finite space), the cosmological equations of relativity indicated that matter was dynamic (expanding like a balloon), fuelled by forces far beyond the power of even the most scientific of men. More to the political point, in proposing the idea of an expanding universe, Fang had drawn on the very idea of Einstein that Mao had seen as the great heresy of relativity: that the universe was ultimately finite. The idea of the cosmos as an infinite propulsion of a perpetual people's revolution had hit a rock.

With the printing of his paper, Fang broke all Party taboos. Marx and Engels were directly contradicted; Mao's cosmic viewpoint was imploded; and the heretical Big Bang theory was laid out in black and white for everyone in China to see. Outraged Party spirits advanced column inches against his science, and a crusade against cosmology was launched. Fang was unmoved.

When Deng had launched the idea of the Four Modernisations in 1975 – with a firm focus on science and technology – the rage unleashed against him had been provoked in part by the fact that science itself had become a cosmic heresy which threatened to unravel the most fundamental tenets of Marx, Engels and Mao Zedong, tenets upon which the logic of the Party depended. As quietly as they could, Party minds who agreed with Deng's direction worked hard to protect the surviving scientists in general and Fang Lizhi, the country's greatest scientist, in particular. Sticks and stones were stayed; and Fang was advised to keep his thoughts to himself. Seemingly deaf, however, to the East Winds that were blowing around Zhongnanhai, in the same year of 1975, Fang Lizhi published yet another paper. This time, he invited a debate on the even bigger question of 'truth'.

From the commanding perspective of outer space, where the earth appeared as a single tiny dot, Fang argued that no theory should be above the theoretical challenge of an individually questioning mind. Neither, he argued, should any idea, 'scientific' or otherwise, be free from the observational test of subjective human eyes. There was no such thing as an 'objectively scientific' question that could be resolved by a quick consultation of Mao's quotations, with any tests limited to a snappy deduction sketched on the back of a Marxist principle. Marx himself had not only emphasized the importance of empiricism but had argued against placing blind trust in an omnipotent 'supreme'. And one of Mao's most famous declarations was that truth could only be discovered from facts. If Marxism, and Mao's interpretation of it, were to be claimed as a science, then its proponents would have to start conducting themselves like scientists, beginning with a more dedicated attention to what was true and what was not. Arguing that if one faithfully followed the Communist logic, no one should be afraid of the truth, Fang even added that it was not beyond the realm of scientific possibility that if everyone were actually allowed to tell the truth in their work together, maybe one day China might even be able to show that there was a dialectical spirit of materialism embedded within the Big Bang.

The matter at stake, advanced Fang, was so important that it went well beyond principle and even physics. It was nothing less than the order of man. The disasters of the Great Leap Forward and the Cultural Revolution had more than proved the point that science without a human mind to ask human questions was a disaster that could push man beyond the edges of survival. Zhang Junmai had been right all those fifty years ago when he had argued that, while the objective powers of science were valuable, without the moral compass of human truth, science was a dangerous thing. Ding Wenjiang, with his idea that scientific truth was an unquestionable absolute, had been wrong. True they had both been doing their best to protect the country from a return to the feudal-imperial past, but by now the lesson should have been learnt: there was not, and never had been, anything wrong with China other than an ancient fear of the people speaking their minds. It was out of the minds of the people's questions that the truth was to be found, not out of a dictatorship that told everyone what to think; and truth being essential to the survival of human beings, China's greatest risk was and always had been the fear of people speaking their minds.

Having been brought back into the fold of the Party's science institutions and advanced to the front of China's bid to make up for lost scientific time, despite his challenging views, Fang was not only catapulted to a higher rank within the University of Science and Technology, but also presented for conversations with leading Western cosmological lights. Fang's ideas turned his lectures into the most popular intellectual journeys in China. Publishing his thoughts both in scholarly articles and in a host of essays and papers crafted for the people at large, he pushed and prodded at the contradictions of science under the single mind of a state. And as Fang pushed and prodded, students in Beijing and other cities began to splash their ink across big character posters, and to plaster them across any and all available walls.

Deng found himself in a dilemma. Scientifically speaking, Fang's logic was hard to argue with. But the question of order a bigger matter. A hundred years of chaos had already passed since the troubling memorial that Kang Youwei and Liang Qichao had presented to the Guangxu Emperor. And while Fang was arguing for truth, an open mind, liberty for individual action, and a heaven within which more than one idea could fly, Deng was counting the bodies of China's rebellious past and calculating the odds of achieving the order that it was the Communist Party's responsibility to deliver. Whatever Marx might have said about empiricism – and whatever Einstein and Fang Lizhi might say about truth, history from the time of the First Qin Emperor onwards had taught that only the firmest grip could maintain a steady state. Lessons from Lenin (who, with his own arguably Mongol background, had presumably inherited the same kind of wolf-like thinking as the people of the steppes) confirmed it. Life under Mao had reminded everyone that being Chinese was about learning to live with contradictions rather than insisting on an absolute truth. And the Republican past before him had clearly shown that the very size of the empire made it impossible to accommodate everybody's voices, however 'scientific' they might be.

But while Deng grappled with the contradictions of science and truth, Fang kept on with his arguments, and other well-educated minds seemed to think it was time for them to stand up and offer their 'truths' as well. All around him, Party minds began to falter. The terrifying possibilities of the unknown seemed to be opening up before everyone's eyes. Why on earth, Deng wondered, could intellectuals never learn the art of keeping quiet?

———

As Deng and his Four Modernisations had advanced towards the Party's pulpit in the early winter of 1978, younger minds had been scribbling down secret thoughts of their own. Aware since the arrest of Jiang Qing that they had been betrayed by the Cultural Revolution, for the last few years they had kept their poems and essays close to their hearts. But in the autumn months before Deng had risen to speak, they began to splash the ink of their anger in big black character posters across a quiet grey wall close to one of Beijing's busiest streets. With little else to do in the long winter evenings, it was not long before Beijing's bored people, torches always at the ready, found them.

Noting that stabbing criticisms of the treachery of the Cultural Revolution supported his own arguments about the need for a more productive future, Deng initially stood back. Indeed, the searing stories of betrayals, tortures and deaths that appeared on television night after night – all attributed to the Gang of Four still awaiting their trial – only emphasised the urgency of reform. Referring to the constitution of the People's Republic, Deng announced that anyone who wanted could write a big character poster: what could be wrong with allowing people to express their views? Instantly famous, the quiet grey wall quickly acquired a name of its own: the 'Democracy Wall'.

Over the weeks that followed, though, the posters began to challenge Deng's call for everyone to unite together in a great new future. 'What unity?' they raged. It was obviously not only Mao's wife and the Gang of Four who had been spitting on the people: it was every Party cadre who had swept up the wealth of the people's labour and put it into their pockets. Bold splurges of ink told of Party cadres raising red pavilions for themselves, and even pulling down historical landmarks that had stood in their way. To which the posters added black strokes of anger at the spying danwei work units, at people being disappeared for daring to speak their minds, and at the imperialistic style of order, which meant that those at the top were always right. Here, there, and everywhere, the reckless ink of the posters shouted out reminders to everyone that where the *ren* respect for human beings was banished, heaven eventually always fell down on everybody's heads.

On 5 December 1978, only weeks before Deng would reach the Party's pulpit and exhort everyone to 'emancipate their minds', a poster appeared that shocked even Deng. Quoting Einstein, it went on to ask a simple question: 'If China is to have Four Modernisations for productivity and science, shouldn't there really be a *Fifth* Modernisation: namely, the voice of the people whose hands and minds will be doing the work, and who will be the only ones in a position to know what's really working on the ground and what is not?' Mistakes, the poster argued, were inevitable, a fact of life. To fear them was to put oneself under the shackles of the imperial past that had always told everyone to shut up. Recklessly, the poster-writer had even signed his name: Wei Jingsheng.

Deng quickly discovered that Wei Jinsheng was one of those young people whom Mao had sent to the countryside in the Cultural Revolution – a city boy who, having lost his education, had reappeared in Beijing years later as an electrician. Proletarian or bourgeois intellectual? Confusingly both, it would seem. But, in Deng's opinion, it did not matter. Wei's argument for a Fifth Modernisation was condemned as 'counter-revolutionary' and Wei himself was detained in Beijing's Qincheng jail. In the spring of 1979 he would be sentenced to fifteen years in its cells.

Meanwhile, back in Hefei, Fang Lizhi, now with a string of scientific successes to his name, was continuing to fire yet more volleys from his lectern, following them up with column inches in a press that was now joining the fray. If China's minds were going to be subjected to the contradiction of a Democratic Dictatorship of the People, led by the members of a Party, how could any Four Modernisations, let alone science, ever flourish? Critics were challenged to a debate, and students were instructed to stretch their thoughts. Relentless in his insistence that minds had to be free, Fang was also ruthless in his attacks on the suggestion that the Four Modernisations could succeed without Wei Jingsheng's Fifth. With every one of Deng's calls for a scientific revolution to propel China up the ranks of the world, Fang fired off yet another riposte to the effect that a narrow-minded attention to technical detail would never unleash a scientific spirit, and that setting targets in the absence of truth would only nurture the risk of lies, with catastrophic failure as the prize.

As the guns were loaded back and forth, Deng, now under attack from both the left and the right, revised his liberal position on the posters: anyone using their ink for counter-revolutionary purposes would be arrested. As winter turned to the spring of 1979 (with the annual April *qing ming* sweeping of the graves of the better loved ancestors; followed by the dangerous 4 May and its sensitive memories of Mr Science and Mr Democracy), Beijing's officials were ordered to tear down the posters on the offending Democracy Wall. Such irresponsible splashes of black on white, Deng declared, had no place in the socialist world. If anyone felt they had something important to say, a more orderly wall would be provided: one where everyone putting up a poster could register their name and their danwei, and take full responsibility for whatever characters they chose to paint.

The Democracy Wall returned to its old grey bricks, and older hearts, sighing once more, stayed at home. The younger hearts, however, took up their pens again. Walls now far too closely watched for anyone's safety, this time they printed their words in pamphlets, and gave them out by hand. Each one was different but there seemed to be two common threads. The first was that the last twenty years had been nothing but a catalogue of the same imperial errors that had been repeated, dynasty after dynasty, over the last two millennia. The second was that man was born to be human. One brave spirit seemed to sum it all up with the observation that it was always the 'inhuman' humans who managed to grab the fruits of everyone's labour and congratulate themselves on their own civilisation; and it was always the 'human' humans who ended up working so hard that they scarcely looked human at all. They were words that carried almost the same price as that paid by Wei Jingsheng: fourteen years in jail.

Spring turning to summer, the pens and the pamphlets went underground, and Deng tried to get on with the business of the Four Modernisations and the pursuit of productivity, including the rehabilitation of once-bourgeois scientists, and the invitation to foreigners to contribute their science and technology to China's socialist future. Recognising the enormity of the task, he reminded everyone that even the greatest river could be crossed only by feeling for stones. There would be advances and there would be setbacks; mistakes were inevitable; some would have to get rich first before others could join them. And while it was important to have a clear goal in sight, it was equally important to understand that a truly successful revolution would take a lot of time.

Meanwhile, the old East Winds continued to blow, occasionally gathering into positively electric storms. Deng's Four Modernisations were described as nothing less than 'peaceful evolution', that conspiracy of words with which a 1950s America had imagined that China could be seduced out of Communism – the one against which Mao had solidly charged every Party mind to guard. Deng's ideas were decried as a treachery that would carry the Party into the clutches of Western capitalism as effectively as any revolution had overturned the imperial past. Aware that he would need to establish some new facts on the ground as quickly as possible, Deng repeated the mantra of the Four Cardinal Principles (keep to the order of the socialist road, uphold the dictatorship of the proletariat, uphold the guidance of Marxism-Leninism and Mao Zedong Thought, and uphold the leadership of the Communist Party); he then scoured the country for more practical ideas.

In 1980 a popular moderniser from Hunan province was appointed general secretary of the Party: his name was Hu Yaobang. In the same year, another moderniser who had recently been Party secretary of Sichuan was invited to become premier of the People's Republic. Famous within Party circles for having rescued Sichuan, China's 'breadbasket', from imminent starvation with an embrace of rebellious peasants who wanted to grow crops on their own plots of land, his name was Zhao Ziyang. With two modernisers at his side, the Four Modernisations as his core objective and the Four Cardinal Principles as a protection against criticism from the left and the right, Deng began to spread his own winds of change.

Intellectuals who had been exiled to the countryside were welcomed back to the city; renegade peasants secretly farming personal plots were heralded as advance heroes of a new 'household responsibility system' which would free everyone from the clutches of the communes. Trade with the West was encouraged for cash returns, and the southern coasts were offered for factories into which the foreigners could pour their science and technology. Of course, the foreigners would not be allowed to spread across the whole of China. But if one applied a little bit of the Monkey King's down-to-earth logic, there was no reason why they could not build their factories behind walls that would keep their capitalist pollution from tainting the revolutionary purity of the rest of the country: *jingji tequ*, as they were announced to the Chinese, 'special economic zones' for the tongues of the West.

With modernisation now being launched across China, Deng Xiaoping looked at the state of the cities. Observing the promising results of the 'household responsibility system' in dismantling the old unproductive communes of the countryside, Deng decided it could become the model for industrial change. Why not adopt the same logic for the factories and put them on to *chengbao*, contracting-out, arrangements that would let a factory head contract out the machinery and keep the profits, as long as he delivered the bulk of its production to the state? Once again, the East Winds raged: with all productivity fixed by Five Year Plans, how could any private production be undertaken without bankrupting the country? And if factories were run for profits, what would happen to the prices? Deng replied that anything could be managed if one just applied a little Monkey King logic. Why not split the prices into two? One, low, price for quotas of goods to be sold to the state straight from the factory gates; and another, higher, price for additional goods that could be bought by people with a little cash to spare, in markets that wanted more.

The Monkey King logic seemingly fit for any purpose, Deng went on to look at the increasingly pressing question of overcrowded housing as well. Reminding the people of Beijing of the privilege and the responsibility of living in the greatest city in China, he noted the revolutionary zeal of the 1950s that had led to a huge leap in the size of the population. It was now time to look at the capacity of the capital to keep up. With the Urban Planning Bureau closed since the bombardments of the Cultural Revolution, and with architectural minds swept away along with almost every other relic of the past, a long-overdue survey of the city and its housing was to be conducted.

Once completed, the survey confirmed what every older Beijinger knew: thousands of chimneys had touched the sky, and the imperial heart of the city had been pierced. The few temples and palaces that had not been converted into workshops and dormitories, or transformed into Party pavilions, were crumbling in the wind. And the sea of yellow and green tiled courtyard houses, once an uninterrupted spread of mesmerising beauty, survived only as lonely puddles in the mud of a now very grey world. To Deng, however, the survey told a different story. Looking at facts rather than fairy-tales, one could see that the question of overcrowded housing could not only be solved, but in solving it, a rather productive new industry might be created as well.

Factories, so indulgently spread across the chequerboard of the old Inner and Imperial Cities, were instructed to sell their central land and premises for a profit, and to use the proceeds to house their workers in cheaper places outside the heart of the city. New homes could then be built so that everyone could get a little more space and the chequerboard could be opened up for those with money to build. Looking at plans for high-rises, relics in the Urban Planning Bureau muttered about the need to protect the low-flying spirits that had swept the city's skies for centuries. But they were easily dismissed: the city needed to accommodate its multiplying population in higher storeys, and no one had seen a spirit for nearly a century. If someone was ready to put money on the street, why would anyone object? The faster the houses went up, the more money would be made. If the cat caught its mice, what difference did its colour make?

The question of housing addressed, Deng then announced that it was high time for Beijing to brush off the dust of its last thirty years, and put a little consuming spring in its step. Shops in the danweis had been all well and good in the past, but given the constant shortages and the changes, why not allow the peasants to bring their produce to an open market, and cut the queues? While they were at it, why not have a beancurd seller on the street as well? Repeating his cat mantra, Deng explained that letting people make a little bit of money on the side was not, after all, such a bad idea. Come to think of it, even though the priests and the fortune-tellers should obviously keep their superstitions out of the city, there was no reason why the temples couldn't open up for a profit-making fair or two. And when festivals came around, why not explode a little shot of profit-making red, and crack a bit of fire? Emancipate your minds!

Beijing's people did not need to be asked twice. Spread out on pavements for popular inspection, eggs and chickens fresh from the countryside flew off the streets. In the shops, even television sets began to come within reach. Temples, whose eaves had long been colonised by pigeons, sprang back to life as markets. Many of them specialised in the sale of what Beijingers had come to call 'the army, the air force and the navy': armies of crickets trained for betting battles, air forces of caged birds offered for heart-conquering songs, and navies of two-tailed fish, flashing their golden scales for luck. It was not long before the army, the air force and the navy were competing with the three new 'must-haves': a watch, a bicycle and a sewing machine. After thirty years of ups and downs, perhaps socialism could deliver something, after all.

With housing under orders, and consumption on the rise, by 1985 Deng was suggesting that Beijing should begin to see itself as a model for the rest of the country. The experience of the last forty years or more had shown that, however important agriculture might be, everybody's future was going to be in the cities. With southern coasts raising factories of modernised production, Beijing should not just catch up but step ahead as well. Before long, a scientist recently returned from a study tour of Silicon Valley, came up with the idea of turning a university village on the outskirts of the city into a special purpose park for computing. China's academics, the scientist argued, were more than ready to start earning some money, and America had proven that when universities and enterprise came together, sparks could fly. The village's name was Zhongguancun. Tracing its roots back to the Ming dynasty, since the 1950s, it had been designated as the site for the relocation of Beijing's earliest universities. Before long it was rising with new businesses – and inspiring the city to start thinking about copying the southern special economic zones with industrial parks of its own.

Beijing now setting a capital standard for other Chinese cities to follow, Deng encouraged Beijingers to raise their sights yet higher. Now that minds had been emancipated, they should begin to think about a more daring dive: out of the iron rice bowl, and into the rushing sea of every man and woman for themself. More of the state-owned and collective factories that could not turn a profit should be cutting their losses and turning themselves over to *chengbao* contractors, foreign or Chinese, who could deliver returns. Meanwhile, workers without a job should try and come up with ideas of their own; and the prices of everything should begin to compete.

Some spirits were very enthusiastic; others were less sure. Life in a money-making city seemed as if it might be a lot more complicated than it had been in the grey old past. Taking their cue from Deng's encouraging speeches, however, the most energetic people rushed ahead, chasing money wherever they could, encouraging government officials to take their courage in their hands and approve a fresh idea, even if the ink of changing government policy was not yet entirely dry. Those who hesitated watched with growing unease as the grey but familiar world of the iron rice bowl changed. Workers on factory floors woke up to find that a *chengbao* contract had turned a comrade with a useful connection to a Party official into a boss. Settling down to the new management, they then found that their hours had been stretched, and the pressure to perform was rising by the day. Many were to be released from their jobs; and almost every older worker,

with or without a job, was to be despatched to more affordable housing beyond the limits of the city. Families who had lived in Beijing
for centuries found themselves cast into an outer-city wilderness that
even the buses could not reach.

Struggling to come to terms with the change in their fortunes,
Beijingers then watched as *hou men*, back doors, suddenly appeared
everywhere. Playing games of *weiqi*, Go, on evening streets, they also
watched as new bosses rushed off to wine-washed banquets. Going to
work in the morning, they passed comrades on the stairway who were
on their way to the airport for officially funded 'study tours' in some
foreign country or another. As like as not, in every case, the lucky
person in question would be jumping into one of the shiny new black
foreign cars that had begun to appear around the city, all with windows
delicately darkened. Soon the apartments of neighbouring officials
were being stuffed with televisions and sofas, or emptied onto carts
carrying the furniture of old lives off to new pavilions where water
and electricity flowed freely, with kitchens and bathrooms that would
never need to be shared. Reaching deep into their pockets for the rising
price of a cigarette, and any other comfort or essential, it was obvious
to everyone on the streets that their own hard work was paying for the
lot: while ordinary people were condemned to the queue, the benefits
of reform were going to those who had found the back doors.

As the gathering possessions and the rising pavilions went from
strength to strength, the price of everything just kept climbing.
Revolutionary righteousness was fading into the mists of memory, and
the edifice of the Four Modernisations was becoming shot with cracks.
What had seemed like a good idea in the beginning was increasingly
looking like a problem. Yes, Deng had warned everyone that they
would have to take a small step backwards in order to get themselves
firmly on the road to the golden age of socialism. But no one had
expected the pursuit of productivity to take on the bitter unfairness of
the imperial past.

———

With Beijing now divided on the question of whether the future could
be both red *and* richer, Fang Lizhi had not given up in his quest for truth.
In 1984, his international prizes propelled him to the vice-presidency

of the University of Science and Technology. But by 1986, across Hefei and other cities, more posters were being splashed across more walls, and the writing on the walls was bringing more and more people onto the streets. Spreading like wildfire across many of China's cities, the protests began to wash up like an eternal tide against the Tiananmen Gate of Heavenly Peace. Discouraging the protests for fear of the violence they might provoke, Fang Lizhi nonetheless welcomed the open minds. The truth was the rock on which everyone's future was grounded, he argued. However hard it might be to hear it, and however unknown or unknowable the answers might at present be, it was the duty of the intellectuals to tell it. Within the Party, East and West winds began to battle, and Deng tried to quell the squall.

Meanwhile, on the people's streets, Beijingers were becoming anxious. Prices were rising even faster than before. And the higher they rose, the quicker everyone rushed to a queue, anxious to stock up on the essentials of life before they slipped out of affordable grasp. Everyone scrabbling for the shops, the tiniest of savings flew out of the banks. At the same time, with labouring hours rising, but jobs under pressure and wages frozen, factory workers turned their sights on the All-China Federation of Trade Unions, the Party organisation founded in the 1950s which had promised (wider scepticism notwithstanding) to look after the workers' interests. Ever-ready with its Party broadcasts, always quick to collect everyone's dues, its energies had never stood up for any of its members and in the recent years of 'modernisation', its eyes had become blind to the racing cost of everything, and its ears had turned to cloth. Brothers united by their labour, the workers decided it was time to stand still and strike.

Recognising the contradictions of a Party-led modernisation, Deng dug deep into the theories of Leninist-Marxist thought and, like the ancient hero Zhuge Liang, looked for the wisdom that would bring two, seemingly incompatible, principles together in the harmonious unity of one. Eventually, he found the answer in Marx's stages of socialism. In the zeal to reach the socialist utopia, Deng declared, China had failed to read the small print. Marx had not suggested that the people could rush from the feudal imperialism of the past straight into socialism. What he had, in fact, said was that one had to pass through the lower stages of capitalism before the great triumph of socialism could be reached. While Mao and the people were to be congratulated on their revolutionary fervour, if true socialism were to be achieved, there was no alternative but for everyone to retrace their steps and create the capitalist industry over which they had leapfrogged in the past. That said, Deng reminded the people that no other socialist state had ever tried to conjure up a capitalist past, that mistakes would be inevitable, and that it might be an idea to take things a little more slowly, perhaps even take a pause. With a number of minds, not to mention factories and prices, already marching forward, it was not clear how this could be done. Obviously, though, the state would not be withering away for quite a while. Belts were tightened, targets were cut, and the Four Modernisations were told to go so slow that it seemed as if they had stopped.

But the factories and the shops did not appear to be listening. Prices did not go down; wages did not go up; and as 1988 unfolded, even those hearts that had embraced the storms of change in the hope of a more colourful future became uneasy.

Then in the summer of 1988, an image of the Yellow River washed across the screens of everyone who had managed to acquire a television set, announcing the beginning of a series that would take everyone back across thousands of years of history. Entitled *Heshang, Deathsong of the River*, just like the Yellow River, it carried its viewers across an epic journey: from floods to famines, from self-strengthening to foreign imperial powers, from Confucianism to Communism, portraying the pent-up rage of the people that periodically erupted into a nightmare along the way. As it told its story, it led, relentlessly, to the conclusion that, at the root of almost every Chinese problem, was the single self-deceiving idea that only those at the top could be right.

Staring at their screens, the television viewers almost fell off their chairs. No eyes watched more closely than the young ones in Beijing's universities. While Deng's dreams had promised a better world, invisible bureaucrats were assigning every graduating talent to a government-appointed purpose, with never a choice about what kind of work they might personally like to pursue. Unless, of course, as it had always been, they were members of the red royal families that could always conjure up the best and most desirable of jobs for themselves.

The past, it seemed, was indeed destined to repeat itself.

In early 1989, nearly seventy years after the 1919 protests that had so boldly paired Mr Science with Mr Democracy, and just ten years after the Democracy Wall, Fang Lizhi wrote a letter to Deng Xiaoping, asking for the release of Wei Jingsheng. Signed by many of his peers, Fang published it openly for all to read. Deng limited his reply to the Four Cardinal Principles: the order of the socialist road, the Democratic Dictatorship of the People, the supremacy of Mao Zedong Thought and Marxism-Leninism, and the leadership of the Communist Party. He also issued orders that the fast-arriving, and now highly inconvenient, anniversary of May Fourth was not to be celebrated with any reference to 'Mr Science' or 'Mr Democracy' but with a call to *ai guo*, love the country. Fang hit back with the simple observation that 'Truth does not distinguish between localities'. In China as anywhere else, he insisted, one should be able to love the country *and* love the truth as well.

Just over a month later, on 15 April 1989, uncomfortably close on the heels of the annual April *qing ming*, grave-sweeping, festival, another veteran Party soul departed: this one, the modernising Hunanese, once-general secretary of the Party, Hu Yaobang. Already set aside by Deng for a failure to crack down on the unrest of 1986, Hu Yaobang's spirit seemed to stand as a heavenly reminder of all that was going wrong.

On 17 April, five hundred students appeared on Tiananmen Square to pay their respects to the man who had seemed to stand a little closer to the people. Over the following two days, on the square and in the streets around, the five hundred became five hundred thousand. University classes were abandoned: replaced with posters, ink and pens. A vigil was taken up opposite the gates of Zhongnanhai. A few days later a 'committee of students' asked for a voice in the newspapers, as well as an open and clear account of the riches acquired by Party officials.

Met with stony silence, a few days after that, a small gathering of students moved to the steps of the Great Hall of the People, the revolutionary monument to the people's proletariat. Digging deep into Beijing's memories of the past, they knelt in an ancient act of supplication to request an audience with the Party's imperial powers. Zhao Ziyang, the other moderniser who had re-revolutionised the fields of Sichuan, once premier and now general secretary of the Party, was abroad, with not a single other Party leader available to receive the students in his place. A reply of sorts was delivered in the form of an editorial in the Party's *Peoples' Daily*, denouncing the 'conspiracy and turmoil on Tiananmen Square' as 'nothing less than a class struggle which is doomed to fail'. With teachers, workers, journalists, and ordinary Beijingers coming out to meet them, the students gathered their courage and began to march to a common cry: *renmin wansui!*, Long Live the People!. As they passed along the roads of the city, shop doors flew open in encouraging applause, buses were brought to a halt, and lollipops and even *renminbi* notes were thrown towards the marchers like votes of support. As April tumbled towards May, the posters only got louder: 'What is Truth?', 'Why can't this poster be published?' and 'Beijing belongs to the people'.

4 May arrived, with its 1919 memories of student calls for science and democracy, and of the awkward fact that so many of those 1919 students had been among the earliest founders and supporters of the Communist Party. Zhao Ziyang, now returned from his travels and talking more openly to a visiting group of foreigners, let it be known that, in his opinion, the students had a point. Back doors should never have become a fact of life; Party officials and new bosses should not have been moving into new pavilions; the press had better and more important things to write about than the empty rhetoric of the past; and at a time of modernisation, questions should naturally be asked. Zhongnanhai shook with shock, but by the middle of May, with Beijing now afloat on a sea of youthful hope, Zhao Ziyang had become a beacon – and Zhongnanhai was beginning to look like a remote and renegade island.

Worryingly for the Party, the students were far from alone. Defying the mothership of the All-China Federation of Trade Unions, a Beijing Workers Autonomous Union also appeared under blazing banners. With twenty thousand members calling for the fat cats to slim down, it seemed as if all the shop floors in the capital were sending someone to turn up in the square. As labour turned up in rising numbers, armies of bookish researchers arrived to join them. Marching under the banners of enterprises that included both state and private production, their slogans pointed not only to a voice for the people, but more specifically to the matter of a constitution, and to a rule of law that would apply to the Party as well as everyone else. Journalists from radio, print and television abandoned the rules of reporting-to-order and joined the crowds, raising their own flags of truth. On 13 May, hundreds of students sat down for a hunger strike. By 17 May, the square was awash with a million hearts seemingly beating as one. Street vendors offered up their wares for free; pickpockets declared a moratorium on theft. As the square swelled with ever-greater numbers, and while the students waited for the Party to come out of Zhongnanhai and have a conversation, everyone sat down to long debates about what it meant to be Chinese.

On 19 May, after weeks of chilling winds blowing across the court-yards of Zhongnanhai, Zhao Ziyang stepped out of the gates. With an understanding that the Party's minds were more fixed, and harder, than anyone on the streets could know or understand, he made his way to the square and the hunger-striking students. 'I am sorry that I didn't come earlier', he apologised, with tears in his eyes. 'Please be patient. The situation is very complicated. It will take time. We can talk. Please eat.'

Later that day, the students abandoned their hunger strike. But as the sun rose the following morning, stronger powers in Zhongnanhai pronounced a martial law, commanding everyone to go back home. Beijing stayed on its streets. Declaring that 'stability is everything', Deng Xiaoping stood the capital's own military garrison down on grounds of a suspected sympathy; the commander of the country's best-equipped and oldest force, the 38th Group Army, had questioned the quality of an order to attack in the absence of war. Replacement convoys of soldiers were summoned from across the provinces to take control of the city, hearts hardened by orders that told them that 'a counter-revolution' had broken out. Alerted by journalists who had broken their boundaries weeks before, Beijing's people flocked to the city's intersections and turned themselves into human barricades. Sleeping on the streets, asking themselves and those around them how the People's Army could turn against its own, stubborn men and women transformed themselves into popular guards. Calculating spir-its were transformed into warm red hearts; and those whose souls had prided themselves on just getting by, began to break into smiles. Army convoys were surrounded by doting grandmothers – even as their drivers looked up to find paper blinds shielding the road ahead from their view. Soldiers in their trucks looked down to see nimble Beijing fingers letting the martial air out of their tyres. As days turned to dusk, anyone venturing out of an evening found the soft breeze of early summer carrying the patriotic voices of ten thousand people singing the tune of the *March of the Volunteers*: 'Arise, arise, arise! Our million hearts beating as one'.

As 3 June moved towards the midnight that would carry it into a day that would forever be remembered as June Fourth, tanks from other corners of the country finally pushed their way forwards. Trucks thick with troops followed in their wake. Called up from the depths of Inner Mongolia, the men had been prepared for war, and told only that a corps of terror was striking at the heart of China. Tanks rolling towards Tiananmen Square, squadrons of soldiers chased young spirits who rushed into the surrounding narrow streets where willow-treed shadows seemed to promise shelter. Bullets flew like arrows; once-beating hearts fell like broken birds; blood ran like ink.

Watching the past appear yet again, heaven might have wept. But, if it did, no one on earth was allowed to see its tears.

PART 5
DOWN IN THE COUNTRYSIDE

When the wind blows, the grass bends.
The Analects (attributed to Confucius, 551 – 479 BCE)

CHAPTER 1

SNOW IN SUMMER

Make a new people.

The Book of Documents (second millennium BCE)

DIRT UNDERFOOT, A whiff of earth in everybody's nostrils, man and nature were once again putting on a spectacular display. Announcing the market in advance, drums had drummed and bells had rung, but by the autumn of 1926 no one in Hebei's Ding Xian had needed to be told when and where it would appear. Near and far, everyone had descended for the day. Bales of straw spread left and right; ruddy apples and warm pears piled towards the sky; proud cabbages stood to command the attention of passers-by. Here and there, chickens scratched in wicker cages, while pigs and piglets grunted in crates; children struggled to keep charge of scrawny goats with minds of their own. Tables offered up mountains of grain: scales ready and waiting for a buyer to appear, as strident voices called out their fare. Woven mats and baskets were presented on the ground for inspection; seeds were spread out for discerning eyes. Worn brown hands clutched precious coins; and every now and then, long and prosperous coats counted strings of cash. Over by a grove of trees, blacksmiths, carters and barbers had set up shop under sheltering branches: shoes for a horse, wheels for a carriage, and a shave for anyone in need. The crowd heaving, few failed to find a familiar face and exchange the age-old greeting of the fields: *chi fan le ma*, have you eaten?

Those who lived nearby had left their village before the crack of dawn. Those coming from further away had walked for a day or more. Some had hit the road with a single pig and a hope. Others, with a little better luck, had pushed their produce in a creaking cart. The richest of all had been carried on the wealth of a horse or an ox, hauling wagons whose wheels turned with little human effort across the bumpy land. But, once arrived, even the tiredest of feet, and the poorest of pockets, knew that they would find a sight to put a spring in their step: jugglers and storytellers for anyone with eyes to see and ears to hear; medicine men entertaining their way to a hopeful sale; letter-writers dashing black characters across white pages. Over by the temple, as always, there was a show of puppets: evil landlords, dark officials and heroic peasants, all caught up in a dance of dramatic delight. For those with a coin or two to spare, the possibilities were endless: *miantiao*, noodles, spun in front of one's eyes before being poured into a bowl of steam; sweet *bing*, cakes, warm from the griddle. And this year, something quite, quite new. All the way from the city of Beijing, and all for free, a group of students and teachers had come to bring the future to the past: lectures with lanterns, conjuring up a magic that seemed to be called science; stories about seeds that burst with bumper crops; promises of new pigs whose fat bellies would dwarf anything known before; and demonstrations of pumps that could cut hours of labour from an irrigating day.

Then, just as the moon was rising – when some thought that heaven must surely have run out of its wonders – an opera appeared with an even stranger tale: the story of a peasant who had learnt to read.

Ding Xian county had not always harboured such high spirits. Set in the heartlands of Hebei province, two hundred miles south of Beijing, it had first appeared as a military garrison under the Tang dynasty's founding emperor, Taizong. Four hundred years later, it had become a county seat, its soft wealth and simple harvest songs poetically captured by a Song dynasty magistrate who was also a scholarly poet. Behind official walls, a Ding Xian county town had risen, home to a succession of tax-collecting and dispute-resolving magistrates. Outside the walls, the county over which the town presided spread across an undulating expanse of fields, scattered with villages, each dotted with the households that brought them to life.

For almost a thousand years, the fields had turned from season to season: feasts and famines had been ushered in by the alternating changes of rain and drought; heaven had smiled and frowned. But in the past few hundred years, the winds of change had brought more than their fair share of trouble. With paltry sums of imperial remuneration, the magistrates had sought an ever-greater affinity with the self-strengthening families, whose wealth was always ready to buy a blind official eye. Taxes had continued to be spread more heavily across peasant lands, and disputes between landlords and peasants were always resolved in the formers' favour. The headmen of the villages had gathered the taxes like bitter harvests, local thugs had backed rent collections with whips, and the additional cost of anyone's shoe-leather used in collecting the payments had naturally been charged to the peasants' accounts.

Preoccupied with the state of the treasury, in the last few centuries, official observations of the heavenly changes had dulled, even as the northern peasants spent all of their energies in trying to deal with the vagaries of the local land and weather. Soils protesting under pressure, forests lost to timber, the clouds seemed to float past without distributing a single drop of rain. Most accepted the changes as part of nature's wisdom – just like the periodic floods, droughts, frost and hail, not to mention the inevitable failures of crops, and the following deaths. Indeed, after millennia of heavenly sliding, even the fact that disputes were typically resolved with a clink of coins was accepted as part of life on earth, as was the fact that if anyone from the fields ever wanted to object, there would always be a ready pair of arms to twist their necks until they saw sense. Those who fell behind with rents, taxes, or both, were naturally forced to go to a money-lending landlord for a loan, with rates fixed by the level of desperation rather than any market, and interest collected on interest as a matter of course. Whenever the harvests faltered, the price of grain would naturally rise. And with the gentry and the merchants placing their bets on the changes, grain acquired by the ton and stuffed into the gunnels of granaries would be held back for as long as possible in order to boost the bumper profits that the inevitable failed harvest would bring. For those who could not afford anything, there was always a patch of land to be sold. And if the land was already gone, then there were the assets of wives and daughters (even sons, if things were really desperate) which could always command a price: an exchange that, as far as the calculating landlords and officials could see, would give the peasant the added benefit of less future expense.

Working without a stop, pouring their sweat into the ploughed furrows of a northern land that had become as hard as metal, beasts of burden had become a luxury which few could afford. Barely earning enough to feed themselves, let alone their families, Ding Xian's peasants had eaten their fair share of bitterness. In a heavenly land of two thousand counties and three hundred thousand villages, each with its own particular troubles with nature, and all with their troubles of landlords and officials, Ding Xian's peasants were not alone. But while nature seemed to have taken a particular turn against the now treeless and exhausted soils of the north, Ding Xian's peasants had often been able to count themselves luckier than some. Remembering the exhortations of Confucius to put oneself in other people's shoes, in parts of Ding Xian county, the gentry had done their best to open up their doors to the peasant poor. On festival days, benevolence had been spread for all to see; and whenever an ancestor merited a celebration, the poorer branches of family trees had been invited to join the lower levels of a feast. From time to time, the White Lotus and other secret societies had even offered hope of serious change – although, in the end, their rebellions had usually come to naught.

But then the foreigners had come, with their cheap cotton and their interfering god, meddling in things they never understood. For a few years, from 1898, it really looked as if the Boxer rebels with their talismans might be able to get rid of them. In the end, however, their boxing fists had failed to match the power of the foreigners' guns, and the price of their failure – levied in time-honoured tradition through ever higher taxes and levies on the peasants – looked as if it would be paid until kingdom come. Remembering a song from the travelling opera that passed through from time to time, peasant minds tilling the fields often dwelt on the thrilling dream of a good official who would free them from the corruption above. But, as the tale itself told, that was a dream that was as likely to come true as snow falling in summer.

Not long after the Boxer rebellion failed, though, a would-be imperial scholar from the most powerful family in the county (one who had failed to pass his exams) had come up with the hitherto unheard of idea of improving not just the lot of his own family, but everyone else's as well. Villages were brushed up for a self-strengthening dream, streets were renamed after the Confucian virtues, trees were planted, and schools began to open their doors to peasant minds. But then, in 1912, the emperor disappeared. Heaven knew where he had gone, but when black clouds of warlords arrived, the scholar with his self-strengthening ideas retreated behind the walls of his courtyards, the villages sank back into their dirt, the schools closed, and an uneasy silence settled over the fields. Plagues of unruly soldiers began to march across the crops. As always, the old hearts sighed: nothing good ever lasted.

By 1918, two hundred miles north of Ding Xian, the eager halls of Peking University had begun to turn their minds to the question of the countryside. Most of the students, like their lecturers, were the sons and daughters of gentry scholars and merchants: a youth whose lives had been blessed with the wealth of their families' spreading lands, even as their protected eyes had failed to see the burden of the peasants' bitterness-eating labours below. Returning from Japan, Europe and America with ideas of revolution in their hearts, they had revisited the comfortable country estates of their youth, and received quite a shock. Where childhood memories recalled spreads of grass blowing in soft winds, minds opened up by studies abroad saw a destitution that their younger selves had missed.

Observing the fields of suffering, most had confidently, and even hopefully, expected to hear a sudden thunderclap of rural rebellion. Hearing only silence, they had reflected upon the past and pondered. The late nineteenth-century revolutionaries had told everyone to 'imagine a people'. But it seemed that the peasants were just a soporific mass of straw who only roused themselves when the harvests didn't appear, at which point, they gathered into brotherhoods of men, hopelessly calling upon heaven to give them a Taiping, Great Peace; and, when that could not be managed, they would dream of 'a good official'. Minds mesmerized by the seasons, senses dulled by the earth, hearts frozen by the hail of rents and taxes: beyond the harvests and the blood brotherhoods, the only thing the vast majority of the population seemed to care about were the wooden gods who ruled their hearts like little demons shouting from their temple heights. No wonder the foreign gunboats had been able to sail themselves into the coastal cities; no wonder the coastal cities had become treaty ports of foreign empires; and no wonder the northern lands of the new Republic were still being carved up into the humiliating territories of foreign powers.

Seeing the students' confusion, in 1919, Li Dazhao, the chief librarian of Peking University (also convenor of Peking University's Marxist Research Society, and a political economist with a passionate interest in the question of what, after all these millennia, it meant to be Chinese) inked a challenge to the students. 'Go down to the countryside and wake the people up' was his suggestion. 'See if you can start to repair the wreckage left by your fathers; and while you are at it, cleanse your own hearts with some purifying labour in the fields.' Elaborating on his words, he explained that while ideas about Mr Science and Mr Democracy might be flooding into China's cities and lapping at the edges of bigger towns, the countryside was still in the dark. Instead of the students following in the ancestors' scholarly examples, it was time that these intellectual flowers started to roll up their sleeves and build the kind of bridges to the countryside that would ensure the peasants would not only be found but never lost again. Peking University's students took up the task. Dedicated to going down to the countryside, the movement was flooded with volunteers, all ready and willing to go and find the missing peasant people, and wake them up. Although, since few, if any, of the students had ever actually spoken to a real live peasant in the flesh, no one was quite sure what on earth they would say to them when they did.

Prepared for the unknown, and fortifying themselves with tobacco and tea, quilts and cameras, not to mention the odd flask of foreign medicinal whisky, the students found that they had arrived not a moment too soon. In 1921, the north-eastern areas of China which surrounded Beijing, Ding Xian included, had once again experienced the disapproving flick of a dragon's tail: no rain, then no harvest, and then nothing to eat other than the bark of a tree – and then even that had run out. Stomachs sank to skeletons; the price of a patch of land, or a wife, fell to a few days' food. In the opinion of some in the cities, it didn't last long – just long enough to winnow out the numbers in the villages, and to sort the wheat from the chaff. Confronted, however, with the stunned faces of those who had survived, the students began to see quite another side to the popular story of an indolent peasant past: less a tale of peasants who had gone to sleep, and more the tragedy of a desperate people who had got lost – if, indeed, there had ever been a time when the bitterness-eating peasants had really been attached to the imperial whole.

Hearts touched, the students looked and thought again. Never part of the walled and gentrified world of Confucian ideals, untutored in the complicated classical language of scholarly minds ('Chinese Latin' as some described it), across the millennia, the long-suffering peasants had tilled the fields for everybody's food, even as they had occupied a silently bitter world of their own. Save, that is, for the moments when, desperate, they had erupted like a storming force of nature, only to be branded as bandits. Really, they were the earliest of revolutionaries who had not just failed to find their luck, but had failed to find anyone who could write their story so that others could read it and understand. And so it was that five thousand years after the time of the Yellow Emperor, these black-haired people were still invisibly tucked away into small villages where the sight of a floating sleeve was never the bearer of any news other than a tax, and where a bus or a train to any other kind of place was donkey-cart-hours away. Waking with the sound of the cockerels, not sleeping until long after the sun went down, this was an invisible world of men, women and children who worked from dawn to dusk for barely enough food to survive.

Thinking even deeper, though, the students began to realise that this was also an invisible world of men, women and children who knew nature like the backs of their hands, and who, while their bowls were never full, had nonetheless kept a song on their lips for as long as anyone could remember, not to mention stories in their hearts to tell their children as hungry bodies tried to sleep. While the peasants could obviously do with a better life, it was the students themselves who had the most to learn. None of the peasants' past had ever been written into a book, and given that the city had never had any use for their knowledge, little of what they knew could even be described in the lofty scholarly language that the city had made its own.

Descending upon the villages in their quest for a nation, Peking University's students received a lesson in what it meant to be a people, and the true meaning of Li Dazhao's words came alive. On closer consideration, the city with its minds was less a citadel of omniscience, and more a corruption of the honest, hardworking man, not to mention a betrayal of the peasant. Conversely, the countryside turned out to be a wealth of buried treasure: man in daily encounters with a wisdom of nature which no city person had any experience of; songs and stories which no city ears had ever heard before. Clutching their notebooks, the students found themselves wooden stools to sit upon, and stroked down every possible fact from the newly discovered world. Meanwhile, astonished at the arrival of a scholarly youth that had never in any peasant's memory shown any interest in the fields, the peasants themselves could only stop and stare. Or at least, the simplest of them stared. Those who had their wits about them took themselves swiftly off to the safety of their homes, confident in their expectation that somewhere at the bottom of all of this was bound to be trouble.

———

As Peking University's students were discovering new rural horizons in the countryside around Beijing, other young minds were finding Chinese peasants in the unlikeliest of foreign fields. One student came across them unexpectedly in France. The youngest son of a Sichuan line of scholars, he had gone, like so many others, to look for China's future in the New World. Accepted at Yale University, Yan Yangchu, or James Yen, as he would come to be known by his English-speaking friends, found himself mesmerised by Woodrow Wilson's ideas that rulers should have principles, that governments should judge themselves by their ability to raise a new and better world from the devastating cinders of the First World War, and that any decisions taken for the people at large should be explained in terms which could be understood by the ordinary man on the street. Desperate to be part of putting such ideas into action, in 1918 Yen volunteered to help the Western soldiers and civilians whose lives had been overturned by war. He soon found himself in France, at the tail end of the Western Front, a member of a delegation organised by the American chapter of the YMCA.

Arriving in France, young American volunteers were assigned to work with displaced Europeans; Yen was sent to look after a corps of Chinese peasants. Masking his disappointment, he remembered that these were men whose desperation had, in 1916, led them to the British recruiting stations of Weihaiwei. From there they had travelled across the seas to dig trenches for a war between countries whose languages they could not speak – traded away by a self-strengthening Republican government looking for loans and personal shares, rather than the return of the northern lands held by Germany, for which the peasants' labour had originally been pledged. It was on these foreign fields that Yen encountered a Chinese peasant for the first time in his life, and on these foreign fields that he came to the same conclusion as the students in Beijing: the son of a scholar had far more to learn from the peasants than anything they might learn from him. Hearts willing to eat more labouring bitterness than he had ever imagined possible, these peasants were men whose only ignorance was of books, and whose stamina and determination put every scholar he had ever known to shame. Before long, Yen's disappointment had turned to exhilaration.

Not only unable to speak English or French, but also unable to read or write the characters of their own Chinese language, Yen decided to give the front-line peasants the education they had missed – on the fields of France. Working in their midst, teaching the strokes of the most essential characters, one by one, Yen gradually gained their trust. As he did so, the unknown stories of a people who had suffered for so long and in such silence began to tumble out like water from a broken dam. Stories of such suffering they would break the hardest heart, they were more than enough to inspire Yen to try to think of how he could make their learning easier. While he might not know what to do with a plough, teaching was something that Yen had been born to.

Listening to his peasant corps, and digging into his own ideas, Yen decided to set aside the textbooks written by scholars, for scholars, and to create a new set of lessons. Written in the ordinary language of the Chinese north from which the peasants came, it would limit itself to one thousand carefully-chosen basic characters which represented the essential reading and writing words of daily life. As Yen began to teach, characters aside, with every lesson, came a torrent of questions: questions about the world whose trenches they had been building, for a start; questions about home; and all of the other questions which, based on nothing more than rumours run amok in the darkness of eyes that could not read, revealed the anxieties of desperate men. With his students studying to the point of forgetting to eat, Yen decided it was also time to start a newspaper. Short and to the point, its four pages of articles opened up everything under heaven, in words that the peasant students could read and understand.

In 1920, with the war over and his peasant students packed on to ships bound for home, Yen returned to China. By 1921 he had persuaded the YMCA to fund a literacy campaign to teach labourers in Chinese cities how to read and write. By 1923, thinking about what might be possible if whole villages of peasants could be taught the magic of the brush, Yen had reached out to like-minded Chinese friends and peers for support in founding what he called a 'Mass Education Movement', the MEM. Lessons would be delivered in the fields and offered at the times of day, and in the seasons, permitted by the farming calendar. Subjects would be chosen which would introduce the peasants to new scientific ideas as well: breeds of pigs which could offer more meat; seeds which would produce bigger yields; and simple pumps which could irrigate dried-out northern fields at prices the countryside could afford. After millennia of being left out of the country's scholarly conversations, China's peasants were finally going to be joined up with the minds of city cousins who were emerging from citadels of learning which most of them had never even heard of.

Not surprisingly, news of James Yen's MEM spread quickly. Volunteers, particularly students, rolled up in promising numbers. Other helpful minds, ones with deeper pockets as well as a few with valuable skills to share, followed in their wake. Then, in 1925, the elderly head of a family in the Hebei county of Ding Xian presented his lands for service. Disillusioned by the competing banners of the early Republic's political parties, and exhausted by a decade of battling against warlords, the elderly Mi Qianshan told Yen that his home county, Ding Xian, had been waiting for decades, if not centuries, or a millennium, for something like the MEM to arrive. Within a year, Mi Qianshan had offered up the entire county of Ding Xian as a labora-tory for the MEM's new countryside.

Peasants were invited to classes not only in how to read and write, but also in how to understand the science of the far-off city world. And with an entire county as a laboratory, the MEM was able to dig deeper into the local earth to find out what was needed than any of its founders had imagined might be possible. Reading and writing were an important beginning, but if the countryside was going to be able to talk to the twentieth-century cities, there was not only a lot of science that needed to arrive, there was also a lot of local, natural knowledge that the MEM's city minds were going to need to learn.

Bubbling with excitement about its possibilities, Ding Xian began to attract the attention of scholarly Chinese minds, including many trained in America. Once on the ground, and gradually getting a better understanding of the countryside – the rhythms of its seasons, the stuff of its soil, the falling of its rains – the scholars began to think about what new ideas might help the peasants find their way to a more heavenly future. Which new breeds of animals? What new crops and seeds? Soon Ding Xian's cabbages were the envy of every market for miles around, and their pigs were winning almost every possible prize. Meanwhile, for Peking University's students – some Communist, but most just believers in their own New Culture way of imagining a people – 'back to the village' became a powerful mantra: chanted not only by themselves, but by some of the most talented minds of the time.

While the MEM had concentrated its thoughts on the Ding Xian pocket in the north, down in the far south, another young scholar had been looking at quite a different county. Youngest son of one of the richest landowners in Guangdong province's Haifeng county, like so many others of his age, he dreamt of 'imagining a people'. In 1917, he had gone to Japan to study. In 1918, his heart had risen to the skies when he heard the news that the old imperialist Russian empire had been transformed into a revolutionary Bolshevik Republic. In 1919, it fell back down to earth with a bang, when the Chinese journalists of the country's *Da Gong Bao* newspaper tapped out the words which told everyone that the imperial powers at Versailles had rewarded the trench-building labour of China's peasants, not with a return of the northern German-held lands to China, but with the transfer of those lands to the rising imperial power of Japan.

Returning to Haifeng in 1921, Peng Pai accepted his family's suggestion that he take up an official position in the county's education bureau. Full of ideas from abroad, he was keen to try out some experiments of his own: new schools, a modern curriculum and young educators whose tasks would include the teaching of revolutionary thoughts on the importance of building solidarity between teachers and their pupils.

With such an imagination, it was not long before Peng was relieved of his official duties. Brothers, uncles and cousins were shocked at the reckless independence with which he had squandered the opportunity of an official career. But Peng rejoiced in his freedom. Looking at all of the things that needed to change, he decided to carry his dreams of solidarity up the local mountain, stand himself at a busy crossroads, and shout out his ideas to every passing peasant. 'Year in, year out', he called, 'you work in the fields until you drop dead, while your landlord sits at home with a book. Meanwhile, selling those you love to pay back a money-lender, you have forgotten the thousand years of labour that the greedy landlords have stolen from your hands.' Of those who had any time at all to stop and listen to something that had nothing to do with the fields (not many), most thought he was mad. Indeed, a number muttered that he sounded like that Great Peace fanatic Hong Xiuquan, the one who had conjured up the Taiping rebellion seventy-five years ago. 'Look where that had got everyone,' they added.

After a few days of talking to thin air, a sympathetic soul named Zhang finally stopped to listen. Taking pity on Peng, he offered him some advice. 'If you want any of these labouring hands to pay attention to your arguments, let alone believe that you might be speaking from your heart, you had better learn the local language. And while you are at it, you should think about trading in your soft silk gown for something simpler, in the rough blue cotton line.' Quick to learn, and desperate to teach, Peng asked his new acquaintance if he had any other advice to give.

That evening, after his own day's labour was done, Zhang returned with a group of his friends and offered Peng Pai an education in the mind of the peasant, with suggestions on how to get the peasants to lend him their ears. 'In a world where rent collectors are nothing but armed thugs,' they explained, 'one where taxes and fees are dreamt up quicker than a cock can crow, where lands are seized without explanation, where talking to an official is harder than getting into the Forbidden City, and where everyone has been taught, with beatings, that obedience is a survival skill, finding a peasant willing to trust an outsider will be almost as hard as finding the eternally elusive good official.' 'But', added one of Zhang's friends, 'you could create a band of brothers which would certainly catch their attention.' Peng was only too willing to take his advice. By the end of the evening, the new friends (Peng the scholar, Zhang and his associates) had agreed to work together, and the Haifeng County Peasant Union was born.

Over the coming weeks, with Peng Pai under the tutoring wings of his new peasant brothers, they walked across the mountains, calling in to every village, and inviting anyone and everyone to come for a talk. Conversations always limited to the evening ends of working days, lanterns were lit, at Peng's expense, and more brotherly spirits were ignited. Within a few months, five hundred brave peasants had found the courage to risk the beatings threatened by officials and landlords, and joined. As a contribution to the new common cause, each advanced a copper coin. Within a year, the Peasant Union had twenty thousand member families. A Peasant Manifesto was inked for all to see. Each member was given a small card testifying to his membership, with a list of the principles by which the Union would abide. Among these, was the capital idea that all of the members would apply their minds and pool their resources for the challenges ahead: land to be tamed, families to be helped, and landlords to be addressed on an equal footing.

Bit by bit at first, and then with something of a rush, the pile of copper coins began to rise. Soon, fields were being turned into open schools, and the Peasant Union was teaching its members the science of accounts. Henceforth, it would no longer be only the landlords who could read the registers of rent. Hills that had been stripped bare over centuries of desperation, were being replanted with trees, and a peasant clinic appeared. Even travelling operas were being organised with new revolutionary stories set to old peasant tunes.

Confidence gathering by the day, the Peasant Union then turned its attention not only to helping the peasants resolve their own disputes – something which the magistrates had rather neglected across the centuries – but to tackling the trickiest challenge of all: standing up to the landlords. Having watched the ways of the magistrates from the courtyard of his own family's power – and having grown up with a landlord for a father – Peng Pai was full of advice. 'Think of them as paper tigers', he said, 'big shadows which will jump in fright if anyone ever really stands up to them'. Seeing Peng Pai resolve seemingly impossible problems, the peasants turned to each other and asked themselves who needed a magistrate if one had a Peasant Union – and what, indeed, could the gentry landlords do if the peasants stood together?

With Peng Pai at their side, drop by drop, the peasants lost their fears. Soon their ideas were beginning to flow like southern water.

'All of our labouring hands,' ventured one, 'trundling individual goods to market, only to find that the landlord-middlemen step in to take the profit. Why don't we make the markets without them, and keep the profits ourselves?' 'So many problems', suggested another 'but so many of us to help. Why not stand together and be the charity that a neighbour might need?' Peng Pai's heart swelled with a warm pride as he saw the very people that he was 'imagining' begin to appear at his side. Introducing a new lesson, he suggested that next time anyone higher up held out a palm to be crossed with silver, the peasants should reply not with a coin but with Sun Yatsen's three simple principles of the people: *minzu, minquan, minsheng* – government of the people, by the people, and for the welfare of the people. Warming to the idea, the peasants' own hearts began to swell. 'If the landlords really cut up rough', shouted some, 'why not take a leaf out of the Crouching Dragon Zhuge Liang's book? We could just pull up the stones that mark the boundaries between their fields, and leave them to jump at each other's throats!'

Bold words shot across the peasants' secret meetings. No one was in any doubt, though, that if they were truly going to become 'a people', then the landlords were going to have to learn some bitter lessons of their own. And if the landlords were going to be learning some bitter lessons, then everyone had better get ready for the inevitable beatings.

But the peasants were as brave as Guan Yu, and all the other ancient outlaws who had since become gods. By 1926, the Peasant Union had spread across Haifeng. Naturally, the landlords branded Peng Pai a 'bandit chief'. But the unionized county of Haifeng was gaining ground, becoming a legend among peasants across the wider province of Guangdong. Everyone was looking with wonder at Peng Pai, and wanting to learn from his revolutionary ideas. With lives as hard as their unknown brothers in the north, and having heard the same travelling opera song, many turned their eyes to the sky and wondered whether, perhaps this time, snow really could fall in summer.

———

While Ding Xian was discovering a wondrous spring in what everyone had thought would be a never-ending winter, and with Guangdong imagining the miracle of a mid-summer snow, up in the old Changsha capital of Hunan province, Mao Zedong was getting on with his own business of finding a foothold in the next revolution. Going back and forth between Peking University's library and the Changsha capital, he was applying a prodigious energy to the possibilities of revolutionary change and to the building of relationships with anyone and everyone who might offer him an opportunity to be part of the advance. Asked to create a Cultural Book Society to promote the Party's literature, he joined up his work with the new efforts of the American YMCA, encountered through the person of the now-returned James Yen.

Hearing about Peng Pai's Haifeng Peasant Union, Mao suggested a few ideas for peasant militia movements in the countryside of Hunan. And when, as part of the Moscow-brokered 'United Front' of the Guomindang and the Communist Party, he became leader of the Guomindang's Peasant Movement Training Institute (the brainchild of Peng Pai, who had joined the Guomindang in 1924) he adopted as many of Peng Pai's ideas as he could. To which, he added the benefit of his own family experience: son of a farmer whose three acres made him a landlord even though he was little more than a rich peasant.

In early 1927, when the Guomindang and the Communist Party were still brothers in revolutionary arms, Mao penned a 'Report on an Investigation of the Peasant Movement in Hunan'. In it, he listed 'fourteen great achievements' of work conducted so far, including: over-throwing local landlords and tyrants, spreading propaganda, igniting brotherhoods of peasants, education, and mutual help and co-operation. As a conclusion, he advanced the idea that the revolution was going to come from the fields. While Chen Duxiu, leader of the Communist Party, followed Marx and Moscow in their belief that revolutions always came from cities, given that nine out of every ten Chinese people were living in a village, it scarcely seemed an unreasonable point of view.

The members of the young Communist Party divided between those who agreed with Marx and the Moscow brothers, and those who thought that, in China, the revolution would come from the fields. One who agreed with Mao was Li Dazhao, once his chief (librarian) at Peking University. But while Li Dazhao and Chen Duxiu stood shoulder to shoulder on questions of intellectual conscience and freedom, Li was unable to move Chen's Moscow-led conviction that it would be the workers labouring under the inhuman conditions of the factories who would bring the revolution to life.

When the Communist dream was smashed in the treacherous Shanghai massacre unleashed by the Guomindang in April 1927, however, the Party began to shift. In the early days of Chiang Kai-shek's White Terror, with Sun Yatsen already dead, Li Dazhao was snatched from his refuge in the Russian embassy by Beijing's warlord and executed. Anyone who looked as if they might be a Communist being chased down, the Party shattered into thousands of individuals struggling to survive. Hounded out of the cities, the remnants of the Communists did their best to find each other and regroup in the countryside. Dreams of a city-led revolution were shattered. That year, the Party moved its annual congress to Moscow, with delegates travelling across the border disguised with beards and hats.

In the months following their return, the battlefield moved to the countryside, with brave individuals from the fields volunteering to take up the lead. Among them, having transferred his allegiance to the Communist Party and vowing that his Haifeng peasants would hold strong against what would obviously be devastating landlord attacks, was Peng Pai. In the southern provinces of Guangdong and Jiangxi, uprisings rose, but the Guomindang's military forces smashed them down. Further up the country, Mao Zedong made his suggestion of an autumn harvest uprising for the fields of Hunan, with a peasant army to be put under his own command. When his uprising fell, he took the opportunity to lead the company that he had acquired into the Jinggang Mountains and build the first of what would become a succession of Communist bases.

Back up in the north-east lands around Hebei's Ding Xian, the shifting fortunes of the Communists, the Guomindang and the warlords had been having an impact of their own. As Chiang Kai-shek's White Terror raged with the support of the northern warlords, the foundations of the MEM had been rocked – with many of Peking University's volunteering students, if not active Party members then at least sympathetic spirits. And then, Chiang Kai-shek had decided that it would be better to leave the north in the hands of allied warlords rather than try to hold it himself, and the remnants of a central government had been swept out of Beijing and off to the Nanjing south. The lands of the north were edging further into chaos, but James Yen and the MEM did their best to hold on to their belief in the possibilities of snow in summer, and work with whatever possibilities they could find.

Ding Xian's future was now a little cloudier, but it had already conjured up a lot of magic, and it continued to work. In 1927, the MEM acquired the additional novelty of a new-fangled 'social surveyor'. Fascinated by the relationship between labour and society, the social surveyor was the son of an American soap-maker who had partnered with a candle-maker to create an industrial fortune: the candle-maker's name was Proctor, and the social surveyor was Sidney Gamble. Gamble had first travelled to China with his parents in 1908. In 1918, he had returned to Beijing with the YMCA, of which he was a devoted member, to apply the new science of social surveys in China's challenging world. By 1925, early surveys around Beijing were being disrupted by the warlords. Gamble, now a friend of James Yen, suggested a study for Ding Xian: Who were the peasants? How did they live? What did they think? And, apart from tilling the fields, what sort of crafting labours did they do? When the survey was completed, the results pointed to a host of practical steps with which the peasants could be imagined into a people. Within a few years, Ding Xian had acquired four hundred People's Schools with classes grounded not on city textbooks but actual village life; fifteen thousand students and a number of alumni villager-students trained to teach; household associations; a youth group; even an association for the very young. Despite the upheavels of the White Terror, the Northern Expedition and the shift of the remaining central government to Nanjing, Ding Xian found a conversation with the county's leaders, and even their support.

The route to the future began to look a little brighter. Friends, relations and alumni pooled their labours, and roads and bridges appeared. Village elders who had lost their way were replaced by younger representatives – not just chosen, but elected, by the village at large. A radio station appeared, full of local news. A *Farmers' Weekly* magazine followed: printed on a single big sheet of paper so that it could be conveniently pasted on to a wall for all to read. In 1929, even as a Great Depression settled in the West, sending dark clouds towards China, a ten-year county plan was crafted, with careful attention paid to Ding Xian's strengths and needs. Weaving hands were organised into co-operatives; trading minds were added to ensure that any profits reached the pockets of Ding Xian's people rather than those of self-strengthening intermediaries along the way. Not long afterwards, diagrams of how elections worked were being drawn on to pamphlets, and scattered around for everyone to consider the wider possibilities of imagining a people in the countryside.

In 1932, the idea of health as a way of life was added. Lighting up Ding Xian like a lantern, it was the brainchild of a man named Chen Zhiquan. Often described as a 'medical bolshevik', Chen had a number of new ideas about how to keep the people healthy – as opposed to the desperate remedies that tried to treat disease. Lessons in public health were held in the open air; the songs of travelling operas were adapted for educational support; ideas about cleaning water wells and washing hands were aired for all to hear. And with no possibility of creating an army of qualified doctors for the countryside – there were not even enough for the cities – villagers were trained to become a front-line in the fields.

By 1933, James Yen's MEM had become the government of Ding Xian. Headquartered in the old Temple of Culture, fêted by representatives from the provincial government above, even recognised as a protected territory by the warlords around, its ideas on everything from cabbages and pigs to teachers and health workers were now flying across the country with wings that no one had ever dreamt of, albeit in skies blackening with the advancing clouds of war.

Ding Xian was not short of company in its trail-blazing adventures. With local Hebei newspapers and magazines covering its story, by the early 1930s, stories of its trials and triumphs were being published by newspapers and magazines across the country, reaching across a much wider world of students and intellectuals. Pockets of Ding Xianism were popping up all over the country, south as well as north – and Ding Xian itself had become a model for a new China. The wildly romantic imagining of peasants as a people was beginning to go beyond a dream, inspiring not just more of the students and intellectuals to roll up their sleeves and offer themselves as volunteers, but even some of the gentry, the merchants and the industrialists.

From the pulpit of Peking University's philosophy department, Liang Shuming (the Peking University professor who had argued that China's greatest contribution to the world was the Confucian idea of man as a virtuous spirit who bent his own desires to adapt to nature) set off in search of a county of his own. Convinced that Confucius' original principles (not to be confused with the Confucian*ism* with which imperial dynasties had raised tyrannies of top-down minds) were critical resources for mankind, Liang Shuming restated the virtues which city scholars should carry to the fields. The *ren* humanity of putting yourself in other peoples shoes; the *yi* integrity of names and purposes; *li* ritual as the remembered chore- ography of common lives; *zhi* knowledge as a pursuit of learning that included investigating 'real' things with one's conscience, rather than mechanically applying the texts of the classics; and the *de* virtue of doing everything so diligently that one would never fail. Principles clear, Liang Shuming raised his own practical bridge between the hallowed halls of city-centred knowledge and the villages that had always sat at the edge, and in so doing, forged a link between the present and the past. Liang's dream was to give the peasants the possibility of creating a governing order of their own: a village life within which everyone would put *ren* empathy at the heart of their values, grounded in the rhythm of daily rituals designed for the common good, and all guided by virtue like the north star. Liang called it 'rural reconstruction'.

Then another scholar arrived, fresh from the London School of Economics. The son of a poor gentry family, who had braved the seas to study the science of sociology, his name was Fei Xiaotong. In London, he had been inspired to look at the different functions of a community and, having understood how they worked, to see how such an under- standing might be applied to change. Returning to China, Fei had gone to the far south-west province of Yunnan, where he had used his learn- ing to write up the stories of China's villages in ways that captivated everyone's imaginations. 'To city eyes, the countryside might seem like a scattered tray of sand', Fei observed. 'But if you look more carefully, you will see that what is actually there is much more of a fabric of threads all woven together.' Battered and torn by centuries of neglect as the villages were, Fei agreed that the fabric was not always easy to see, but if only everyone would take the time to look, they would still find a warp, a weft and a pattern. And recognising that there was still a pattern, why on earth would anyone want to add a bloody revolution to the miseries of the earth?

Looking at the factories now sprouting across the cities, and at the industries sweeping up migrant hands, Fei Xiaotong addressed himself to the Guomindang, whose power now spread across so much of the land. 'Stop parroting the West', he argued, 'anyone with eyes to see can tell that it is a world obsessed with cities which behave as if the countryside was a cosmic mistake and assume that man, better made for factories, has nothing to do with nature.' Then, listening to the Communists and their Marxist theories, he turned to offer them an honest opinion as well. 'Stop chattering about 'class' as if everyone lives in a textbook, and look at facts on the ground.' And then he addressed himself to by far and away the vast majority of the people: the men and women who were neither on the Guomindang right, nor the Communist left, but were standing in the middle hoping only for a wider security with which they could return to peaceful lives: 'Roll up your sleeves, brush off your dusty Confucius, and start thinking about how to build a truly Chinese world where everyone can live together, without forgetting the blindingly obvious truth that nothing worth having can be achieved in a day or even a night.' Cities could rise, but no one should forget that China and its people were grounded in its fields. And if the fields and the people were to survive, the trading minds harboured in the cities would need to co-operate with the peasants, including helping them to find a way to raise some manufacturing possibilities in the countryside, while ensuring that the peasants could profit from the wares of their own labour.

Printed on the pages of newspapers up and down the country, news of Ding Xian's triumphs, Liang Shuming's Confucian journey, and Fei Xiaotong's sociological remedies spread across the land, all described as 'rural reconstruction'. North and south, the future of the rural world became the centre of almost everyone's attention. And as the population read its newspapers, there arose an increasing understanding that the biggest problem of all was the fact that the cities and the fields had been pulled apart – and in that process, the ability of the countryside and any peasant to earn a livelihood was rapidly disappearing. Crops were being farmed for exports and cash rather than food; cotton cloth and crafts were being surrendered up for copper pennies before being sent on to the cities by traders, who were the only ones who made a profit. With the peasants working every hour that any god could give them, it seemed that only those who could find their way into one of the rural reconstruction projects, would be able to change their fate.

For James Yen, Liang Shuming, Fei Xiaotong, and all the other 'intellectuals', including the Peking University minds, rural reconstruction was not just a question of the survival of the peasants – nor even just a matter of imagining a people from a scattered tray of sand – it was a matter of creating the foundations of a country which would include both cities *and* the countryside, and where each could learn from the other. And unlike the millennia of the past, the new intellectuals would not be stroking coded characters of disapproval onto scrolls of paper, but would put their own shoulders behind the ideas. Bit by bit, and drop by drop, the dream began to take shape. Here, there, and in more places than one could have ever imagined, rural skills and city minds began to come together. Rural co-operatives, for manufacturing and trade as well as farming, sprang up like bumper crops, all organised by the people themselves. Village hopes began to rise with hosts of enterprising ideas; even as those in the cities began to imagine a different future. It was a stubborn dream of snow in summer: one that almost came true.

Meanwhile, down south in the Jinggang Mountains, while news of James Yen's educating ideas and Ding Xian's prize-winning pigs no doubt reached Mao's ears, it was the dream of a Communist state which had taken hold – with Peng Pai's idea of Peasant Unions an inspiration, but the lessons of the First Qin Emperor as a guide. Peng Pai's idea, but without Peng Pai. Arrested at a secret meeting in Shanghai in 1929, the desperate attempts of Zhou Enlai to rescue him failed. On a late summer's day, refusing even under torture to give up his dream, the great heart who had led his peasants not just to imagine snow in summer but to make their dreams come true was executed by the Guomindang.

In that same year, Mao Zedong carried the kernel of Peng Pai's ideas from the Jinggang Mountains to Jiangxi, to a bigger base spread across thirty thousand square kilometres of mountainous land that would become China's first Soviet Republic. Not the vast flat land that he would later find in the north, but home to three million, mostly peasant and widely scattered, people. And then in 1934, while others up and down the country were trying to imagine a people, and with the battle for the 'survival of the fittest' raging between the Guomindang and the Communist Party, not to mention those within the Communist Party itself, the Party decided it was time to march on.

CHAPTER 2

LEAPING AHEAD

Discover truth through practice.

Mao Zedong, 1937

THE RED HEART ARRIVED in Liu Lin village on a late winter's day, disguised as a donkey driver. Of course, whispers of a Communist army had floated in before: the one that was supposed to be dividing up heaven and earth into equal pieces for the poor. But in these dry lands of yellow earth far from anywhere, truth and hope were always hard to tell apart.

As ragged as the poorest of the villagers, the donkey driver found a shelter at the fraying edge of the village caves, where the meanest of the dwellings tumbled into the fields beyond. Over the nights and weeks which followed, smuggled glances led to tests of cautious words until, eventually, everybody at the bottom of the pile knew exactly what colour he was. With the landlords' militias scouring the countryside on full Guomindang alert for any cunning Communists, one couldn't be too careful. Like-minded souls carefully identified, in the dark corner of a field, under a moonless sky, the donkey driver revealed himself as a revolutionary from Xi'an. The whispers were true, he murmured in a tongue that was clearly not from the fields. 'There is a Red Army and it is on its way. Tell no one except the poor. If you want to help, organise yourselves into a peasant union and create a company of rebel soldiers of your own.'

Over the months that followed, whisper by whisper, bravely independent spirits conjured up a Peasant Union from the fields, together with a company of rebel soldiers they could confidently call their own. It was not long before treacherous ears reported events to the landlords sitting behind their fortified county town walls, and no time at all after that before the landlords' militia appeared in the fields with their spears and swords. But, with the donkey driver always behind them, the company of rebels was prepared. As so often across the past, the dazzling exploits of the Crouching Dragon Zhuge Liang, and the heroic stories of the *Outlaws of the Marsh*, had been scoured for strengthening inspiration. With only wood for weapons, bayonets and rifles had been carved and covered in silver paper to make them glint menacingly in the sun. With only fireworks for gunpowder, firecrackers had been hurled over the walls of the officials' courtyards in the dead of night, attracting a returning fire which, just as in Zhuge Liang's battle of the borrowed arrows, sapped the ammunition and the spirits of the landlords' side.

At one point, the chairman of the Peasant Union was captured and taken to the county town, where he lost his head to a warlord's sword. But the Union stayed strong. By the end of the following September, battles fought and won amidst the corn, Liu Lin's land and that of its neighbours was sitting under a new heaven – one where the poor could till the fields without having to pay taxes, or even rent, where justice was free for all, and where not a single landlord could be found.

By the end of the year, the donkey driver was gone. By night, he had helped them plan not only their defences but their future. By day, he had put his shoulder to the plough with the best of them. When a fragile field had slid off its precarious slope, he had been the first to offer his ideas and his labour to try to restore the loss. If a family had needed a helping hand, he had been there before they had even asked. At every meal, he had eaten the same cabbage as everyone else; and if there was ever any corn, he had never, ever, taken a grain more than the rough hands next to him. When he had left, he had taken only one gift, the simplest of all to give for those whose home it was: a hand-sketched map of the lay of Liu Lin's land and that of all of the surrounding villages, including every secret path. 'I will be back', he promised, 'and when I return, I will not be alone.'

The 'drop by drop' approach taken up by James Yen, Liang Shuming, Fei Xiaotong and the Peking University minds had worked well for a while. But the tides of the time had been unwilling to wait. In July 1937, the Japanese army had swept across the north of China, and into its county towns. With no troops to protect them, as the Japanese poured through the northern gate of Ding Xian's county seat, the MEM workers and everyone else who wanted to follow them, had picked up whatever they could carry and clattered out through the gate at the south. Like brothers and sisters in the cities, each had to make his or her own choice about where to go. The options were narrowing: by August, Shanghai had become a muddy battlefield of a second war with Japan; by the end of the year, having lost Nanjing to a Japanese massacre, the Guomindang would be moving to the central cities of Sichuan.

For anyone ready to convert to the Party's faith, Yan'an always offered an open door. Many of the MEM members sympathised with the Communist idea of equality, and few were fans of a Guomindang whose self-strengthening seemed to have engulfed its forces in clouds of corruption. But the rising stories of Mao's battles with other Party minds – and worrying whispers about the purges of those daring to question Mao's ideas – were as disquieting for the MEM sympathisers as for others. Unsure, many decided to stay within the guns of the Guomindang's world. Once again, Chinese minds divided: some made their way to the Shaanxi plains around Yan'an, hoping that Ding Xian's lessons could be taught in the new Communist world. Others, including James Yen and many of the MEM's organising volunteers, followed Chiang Kai-shek to Sichuan, eventually landing in the inland port of Chongqing that, by the end of 1938, had become the latest capital of the country.

James Yen and his followers might have congregated in the industrious city of Chongqing, but none of them had given up on their dream of a new countryside. Soon, they dug themselves into the county of Beipei, close to Chongqing, and tried to build yet another new world. Peasants were taught to read and write, new breeds of pigs were raised, new seeds were sown, better pumps were installed for spreading water, schools were opened for all, health was taught as a way of life, and co-operatives were created for rural industry, with markets added for peasant trades. Beipei became Ding Xian all over again – with the added ideas of Liang Shuming's rural reconstruction and Fei Xiaotong's rural enterprise sown deeply into its soil. Although physically located within the territory of the Guomindang, few of the MEM adherents had any attachment to Chiang Kai-shek's version of the national dream. Tired of disasters, weary of broken promises, they were also shocked at troops who seemed to see the Chinese people as their own personal property as well as at a government now suspiciously scrutinising every word for subversion; they were also worn out by the daily assaults on what anyone could say. From time to time, some even wondered whether the future might not be better in Yan'an after all. Indeed, for many of those brave enough to touch the banned pages of the Party's propaganda or tune into its secret radio signals, Mao's thoughts on New Democracy began to seem not so bad. 'An enlightened and progressive China', he promised. Well, everyone could do with that. But this was the stuff of evening conversations, those moments when, after a long day's labour, Chinese hearts would ask themselves the age-old question: what did it mean to be Chinese, and where on earth was heaven?

Then, as the Second World War finished, America poured its dollars into the Guomindang's lap, not only to fight the Communists but to support the idea of rural reconstruction which was now seen as the best means of saving China. James Yen and others like him sighed. While dollars were always helpful, it was not money that China's countryside needed: it was a sympathetic bridge between the rural and the city worlds – and time. In any event, with corruption now rife across the Guomindang's Republic of China, the chances of those dollars being used for much other than strengthening the pockets of individual officials seemed slim. With the best will in the capitalist world, once again, it looked as if the peasants and the villages were going to find themselves at the bottom of the pile.

With the civil war now resurrected, the rural reconstructionists raced, like the ancient Nüwa, to shore up as much of a heavenly countryside as they could before the black skies collapsed on to earth. With whatever narrow threads of energy left to them, a few took the time and gathered up the courage to tell Chiang Kai-shek why they stayed in a countryside controlled by his troops. It was certainly not because they believed in the Guomindang's censorship or revelled in its corruption. They stayed because, while they might not be able to say whatever they wanted, unlike the whispers that they heard from Yan'an, their hearts still had the freedom to be silent.

In 1947, two years after the war with Japan had ended, and as competing ideas about order became the central theatre of China's post-war battles, Mao surveyed the landscape from his Yan'an caves. A lot had changed. After Japan's surrender, the northern Chinese lands that it had occupied were picked up by Russia's Soviet Republic. Eventually, long after any movable industrial parts had been expatriated to Moscow, Stalin turned the territory over to Mao. With the change in jurisdiction, the Chinese Communist bases in the north now included some of those MEM members who, disillusioned with the Guomindang, had decided to stay where they were and look for their future with Mao. Meanwhile, the 8th Route Army, whether in companies of troops or as individual donkey drivers in disguise, had spread out, not only fighting against the Guomindang for territory, but also actively reaching out to capture peasants, body and soul.

Every successful battle seemed to open up fields of possibilities. Peasant unions and rebel soldiers had united in the creation of a new heaven and a new earth. Where stories ran riot about Guomindang troops ransacking granaries and trampling across fields, every 8th Route Army soldier was a Guan Yu guardian, straight out of the magical stories of the past. Famous for fighting fiercely on the side of the poor, they conquered land from the landlords, and were said to be redistributing it to the peasants, even helping them plant their corn as well. Where the Guomindang's troops scorched the earth in a desperate attempt to flush out Communist spies, every 8th Route Army commander was a Zhuge Liang Crouching Dragon who scoured the landscape for any and every possible means of winning a battle without harming the people at large. Rumours that muttered otherwise were nothing but Guomindang lies.

Not surprisingly, with new models of old brotherly heroes, stories were told of how many peasants, men, woman and children, were willing recruits. Eager to do anything to bring about a new and better heaven, no task was too burdensome. In the dead of night, barefooted bands of brothers (men who knew the lie of the land better than the backs of their hands) climbed up poles and cut the Guomindang's communicating wires. By the light of day, from the vantage points of their fields, peasant eyes observed Guomindang troops moving this way and that, and when they got back to the village after the sun had gone down, they whispered what they had seen to brothers who were now messengers for the donkey drivers. Nothing was too daunting to learn or discover. No one, not even a child, was too young to become a hero.

With Moscow adding capital support, field by field, county by county, the north of China turned red. And when, on 1 October 1949, the Party's radios reported the magical story of Mao Zedong waving to the people from the terrace of Tiananmen's Gate of Heavenly Peace, and announced the dream of a People's Republic of China, the fields exploded with joy. Strings of firecrackers crackled like guns, children raced around like miniature airplanes, pedlars appeared from nowhere with threads of fruit, and everyone put on their best blue cloth.

Not everyone, however, rejoiced. In November 1948, with the Communist flag firmly planted on northern soil and Mao's troops turning south, Zhou Enlai had sent word to Sichuan that James Yen, and every other patriotic mind, would be welcome in the coming People's Republic. Yen, more suspicious than ever of Mao's darker ideas, set sail for America. Once again, the MEM members and followers divided. Many followed the Guomindang to the refuge of Taiwan – not because they wanted to live in the corruption of the Guomindang's orders, but because they thought that the Guomindang might be the lesser of two evils. Others decided that, red or white, China was China, and it was hard to be Chinese anywhere else. Yan'an was full of friends from the past: surely things could not be that bad. When the dust settled, wouldn't everybody realise that they were all pursuing the same dream?

Waking up to the new dawn of the People's Republic, it seemed as if the sun was going to shine over every rural river – so Ding Ling's stories told. If the Party's land-reforming cadres did not arrive today, they would certainly be coming tomorrow. And once they arrived, the 'autumn accounts' with which landlords had once terrified their tenants, would be settled to a different tune, with all of the land divided up and shared out, and everybody treated the same. After thousands of years of tyranny, the days of tilling somebody else's fields looked as if they would finally be over.

Gathering together the land-reforming experiences of the earliest Chinese soviets, incuding Yan'an, Mao marshalled his thoughts on how best to proceed. Like all Great Men, he began by consulting the past. The old idea of a hierarchy of four occupations – *nong* farmers, *shi* scholars, *gong* artisans, and *shang* merchants – had obviously become confused. The *shi* scholars had risen to the top of the pile, eventually becoming lords of lands that they did not farm themselves, and then rushing off to the city to live new lives of ease. The *shang* merchants, pushing their own way upwards, and trying to become *shi* scholars in the process, had turned the countryside on its head, and then torn off to the cities for an even more profitable life. Left behind in the countryside, the *nong* tillers of the land had fallen to the bottom of the heap. Meanwhile, and depending on the quality of their skills, the artisan *gong* had gone in all directions – some up, some down, and some staying where they should have been: an industrious rung above the unproductive merchant *shang*.

It was time to wipe the imperial slate clean – and what better cloth to use than the scientific logic of Marx. Applying the simple divides of class, rather than the more difficult idea of imagining a people, the countryside was reconstructed again. First on Mao's list were the idle landlords, those who had lived off everybody else's labour. They now belonged so far down the bottom of the pile that one really shouldn't worry if some of them fell off. Good riddance to them. *Chi shenme, huan shenme*, as the old wisdom went: you get as good as you give. Then there were the 'rich peasants', those with a bit of extra land that they rented out to others while tilling a lot of the fields themselves. They should go down to the lower levels of the pile, just above the idle landlords. After that, there were the 'middle peasants', who worked their own land. Obviously, they should be a cut above the rich peasants. Then came the 'poor peasants', tenant farmers and others who worked for a wage. They should sit just above the middle peasants, quite close to the top, and be given a piece of land of their own. And then there were the 'hired hands', those with nothing to their name but their labour. Reaping the greatest rewards of all, they would now get a piece of land of their own, and rise to the top of the pile.

With class now in control, redistribution was the order of the day, and not just of land and status. Anyone who had possessions beyond a wok or a pot was told to gather them up and be ready to share them out equally in order to restore, even if only in the smallest way, the great injustices of the past. Not, of course, including the animals and the ploughs: they would be put in the fields so that the Party's land reform teams could somehow work out who should be able to use what, and when.

Over the course of the next three years, the Party's land reform- ing cadres worked their way across China's vast lands, visiting almost every imaginable corner, no matter how remote. It took a while: as Mao Zedong had once said, 'when night falls in the east, the west is still lit up; when darkness covers the south, the north remains bright'. By the time they arrived in some villages, they found that the villagers had already executed a rough justice of their own. And in many places they found themselves obliged to right not just the wrongs of the past, but recent ones as well: strong voices who had put themselves at the top and pushed the weakest out, and local thugs who had decided that anyone who owned any land at all, even if it was small or as unyield- ing as rock, should be instantly despatched to another world. There was a lot to teach, and a lot to learn. With the landlords toppled from their perches, many of the peasants could scarcely stop from pinching themselves: had snow really fallen in summer? Others, however, were convinced that it could not last: surely, it would only be a matter of time before the sky changed, and the landlords, whether alive or as the hungry ghosts of the dead, would come back, grab their land, and give everyone a beating.

Meanwhile, there was a whole new language to learn, with the lexi- con of class rankings replacing the old Confucian relationships, and fixing everybody into new revolutionary places. Naturally, everyone wanted to be a poor peasant or a hired hand: heroes, who were entitled to the best redistributing returns. No one wanted to be a rich peasant: condemned to a cloud of suspicion, it was not much better than being a landlord. Being a middle peasant seemed alright, but it was a bit too close to the dangerous rich peasant status for the liking of most. These challenges aside, it was also clear that not everyone in the coun- tryside was celebrating. Rare surviving landlords and rich peasants were quivering in their boots: lucky to escape with a bashed-up body, millions of their peers had died in the rages of anger that had been poured upon their heads. And then, according to the Party, there were the counter-revolutionaries hiding in the straw of village life: men and women whose hard hearts secretly yearned for a return to the past; bad elements who worshipped wooden gods; and those who harboured subjective dreams about the original rural reconstruction. They would clearly need to be rooted out.

Trained to find the enemies of the people, and guided by quotas from the top, the Party's work teams organised the villagers into meetings and instructed them in the Yan'an arts of struggle and self-criticism. It was soon clear to all, though, that truth was not an easy commodity – it usually took a beating to bring it out. But to many, it seemed the truth was just the icing on the cake: an important question of justice, obviously, but once the bad elements had been settled at the bottom of the Democratic Dictatorship of the People, where they belonged, they would be cleaning pigsties, sweeping the streets and carrying anything and everything that the village leaders ('on behalf of the people') might require. The really important thing – the magical snow-in-summer thing to which every once-downtrodden heart should be directed – was the fact that each peasant would have a piece of land which he could call his own. Backs applied to the hoes and the ploughs, horses available to lend a hand, with everyone expected to help everybody else, and the fields about to be washed with plenty, surely everything would soon settle down.

Installed in his spreading Zhongnanhai courtyard, by the early 1950s, Mao was receiving regular reports about the affairs of the country-side. The early achievements had been highly encouraging: red flags waving as far as the eye could see, landlords tamed or eliminated, land for everyone who deserved it, and harvests rising. Under the guidance of the Party's workers, peasants had even elected their own village leaders, to replace the tyrants of the past.

But looking at the bigger picture, Mao was a little concerned. While many people should have been satisfied beyond their wildest dreams, as the seasons turned and the meetings continued, there seemed to be a lot of fussing about who got which piece of land, and whose fields were weeded first. There was also a lot of complaining about class-classifi-cations. Not to mention a lot of revelling in thoughts of new clothes. As if that were not enough, there was also a lot of whining about 'too many meetings', even as everybody wanted to have a view of their own. New Democracy was where the will of the people was protected by the guidance of the Party. But somehow the peasants had got the wrong end of the stick and were launching themselves into a kind of 'extreme democracy' where everybody chattered about their personal opinions, and no one gave the blindest bit of notice to the revolutionary principles at stake.

It was not long before Mao reached the conclusion that the peasants were incapable of understanding that what had been achieved was not about satisfying the individual wills of hundreds of millions of Chinese people but about creating a greater revolutionary will of the people at large. Fields and donkeys were as nothing compared with the prize of a truly socialist world where everyone would eventually own everything, and even the state itself would wither away. Seeing selfish subjectivism in every direction, hearing the constant refrain of peasants wanting nothing more than to create their own personal paradises on earth and in so doing constantly criticizing everything, Mao came to the conclusion that it was time to move the revolution on. The peasants needed to understand their place in the new China: a China which not only had to attend to its affairs at home but which, in the battle for the survival of the fittest state, also needed to ensure that it was strong enough to keep any imperialist foreign powers out.

As Mao worried about the quality of peasant minds, his thoughts naturally turned to the fact that the country's power to defend itself among the endlessly competing nations of the world would now have to come from the cities and their industries. If the city industries required for China's 'survival of the fittest' battle were going to be able to grow, it was the countryside that was going to need to fuel and feed them. True, Fei Xiaotong and the original rural reconstructors had been playing around with manufacturing co-operatives in the countryside, but these were nothing more than chicken feed in the bigger scheme of things. Given the fuzzy and rather selfish thinking that was going on in the villages, the Party was going to have to have to deliver some bigger change. Step-by-step was the answer: better not to panic the peasants with too much information in advance. Old habits die hard, and even revolutionary peasants would need time to get used to the rather contradictory idea of an order in which the peasants who had battled for the revolution were now to devote themselves to the industrial success of the cities.

The first revolutionary step would be for the peasants to pool their land into mutually helping and very local 'co-operatives'. With this achieved, and with everyone's confidence won, the second step would be to ask the peasants to express their revolutionary gratitude by selflessly folding the co-operatives, and their own land, into bigger collectives: still local, but now under the county governments of the Democratic Dictatorship of the People rather than the old villages and their heads. Obviously, quite a few people were going to mutter about the loss of land so recently acquired, and at such a human cost; but those who did would simply be revealing themselves as just the kind of bad elements that needed to be eliminated. With the collectives organised under local county government, the need for a third step would then become obvious: with a little better organisation, the collectives could be pooled together into vast 'communes' for economies of scale. Scale achieved, the communes would be able to manage themselves, and the wasteful job of local county government would disappear. The state would start to wither away, and Marx's utopian dream would begin to appear.

Clear about the broad direction required, Mao looked at the maps and started to think about a plan. As far as he could see, the ancient foundations were encouraging. Two thousand years after the First Qin Emperor, the faint traces of his commanding genius could still be seen in the ancient grids of central power which had been flung like a net across the country at large: a patchwork of twenty-five provinces, each with a capital of its own, thousands of counties and towns, and hundreds of thousands of village settlements spread across endless fields. To any keen Chinese eye, the order was clear: the provincial capitals had been the seats of imperially-appointed governors; the county towns had been the seats of imperially-appointed magistrates, supported by a loyal gentry; and the village settlements had been, and still were, where the majority of China's now six hundred million men, women and children lived – all bound together in groups of households, with each one guaranteeing the obedient peace of all. Truly, thought Mao, the First Qin Emperor had done more for the Chinese people than any other emperor since.

In the intervening millennia, however, the clarity of the Qin genius had become muddied by far lesser men. For a start, the tight central control which the First Qin Emperor had so wisely insisted upon had gradually been eroded until the provincial governors and the gentry were doing whatever they wanted, taking care only to ensure that the fiction of the simple Confucian ideal was maintained at the top. In such a world, it was hardly surprising that everyone else had fallen to thinking only about themselves: families in the fields weaving cloth to sell to others for extra handfuls of coppers; artisans making all sorts of frivolous gadgets; merchants leaping at the chance to sell anything they could get their profiting hands on; and even scholars jumping on the bandwagon. With all of that going on, it was even less surprising that under the Manju Qing, messy market towns had further clouded the simple order – hundreds of them by the time the first revolution had exploded in 1911. But by that point, the wisdom of the First Qin Emperor's genius had been well and truly lost. Then had come forty years of Republican chaos: warlords everywhere, and Guomindang variations on self-strengthening mixing up farming and trade. Factories had been scattered wherever an individual mind chose to put his ideas or his money, and a number of peasants had ended up dabbling in industry, whether at home or in the cities, instead of minding the fields.

It was as clear as crystal that the picture was not only wrong, but dangerous. After one hundred years of humiliation at the hands of the imperial powers, even a half-educated schoolboy could see that the countries of the world were engaged in a bitter battle which only the fittest would survive. Likewise, any half-educated schoolboy could tell you that the deciding factor in this battle would not be how many fields one had, or who had them, but whether or not those fields, together with any ponds and seams of minerals, were marshalled for the collective good. The 'collective good' was, of course, the delivery to the cities of the harvesting surpluses necessary to fuel the industrial productivity on which China's strength – and survival – would depend.

Contemplating the facts on the ground (and drawing on the experience of the bigger Russian Soviet brothers, not to mention the ancient Halls of Light), Mao was persuaded that the solution lay in the creation of a new Party-led central government commission which would be charged with building the urban industrial triumph required for survival. The same commission would also decide, in meticulous detail and on a five-yearly basis, exactly what everyone, in the countryside and the cities alike, needed to do to make it happen. Order and production would go hand in hand, all under a Five-Year Plan.

The most important and urgent questions were how to increase the harvests as quickly as possible, and how to get them transferred to the cities at as low a price as possible, so that industry could rise. Production quotas for grain, the most essential harvest, seemed to be the obvious answer. Given that the peasants were still at the earliest stage of farming their own land (not to mention stubbornly insisting on getting the best prices), while they might be allowed to keep other produce for their own family needs, all sales of grain would need to be made to the central state itself. That should get the harvests up, and keep the prices down.

In 1954, the first Five-Year Plan was put into action. With the stroke of a central brush, Mao instructed his lower Party officials – and the lower Party officials instructed those in charge of the villages – to inform the peasants that, while they could keep the land they had been given, from now on, they were going to work in co-operatives. Not the old kinds of co-operatives where villagers organised themselves, selling their produce on messy rural markets, but new ones, organised by the Party, with everybody's grain, as the most important crop, sold only to the central state. While they were at it, the officials should tell the peasants what grain quotas every village would have to meet, and the prices they were going to be paid. Lots to do, no time to lose, the revolution was only just getting started: a 'little leap forward' should do the trick.

As might have been expected, reaction in the fields was mixed. The old poor peasants were rather enthusiastic, unable to believe their luck that someone else would take on the job of organising everyone to help each other. Conversely, the old middle and rich peasants were rather upset by the loss of the power to set the terms and prices of their own grain. Once they had got over their initial shock, however, many started trickily seizing on the details. 'How much of our fields do we have to turn to grain?' was a common question. 'If this is a democracy, why do we have to join a co-operative?' was another. Trickiest of all, though, was the question that only the cleverest asked: 'If everyone has to contribute their fields and produce to a quota fixed by Beijing, whose land is it anyway?' Mao began to see that it was not just the bourgeois city intellectuals who had a lot to learn.

By and large, the Party officials and village leaders patiently explained the logic of helping a neighbour – and the necessity of defending China in the wider battle of nation states. They also reminded everyone that they could still keep a small plot for their own family needs. But with the questions continuing, some of the Party officials and village leaders found themselves pushed beyond the limits of their patience. With many peasants unwilling to join the co-operatives, the most stubborn heads were dealt a beating. And in the new registers which the Party had taken to keeping, a little black question mark was placed by every name which raised an inconvenient objection or just refused to join: a clear sign of a clandestine counter-revolutionary. More meetings were held, the arts of struggle and self-criticism were practised over and over again, and for those who really could not learn from their mistakes, punishments were to hand.

Strengthened by the struggle sessions and the punishments, the powers of the Party's local cadres seemed to climb. But quieter questions began to whisper on a few suspicious people's lips. One was the obvious query about why, given that the revolution had been won by the peasants from the fields, it was the cities and their industries that were going to get the benefits of the grain. Another (noting that the peasants – who, after all, were really supposed to be the new rulers – were going to submit themselves to the greater will of the people, and that the Party was going to decide what that greater will was) mischievously asked who the Party was going to answer to. The natural response to the first question was that the peasants still had a lot of lessons to learn. The answer to the second question was a sharp and simple snap that over the last five thousand years, heaven had never submitted to anyone. 'But if that was the case', persisted the thickest minds, 'why had there been a revolution at all?'

———

Summer turned to winter, winter turned to spring; seeds were sown, fields were ploughed, and soon a year had passed. By 1955, the first of the three steps – the creation of nearly a million new co-operatives – had been taken, and the principle of mutual assistance for a greater common good had been repeated. But, still clinging on to the idea of individual plots of land for their own household needs, the peasants had once again managed to miss the point. Their petty ignorance was reflected in less-than revolutionary results. While the co-operatives' grain harvests were promising, they were as nothing compared to the bumper crops of the other produce – from apples and potatoes to chickens, ducks and eggs – which the peasants' individual plots sent off to market.

Getting a little impatient, Mao decided to move things along to the second step (collectives) as quickly as possible. In the same year, 1955, he issued an updating announcement in the name of 'the people': it was time for the peasants to concentrate all of their energies on production, rather than worrying about their own individual marketing. From now on, they should selflessly contribute all of their land to a host of new collectives, with Beijing deciding what they would need for their own consumption – after a careful consultation of what the cities and their hungry industries required. And for the avoidance of any tricky doubts, 'land' would include not only the fields, but also any orchards, chickens and ducks.

This time, there were a lot more questioners in the meetings. But after some sharp 'clarifications', the majority bit their tongues. Following up on the logic of the collectives, in 1956, Mao decided that it was time to close everybody's markets. Appearing as regularly as the seasons, part of the rhythm of everybody's country life for centuries, the peasants could scarcely believe their ears. Mouths opened, ready to complain. But then Mao's city suggestion that a hundred flowers should bloom had ended with the brutal Anti-Rightist campaign – and three hundred thousand city intellectuals, 'rightists', arrived in the countryside. And those were just the ones who had survived. The fate that awaited anyone who could not keep their revolutionary tongue under control was plain for all to see. Party officials at all levels made sure that the new position was clearly communicated to the villagers at the bottom: even the most constructive criticism was going to come at a cost so high that nobody would want to pay it. And there would be a particularly punishing cost to any local Party official or village leader who failed to keep a firm lid on local opinion: yes, there had been a revolution but now that up was down, and black was white, the old idea of obedience had to be restored – obedience to the Democratic Dictatorship of the People, of course.

Back in Beijing, Mao, impatient to fuel the industrial revolution with bumper crops from the fields, decided to crack on to the third of the steps. Time to gather the collectives into even bigger 'communes'.

Local government would disappear and, just as under the First Qin Emperor, every household would work in production teams, organised under production brigades. Henceforth, regardless of local land conditions, production goals, crop choices and farming methods would be set by the central mind of the Party and its government, rather than by the individual peasants on the ground. Irrigation systems would be stretched as far as the eye could see; wells would be dug to sparkle like subterranean stars; dams would be raised to tame rivers; roads, canals and bridges would be built to speed the greater harvests up to the cities.

With the lessons of the Anti-Rightist campaign still fresh, complaints were few, and those who dared to express contrary opinions were quickly struggled straight. In 1958, a second Five-Year Plan was announced, and the revolutionary idea of a *Great Leap Forward* was announced, with the twin goals of catching up with Britain's steel output within fifteen years, and firing the furnaces of industry with a doubling in the peasants' production of grain. Just to make sure that everybody could give their full attention to the targets set, communal kitchens would also be created so that nobody else would have to cook. 'More, faster, better, cheaper' would be the slogan of the day. With these efficiencies in place, the countryside would deliver mass bumper harvests, and any inconvenient outbursts of local nature could easily be contained. China's industrial productivity would rocket: more grain to feed the cities, and with the communal kitchens feeding the people, everyone's woks and pots could be fed into local furnaces, which would increase the national output of steel as well.

Every official was aware that Mao expected revolutionary harvests. They were also aware that, in the Party scheme of things, their zeal would be matched against that of their peers, and their personal futures would be held to ransom too. Encouraged by strong crops in recent years, many Party cadres in the countryside saw an opportunity to make their revolutionary careers fly. Clear as to Mao's expectations, when Beijing asked for local estimates, almost all of the officials decided to demonstrate their Communist credentials with a robust embellishment of the harvesting volumes they expected to achieve: what harm could a little confidence do?

As the 'estimates' were delivered, the old heavenly facts – that nature was rarely predictable, and that bumper harvests tend not to come in strings – were conveniently set aside. Also set aside were the more revolutionary facts that a number of peasants were now being despatched to the cities to build new industrial factories, not to mention the raising of the triumphant ten-year anniversary monuments in Beijing. Across the communes, Party cadres took the estimates for fields expected to produce five hundred kilos of grain, and bumped them up a bit. Up in the county towns, Party officials, just as keen to establish their revolutionary credentials, and with the added advantage of a city thinking that believed that nature always had room to stretch, added a zero, here and there. Further up in the provincial capitals, higher Party officials, keenest of all to bask in the revolutionary sun, and furthest away from any inconvenient idea of what nature could really do, doubled everything. By the time the estimates arrived in Beijing, the scale of their ambition would have been seen as preposterous by anyone who had ever spent any time on the land, or indeed anyone who had not been petrified into silence. But no one on the land was asked for their opinion. Planning the strategy that would enable China to catch up with imperialist Britain in fifteen years required only the clearest, and most objective, of city minds.

Estimates presented, the quotas were set, central purchases were made at the new low prices, and the grain was ordered to be loaded onto trucks and boats. From there it would travel to the cities, whence it would either be distributed for urban consumption or loaded again on to ships bound for other foreign countries who would pay an industrially-valuable US dollar price (or to the Soviet Union as part of an early deal for Moscow's support). As trucks began to move the vast volumes of grain out of the countryside, villagers and lower level officials who had not been privy to the higher-level embellishments raised surprised eyebrows. Some even dared to question whether there would be enough grain left in local granaries to feed the peasants themselves. Needless to say, the questioners were put firmly into their obviously counter-revolutionary places, and the loaded trucks and boats continued to move out. Mao was ecstatic. All it took was a bit of revolutionary fervour and the Chinese talent for working hard: catching up with Britain in fifteen years? With this kind of zeal, they might manage it in two or three.

By the early months of 1959 though, a cold dawn of truth began to spread from under the moonlit facts – at least to the Party officials in the countryside. In the communal kitchens, food was now running out before the last peasants had got to the front of the queue. And in many parts of the country not only were the villagers getting hungrier by the day, but quite a few bodies seemed to be tumbling by the wayside. Still eager to make their numbers, the officials put the early deaths down to an unfortunate run of natural events, and turned their attention back to pushing the limits of production in the fields. The peasants were exhorted to 'dig deeper, irrigate better, sow those seeds whose packages carry the biggest promises of yields – and sow them closely'. To which was added an instruction for the commune leaders: 'Whatever you do, make sure that when the next time comes for the trucks to be loaded, by hook or by crook, and regardless of the tears of any hungry onlookers, the quotas are met.'

Already wobbling on weak legs, day in, day out, the peasants were sent back to the fields to force the earth into revolutionary action. Following planting instructions from the top, almost no one had the stamina to argue that many of the new ideas were taking everybody backwards, rather than leaping anything ahead. At the end of every day, exhausted by labouring targets fixed for men who were eating enough to work – and disheartened by planting seeds so closely that they would never be able to grow – the peasants could only join the communal kitchen queues and hope that whatever was left in the pot would be enough to carry them through to another day.

It was never enough. Up in the Shandong north, the peasants returned to that desperate diet of the worst of the imperial times: tree bark and chaff. In other parts of the country, they foraged for whatever might keep the aching pains in their stomachs at bay: roots, wood, grass, and any and every insect, whether it crawled, or jumped, or flew. Dogs no longer barked, chickens no longer clucked; children stopped running. In the most unfortunate of counties, whole villages became hungry ghosts. Those who had a breath of life left in them began to whisper rhymes as old as the Ming dynasty: tales of times of famine, when beggars were so poor that they had only children left to sell. This time, in their desperation, some would even eat their dead.

In April 1959, the bureaucratic government of the Democratic Dictatorship of the People quietly sent a report to Mao noting that twenty-five million people across fifteen provinces did not have enough food to survive. Mao observed that this must be a temporary crisis – an understandable problem when transforming such a big country with so many mouths to feed, and one that the local officials were surely more than capable of fixing. 'No need to reduce the amount of grain that the state is procuring for the cities', he commanded, 'the revolutionary spirit of the peasants will sort it all out in the end'. Down in the countryside, each commune became locked in its own official secrecy. With every Party official acutely aware that Mao was counting on them, most decided to bury the mounting evidence of the human costs of their revolutionary fervour. It was not easy. Dead bodies, mounting by the day, were demanding to be buried in the dark of night. Meanwhile, starving individuals kept trying to make their way to buses and trains, hoping to find food elsewhere, and seemingly oblivious to the fact that if anyone outside knew what was going on, their local officials would lose their jobs – or worse. Worrying round the clock, the officials came up with the idea of 'dissuasion' stations to round up the complainers before they could leave. Prison cells were stretched to hold the most unco-operative complainers until they could see sense – or until the prison's food ran out; in which case, the problem was solved.

A rather bigger problem, however, was the mountain of counter-revolutionary letters, which clearly had to be stopped. Missives to friends and relations, some even recklessly addressed to higher Party officials in Beijing, they included desperate alerts of what the people of the individual communes assumed was just a local disaster, with each of them begging those outside and above to come and help. Reading all the mail was obviously an impossible task, but the postal service could easily be suspended. In some parts of the country, peasants who had not understood their place in revolutionary history rose up in riotous anger, and had to be beaten into silence. (On the positive side, this did mean fewer mouths to feed.) As if all of that was not trouble enough, from time to time an individual official or a commune leader would begin to get cold feet and think that it might be time to own up to the over-estimates. Only heaven knew how such subjectivists had managed to survive this long. With the power to bring the hounds of hell down from Beijing, they were beaten like the drowning dogs they clearly were. Casting aspersions on excellent situations, could they not understand that there was a bigger revolutionary truth at stake – not to mention a number of official careers and lives?

———

By the end of 1959, with Mao describing the Great Leap Forward as a uniquely Chinese combination of Marxism on the one hand and the First Qin Emperor's wisdom on the other, some of his comrades were feeling uneasy. As hunger touched Beijing, a few of the most senior leaders made disguised visits to their *lao jia*, old rural family homes. Seeing once-lively villages worryingly quiet, and with relatives willing to whisper behind the walls of their homes, they soon understood that hunger was stalking the fields. Delicate questions were asked and anxious local officials conjured up the better-fed people from the dying ranks to put on a reassuring display. But, eventually, even the most imaginative of officials began to run out of steam. By the spring of 1960, it was crystal clear to those in the senior echelons of the Party (as it had been clear to almost everyone in the lower ranks for the last two years) that China's countryside was engulfed in a mass famine. It was also clear that the people's desperate cries for help had been smothered by the very same men and women who only ten years earlier had been revolutionary heroes.

Astonished at the ability of the people to eat so much bitterness in so much silence, some noted that if China had been like any other country in the world, the troops would have had to be sent in long ago. Others replied that if China had been like any other country in the world, Party leaders who had faced hails of bullets on fields of war would never have trembled before Mao like a herd of sheep. Not all of the local officials, however, had stayed silent. While many in the countryside battled to keep the truth separate from facts, there were, as there had always been, heroes; and in Beijing, a handful of brave Party comrades finally forced Mao to acknowledge that something would have to be done. By the summer, the flow of grain from the countryside to the cities began to slow, and the courageous comrades began to enquire into the causes of the nightmare on the ground.

In the end, the enquirers concluded that it was all the product of 'five winds', each of them contagious. The first was a 'communist wind', which had stripped the peasants of even their pots and pans. The second was a 'commandism wind', which had seen local officials rise as gods. The third was an 'exaggeration wind', which had transformed so many wild dreams into paper facts that no one had any idea what was really going on. The fourth was a 'chaotic directives wind', which had every bureaucrat tripping over his own orders in an attempt to defeat the logic of nature. And the fifth was the 'cadre privilege wind', which meant that, at the end of any day, the soup ladles were always firmly in the hands of the Party's officials: men and women whose bowls were always filled first, and to the brim, regardless of how many hungry mouths were standing behind them in the queue.

Within a year, the courageous comrades had succeeded in putting a question mark over the communes, and Mao was under heavy pressure to think again. But the revolution was not finished with the countryside yet.

CHAPTER 3

WINDS, AND MORE WINDS

These creatures in the world below were compounded of
the essence of heaven and earth; nothing that goes on there
should surprise us.

The Jade Emperor to his ministers in the Treasure Hall of
the Holy Mists of the Cloud Palace; *Journey to the
West*, Wu Cheng'en (seventeenth century)

LONG BOW VILLAGE was asleep when the brigade office fell.
Momentarily unifying under a single banner in the spring of 1969,
the Red Guards from the cement plant, the Rebel Regiment from the
railway repair shop, and the Mao Zedong Thought Red Guards from
the middle school – all of them supported by a motley young crew
from the nearby power station – broke down its door with little effort.
A quick shine of a torch over the obvious hiding places, and the seal
which held the stamp of the brigade's power had been seen, seized and
carried off to a new home in the pocket of the youngest and least obvious suspect. Mission accomplished, everyone went home to bed.

Over the following days, news of the 'power seizure' travelled fast,
and the rebels found themselves in rising demand: other brigades
were ripe for a takeover and there was also the bigger prize of the
commune itself. Before long, the villages of the Taihang mountains in
the Shanxi north were locked in so many cultural revolutionary battles
that nobody knew which way was up. Loyalists defended the old guard;
young rebels fought for a new one; both old and new accused the other
of betraying the revolution. Few, if any, of the onlookers could tell who
was right or wrong.

If the truth be told, the holders of both sides of the lines looked
suspiciously like the great-grandchildren of the old feuding families
whose battles for local power had been tearing the village apart for
centuries. A hundred years before, one of their feuds had divided the

village into a north and a south. Even when the north of the country had gone to war (Guomindang against the Communists; everyone against the Japanese) they had continued to prosecute their old enmities, albeit against the backdrop of bigger battles. Then had come the Communist revolution and the struggles against anyone who looked like a landlord. Although both sides had lost a lot of their richer numbers in those battles, poorer relations seemed to have picked up the cudgels, opening up yet another generation of struggles. In the early years after 1949, the fights had been about whose new fields should be irrigated first. A decade later, they had graduated to the often life-and-death question of who should hold the soup ladle in the communal kitchens. Things seemed to have died down a little in the years that followed the Great Leap Forward, but then there had been that wife-snatching incident a few years back (more of a bride-to-be really, but jealousy ran too deep to be mindful of such fine distinctions): that obviously hadn't helped.

And then heaven had sent down troubles all of its own. Who would have thought that a *Cultural* Revolution would come to the countryside? Surely something like that belonged with all those battling intellectual brushes back in Beijing? But somehow, like most bad things, it had found its way to the fields. Investigating work teams had descended from the county town to inspect the old 'bad elements' and 'class enemies' and, before anyone knew it, new revolutionary whispers were blowing all over the place.

The first whispers had pointed to brigade team leaders who had become too big for their sandals: punching others to make a point, while cooking the village books on the side themselves. Then the counter-whispers had followed: pointing to rebel heroes who had hidden Guomindang pasts, or even secret Japanese connections. Was Whiskers Shen really a man who could be trusted? And what about Little Shen, was he the solid revolutionary that he pretended to be? The mass meetings had only made things even more confused: points and counterpoints scattered in all directions, jumbling up not only the present and the past, but the real and the imagined as well. Blasted out on loudspeakers, directives from Beijing had been hurled by the left and the right, each convinced that the magic of acoustics transformed their own particular black into white. Opposing positions had plastered their posters across village walls, one on top of another, with each layer covering up the bad ink of the one before. And then the clubs, spears and knives had appeared, with battles breaking out on the threshing floors of the granaries, and sacks of grain becoming spoils of war.

The shop floor of the nearby railway commandeered, machine tools were now turning out artillery and shells. Anyone who could hid behind their doors. Those who tried to keep up with the times found themselves having to change the scores by the day. One day, the Mao Zedong Thought Red Guards were holding the railway yard in an alliance with the May Fourth Regiment (whoever they were); the next, the Rebel Regiment had seized the middle school, and were advancing on the railway yard. Every now and then, someone's ink would run dry – or the shells would run out – and a strategic retreat would have to be made to the county town. Once in a while, the loudspeakers would succumb to a technical fault, which made it harder to know who was up and who was down. But at least the village could get some sleep: heaven had not completely lost its heart.

It all started with the 'Four Clean Ups' in 1961 – Mao's idea of cleaning out the bureaucrats who, in his opinion, were the biggest problem. But, of course, that was yet another one of those good ideas from the top which always seemed to end up badly in the fields. After the Great Leap Forward had floundered in famine, more individual leaders, some disguised as peasants, had smuggled themselves into the countryside to find out what was really going on. Apart from the discovery of the five winds of communism, commandism, exaggeration, chaotic directives and cadre privilege, the reports that returned to Beijing showed that there were other reasons to worry as well. Not only was local peasant knowledge still being ignored but the commune leaders were putting themselves above the people in ways that were threatening the revolution itself. Those in charge of communes close to cities had taken to farming their own personal plots of land and selling the produce on nearby black markets. Others, further away from the city's black temptations, had traded chickens for back door payments, confiscated grain from out-of-favour peasants, awarded themselves more work points than their labour merited, and gambled with commune funds. Whether near to the cities or far away, a number had even taken up the old world practice of buying child brides. With friends and family aiding and abetting, and few peasants daring to raise a subjective flag of objection, was it really any wonder that the commune leaders had become new local emperors?

While Mao might have lost his footing on the Great Leap Forward, it seemed that his warnings of the rise of a new bourgeoisie-gentry had been sharply on the mark. True, Zhongnanhai had divided over the communes in the aftermath of the famine: should they be the only means of farm production, or would productivity be higher if the peasants were allowed to keep some land on the side for themselves? But one thing everyone had seemed to agree upon was the importance of cleaning things up.

Since the bourgeois rot obviously included bureaucratic spirits in the cities, tens of thousands of officials were despatched to learn the lessons of manual labour at the hands of the peasants. At the same time, it was agreed that the local officials needed to be taught some lessons about the duties of a revolutionary spirit. Commune accounts should be subjected to the harsh light of an outside scrutiny, work points should be clarified (how many points for how much work), commune assets should be ticked off against inventories, and the granaries should be inspected against actual levels of production.

As ever, opinions had differed, deeply, over how all this was to be done – and by whom. For the senior leaders (still the same old 'foot-draggers' as far as Mao was concerned) this was a delicate matter that should be managed by the Party itself ('internal housekeeping'). But for Mao, the matter was far more important than a famine – it was the rise of a new bourgeoisie, and as such it went to the heart of the revolution, requiring nothing less than the purging energies of the mass of the people at large. This time, the senior leaders seemed to win, and Mao, rather surprisingly, lost. Party work teams were despatched to investigate communes across the country, and the masses with their inconvenient energies were either herded into the fields, or called to attend endless meetings where their criticisms could be safely batted in other directions: particularly towards the reserves of old landlords and other bad elements who could be recalled to another round of struggle. And if ever the reserves of old class enemies ran low, new class enemies could always be found. Senior Party leaders congratulated themselves on keeping the heat down; Mao muttered that the only way to really solve the problem would be to let the masses off the leash.

Meanwhile, skulking in his Zhongnanhai garden in 1963, Mao consulted the landscape and came across a model northern commune by the name of Dazhai. With a truly revolutionary leadership and workers, it seemed to be a commune that had genuinely transformed its fields into a miracle of production. Terraces had been laid like slanting walls, tunnels had pierced perpendicular cliffs, dams had blocked rivers to drain new lands; even mountains were said to have been moved. Noting the proud sweep of red flags flying above its fields, Mao invited its leader – clearly someone who understood the importance of revolutionary science and its power over nature – to stand by his side. And with the revolutionary man standing by his side, he then invited the heads of every other foot-dragging commune to come and 'learn from Dazhai'.

When not praising Dazhai to the skies, Mao also watched as his new rising star, Lin Biao, set about telling the story of the revolution's success. A man of towering military credentials, and a comforting supporter during the criticising assaults from the bureaucrats at the end of the Great Leap Forward, in 1963, with a stroke of propaganda genius, Lin suggested the idea of a soldier in the People's Liberation Army as a revolutionary hero to raise the people's spirits. Named Lei Feng, he was described as a truly red heart who never failed to put others before himself. Revolutionary resolve was indeed strengthened when the people were informed that he had died at the age of only twenty-two, in the line of duty: struck down by a telephone pole which had been hit by a reversing army truck. Lei Feng's diaries were distributed into the hands of Mao's adoring public, with a personal inscription written by the great red sun himself, to the effect that it was the People's Liberation Army which had the most to teach the people (presumably including the rest of the foot-dragging Party as well). A Party wind (the exaggeration wind, perhaps?) then carried Lei Feng's diary down to the countryside, accompanied by a fervour of revolutionary work teams to help keep the endless meetings awake. A year later, Lin Biao followed up his success with a collection of Mao's quotations – binding them into a *Little Red Book*, initially for distribution to the troops and then offered to the wider masses. But by 1965, exhausted eyelids were drooping once again, and after the work teams had gone back to Beijing, few in the countryside remembered their lessons. For those who did manage to pay attention, however, it was clear that some important writing was beginning to appear on the wall.

———

While the peasants were being taught about model revolution-aries, from 1963 the city youth were being told that they should be learning from the peasants. Arguing that books were a simple, and ultimately damaging, form of education, Mao had suggested that the city students should advance their studies through practical labour in the countryside. 'Bad class' students (those studying under the shadow of their parents' mistakes) listened particularly attentively. Relegated to the bottom of every lesson by their teachers, their backgrounds had condemned them as permanently 'bad eggs': runts of a litter whose higher-born, 'red class', peers were wholly justified not only in push-ing them into lonely corners, but kicking them as well. Hearing Mao's suggestion of countryside studies, the desperate ears of the bad eggs seized upon what seemed to be a promise of redemption: volunteer for the fields, and finally get to bask in the warm rays of the Great Leader's revolutionary red sun. Hands had been quickly raised, and over the next few years, the villages had been invited to welcome a number of student volunteers – whether they wanted them or not.

It had not been long before the student volunteers realised – like the earliest sudents who had gone down to the countryside forty years before – that they had a lot to learn. In a world of mud and flies, few lessons from the classroom held any value. As far as life in the fields was concerned, the only marks that mattered were work points; and the peasants were far too busy trying to survive themselves to have any time to show city youths what to do. Some of the students managed to get themselves into schools – as teachers of muddy village children. Most, though, were set to the muckiest of tasks: carrying the stinking buckets of ordure that no peasant ever really wanted to touch, and which surely even a pair of soft city hands could manage. From time to lucky time, some were invited to tell an evening story to leaders of villages who had never seen the wider world: tales of tall buildings, which frankly beggared belief, and stories of Mao, the Great Leader, waving from the terraces of the Tiananmen Gate of Heavenly Peace: a god who, the students assured everyone, was really a man. Summer turned to winter, winter turned to spring and, desperate to prove that they were better than the bad blood of their parents, the bad class students pushed themselves to eat the labouring bitterness on which the countryside survived.

In the late summer of 1966, letters arrived from parents in Beijing with news of a Cultural Revolution and of a new, elite, army of young Red Guards which had adopted Mao as their commander and was 'bombarding the headquarters'. With the Party citadel of Zhongnanhai seemingly unscathed, the students in the countryside were as confused as their city peers as to where and what the headquarters were. But as the months passed and more letters arrived, it seemed that schools and universities had somehow become battlefields; and in the ensuing chaos, the very teachers and professors who had pushed the bad class students to the bottom of their schoolrooms had been revealed to be treacherously bad elements themselves – in disguise. Remembering teachers who had battered their knuckles with rulers, and stung their hearts with class enemy taunts, many of those who read their parents' Cultural Revolution news thought that it was not before time. Some even wondered if they would now be able to go home. But as they read to the end of the letters, they found that Mao was calling upon the Red Guards to wage a war of 'perpetual revolution' and launch a campaign against the 'Four Olds' of customs, culture, habits and ideas. Hard as the countryside might be, their parents told them, they were better off where they were.

As the summer of 1966 turned to winter, the letters told of a twist. Somehow the Red Guards had split into two, and started to fight each other – and then a new front had opened up altogether. This one was not led by the usual 'red class' vanguard, but by groups of students, from middle schools as well as universities, who had picked themselves up from the bad class floor, and launched a defiant rebellion against red classmates who had once been their tyrants. Expecting the next lines of the letters to tell them that the bad class upstarts were being rounded up by the army, they were astonished to read that Mao was encouraging them. In the perpetual revolution, Mao was now calling time on the idea that the red class students were the only natural revolutionaries, and urging the rest of the city youth to rise up in the name

of the oppressed masses – whoever they were – and against incumbent powers of any and all descriptions. 'Call it the Great Democracy',
Mao said. Taking him at his word, the bad class students still in the
cities had apparently done just that, calling themselves the *Rebel* Red
Guards. With Mao now supporting a revolution of all against all, ink
was suddenly free, posters could be plastered everywhere, and every
student of every faction could chase down every counter-revolutionary in disguise, whoever and wherever they might be. They could even
have the trains. According to Mao, China was a big country, and the
trains were there to serve the people; the students should be sharing their revolutionary experiences with whoever they liked, and the
carriages could take them wherever they wanted to go.

Before the year of 1966 was out, the bad class volunteers no longer
needed letters from home to tell them what was going on: waves of
Red Guards and Rebel Red Guards were washing up in the countryside's county towns. Already on the ground, and for once in a position
to steal a march on even the reddest of the good class elements, the bad
class youth were determined to make their mark. Ink pots at the ready,
they splashed paeans to Mao in every direction. Alert to every shifting
loyalty in the villages, they also offered their services to turn the old
wrongs of the countryside upside down. With trucks and loudspeakers
regularly commandeered for official revolutionary purpose, it was not
long before 'power seizure' winds were beginning to blow across the
fields.

When the cities exploded in youthful rage, the peasants had done their
best to continue their essential hoeing, planting, weeding and harvesting, in the silence of the fields. But with new waves of city students
being carried by the trains to provincial cities, and then catching carts
and trucks to county towns, the countryside suddenly found itself
caught up in the heat. Paper and ink available on demand by official
decree, wherever the students went, big character posters followed in
their wake. When the posters went up, many of those in the countryside who felt badly treated by the recent revolutionary past suddenly
saw an opportunity to turn the tables. Old scores could be settled in
new directions, and, hardly believing their luck, those who had lost

earlier battles, began to hope that past wrongs might now be righted.

As the months moved on, though, the stories from Beijing began to acquire a much darker air. The score-settling in the capital had now apparently turned to war, with university campuses and city communes becoming battlefields. Factories were burning like fires, while struggle sessions, power seizures and torture had become daily facts of life. Any and all education had been thrown out of the schools, and, with everyone busy with the perpetual revolution, productivity had come to a standstill. As the red ink continued to splash down from Beijing, the peasants began to get concerned.

They were not alone. Up in the revolutionary capital, even the inhabitants of Zhongnanhai had been wondering how long their portals would be able to stand strong. Eventually, the People's Liberation Army was asked to put out the rebellious storms, and Mao agreed that all of the students who were ticking like bombs in the cities (in middle schools and universities alike, not only in Beijing but across the land) would have to go. 'Go where?' the bureaucrats had asked. The peasants could scarcely believe their shocked ears when news of the answer trickled down to the fields: 'to the countryside'.

What had been an eager countryside adventure for the Red Guards in the early seasons of the Cultural Revolution became more of a punishment when the Party announced that every youth now had to leave the city. It was one thing to sweep down into the fields on a train and a truck, knowing that you could go home at the end of a week – but quite another to find that you were going to follow the bad class students into a rural exile that might never end. But Mao had spoken, and the People's Liberation Army had backed him up – although with the busybody bureaucrats still at large, many wondered whether Mao, the leader of their student hearts, was really free to speak his own mind. Across the cities, work teams were summoned to scour the academic registers, and the name of every student, from middle school through university, was matched with an individual village and told to be ready to go. Well, not quite every name. Single children who could point to dependent parents would be allowed to stay, as would older students who could show that they already had a job. Not to mention, of course, the sons and daughters of parent-cadres who had, in all the chaos, managed to keep their official positions of power. For the rest, however, bags were packed (clothes only; books, banned, were only for the bravest pockets) and trains were boarded.

With stories of countryside hardships having filtered back to the cities in letters, and with no one able to tell the new wave when, or even whether, they would ever be able to come back, many students left with heavy hearts. Others, built of sterner stuff, imagined themselves as new Lei Fengs: models of Mao's revolution, ready to go and serve the peasants with all of the lessons that a city could teach.

No sooner had the students' soft shoes touched the country mud, however, than they realised that the travails of the past were just the beginning. While it seemed to have escaped the notice of the powers in Beijing, once on the ground it was obvious that there were only so many people that a field could hold, let alone support. How on earth could eighteen million students be squeezed into a countryside that was already buckling under the revolutionary strain? The brigade teams were already hard-pressed to match work points with enough of the basic food on which everyone depended. And while teaching seemed the most obvious job for the students, places were in short supply. Generally speaking, a village had only one school and one teacher, and in many cases, that one place had already been taken by the 'bad elements' who had been first to arrive. True, there was always a need for someone who could count and read well enough to keep the village books, but all the villages in China could not find room for the ocean of students who were being sent in their direction.

As the students struggled to absorb the enormity of their new situation, for the most part, the peasants tried to do their best: squeezing harvests to feed the millions of extra mouths; making do, themselves, with less. Helpless in the face of nature, early student dreams of Lei Feng heroics were quickly dashed. Exhausted before the farming day was done, plagued with lice, sleepless with the shock of a life without family or the surviving entertainments of the city, few were able to till the land to any noticeable effect. Even fewer were left with energy for any of the other tasks which needed to be done just to survive. When new buildings were grudgingly put up to accommodate the students, it was the peasants who had to raise the bricks. Not surprisingly, the buildings looked much more like granaries than living quarters – the villagers were looking ahead to more productive future uses, and hoping that the students would not be staying long. They were not the only ones.

For their part, the students, some as young as thirteen, others old enough to have been graduating if their worlds had not been turned upside-down, looked up in dismay at the countryside's endlessly boring skies. Pitched battles prompted by periodic power seizures offered occasional opportunities for action and glory, but as far as the students could see, the results were only ever yet another reshuffling of local interests. Obviously, the outcomes were important to some-one at the top – and the diversions were certainly welcome – but in terms of a revolution, nothing ever seemed to change the lot of the peasants below. From time to time, electrical faults and damaged limbs offered some the possibility of applying the elementary principles of city knowledge and experience. Once in a while, peering at the earth beneath their feet, and scouring the memories of past biology lessons, one or two even managed to unravel the mysteries of unco-operative soils. But revolutionary purpose was hard to come by, and time in the fields passed as slowly as eternity. Up before dawn, to bed before dark, not much to eat, no books to read, no films to watch. There was only the squawk of a loudspeaker for any kind of broadcast, with 'The East is Red' replayed over and over again. Either that, or yet another exhor-tation to 'learn from Dazhai'.

In April 1969, parental letters announced the end of the Cultural Revolution. But as far as the students in the countryside could see, their parents had been misinformed: there were even more power seizures going on in the communes than before. A few months later, more letters arrived, this time announcing the fall of Mao's desig-nated successor Liu Shaoqi (author of *How to be a Good Communist*, now apparently found to have been a treacherous wolf in Party cloth-ing), and the rise of his successor, Lin Biao. Still loyal to Mao, student hearts broke at Liu Shaoqi's betrayal and hoped that Lin Biao would be a more worthy successor. But none of it made any difference to the monotony of their imprisonment on the land. Out to the fields and back again, day in, day out, with only blaring loudspeakers and the odd pitched battle to punctuate the peace: when would it ever end?

Everyone looked for an edge or an opportunity that could carry them back to the city; few found one. From time to time, a 'lucky' soul (almost always someone from one of the reddest families) managed to swing the ailing parent or the miraculous job that could secure the coveted chops and approvals required to get them back home. No one believed the bit about the parent or the job – one way or another, there was always a *hou men*, back door, at the bottom of it all. But it didn't really matter. With the city and home a fading memory, and nothing but cocks crowing, seasons changing and endless boring meetings to mark the passing of time, no one believed in anything very much any more.

And then, in 1972, letters arrived that sank the students' spirits even further: Lin Biao, the military man who had replaced Liu Shaoqi as Mao's designated successor, had turned out to be nothing but a 'renegade and a traitor' himself. The news was so big that the peasants heard it on their grapevines even before it hit the village meetings. Two traitorous men discovered to be standing at Mao's right hand in the course of just a few years? Confused, the peasants asked the students what on earth was going on up in that heavenly Beijing. Cast adrift from a city which had once been home, now as perplexed as anyone else, the students could only shrug their shoulders with the rest of them. Nothing made any sense anymore.

With the fall of Lin Biao, the students' dashed dreams now turned to strategies for escape. Distance and money were not the only obstacles. There was also the *hukou* net of official registration that continued to cloak the country, just as it had in the time of Qin. Now registered as rural residents, like the peasants, if they wanted to shift from the countryside to the city they would have to get a clutch of approvals which only the best connected could secure. With a bit of luck and courage, and a lot of persuading dinners for those in positions to help, one could probably smuggle oneself into the city. But without a ration card and a job, staying there would require the co-operation of a lot of family and friends: family to keep them in food, friends to keep their silence. With every passing year, the redder classes of students pulled every possible family connection to make it back to the city. And up and down the country, every other family scrimped and saved to find the money to cover the costs of the favours.

While a number made it back, many were left behind with a rising fear that they would never be able to leave – that, and an anger which ate deep into hearts which now sensed they had been betrayed. Education had become nothing but a memory, and the only hope of a job if they ever made it back to the city would be that of a labourer at best. What if they never made it back? As far as they could tell, they would never see their families or a city again. Left to their own desperate thoughts, some threw themselves into wells. Others cast their minds back to the giddy heights of the Cultural Revolution and wondered what on earth had happened. Yet others, in the depths of their misery, began to look again, beyond Liu Shaoqi and Lin Biao (the so-called 'wolves in Party clothing') to Mao. The peasants were right: what on earth was going on?

When Zhou Enlai had died in 1976, and Tiananmen Square had been flooded with a hundred thousand Beijingers, more letters arrived in the countryside, describing the crowds that had overwhelmed the standing guards, all of them demanding an end to the counter-revolutionary terror of the 'Gang of Four'. The still stranded students knew exactly what that was all about: the crowd had clearly included a lot of smuggled returnees from the countryside, the angry flotsam and jetsam of a lost generation of youth. If they could have made it out of the fields, they would have been at the square themselves. Living lives without an education, employed in factories, or not employed at all, those 'lucky' ones had obviously reached the same conclusion as their student brothers who were still in the countryside: they had all been nothing but sacrifices in a greater battle of heavenly tigers. And as sacrifices, like thousands of years of other Chinese, they had never stood a chance. No wonder the anger of the crowds had known no bounds.

This time, though, the winds carried on changing. And changing so quickly that in September 1976 the students in the countryside got the news of Mao's death direct from local Party officials before any letters appeared. In October, reports arrived that the Gang of Four had been arrested and finally 'smashed'. Deng Xiaoping, now restored as vice-premier, had called a formal end to the Cultural Revolution, and then promised 'Four Modernisations'. Given that the Four Modernisations would obviously need some educated minds, the students wondered if, perhaps, they might finally be released. It almost seemed too much to hope for. Indeed, for many, it was. Thinking through Deng's modernising ideas, the still stranded students soon realised that time had passed and left them all behind. After a decade or more in the countryside, even if they could get back to the city, what could they possibly have to offer anyone? But now, at least, it was official: they had been betrayed by a Cultural Revolution which had been nothing more than Mao's wife spitting on her enemies. In December 1978, when rumours filtered back of Wei Jingsheng's poster asking for a Fifth Modernisation, a voice for the people, the students could not have agreed more.

While the Four Modernisations gathered pace in Beijing, gusts of change began to appear in the countryside as well. Whispers started to circulate that individual peasant households might be given plots of land to farm for their own account. If it was true, it wasn't a moment too soon. After a decade of calls to 'learn from Dazhai', not to mention the turbulence of the power seizures, few of those in the countryside felt any better off than they had been before the Great Leap Forward – and most seemed to think that things had gone distinctly backwards. Without a patch of land to call their own, and under the constant gales of commandism, chaotic directives and cadre privilege, many peasants had reached the conclusion that it didn't really matter what they did; and actually, given the exhaustion of the soil, less would probably anyway be more. Feet dragged to the fields as slowly as they could, hoes were cast aside as soon as the afternoon sun gave the slightest indication that it might be winding down. Up and down the country, still under productive pressure from the top, brigade team leaders struggled to marshal their troops to push for yet another bumper harvest – and largely failed.

Here and there, however, seeing the exhaustion of the fields and the desperate fortunes of their families, brotherhoods of men had begun to meet together in the dead of village nights, sealing secret pacts to change their fate. While the Party might have put the fields under the iron will of the communes, these brotherhoods decided that if they didn't start separating out some plots of their own soon, everyone's futures – and all of their ancestors' wisdom – would be lost. Aware of the counter-revolutionary risks they were running, the brotherhoods agreed that, if the worst came to the worst, each surviving member would look after the families of the fallen.

But then Deng Xiaoping had come searching for ideas that might restore the harvests of old, and the secrets of their plots had become harder to keep. By 1979, their treachery had been outed; but retribution failed to fall. Instead, with a leap of Monkey King logic, the Party secretary of Sichuan, Zhao Ziyang, had suggested to Deng that the rebellious peasants might have hit upon the very solution he had been looking for: a household responsibility system for the fields.

Deng had been quick to grasp the possibilities. Henceforward, the communal grain quotas would be divided between the peasant households. Each household would be given an individual plot of land from which they would have to deliver up their share of the quota, but from which they would also be allowed to keep any surplus, whether as food for themselves, or to take to the side of a road and start a new local market (or better still, load their produce on to a borrowed donkey and cart it off to the better prices of a nearby city or town).

Many rejoiced, but not all. And as always, everyone had their questions. The most common questions were: 'How will the land be divided?' and 'Who will do the dividing?'. Others included: 'What will happen to the animals and the tools?'; 'What will happen if your particular plot of land can't deliver its yields?'; and 'What is going to happen to the communes?' And while a number of the stranded students had by now given up and resigned themselves to life in a village, many continued to ask their own now-dull question: 'When can we go home?'

The obvious answer to the dividing of the land was that the people would do it themselves – through the brigade team leaders, of course. Smiles fell a little at the mention of the brigade team leaders being involved, but any kind of new spring was better than the long winter that the communes had been. As far as the question of the communes was concerned, Deng promised that they would be faded out: their bureaucracies would be turned into new 'township' governments which would sit between the governments of the counties and the leadership of the village. Some thought it looked as if everything was going back to the past. But if the peasants could once again decide how they were going to farm the fields, why should anyone complain?

As for the students, they had already had their answer in 1978, when Deng had finally acknowledged that they were right to want to come home. Indeed, he had added, it was also time that the peasants were released from the burden of looking after them. But the Four

Modernisations had not yet got sufficiently off the ground to create the city jobs and apartments that would be required. Just a little bit more patience, Deng urged, and they would eventually be released.

The biggest gusts of change were in the south, under the strength of a supporting gale from Beijing. 'Household responsibility' was indeed an important contribution to the Four Modernisations but if China was going to recover its productivity, more would be required. Once again, Deng scoured the past for inspiration, and consulted every element of the present for ideas. As he scoured and consulted, he found himself looking at the wider lands of the Chinese civilisational idea: the renegade province of Taiwan; the Malayan island of Singapore to which numerous boat-borne Chinese had floated off across the centuries before; and the lost rocks of Hong Kong. Looking at all of these outposts of Chinese, he saw that a host of modernisations had been already achieved with the help of some 'special purpose' ideas. In Taiwan, special parks were bartering low wages for Western technology; in Singapore, overseas Chinese were trading on family ties across vast sweeps of Southern Asia; and in Hong Kong, not only had one of the world's greatest markets been created, but, in a stroke of genius worthy of the Monkey King, it had also been successfully separated from any reckless Western ideas of democracy. Oddly enough, the separation had begun as a British idea.

Looking again at the map of China proper, Deng saw a southern coastal countryside full of modernising opportunities. Studded with old ports that had once been lost to foreign treaties, it was also a land of fishermen who had since seen limited trade, and a hinterland packed with peasants. With the southern coast so close to the rising markets of overseas Chinese, special purpose possibilities seemed to be everywhere. With Hong Kong at its fringe, the southern east of China's mainland should be able not only to tap into a harbour which traded with the world's imperial capitalists, but also find a way into the currents of the overseas Chinese anchored in Singapore. Far away from Beijing, and full of fields, the coastal hinterlands could easily be fenced off as parks without the Communist Party having to change its colours. True, Hong Kong and all the other overseas Chinese ports were full of traitors from the imperial past, not to mention escapees from the more recent revolutionary present, but the wealth of the overseas Chinese was a pearl of a prize that any crouching dragon would take.

By the end of 1979, four locations had been carefully chosen to host a set of new 'special economic zones'. One of them came with the rather unprepossessing name of 'deep ditch': Shenzhen. Name aside, however, Shenzhen, like all of the new zones, offered two invitations: one, to the capitalist-imperialist West to send its science and technology; the other, to overseas Chinese relatives to send back any spare cash which they might not need and give their mainland cousins a helping hand. For many of the peasants tilling the chosen fields, it suddenly seemed as if snow might once again fall in summer. From Shenzhen's deep ditch, a walled city of factories rose; well, more of a clutter of fences around a constantly expanding construction site, but within the fences were construction and factory jobs for lucky recruits. Across the surrounding villages, families found that long-lost relatives with money began to reappear like dreams. Within a few years, Shenzhen had grown so big that it was jumping its walls, with factory owners offering jobs to anyone, and always eager to lease yet more fields on which to spread their greater productivity. When those who wanted to work on a production line, but did not want to lease their fields for factories, began to worry about how they could hold down a job *and* till the fields, the special economic zones were granted a magical dispensation which allowed local peasants to hire peasants from other parts of the country to come and do their work.

Within a few years, as Deng had hoped, the communes around Shenzhen were all but relegated to the past. The villagers found themselves spoilt for productive choice: Buy a tractor to rent out for a fee? Rent out a village fish pond? Open a brick works? The possibilities seemed endless. And as the southern coasts took to modernisation like ducks to water, many across the rest of China's countryside began to wonder how they could catch up with the future too.

———

Scouring the countryside for inspiration, Deng soon found that pockets of prosperity were breaking out all over the place. The greatest number seemed to be in the provinces around Shanghai, with the most successful of all in a long-forgotten place called Wenzhou.

Sitting on a south-eastern coast of rocky hills, Wenzhou was a land of towns and villages screened from the rest of China by the Yangdang mountains, and threaded into the waters of the East China Sea by a fringe of tiny islands. In ancient times, before the period of the Warring States, it had been home to the independent people of the Yue. With long subtropical summers, its local breezes had always been quick to conjure up typhoons; and with little flat land, it had been the despair of emperors dreaming of settled fields.

By the time of the Song dynasty, the Wenzhounese had been stubbornly insisting on a more practical school of heavenly thought which was as happy to trade as to farm. There was even a tale that one of the emperors had once resorted to exchanging Wenzhou's people with those of a poorer province, in the confident expectation that this would finally rid the Wenzhounese of the pernicious trading idea. But the Wenzhounese had won – the trading ideas were simply transplanted to a whole new part of the country, while the new arrivals in breezy Wenzhou were quickly converted to markets.

By the time of the Ming and its idea that everybody stick to the fields and villages, Wenzhounese sons were already spread across the country, and the local hills and mountains were as unlikely as ever to become fields; the Wenzhounese had had no choice but to defy the imperial wisdom of the day, trading in the shadows of family networks, supported by private paper for money. At the end of the Ming dynasty, few were surprised when the Wenzhounese had emerged as supporters of those members of the Donglin Academy who argued that the 'investigation of things' required on-the-ground human judgement rather than an iron-clad reading of the classical Confucian texts. Even during the times when the Ming (and later, the Qing) had cleared the coasts (the Ming to put an end to the disruptive trade with foreigners; the early Qing to put an end to the Zheng family of Ming pirate-loyalists) the inhabitants of Wenzhou had either climbed over the Yangdang mountains to manage their domestic trade routes, or taken to their boats with bundles of cash and hulls full of crafts and settled in other parts of the world, trying as best they could to keep a connection with those they had left behind. Naturally, secrecy had become an essential trick of their trade.

By the time of the Qing, Wenzhou's networks had spread across the country and abroad, supported by a long-established system of private paper, issued like money to cover the trades. And when the 1911 revolution had pulled the rug from under the Qing floor, the Wenzhounese found themselves in their element. Cash-rich families extended credit north and south, with overseas brothers ready and willing to support any sons who wanted to try their luck abroad.

But all that was long ago, before the revolution and its communes had flattened everything to the uniformity of a Five Year Plan. Or was it?

When the Communist Party had held its first Congress in 1921 in nearby Shanghai, the Wenzhounese, always quick-witted, had formed an independent local branch of their own; naturally, it funded itself with contributions from local factories. When, in 1949, Mao's branch of the Communist Party captured the country, the local Wenzhounese Communists simply bent with two winds: receiving central orders from Beijing, but applying them in the breeze of local conditions. As Beijing changed the countryside's co-operatives into collectives and communes, each new central directive was translated as yet another request for increased yields – with similar central edicts, directed to the factories of Wenzhou's towns, being interpreted as well-meaning, but misguided, thoughts on how to improve local production. Naturally, central work teams had made inspecting appearances, but these had been regarded as temporary obstacles to endure – certainly not reasons for a fundamental change of heart. Of course, every now and then a local leader had to take a fall for the benefit of everyone else. But such ccasional sacrifices – struggle sessions and stints in jail – were seen as investments in keeping Wenzhou's productive ship afloat, with every act of official selflessness rewarded with a higher share of the profits.

Over the following two decades, Wenzhou continued to play its age-old game of central cats and local mice. As fields were tended for public display, a significant manufacturing underground was maintained, with factories quietly subcontracting to family homes, traders silently plying their wares across family connections laid centuries before, and deals sealed in the dead of night by men who were born blood brothers. Deng Xiaoping might have been astonished when Wenzhou announced its ten thousand town and village enterprises.

But for the people of Wenzhou, and all of those who traded with them, it was nothing more than the sharing of a well-kept secret.

Shenzhen had its special purpose, and Wenzhou had its secrets. After decades of tilling the fields, by the 1980s, peasants in other parts of the country were beginning to search for their own modernising opportunities. With many villages hundreds of miles away from either a city or a coast, and without the benefit of Wenzhou's centuries of networks and experience, it was not easy. But casting their minds back as far as they could possibly go, it did not take them long to realise that no one in the countryside could think of a time when an official had not been interested in a profit. And come to think of it, no one could remember a time when a relationship with an official had not been worth its weight in gold. With the communes being broken up, and with the leaders of the communes and the brigade teams going off to join the new township governments, a number of bright minds looked at what was being left behind and wondered. The chicken coops, orchards, saw mills, cement plants and repair shops which had all once served the communes were now being sold off for a song. Indeed, most of them had already been earmarked by officials thinking about their own personal 'modernisation'. But with government jobs on offer in the new townships, many surmised that the officials might appreciate a village partner: someone who would be willing to buy up local productive assets at the songs they were being sold for, and share the future returns. In that way, the officials would be able to pursue their own bureaucratic futures, and everybody could get a foot in the game.

Not everyone was keen. Particularly unenthusiastic were those who watched from the sidelines and saw chickens being swept up into other people's hutches, the incomes of the saw-mills disappearing into somebody else's pockets, and orchards tumbling into a neighbour's ready hands. It seemed that everyone who wanted to be anyone was arming themselves for modernisation, with the arms the stuff of daily life: 'twenty-shot pistols' of cigarette packs, 'hand grenades' in the form of bottles of wine, and 'explosive satchels', full of the biscuits which always smoothed the course of the countryside's trade. Watching the fruits of thirty years of bitter labour vanish into dust – to say nothing of all the struggle sessions and the fallen bodies – hearts as cynical as the stranded students asked themselves some questions. One of the most obvious was: 'If we have all been working for the same kind of work points all this time, how come some of us can afford to buy the very means of production themselves?' Equally obvious was: 'Who's paying for the cigarettes?'

With the leaders of the communes and the brigade teams now busy with the new bureaucracy of the townships (not to mention personally productive enterprises on the side) and with the old idea of 'to each according to his work' well on its way to becoming 'to each according to his enterprise' it was difficult to find anyone who had the time or the inclination to answer. Old hearts sighed. Gone were the days when someone would help out a neighbour without charging a fee. At this rate, 'household responsibility' or not, it wouldn't be long before the peasants were working for someone else again, and city fat cats were appearing to buy whatever they could: where on earth had the revolution gone?

The peasants were not the only ones with the questions. Watching the transformation of the countryside, the still stranded students who had lost their youth to Mao's revolution, now adults in their twenties and thirties, could scarcely believe their eyes.

On 1 October 1980, those once-students who had not already managed to smuggle themselves back to the cities were, in principle and subject to the paperwork, finally to be allowed to return. But after all this time, not everybody wanted to go: some had married in the countryside, and could no longer leave; others had come to the wistful conclusion that with no possible qualifications for any kind of city job, the past was better off left as a dream.

Those who did go home, found themselves greeted by shiny new posters carrying visions of a high-rising city world, and the sight of heavy trucks shuttling backwards and forwards along rapidly-building streets. Remembering the old posters that had once carried images of revolutionary workers, and recalling the open streets in which their own dreams had once roamed, many of them wept. Picking up their pens, they began to write the stories and poems of everything they had experienced and seen. Careful to keep their scribblings underground, they were more than willing to share them with each other, and with the handful of outsiders whom they felt they could trust.

In 1986, and again in the spring of 1989, they would find their way to Tiananmen Square, hoping against hope that heaven would finally be ready to listen. For over twenty years, they had leapt forwards, only to find themselves thrown backwards, and all for somebody else's dream. If snow were ever going to truly fall in summer, something would have to change.

PART 6
GREAT MAN

The sage assesses the affairs of the age and prepares himself in response to them.

Han Fei (280–233 BCE)

CHAPTER 1

FULL SPEED AHEAD

He perceives the laws of Heaven and Earth; He discerns
the ways of demons and gods ... his mind clearly orders all
planets and stars.

Journey to the West, Wu Cheng'en
(seventeenth century)

IT WAS NIGHT WHEN the special train pulled out of the railway
station. Wrapped in the winter of early 1992, the streets around
stood silent. Few had noticed the dark cavalcade of cars that seemed
to glide through the dusk; and no one had witnessed the large family
make its way to the waiting platform. Except, that is, the appointed
sentinels of the People's Liberation Army and the escorting five-star
general. 'A holiday in the south,' was all that the Party had been told:
much deserved and long overdue for the small spirit upon whose
personal energies everyone in China had come to depend. All other
engines stood down for the night, the carriages of the special train
pulled out of the station and, picking up speed, chugged devotedly
down towards the Yangzi, leaving the sparkling stars of Beijing's
ziwei purple enclosure behind. By morning, the first of the carefully
planned destinations had been reached: the accidentally revolutionary
city of Wuchang (sister of the old Hankou; both now part of the much
bigger industrial powerhouse of Wuhan).

Standing on the platform, waiting for the doors to open and the
greatest of the surviving revolutionaries to descend, the small group
of high provincial officials assumed that their task was to wish him and
the sixteen other members of his family a happy holiday. By the time
the slight figure had climbed back into his carriage twenty minutes
later, they knew that a holiday was the last thing on his mind. Feet
barely touching the ground, his parting words had been sharper than
a north wind: 'Do more, talk less, cut the boring meetings, drop the

427

endless reports. And next time I see you on television, you had better be talking change.'

As the special train sped off down the line, bound for Guangdong, the momentarily speechless officials gathered up their wits and reached for their phones. Wires charged with electrifying currents, the urgent message to their southern colleagues was short and simple: watch out, this is not a holiday – a revolution is on its way.

––––––

Time had passed slowly since the flaming summer of 1989: productivity had slowed, and even the miracles of Wenzhou had dulled. Stunned into silence, young and old, workers and intellectuals alike, the people had retreated from Tiananmen: the gate which had become a square, the place which had once stood for communications between heaven and earth. Zhao Ziyang (Deng's premier and once-annointed successor, who had become general secretary of the Party) had been retired to his own courtyard: a courtyard with a curtain drawn across it, in case anyone dared to think about a conversation with the man who had clearly been responsible for encouraging the bourgeois student spirits which had nearly brought heaven down on the Party's head. Within the Party, criticisms and self-criticisms had been made, all in true Yan'an style. Trained in Moscow, Zhou Enlai's adopted son, Li Peng, had succeeded Zhao Ziyang as premier, becoming the leading light of the left-leaning East Winds. A new general secretary (and anointed future president) had been appointed in the form of a safer, if less heroic, pair of hands, belonging to a southern engineer named Jiang Zemin: a man who had risen through the ranks of the Party to become Minister of Electronic Industries, and then a loyal Party Secretary of Shanghai.

The battle for Communist supremacy had been hard and fought beyond China, across the wider Communist world. While the Party had managed to defeat the threat of Tiananmen, many thought it had been touch and go; by the end of 1989, Hungary had given up its socialist senses, East Germany had lost its wall, and Romania's people had despatched their own general secretary, Ceausescu, to another world, with a simple bullet of justice to the head. Then Moscow – the red star that had set the Party on its early course – had been captured by soft hearts whose *glasnost* openness had been causing havoc for years, and whose *perestroika* fiddling had already pulled the rug of power from under the feet of the once almighty Soviet State. Scarcely credible to the Party faithful in Beijing, by 1991, Lenin's Russian dream had simply vanished in a puff of faint-hearted smoke.

Behind the gates of Zhongnanhai, the biting East Winds had once again gathered in whispering corners, before raising themselves into full-blown gales of leftist virtue. Directed towards Deng, they even included gusts from Deng's own appointed successor, Jiang Zemin. 'The storm', they grumbled, 'has been a long time coming. And if everyone had been on their Leninist guard, the Party would have addressed the risks long before.' Some pointed to that ill-fated day in December 1978, when Deng had taken command of the Party pulpit and announced that everyone should emancipate their minds. Others insisted that the weather had changed long before that: in the after-math of the Great Leap Forward's famine, when weaker Party spirits had lost the courage of their revolutionary convictions in their rush to get the harvests back. One or two argued that the gathering clouds of havoc had been there from 1949. Others suggested that they had been there long before, from the Yan'an days or even the earlier Jiangxi Soviet: all part of the primeval struggle between the true revolution-aries (those who understood the need to master stubbornly subjective minds) and the bourgeois liberal intellectuals (those who were simply playing revolutionary games).

Whenever it started, the East Winds had argued, it could no longer be ignored. While Deng might blame the students' counter-revolu-tion on the Peaceful Evolution conspiracy of the American capitalist West, everyone knew that the real question was about the Marxism-Leninism-Mao Zedong order of the Communist Party itself. What were the Four Modernisations, other than a treacherous capitalist shot of bourgeois liberalism across the bows of the striving socialist state? What was 'productivity', other than an old imperialist trick designed to distract attention from Marx's central point of class struggle? Exactly what kind of Leninist discipline had anyone expected to see when Fang Lizhi and the other intellectuals had been welcomed back into the fold and then sent off on hundreds of scientific journeys to the West, only to return with the treacherous sutras of capitalism? Had anyone really thought that the bureaucratic delusions of household responsibility for peasants, and *chengbao* contracts for the factories, would not bring back precisely what Mao had predicted: wine-soaked bosses, rising pavilions, runaway prices and panic in people's hearts – not to mention an entire revolution betrayed?

'For that matter,' the East Winds continued, 'who, or what, was Deng Xiaoping?' 'Revolutionary hero, in the mould of the great self-strengthener, Zeng Guofan? Heaven help us.' 'Rising sun, in the footsteps of Mao Zedong? Well, only in the sense that his black and white cats had almost brought down the same heavenly catastrophes as the Great Leap Forward.' Truth be told, the revisionist Deng looked a lot more like the Monkey King whose own *Journey to the West* had created all that chaos in heaven. *Bian!* with his magic stick, and a sudden directive had appeared declaring that the only thing which mattered in socialism was getting rich. *Swoosh!* with his cloud somersaults, and state-owned factories had been left to flounder in the mud, while towns and villages threw up untamable enterprises, and southern coasts went back to being temples of foreign factories. *Flash!* with his spells, and suddenly everyone was rushing to multiply productivity four times in ten years. And all the while, Deng had been mesmerising everyone with his endlessly repeated Four Cardinal Principles (keep to the order of the socialist road, uphold the dictatorship of the proletariat, uphold Marxism-Leninism and Mao Zedong Thought, uphold the leadership of the Communist Party), as if a mantra could defend anyone against anything, particularly the perilous charms of the capitalist West.

By the November plenum at the end of 1989, fired with the confidence of impending victory, the East winds had regained control of the pulpit. Declaring that weeds of bourgeois liberalisation had, once again, risen within the ranks of the Party, they announced that it was time to root them out. And then, echoing Deng's own insistence that stability was everything, they set out their principles for revolutionary order: any and all ideas of markets would need to give way to the primacy of the Five Year Plan; the rush for productivity would need to be braked to slow; and the coasts, with their special economic zones, would just have to cool their heels.

Deng was not surprised. In fact, he told himself he should have seen it coming. Zhao Ziyang had let his foolish heart blinded him to the responsibilities of socialist power with Chinese characteristics. Talking, as they had done in the early years, about the respective importance of 'democracy' and 'law', Deng had assumed that Zhao understood them in the same way as himself: 'democracy' as a once-and-for-all revolutionary choice in favour of a Communist Party which would thereafter be trusted and left alone to take the right decisions at the right time, and whatever the circumstances ('democratic centralism'); 'law' as an improvement in the clarity of rules for bureaucratic efficiency – and certainly not something to be allowed to threaten the essential mechanics of the revolutionary Party ('the socialist rule of law'). How could he have known that Zhao was dreaming of the kind of democracy that would let every speck of sand in the tray stand up and say whatever it wanted, let alone of a law that would want to put itself above the Party's guns? But he should have realised that a man like Zhao would easily be carried away by those imperially-capitalist liberal winds. True revolutionary hearts would never have been so easily fooled. Popular voting was a fuzzy kind of thinking which would never have won the revolution, capitalist law was nothing but bourgeois liberalism unleashed; and mixing up mind emancipation at the top with subjectivity on the ground was a surefire recipe for disaster: with that kind of confusion the Party would not even have made it to 1949. But misguided though Zhao may have been, none of his mistakes changed the fact that ideas that failed to feed the people were never going to deliver the socialist utopia that Marx or any of them had dreamt of; nor did they change the fact that feeding the people was not a betrayal of Marx.

Listening politely to the pulpit pronouncements of the left, Deng acknowledged that mind emancipation was a challenge, and that the most vigilant of the Party's present-day spirits would be required to ensure that the ghosts of the past stayed buried. No one wanted the Dictatorship of the People to be betrayed, as the 1911 revolution and its National Assembly had been betrayed by Yuan Shikai and the following warlords. But it was for this reason that he had set the Four Modernisations under the careful guard of the Four Cardinal Principles, and why he had so firmly resisted Wei Jingsheng's counter-revolutionary call for a Fifth Modernisation. And as everyone could see, his prudence had been rewarded with an ultimate triumph over the counter-revolutionary treachery of Tiananmen – something that the Moscow brothers, with their *glasnost* and *perestroika* had obviously failed to achieve. Unlike Russia and Romania, here in the Chinese People's Republic, the proletariat was still a dictatorship of the people under the leadership of the Party: how else could they have kept the Party and avoided Ceausescu's terrible fate? The Communist Party was still leading: weren't they all still in power? Marxism-Leninism and Mao Zedong Thought were still the lexicon of everyone's ideas: would anyone in the Party dare to put forward a single idea without grounding it carefully in the Communist classics? And for those who were paying attention to facts on the ground, in the lands of the Chinese People's Republic, the socialist road was still advancing – or at least would be if those East Winds would stop their whining.

His opinions expressed, and his steam gathered, Deng then pushed on to make his points about China's socialist future. Since 1958, far from catching up with Britain, China had fallen down to the level of Ouagadougou (Africa, for those who needed to consult their maps). Markets were not the exclusive prerogative of the capitalist West, even as planning was not the exclusive prerogative of socialism. If anyone was casting an anxious eye over their shoulders towards a crumbling Moscow, the lesson they should learn was that the shift towards the kind of productivity that could compete with the West needed to be faster, not slower – albeit tightly controlled by the leadership of the Party. There was a train in the station, ready to take China and its socialism to a glorious future. If everyone didn't jump on it, quickly, the opportunity would be forever lost. At stake was nothing less than the survival of the Party's dream.

But Deng's observations fell on ears deafened by their own sense of triumph. Rounding on his recollections of the past (and keeping their remarks to the secret recesses of the inner Party, lest any outside spirits should get confused), the East Winds replied that the only real problems the Party had had in forty years of successful revolution were Mao's Great Leap Forward and the Cultural Revolution. In the Great Leap Forward, Mao's excessive ambition had 'drained the ponds of the collectives, in a pursuit of flying fish'. But before that, everything had been plain sailing: a golden age where the necessary battle against bourgeois liberalism had stood shoulder-to-shoulder with the taming of markets by a planned command. As for the Cultural Revolution, even men like Mao could make a mistake: '70 per cent right and 30 per cent wrong', as Deng himself had once put it, was not a bad verdict in the scheme of history. A couple of mistakes did not change the logic of a revolution. It was time to go back to the socialist basics.

'Socialist basics?' Deng repeated, in an effort to control his temper. As far as he could see, the East Winds didn't have a clue. Zhongnanhai had simply gone back to being that Yan'an cauldron of bored wives with nothing better to do than tell tales and stir up trouble – if, indeed, it had ever really been anything else. With thoughts like these, the Party would become the centre of nothing but its own hot air.

Retreating to the quiet of his own company, and reflecting on the urgent need for fast action if the train was going to keep moving ahead, Deng decided that the solution was not going to be found in the classically Communist corridors of Beijing. Thinking about it, he told himself that he should have seen that earlier as well. When had anything sensible ever come out of a central cave? Across the story of China's time, wisdom had always come from the provinces – the places where men were men, and truth was always based on practical facts. Say what they would about the capitalist fringes of the coast, it was in cities like Shenzhen and Shanghai where the future would be found. Of course, there would always be a need for a centre to make sure that everyone ultimately pulled together. But the trick was for the centre to make sure that the provincial spirits aligned, without disrupting their energies.

It was, Deng acknowledged, a difficult balancing act, one at which successive ancient dynasties had spectacularly failed. The ancient Zhou had let everything drift apart; the First Qin Emperor had pulled everything too tightly together. The failures of the Zhou had been followed by a war of all against all conducted over more than two hundred terrifying years. And while the collapse of Qin might have led to the glorious Han, it had also ultimately opened the way to the Yellow Turban rebels and the Three Kingdoms which had in turn opened the gates to successive waves of conquering barbarians tearing down from the steppes. The lessons of failure had been repeated again and again across the last fifteen hundred years; it was time that China learnt them. What was required was a protection from overzealous local spirits and foot-draggers alike. And if the younger Party leaders were not up to it, then Deng himself would pick up the reins, and make the balance work. Fortunately, he reminded himself, in 1978, he had taken a very early step to protect against any risk of a return to the central madness of the Great Leap Forward by separating the country's provincial 'kitchens' from Beijing: allowing the governments of each province to collect their own taxes and balance their own budgets. If the East Winds were going to go on strike and insist on centralism, he would just have to go down to the provinces and get the kitchens on his side.

From 1990, Deng took himself off on repeated journeys to the south. Staying away from the capital for ever-longer periods of time, the less centrally opinionated and far more practical Shanghai became a particularly preferred retreat. Happy to be left in planning charge of the Beijing headquarters, the East Winds thought he was right to take account of his aging years and seek the solace of a quieter, and certainly warmer, provincial climate. They were all getting old. It was time to bring some younger spirits into Zhongnanhai: left-leaning ones, of course.

Once in Shanghai, though, Deng had no interest in wasting his time on rest. Turning quickly to a search for more emancipated minds, he had soon found one in the person of a rehabilitated one-time rightist who had become the Mayor of Shanghai: a man by the name of Zhu Rongji. Keen to ensure that the wider body of provincial spirits across the country would also be able to grasp the urgent need to act, Deng had then picked up a pen – and a pen-name – and swept every willing journal with articles arguing for a clear-sighted understanding that whatever strengthened the productivity of the nation would naturally be socialist, and that capitalism did not have a monopoly on energy and imagination – unless of course socialism chose to bind its own feet. Zhongnanhai plugged its ears to the articles, and the lily-livered Jiang Zemin called for a 'great wall of steel' to defend China from America's dream of Peaceful Evolution.

The provincial spirits, however, had heard Deng's clarion call and, picking up pens of their own, they argued that unless socialism was grounded on *provincial* production, both the Party and its people would remain in the trenches of the poor. In 1991, using his remaining Party powers, Deng then waved his Monkey King stick and '*bianned!*' Zhu Rongji up to Beijing as deputy premier of the nation at large. The East Winds regrouped, and launched an inky campaign against the dangerous rise of a 'one-voice hall' (Deng) and a return of the ancient fiefdoms of the Zhou state (the provinces) with their feudal lords (the provincial leaders) whose ambitions, they argued, would ultimately collapse heaven on everyone's heads.

With nothing less than the prize of socialism at stake, Deng decided to retreat to the past himself. Drawing on his own guerilla youth, and emulating the Crouching Dragon Zhuge Liang, he looked at the landscape, meditated on the changes and waited for the *dao* way to appear. When, in January 1992, the stars seemed to be perfectly positioned, Deng decided to storm the pass of central Party opinion by climbing on to his special train and advancing under the cover of a holiday to the farthest fringe of the southern coast. Once in Guangdong, he swept off to the specially productive zone of Shenzhen, by now a forest of factories with an advancing line of skyscrapers, and declared it to be a beacon of the future. Addressing the whole of the country through the southern crowds, he then went on to explain that socialism was really three things: it was whatever promoted socialist forces of production; it was whatever strengthened the power of the socialist nation; and it was whatever raised the people's standard of life.

To this, he added the observation that in a country as big as China you could not always expect life to be calm and steady, and when a rare Darwinian opportunity arrived to leap ahead in the bitter battle for the survival of the fittest, you had to seize the moment and '*jia you*' – speed up!

It would be more than two months before the East Winds unlocked the Party newspapers and allowed them to print not only the story of Deng's travels but also the headlines of what he had said. But before the end of the year – having marshalled the strongest of the provincial leaders and ensured that the biggest stars in the People's Liberation Army were on display – Deng finally recaptured the headquarters. It was 1992, a year in which the Party would convene one of its five-yearly Congresses. Always the occasion for a review of what the state of the nation would be over the coming five years, this one, the fourteenth since the founding of the Party, had been especially designated for the announcement of a new, 'third generation', leadership, to follow after Mao and Deng. Once again, Deng rose to the pulpit. Having made sure that the pews were stocked with provincially-emancipated minds which were also clear that there was not an inch of space for any bourgeois liberal tendencies, he snatched a triumph from the winds of the left. Applauding his vision, the congregation congratulated him on the 'tremendous courage' that he had displayed in opening up both 'a new understanding of Marx' and 'an advanced way forward for the Party'.

As praise poured upon Deng's head, the Party acknowledged that socialism depended on developing the economy as fast as possible, and that productivity was indeed the measure of progress. Resolutions agreed that nine more coastal cities would be opened up, and productivity would be quadrupled by the year 2000. Guangdong was to be given the honour of catching up with the small fire-producing dragons of the Chinese influenced East (Taiwan, Singapore, Hong Kong and South Korea, which while technically not an outpost of Chinese, had been loyally following the Chinese idea for over a thousand years). Even Jiang Zemin, hitherto a rather disappointing successor-in-waiting, agreed to board the train and push things forward faster. In fact, softening to the notion of a Party-led prosperity, Jiang even offered Deng a new mantra to smooth the difficult edges of socialism-as-riches: 'the socialist market economy'. Of course, as Deng knew better than anyone, the idea of a socialist market economy was, like all great goals (and Daoist visions), something of a contradiction: a river of rapids to be crossed in itself. Working out what it actually meant would take years of careful stone-studying. But surely that was what mantras were for – to keep you going. The important thing was that Jiang Zemin had finally boarded the train, with a grasp of the ancient wisdom that all journeys of ten thousand miles had to start with a single first step.

Bearing the enormity of the journey in mind, Deng also noted that, disappointing though this would be to many, even if they advanced at a relatively fast pace, the Party would have to accept that the primary stages of socialism would not be completed until 2050. Marxism-Leninism and Mao Zedong Thought had been secured, as had the Democratic Dictatorship of the Proletariat, led by the Party, with everyone firmly committed to the socialist road. But, as he had noted in the late 1980s, in their zeal to race ahead, the Chinese people had skipped one of the early stages on the road to socialism: the capitalist one that was necessary to pave the way for the final utopian triumph. Going back to cover the lost ground was going to take longer than he had originally thought. No one should worry, though. The winds had changed, the course was now clear. After Tiananmen, no one was in any doubt that while there would be 'relaxed controls on economic matters', on political matters, there would be 'tight controls'. *Liu si*, June Fourth, was a never-to-be-mentioned-again 'political incident'. And in order to ensure that it never returned, the memory of that Tiananmen day would be erased from everyone's minds. In its place would rise the story of 'one hundred years of national humiliation', starting with the Western gunboats that had appeared in 1841, and overcome by over 50 years of patriotic Party sacrifice that had kept the foreign barbarians at bay: call it a 'Patriotic Education Campaign', suggested Deng. To be launched across the country, its texts would take the form of books for schools and children, with newspaper editorials for adults, and museums and monuments to remind everyone, young and old, of both the heroic battles which the Party had fought and of all the great humiliations suffered. Etched into the very rock of the country's architecture, the monuments would stand forever: just like the inscriptions with which the First Qin Emperor had announced his achievements to heaven, carved on the rocks of the great Mount Tai.

Listening to Deng's promises, not all of the East Winds buried their reservations about high-speed socialism. But everyone finally agreed to reach out across the river and at least look for the same kind of stones – socialist production, a strong socialist nation and higher standards for daily living – that would deliver the great dream of Marx and Mao. Suddenly, the dream that had been floundering only a year before, had, with Deng's indomitable spirit, and with Zhu Rongji's capable Shanghai support, found its feet. By the end of 1992, picture postcards of Deng's southern holiday were being printed in spreading newspapers, with many people pasting them on their walls. Productive spirits were rising once again. By 1994, there were even encouraging signs of speed.

The fastest-growing bamboo shoots, and the easiest to see, were in Shenzhen. Purpose-built for productivity, the special economic zone had become the immortalisation of Deng's productive ideas: full to bursting with factories, complete with special purpose dormitories so that everyone could sleep close to the job. Armed with Deng's calls for mind emancipation and speeding up, hundreds of thousands of eager hands had already flocked there by the end of the 1980s. And empowered with the Monkey King idea that the use of the people's land was really a right in itself – one which could be bought and sold without ever affecting actual ownership – the factories and dormitories had now swept across the flimsy fences which defined the special economic zone, and flooded the hinterland beyond. Villages had given up the ghosts of their ancestors; fields and fish ponds had fallen to bulldozers; and what had once been a fishing fringe of thousands had became a socialist landscape of four million newly productive people. Most of the new people were migrants who, with the special purpose powers granted by Deng, had managed to storm the *hukou* household registration barriers designed by Mao to keep the country cousins in the fields.

Throughout it all, the People's Liberation Army had been a powerful source of support. With the Party clear that socialism was not just about defending the nation from outside threats but also strengthening it from within, their forces had long been volunteered to help with the task of socialist construction. Fresh from rebuilding the northern steel city of Tangshan (after the earthquake which had eerily shattered the city, six weeks before Mao's death), a crack corps of officers and soldiers had become an instant body of civil engineers and construction managers. Called down to Shenzhen, the army had then swiftly raised pavilions of production and power as far as the eye could see. The factories had then been furnished with automatic equipment capable of carrying out orders with optimal efficiency: no messy subjective thinking required. Dormitories had been raised in scientific rows, efficiently designed just to cover the sleeping hours of the workers, with no need for anyone to waste time or space in accommodating inconvenient families. Watching the speed of the army's progress – and always quick to see an opportunity – Hong Kong's land-hungry *da ban* big bosses (*taipans*, to those who spoke in Cantonese) had even put forward plans to develop vast areas in a single leap. When local planning bureaucrats pointed out that Shenzhen had reached its limits, Deng waved his magic stick to *swoosh!* the limits away.

By 1985, the army had raised up China's first skyscraper; by 1989 Shenzhen was beginning to look like a real city, which, in 1990, with a declaration from Beijing, it duly became. In 1994, refreshed by the bracing breeze of Deng's 1992 visit, and with the help of an eager Hong Kong Chinese engineer, Shenzhen then emancipated its own mind and launched a new urban revolution as well. Blazing a way through hills and mountains, leaping across rivers, new roads rushed out of the city like hungry dragons, stretching the city's limits far and

wide. Villages fortunate enough to find themselves licked by the dragons' flames, exploded like stars into industrial zones, each (just like the
villages of Wenzhou) with their own particular productive idea: shoes,
lights or whatever else the outside world might want. Everything had
all happened so quickly and over such a vast area, that many wondered
what to call it: was it a city or a state? Or was it something else entirely?
But revelling in the roaring socialism that it was producing, no one on
the ground had any time to worry about the niceties of names. In the
end, they settled for a description pulled out of the geography books:
the Pearl River Delta.

Further up the coast, the once foreign emporium of Shanghai looked
down with envy at Shenzhen's new socialist credentials. The most sparkling of imperial China's treaty ports, this was the old *Shanghailand*
that had once observed no other laws but its own. From 1949, its
decadent past had brought it nothing but shame. After forty years of
distrust, however, Deng, the crouching dragon, had looked at the city
with new eyes, and seen the possibility of something quite different.
Refreshingly far from Beijing, it was already a port and a city that sat
near to the sea. Divided by the wide Huangpu tributary river mouth
of the Yangzi, it had both a central Puxi, west bank that held the cities
greatest assets, and a wide eastern area, Pudong, that had scarcely
been touched; it was also surrounded by energetic provinces. Like the
southern lands around the Pearl River, this was a geography that had
the power to transform not only its own productivity but that of the
entire Yangzi River delta as well.

By 1992, new construction enterprises (among them, many founded
by army veterans from Shenzhen) were already advancing onto
Pudong's mudflats. By 1994, a *Pearl of the Orient* television tower
touched the skies, while bridges stretched to connect the city under
the sparkling banner of socialism. As with Shenzhen, more roads
set off like dragons, carrying torches to light up not only the lands
of surrounding fields, but those of whole cities and provinces which
spread all around. Suddenly, ancient towns whose crafting treasures
had once floated up the Grand Canal to the Ming and Qing heavens in
Beijing found new fortunes of opportunity lapping at their feet – even

as the villages of Wenzhou, now openly displaying their productive powers, found a vast port ready to hand.

Watching images of flashing dragons and rising skyscrapers on evening television, hundreds of other cities across the country, not to mention tens of thousands of towns, entreated the approving powers above to grant them the official chops required for special zones of their own. Some succeeded; others failed. But in the prevailing spirit of mind emancipation, even those who failed decided to go ahead just the same. And out in the fields, tens of millions of eager hearts picked up bundles of hopes and clothes, and decided to create their own opportunity by storming the passes to the cities. For many, *hukou* registrations came to be seen as nothing but a temporary inconvenience which would surely soon be 'disappeared'. The country cousins rolled into the new city world like a tide.

Upon reflection, it had all happened just in time. On 1 October 1995, television images of Deng Xiaoping observing the fireworks of the forty-seventh anniversary of the founding of the People's Republic of China showed everyone that, at ninety-one, his light was finally fading. But as Deng moved into the shadows, Jiang Zemin found that the waters of the Party's river were rising fast around him. Once again, prices were soaring to the skies, while state-owned factories were sitting on mountains of debts. It seemed that without Deng's personal power to keep them in check, the provincial energies had run away with themselves. But in the absence of anyone with Long March credentials, how was the Party going to calm them down without risking another sinking of the productive socialist ship? Fortunately for Jiang Zemin, Zhu Rongji, rewarded by Deng with a promotion from mayor of Shanghai to vice-premier of the state, was there to take the blame.

Jiang Zemin was clear that finding the next stone to cross the river was going to take more than a holiday postcard – just as he was clear that the East Winds which had been temporarily becalmed by Deng could easily gather themselves up into another gale: one which he might struggle to command. Already at the end of 1994, looking for a personal *pai banzi*, do the deal, strength, Jiang had invited loyal Shanghai powers to join him in the Politburo height of Party authority, in a bid to bolster his support in the rather frightening courtyards of the central Party's families. Thus reinforced, Jiang had then managed to secure a Party resolution to reiterate the old Leninist principle that centralised decision-making was everything. With central power clarified, he followed it up with a confirmation that, as general secretary of the Party, chairman of the Central Military Commission, and president of the People's Republic of China, he was the *hexin*, core, of everything.

With the full force of the Party's order now behind him, Jiang decided to make it clear that, while he had not had the privilege of standing shoulder to shoulder with Mao on the Long March himself, he was nonetheless a true inheritor of the ancient skills with which Yu the Great had tamed the lands. The Leninist institutions that he had inherited would not just be nourished, but strengthened. The Party's principles of Marxism-Leninism-Mao Zedong Thought would be tightened. Anyone likely to cause trouble would be asked to step outside. Looking back to the strategies deployed by rulers of the past, he also noted the virtues of campaigns against corruption – campaigns that provided a leader with a convenient whip with which to beat down any unruly weeds of critics, and also the power to sort out any self-strengthening excesses. As ever, it was simply a matter of whispering a troublesome name and then, not only would the individual weed disappear, but the waves of shock would ensure that any other weeds would be quick to step into line – or leave the country. That should be enough to keep any awkward voices at bay.

Jiang, however, had forgotten that everyone had read the same history books, with many of them doing so at the far more frightening feet of Mao. As the fourteenth Party Congress neared the end of its five-year term, the East Winds leapt ahead of him. Presenting a carefully inked ten thousand character memorial, they declared that the socialist state was disappearing, and that a new bourgeoisie was advancing up the productive ranks. They also argued that, thanks to Deng's love of studying the treacherous West, a new insurgency of stubbornly subjective intellectuals had been gathering, all steeped in the technical aspects of Western wealth-creation, and very likely harbouring bourgeois liberal ideas as well. It was, they argued, nothing more nor less than another battle in that endless American campaign for Peaceful Evolution. And with the intellectuals dedicating themselves to their own subjective opinions, China was at risk of being colonised by undisciplined Western ideas that had no concept of the pivotal importance of leadership by a Party.

Jiang bravely refused to listen. The East Winds then decided to pick up a trick from Deng, and step on to a train of their own. This time, though, the train was not bound for the south, but for the industrial heartlands of the north-east, where men who had once worked for the Party state were not only losing their jobs, but their iron rice bowl pensions as well.

With Deng's dream, and everybody's productive futures, at stake, it was not long before a countervailing force of right-leaning 'West Winds' rose up behind Jiang. Representatives of the more productive provinces, they were determined to continue their rise – and, over time, to secure their gains with the additional protections of democracy and the rule of law (protections which they argued even Marx himself had advised).

Carefully tutored by Deng in the critical necessity of avoiding any discussions of either democracy or the rule of law if productivity were to prevail, Jiang now found himself caught between an East Wind left (which wanted nothing to do with wealth-creating productivity), and a West Wind right (which wanted wealth-creating productivity, but insisted on having the twin demons of democracy and law as well). Like so many before him, Jiang turned back to the past for inspiration, and hit upon the old idea of a personal school of theorising brushes. Finding a committee of supporting minds – sensible ones which understood the importance of having both productivity *and* a disciplined obedience to the Party – he armed them with a free flow of ink, and commanded them to come up with a definition of socialism that would defeat both of the storming winds: East and West alike. 'Take your time', he said, 'but not too much of it'.

As Jiang's brush committee set to work on the definition that would square his circle, the ink-hurling continued. In early 1997 Deng Xiaoping finally died. The battling brushes paused for a moment's reflection and Jiang Zemin, still firmly at the helm, stood up to declare that he would work as hard as any of the Great Men who had gone before him. As he spoke, the hands of a long-ticking clock moved towards the midnight hour when, on 1 July 1997, the imperial British rule of Hong Kong's island rocks would run out. This was the eager-ly-awaited date when the magnificent market which sat off the shore of Guangdong would return to China, carrying some of the world's most potent capitalism in its bags. The return had been conditional upon a fifty-year 'One Country, Two Systems' compromise, grounded in a treaty with Britain and supplemented by a 'Basic Law' that clearly seemed to think it would become a Constitution; but the important thing was that the Party was throwing off one of the last humiliations. With Deng departed, it was Jiang Zemin who rose to welcome the people of Hong Kong back to the heartlands of China and, in so doing, to herald the triumph of the Chinese nation over 'one hundred years of humiliation'.

By the time the Party came together at the end of 1997, for the fifteenth five-yearly Congress, Jiang and his committee of brushes thought they had finally found a definition of socialism that would knock the stuffing out of both of the battling winds. Its name was not exactly elegant – but this was, after all, the Communist Party, and not some salon of scholarly minds. The key was a new 'science of Deng Xiaoping Theory', grounded in the idea of 'one centre and two basic points'. The 'one centre' was *jingji fazhan*, spreading economic development. As for the 'two basic points', the first was Deng's familiar Four Cardinal Principles' (keep to the order of the socialist road, uphold the dictatorship of the proletariat, uphold the supremacy of Marxism-Leninism-Mao Zedong Thought, and uphold the leadership of the Communist Party); the second was Deng's 'mind emancipation'. Armed with such scientific clarity, who could fail to distinguish between those ideas of Marxism that were truly Marxist, and those ideas of Marxism that were actually devilishly anti-Marxist ideas in disguise? In short, the central task was economic development, with every problem to be solved by the power of the Party, coupled with a heavy dose of more economic development, and, where necessary, a spoonful of Monkey King logic as well.

Standing tall in the Great Hall of the People, Jiang Zemin presented the new Deng Xiaoping Theory to the Party, with onward broadcast to the masses. Also charged with appointing a new Party leadership, he took the opportunity to strengthen his own revolutionary credentials. Always the late-coming engineer rather than a pioneering Long Marcher, he decided to polish his position with the appointment to the Politburo of some of the sons of the Party's greatest founders. While Deng had always insisted that the Party should on no account perpetuate its own 'aristocracy', the invited sons were only too happy to continue the family tradition. Others, remembering Deng's words, looked up at the skies in consternation. Casting their minds back to the early centuries of the Zhou dynasty and to the fiefdoms of families that had been spread across a land which had ultimately fallen to their battles, they lost no time in calling the sons 'princelings'.

When the new Politburo members rose to take their places, the third generation leadership of the Communist dynasty was not only younger than its revolutionary forebears (and if the newspapers were to be believed, a lot better educated) but a sparkling combination of some of the country's most exceptional Party talents and the descendants of some of the Party's greatest family lineages. What the third generation leadership actually thought, however, about anything, was not much clearer than the scientific 'one centre and two basic points' of Deng Xiaoping Theory. Apparently, they had found an answer to the losses and debts of the state-owned enterprises – a solution which was supposed to sort out everything else as well. The biggest and most important of the state-owned enterprises were going to remain the property of the people: as Jiang Zemin had correctly observed, how could China be a socialist country if it did not own the core means of its production? The smaller, and less important, ones were to be allowed to emancipate their minds by experimenting with ideas which had once been seen as monopolies of the capitalists, but which, since the unveiling of Deng Xiaoping Theory, were now understood to be available for anyone and everyone to use under the helpful mantra of the 'socialist market economy'. Still not quite clear about how exactly a socialist market economy was supposed to work (no one really was), most cadres decided that it was time to transform whatever state assets they could into more productive 'companies', with themselves and their families as shareholders.

For those on the podium of the Party (and all of those, friends and relations, who stood behind them), the stones were clearly lining up for a heavenly crossing of the river. Outside the Party, though, a number of intellectuals saw the stones as something more like rapids. Intellectual minds divided, as they had been dividing since Deng had declared the Four Modernisations (as indeed they had been dividing since the time of the shamans). On one side, were those who had chosen to follow a Party which they felt had made mistakes, but was learning its way to a better future. On the other side, were those who wanted the freedom to look for other answers, whatever they might be.

The divide had been particularly acute after the shock of 1989 had been followed by Deng Xiaoping's 'southern holiday'. Many of those who, in the 1980s, had dreamt of Wei Jingsheng's Fifth Modernisation, had begun to think that they, and everyone else, might be better off following Deng and his mind-emancipating economic development: it might take a little longer to get to the ultimate utopia, they had reasoned, but Deng seemed to be on a genuinely progressive track and perhaps such an ambitious revolution really did need both a strong nation, and time. But as economic development had come to be raised to the pantheon of the gods, with every problem supposed to be solved with more economic development, more Party power and, where necessary, another dose of Monkey King logic, a number of intellectuals had increasingly argued that the Party was building up the same kind of 'human portents' which had brought down the First Qin Emperor and had been periodically rocking the Chinese world ever since. Hard though it might be to achieve, they argued, there was no getting around the fact that for a state to be strong, heaven had to be able to listen to its people. Western democracy was clearly flawed but it was not the only model; and heaven could not listen to its people if its laws had been hijacked by a gun.

The critical logic of the questioners was hard to fault: having watched the fields of the revolutionary past being so quickly concreted over for cities of glittering dragons and trains, those left in the mud naturally wanted to know what had happened to the socialist dream. Deng had not only brought back the bourgeois bureaucracy which Mao had fought so hard to resist, but in the process he had managed to recreate the age-old, 'never-left-out' class at the top – the one that always managed to appropriate the profits of any opportunity that ever opened up. You could dress it up as black and white cats if you wanted, they argued, but China was now repeating old imperial lessons that it surely should have learnt by now. The floods of peasants migrating to Shenzhen and Shanghai were simply Hankou all over again. And the currents of cadres pursuing their own personal modernisations were nothing but reincarnations of nineteenth-century self-strengtheners without a belief in anything or anyone other than themselves. And as for 'modernisation' – well, that was nothing but a euphemism for the fact that the people's property (the state-owned factories and the land) was once again disappearing into private pockets as fast as it had ever done in imperial times before.

One mind that was particularly shocked at the speed with which Deng Xiaoping Theory was converting the Communist revolution into a new age of imperial feudalism was that of a forthright intellectual by the name of He Qinglian. A historian-economist editor of a Shenzhen newspaper, in 1998 she decided that it was time to call the colour of the cats. 'The bureaucrats', He Qinglian observed, 'are using their official positions to enclose a people's property that has been won with blood, and then siphoning off everything worth having into their own personal accounts.' 'In the cities', she added 'the People's Republic is being left with the cost of supporting the loss-making carcasses of factories, not to mention paying off workers who have lost their jobs, while Party-appointed cadres are taking the productive assets off the public stage and walking away with the profits.' 'Meanwhile, in the countryside', she continued, 'a new bourgeoisie of self-strengthening peasants has emerged, turning once-fertile fields into factories, and, just like the old scholar-merchants, floating themselves off to the cities to enjoy their new-found fortunes.'

Gathering her thoughts into a book, He Qinglian went on to set out her view that it was all rather reminiscent of seventeeth-century England, only with the added Chinese characteristics that the feudal families and secret societies were of an industrial scale. Red leaders and bureaucrats got rich, and in order to keep the gains coming, they passed on new opportunities to their children – even as they declined to open up the Party to any further reforms that would enable outside eyes to check the size and origins of their wealth. Prices of state assets were being fixed low enough to ensure that property could be transferred into their hands, and once that was accomplished, the prices were then being allowed to soar, so that profits cascaded into their own accounts. This left those who had not managed to make the same self-strengthening leaps – anyone who was not an official or related to an official by birth, marriage or mutual bonds of blood – out in the cold. The piles of profit were then being thrown at more of the fields to convert them into cities. As if all that wasn't bad enough, given that the fastest growing possibilities were on the coast, cash from all over the country was pouring into the cities of the east. With such an imbalance, even the ancient Nüwa would have struggled to keep the pillars of the skies from crashing down and dangerously tilting the country off its axis. Industries that Mao had painstakingly tried to relocate to the country's interior were now crumbling. Indeed, the whole of China was being deliberately marched backwards towards a so-called 'primitive stage of capitalism' that would have shocked both Marx and Mao. Meanwhile, the Party had become a secret society all of its own. Not surprisingly, China's people were becoming more unequal by the day. If someone did not pull up the never-left-out class by its roots, and soon, it would take all of China down with it, just as it had always done before.

Keen to retain the talents of the scientific intellectuals, Jiang Zemin was willing to let a few flowers bloom. But in the face of He Qinglian's assault, he retreated to the firmer footing of Leninist discipline, and took the opportunity to remind everyone that China was still a revolutionary socialist state under the constant threat of Peaceful Evolution from an ever-imperialist West. The verdict of history (according to Jiang Zemin, and now supported by the textbooks of the Patriotic Education Campaign) was clear. The Republic's flirtation with a national assembly in 1912 had been a disaster: pointless arrows had been hurled in every direction, Sun Yatsen's protégé-premier, Song Jiaoren, had fallen to an assassin's bullet, Yuan Shikai had dressed himself up for an imperial role, the provincial fiefdoms had protested, warlords had stepped into the breach, and then a nationalist Guomindang party had turned itself into a bunch of industrial-militarists and nearly sold the country up the capitalist river. Conversely, the Party's founders had sacrificed life and limb to fight the Guomindang. In the face of appalling odds, they had applied Marxist principles of socialism and Leninist principles of organisation to rescue China not only from capitalism but from the imperial foreign powers with which capitalism so regularly marched. Times had been tough, some of the Party's bravest hearts had fallen, the people had had to eat a lot of bitterness, but with the road so painstakingly prepared by Mao, Deng Xiaoping had been able to arrive on the horseback of mind emancipation, and the possibilities of a socialist market economy had been miraculously discovered – on which the Party was now building a strong and productive socialist future. It was as worthy a triumph as any of those of the Great Men of the ancient past.

Having summed it all up, Jiang went on to declare that, against all the odds, the Party had succeeded in creating nothing less than a 'socialist spiritual civilisation'. This having been so miraculously achieved, the ink-splashing intellectuals had a collective duty to craft their characters in ways that would promote the people's 'socialist harmony' – just as Mao Zedong had put it so clearly in Yan'an. The hurling of subjective opinions was putting everyone's future at risk: it was time to stop. The reckless intellectuals were banned; and those who refused to listen to words of warning were threatened with the prospect of a stay in Beijing's Qincheng jail. He Qinglian remained at liberty, but her works were cut down to a more acceptable size, and the question of her future acquired a clear black mark.

As the intellectuals were learning their lessons, Jiang suggested that it was time for all of China to reconsider and reflect upon the better traditions of its Confucian past. Specifically those Confucian values of an orderly and productive *jia*, family, guided by *li*, ritual, and *yi*, integrity: principles that meant that every individual kept to their particular place, with the fatherly heads of everyone always at the helm. What China needed was more *gao suzhi*, high quality, individuals – people who would be scientifically fit to advance the spreading economic development, accepting the Party's leadership of everyone into a harmoniously unquestioning future. What the country did *not* need were selfish individuals of the low-quality kind who could not stop themselves from asking questions – a recklessness which was a risk to all. Confucius had been on the right track when he had suggested that man should cultivate himself. But the First Qin Emperor had also been right: left to his own devices, man was an unreliable creature at best. Fortunately, socialism, with its emphasis on scientific facts and objective thought, was able to light the way. With enough high quality people, the revolution would be unassailable. But let the weeds of the low-quality people creep in, and heaven would fall down on everyone's heads.

Jiang Zemin's views clear, every institute of learning, high and low, was instructed in the critical importance of the high quality people, goals. To help everyone remember how they were supposed to be thinking, four new 'must haves' were announced: lofty ideals, a sound morality, immaculate discipline and the knowledge required for a new productive world. All four had the historic endorsement of 'what Confucius must have thought'. Sadly misunderstood at various points in the revolution, Confucius was now to be recognised as one of the greatest minds the world had ever known. The direction clearly (re) set, newspapers and television channels were commanded to take up the task of shaping a higher quality of popular views. Advertising billboards were designed to inspire the higher quality virtues and launched like banners across every city and would-be city. As one expert on the idea so helpfully explained it: 'If a factory strives to produce high standard products, how much more important for a state to ensure that its people should meet high standards too.'

To make the point crystal clear, when ten thousand 'meditators' assembled in front of the gates of Zhongnanhai in 1999, Jiang Zemin met them with the full force of the state's security. A new generation of Taiping Great Peace fanatics, now inspired by the combined dreams of Buddhism and Daoism, they were men and women who had taken up the banner of a dharma wheel in action, calling themselves the *Falun Gong*. With most of them retired – and all of them seemingly determined to use their time to make some kind of point about a power greater than the Party, Jiang followed up the security with arrests. Declaring that China was under the threat of a new form of 'spiritual pollution', he then outlawed any and all superstitious forces that dared to threaten the *gao suzhi*, high quality, of the people. Every channel of education and information, from schools to newspapers, television channels to museums, was mobilised. No one was left in any doubt as to his or her duty to shun the Falun Gong as well as any other 'other world' idea. The hundreds of thousands who failed in their duty found their way to one of the many *laogai*, reform-through-labour, camps, situated at the harshest edges of the Communist empire, not least in the deserts of the north-west.

In 2001, the historian-economist He Qinglian stood up again: this time arguing that the state was not a god, and economics was about subjective human beings rather than objective science. With the forces of the Party now very clear about the risks of spiritual pollution, and with her own card clearly marked, He Qinglian found herself under the sharp chill of Mao's long shadow. Unable to keep her silence, she left her homeland for the 'lower quality' country of America, where she could safely speak her mind.

Once again, the intellectuals divided. Some decided to follow He Qinglian, if not out of the country then at least into the retreat of more academic studies. Some determined to keep up the battle, but to take a bit more care in what and how they wrote. The greater number, however, decided that, with the Party's position so clear, and with spreading economic development now beginning to look as if it could work, it might finally be time to take up Deng's ideas on mind emancipation and start to think about how productivity might be profitably pursued under the leadership of the Party.

Among those who decided to apply their talents to the market, many recalled the early days of Deng, when a seasoned Party veteran had compared the creation of the socialist market economy to building a birdcage. Explaining that free market principles were the bird, and the socialist plan was the cage, the Party veteran had gone on to note that it was all about the physics of flight and the structural engineering of cages. Build the cage too small, and the bird would not be able to fly at all. Make the bars of the cage too wide, and the bird would fly away and leave it empty. This was obviously a science that would require truly great minds. Ready to serve the people, the market intellectuals flocked to the side of Deng's capable disciple, Zhu Rongji, now premier, and to the Communist dynasty's formal resurrection of the ancient Hall of Light: the 'National Development and Reform Commission'.

Reassuringly supported by a high quality body of loyal intellectuals, Jiang Zemin and his Politburo were able to get back to the business of crossing the river by feeling for stones. But as Zhu Rongji and the new Hall of Light tried to work out how the socialist market economy would function, it was soon as clear as ever that nothing was going to be easy. Comparing the sorry situation of the state-owned factories (iron rice bowls, mountains of unwanted production, towering debts, and now losing even more money than ever) with the rising energies of the newly private enterprises, they decided that the only hope was to move forward faster: get on with splitting up the state-owned enterprises, sell the loss-makers to any buyers they could find, and rescue those which were too important to give away. Wherever possible, this should be achieved by learning from the Western science of markets that helpfully seemed to say that it was always better to use other people's money (with Hong Kong's stock markets offering an obvious pool of funds). While they were at it, they should also offer the best of the new private spirits an invitation to join the Party. 'Capitalists into the Communist Party?' a sharp East Wind shrilled. 'Not capitalists,' explained Jiang Zemin patiently, 'entrepreneurs – who, just like the cats, can always be black or white'.

In 2001, the entrepreneurs were welcomed into the Party as 'advanced productive forces', to clapping applause. Whispering offstage, a muttering of low quality voices noted that it was not really much of a change: given that it was the officials and their families who had been buying up the people's assets and turning them to a profit, the Party was already awash with entrepreneurs. Oblivious to the humour, Jiang Zemin stood up to note that, with all of the complications involved in building a socialist market economy, the Party ought to extend Deng Xiaoping's estimate of how long it would take to get to socialism: add another fifty years, say 2100. After all, in the greater scheme of five thousand years of history, being becalmed in the capitalist stage for another half century was surely not too much of a price to pay for the ultimate utopian ideal. Other muttering voices (of the lowest quality) suggested that far from marching towards a Marxist utopia, the Party seemed to be privatising *itself.*

In October 2002, the third generation of the Communist dynasty gathered again, this time to launch the Party's sixteenth Congress. Once again, Jiang Zemin advanced to the centre stage of the Great Hall of the People to announce the state of the nation for the next five years. After two terms of five years at the helm, he was also going to welcome a new 'fourth generation' of leadership to the top.

Accepting the praise of a grateful Party – as much for his helpful clarification of Communism as for the powerful forces of production unleashed – Jiang then handed over the general secretaryship of the Party to his vice-president, and fellow engineer, Hu Jintao.

Before leaving the podium, however, Jiang took the opportunity to declare that 'the strategic adjustment of the economic structure has been crowned with success'. Couched in such objective terms, it was not immediately obvious to everyone in the audience what he meant – certainly not to those watching from home. But the word 'success' was a clue, as was the uniform ripple of applause that seemed to confirm that this must be something good. Continuing, Jiang Zemin noted that there were still some problems: a countryside that had decoupled from the cities; a western hinterland that had somehow got separated from the coastal east; a few people who did not have a job; and some inconvenient 'climate events' that nature was inconsiderately throwing in everyone's way. The problems deftly filed into individual boxes, Jiang Zemin then went on to restate the *jingji fazhan* spreading economic development cornerstone of Deng Xiaoping Theory. To which he added, with a final revolutionary flourish worthy of Deng himself, that the Party would now proceed to deliver a quadrupling of socialist production by 2020. With obedient Party clapping ringing in his ears, Jiang then unveiled his own addition to the pantheon of Chinese Communist Party thought: the Party should 'represent advanced social productive forces; represent the progressive course of China's advanced culture; represent the fundamental interests of the majority'. With the artistic elegance of an engineer, he skilfully named his contribution the 'Three Represents'.

Those still watching on their televisions at home were, by now, scratching their heads – with most deciding that the 'quality' of their minds was obviously not high enough to keep up. Looking closely at the screen, though, it seemed that even those sitting on the highest-quality Party seats were struggling to see the point: Three Represents? Representing who? And representing what? Some decided that it must be about representing everybody and everything. Others said it was particularly about representing new classes of entrepreneurs and intellectuals (those who understood that working with one's mind was not about asking dangerous metaphysical questions of 'why', but about responsibly focusing on the essential scientific point of 'how'). Yet others said that it was really all about creating that Western idea of a large middle-class of people who could hold everything together while the top was still feeling for the stones. 'Isn't class struggle a thing of the past?' asked some of the more confused minds. 'That's right', replied others who had been quicker to get the knack of the new: 'this is class without the struggle.'

When, in the spring of 2003, Hu Jintao joined Jiang Zemin on the podium of the annual meeting of the National People's Congress as the newly appointed general secretary of the Party and president of the country, it was clear to all that something was missing. Jiang had passed on the leadership of Party and State – but kept the all-important command of the Central Military Commission under his own personal wing. With only the most tenuous of links to Deng Xiaoping, and none at all to the princelings, it was clear that Hu was going to have a struggle on his hands to wrest the guns of the Party's power from his predecessor. But observing Hu's relative youth, noting his engineering background and decades of work in some of China's toughest inland provinces (not least Tibet at the time of Tiananmen), and looking at the increasingly worrying state of the peasants, some thought that even though the withheld leadership of the military was a problem, there was a lot that Hu could do to get things on a smoother track – particularly in the countryside.

Over the previous few years, while the advanced forces of production had been speeding ahead in the coastal east, peasants in the listing landlocked west had been floundering in the mud. Anyone who could, had smuggled their way through the border controls of *hukou*, and rushed to the coastal east; willing to eat any bitterness in order to keep aged parents and young children afloat in village homes, they had taken the riskiest of jobs at the poorest of pay. In some provinces and districts, so many had left their homes that entire villages had been hollowed out, leaving an 'army' of the oldest and the youngest to keep the countryside going.

Not all of those in the countryside had left, however. Some, particularly those able to serve the local officials, had stayed to see what more might be done with Deng's Monkey King logic, transforming any remaining relics of the socialist landscape into an entrepreneurially personal profit. Rights which the peasants had been given to 'use' the land for their individual household responsibility plots had been a particular object of interest: thirty years long, and with any underlying ownership being held by the Party state, they offered obvious opportunities to persuade village heads and their committees that the land which the peasants were 'using' should be redistributed to a more productive cause. Of course, the peasants were complaining. But as Deng had explained so carefully, and Jiang Zemin had confirmed, this was all for the far greater cause of an eventual (now 2100) socialist utopia for all. Meanwhile, an increasing number of local officials had been making contributions to their own self-strengthening treasuries by raising taxes, levying fees and looking for any other opportunities to convert the public assets of their neighbourhoods into a personally productive wealth.

Transfers of land rose to the skies, and cash began to circulate on a scale not known since the rise of the self-strengtheners at the end of the nineteenth century – or the trading fortunes of the Ming. As in the past, the circulation was largely limited to the hands of those whose official positions gave them the power to approve a transfer, including of course, families and friends. Obviously, one could not expect the peasants to understand the greater importance of the exchange, and heaven forbid that anyone should see bundles of cash changing hands and get the wrong idea. Scratching their heads for a way to trade land for cash without the risk of inconvenient questions, some suggested that a solution might be found in the popular game of *mah jong*: with everyone in China a skilled player, it was just a matter of a would-be buyer intentionally losing, and then showers of cash could be transferred from one playing hand to another.

As the officials, the self-strengtheners, the families and the friends pulled their chairs forward for the game, chill winds began to blow across the precarious fortunes of the fields. With the communes long gone and modernisation racing ahead all around them, the peasants were struggling to survive. Lucky ones found themselves staring at a stubborn soil that, after decades if not centuries of exhaustion, was once again failing. Unlucky ones were evicted to make way for a factory or a town. Educating children had become an unaffordable dream: even if a school had been built in a neighbourhood, admission and attendance required a host of supplementary fees. The cost of admission to anything but the barest of hospitals was a crisis that would always plunge a family into debt. And whenever an official knocked on the door, everyone knew that it could only mean yet another demand for a tax. Poor, sick and desperate, once again, as in the imperial past, the peasants began to band together in brotherhoods. And, once again, they found themselves confronting the organised forces of the officials and self-strengtheners: battalions of thugs who had been deployed for centuries to keep the countryside under control. Now, however, the thugs were operating not under the name of an emperor, but under the banner of a Party order which Deng Xiaoping had called Stability Maintenance. This was no imperial tyranny but a single heart, beating as one, with anyone whose heart wanted to think otherwise necessarily needing to be 'harmonised.' Any and all opposition was just an irresponsible splash of spiritually polluted minds. And, as in the Great Leap Forward, anyone who dreamt of smuggling a hopeful plea for help out to a higher authority would find that it was either buried or returned with a punishment.

By 1999, things had become so bad that a rare good official, by the name of Li Changping, took his career into his hands and wrote a letter to the premier, Zhu Rongji. 'The peasants' life is so hard', wrote Li Changping, 'the countryside is so poor, the soil is in such a desperate state; the township governments have not only bankrupted themselves but the peasants; and the peasants are being held hostage to the rampant ambitions and buried debts of local officials who have modernised nothing but themselves.' 'It is', he declared, 'time to tell the truth.' Investigation teams were sent down to Li Changping's particular corner of the countryside, but the cats had scarpered, leaving only a few black rats of thugs to take the blame. Published by a brave southern newspaper, however, Li's letter began to circulate widely, and in 2002 it was converted into a wildly popular book entitled *Telling the Truth to the Premier.* As the countryside stayed in the mud, other reports began to rise: some so much blacker than Li Changping's that no one in the Party wanted them to see the light of day.

By the time that Jiang Zemin finally stepped down as general secretary and president in March 2003, the state of the peasants in the countryside had become so desperate that hope was daring to spring. Surely the Party would do something to save the peasants who, after all, had been the ones who were supposed to have won the revolution in the first place. Like a loyal son, rising to the pinnacle of power, the new general secretary and president Hu Jintao rolled out Deng Xiaoping Theory in deference to the greatest of the recent ancestors, and the Three Represents in an act of filial piety to his 'godfather' Jiang Zemin. Hu lingered longest on the last of Jiang Zemin's trinity: 'the fundamental interests of the vast majority of the people'. Deng was right, declared Hu, to recommend the Four Modernisations; but everyone should always remember Mao's three revolutionary musts: modesty and prudence without arrogance, plain living and hard struggle. Standing beside him on the podium, newly appointed as premier, was the kind face of Wen Jiabao: a geologist by profession, but far more striking as the man who looked like everyone's favourite grandfather. Once again, some began to dream of snow in summer.

No sooner had Hu and Wen taken the reins, than it was clear that heaven had already secretly struck its moral judgement on the events of the recent past. A mysterious and deadly virus had been spreading across the countryside; flagrantly disregarding the *hukou* barriers, it was now jumping from the countryside directly into the cities. There had been whispers about a strange disease among the peasants for quite a while, but those in the higher-up towns and cities had been too busy burying facts to listen. Already in 2002, the virus had gripped the lungs of a number of southern peasants, squeezing them to an early death. While some brave hospital brushes had reported the cases, local officials had buried the news along with the bodies – worried about Stability Maintenance, in light of the fact that many of the dead had been turned away because they could not afford the deposits required for a bed.

In early 2003, quiet burials had become a little more difficult when visiting doctors from Hong Kong became infected with the virus, and carried it home, where it was given a name: SARS. Then in early April, less than a month after Hu Jintao had assumed the mantle of power, the virus suddenly jumped all boundaries of brush control when a reckless doctor of some seniority (retired, of course) informed the television networks of the central state and of Hong Kong that the virus had taken hold of hospitals in Beijing. The origins of the infectious agent, it turned out, were to be found in an ever-expanding population of pigs and poultry reared on tiny plots of land by peasants who, looking for their own place on the self-strengthening bandwagon, had been trying to keep up with the cities' rising demand for ever-greater quantities of pork and duck. Having made the leap across the species, from there, the virus had jumped but a few inches to the peasants themselves who, rearing as much livestock as they could on tiny patches of land, had been living cheek-by-jowl alongside their charges. Whether or not SARS was a strike of heavenly anger, it was clearly a sharp rebuke to Deng Xiaoping Theory and its central idea of spreading economic development, supported by two basic points: one of which (mind emancipation) had encouraged everyone to do whatever they could to get rich; the other (the Four Cardinal Principles) had ensured that the Party's powers were beyond the questions of any human voice.

Shocked at a natural disaster that was clearly man-made, Hu Jintao and his premier, Wen Jiabao, immediately launched a 'People's War' against the latest heavenly disorder. Thousands were quarantined: whole villages in the countryside, and entire apartment blocks in the most affected cities. Productivity plummeted. Some of the most advanced productive forces railed against the interruption to socialist growth; conversely a number of left-leaning intellectuals argued that it was time to slow the pace down to something a little more human, and while they were at it, time for the Party and its state to start listening to the people at large.

The war on SARS was eventually won. But when the (official) numbers were counted, five thousand Chinese had been infected, and three hundred and fifty lives had been lost (not including another two hundred and ninety-nine others who had died on the outlying rock of Hong Kong). The country's socialist civilisation had been humiliated. Hu and Wen stood up to say that Deng's *jingji fazhan* economic development remained the primary goal, but that the territory over which it was to be pursued would now be officially expanded to include the countryside. Henceforward, the peasants were to be at the forefront of the Party's paternal concerns. At the end of 2003, Hu Jintao went one step further, quoting the words of one of Confucius' greatest disciples to say that 'the people are the root of any power'. Now seemingly reading a lot of the classical texts, a year later Hu Jintao went on to embrace Confucius outright. Once banned, the ancient scholar was now well on his way to becoming part of the Communist dynasty's pantheon. Quoting from the texts that had become the architecture of imperial thought, Hu declared that not only should society be ordered, but it should be a harmonious whole as well.

While Hu Jintao was reading his books, two recklessly intellectual brushes in the provinces decided to travel across the countryside and see for themselves what was going on. Gathering up their life savings, they travelled across fifty villages in what had, over the last century, become one of China's poorest provinces, Anhui. Their social survey completed, they then wrote it up in a book entitled: *An Investigation into the Lives of Chinese Peasants*. The lines of their text described in painstaking detail the taxes and fees which were cannibalising the peasants; its pages bled with the stories of their miseries. Like sheep under the power of official wolves, the peasants were being ravaged by taxes, raped by transfers of their land, and whenever they dared to protest, they were being arrested so that the stability of the socialist order could remain undisturbed. Thoroughly grounded in objective research, but outrageously subjective in spirit, the book spread like wildfire: initially openly, and then, when the organising principles of socialist harmony banned its polluting poison, in the underground market of ideas.

Over the next three years, Hu Jintao and Wen Jiabao applied their energies to improving the lot of the peasants. Seeing the obvious solution as more economic development, plans were announced for a New Socialist Countryside'. Roads were quickly forged in every direction, in the hope that blazing dragons would follow in their wake. Power stations were swiftly raised for everyone's electrification. Schools and hospitals were ordered to be built, immediately. Taxes on peasants were to be cut – with the costs of the cuts to be covered by the local governments. Meanwhile, Stability Maintenance was to remain the order of the day.

Commanded to deliver results in double-quick time, and not sure where to get the cash from, many of the village heads and their committees looked at the land use rights which were floating above the fields, and decided that their only choice was to sacrifice a few more peasant plots to generate the money required for the greater good of all. Others, with even more emancipated minds, decided that it was time not just to sell a few fields, but to jump right into the sea of the city, and get into the business of building towns. In terms of getting rich quick, it seemed a reasonable solution: with cities having become treasures of industrial production, over the last twenty years, the act of building offices and shopping malls had become a very important source of productive value – not to mention the added productive benefits of building roads and accompanying airports.

Before long, village heads and local mayors were becoming construction entrepreneurs, rewarded for city-raising success. The countryside was on the move: the more ambitious villages became small towns, and the more ambitious small towns set off to becoming bigger towns, if not small cities. Every now and again, a growing village or town would find itself colliding with a bigger city. When that happened, the bigger city just expanded its boundaries – and the price of everyone's land went up.

But not everyone hit the jackpot. A lot of the ambitious small towns remained works in progress: sky-rising pavilions in the middle of nowhere, they hung, suspended, somewhere between a dream and a nightmare.

Meanwhile up in the capital city of all, Beijing had beaten the rest of the world in a bid to host the 2008 Olympics. A model for the country's cities, every possible productive energy was being harnessed to turn the luck of Beijing's Olympic draw into a socialist triumph that others could copy. With so much to do, and so little time in which to do it, the urban planning bureau, once preoccupied with protecting the flight paths of ancestral spirits and still stuck in a dusty corner, was easily overlooked. Greater men, clear about the need to build a lot of storeys, looked at the big old chequerboard squares of Beijing's once Imperial and Inner cities, and offered them up to self-strengthening enterprises, state and private, who could develop them, one vast block at a time. Architects seemed an unnecessary complication: hard to find, they were easily replaced with a 'cut and paste' click of a mouse to reproduce the same building over and over again, with a thoughtful adjustment of the 'hat' on top, just so that everything didn't look *exactly* the same. Roads were raced into existence; and as more and more cars began to appear, rings of roads were wrapped around the city to try and speed things up. Meanwhile, water and power, essential for both production and consumption, were assumed to be as endless as the heaven that obviously supplied them: a heaven that would also naturally clean up the rubbish as well.

Inconvenient planning and architectural voices silenced, clouds were now pierced on a regular basis, with any and all of the spirits' ancient flight paths permanently cancelled. The new ring roads notwithstanding, roads spread and then jammed. While profits beckoned tantalisingly at every turn, tempers began to fray. Once-distant villages were swept into the city, ten at a time. Distances between everywhere got so big that bicycles could not possibly keep up. New cars poured on to exhausted roads, ten thousand by the month – with each new ring road inconveniently creating a whole new city within the city, even as the original Beijing was still struggling to find itself. More productivity, and more people, needed more water and power. But the wells of the city had long ago run dry, and more power would require new power stations, with new power stations requiring a lot more coal.

As the capital grew like topsy, more and more hands were needed on deck. The most preferred were the revolutionary kind: those willing to work for the socialist dream, with only the most modest demands for cash. With everyone in the city jumping into the rushing sea of enterprise, though, such revolutionary hands were now in short supply. But out in the Communist countryside there was still a seemingly endless reserve of peasants, all desperate for a city job. Equipped with their labour, any city would be able to rise without bounds. More *hukou* barriers were temporarily bent, and the dust and smoke of destruction and construction soon filled the air. Office blocks, residential compounds and shopping malls were anchored in every imaginable spot; pavements were dismissed as a waste of space; and the old willow trees that had wept across the past were liberated from their roots.

By 2006, hundreds of cities across the country, new and old, were racing to follow Beijing to the dizzying heights of a 'global city'. No one was very clear what exactly a 'global city' was but, copying Beijing, one couldn't go far wrong. Up and down the country, no matter how far away they were from the capital, ambitious mayors threw themselves across every imaginable river to get to the global city dream as quickly as they could. The people's air, land and water – not to mention the peasants – were all commandeered for the cause.

Watching the rise of the cities, and the spread of re-organised state-owned enterprises (many of which, now flushed with the cash of offshore markets, were expanding so fast that the Party's bureaucracy was struggling to keep up with them) more reckless brushes began to protest. China was returning to the world of feudal lords that had collapsed the ancient state of Zhou. Whether they were the offices of city mayors or the towers of now-revived state-owned corporations (or indeed the palaces of those whose wealth had rocketed with the profits pocketed by sending public assets to market in Hong Kong), the headquarters had been commandeered by the same never-left-out class that always seemed to come out ahead. Pointing to the clutch of names at the top, a bunch of particularly irresponsible brushes splashed their ink at the rise of a red aristocracy whose families had captured the people's wealth.

The blackest of the brushes were harmonised with jail sentences; and a popular intellectual magazine that told a more subjective version of the Party's history was relegated to the bin. But it was not long before the ripples of anger repeated themselves within the Party itself. Left-leaning East Winds rose up again, shouting that the Party had gone so far and so fast that it had given up the hard-won revolutionary gains, and was handing the country back to the Western imperial capitalists. West Winds – now armed with the riches of socialist success, and anticipating the benefits of a continued national strengthening – rose up in even bigger gales to argue that the only way to solve any of the problems was to keep moving forward. Faster.

In October 2007, the Party gathered once again, this time to convene its seventeenth Congress. Like his ancestors before him, Hu Jintao faced the not uncommon revolutionary challenge of presenting a united Party front to the masses, even as war had broken out within the Party's own ranks. Having scoured the classics of the Party's texts, Hu delivered a report that was crafted in the most objective and harmonious of terms. Socialist culture was thriving, he reported; the people as a whole had a *xiaokang*, relatively comfortable, standard of living. To which he added that there were, of course, problems to be addressed. Carefully listed in the dull language of the Party's objective thought, the problems did not, however, seem to be so grave that they would stir up any human portents. 'Some' Party cadres were not quite straight – but Hu explained that they were only a 'small number'. All in all, socialism was still defined by Deng's ideas of 'productivity, nation-building and living standards'; the route to success was still Deng's central point of *jingji fazhan* economic development and his twin pillars of the Four Cardinal Principles (by now fairly easily summarised as 'leadership by a single top-down Party mind') and mind emancipation. And Jiang Zemin's Three Represents were still there to lead the way.

To these foundations, Hu Jintao added a new principle that ought to finally fix any residual theoretical problems with a great advance in Marxism-Leninism-Mao Zedong thinking. The new principle, Hu declared, would 'take development as its essence, put the people first as its core; take comprehensive, balanced and sustainable development as its basic requirement; and employ overall consideration as its fundamental approach'. Its name, Hu announced triumphantly, was Scientific Development. While the trained minds in the Great Hall of the People managed to keep their eyes open, most of those sitting in the aisles of their television homes couldn't help but fall asleep.

Oblivious to the fading energies of his audience, Hu then went on to point out the revolutionary virtues of the new principle. Unwavering in its pursuit of a socialist society that would realise the full potential of man, Scientific Development was quintessentially Marxist. Tightly managed, it was also a beacon of Leninism. Putting, as it obviously did, the revolutionary triumph of the Chinese people at the forefront, it was also pure Mao.

For those concerned with theory, the idea of Scientific Development seemed to have successfully managed to say something, while leaving the disputed terrain of the past largely unchanged. For those concerned with the practical world, whether within the Party or outside, its value depended on where they were sitting in what, to quote the historian-economist He Qinglian, was rapidly becoming a 'runaway train'. In first class, the Party, flanked by its advanced productive forces of entrepreneurs and scientific economists, was settling down for a comfortable journey. In the soft seats, the supporting middle classes could take confidence in the fact that the train would keep going long enough to get them to their destinations. On the hard seats, the lower classes, struggling to make ends meet, were getting anxious about the rattling. And anyone who had lost their job, or who had smuggled themselves into a city with nothing to call their own, was either clinging on at the *hukou*-less edges or, in the case of those whose land had been sold from under their feet, had already been thrown off the train.

On 12 May 2008, obviously frustrated, heaven expressed its loudest opinion yet. As Beijing sat down to an early afternoon, somewhere off in rural Sichuan an earthquake shook with such a tremor that even the capital's seats moved. For a cluster of remote rural Sichuan counties, the floors of their lives completely disappeared. Premier Wen Jiabao and the People's Liberation Army advanced to the front. Lei Feng-like heroes were filmed in action (even truer heroes appeared in their thousands, but not belonging to the army, they were missed by the cameras). Thousands of survivors were rescued; but many more thousands died.

As the dust began to settle, it seemed that the greatest losses of life and limb had been in the buildings put up by those with official connections: the schools and the hospitals raised in the rush for the New Socialist Countryside – the ones where the profits had been pocketed by local self-strengtheners. It was even rumoured that a stubborn and subjectively-minded geologist had sent a warning of an earthquake to the offices at the top; but as with so many other reckless letter-writers, his words had hit the dust. Once-tamed brushes began to dip themselves into the internet ink, posting daily updates of the names of the dead, and offering a voice to families whose children had been lost to the corruption of socialist speed. The people's *Xinhua*, New China, news agency reported over sixty-nine thousand dead. Everywhere, heads were dipped in sorrow, hearts wept with grief, and the forces of socialist harmony began to roll into controlling action.

As the months passed, Deng's glittering train picked up its speed once again, and attention returned to Beijing, where, at eight p.m. on the eighth day of the eighth month of 2008, the city exploded. Across the world, human breaths were whisked away as the Olympic Games opened with the words of Confucius, and the greatest man-made spectacle on earth unfolded. Fireworks put the footprints of mankind in the sky. Carefully choreographed dancers stepped out images of China's greatest inventions, from the Confucian ideal to paper. The planet appeared as a vast metal ball, covered with acrobats who, with a quick cloud-somersault tumbling, transformed the whole into a glowing Chinese lantern: red, of course. By the end of the Opening Ceremony, the Confucian principles of heavenly order had been displayed for all to see. Over the following weeks, almost every symbol of heaven-sent luck and Great Man-delivered triumph was unleashed; medals cascaded from the skies.

By the end of the games, the socialist market economy seemed to have delivered the kind of golden success which other countries could only dream of – with the point now deftly made that such successes were obviously built on the innate wisdom of a heavenly civilisation burnished over thousands of years.

Within a month, the truth of that point seemed to be spectacularly confirmed by the shock of an astonishing collapse in the capitalist numbers of the Western world. 'A global economic crisis', according to the headlines of the foreign papers, and echoed by the shaking voices of Western bankers who seemed to be at the forefront of the crash. 'Global?' asked the Party – 'surely, what you really mean is just 'the West'.'

CHAPTER 2

NATURE'S TRAILS

The world is a holy vessel. Let him who tampers with it, beware.

Dao De Jing, Laozi (sixth century BCE)

THE WIND AND THE rain had been pouring in all day. By the early August afternoon of 1975, the skies were so dark that it could have been dusk. At midnight, the heavens above seemed to have turned into a storm of so much water that it could have been day. But by then, no one in the old Henan district of *Yicheng* was thinking much beyond sandbags. Battered by winds, drenched by the rain, a place of desperate men, women and children stood shoulder to shoulder in a race against a tide of water that was lapping at the top of the local Banqiao dam. Higher and higher they piled their sandbags, but as high as they went, the water just kept rising. At one a.m. the sky suddenly cleared and the stars emerged. An excited spirit shouted that the waters were receding, Yicheng was saved! And then, within the time that it took for a head to turn, a flash of lightening struck from above, a stroke of thunder clapped, and another voice screamed the last words that Yicheng would ever hear: '*he long dao le*', the river dragon has come!' Rearing its head as high as the sky, a mountain of water roared across the dam, and flung itself down upon everyone's heads.

For eighty-five thousand souls, the world came to an end that night. The river dragon did not blink. Breaching banks without a pause, its heavy coils rolled like tides across the fields of the wider land. Surrounding towns and villages became instant islands in an ocean; lower-lying settlements were swiftly swallowed into watery graves. Finding themselves afloat, hundreds of thousands of surviving souls clung to passing branches and gripped the tips of roofs which had suddenly become rafts. Over the days that followed, marooned others clung to life by stripping trees of all their bark and chewing on the leaves, while those afloat snatched at passing pumpkins and floating pigs. Then, under the hot August sun, the watery fevers followed. When the river dragon finally departed two weeks later, he left the sacrifices of one hundred thousand corpses rotting in sodden fields now baking in the heat. Cut adrift from the rest of the earth, eleven million people lost their homes, with hundreds of thousands ravaged either by the following fevers or the poisons of the floating food.

Henan hearts never forgot the river dragon's rage, but the Party's Propaganda Department ensured that few others would ever even know that it had happened. A miracle of socialist construction, the Banqiao dam had been built in 1951, to hold back the waters of even a one-in-a-thousand years appearance of the river dragon: an 'iron dam' which even the wildest forces of nature would not be able to move. But the dragon which appeared on the 'qi-ba-wu' seventh day of the eighth month of 1975, had been unmoved. Counting time by the cosmic calendar, he had been asleep for the last two thousand years.

Water: the first of the 'five elements'; the stuff of the rains and the rivers which had been the most constant threads in the twisting life and death fortunes of the Yellow River's people and their heartlands. When ancient dry days had turned to cloudless months, or when deluges of storms had washed the river over its banks, hunger had gnawed at the feet of the black-haired people, and anxious emperors had summoned their shamans. The shamans had then consulted the oracle bones for news of heaven's intentions, and raised sacrifices to the skies. And when the monstrous Gong Gong had reared the river up, flooding the fields beyond human endurance, the ancient Great Men, Yao and Shun, had not only carried on the sacrifices, including appeals to the ancestral Yellow Emperor, but also dyked and dammed as hard as they could to protect the heavenly lands. And then Yu the Great had spent thirteen years surveying the vast twists and turns of all of the rivers. Tracing their terrains right up to the spirits of their mountain sources, he not only charted every depth but classified the surrounding soils. The survey completed, Yu then divided the lands into nine provinces (each with their own specific sets of commands for taming the disorders of nature) and turned the ordering of the Yellow River's heartlands into the heavenly duty of man.

Such was the determination of Yu the Great, that the Yellow River had indeed bided its banks for a while, as had the smaller rivers which washed across the expanding territories of the Yellow Emperor's people. But within a hundred years, river dragons were rearing their heads again, with those of the Yellow River being particularly troublesome. Hiding in the muddy waters from which the river took its 'yellow' name, they seemed to see its sandy banks as nothing more than an invitation to jump as high as they could. Looking more closely at the depths, though, and listening to travelling tales of higher mountain waters which flowed as clear as a mirror, later minds would wonder whether the dragons themselves might have been composed not of water but of silt: the silt of the rich yellow earth of the plains through which the river flowed.

Certainly, grains of sandy soil been swept by the river's waters like harvests since ancient times, settling on to the bed of the Yellow River that simply rose and rose. From time to time, they had reached such a height that the river was forced to change its course completely. Oddly enough, this happened particularly in those places where a lot of trees had been cut down, or where the natural course of the river took a sharp turn. As successive emperors peered at the problem, some (particularly those of the shaman tradition that insisted on looking at the patterns of the earth, rather than serving the taming will of man) wondered if it would not be better to let the rivers wander at their own will, possibly even letting the trees stay rooted in the ground as well. But the imperial scholars were of the opinion that dykes and dams were a better proposition. Scholars and peasants alike, though, agreed that it would take a Great Man Emperor indeed for the waters of the Yellow River ever to run clear.

Centuries, if not millennia, passed; the people and their harvesting fields grew and spread. Forests fell to timber, and the earth dried. Some of the Yellow Emperor's people decided to push south into other lands, looking for more water and more fields. By the time that the First Qin Emperor unified the world of the Warring States in 221 BCE, the lands that barbarians were beginning to call 'China' had stretched to embrace many more rivers than the Yellow River alone. Some were simply tributary branches of bigger rivers. Others seemed to fall from the mountain heights of newly conquered central lands. One was a torrent of a force that seemed to roar out of mysterious mountain reaches in a higher west, before meandering across lands that had been home to the once-independent states of Ba, Shu, and Chu – reorganised and renamed by Qin as the heavenly provinces of Sichuan and Hunan.

Almost as great as the Yellow River, this mighty torrential force had come to be known by two names. To those who lived their lives along the banks of its higher reaches, it was the *Chang Jiang*, the Eternal River. To those who lived in the fishing villages around its mouth on the eastern sea, including the early village of Shanghai, it was the Yangzi: said to have been so named after the glittering Yangzhou city under whose shadow those villages sat. While the lands through which the river passed were not composed of quite the same fine yellow soil as that of the northern heartlands, as forest after forest had been felled to make way for new fields, and as the roots of the trees had shrivelled and died, the earth had begun to float like dust into its waters. Nobody called it 'yellow', but the mud was clear for all to see. And every now and then, just like the Yellow River, watery dragons would also leap out of their beds and change the course of its journey. Emperor after emperor would try to tame the Yangzi, as they would try to change the course of almost every other river that washed across their lands. And while they were taming, here and there, they added a few imperial refinements, in the form of canals carved into the conquered southern lands, so that the many smaller rivers of this new region could be joined up into rising tides of trade. Eventually, in the early 600s, the Sui had completed their Grand Canal, uniting the original farming north – now a little dry and unadventurous – to the newer south, a place where rain and rivers had always flowed like silver, and where quick hands readily turned the treasures of nature into a glittering trade of crafts.

Hardly surprisingly, in both north and south, while emperors tamed and quick hands crafted, the building, repairing and re-building of dykes, dams, irrigating ditches and various riverine diversions became part of the labouring peasant life. As natural as tilling the fields, felling forests and soldiering in wars, they were tasks like any others, requiring a back-breaking labour which depended on nothing more nor less than a *chi ku* ability to eat the bitterness of suffering and pain.

By the time Mao Zedong ascended to the eaves of the Gate of Heavenly Peace in 1949, nearly four thousand years of river-taming had passed. But with decades of ravaging warlords and civil war (not to mention a war with Japan fought on Chinese land), once-settled peasants had been transformed into desperate wandering refugees, and river dragons had been left not only in charge of their own destinies, but those of the surrounding fields as well. Dykes, dams and irrigating ditches had fallen into disarray; waterways had become clogged with the debris of everyone's battles; and rivers that breached their banks had been left to pursue new channels. The fields (heavily contested prizes of war endlessly trampled on by troops of varying colours) had turned to mud. Wherever possible, peasants, dependent on the earth for their food, had made attempts to make do and mend. Working on their own, against all the odds of warring man and nature, they had often struggled in vain.

Looking at the Great Man task of taming nature, like every emperor before him, Mao was quick to see his duty. He was also quick to see how, in a wider world that followed the logic of Darwin's idea of the survival of the fittest, his responsibility for the land dovetailed neatly with his duty to build a nation which would not only *survive* but which would find its place at the top of the tree of the world's fittest states. Declaring that China would leap ahead of Britain's steel production in fifteen years, Mao announced that the tamed forces of nature would deliver the energy required for a productive triumph. Washed with obedient waters, the fields were to yield vast harvests; fired by the torrential power of fast-descending rivers, electricity would fuel the furnaces from which the necessary steel would be produced to deliver a great industrial future: a Great Leap Forward.

Gathering his people together for what he saw as a new campaign in the war of orderly man against the *ziran*, just as it is, wilderness of nature, Mao organised the peasants into armies of communes, each divided into companies, platoons and brigades. Then, in 1958, declaring that 'great courage brings forth great yields', he unleashed the full force of his peasant troops against the combined challenge of the rivers and the fields. Looking at the rivers, his mind then turned, like the minds of all Great Men, to the essential matter of dams.

The raising of electric power from water, along with the watering of fields and their protection from floods, was a critical pillar of the earliest planning. To assist the Party in its cause, Mao had already called upon the skills of the big Russian brother whose engineers had built a raft of dams across the Siberian rivers of its own, Russian, Far East. In 1955, however, keen to show that the younger Communist brother could also raise an engineering triumph, Mao announced a proposal worthy of a truly Great Man: *Sanmenxia*, the Three Gate Gorge. A parade of forty-six cascading iron walls to be strung along the Yellow River, its mighty centrepiece was a damming of the 'three gates' of a mountain gorge that, legend had it, Yu the Great had once opened with an axe. Once completed, billions of kilowatts of electrical energy would be unleashed for productive purpose, and millions of Chinese lives would be protected from the periodic rages of the watery dragons. There was even a promise that the ancient prediction – that the waters of the Yellow River would run clear when a Great Man ruled China – would finally come true. In the process, one million mu, 670 square kilometres, of fertile land would have to be flooded to create the reservoir necessary to underpin the dam, and two hundred and eighty thousand people would have to be relocated to another quarter of the country. Nothing but the usual revolutionary sacrifices to be made for the greater good of all.

From the moment that the Sanmenxia dam was first proposed, though, one impossibly subjective mind insisted on advancing a less than helpful 'expert' opinion. A hydrological engineer by the name of Huang Wanli, this was a man who had surveyed thousands of kilometres of the Yellow River and its surrounding lands. Having done his surveys, Chen advanced the view that while Russian engineering principles might work for rivers passing through Siberia, they could not possibly be applied to the Yellow River. Siberia was a land of clear-watered rivers that passed through untouched forests, with hardly any people to speak of. But the Yellow River was one of the muddiest rivers in the world, passing through a terrain which had not only been heavily deforested, but planted with millions of human beings instead. The risks of any dam getting silted up with mud were far too great. To which, Huang Wanli unhelpfully added that the costs of any failure would not only be counted in the loss of Mao's dream of leaping forward: they would be counted in a toll of millions of lost human lives.

Not to be defeated by a reckless expert opinion, the Party leaders who had commissioned Sanmenxia pointed to fine engineering designs which showed hundreds of thousands of silt checks, not to mention a set of plans for extensive reforestation. But the hydrological engineer was stubborn, and in 1957, he was despatched to a *laogai* labour camp where, like all of the other subjectively-opinionated intellectuals, he could reform his opinions through bitterly hard work. Inconveniently, at about that time, the Banqiao dam in Henan had begun to develop a few cracks. With the Russian engineers' assistance, the cracks were filled with concrete, and Banqiao was declared to be an iron fortress that no waters would be able to break. The news about the cracks was buried, and with the disruptive subjective opinion also out of the way, the Great Man project of Sanmenxia could begin.

Dams settled, Mao then turned his mind to the rice and grain that were to fuel the Great Leap Forward. Details of the agricultural plan having been forged in the garden of his own courtyard in Zhongnanhai, Mao convened a meeting of his lieutenants to explain the fundamentals of farming. Traditional principles, he explained, were little better than any other counter-revolutionary superstition that needed to yield to science: only seeds that promised the greatest yields should be planted; any and all planting was to be close and deep; and as many crops as possible were to be squeezed into the clearly lazy seasons.

The peasant army was a little surprised at the strange instructions, and some brave spirits dared to raise their hands in questions. But the majority of the questions, like the earth itself, were soon overturned. As the more stubborn questioners were swept off for struggle sessions, most of the peasants concluded that silence was the safest policy. Perhaps, dreamt some of the more hopeful minds, Mao's towering spirit had mastered the art of squeezing grain from a stone. Eventually, everybody had picked up their hoes, but it was not long before they struck the very kinds of problems they had expected. With soils already thin after centuries of toil, and with the earth of mountain slopes having never been very thick, in many places, the hoes found themselves striking rock. When the time came to harvest, it turned out that the lessons of their fathers and the ancestors had been correct: where too many seeds are planted too close together, everything gives up the ghost of life.

With an industrial revolution to deliver in fifteen years, and a Great Leap Forward to achieve, commune leaders were told that, whatever the problems, no prisoners were to be taken: nothing less than a total victory over nature was required. Commanding the peasants to redouble their efforts with revolutionary zeal, war was then declared on the tea bushes, orchards and any surviving stands of forests and trees that were obviously occupying valuable places in the soil. Meanwhile, a supplementary campaign was introduced to address 'four pests' which had sprung up like foes. Rats and sparrows were eating the grain from under everybody's noses; while flies and mosquitoes were refusing to give up a war of their own which they had been waging against man for as long as anyone could remember. Armed with catapults, hungry children were unleashed into the fields. Equipped with pots and pans as drums, their even hungrier parents and grandparents followed them. The catapults scored heavy victories over the rats; the pots and pans managed to force the sparrows into a perpetual flight that eventually, so the story was told, they dropped from the skies with exhaustion. And with workpoints offered as a reward for the flattened remains of the enemy flies and mosquitoes, even fingers and thumbs seemed to deliver a few victories of their own.

But by 1962, somehow nature seemed to be winning the war. Apart from the messy matter of local leaders overstating their estimates of production and the following havoc of a human hunger which had reaped harvests of peasant souls, it turned out that rice and grain really couldn't be grown on rock – and even where the rocks were clothed with a film of soil, the soil itself simply turned to dust. 'Plant as deep and as close as you like', the soil seemed to taunt them, 'but I have nothing more to give'. Successes on the front of the four pests notwithstanding, it seemed that nature was a trickier opponent than even Mao had reckoned: wherever the familiar foes were vanquished, nature simply replaced them with squadrons of cockroaches and locusts, all marching in to fill the vacuum created by the others' defeat.

Yet another inconvenient expert told Mao that even man himself was becoming a dangerous force of nature. From a challenging four hundred and sixty-five million people in 1949, by the early 1960s, China's population had reached six hundred and fifty million – with every indication that it would reach eight hundred million by the 1970s. Growling that 'no one had ever heard of there being too many people', Mao silenced the 'expert': not just a reckless rightist, but obviously a sympathiser with the bourgeois imperialist ideas of Ma-er-sai-se, the British Thomas Malthus. In his heart of hearts, though, Mao began to wonder. Obviously, the results of the imminent, 1964, census would have to be suppressed; and a lot more grain and rice were going to have to come from somewhere. Either that, or the size of the people would have to be cut.

Scanning the socialist countryside for better news, in 1963, Mao's attention had been caught by the Dazhai commune in the northern province of Shanxi. Named Dazhai, Great Outpost, after its closest town, it was also a *da zhai*, great outpost, in terms of spirit as well. Set in the Shanxi heartlands of the country, the land had been hoed and ploughed since the earliest of Chinese time, with rolling hills losing their forests and a bumpy earth tilled until it had turned to dust. Long and cold winters, often without a hint of rain, had not helped, nor had the short summer heatwaves with deluges of monsoon rain that regularly swept the rich loess topsoil into the Yellow River, ushering in the floods that always carried destruction and famine in their wake. Into this natural nightmare had stepped a true revolutionary spirit: a once-peasant who had become the local commune's Party secretary. Determined to snatch victory from nature, he had marched his brigades out across the rebellious land – thousands of peasants at a time. Labouring day and night regardless of the seasons, supported by singing loudspeakers, and spurred on by the promise of work-points, within three years 'Dazhai man' finally seemed to have conquered the earth. Trees – with or without fruit – had been felled. Stubbly hills had become terraces of rice. The dusty earth had become sweeping fields of grain. Everything was being washed by man-made streams. And wherever a stubborn mountain had tried to stand in the way of newly irrigating waters, a man-made tunnel had pierced its heart.

Enchanted by the doughty Party secretary's spirit, Mao compared the triumph of his feats to the ancient story of *Yu Gong Yi Shan*, the foolish old man who moved mountains, which told of a man who had insisted on moving two view-blocking mountains, one shovel at a time. While his neighbours mocked, the old man, helped by his loyal family, kept going until, one day, heaven itself took pity upon him and sent down a pair of immortals who moved the mountains out of his way. By the end of 1963, Mao had decided that everyone should be learning from Dazhai. Party secretaries responsible for communes across China were told to march delegations from their own communes to the Shanxi heartlands, to witness the art of successfully waging a war against nature. Led to the top of Dazhai's Tiger Head Mountain, the results were clear for all to see. Revolutionary armies of men, women and even children, were spread out like ants; and vistas of rice and grain appeared in breathtaking displays. It was clear to the visiting delegations that the straggling efforts of their own muddled fields were nothing but a personal disgrace.

With other communes eager to learn, Dazhai's triumph became the stuff of everyone's dreams: how to move mountains with thousands of hands; how to turn selfish slopes into yielding terraces; how to carve dykes in every direction. And, most important of all, how to make sure that the peasant-soldiering troops kept their socialist productivity high.

Returning back to their very different quarters of the country – from flat plains to high mountains, from deep jungles to watery lakes and marshes – no one could forget the visions of Dazhai's terraces. Nor could they forget Mao's new mantra: 'learn from Dazhai'. Inspired and shamed, the Party secretaries pushed their communes and their lands ever farther. In the north, more of the grasslands were set to the plough. In the western south, ancient forests were felled for rice. In some places, the earth was piled into mountains so that terraces could be created. In others, lakes were drained and filled in with rocks, sand and earth, so that key crops of grain and rice could be grown where self-indulgent fish had once swum. At the extreme edges of the empire – in the remotest deserts, forests and steppes, to which the worst of the rightists were typically sent – man and nature were pushed to the end of their endurance and beyond. Every inch of land was turned to productive purpose, and the very veins of the earth were plumbed in an effort to find more water with which to wash the fields. With wells being dug deeper and deeper into the water table below, many of them ended up hitting rock. As the Party secretaries continued to bark their commands, the peasants watched as nature yielded: flocks gave up their sheep for grain, primeval forests burned like tinder, lakes made way for crops, and ancient oases were transformed into desert dust. Questions and tears were everywhere. But few dared to interrupt the objective advance of the revolution.

––––––

While the peasants wasted their tears on the smaller matters of life, Mao was soon required to turn his attention to a rising storm in the relationship with Russia, complicated by America. It was a storm that, on the face of things, seemed to have little to do with nature. In the end, however, it would be nature that would pay the price.

After Nikita Krushchev – with Stalin on his mind – had raised the uncomfortable matter of personality cults in the middle of the 1950s, Mao had come to see Russia as an overbearing older brother who needed to be put in his place. Keen to burnish his own Communist credentials in the aftermath of Second World War, which had left a number of regional loose ends, Mao was equally keen to push both the Chiang Kai-shek supporting Americans out of Asia, and to resurrect a greater level of respect from neighbours, who seemed to have forgotten about the ancient *tianxia*, all-under-heaven, idea. Korea and Vietnam offered particular possibilities. With the Korean peninsula now divided into a Communist North and an American-influenced South, Mao had encouraged Kim Il-Sung, North Korea's leader, to defend himself from the American threat by aggressively snatching at the South. Within three years, Mao had lost up to a million revolutionary soldiers to a North Korean cause that failed to do more than keep the status quo; in the process, he had acquired a *tianxia* protecting obligation that would last long after his own life. At the same time, the Party's past dependency on Stalin's funding had developed into a state-to-state relationship in which China would exchange grain in return for Russian technical know-how which would strengthen the country's industry and arms – a relationship that would cost China's peasants dear. But as Krushchev insisted on denouncing Stalin's cult of personality, the relationship between Moscow and Beijing cooled: the military technology transferred was less than had been expected, and Mao sensed a rising Soviet concern to contain his revolutionary ambitions in the rising Cold War that was spreading across Asia and the wider 'third' world.

Foot-draggers that they were, it took Mao until 1961 to get his own Party comrades to declare the Russian Communist Party a gaggle of revisionists, traitors to the ideals of Marx and Lenin. Soviet Russian engineers and loans were withdrawn and a new cold war emerged between China and Russia. Mongolia, the vast northern land whose borders separated Russia from China and whose loyalties had been lost to Moscow from the early 1920s, became a military buffer, stuffed with Soviet rockets. Even then, the Party comrades failed to see that the threat was not limited to Russia but included America as well. With China exposed to the north, the south, and along its coasts, Mao managed to secure some contingency planning for war.

Then, in the summer of 1964, a ticking timebomb to the south exploded. From 1884, when the French had defeated the Manju Qing army and destroyed the Fujian fleet in a single hour, Vietnam had become a hotly disputed territory with the West. In 1940, it had

been invaded by Japan; by 1944, the Guomindang were supporting
the American-led West in a mission to oust the imperialist Japanese
from its lands. In 1950, Vietnam had briefly divided into an independent Communist North and a weak French South, after which a
decade of compromises between an American-led West and a Soviet
Union-led East struggled to keep Vietnam at peace. But in 1964, the
United States collided with the Russian-supported North Vietnamese
in the Gulf of Tonkin, and even the foot-draggers understood that the
competition of Russian and American forces on China's southern land
and sea borders was a risk. The fact that the Great Leap Forward had
failed to catch China up with anyone just made everything worse.

Looking closely at his maps, Mao decided that if China was to become
the fittest state of all, more assaults on nature would be required. By the
end of 1964, with the help of the surviving scientists, the first of China's
atomic bombs was tested, at Lop Nur, on the edge of the Taklamakan
desert: remote, but close enough to the Soviet Union's Central Asian
Republics for the impact to be felt. By 1965, having explored his own
inner crouching dragon, Mao more quietly launched a 'Third Front'
which would see every industry vital for the survival of the People's
Republic carried to the sanctuary of the country's mountainous centre:
Sichuan. *Kaoshan*, close to the mountains; *fensan*, dispersed; *yinbi*, hidden.
The Third Front and its industries would be spread out across places
where no boats could ever land and no planes would ever be able to
see what was going on below. With plenty of mountains that could
be pierced with tunnels, the movements of production could easily be
hidden; surviving forests could screen the skies; and seams of locally
abundant minerals and metals would be able to fuel both construction
and production. Armed with such advantages, an entire new world of
industry could be conjured up from the midst of the wildest nature.

Advancing to the new Third Front, the People's Liberation Army
was given the task of building the roads, railways and bridges that
would carry productive machines out of their industrial city homes
– and of blasting open the tunnels that would hide the final destinations from any prying eyes in the sky. Workers and students were
commanded to follow, so that new forests of chimneys could be raised
within the mountains. Smoke-emitting funnels peeped out from places
where no airborne bomber would think to look; rocky cliffs housed
coal-powered generators. Perpendicular gorges became powerhouses

producing steel, chemicals, tanks, cars and planes – all with the grey clouds of their energies hidden behind the mountains. River banks became hosts to furnaces of iron and steel, planted where chemical and metal waste could pour smoothly into the waters below, and so carefully located that if ever there were an accidental leak of a brightly-coloured substance, no enemy would ever need to know.

The anticipated war with Russia never happened. But by the time that Mao died in 1976, the mountains of Sichuan had been tamed to host the industry of man. And when Deng Xiaoping resurrected the idea of the Four Modernisations in 1978, no one looked forward to increasing industrial production more than the invisible industrial-military installations scattered across the remote mountain areas of Sichuan. Equally enthusiastic were a number of self-strengthening individuals who, soon to be liberated from the mountainous communes, would be free to explore their own industrial possibilities in the heart of nature's silence.

As Mao was devoting his energies to the possibilities of man at war, the old matter of dams raised its head again. The Sanmenxia dam had been ordered for construction, but by 1962 it was clear that things had not gone entirely to plan. Once raised, just as the hydrological engineer Huang Wanli had so expertly predicted, vast quantities of Yellow River silt had not only built up against the dam itself but were backing up along the length of one of its tributary rivers. With the silt rising higher by the year, there was a risk that the tributary river might breach its banks and flood the once imperial city of Chang'an – now the industrial city of Xi'an. Battalions of hydraulic engineers were thrown at the problem, but the silt refused to retreat. At one point, with no Russian engineers left to lend a helping hand (and with a number of other things on his mind), Mao suggested that if nothing could be done, the mighty dam would simply have to be dynamited into dust. Anxious engineers prevaricated, and the backed-up waters flooded the surrounding land with rising water tables adding salt. In the event, the loss of Xi'an was averted by drilling silt-liberating holes into the walls of the dam: so many holes that while the great dam itself survived, by the late 1960s, it was good for neither power nor controlling floods. Meanwhile, the salt stayed in the soil, destroying crops for years to come.

Not to be defeated by a failure or two, Mao was keen to find an opportunity for a socialist success. With a steady flow of objectively minded hydraulic engineers always eager to please an emperor, new proposals were submitted. One was for a mighty dam at Gezhouba, on the Yangzi. Another was for an even greater dam, slightly higher up, at the Yangzi's Three Gorges. The idea of a dam at the Three Gorges was a great temptation. Sun Yatsen had first suggested it, and Mao had often dreamt of it – even immortalising his dreams in a poem that had been learnt by schoolchildren up and down the People's Republic. In the event, it was reluctantly decided that Gezhouba would go first and pave the way. But the dream of a dam at the Three Gorges was simply biding its time.

While Mao eventually followed all of the other Great Men up to the ancestors' skies, the dream of a Three Gorges dam had acquired a life of its own. After years of reports and discussions within the inner recesses of the Party, by the beginning of 1989 a plan for the dam had finally, and rather quietly, been approved by Deng Xiaoping. All that was required was a final rubber stamp from the annual spring meeting of the National People's Congress – the representative body of the people that was designed to be a truly objective voice. With the Four Modernisations now underway, however, things had changed a little from the days of Mao. Not least, Chinese experts were travelling abroad to learn from foreigners, particularly those in America. As the scientists travelled, they were often accompanied by journalists instructed to cover the story. At one point, one of the accompanying journalists – an engineer who had changed her trade – found herself passing through Hong Kong, where she read an anxious story about a dam in a local newspaper. Headline news in Hong Kong, the story had failed to make the back pages of the Party papers at home, even though the dam was in the heart of mainland China. The journalist's name was Dai Qing, and the fearful story was about the risks of a proposed Three Gorges dam.

Rumours that Mao's dream of a great dam at the Three Gorges might be resurrected had been whispered at home for some time. Realising that the rumours had become a fact – and that the outside world was highly informed about its risks – Dai Qing decided that she would investigate things on her own. When she returned to Beijing, she found her way to other Chinese who had heard the same news on their travels abroad. She also found her way to Chinese government officials and scientific experts who had been directly involved in the Party's preparations, and were themselves becoming increasingly concerned. Two kilometres wide, with a man-made reservoir whose watery dragon would soon swallow nineteen cities, three hundred-odd towns, a thousand villages and vast swathes of farming land, not to mention the homes of over a million people, the scale of its imagination defied even the greatest of the First Qin Emperor's works.

Piecing together a picture of the risks, Dai Qing suggested to her new-found friends that they compile a set of expert opinions and factual documents which could check the Party's calls to 'conquer nature!' More importantly, she added, such a book of documents could clarify the precise technical and human problems of a Three Gorges Dam in words that the representatives of the National People's Congress could understand. True, the National People's Congress had always followed the objective order of the Party, but a lot had changed since the death of Mao. Perhaps it was time for the men and a few women who technically had the power of a final say on everything (at least under the formal terms of the Chinese Constitution), to get a little homework.

Prepared and circulated to its intended readership, Dai Qing's book, entitled *Yangzi! Yangzi!*, found its mark. Discussions with the representatives arriving in Beijing for their annual meeting showed that they were beginning to echo the opinions of the book's contributors with questions of their own: 'What about the silting that builds up behind a dam and puts at risk the very lives which the dam is supposed to be saving?' 'What about the million people who would have to move their homes?' 'What about the already-disappearing *baiji*, white dolphin, that would have no waters left to swim in?' 'And what about the treasures of the old Chu state on whose ancient lands the Three Gorges sit?' To all of these questions, yet another expert added the very inconvenient observation that the Yangzi River was perched upon a geological fault line that made every dam constructed on its saddle a risk. Not only a risk of provoking the very flooding which the dam was supposed to prevent, but a risk of triggering an earthquake as well.

When the formal report on the Three Gorges Dam was delivered for its anticipated approval, the harmonious ritual of the National People's Congress was interrupted with a host of unscripted questions. The microphones of the questioners were quickly cut. Answers to the most persistent questioners were then issued in the corridors – all grounded on the strengths of Party science. To these were added lectures on the objective decision-making that was required of all true supporters of the Party's continuing revolution. And as far as the question of silting was concerned, that was clearly just a problem of cutting down too many trees: nothing that a quick planting of forests couldn't handle, and nothing to do with dam-building at all. The same went for the argument that the sewage of factory waste would get caught up in the dam: the factories would just have to be told to clean up. As for the now million-odd people who would have to move their homes, surely such self-sacrificing virtue had been displayed from the time of the Qin, if not the Shang: it was all part of what it meant to be Chinese. And as for the truly rightist arguments that the archaeological treasures of Chu would be washed away and the *baiji*, white dolphin, might disappear – well, relics of the past could always be put in a museum, or an aquarium. It was time to move on.

To those at the top, it was clear that the revolutionary discipline of the National People's Congress, like everything else in a 1989 spring of troublesome anniversaries, was experiencing a temporary lapse. It was ten years since the imprisonment of Wei Jingsheng, the dangerous spirit who had called for a Fifth Modernisation, and the astrophysicist Fang Lizhi had just had the audacity to send an open letter to Deng asking for Wei's release. As if that was not enough, it was seventy years since the original May Fourth science and democracy protests had exploded in Beijing. With so much bourgeois baggage in the air, how could anyone hope to get anything done? By the time the National People's Congress came to a close, it was clear that no vote was going to be taken – or at least, not one that could ever be officially recorded. Within a month, the streets of Beijing had become a river of banners: all asking why, after so many millennia, the truth about anything could still not be told. And then June Fourth silenced everyone. On 14 June, with *Yangzi! Yangzi!* now banned, Dai Qing was arrested. Like many of the other reckless intellectuals, some of China's greatest scientists began to make their way to a voluntary exile in the West.

It would take a little time for the Party's dam-building confidence to rise again. But Zhou Enlai's adopted son, Li Peng – a Moscow trained specialist in hydroelectric engineering – had recently been appointed premier; naturally, he was keen to ensure that the vision of the great dam did not die. In the spring of 1992, with the changes seeming a little more auspicious, Li Peng returned the dam designs to a chastened National

People's Congress for a more obedient vote. This time, the rubber stamp was successfully secured, and armies of engineers were deployed to bring the dream to life. Five years later, in 1997, Jiang Zemin was able to rise to the Party's podium and announce the completion of the first stage of the Three Gorges dam. Declaring it to be a victory for the spirit of the 'foolish old man who moved mountains', he repeated the eternal Great Man cry: 'Man must conquer nature!' Four years later, with a successful bid for the Olympics under Beijing's belt, the schedule for the dam's completion was accelerated – so that it could be ready to demonstrate its revolutionary streams of energy for all the world to see.

Back in the countryside, after Deng's announcement of the Four Modernisations and his call for mind emancipation, few had been idle. As the communes had been transformed into township governments from the early 1980s, commune leaders had become mind emancipating township officials with a host of useful powers. Among the earliest and more unusual of these powers was one that put them in charge of the reproduction of man. While Mao had chosen to ignore the problem of an expanding population, by the time that Deng returned to Beijing in 1976, the number of China's people had leapt to a shocking eight hundred million, with no sign of slowing down. In 1979, Deng had introduced a 'one-child' policy: one child in areas where there were more buildings than fields; two for those areas where there were more fields than buildings. Requiring an army of officials to enforce the policy, it had been obvious to those in local government that the townships and their new officials would be perfectly placed for a heavenly control of human reproduction.

The powers of the townships, though, went well beyond procreation. Indeed, the most officially appealing of the townships' powers was that of approval over which of the old pieces of industrial production went where. With everyone looking for pockets of profit, chimneys of all descriptions had begun to spread across the land. From coal washing and coking plants, zinc smelters and steel furnaces, to cement factories, sawmills and repair shops, the advance of the chimneys had been less like that of slow-growing forests and more like wildfire. With local cash reserves low or non-existent, and every penny needed for profits, the trick had been to get the furnaces of production firing on any and all of the rickety cylinders that were lying around. Engines that should rightly have died years before were resurrected to splutter into the future, regardless of their soot. And with roofs and insulation an unnecessary expense, plants and smelters were left to exhale in the freshness of the open air. It was not long before the fields of grain and rice were covered in soot – and not long at all before rivers were running with the sulphurous slurry of coal. When newly enterprising villagers added peach trees and lettuces to their farming patches (not to mention water-drinking animals), the peaches, the lettuces and the animals ended up black as well. Busy with mind emancipation, though, the colour of nature was not considered to be the greatest of man's concerns. And while some of the villagers were unhappy about the changing taste of the air (and the water), everyone was encouraged to get on with the new art of making money.

Townships that were close to the booming coastal zones of the south offered some of the greatest opportunities. Observing the peasants struggling to farm their fields *and* work in the factories as well, local officials conjured up a mind-emancipating solution. With the old communes a fading memory, the chemical fertilisers that had been developed for their use could, for a fee of course, now be offered to a new generation of individual farming households. Indeed, with new, self-strengthened, fertilizer factories coming on local stream, the substances would be available in even greater volumes and strengths. Local officials became experts in the new magic: 'Just apply it in industrial quantities to make up for the loss of the nurturing human touch, and the fields can be left to farm themselves.'

Up in the north, the peasants were staring at quite a different challenge: a dry soil which had not only become so exhausted that it seemed to have no more nutrients left but which, in many areas, was now desperately struggling to hold the deserts back. Looking at the problem, their own local township officials saw the same solution as their southern peers: chemical supplements to give the dust a boost. Concoctions of phosphorus, sulphur and zinc boosted with chemicals were swiftly ordered. Not everyone could read the instructions – and to the officials who could, they seemed unnecessarily complicated. Instant experts, the officials recommended that everyone just spread the powder in all directions, and let it do its work. And if it didn't work quickly enough – or if your fields had more rocks than soil on them – then, obviously, you needed to spread some more. Up and down the country, from the watery south to the dry north, fields (and rocks) were fed as they had never been fed before. And when it rained, the rain washed the chemicals into the rivers, and down into the tables under the earth. That way, everything got a shot.

Time passed, the Four Modernisations continued their promise of wealth creation, and by 2000, the countryside was reaping an industrial harvest – of sorts. Flush with hope and anticipation in the early years of Deng's productive revolution, after almost a decade of racing ahead, the peasants had found that fields sprayed with the new chemical fertilisers were struggling. More and more of the chemicals had been sprayed all over the place, with their compounds regularly strengthened, but the crops remained stubbornly in the dumps. Peasants looking for answers of their own began to look again at the countryside that had changed so quickly all around them. Many pointed to the forests of chimneys belching out oceans of smoke. Some, particularly those whose fields fronted onto rivers, pointed to sewage pipes that washed the waters with streaks of red, orange and yellow, and from time to time turned the rivers completely black – save for the layers of milky white froth that periodically appeared. Turning to their village leaders and township governments, some dared to suggest that it might be time to call a halt to the chemical destruction.

But by now, the factories of the town and village enterprises were also struggling. Constructed from the local tangles of pipes and smokestacks of the communal past, few had modernised themselves beyond the idea of getting rich. While the special economic zones of the eastern coasts had acquired more money, more science and technology and more demanding Western markets, everywhere else in the countryside had fallen further behind. Local township officials had begun to worry. Since many town-ships and local officials had, directly or indirectly, become owners of the factories, poor profits were a problem – not only for themselves but for the local government finances which were buoyed up by the revenues of their production. Looking anxiously at the performances of next-door neighbours, township and village leaders decided they would need to do whatever it took to keep their own local income rising. Sooty opportuni-ties and mines relocating from places, in China and abroad, that did not want them, were accepted with alacrity. And if ever a gaggle of villag-ers had an opinion, the leaders were always quick to point out that one village's loss was always another's gain.

While soot-covered fields and black rivers running with sludge had once seemed to be a mild inconvenience, as time went on, some of the peasants began to wonder whether there wasn't more to the darker colours than met the eye. Hacking coughs and unseasonal colds seemed to have taken up permanent rural occupation. In some parts of the country, the problem went well beyond coughs and colds. Here, a number of infants began to be born blue; there, other babies arrived with twisted hands and feet, not to mention minds that seemed to struggle to keep up. In many places, older adults, instead of living longer, seemed to fade well before their time; breath shortened to a wheeze, they were also wracked by pains which no one had ever had before. Those who could afford a trip to a county town clinic (or whose families were brave enough to take out a loan for something higher up) came back with faces longer than a pole. Lungs riddled with sulphurous water; kidneys, stomachs and throats attacked by arsenic and mercury; their bodies were now being ravaged by cancerous cells. Treatments, they were informed, might be possible – but they would require levels of modernisation and cash that the countryside had yet to achieve.

In the early days, dismissed by local officials but still hoping for some sort of a solution, the peasants covered their sleeping faces with wet cloths to keep out the worst of the fumes. They also saved up their money for shop-bought bottles of water, trusting that it came from cleaner rivers than their own. With many worried that no one in the outside world would speak to them if they understood what cauldrons of death and destruction their villages had become, everyone did their level best to bury their fears. Some tried to appeal to the local factory workers and miners to stop the destructive production. But many of the labouring hands were migrants from other, even more desperate, corners of the countryside. Replying to the appeals, the migrants explained that if they had any hope of earning the cash of life anywhere else, they would certainly carry themselves off to eke out an existence in another part of the land, but survival was a battle for everyone, everywhere. Listlessly lying down to die, desperate wives, husbands and children turned their gaze to the smoke stacks and the sewage pipes, and remembered that it had not always been this way.

As the threats of death became clear sentences, relatives and friends inked brave appealing letters to township officials, begging them to close the factories. Clear, however, about their duty to follow Deng's exhortation to spread economic development under the leadership of the Party while emancipating their own minds, the officials replied with denials and disdain. To which, they added scientific questions so difficult that there was probably not anyone, even in a city, who could possibly find an answer, let alone a peasant. 'You say that this particular chimney or sewage pipe is killing your father', the officials challenged, 'but where is the link between the two? The hills and the plains are full of factories, and the air which passes over your heads has come through a lot of other places before it has got to here, not least the state-owned industrial plants in neighbouring townships and counties. How do you know the problem is not coming from them?'

Anyone who could, left. And as those who stayed behind watched their hopes vanish in puffs of red, orange and yellow dust, some decided that perhaps their only chance was to speak their own truth and call their homes by their proper names: cancer villages. The township government might not like it – it certainly wouldn't help in attracting new money for enterprising investment; and official careers would be bound to suffer. But the speakers of the names were too far advanced on their way to another world to care. And, anyway, if the god of war and great protector of the weak, Guan Yu, was on the peasants' side, the officials would eventually be going down to the hells below. Up in Beijing, a few brave voices tried to spread the truth of the peasants' misery, but somehow the airwaves were always stuffed with happier tales.

———

With the countryside collapsing under the weight of its many miseries, families and friends of the officials soon started to board the softer seats of the country's trains and make their way to the cities. Settling in the comforting compounds of suburban villas, they looked around at their new surroundings and congratulated themselves on having left the choking chimneys behind them and joining a modernised world where everyone's water was clean. Keen to explore the treasures of their new home – and to emulate the 'high quality' of the city's middle classes – they then climbed into newly-purchased cars, and took themselves off to the rising temples of consumption, where fountains of water, redirected from the fields, played like music, and every luxury in the world could be found.

New homes acquired air conditioners; televisions and washing machines were added. And when winter came, coal by the cartload was burned in someone else's backyard, to power the electricity that would keep them invisibly warm. With so many people flocking to the urban dream, more coal and more cities were obviously needed – it was only a question of finding the space. Here, there, and everywhere, new citadels rose. Up in the spreading Gobi desert of Inner Mongolia, now home to some of the fastest money-making speed in the country, someone stretched their imagination, and within the blink of an eye, a shimmering city appeared in an area dedicated to the production of coal; it was named 'Ordos', after the spreading palaces of Chinggis Khan that had graced it in less sandy times. In the rest of the country, township officials looked again at the peasants' land use rights to see which fields could be liberated for yet more productive urban purpose.

For a while, the cities seemed to sparkle like magic, certainly for the 'higher quality' middle classes: safe-to-drink water on tap, food wrapped up in shiny plastic packages, cool cars to smooth even the shortest journey. But as always, the superstitious rumours were quick to catch up, particularly in the dry and dusty north. Hundreds of cities were said to be sinking because too many wells had been dug. Others were falling victim to dust storms, unleashed by the rages of fallen forests. Those already full of industrial factories had also become home to plants that were burning coal at tonnes a minute in a bid to keep up with rising demand. The countryside's clouds might have been left behind, but it seemed that the cities had clouds of their own – stealing all the bright blue skies and blocking the rays of the sun. Looking with sharper eyes at their new urban habitats, some even began to whisper that the vegetables which were wrapped up in such shiny plastic came from the same black fields, washed by the same black waters, which everyone from the countryside thought they had safely left behind. Others replied that there was always someone wanting to rain on a fortunate person's parade – chatterboxing gossips who just couldn't appreciate the value of the *gao suzhi*, high-quality, city life.

As time went on, though, more began to wonder. Measured in square metres of housing, television sets and washing machines, life in the city was certainly much better than it had been in the country-side. Schools, roads, buses, even metros, were bustling; shops sparkled; restaurants were full to the brim, and the cracking sound of celebrating fireworks was never far away. According to the newspapers, even life itself had got longer. But here and there, it seemed that not everything was quite right. Shining new industrial plants regularly appeared out of nowhere, stuffed full of modernising chemicals – and before one knew it, suddenly everyone in the neighbourhood knew of a child who was struggling to breathe. Everywhere, the rain began to take on a special metallic quality: washed with the acid of production, some said. Even the meat and the vegetables which appeared so temptingly on city plates turned out to have a poisonous sting, turning stomachs and sending people rushing to a hospital – where questions about the food led to a rather resigned shrug of doctoring shoulders and a new medical mantra: 'we get a lot of that, these days'. Meanwhile, as the cities continued to spread, once-smooth roads began to slow to little more than mobile parking lots, belching out yet more clouds of smoke.

Certainly, there didn't seem to be much sun anymore – and what sun there was looked dimmer than the moon. Even the clouds had changed: now harder to see in the grey cloak which shrouded everything, they were no longer soft balls of floating cotton, but menaces that concealed the grit of production in their misleadingly soft folds. Coughs and colds were everywhere; few could escape the nagging doubt that something worse might be lurking within. For the young, the old, and the un-revolutionary weak, even the breath of life was becoming a bit of a struggle. One way or another, Mao had got his forests of chimneys – but unless there was a good stiff wind to blow away the fog, it was getting harder to see them.

On 12 May 2008, as Beijing counted down the last days to the Great Man spectacle of the grandest Olympics the planet had ever witnessed, eleven miles below its surface, the earth quaked. Spreading across 155 miles of a geological fault line under the province of Sichuan, the epicentre of the quake was a world of villages and county towns spread across the hills and valleys of the remote Ngawa region: once part of Tibet, and still scattered with people who traced their ancestry to the Buddha-jewelled mountains of the gods.

As broken hearts asked the skies why loved ones had been taken from them, a few expert voices ventured to ask a question with a past: why had the Three Gorges dam been built across a Sichuan land which was threaded with a fault?

The Long March 1934 - 35

Route of First Front Army

Routes of minor CCP commands

KAZAKHSTAN

R U

M O N G

INNER MONGO

KYRGYZSTAN

XINJIANG AUTONOMOUS REGION

Ili River

Tri Mountains

TIBET AUTONOMOUS REGION

NEPAL

BHUTAN

ARUNACHAL PRADESH

BANGLADESH

INDIA

MYANMAR

LAOS

Bay of

Bengal

THAILAN

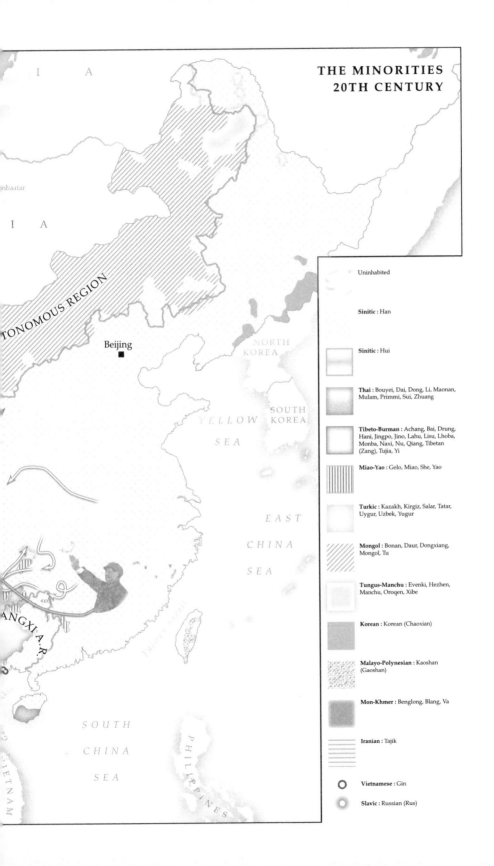

THE MINORITIES
20TH CENTURY

Beijing

I A

I A

nbaatar

TONOMOUS REGION

NORTH KOREA

SOUTH KOREA

YELLOW SEA

EAST CHINA SEA

ANGXI A.R.

SOUTH CHINA SEA

PHILIPPINES

VIETNAM

Uninhabited

Sinitic : Han

Sinitic : Hui

Thai : Bouyei, Dai, Dong, Li, Maonan, Mulam, Primmi, Sui, Zhuang

Tibeto-Burman : Achang, Bai, Drung, Hani, Jingpo, Jino, Lahu, Lisu, Lhoba, Monba, Naxi, Nu, Qiang, Tibetan (Zang), Tujia, Yi

Miao-Yao : Gelo, Miao, She, Yao

Turkic : Kazakh, Kirgiz, Salar, Tatar, Uygur, Uzbek, Yugur

Mongol : Bonan, Daur, Dongxiang, Mongol, Tu

Tungus-Manchu : Evenki, Hezhen, Manchu, Oroqen, Xibe

Korean : Korean (Chaoxian)

Malayo-Polynesian : Kaoshan (Gaoshan)

Mon-Khmer : Benglong, Blang, Va

Iranian : Tajik

Vietnamese : Gin

Slavic : Russian (Rus)

CHAPTER 3

THE EDGES OF ORDER

In the Great Unity ... there is no division into national states
and no difference between the races. There will be no war.
Da Tong, The Great Unity, Kang Youwei (1858–1927)

As an early March sun separated night from day, the jewelled
peaks of the Himalayan Mountains pierced the early morning
mist. Waking to the dawn, the snow lions of the Potala palace roared
their *sunyata* silence of emptiness, courage and truth – a roar so quietly
powerful that it promised a freedom from the *samsara* cycle of deeds and
consequences. The palace itself, perched on the red Marpori mountain,
gazed out across the *Kyi* River, towards the *Che-la* mountain pass: the
path by which the Dalai Lama had walked his way to India. Nearby, as
the glint of the early light spread, two golden deer appeared, kneeling on the roof of the Jokhang Palace. Soft noses raised towards the
dharma chakra wheel of the Buddha's searing sight, gentle ears silently
listening, they were a reminder to all that the Buddha-nature lives
within the meekest of human forms.

The sun rising a little higher, now dusting the sky with the soft
red of a rose, the world below awoke. Monks wrapped in saffron-co-
loured robes began to hum their meditating mantras, filling the icy
air with the warm breath of a thousand searching souls. Crawling
pilgrims added their own peregrinations, touching prayer wheels as
they passed. And as the prayer wheels turned, each searching heart
added its own softly muffled mantra to the wider air: '*om mani padme
hum*'. Six syllables which any mind could translate as 'behold the jewel
in the lotus', or some such simplicity, but which, for deeper minds with
the humility and self-discipline to search, held ideas as big as oceans:
the jewel as the enlightenment which comes from the heartfelt pursuit
of wisdom; the lotus as the flower which blossoms in the muddy waters
of life; and all real meaning to be found in the dedicated pursuit of an

understanding which can never be captured in the simple language of a mantra's spoken words.

With the day now gathering its energies, a wide blue sky ushered in a caravan of clouds. Soon a forest of advertising boards caught the light. The biggest of the boards declared the power of a rising China Telecom across the ancient Barkhor Square and, at 11,500 feet above the sea, the highest service in the world. Shops began to lift up their shutters, and in the Chinese characters of the Yellow River heartlands that had always insisted on a greater unity, goods were proclaimed for sale. Within the lanes around the square, solid white walls caught shadows of light, prayer flags flapped in a breeze and busy stalls began to come to life. Miniature Buddhas vied with tempting trinkets, all carried up to the meditating heights from the productive energies of southern Wenzhou. Incense, rising from humble burners, spread in every direction; pool tables, recovered from their late night entertainment, were dusted off for a new day of play. Street cleaners, gathered in battalions, stepped around the clutter of construction, meditating on the dust to be swept from all around. The sun now higher, the whitest of clouds drifted across the clearest of skies, and clutches of southern tourists began to appear, rushed to the summit by the highest of trains. Stepping into the Lhasa city of the gods, they clicked the lenses of their third eyes across a feast of sights, advancing through the streets as fast as their mobile phones could carry them.

Deep in the Potala palace, the blue Akshobhya Buddha stared into the emptiness of eternal space, with the light of understanding. Blue, like the colour of water that carves through solid rock without violence, which hardens like the sharpest of intellects when frozen, and then softens to a free flow when it realises the liberating wonder of wisdom.

A few miles away, at the foot of the Gambo Utse Mountain, the doors of the Drepung Monastery stood open, and hundreds of monks began to walk to the heart of Lhasa. Hearts burning, their minds were meditating on the memory of the time – forty-nine years ago to the day – when the Dalai Lama disappeared into an exile from which he had never returned. In a few days, the old Barkhor Square, once home to the gods, now home to the Wenzhou trinkets, would explode into balls of fire. Soldiers would march in pairs; knives would appear; batons would strike; and an acrid smoke would fill the air. Below the Potala

Palace, 'Beijing Street' would flood with tears of gas and screams of anger. And the *Kyi* River would continue to flow – along with the blood of days that would stretch into a seemingly eternal night.

It was not meant to be this way.

When Yu the Great had mapped the heavenly heartlands four thousand years before, the order of China's settled world had been painted everywhere. It was greatest, of course, at its central heart: the place from which the patterns of nature had first been observed and where the Yellow Emperor had brought together the myriad tribes. The patterns having been transformed into a civilising plan for the harmony of heaven and earth, conducted by a heavenly people who understood the importance of taming themselves, the resulting idea of order had been stretched and the further it had been stretched, the more it had naturally dissipated. At the edges of order, walls had been raised to mark the boundaries of human civilisation. But, like so much else in the cosmos, they had been subjected to the energies of chaos, particularly the chaos of a barbarian world with no civilisation at all. Observing the wonders of the settled world, though, some of the barbarians had come to see the order of the heavenly plan as a model for all. Taming themselves into *ren*, human beings, they had learnt that it is only by cultivating himself that man can transform chaos into order. And they had learnt that, where an individual barbarian ruler could tame not only his own heart and mind but the hearts of his people, he could even become a descendant of the Yellow Emperor himself.

With a number of barbarian rulers attempting to emulate the civilisation of the settled world, though, and others being persuaded, the borders of the heavenly heartlands had gradually extended until they covered what seemed to be almost all the world. And with the best of climates and soil – best not only for producing harvests, but also for cultivating the orderly qualities of man – it had become clear to the Yellow Emperor's descendants that the civilising splendour of the settled lands was a gift to those with the misfortune to have been born outside.

Of course, there have always been stubborn spirits: wolves and dogs who preferred the wild. Far too primitive to understand the

responsibility of man to order nature, these were people who naturally kept to their chaos. But not all barbarians were the same: while
starting as wolves and dogs, some were eventually able to appreciate
the wisdom of the civilised settled ways. Conversely, not all of those
born in the Chinese lands were civilised: even some of the purest
descendants of the Yellow Emperor behaved in such an animal manner
that they could really only be barbarians at heart. As with everything
else in the settled, ordered, world, the important thing was to name a
thing after its nature: call a dog a dog, and a wolf a wolf. Just as you
would call a true father, a father; a true son, a son; a civilised man
who had mastered the written word and the Confucian virtues, a *junzi*
gentleman; and the man responsible for conducting the harmonies of
heaven and earth, the Son of Heaven, ruler of all. Just as you would
call all those who failed to understand the secrets of an orderly society,
barbarians. And in a world where natures and names were plain for all
to see, but where stubborn wolves and dogs could not be trained to
see the importance of order, a Son of Heaven ruler should not hesitate
to take the sterner measures required for everyone's all-under-heav-
en-harmony – whether the measures took the shape of a wall or a war.

It was not easy, even within the heavenly lands. While the Yellow
Emperor's true descendants had settled to order, many others had
insisted on carrying on with their tribal ways. They had not only
tramped around with their muddy feet but addressed themselves
directly to heaven whenever they felt like a conversation. Beyond the
boundaries of the heavenly civilisation, it had become clear that there
were hosts of uncivilised lands where the people never stopped chattering to heaven, whether or not heaven was interested in what they
had to say. From the north, they appeared as wolves on horseback,
descending like raging winds to sweep away the precious treasures of
harvests, iron and silk that the settled world produced. To the south,
myriad others, from wandering tribes to small settled states, kept to
their forests and mountains, joined from time to time by wilful hearts
who, born into the ordering reach of the heavenly cities and fields,
inexplicably insisted on looking for heaven somewhere else.

Time passed, and towards the end of the last millennium BCE, with
reinforced walls to the north, the iron will of the First Qin Emperor
pushed down to newly-discovered oceans of the south: imperial armies
were mustered, and stubborn spirits were pushed over mountains,

across rivers, into remote rain-filled forests and off to the south-western edges of the land. With northern walls in disrepair after their own rebellion, the Han then found themselves struggling with the steppe north and, in trying to manage the horseborne hordes, found themselves stretching heaven to the far west, traversing deserts and mountains once thought to be natural boundaries and now found to be oases of barbarian city-states waiting to be civilised. But just like the unruly elements of nature, the barbarians were tricky beasts with complicated webs of their own relationships and packs of arrowmen who coveted the treasures of the settled land with little understanding of either the *tianxia* order or the heavenly mandate upon which that order depended.

Far less organised, and without any horses, the southern barbarians were a little easier to deal with, although still quite tricky. Every time new dynasties, including the Han and the Tang, re-traced the steps of the First Qin emperor to the south, they found yet more of them. Hidden, and always muddy, some of them even seemed to include the descendants of spirits who had inexplicably left the lands of the Yellow Emperor for the swamps of the south. More armies were advanced, more forests felled and as each forest fell, the armies raised fields across lands that were obviously not occupied by any being that could possibly be described as a *ren*, human being. From time to time, progress was made: finally seeing sense, some of the tribes eventually settled down beside the Chinese peasant armies. For every tribe that settled, though, there were many others that ducked and dived: looking for pockets of wild freedom, whether in the darkest depths of the wettest forests, or in the nooks and crannies of mountains whose stern and rocky faces would challenge any standing army. Even when confronted by the clearly superior forces of order, some of the tribes astonishingly fought back. Battles were fought, seemingly to the death, only for others to appear from the midst of nature's chaos to take up the fight.

While the northern barbarians required an almost constant state of war, eventually the officials of the Ming dynasty hit upon a solution for the south: 'train the tribes to manage themselves'. Casting around for individual tribal men who could learn to appreciate the power of the brush and the value of the settled field, the officials made their selections. Individual tribal leaders were appointed as *tu di*, local chiefs, and rewarded with heavenly titles to note their evolution to the civilisation of man. The only price of the title was a dedication to unity.

The conquering Manju Qing, like so many earlier others, appreciated and embraced the wisdom of the *tianxia* idea; but like the Zhou over two thousand years before them and other northern conquerors in between, they also saw room for a few steppe improvements. Encountering the southern tribes as they swept the land searching out Ming loyalists, they adjusted the Ming solution for the south: local chiefs were replaced with imperial officials, and Kangxi issued a Sacred Edict that proclaimed sixteen virtues of settled Confucian values to the remotest corners of the conquered world. 'Esteem filial piety' had been the most obvious of the virtues, with others including 'respect farming, wipe out strange beliefs, embrace the correct doctrine, elevate customs and manners', and, naturally, 'guard against sheltering those who dare to disobey'.

With the south under a better order, and with the north more a matter of dealing with cousins and distant kin, Kangxi then took tactical advantage of a split within the Mongols to create a biddable 'Inner' east, whose Mongols would be able to bend to the settled idea, and a wilder 'Outer' west, whose Mongols might take a little longer to turn. When the Tibetans (whose reincarnating Dalai Lama had long been spiritual advisor to the Manju, as he had to the Mongols before them) asked Kangxi to help them rid themselves of the tribe of Zungar Mongols from the Outer west, Kangxi generously left a pair of *amban*, resident advisors, to keep a protective eye on the city of the gods, and on the Dalai Lama.

With Tibet seemingly restored to peace, Kangxi's son, Yongzheng, then turned his army back to the south and spread Confucian schools across the tribal areas of the surviving forests. The Manju having brought additional, steppe, ideas, Yongzheng saw the process as the taming of the tribes to the order of the Son of Heaven, supported by the disciplines of the Manju hunt, including 'storing wealth among the people'.

When Kangxi's grandson, Qianlong, took up the reins, there were still a lot of lands that had not, yet, been tamed. Following his grandfather's example, Qianlong launched Ten Great Campaigns. At the north-west edges of order, he finally defeated the Outer Mongols. With that success under his belt, in 1768, he marched his troops on to bring the Turkic lands of the Uighurs (those barbarian warriors who had once held the Tang dynasty's Chang'an to ransom) into the empire of the Great Manju Qing, adding a few oasis states for good measure. As Qianlong conquered, he settled the new lands with garrisons of soldiers, each charged with covering their costs by farming the oases of the fragile new frontier. Turning to the south, he then swept up the remaining unruly tribes across the south-west, pausing to pick up a few neighbours as well.

It was a shock, therefore, when, in 1855, Qianlong's descendants found that a band of Chinese Muslims had risen up in the south-west provinces. At the height of the Taiping rebellion, and with the barbarian Western devils pounding the ports, it could not have happened at a worse time. Astonishingly, the Chinese Muslims had not only dared to raise a 'Panthay' rebellion, but had gone on to declare an independent sultanate in the Dali city of Yunnan province as well: who on earth did these upstarts think they were? Investigating things, the Qing found that the rebels were descendants of Muslim traders who had arrived on caravans of trade from the lands of the tribute-paying Miandian, Burma, and that their leader was a Chinese-born man, once known by the civilised name of Du Wenxiu, who had then transformed himself into a sultan – and assumed the obviously barbarian name of Sulayman ibn Abd ar-Rahman. Battles followed across towns and villages. The rebels even besieged the capital of Yunnan province, Kunming. Eventually, a peace of sorts was restored: but not before a million Muslims had been despatched to another world, a host of survivors had fled across the barbarian Burmese border, and a pacifying passage of twenty years had had time to work its charms.

Unfortunately, as the nineteenth century advanced, the Muslim problems were not limited to the south-west. In 1865, up in the Kokhand north-west (present-day Tajikistan), a Tajik leader snatched away the Kashgar oasis-state that Qianlong had captured, and declared it to be an independent Islamic kingdom of Kashgaria. Qianlong's descendants managed to get it back. But it took twelve long years, during which the greed of the barbarian Russians started to fray yet more of the north-western edges into states of unrest. Eventually, a treaty got the Russians under control (the Ili Valley secured in return for a pile of silver and a right to trade). The rebellions were then successfully silenced by converting the frontier garrisons, farmed by the army, into the clear black lines of a more governable territory whose name corresponded perfectly with the change of facts on the ground: *Xinjiang*, the new frontier.

By then, however, it had not just been the barbarians in bordering lands who were causing trouble – the far-off European and American West, as well as the nearby Japanese, had become a problem too. Wherever they could, the Westerners and their Japanese lapdogs used the bordering lands, of barbarians and neighbouring tribute-payers alike, as channels for attacks of their own.

In 1884, down in the deepest western south, *Faguo*, France, occupied the once *tianxia*-observing and tribute-paying Vietnam; when the Manju Qing's army responded to Vietnam's calls for protection, the French smashed the Fujian fleet to bits. Ten years later, the sea-neighbouring Japanese stepped in to the north: gunning the re-built Beiyang navy to pieces off the Yellow Sea coast of Shandong's Weihaiwei. With that victory under their imperial belts, as the price of peace they ended Korea's ancient payment of *tianxia* tribute, replacing it with an expanding protection of their own; they also insisted on the island of Taiwan.

And then the Qing found themselves caught in a Great Game war between the British lion in neighbouring India and the Russian bear across the old Mongol north-west, with the Himalayas in both of their imperial sights. In 1903, a British madman by the name of Francis Younghusband had advanced the Union Jack, with its maxim guns, into the lama lands of Tibet, wrapping the Buddhist kingdom in a British 'protection'. Fortunately, the heavenly province of Sichuan had been able to pull the eastern edges of Tibet into its own embrace. Confronted with so much meddling in so many directions, however, the now-crumbling Manju Qing decided that it would be a good idea to make it clear that all of the Mongol lands, Outer and Inner, were theirs.

By 1905, after a war between Russia and Japan fought on China's lands in the north, and won by the Japanese, the Manju Qing's lands and their *tianxia* tributaries had become a giant feast being eaten by everyone.

———

Heaven, however, still had some unsettled questions. When the intellectual rebels of the late nineteenth century argued for revolution, much of their energy was focused on the fact that the Manju Qing had been barbarian conquerors, unfit and unable to rule. Discovering the old Hunanese text, the *Treasures of Chu*, seeing the tyranny of a Qin idea of unity that had destroyed other, independent, minds, Tan Sitong urged true human hearts to rise against them. To this, a Hunanese friend of Tan's, by the name of Tang Caichang, added that in the battle for independence, origin was all. Pointing to the West's new science of anthropology, Tang Caichang declared that the world was divided into races, and while Westerners concentrated on the colour of someone's skin, it was obvious to any Chinese that race was not just a matter of a hierarchy of colour but a hierarchy of civilisation as well. The Manju Qing were clearly not civilised Chinese; not only was their skin a darker colour, but no amount of Confucian learning could disguise the barbarian origins of the hunt-on-horseback idea with which they ruled.

True, Tang Caichang continued, the West had placed themselves, as 'white' Caucasians, at the top of the racial tree. But this was just a historical error on the part of a people who lived too far away from the civilised lands of China to know any better. Any 'top' should naturally include the Chinese (who the West had unfortunately labelled 'yellow'). And, being at the top, the Chinese should obviously be distinguished from the lower levels of darker brown and black who (as the West had so scientifically proven) were a lesser human race. Of course, being near-sightedly focused on their own 'brown' Indians and 'black' Africans, the Western scientists had not noticed that the inferior 'brown' races also included the 'brown' Manju, and the Mongols who had preceded them, as well. It was really all just as the descendants of the Yellow Emperor had always known: the world was divided between the forces of civilisation in the heavenly lands, and the barbarians in the bestial wilderness beyond. The colour of a people's skin was just nature's way of illustrating this obvious and universal fact.

Tang Caichang having made his points, when Sun Yatsen had invited the student rebels to join him at the end of the nineteenth century, he was quick to see the importance of the racial question – not just in terms of the barbarian status of the Manju, but in terms of the inevitable havoc that confused Western minds would wreak if they became involved. Referring people to the opinions of a returned scholar, Yan Fu, who had translated many of the foreign works, Sun Yatsen noted Yan's warnings on the lessons to be drawn from the devastation of the brown and black races in India and Africa by the West. 'They will enslave us', Yan declared, 'and hinder the development of our spirit and body … [If] the brown and black races constantly waver between life and death, why not the four hundred million yellows?' Yan Fu was right, Sun declared: 'What if those Westerners, in their barbarian ignorance, mistakenly applied the same kind of treatment to the 'yellow' Chinese people who have been hijacked by the brown Manju, as they would naturally apply to the inferior Manju themselves?'

Listening to Sun Yatsen, anxious Chinese minds began to contemplate the dreadful possibilities of extinction. But Sun had a solution. 'It would all be fine,' he argued, 'if the true descendants of the Yellow Emperor explained that they were not just an amorphous mass of black-haired people living under the Manju Qing, but a single, pure, race with a common blood as well as a distinctive common language and belief: four hundred million men and women who, originating from a Great Man Yellow Emperor thousands of years ago, had devoted millenia to developing and personifying the civilised idea of a *ren* humanity.' 'Yes', Sun conceded, 'they had failed to take the superficial step of proclaiming themselves a nation state – but this was just a sign of their higher evolution: any patch of land could call itself a state, but only the people of truly Great Men could be called a civilisation.'

As he explained the situation, Sun Yatsen also reminded everyone that, one way or another, and over the great stretch of Chinese time, a number of other mingling races had found their way into the Chinese lands: a few million Mongols, a million Manjus, a few million Tibetans, and over a million Mohammedan Turks. These were to be distinguished from the 'Han' descendants of the Yellow Emperor. The Han were the people who had transformed the original wisdom of the *ren* humanity into a Confucian culture, predicated on an idea of 'self-cultivation.' And, with the transformation having been accomplished under the Han dynasty, naturally the people had taken the name of 'Han' to describe their race. Ignoring the Hunanese dream of a separate identity of their own, Sun declared that it was now time for the 'Han people' to rise up as the superior race they were and throw the brown Manju barbarians off their perch. When, in 1911, an accidental bomb had gone off in Wuchang, it seemed that was exactly what they had done.

When the Manju Qing empire was brought to an abrupt end, many of the barbarians at the edges of the empire assumed that they were as free as the Han. High up in the Himalayan mountains – and with the eastern edges of the Tibetan empire having already been eaten away by China's neighbouring Sichuan province – the thirteenth Dalai Lama declared that his people should assert their freedom not only in the next life but in this one too. Chinese troops, not yet sure what the shape of the new Republican China was to be, stood up to hold the Tibetan territories that had surely come to be under the authority of the Qing. But in the confusion of the moment, loyalties wavered, and the battle was lost.

Similarly, when news of the accidental revolution reached the tribute-paying Ulaanbaatar, capital of Outer Mongolia, its Buddhist leader was declared Great Khan of the Mongol nation, and a statement was issued to the effect that any submissions of the past had been nothing more than the repayment of old debts to the Manju cousins – debts which were on no account transferable to any Han Chinese. Looking at the declared independence of the Outer Mongol cousin, Inner Mongolia was then torn between Buddhists who were keen to return to a great Mongolian Khanate, and the ambitions of a group of Inner Mongol princes who hoped, like many of their predecessors, to find a better future for themselves in a stronger China. To which was added the complicating detail that the Inner Mongol lands were already home to a large number of Han Chinese who had been flocking north for decades, if not centuries: escaping the collapse of their own overburdened soil, they had settled new fields and trading towns on what had once been pure Mongol grasslands.

There was just as much chaos and confusion within the heavenly lands themselves. When Hunan province, the old state of Chu, declared its independence, other provinces followed suit, each rising up to throw off the Manju Qing. They were not alone. Seeing an opportunity to secure their own independence, a number of old barbarians also rose up to claim states of their own: in the lower south-west, a tribe to the south of Yunnan declared a kingdom of Sipsong Panna, Xishuangbanna to the Han Chinese. Meanwhile, watching their Tibetan and Mongol neighbours, individual groups of Turkic people in the north-west (including, the Uighurs) tried to shake the soldiers of Qianlong's garrisons out of what had become Xinjiang province. Fortunately for the young Republic, a wily once-imperial official with military ambitions of his own was quick to turn his coat from the

ousted Qing to the new Republic and hold the Uighurs in their place –
but it had been touch and go.

Within a year of its revolution, the fledgling Republic split. Educated
minds immediately thought back to the opening words of the *Romance
of the Three Kingdoms*: 'The Empire, long divided, must unite; long
united, must divide.' Fears rose, not only of a new Three Kingdoms but
of another devastating period of Warring States. Newspapers exploded
with opinions, divided between those who wanted a 'China proper' and
those who wanted something 'greater'. Given the recent revolution of
their own, and given Confucius' exhortation to always put oneself in
other people's shoes, for those who wanted a China proper (seemingly,
a minority) the situation was simple: just ask the Mongolians, the
Tibetans, and everybody else, what they want. But those in favour of
the 'greater' idea (far more in number, or at least far more vociferous)
argued that any idea about simplicity was dangerously misplaced. The
Han, with their greater civilisation, were obviously capable of developing the requisite national consciousness and political understanding
required to survive in the new twentieth-century world of sovereign
states. But the Mongols, the Muslims and all the other rag-tag barbarians who had ended up in the heavenly lands were nothing but simple
animals, with no idea at all about the stakes and risks involved. And
while these particular animals might be simple, there were greater
beasts prowling around on the outside – Russia, Japan, Britain and
the rest of Europe, not to mention America – which were extremely
dangerous. The lesson of the past sixty years had been clear: the territories of any lesser races not held with an iron Chinese will would
not only be lost, but would be used by the greater Western barbarian
beasts as a springboard from which to try and capture the Chinese
heartlands as well. As for Confucius and the old *ren* idea of putting
oneself in other people's shoes, well that belonged to another time;
obviously, the world had changed.

Once again, Sun Yatsen came up with a reconciling suggestion. If the
survival of China as a country, and the Chinese as a people, depended
on the securing the unity of the many lands and people within the
greater borders established by Kangxi, then the idea of a single Han
Chinese state would need to be adapted in order to embrace the other
buffering races, and their territories, as well. Not one Han race alone,
but five races, as one great *guojia*, state family, led by the superior Han,

whose civilised sense of responsibility would ensure the unity upon which, as emperors from the earliest of times had understood, the security of all depended.

With things a little clearer, the new Republic of China reached out to the edges of the old Manju empire and read them a series of revisions to their independent dreams. Tibet would just have to remain divided, with the eastern part of its Kham province now obviously a part of Sichuan. Mongolia would also have to stay in two pieces – at least until Outer Mongolia could be persuaded to change its independent mind. And if the Inner Mongolians were stupid enough to keep raising objections about independence, someone should explain to them that under the new Republic of China, anyone from any of the five races could become President – as long, of course, as they had the right qualifications. As for Xinjiang, well, fortunately it was already in the hands of a loyal militarist, so there was no need to have a conversation at all. And as for the southern tribes, without any armies of their own, and not much of a voice, they would just have to accept the fact that they were a people whose time had long gone. Unfortunately, they had missed out on a lot of the civilisation, but they would be welcome to join the unity of all.

The security of China's borders was, however, not the only battleground of opinion. At the turning century's troubling time of change, many of the Han Chinese were concerned to find a common purpose and identity that could pull everyone together. 'What did it mean to be Chinese?' had been a hard enough question to answer in 1279 when the Song had fallen to the Mongol Yuan; but after the rise and fall of the Ming, after the hunts of the Manju Qing, after the ravages of the Western barbarians, and with the accidental, 1911, revolution lost to warlords, it was a question which had only got harder. Some, a little vague on the present as well as the past, suggested that Buddhism was the obvious glue. They were soon set straight with the observation that sprinkling holy water over a people who had long ago set aside the idea of the Buddha for the strength of the family could only be a remedy of the desperate. Others suggested that the common thread was origin: a common ancestor in the Yellow Emperor who had not only sired the people who became the Han but had probably sired many of those who, after five thousand years of migration and commingling, had not only got a little darker but had also got lost. Yet others pointed out that, while the idea of a common Yellow Emperor ancestor might cover the tribes who had been pushed from north to south (even, at a pinch, covering some of the Manjus who had been sitting quite close to the heartlands before they became the Qing), it would be extremely difficult to stretch his progeny to include the Tibetans, the Mongols and the Turkic Uighurs. Others, digging deeper into history, pulled out stories of princesses offered up for tribute-generating alliances, and argued that the Yellow Emperor's blood was probably running through the veins of even these unlikely barbarians as well.

Some were convinced; others were concerned. 'Yellow river, yellow emperor, yellow people', the great reformer Liang Qichao observed, 'it all seems to add up to some idea that yellow is our operative identity, with a serious risk that the rest of the world will simply laugh.' After a long time arguing, however, someone else suggested that these kinds of questions were natural for a new nation. To which, Li Dazhao (Peking University's chief librarian and the political economist who had been driven by the question of what it meant to be Chinese) observed that the questions which were being debated were really part of the wider challenge of 'imagining a people'. Scattered like sand, and with an illiterate majority of peasants cut loose from the written civilisation of the intellectual scholars and imperial classes, the question of precisely what it was that united even the pure Han had obviously yet to be answered. If the Republic was to be known as China, then it was time to go out of the city and down to the countryside to find the real 'Chinese people' – including *all* of the various races.

While they were at it, Li Dazhao added, they should take the time to find everybody's stories – those of the pure Han *and* the tribes – and weave them together into the colourful fabric of a new and greater whole.

The early Peking University students had indeed gone down to the countryside – in the company of many rural-reconstructing others. Waves of warlords had also spread out, as had some of the barbarian foreigners, particularly the Japanese. By the late 1920s many were suggesting that if one were going to weave everybody's stories together, it might be an idea to include an extra strong thread for the fierce tribal spirit of the Mongols and the Manju – a spirit which the Chinese 'sheep' had either never had, or, if they had ever had it, had obviously lost. Having been held in the noose of a Manju hunt for so many centuries, it was high time they learnt the value of an inner barbarian nature: clearly a strength which the imperialist West and the Japanese had managed to retain. When Mao and his fellow Communists slipped out of the Guomindang's net and set off on their Long March in 1934, it was a thought that many carried in their hearts. And it was on the Long March that the Party would be confronted with living evidence of the fact that the Chinese lands included more than the Han.

Leaving southern Jiangxi province in October 1934, the eighty-six thousand Long Marchers initially walked west. Keeping to the shadows of the wilder world, they first crossed the southern bottom of Hunan, and then continued on across the upper tip of Guangxi, into Guizhou and then through the eastern edges of Yunnan, from where they turned north, to Sichuan. Walking across the mountains of Sichuan and further west on to the grasslands of Tibet and then into the deserts of the north-west, they had traversed some of the wildest lands in China's world, and met tribes of people who had only been seen as strange creatures in imperial picture-books. In Guangxi, a land dotted with strange hills like spires, they encountered groups of people known as the 'Miao' whose story, told through their own many different languages, described an ancient flight from their original home in the Yellow River north. In the tropical rainforests of Yunnan, they encountered the Yi, another group of people with many different languages who prided themselves on having ancestors who had battled against the ancient Zhou. Proceeding across the Jade Dragon Snow Mountain – and shivering through the vast and empty Tibetan highlands – they occasionally met wandering pockets of nomadic Buddhists who had little or nothing to share, but far more frequently found themselves victims of the hostile arrows of invisible Tibetan warriors, who were keen for them to leave. Entering the wastelands of the deserts, they then found themselves at the mercy of quite another nature, punctuated by Islamic oases shot with the divided loyalties of far-off Central Asian lands.

Often desperate, and dependent at every step on the refuge and shared food offered by people who had no wish to be part of Sun Yatsen's 'five races, one family' idea, the Long Marchers discovered an entirely new world. Freed from the flatness of the picture-books, the 'tribes' suddenly appeared as real human beings. Some were inclined to be friendly; others not. Lives hanging on the hospitality and local knowledge of those who were helpful (and shocked at the encounters with those who were not), this encounter with other races led to some to imagine a truly new China, one which would live at peace with the tribes which the imperial dynasties had wrongly tried to bury. Others, however, saw nothing but a world of uncivilised people simply waiting to be tamed. For his part, Mao, with a weather eye on victory, however it might be achieved, promised that old injustices would be redressed and the tribal brothers – to be described as *minzu*, minority peoples – would be given the right to choose exactly what and whose people they were.

The tribes were not the only different people the Long Marchers encountered. Others were pockets of people whose voices seemed to be Chinese but who owed their greatest allegiance not to Confucius but to Mohammed. They called themselves the Hui. Long Marchers who had read their schoolbooks remembered that some of them were the descendants of early Arab traders who had arrived in the southern coastal ports of China from the later times of the Tang dynasty, while others were descendants of the *semu*, the coloured-eyes, brought by Kublai Kan from the Persian end of his cousins' Mongol empire, to supervise the conquered, and not-quite trusted, scholar officials of the Song. Whether their ancestors had arrived from the south or the north, the men had married Chinese women and, insisting on living in Quran-reading communities, had followed the river routes of trade, looking for places to settle. Some had made their homes in the southwest, where markets spread along the soft borders with Burma and Vietnam; others had settled in the north and west which were home to people who traced their origins to the steppes. The Hui were not a people in the sense of having their own independent language and geography, but they certainly had a different idea about life in both this world and the next. Accepting their hospitality and listening to their dreams, Mao made them the same promises of a truly new China: a People's Republic that would live at peace with any and all other people, all of whom would be free to choose their futures.

By the time the Long Marchers came across the last groups of Hui, however, in the Ningxia north-west, Mao was also floating another idea. Tales had reached his ears of Hui warlords who had allied themselves with units of the Guomindang, themselves allied with renegade forces of loyalist White Russians, all intent on smashing an 'East Turkestan Republic' raised in Kashgar by Uighurs – with Moscow's support. Contemplating the invisible currents of energy sparking in the Muslim world, Mao cast his mind back to his own studies of history, and remembered a man called Ataturk who had recaptured the Turkic remnants of the lost Ottoman empire from the Western imperialists. Once in Yan'an, and struck by the possibility of strengthening the Party's army with Muslim forces, Mao invited other groups of Hui to raise a 'Mohammedan Red Army' – and then gone on to think about what other pockets of desperate people might be willing to stand beside his Communists in the hope of a future independence. The Inner Mongols were one possibility: now caught between Chiang Kai-shek's Republican China and the new Japanese 'Manchuria' which, established in 1931, was increasingly devouring neighbouring lands. The Xinjiang Uighurs, whose attempts at raising an independent East Turkestan had been smashed by the Guomindang, were another.

The right of a people to choose their destiny became a Party principle. Mao assured the most loyal of the *minzu* minority groups that, in the event of a Communist victory, a successful and grateful Party would reward them with autonomous areas of their own, named after their people and united with the Communists by the common battling desire to be free. In 1944, the Uighurs lost a second attempt at an independent East Turkestan to the superior forces of the Guomindang and their allied warlords. But in 1945, the Russian brothers snatched both Manchuria and the neighbouring east of Inner Mongolia from Japan, and, two years later, in 1947, offered the lands to Mao. Mao then declared that the people of Inner Mongolia should be the first of the promised self-governing areas: the Autonomous Region of Inner Mongolia.

The idea of groups of independent *minzu* people was as intoxicating for some Party members as for the various minzu themselves. But as

revolutionary victory approached, senior Party minds began to wonder
what exactly a future Communist government would do with pockets
of minzu freedom. In an ideal world, promising them the power to
choose what they wanted to be was laudable. But in the real world,
where only the fittest survived, and in the lands of China, where any
new Communist state would be immediately faced with just the same
kinds of foreign imperial threats that the Qing and the Republicans had
had to battle before them, was such a promise really practical? 'If we
offer them a choice, won't we be encouraging them to accept?' asked
some. 'And if they accept, won't we find that our borders have suddenly
frayed into nothing but an open invitation to anyone to invade?'

Other Party leaders, less sympathetic to the minzu dream went
even further: 'Who on earth are these *minzu* peoples anyway?' 'And
why shouldn't they be evolving like everybody else to the higher level
of socialist man?' When the questions were answered with the point
that promises made would have to be kept, the questioners responded
with the sharpness of a people who had battled bitterly for their own
survival. Having been so long in the grip of the Manju Qing's hunt,
not to mention having become part of the board of a Great Game
played by the imperial powers of Russia and the West, surely they had
been hoodwinked too many times by other people to treat a promise
with care.

Unaware of the inner battles of the leadership, the wider body of
the Party's membership noted that when a provisional Constitution
entitled 'The Common Programme' was announced in late September
1949, declared everyone to be equal, with each group destined to
govern themselves within the wider embrace of a bigger, united
family. The idea of equality still seemed to be standing firm when
Mao Zedong rose to the eaves of the Tiananmen Gate of Heavenly
Peace two days later, on 1 October 1949, to declare the founding of the
People's Republic of China.

But behind the scenes, stronger winds of ruling reality had already
taken charge. 'Minzu choice', they had successfully argued, 'is nothing but a slogan for a fractured past – not at all a principle on which
a unifying present can be built.' To which they added that it would
be better not to make a public announcement on the point: the truth
could always be hidden in the detail. It was clear, however, at least to
everyone who counted at the top, that it was the Han Chinese who had

sweated blood and tears to deliver a successful revolution, and it would be under the Han Chinese that everyone's future would be found.

Well before 1949 was out, the Party, learning from the past, began to tighten a grip around the difficult edges of the old Qing empire worthy of a Manju hunt. In the summer of 1949, the First Field Army of the People's Liberation Army advanced to Xinjiang to relieve the Guomindang of their posts, and liberate the people. In late August, the leaders of the (failed) Second East Turkestan Republic were invited to a conference in Beijing. Thanked for their great service to the people of Xinjiang and China, three days later, they boarded a plane to return home. Neither they nor the plane ever arrived. In December, three months after replacements accepted an invitation for Xinjiang to join the People's Republic of China, Beijing announced that the original plane had crashed 'somewhere over Lake Baikal'. It was one of those twists which, as everyone living at the north-western edge of China's lands knew, was rarely a matter of fate.

And then, in the early months of 1950, the People's Liberation Army marched from Xinjiang to the Tibetan Plateau, across Himalayan lands that included a corner of a newly independent India. Severing the Lhasa capital from the entire Tibetan east, the army declared that the Tibetan people had returned to the motherland of the People's Republic of China. Setting off to build a hidden Himalayan highway between Xinjiang and Tibet – through India's Aksai Chin – the highest ranking military officer left instructions for the sixteen year-old Fourteenth Dalai Lama to send an envoy to Beijing to sign a seventeen-point agreement for peace. All typed up, and not open to negotiation, the 'agreement' stated that Tibet would be given a right to 'exercise autonomy' and that 'nothing would change in the political system of the Tibetan lands'. Advised by the Commander of Tibet's tiny army – and remembering a desperate prophecy of death and torture left by his predecessor – the young Dalai Lama signed. Within months, the streets of Lhasa were occupied with thousands of soldiers from the People's Liberation Army, all waving images of Mao and proclaiming the liberation of Tibet. Dazed, Tibetan monks and people had asked: *liberation from what?*

Back in Beijing, with the Party's provisional constitution having announced that the *minzu* people would not only be equal but would be able to govern themselves, attention now turned to three longstanding *minzu* questions which had not yet been answered. The first was how the *minzu* were going to govern themselves while also sitting under the Han Chinese. The second, a much older question, was who the *minzu* people were. And the third, which would probably need to be answered before the second and the first, was where exactly the various *minzu* were to be found.

In 1951, a Central Institute for Nationalities was established, populated by anthropologists and sociologists who had chosen to stay in the mainland under the new People's Republic. In 1954, they were secretly set to the task of finally working out the answers to the minzu questions – as quickly as possible. A little at sea, given the enormity of the task and the short timetable, the social scientists turned to the Russian big brother for ideas, and to their own books for facts. From Russia, they took their lead from a set of 'nationality principles' that Stalin had applied to the vast Central Asian and Far Eastern empire of the Russias when it had been reconfigured into a 'Soviet Union'. For books from home, they buried themselves in the surviving imperial libraries of the Song, Ming and Manju Qing picture-books – works compiled by successive emperors, each keen to compliment themselves on the many and varied colours of their lands.

Typically intellectual, however, the anthropologists and sociologists were just too slow. With a new People's Republic to run, and promised *minzu* autonomies to be created in some form or another, the Party had no time to wait for a scholarly text. A snapped census was suggested: if the imperial picture-books couldn't provide easy answers as to who was who, why not ask the *minzu* people themselves? Unfortunately, when the results of the snap census were compiled, it became clear that the people were no clearer than the picture-books. Most of the respondents had struggled to even understand the questions, and four hundred different groups (two hundred and fifty in Yunnan province alone) had popped up with a claim to be some kind of *minzu* or other. Obviously, the respondents hadn't studied politics or any other of the social sciences. With the respondents lacking the education necessary to produce responsible answers, the researchers were instructed to go out across the country and find the answers out themselves. 'Learn the languages, pick up the history and deliver your considered scientific opinion', they were told. 'And no need to worry about how long you will be away – a few months should be enough.'

The researchers did their best but, however bright they were, and however hard they worked, they could never have done enough. There was not one neat migration but layers of migrations over thousands of years. And the tribes had not just moved from north to south, but from east to west, and often back again. To make things worse, as far as the researchers could see, the idea of four hundred different groups was, if anything, a gross over-simplification. 'Local chiefs' had regularly simplified complicated tribal origins in a bid to get and keep imperial titles. And when the Manju Qing had sent central officials to replace them, the new officials (observing at first hand the more natural lives and beliefs of the tribes, acclimatising themselves to the softer life, and concluding that the less the centre knew, the easier things would remain) had insisted that, in the interests of imperial comprehension, the facts of origin should be simplified even more.

As the scholarly researchers researched, the fact that the origins were complicated soon became clear. But from what they could see on the ground, sorting them out in anything less than a lifetime would be impossible. Even the languages couldn't help: far from being able to identify a handful of common and learnable tongues, the scholars were struggling to come across any common chatter at all. Thrust into the fog of five thousand years of complicated tribal histories across a vast geography, and with only months to find their way, they were close to drowning, when an impatient Beijing recalled them. Having taken far too long, the fussing intellectuals were told that the messy matter of who was who was being transferred back to the Beijing bureaucrats. Far from the field, they would have the objectivity that only official training, and distance, could provide.

Poring over their tea leaves, the Beijing bureaucrats came to the conclusion that, rather than worrying about reading everything, labours could be saved if they availed themselves of the practical assistance of a nineteenth-century British cartographer (and Major General) by the name of Henry Rodolph Davies. Having been charged with charting the boundary between British imperial Burma and Qing China in the early 1890s, the Major General had helpfully left his maps and definitions behind for Chinese posterity. With colonial clarity at their fingertips, the bureaucrats were able to deliver their verdict on the *minzu* situation in the commendably efficient space of only six months: fifty-six identifiably different groups in the Chinese lands, including the pure race of the Han. True, there were a lot of others who *claimed* to have more of a tribal difference. But they were obviously victims of a 'false consciousness': after so much time in the trees, they had obviously lost track of the links that related them to other tribal cousins. So what if their ancestors had always argued that they weren't the same? Ancestors could be just as mistaken as descendants. And as for those who argued that they had to be different because they spoke a different language, that was neither here nor there. Obviously the past had created a terrible mess; and while some might find it difficult to understand the languages of the long lost relatives with whom they would now be reunited, that was nothing that a little language training – and a lot of political education – couldn't cure.

Names were named, and by squeezing thousands of strands of difference into a manageable fifty-six, everyone was put in their places, and named. Even at this dramatically pared-down number, however, there were clearly far too many *minzu* for each to be given its own autonomous region. Which ones to choose? How to make sure that the chosen few were clear both about the meaning of autonomy within the greater Chinese family, and about their own responsibilities for unity? And how, given the essential importance of unity, were 'autonomous' decisions to be made? In 1954, a new Constitution had helpfully made a start by declaring that national autonomous areas would – as and when they were established – be inalienable parts of the People's Republic of China. Behind the scenes, desperate bureaucrats tried to work out the devilish details.

Eventually, it was decided that a small number of very big groups would be rewarded with a region – roughly the size and status of a province. Beyond these fortunate few, the majority of the minzu groups would receive smaller privileges of autonomous prefectures (cities, towns and surrounding areas) or autonomous counties (villages, smaller towns and surrounding areas). At the same time, everyone would have to recognise that some of the areas (particularly in the messy south-west) would have so many different *minzu* that it would be better just to give them the name of the biggest group, rather than worry about the details: China might be a big country, but if one took out the mountains and the deserts, and factored in the number of people, everyone was really rather squashed in. There was also the fact that, with the Han people being far more numerous than any of the other races across the heavenly lands, whatever they were called, many of the autonomous areas would naturally be home to much bigger numbers of Han.

Turning to the question of the meaning and responsibilities of autonomy, it was obvious that these would need to be understood in the bigger picture of the wider Chinese family – with unity as the ordering principle of all.

As for how decisions would be made *within* the autonomous areas, well naturally the minzu should benefit from the broader principles of socialist democracy, including the leadership of the Chinese Communist Party, under the Democratic Dictatorship of the People. Just as in other areas of the country, local people's congresses would be created, with locally elected members proportionately reflecting the colours of the (recognised) *minzu* groups living in the relevant area (including the local Han). Not everyone was happy and quite a few had their questions: 'Won't there be a risk that in some places the numerically greater Han Chinese will actually be running the autonomous regions?' 'Well', answered those in charge, 'with so many small groups of different *minzu* people and with so many Han, some of the *minzu* colour is naturally bound to fade – but, as man moves towards the realisation of a unity that is both socialist and Chinese, surely this is only to be desired.'

Returning to the more difficult question of exactly which others, beyond the Inner Mongols, would get the rewards of the big autonomous regions, in the end, it was events which settled the selection. In 1955, anxious about tempers raging across the wild Xinjiang northwest, Mao decided that things might be easier if the various groups could be divided even further. Separating out the biggest group (the Uighurs) from the many, generally Turkic, others (Kazakhs, Kirghiz, Tatars, Salar, Uzbeks, not to forget some lost remnants of the Cossacks), he created a Xinjiang Uighur Autonomous Region. Three years later, it seemed appropriate to give the better-behaved Hui a place of their own, as well. That was a little hard to do, given that they were scattered everywhere across the country. But the Hui of Ningxia Province (sitting below the western stretches of Inner Mongolia at the entrance to the corridor which led to Xinjiang) seemed to be as good a candidate as any: being a group who had supported Mao and the Long Marchers on the latter legs of their journey, it seemed quite right that

they should get an autonomous region of their own. With three autonomous regions now settled in the north, Party thoughts then turned to
something that would balance things in the south. Looking at the map,
the obvious answer was the biggest of the southern minzu groups, the
Zhuang. Notifying them of their selection, an autonomous region was
created for them in the misty mountains of Guangxi.

With all of that settled, each autonomous region was to be given a
'chairman' (just as each of the Han provinces had their 'governors'),
selected from the relevant minzu minority and invited to sit visibly
at the top. And just to make sure that the minzu remained clear about
the importance of unity, Mao applied the same principle to them as
he applied to every province in the country: behind every chairman
(as behind every provincial governor) would sit a Communist Party
secretary. Selected from Beijing, and almost without exception Han
Chinese, it would be the Party secretary who would hold the unifying
power.

With the first four autonomous regions now appointed, as well as a
host of smaller autonomous prefectures and counties, attention then
turned to the unifying principles of socialism under which everyone
would live. The most fundamental was ownership of the land. Begun
in earnest in the early 1950s, the reforms which gave every individual
peasant a pocket of his own land were already hitting trouble among
the most backward kinds of *minzu* – stubborn people who insisted that
their lands had always been held by all of them together and could not
possibly be divided. Moving on to the collectives and the communes
should have been easier (after all, wasn't a collective just another kind
of common land?). But the minzu had fussed again, this time arguing that if the land was asked to do too much, and if the people who
farmed it were forced to follow the ideas of a single top-down mind,
it would not be able to support anybody. Then there was the question
of Tibet: with so much of its land owned by the monasteries, someone
was going to have to talk to the monks.

Mao had originally been willing to give the Tibetan people the time
they needed to adapt to the new state of affairs. But by 1957, the revolutionary transformations in the Sichuan-bordering east of Tibet had

gone a little faster than planned. Local Party officials, first keen to divide the land, then just as keen to put it into collectives, had whipped up storms of local zeal. The monasteries and their lands had been folded into the people's property; monks had been returned to a lay way of life; herders arguing for nature had been trampled underfoot; and any and all other inconvenient Tibetan minds were now being denounced as feudal rightists and swept into jail.

Uneasy at the news that was reaching Lhasa, but without any idea of how to deal with the Chinese – and with no help from any other barbarians near or far – the young Dalai Lama pinned his hopes on a rather surprising declaration by Mao that he was an ardent admirer of Guan Yin. Given that the goddess Guan Yin was not just the goddess of compassion but had been inspired by the greatest of the Buddhist bodhisattvas, Avalokitesvara (the bodhisattva of which every Dalai Lama is a re-incarnation), this seemed to offer some grounds for optimism. But while the young Dalai Lama hoped for a meeting of minds, the eastern monasteries and temples were falling to the Party's land reform, and the tempers of the eastern Tibetans were exploding.

In 1958, Buddhist scholars tried to calm the rage by encouraging monks to rebuild their temples in their hearts, rather than on what were now heavily contested lands. Clear that what was at stake was the future of Tibet, the monks were unwilling to yield. By 1959, the news reaching the Dalai Lama was even more worrying. The Great Leap Forward, declared in China the year before, was now not only leading to famines in Sichuan but had taken a grip on the eastern Tibetan province of Kham as well. Waves of eastern Tibetans began to flock west to Lhasa; saffron furies erupted in the city of the gods; and Chinese guns trained themselves on the people on the streets. Skies darkening for a storm, the Dalai Lama's advisers persuaded him to gather himself up as the hope of his people, and find his way to the sheltering slopes of Himalayan India. Meanwhile, fearful that the Dalai Lama was in danger, in the days around his departure, thousands of Tibetans gathered to protect him. In the ensuing encounters with the People's Liberation Army, two thousand Tibetans died. When news spread that the Dalai Lama had left, remaining Tibetans found themselves adrift in a world that had lost the beating heart of its Buddha: eighty-seven thousand others set out across the mountains to follow him.

With the Dalai Lama gone, and the seventeen-point agreement obviously broken, as far as Mao could see there was no reason why the Himalayan kingdom of the gods could not now bow to the unity of the Chinese family. And with India having treacherously offered the Dalai Lama refuge, it also seemed appropriate to rename sixty-five thousand square kilometres of neighbouring territory that the imperial British had once marked off as being part of India, as a new 'Southern Tibet'. Meanwhile, with the People's Liberation Army now firmly in command, the Great Leap Forward began to jump across all the Tibet lands. And as the Great Leap Forward jumped, Tibet exploded. Rebel monks fell in their thousands to the new military power, condemned, like so many other subjective spirits, to *laogai* camps of labour. Eventually, as in the other minzu regions, a Democratic Dictatorship of the People was declared – and a war of the classes was unleashed to set anyone who tilled the land against the 'landlord lamas'.

In 1962, having stayed behind in Tibet, the Tenth Panchen, Great Scholar, Lama (the highest ranking Buddhist teacher after the Dalai Lama) bravely stroked a secret memorandum to Mao: 'Two thousand five hundred monasteries have been reduced to a pool of seventy, and the army has declared war on the people of Tibet.' 'When', he asked, 'will it ever end?' Describing the memorandum as the 'poisoned arrow' of a separatist enemy, Mao despatched the Panchen Lama to Beijing's Qincheng jail. In the same year, the People's Liberation Army was sent to insist upon the borders of the new 'Southern Tibet', pushing into the lands of India's Arunachal Pradesh and battling across the region of Aksai Chin. The ensuing war between China and India lasted only a single wintery month, at the close of which Aksai Chin had been firmly embraced within the People's Republic of China.

In 1965, with the border fixed and the Great Leap Forward having run out of steam, Tibet became the fifth, and last, autonomous region. Led by a Beijing-educated Tibetan chairman, it was naturally ruled by a Han Chinese Party secretary (a general in the People's Liberation Army). Not long after that, the battle against the 'Four Olds' was carried up to Tibet, and a Tibetan Red Guard was created, charged with ushering in a Cultural Revolution of its own. A thousand years of Tibetan Buddhist relics – monasteries, images, prayer wheels, bells and books – all went up in flames. Every religious observation was abolished. The Tibetan language was 'simplified' to the point that many no longer recognised it. Posters of Mao were placed in every household. Rebellious hearts were exposed to the cleansing education of struggle sessions. And, as elsewhere, although a little later, communes followed. Asking why Mao could not be satisfied with the secular world and leave their Buddhist hearts alone, thousands of Tibetans threw themselves into yet more uprisings. Their questions answered with bullets of unity, they were buried in graves that they were forced to dig themselves.

By the time the furies of the Cultural Revolution blew themselves out, the *laogai* labour camps had become a feature of the Tibetan landscape, even as the landscape had fallen under the familiar taming order of the heavenly Great Man. Treasured for the glittering minerals hidden within the veins of its earth, even before Deng announced his Four Modernisations in 1978, Tibet was already being excavated for its temporal wealth. Uranium discovered, its distant plateaux then became natural sites for exploding tests of nuclear power. Above the ground, forests were flattened and rivers were beginning to dry; across the grasslands, soil turned to dust. Mines were becoming towns, rivers were charged with radioactive energy, and the detritus of nuclear experiments was being buried underground. By the time that Deng departed to the next world in 1997, the taming of Tibet's nature had become an industry all of its own.

As the socialist dream set Tibet alight in the west, across the arc of the north, the Inner Mongols found themselves battling against similar storms of change. Guided by shamans and raised with Buddhism, the Mongols also saw themselves as the children of a Tengr sky and a grassland mother – led by the totem of the wolf. Swept with oceans of grass, the vast steppe might seem to offer life to endless numbers of hungry mouths, but every Mongol knew that wild winds, poor rains and heavy snows made the grass a fragile support. Stewardship was everything. Storming horses, grazing gazelles, wandering yaks, greedy goats and sheep, even ravenous marmots and rabbits, all had their place, but only if each group of creatures kept to their individual limits within the 'Big Life' of nature. Hunting in cunning packs, culling the greediest of mouths, it was the wolves who kept the natural world in order. And man? Well, trained to see himself as answerable to the Tengr sky and the grassland mother, and tutored by the wolf, man could perform a similar role. Indeed, learning from the wolves, man and horse combined could even become a worthy opponent, ensuring that the hunting packs of wolves would, like the groups of every other species, keep themselves within the limits of the land. But to earn his place at the top, man-on-horseback had to keep himself and everyone else on a constant move, ensuring that no heavy herds of anything were ever able to stay so long on any patch of grass that it could be trampled into deadening clutches of mud.

To the Mongols, this was all a simple 'grassland logic'. But while the logic was something that even a Mongol child could grasp, it took a true man to master the actual forces of mind and body required to keep up with the wolf. Even after thousands of years of living at the edges of the Mongol world, few Han Chinese had managed to understand it. At home in a world where forests were flattened for fields, where nature was ordered for bumper harvests and everyone was part of a family within which they were constantly told not only what to do, but exactly how to do it, how could they ever understand? Chinese scholars might sing the praises of nature in their books and paintings, but the nature they praised was an abstract idea of an ancient golden idyll that had very little to do with the reality of the natural world. Keeping to their studies, the scholarly Chinese had turned themselves into a herd of highly educated sheep. Perhaps it had been different thousands of years before: perhaps everyone had even come from a single sky. But if that was the case, the Chinese had clearly lost that early wisdom: settling on their fields, they had come to hear the cry of a wolf as the wail of a hungry ghost. Scratching at their yellow earth, they had become a people who grasped at patches of land, without ever understanding the bigger sweeps of life. And ordered in their families, imperial rulers had come to see them as little more than units of production – an idea that they had, largely, followed. Obviously it had not worked: when things had really begun to unravel in the nineteenth century, the northern Chinese had flocked to the Mongol grasslands. But even then, they had not come in search of the lessons of the wolf: having exhausted their own fields, they were simply looking for fresh lands to farm.

By the early 1950's, with Stalin having swept up the Inner Mongol lands in his iron fist and then turned them over to Mao, and with the

Chinese people in need of as much grain as they could find, the trickle of Chinese sheep become more of a trampling herd. As in Tibet, land reform and the collectivisation of everything was conducted under the unifying guidance of the Han big brother. Beneficiaries of the first of the autonomous regions, with a clear promise of a land of their own, the Inner Mongols were shocked to find themselves first forced to divide up their grasslands with fences, and then ordered to plant sheds on the grasslands, and then settle everything under the command of commune leaders who had never even seen a wolf, let alone dreamt of one.

But that was only the beginning. The ravages of the Han's Great Leap Forward not only turned the grasslands into communes – complete with militarised production brigades – but transformed the trampling herd of Chinese sheep into a flood that threatened not only the Mongols, but the very force of nature itself. This time, a torrent of people flocked to the grasslands in desperate search of lands that could be turned to grain. Desperate descendants of that misguided ancestor they called Yu the Great, the migrants put up more fences and sheds, diverted rivers, felled trees and pierced the ground with wells. And as their madness reconfigured the landscape of the wolf, their Great Man attention turned to the wandering yurt-like *gers* in which the Mongols carried their nomadic lives. Declared to be barbarian, the *gers* were replaced with immovable boxes built from bricks and tiles, each adorned with one of the chimneys that seemed to follow the Chinese wherever they went.

As any wolf-child could have told them, it was not long before the horses got tangled up in the wire fences and the sheep spread like clouds. Before much longer, the grass, on which everyone's survival depended, turned to mud. But, freshly arrived from southern fields to teach the Mongol brothers how to farm, the Han leaders of the production brigades dismissed the complaints as the dying gasps of a backward world. And when the Inner Mongols continued to complain, their, Inner Mongol, chairman was denounced as a rightist: no matter that he had been a member of the Chinese Communist Party since 1925. Complaints turned to protests, and more Mongols – monks and herders alike – were denounced, this time as criminal 'separatists'. Time and again, the Inner Mongol chairman begged Beijing to remember Mao's promises of autonomy; and each time, Beijing replied that autonomy was only autonomy within the greater unity of the Chinese family.

When, in 1966, the Inner Mongol chairman finally realised that the idea of 'autonomy' was nothing but a trick of the text, the Party brothers rounded on the Inner Mongols as ungrateful dogs, unworthy to call themselves even cousins of the Chinese. At which point, a special force of the Cultural Revolution was unleashed to root out the dangerous separatist enemies looking for an independent state. With Soviet Russia now an enemy – stuffing missiles into Outer Mongolia, now known as the Mongolian People's Republic – Beijing unleashed the terror of its Cultural Revolution upon Inner Mongolia's two million heads: excruciating tortures that left hundreds of thousands crippled and maimed, deaths beyond anyone's imagination and a toll of the disappeared which was almost as great as the dead.

The principles of unity now clearly established, a flood of Han students was sent to the grassland 'countryside', charged not with learning from the nomads but with learning from the commune leaders who were settling the nomads on the fields. Meanwhile, the borders of the Inner Mongolian Autonomous Region were redrawn to ensure that the surviving Mongol voices were in a more harmonious balance with the surrounding provinces of the Han. Exhausted by its own rage, Inner Mongolia's Cultural Revolution eventually died out, although it would be a long time before the Han students went home.

No sooner had the Cultural Revolution died away though, than another Great Man idea appeared: the Four Modernisations. Large areas of grassland were set aside for mines, cities and their attendant industries. And in the race to get rich quickly, war was declared on the wolf. The bravest of all defenders of the Big Life of the grasslands, the very totem of the Mongols, there were few things that the wolves feared, but one of them was the explosion of gunpowder. Seizing on this useful fact, the Han modernisers armed themselves to the hilt. Realising that few of their number were very good shots, they recruited dead sheep to their cause: wiring them up with explosives so that hungry wolves would be blasted to death, without anyone needing to raise a gun.

By 1989, Inner Mongolia was on its way to a modern future: the wolves had been defeated, and the big life of Inner Mongolia's grasslands was almost dead. With so many Han migrants, the Mongols could no longer be described as the majority of Inner Mongolia's people. Cities rose, and memories of a very different past were buried. Secretly, broken

Mongol hearts wondered whether their world might have been saved if the wolves could somehow have become masters of the brush. Out on the steppes, however, men who had once ridden with the wolves wiped away their tears and remarked that, without the grasslands, Beijing would soon be feeling the dusting sting of sandstorms. But by then, of course, it would be too late for everyone: wolves and man alike.

As the Tibetans and the Mongols battled, the changes of the People's Republic were also reaching into the north-west lands of the Turkic tribes, including the 'new frontier' of Xinjiang province. A world of mountains whose white glaciers dropped into oasis valleys, Han adventurers had long been tantalised by its surprising green pastures. To those whose ancestors had lived there, however, this was a world where everything sat on the edge of a vast and hungry desert: seed too many fields and the soil would turn to sand.

From 1950, Xinjiang's people were offered supporting hands to help them build the socialist dream. Engineers from the big Soviet brother were invited to help open up the seams of the earth. A Xinjiang *Bingtuan* Production and Construction Corps, a military-led division of Han settlers, was put in charge of almost all farming (including a thirsty cotton spread across the valleys) and given responsibility for planting factories as well. Schools taught children that the heroes of the Uighur past were no better than bandits. Scarves of Islamic modesty were banished. And then, as everywhere else in the great Chinese family, land reforms first swept out landlords, and subsequently pushed the 'liberated lands' into collectives. In the accompanying class wars, landowners, moneylenders, mullahs and traders across the roof of the world were all renamed as 'sheep' and 'goats'.

Few, if any, Uighurs believed that the socialist future was going to be any different from the imperial past. In 1957, Beijing's Anti-Rightist campaign reached up to Xinjiang: Uighur homes were stripped for searches; Uighur men disappeared into the night. Then, as the Great Leap Forward loomed, the fragile lands were put under more ploughs than anyone could ever have imagined, and the seams of the earth were opened up for yet more mineral prospects. As Uighur hearts cried, loudspeakers, installed on every corner, rejoiced in the fact that the

Chinese and the Uighurs were now one very big family: as if anyone needed reminding.

Up in the Altai north, stronghold of previously attempted East Turkestan Republics, anger had grown to rage and, in 1959, the rage exploded into rebellion. When the rebellion was successfully flattened by the People's Liberation Army, rumours whispered that Mao had expressed his gratitude for a mountain of dead Uighur bodies which could be used to fertilise a hungry soil. As elsewhere in the minzu world, rebels who survived were sent to *laogai* labour camps – and anyone suspected of any subjective sympathy was 'migrated' to the south of Xinjiang.

With Uighur history officially condemned as a counter-revolutionary force, Uighur parents whispered the stories of past heroes into their children's hearts. Tales were told of lions who had once swept across the roof of the world, carrying the trades of all; and of men who had offered their fighting courage to the sheep-like Tang, and who, even in their own conquest, had never given up the fight. Brave rebels across the ages, their numbers included not only hardened warriors, but women with a beauty and courage which matched the land. Of these, none was braver or more beautiful than the great Iparhan. Captured by a Manju Qing general, she had been given to the Qianlong emperor as a 'fragrant' concubine. Captivated, Qianlong offered to recreate her lost Uighur world in the Imperial City. Chinese schools taught of her returning Qianlong's love, but every Uighur heart knew that she had never yielded: threatening to starve herself to death, she had spurned the counterfeit paradise; reluctantly agreeing to live on, she had insisted that her corpse be buried in her homeland. Smitten, Qianlong had agreed – and kept his word.

When the Cultural Revolution arrived, its furies were trained to find every treacherous Uighur heart suspected of harbouring a separatist sentiment. In Xinjiang as elsewhere, the Four Olds were set to flames, with any surviving scarves of Islamic modesty added to the fire, followed by books of prayer. Enemies of the Han people were burned in hells of oil; and more and more of the fragile valleys were set to crops of cotton. An already steady flow of Han migrants (one that now included shocked waves of exiled Rightist intellectuals, sent to reform themselves by smashing up Xinjiang's rocks) was followed by a tide of city students despatched to man the fields.

Nature collapsing, smoke rising, coughs hacking, hearts breaking, few Uighurs noticed when Mao exploded his first atomic bomb
in 1964, on the Lop Nur edge of the Taklamakan desert and close
to listening Russian ears. Being a land of barbarians, it had not
occurred to him to put up a protective fence or tell the Uighurs
of the risks. Wandering camels and Uighur shepherds found themselves scorched with cosmic dust – and over the years that followed,
thousands (perhaps two hundred thousand) were kissed to death
and destruction by the spread of the radiating power. In 1968 (with
Russia and China now in a cold war of their own), Moscow helped the
Uighurs rise again in a struggle for an independent East Turkestan;
again, they lost.

Across the next twenty-five years, and with the rise of Deng's Four
Modernisations, the Xinjiang Production and Construction Corps
continued to tame the lands, expanding its industrial activities, and
raising new cities as it went. Rebellions were met with arrests and
executions; suspicions of separatist sentiment were followed with
torture. And when, in 1991, the collapse of the Soviet Union relaxed
Russia's grip on the wider Turkic people at the edges of Xinjiang's
borders, instead of thinking again, Beijing simply tightened the noose
within which the Uighurs were held.

And then there was the south. With waving coconut palms and tropical rainforests, all watered with mists and washed with torrential rains,
these were very different lands. Unified for harmony, however, the
same taming forces were unleashed. Stands of coconut trees were first
divided for land reform, and then reunited for a collectively greater
productive power. Superstitious spirits who dared to argue that the
trees had a life of their own were despatched to another world, or a
laogai labour camp, before they could do any real harm. The Great
Leap Forward brought neighbouring brigades of Chinese communes
in search of the farming possibilities of a tropical jungle – although
eventually they had been obliged to admit that growing grain and
herding sheep was really not a possibility in the tropics. Surviving
coconut trees, seen as far too idle, were replaced with a more productive rubber; mountains were terraced with rice.

As once-magical rainforests fell to make way for greater production, hanging gardens and sacred groves followed suit. Without their ancient homes, eagles and tigers scattered in all directions, peacocks and pheasants disappeared, and any of the shy snub-nosed monkeys who had managed to hang on to their branches quickly found their heads on the plates of hungry men. Meanwhile, the descendants of the elephants that had fled from the Chinese north thousands of years before lost their final sanctuary.

The people who survived the Great Leap Forward lived to find themselves beaten down in the bitter battles of the Cultural Revolution, even as ancient spirit-gods, who had watched over the fortunes of animals and humans alike since time began, were pulled from the skies, and trampled on the ground. While the silenced tribes watched open-mouthed as their world died, Mao observed that 'battling with nature was a boundless joy'. The tribes themselves would come to call it the 'age of wild ghosts': a time when the fragile boundaries between the living and the dead all but disappeared.

When the Cultural Revolution eventually blew itself out, and Deng Xiaoping ushered in the Four Modernisations, even the Communist Party had to admit that something precious had been lost. Soils struggled to death in a land that had once seemed boundlessly fertile; climbing wisteria and tropical orchids were giving up their ghosts; groundwater was being sucked into the greediest tree that anyone in the rainforest had ever seen: rubber. Not only had much of the ancient forest fallen – and much of the newly planted forest failed to thrive – but even the once abundant torrents of rain, and the watery mists, had begun to fade away in protest.

Then, on a summer's night in 1975, a Yunnan village exploded. Hard on the edge of Vietnam, and flat on a route that had once carried traders across a southern Asian sweep from Bengal to Malaya, its name was Shadian. The explosion was triggered by a simple misunderstanding: with the Cultural Revolution having faded, a gentle population of Muslims had assumed that it would now be safe to revive a mosque that had been smashed by the Red Guards. But while the Cultural Revolution had come to an end, no official had been willing to approve a resurrection of the old superstitions. The Muslims had become rebels, and fighting broke out on the village square. Remembering the Yunnan troubles of the Manju Qing, the Party rushed heavy cannon and artillery to the scene – and then commanded MiG jets to sweep the streets with rockets. Before anyone had time to say their prayers, Shadian had been reduced to rubble, a thousand people had lost their lives, and a small pocket of the Muslim world had been shot to kingdom come. A few years later, in 1979, apologies were made and a number of new mosques were offered in a bid to make amends. But in many parts of the country, Muslims quietly observed that, whatever was going on in Beijing, they would stick to Islam: whichever way the Chinese winds blew, the Quran never changed its mind.

When Deng Xiaoping arrived at the head of the Chinese Communist Party's family, it was clear that if the Four Modernisations were ever going to flourish beyond the Han heartlands, a lot of damage would need to be repaired. Privately acknowledging that thirty years of social-ism had delivered more feudalism than progress, the Party offered to loosen the noose of unity, and give autonomy a bit of space to breathe. Here and there, in the corner of a corridor, some senior Party members even whispered that it might be time to face up to the fact that it might not actually be possible to get the *minzu* minorities to relinquish their foolish dreams of gods, wolves, spirits and Islam – at least not in this life.

Talks were offered to the still-exiled Dalai Lama, on condition that he return to Tibet. Declining, the Dalai Lama, nonetheless, sent a dele-gation of his own to explore the facts on the ground. Arriving in Tibet, his 'eyes and ears' saw a shattered landscape and a desperate people. The worst of their fears were confirmed.

Rising to an American podium some years later, on 21 September 1987, the Dalai Lama gently reminded his audience (including the distant but acute ears of the Chinese Communist Party) of a thou-sand year-old pillar which, still standing in Lhasa, had been inscribed with the words of a treaty between the Manju Qing and the Tibetans: 'Tibetans will live happily in the great land of Tibet, and the Chinese will live happily in the great land of China'. The Dalai Lama then went on to ask the powers of the mortal world to embrace the land of the gods as a 'zone of peace'. Within weeks, Buddhist monks were reck-lessly chanting dreams of an independent Tibet. The chants turned to protests, the protests turned to arrests, beatings and spectacles of trials – all of which fuelled further furies, not only in Tibet but across the neighbouring lands of Xinjiang.

By early 1989, the protests began to wash into a wider Beijing spring that was marked not only with marches in the capital of the country but in Lhasa and in the Urumqi capital of Xinjiang as well. For a moment, Tibetan and Uighur hearts dared to hope that Wei Jingsheng's dream of a Fifth Modernisation – the voice of the people – might be possible for all. But even before Beijing's students had settled down for their hunger strike in Tiananmen Square, in Tibet and Xinjiang alike, the protests had been followed by yet more arrests, more beatings and more spectacles of trials.

By the time that Deng Xiaoping boarded his train in 1992, China's edges of order were fraying, badly. Minzu hopes having been dashed across the land, once again heaven was offering its opinion through ravages of nature that confirmed the worst of the minzu fears. Up on the now-muddy Inner Mongolian grasslands, it was not only wolves that had become hard to find but even the gazelle (although in the rising dust, some argued that it was difficult to see anything). Tractors, motorbikes and chain-link fences had killed off the horse-borne herders, and with them had gone the strength of the Mongols' once-legendary horses. Green grass had been replaced with a yellow stubble and, as the herders had predicted, sand storms had risen up and raced down to Beijing. Meanwhile, across in Xinjiang, as the Xinjiang Production and Construction Corps expanded its industrial and agricultural empire, cancers were eating into the lives of the Uighurs and the desert was stretching its sandy fingers ever further into once-green valleys. Up in Tibet, the white glaciers of the Himalayas were melting, and the Tibetan grasslands were, like the grasslands in the Mongol north, turning to dust.

Down in the tropical south-west, rubber having failed to meet its quotas, anxious officials were redirecting production to the pleasing of tourists, with Miao minority dances. Sun-kissed girls sparkled to order in headdresses of silver, and colourful skirts swirled with tinkling bells, all reminiscent of the romantic pages of the old imperial picture books. But a few surviving older minzu stubbornly refused to give up stories of an ancient past which they had tried to tell the researching anthropolists and sociologists so many decades ago. 'There was an epic flight', they insisted, 'from ancient lands of ice and snow which had once been ours'. Full of fantasy, their tales told of brave journeys across treacherous mountains, of leaps across rivers and of the discovery of a cinnamon sea that, even with all its beauty, had been only a shadow of the wonderful world they had been forced to leave behind. Recounting their tale, some even pointed stubbornly to poems etched on the cliffs of Sichuan: the desperate words of other fleeing tribes, who had made it that far but not beyond, standing like cries across the ages.

Declining to accept the Party's account of their people as one of many tribes who had been civilised by the Han, the descendants followed up with an ancient story that explained it all. A long, long time ago – almost as long ago as the days of the Yellow Emperor – two brothers had set off on a journey, each one carrying a book. Sleeping in the wild one evening, the brothers' makeshift camp had been attacked: possessions scattered, the older brother had lost half of his book; the younger brother had no book left at all. For some time, the brothers had continued on their journey, but eventually they had gone their separate ways. Armed with half of the book, the descendants of the older brother had raised an empire on the power of the written language, and eventually become the Han. Without a book at all, the descendants of the younger brother had kept the power of their own ideas and speech but lost the key to a written language: they had come to be known as the Miao. Most scholarly minds sniffed at what was obviously a foolish fabrication. In the 1990s, however, a Chinese scientific researcher announced that the earliest inhabitants of the Yellow River were, in fact, the ancestors of the Yunnan Miao. While the Han Chinese were astonished, the Miao themselves were not surprised at all – they had been telling the Han that the heavenly lands had originally been theirs for as long as they could remember. By then, however, there was little to be done: the past was gone, and what did it matter who had originally been who?

While the foolish minzu minorities kept clucking about their pasts, the Great Men of the Party were looking to the future. In 1997, with Jiang Zemin now at the helm, a grand plan was unveiled to unleash the true productive potential of the failing edges of order, and, in so doing, to finally bring their superstitious people into the rising triumph of the modern world. The name of the plan? 'Develop the West'. Up in the north, across the arc of Inner Mongolia, Ningxia and Xinjiang, a necklace of new industrial parks-cum-cities was promised: a 'Northern

Shenzhen'. As for Tibet, a high-speed train was announced, one that would whisk productively touring Han Chinese right up to the dizzying heights of the new market of the gods.

By the year 2000, Develop the West was spreading its civilising energies as fast as Deng Xiaoping's train had sped south. Modernising eyes, Chinese and foreign alike, lit up at the prospects, even as many of the hearts at the edges of China's order sank. Looking at the speed at which the fragile Tibetan world was unravelling – and meditating on the Party's anxious concerns about the security of China's borders in that constant battle to survive – the Dalai Lama suggested a 'middle way': one where Tibet would remain within the iron borders of China, but would be given the freedom to pursue its own dreams. To many who heard his words, it didn't seem so different from Mao's original promise of 'autonomy'. But His Holiness was dismissed as an incorrigible separatist and a danger to all. Tibet was wrapped even tighter into the Chinese family, and foreigners hoping to trade with the bigger empire were reminded that unity was everything.

The Tibetans, however, were not the only barbarian people to speak out; and the Dalai Lama was not the only voice. In the lands of Xinjiang, a stubborn woman emerged from the desert on the back of Deng Xiaoping's Four Modernisations: her name was Rebiya Kadeer. A picture-poster of what a Uighur with a high quality productive mind could do, Rebiya had built a trading empire of such success that, in 1992, she had been elected to join the National People's Congress. Having become officially responsible for representing her people, she decided it was time to tell the tales of what had been happening to them in recent years. Rebiya's stories included the tale of a 1997 rebellion that had become a massacre in Yining, a city known by the Uighurs as Ghulja. They also included the hitherto unreported tragedy of an earthquake that had struck the village edges of Kashgar in the same year, burying thousands of Uighurs. In 1999, having chosen to put truth above unity, Rebiya and her tales were relegated to the dark corner of a prison – yet another incorrigible separatist who had abused the generosity of the Party, and whose freedom could only spell a danger for all.

Certainly, there was danger. As the Uighurs found themselves in an ever-tightening noose, they fought with every ounce of Quranic conviction for the independence which they believed should be theirs.

As imperial Beijing gave way to a new Republican order, camels continued to meander past the walls of the city, even as trams and cars jostled within its walls.

After the 4 May demonstrations in 1919, protests continued in what would be known as a 'May Fourth' movement; this image was taken on 29 November, by American Sidney D. Gamble.

Hu Shi taught philosophy at Peking University: 'The world is built little by little, a bit at a time. But even the little depends entirely upon the energetic contributions of you and me and the other fellow.'

Cai Yuanpei (second right) transformed Peking University into a storm of ideas; pictured here in 1933 with George Bernard Shaw (second left), Song Qingling (Sun Yatsen's wife, also a revolutionary; centre), and the towering author, Lu Xun (far right)

Chen Duxiu: founder of the magazine New Youth; author of the call to throw off the bonds of old ideas; Dean of Peking University under Cai Yuanpei; co-founder of the Chinese Communist Party.

Li Dazhao: Peking University's Chief Librarian under Cai Yuanpei; author of the call to youth to 'go down to the countryside'; co-founder of the Chinese Communist Party.

Chiang Kaishek (Jiang Jieshi), successor to Sun Yatsen as leader of the Guomindang; in 1927, his Shanghai massacre of Communists triggered a civil war which he fought alongside a growing war with Japan; his 'New Life' movement promoted social morality as a counter Western individualism.

Like the last Tsar, who fought a battle with Japan on Chinese territory, Stalin saw China as a critical buffer against Japan; Mao saw Moscow's favour as essential to success within the Party and between the Communists and the Guomindang.

Ding Ling, the author whose very human works made her both a heroine among early Communists and a prize in Mao's propaganda battle against the Guomindang.

Mao Zedong with revolutionary intellectuals at the Yan'an Forum on Literature and Art, 1942; Mao's declaration that 'subjective' literature and art were to be subservient to 'objective' science led to a purge of many of the intellectuals who had built the Party.

On the fields of WWI France, James Yen (left) discovered corps of Chinese peasants and taught them to read. On returning to China, he founded a 'mass education movement' (MEM), and launched a rural reconstruction experiment in Ding Xian.

After a succession of land reforms, the Great Leap Forward organised the peasants into communes and sent them out to till the land on an industrial scale: 'more, faster, better'.

In 1958, the Great Leap Forward was heralded with new technology, including the *Dongfanghong* tractors which promised a triumph over nature.

Mao's Cultural Revolution was energised by an angry youth which organized itself as Mao's 'Red Guards'; soon the 'Red Guards' were followed by 'Rebel Red Guards' in battles that many would describe as a form of 'extreme democracy'.

Inspired by the heroism of Lei Feng, China's youth, including the soldiers of the People's Liberation Army, saw the quotations contained in Mao's Little Red Book as mantras.

In 1978, big character posters appeared on a wall in Beijing, splashing the anger of a youth betrayed by the Cultural Revolution; one poster called for a 'Fifth Modernisation', the voice of the people.

Fang Lizhi, the astrophysicist whose work made him one of China's greatest scientists, and whose pursuit of truth put him on a collision course with Deng Xiaoping and the Party.

In spring 1989, Beijing's students appeared in Tiananmen Square, asking for a voice; by late May, students had arrived from across China; on 2 June they would be joined by three friends: Liu Xiaobo (smoking, left), Hou Dejian (centre) and Zhou Duo (right).

Deng Xiaoping called for
Four Modernisations and
leapt the country forward
with Special Economic
Zones; resisting the idea
of a Fifth Modernisation,
he saw Tiananmen Square
as a protest too far.

After the failure of the
Great Leap Forward
and the chaos of the
Cultural Revolution,
Deng Xiaoping set out
to modernise China with
'mind emancipation';
Shenzhen's Special
Economic Zone became
a laboratory for the
'socialist market economy'.

Jiang Zemin (right) was Deng's third choice as successor and relied on princelings and private enterprise for support; Hu Jintao (left) followed Jiang, but, without a Party family, he struggled to assert an independent authority.

Dai Qing's book *Yangzi! Yangzi!* challenged the Three Gorges Dam and took the NPC by storm; in the silence after Tiananmen, the Dam was approved and Dai Qing was arrested.

Once the Dalai Lama's residence, home to the blue Akshobhya Buddha, the Potala Palace stands on the Marpori mountain which represents the Bodhisattva Avalokitesvara, known in China as the goddess Guanyin.

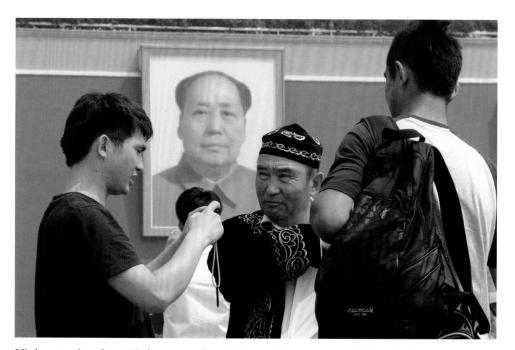

Uighur tourists from Xinjiang standing in front of the portrait of Mao that faces Tiananmen Square; in October 2013, a 4x4 gunned its engine for the image, exploding into a ball of flames.

Miao dancers from the Guangxi Autonomous Region in the south, gracing the opening ceremony of the 18th Shanghai Tourism Festival.

As Mayor of Chongqing, Bo Xilai exhorted the city to 'Sing Red', while making his own cloud-somersaulting leap for the leadership; pictured attending the closing ceremony of the NPC in March 2012.

In late 2011, Wukan's 13,000 villagers first battled for their land in the southern province of Guangdong; losing a leader to a death in police custody, they battled again.

In March 2014, a sunflower protest was launched in the renegade province of Taiwan; protesting against a cross-straits agreement negotiated by the Guomindang, they insisted that Taiwan and the mainland were two countries rather than one.

From September 2014, Hong Kong's students occupied Central in a battle with Beijing about the meaning of 'one country, two systems' and the meaning of the rule of law.

Xi Jinping leads the Politburo Standing Committee in strict order of formal rank; Xi is immediately followed by Li Keqiang, the Premier; sixth in line is Wang Qishan, powerful head of the CCDI.

Declaring that the world has entered 'an era of large scale development of oceans and the poles', Xi Jinping is keen to construct a 'maritime power'.

Astonishing journalists with her plastic finish and long black hair, Jia Jia will be slower to enter into mass production than more industrial models: her creators are working on the laughter and tears that will bring her to life.

Already in 1997, the Party had launched a 'Strike Hard' campaign against Xinjiang and Tibet, charged with smashing anyone and everyone who insisted on 'telling truths from the past.' But Strike Hard notwithstanding, in Xinjiang, explosions on buses – rarely reported and largely buried – became regular occurrences, as did a number of equally buried assassinations and plottings, disturbances and riots, poisonings and carefully placed bombs. More Strike Hard campaigns followed. In 2005, Rebiya was eventually released into the custody of a complaining America. As she departed, Hu Jintao, the new head of the Communist dynasty, once Party secretary of Tibet, stood up to remind everyone about the importance of unity: the Han were not to be separated from the minzu minorities, and the minzu minorities were not to be separated from the Han.

By the time the Chinese family prepared to welcome the world to the Olympics in the early months of 2008, hearts from the most stubborn edges of order were mustering whatever voices they could. From the desperate lands of the Uighurs came a host of plots, imagined and real. And from Lhasa, the city of the gods, came the chants of a swelling tide of Tibetan monks that gradually rose to a crescendo of *Bo Rangzen*! Free Tibet! By 14 March 2008, the streets of the city of the gods were burning with anger and pain.

It was not meant to be this way.

BOOK III
WHAT CAME NEXT

Those who rule are supported by those who are ruled. This is a principle accepted by the world.

Mencius (372 – 289 BCE)

PART 7
HOW MANY SUNS?

In the era of Yao, ten suns rose all at once;
Yao ordered Yi to shoot nine down.
> *The Classic of Mountains and Seas* (fourth century BCE)

CHAPTER 1

THE HEAVENLY PARTY

He who wished to bring order to the state first harmonised
his family, and wishing to harmonise his family, he cultivated
his person.

The Great Learning, Confucius (551 − 479 BCE)

D USK FELL EARLY ON the mid-November evening of 2012.
Streets cleansed of all but the most important of passages, a
muffled silence had descended. Mao Zedong's spirit peered out from
his portrait, still suspended from the Gate of Heavenly Peace. Calm
though his features were, however, an air of nervous anticipation
seemed to hang in the late autumn chill. With all thoughts, near
and far, fixed on the outcome of the Party's eighteenth Congress,
the attentions of those nearby were set on the blazing lights of the
Great Hall of the People and the movements of the heavenly Party
within.

After a year of carefully negotiating the parting script, the moment
had come for Hu Jintao, leader of the fourth generation of the
Communist dynasty, to stand at the Party's podium and make way for
a younger brother: Xi Jinping. The ascent of a new star was never
easy, and the vermillion walls of Zhongnanhai had tried to keep the
rising squabbles secret. But as with imperial families across China's
ages, there had been so many squabbles, and some had been so loud,
that whispers of disharmony had eventually floated out on somebody's
vapours; and floating out, they had naturally landed in earthly ears. So
many squabbles, it was a miracle that it had not all ended in a war. And
so many factions, each with so many different strands, that whispers
alone made it difficult to work out what was really going on. Certainly,
some of the tales were so shocking that it seemed to some as if the
Monkey King himself was in charge.

At one point, Xi Jinping had disappeared from sight. Rumour-mongers suggested that he had locked himself up with his Party godfather, Jiang Zemin, refusing to budge unless and until he was given all three of the highest Party powers (not just general secretary-ship of the Party and presidency of the country, but chairmanship of the Central Military Commission as well). Others, closer to the central stage, said that he was simply recovering from taking a heavenly chair in the back – wielded, like a heavenly cudgel, by a competing contender in a rage. It was all just as the Jade Emperor had once observed: 'Made up of the essence of both heaven and earth, nothing that goes on among these creatures in the world below should surprise us'. Calmed with honeyed promises, tempers had finally been contained and, on an early November day, the Zhongnanhai squabblers had been coaxed underground, into the secret passage that would sweep them under the Avenue of Eternal Peace and up to the bright lights of the Great Hall of the People. Above-ground, black-winged saloon cars would glide across Tiananmen Square, revealing a movement in the ordering will of heaven to the waiting hearts of earth.

Emerging on to the star-lit stage of the Great Hall itself, the sequence of the squabblers' appearance had been all that any Party eye, or even the televisions at home, had needed to understand the ranks: first came Xi Jinping – obviously the new son of the Party's heaven; next, Li Keqiang, the man who would clearly be premier; then the five other successful squabblers who would serve along their side. The unity of heaven and earth now clearly displayed through the highest levels of the Party's Politburo, the seven men then left the stage. As they made their way back through the underground passage, on the earth above, the same black-winged saloons ignited their engines, would trace the path of the celestial rulers back to the velvet portals of Zhongnanhai – with only a tail light to hint that heaven had truly touched the earth.

It had certainly been a long march for everyone. Not just for those who had reached the top, but for all of the other Party members who had taken part in a journey that, one way or another, had taken much of the last thirty years. Thirty years in which the lectures of the Party's

founding ancestors had never been far from their side. And thirty years
of inner Party battles in which everyone had had ample opportunity
to contemplate the extraordinary relevance of the lessons of China's
ancient past. Some said that one could trace the text of those years
across the rhyming lines of an epic Song dynasty poem about the *weiqi*
game of 'Go' – that wooden board of squares on which two players
armed with opposing piles of black and white stones set down their
pieces one by one in a bid to encircle the other and win.

They seemed to have a point. In its opening words, the poem
described the early years of the recent succession to perfection: 'While
the etiquette of guest and host had been thoroughly observed, facing
each other, the opponents had become like barbarians and savages'.
Warming up to the ambitions aroused by the game, the Song dynasty
poet had then uncannily described exactly what had been happening
over the past five years: 'Dragons and snakes had raced, ghosts and
spirits had laboured, fire and smoke had risen'; even the observation
that 'Palaces had been plotted, tigers had been ridden, and flags of
armies had been raised' had been faultless. And the description of
calculating hearts could not have been closer to the mark: 'Truth and
deceit had been blended together, slandering and cheating had been
woven through speech, rotting bones had been called oracles, righteousness had been squeezed by profit'.

Across it all, precisely as the poem had observed: 'The past had
been used to observe the present'; and just as today: 'Family and state
had advanced together, in the extreme'. Nor was it just the past and
the present in terms of human ambition: threaded across the past was
that impossible conundrum of reconciling the contradictions of Laozi
and Confucius. Laozi, who had cryptically observed that the 'Way is
great'; and Confucius, who had offered a guiding set of principles, and
then unhelpfully added that 'Talent is difficult to come by'. Hardly
surprising that the journey from the past to the present had been
such a challenge. Indeed, one could scarcely believe that the poem's
author was not writing about the facts of the last few months when he
had written: 'About to rise, plunging falls had followed; everyone had
known that when one meets the blade of a knife, not a single hair of
an error can be tolerated'. Written in the eleventh century, who could
tell how many times the truths of the poem had been repeated in the
thousand years that had passed since then. And who on earth could

have imagined, back in the revolutionary ranks of 1949, that in 2012, the Party's very own spirits would be reading its lines again.

The latest Son of Heaven, Xi Jinping, was born in 1953: the son of a father who had thrown his heart into the earliest heroic years of the Communist Party. Xi had been raised on the battleground of Mao's Zhongnanhai. Like those of so many of his peers, his father, Xi Zhongcun, had been purged to a tractor factory in the mid 1960s, not far from the ancient Zhou capital at Luoyang, in present-day Henan. As the Cultural Revolution then wreaked its havoc, the young Xi's father had been swept off to jail – and Xi had stepped into the angry tide of Red Guard youth, deftly navigating the raging battles until he was leading a production team of his own. When the Cultural Revolution had blown itself out, Xi found his way to the newly re-opened 'red and expert' doors of Beijing's Tsinghua University. By the time he graduated, Deng Xiaoping was ushering in the Four Modernisations, and Xi's father had been resurrected to the constellation of Party leaders: placed in charge of the southern province of Guangdong, far from the smouldering factions of the Party family in Beijing.

Setting his sights far into the future and firmly on the top of the heavenly Party, the young Xi Jinping decided to place himself first at the feet of a Party general. Gaining experience at the military wing of the centre, Xi had then consulted the past, looked at the seasons, and remembering the words of an old Tang dynasty maxim, 'No experience at the local level, no nomination for the centre', declined the spoiling comfort of a princeling's desk in Beijing in favour of a lowly official post in a county town that few of his peers had ever heard of, and to which none had any desire to go. The lowly post had had its fair share of local dragons and snakes, from which Xi learned his lessons; it had also had a number of ghosts and spirits, who were more than willing to offer their advice.

More experience gained, Xi then consulted the winds of change – which, in the 1980s, were blowing firmly south. His father having persuaded Deng to look more closely at the special economic zone possibilities of Guangdong, Xi found himself a position in the nearby province of Fujian. Still learning, Xi watched as Deng struggled to tame the Four Modernisations. On the Fujian coast of Xiamen (once known as Amoy), a sparkling special economic zone had been raised – only to find that a smuggling nest of official vipers had reared its ugly head. And when in 1996 the old Guomindang, still ruling on the renegade island of Taiwan, announced that they were going to launch themselves into a sea of democracy, Xi, now higher up in Fujian's government, watched as his olders and betters launched a volley of angry missiles across the Taiwan straits – and as a prowl of American aircraft carriers nosed their way through the separating waters, in an imperial show of silent warning.

Painstaking in his attention to detail, exercising the utmost care when feeling for river-crossing stones, Xi's advances eventually attracted the approving attention of the then Party secretary and President, Jiang Zemin. In 2002, he was offered the position of governor, and soon afterwards Party secretary, of the neighbouring province of Zhejiang. A rollercoaster of a province – home to Wenzhou, close to Shanghai, and never far away from a typhoon – Zhejiang was already one of the fastest, and loosest, of China's dragons. Xi took care to watch his step. With Hu Jintao and the third generation of leadership moving into a ten-year period of office, and with new retirement limits set by Deng, it was now clear that he had ten years, and ten years only, to reach the top. Hu Jintao had already gained the summit of power in 2002. If Xi failed to take the prize in 2012, by 2022 he would have passed the sixty-eight-year limit on the age at which leaders could take up a post.

Looking at the *weiqi* game-board, consulting the past and its lessons and the present with its changes, Xi watched for possible openings. Once again, 'racing dragons and snakes' were meticulously observed and 'ghosts and spirits' were approached for their advice. In 2007, after the Party secretary of Shanghai tripped over his own corrupting ambitions, Xi's diligence was rewarded: Party secretary (far more important than the governorship of anywhere) of the great Shanghai municipality that reported directly to Beijing. It was a position that offered a direct route to the Politburo. Within a year, Xi Jinping was in pole position for the final ascent to the top: not only admitted to the highest, Standing Committee, level of the Politburo, but vice-president of the country itself – with the added honour of leading the Central Party School which, since the time of Yan'an, had always trained the Party's highest minds.

Xi Jinping was not, however, the only tiger clawing his way to the top – nor even the only prince. As Deng had rebuilt the Party, and as wealth had become a productive possibility, many a red heart – Party prince and commoner alike – was looking up at the promise of the socialist sky, and fixing their sights upon the heavenly ladder. With their mettle forged in the hottest furnaces of the Cultural Revolution, the toughest were always likely to be those cubs who had learnt their lessons in the brutal heart of the Party's family factions – and the toughest of those would presumably be the ones who had learnt alongside their fathers in the *laogai* labour camps. Indeed, in 1976, when Deng tried to repair the damage of the Cultural Revolution's storms by rehabilitating parents with positions of power, many felt that the young cubs had paid a high enough price for the terrors of the past.

While Xi had guided himself by the proverbs of the imperial past (particularly the one about gaining local experience), most of the other young cubs had been more than happy to accept the soft seats that would keep them in the comforts of Beijing and close to the central pulse of Party power. It was a simple mistake: with so much change in the air, most assumed that the old imperial ideas had ceased to apply in what would surely be a new kind of socialist world.

Most, but not all. Four years Xi Jinping's elder (born in 1949), Bo Xilai had been born to Bo Yibo, a man who had swum with Mao in the waters of the Yangzi River – and become one of the 'eight great immortals', the early Party leaders who fell foul of the Cultural Revolution and had been rehabilitated by Deng in the late 1970s. Imprisoned at seventeen for nothing more than being the son of his father, when Bo Xilai returned to Beijing in his mid-twenties, he was offered the solace of a research position in Zhongnanhai. Like Xi Jinping, though, Bo sensed that the battle for the top would require a greater grasp of the country at large.

Springing himself from the gilded cage of the capital, Bo Xilai also went to a dusty county town that no one had ever heard of. Unlike Xi, however, from there he turned north, making his way, in 1990, to the port-city of Dalian, part of the old Manju lands that had become the present-day province of Liaoning.

Dalian was a place that had been at the heart of many of the ravages of the past. Pushed and pulled between tugging imperial powers at the end of the Manju Qing, in 1931 it had been wrapped up by the Japanese into the new Manjuguo, Manchuria, and transformed into an industrial powerhouse. Returned to Republican China at the end of the

Second World War, it had then changed its industrial colours to serve the Communist Party's state-owned enterprises, SOEs, only to fall to Deng's modernisations with the rise of a more enterprising south; the SOEs had collapsed. Many, observing its tattered glory, would have seen a bedraggled city best left alone. But Bo Xilai and his father saw the possibilities of applying the same kind of Monkey King magic that Deng was launching in the softer south, only this time for the popular benefit of a neglected industrial north.

While Xi was carefully feeling for stones in Fujian, Bo Xilai became mayor of Dalian, and in so doing, found himself a magic stick of his own. Waving the stick to trade favours across family, friends and Party, he strengthened the forlorn Dalian like no other Chinese city of its size. *Flash!* and an expressway leapt up to link the city to the future. *Swoosh!* and spreading boulevards appeared, washed with colour-changing fountains, and serenaded with musical notes broadcast from the controls of his personal office. Over the next ten years, while Xi Jinping scoured the lessons of the past to avoid the errors of the ancestors, Bo Xilai repeated the races of the dragons and the snakes. Riding tigers, plotting palaces, raising questionable bones as oracles, he 'advanced the family and the state together, in the extreme'. Dalian was transformed, but those outside his family began to wonder whether virtue had not been squeezed by profit.

Bo Xilai expected his northern magic to result in a shower of promotions. But enemies had been made, with some even repeating Confucius' observation that 'true talent is difficult to come by'. Bo Yibo, the father, however, was standing by, and the Party's propaganda resources – very sympathetic to Bo Xilai's past – were commandeered to change opinion. In 2001, when the Governor of Liaoning province fell to a sudden scandal, Bo Xilai was ushered into the post. From there, in 2004, he was able to leap back to Beijing, as the head of a ministry. With another leap in 2007, he found himself in the wider ranks of the Politburo. But the leaps fell short of Xi Jinping's attaining bounds, and without a coveted seat on the Standing Committee of the Politburo, the two were not quite neck-and-neck. Bo Xilai cast around for catching-up possibilities, but by the end of 2007, he found himself denied the coveted vice-premiership and offered the snub of a position as Party secretary of Chongqing instead. Not at all the *pai banzi*, do the deal, leap which would carry him to the top position in 2012 – but perhaps a platform from which he could conjure up a set of changes which might, just possibly, cloud somersault him to the front.

Chongqing, once the capital of Sichuan province (once, indeed, Guomindang capital of all), had recently been expanded and raised to become one of four great municipalities reporting directly to Beijing, with a 'greater' population of thirty-three million Chinese heads. It was also a city of debilitating heat, monsoon rain and organised brotherhoods of crime, with so many waves of unemployed refugees from the Three Gorges dam that it would make even a black heart weep.

Looking at the *weiqi* game-board, and facing his opponent with as much grace as he could muster, Bo knew that every advance would now require a savage battle. Given the scale of the challenge before him – the terrain to be covered and the short time to hand – the only obvious spirit who could help him was the ghost of Mao Zedong. Not just Mao, the master tactician who had wrought endless victories from the jaws of defeat (although those were obviously useful lessons) but Mao the great glowing sun who, when challenged by the Party as a 'cult that had gone too far', had risen above the factional fray to directly command the hearts of the people at large. True, it had taken a Cultural Revolution, but hopefully this time it would not come to that.

With the clock now ticking, and only five years to go before the career-defining 2012, Chongqing was launched into an eye-catching extravaganza of initiatives that would not only capture the attention of the Party's greatest leaders (those who would decide which contender would be invited to take the helm) but also the hearts of the people as well. Drawing on the family favours and princeling confidence which had stood him so well in the past, once again Bo picked up his magic stick, and as he had done with Dalian, *swooshed* Chongqing into the future. Ignoring the shrouds of almost perpetual fog, and the cauldron of heat, he poured so much concrete into the Jiangbei city centre that it began to look like New York. Aware that only the strongest of headlines would catch Beijing's attention, he also pulled his toughest Dalian policeman to his new Chongqing side, declaring a war on anyone whose money insisted on having a mind of its own. The rich found their assets redirected to Chongqing purpose. Complaining officials were despatched to the countryside. And any lawyers contemplating taking up anyone's cause were reminded that the font of all justice lay with the Party secretary (with any disagreements to be settled in jail).

Chongqing advanced to become the fastest-growing city in the world, with further distinction when PLA generals were invited to participate in local military games. Headlines glowing, Bo then announced some improvements for the benefit of the masses at large, particularly those hanging on for dear life to the hardest seats of Deng's runaway train: a 'red gdp' to give everyone a share in the municipality's SOEs, and a nostalgic return to the sound of songs which had once put a spring in the step of revolutionary hearts. 'Sing red!' Bo declared. With no need for any further encouragement, the men and women in the hardest seats joined in a chorus whose high notes could be heard even in the gardens of Zhongnanhai.

After only three years of Bo's magic, by 2011 Chongqing had leapt to become the greatest model of China's cities, and Bo's Monkey King magic had captured a number of imaginations. With only a year to go before the leaders of the heavenly Party announced their successors, Bo Xilai confidently expected a reward. But the Party was divided. Some were mesmerised; others refused to be fooled. Hu Jintao, no scion of a princely family, and shocked at all of the heavenly havoc in Chongqing, was watching in stony silence. Having spent so many of the last few years proclaiming the ancient principle that 'the people are the root of any power', and insisting that 'society should be harmonious', it was hard for him to argue that Bo and his red songs were anything other than a *tianbao*, treasure, sent directly down from heaven. Equally, it was hard to avoid the fact that Bo Xilai had created a personal fiefdom as challenging as anything in the ancient Zhou past. It was even harder to ignore the military games that Bo personally hosted in Chongqing – and with them, the nagging fear that he was preparing the way for another Cultural Revolution if he did not make it to the top.

Xi Jinping began to wonder if he had been outfoxed. 'Observing the etiquette of guest and host', in late 2011, he decided to pay a visit to the reddest-hearted and fastest growing city in the world (and the personal fiefdom of his would-be rival) to see for himself what was going on. As shocked as Hu Jintao, but with a far greater personal stake in the game, Xi Jinping quietly complimented his opponent on the wonders of Chongqing and the joy of being so red.

As 2012 appeared on the horizon, and as the tigers faced each other on the mountain of power, the wider ranks of the Party were also getting ready for a change. After years of trying to tidy itself up after the disasters of the Great Leap Forward, the Cultural Revolution and the Gang of Four (not to mention the Tiananmen events of June Fourth), Deng had re-organised the Party to a point where concensus was a principle for decision-making and (particularly important not only for everyone's careers but for avoiding the tyranny of another Mao) it was accepted that no one would be eligible for a new position after the age of sixty-eight. Accordingly, 2012 was not only a year that would usher in a new son of the Party's heaven, it was also a year when there would be an unprecedented exodus of older leaders, with the ranks opening up for an almost entirely new sweep of Communist Party officials as well.

The oracle bones having been clear about the change for a few years, as Xi Jinping and Bo Xilai had been plotting their final triumphal moves, everyone else in the Party had also been playing their own personal games of *weiqi*. With an official office now worth its weight in gold, every platform of promoting possibility had been explored, both inside and out. And in all the exploring, everyone's attentions had naturally turned to the palace of all promotions: the outwardly invisible department of the Party that was responsible for organising everyone's appointments and which, unsurprisingly in the earthy language of the Party, was simply called the 'Organisation Department'. Rising from a horde of personal files painstakingly compiled since the time of Yan'an, over the previous decade, the Organisation Department had been transformed into a powerhouse of personnel intelligence unmatched in any of the four quarters of the world. In the process, it had become so big that it now commanded a vast Beijing building of its own. Such was its power over each Party position, and over the files of everyone's past, that every official aspired to have a friend or a relation who worked there – and no-one whose future it governed ever needed to ask for its address.

Some said that the Organisation Department was, like so many other institutions of the Party, entirely Lenin's idea, born of the scientific need for an all-powerful Communist machine which could direct the many strings of its own orchestra without a single stumbling fault. Others said that Lenin had simply copied the idea from his Moscow ancestors, who had got it from Chinggis Khan and his conquering Mongols. Yet others argued that the Mongols had got it from the Chinese officials of the Song dynasty Chinese when they conquered the empire in the thirteenth century. From where had the Song dynasty Chinese got it? From their own ancestors, of course – right back to the state of Qin and its idea of cloaking the country in a grid of iron. From where had the Qin got it? Probably from being an ambitious dust bowl in the western back of the sparkling Zhou's beyond. Wherever it might have come from, in the years after the Tiananmen 'incident' in 1989, the Organisation Department had been tightened and polished like never before.

With so many careering fortunes at stake, when the soft 2011 Year of the Rabbit jumped into the 2012 celebrations of a new Year of the Dragon, it was not only the families and friends of Xi Jinping and Bo Xilai who were concentrating on the upcoming Eighteenth Party Congress. Nor was it only those who had dreams of serving from the centre. Out across the country, with thousands of Party-powered jobs about to open up within the provinces and the counties, everyone who was anyone was in hot pursuit of a heaven-sent fortune. And, just as in the capital, it was clear to all that the beneficiaries would not only be those who got the jobs – and, of course, their extended families – but also those who were able to ease a personal protégé into the kind of position that could provide a lifetime of reciprocating favours. In a land where every Party official, high or low, was some sort of emperor, everyone was looking for a horse to back.

With no one in any doubt about the stakes, and with winter now yielding to spring, for those in the Party's Organisation Department, heaven seemed to have already arrived. Filing cabinets were groaning so heavily under the weight of highly qualified candidates that it was plain to all that for most positions there was an embarrassment of choice: obviously, it was just a question of listening to the finer qualities of persuasion. Clear about their orders for years, suddenly godfathers, fathers, grandfathers, blood-brothers and every other qualifying kin from across the realms of heaven and earth, were all sent into a final frenzy of competitive action. Private rooms in restaurants were discreetly booked (with restaurants now filling to the rafters); flattering gifts were offered with the delicacy of afterthoughts; flowers were ordered to perfection; telephone lines were stroked with assiduous attention. And in the race to accumulate the mountain of favours necessary to swing a heavenly Party mind, there was no possible official desire on earth that would be too hard for the most determined candidate to satisfy.

Of course, it was not quite that simple. True, there was an embarrassment of technically qualified candidates; and, true, the favours on offer were extremely appealing. But there were other matters, and pressures, to consider. With the battle for heaven raging above, few were in any doubt that the future of the Party was also at stake: Left or Right? With the glittering train racing full speed ahead to a socialist future which now included the creation of a missed capitalist past, not everyone could tell the difference anymore. But across the years of Hu Jintao's leadership, it had also become increasingly clear that the fuzziness of the past might not be able to continue into the future.

The importance of the question was felt well beyond the Communist Party. As the business of business, private and state-owned, had come to depend on the Party, it was not only the future of the Party that was at stake but everybody's economy as well. Indeed, while Xi Jinping and Bo Xilai had been battling it out for the top job, businesses across the country, including those investing from abroad, had been reaching deep into their pockets to entice the princelings and other well-connected Party spirits to join their corporate ranks. With the positions of the princelings and the well-connected Party spirits dependent on the politics of the Party, there was barely a business in the land that did not have some kind of stake in the game. If the Party lurched towards Bo Xilai and his Maoist left, while Bo and his family might reap a giant harvest, would the wider princelings and well-connected Party spirits still be able to hold their value, or would some sort of avenging 'Cultural Revolution' be unleashed to show everyone that Bo was in charge? What if the Party veered towards Xi Jinping? Would he be able to hold the levers of the glittering train steady or would he tilt them to one side? With so little known about the personal opinions of a man who had always upheld the highest Party etiquette of secrecy, who could know which way he would go if he tilted: Left or Right? And whichever way he went, what sort of a reckoning might follow? To this, some replied that change would have to come at some point or another – and if blood were not to be spilt on the streets, the sooner it came, the better.

Others pointed to the diamond-studded skeletons in everybody's closets and said that change of any kind was the last thing anybody needed. What if Xi Jinping tried to hold the tiller steady but Bo Xilai decided to throw a monkey king's temper tantrum and unleash the disgruntled 'sing red' populace to tip everything upside down? Those who remembered the Cultural Revolution, shuddered.

———

Braced for the usual rollercoaster of a dragon year, few, however, were prepared for the rocket that February 2012 would explode in the fiefdom of Chongqing. Xi Jinping seemed to be best prepared for the pole star position, but with red hearts loudly singing Maoist choruses, some were expecting Bo Xilai to make a last minute cloud-leaping sprint for some kind of Party pinnacle. Others, well ahead on the *weiqi* board, wondered whether the whole game might not change completely if Bo got his way. Impatient eyes turned to the advancing March meeting of the National People's Congress. This was not the formidable heavenly eighteenth Congress of the Party which would, as always, follow in late autumn, but the annual spring grandstand of three thousand carefully (s)elected delegates, which the flamboyant Bo might well try to turn to some Monkey King advantage.

Chinese New Year banquets only just digested, Party mouths dropped in shock when, on 6 February, the internet flashed out a story which even the Jade Emperor might have found difficult to believe. Fleeing from the Chongqing court of his master, Bo Xilai's Dalian policeman had apparently appeared at the guarded gates of the American consulate in nearby Chengdu begging for protection, hotly pursued by a squad of armoured vehicles with official Chongqing registration plates. Bo Xilai's offices made a quiet announcement to the effect that every valued employee needs a 'vacation-style therapy'. Meanwhile, the internet followed up with yet another explosive story: after a brief spell of American hospitality, the Dalian policeman had been returned to the Chinese world and was being escorted to the Beijing capital by Party powers – in the security of a commercial airline, for fear that Bo Xilai's dark Chongqing forces might shoot down any private plane.

As the masses struggled to keep up with the pace of the story, Bo Xilai quietly boarded a flight of his own, and paid a personal visit to the 14th Group Army, based in the Yunnan capital of Kunming and the unit whose earliest roots had been nurtured by his father at the time of the Long March. 'Cherish the memory of the revolutionary ancestors', he was said to have remarked. A few weeks later, a flurry of Chinese whispers tickled the sharper ears of the country at large, murmuring that the army had contemplated a coup.

Curiouser and curiouser. Minds now turned with even greater excitement to the looming date of the National People's Congress. Although technically the highest power in the land, no one was under any delusion that its rubber-stamping delegates would be dealing with any of the important matters of Party succession. But after the events of the previous few weeks, hopes were high that Bo Xilai might make a pulse-raising appearance; and many wondered whether Hu Jintao might take the opportunity to pass a judgement.

For two weeks, the delegates shuffled dutifully in and out of the Great Hall of the People: work reports were chanted, duty-bound votes were counted; and no one said anything so interesting that microphone communications needed to be cut. There was a moment of excitement when Bo Xilai met the Press to explain that even heavenly heroes could not always be sure that their friends could be trusted – and went on to call for an assault on the capitalist devils who had captured the high ground. Then, just as the short grandstand seemed to be over, Wen Jiabao, the outgoing premier, popped his head above the parapet and unleashed a quiet observation that stopped almost everyone in their tracks. 'China is facing unprecedented problems', Wen noted. 'And unless deep and widespread change takes place within the Party, the Cultural Revolution could easily happen all over again.'

The following day, Bo Xilai was dismissed as Party secretary of Chongqing. A month later, he was suspended from the Politburo. But long before that, he had disappeared, and would not appear again until well into the following Year of the Snake. By which time his wife would have astonishingly confessed to the murder of an unknown foreign-devil businessman who had become a family friend, and Bo himself would have been charged with a dazzling display of corrupting crimes.

Back at the frontline of the Party's succession, as spring turned to summer, the myriad of interlocking races for the heavenly positions moved into their final laps. Long-distance runners worked overtime to make sure that promised positions stayed on track. Outliers who faced the bitter prospect of being an 'also-ran' pulled on every favour-fuelled lever in reach. Godfathers were kicked into overtime, fathers and grandfathers were told to dig deeper into the webs of their relationships; in desperate cases, they were instructed to wake up the near-dead, if that was what it would take. As hopeful candidates put the final touches to long campaigns, the provinces began to arrive in Beijing. Hotels were stuffed to the gunnels, and patient officials in the Organisation Department waited for the prices of their favours to go up. Gifts rose to the skies: from fortunes of apartments at the higher levels, to overseas school fees, must-have watches, and vacations in the lower ranks. Promises flowed like fountains, and even the smallest of favours, embellished and amplified to keep up with the times, were dredged up from the past. And in every corner of the capital, the personal assistants to everyone-who-wanted-to-be-anyone were keeping minute-by-minute mobile tallies of where their own particular player was standing, and whether or not any other horse had somehow managed to storm ahead.

With all eyes on the race, summer arrived. Bo Xilai's wife suddenly appeared in a court, calmly admitting to a cold-blooded cyanide poisoning – even though a quietly spoken forensic expert had dared to make an off-the-record observation that the evidence did not fit. A death sentence, suspended for life, was gratefully accepted by the penitent confessor. Once again, China's internet ignited with speculation. Most of the posts were of the opinion that if the Party ever presented something as fact, it could be reliably assumed to be untrue. Some suggested that the softly spoken woman who had made the court appearance was nothing but a body-double. Conspicuous in his absence, Bo Xilai was assumed to be in the bowels of the Party's prisons, while the Party's tigers were battling over what to do.

Up in the inner sanctum of Zhongnanhai, however, with nothing short of the heavenly future of everything at stake, everyone's tempers were exploding. What had started as a fundamentally family affair, had now managed to mix up the next generation of Party leadership with the perilous question of what kind of a Party it was. Given that Xi Jinping and Bo Xilai were princelings, neither the question of the succession nor the matter of the madness in Chongqing could be separated from the Party's battles of the past. And the Party's battles of the

past could not be settled without slandering someone else's parents
– and bringing in all of the politics of power. In the light of the treacherous shoals of Party history, was Bo Xilai a hero, a traitor or a victim
of a Cultural Revolution that had torn up everyone's sense of right
and wrong? If Bo was indeed a traitor, could the Party really sacrifice
the son of a man who was one of its 'eight immortals' – and what,
given the popularity of his 'sing red' campaign, would happen if it did?
Underneath these family dramas, sat the question that had haunted the
Party since Tiananmen, and arguably since the caves of Yan'an: what
kind of a Party should it be? After the travails of the last thirty years,
was it really practical to assert that the Party was the guarantor of a
Democratic Dictatorship of the People? And if it was not, could the
Party ever become accountable to the people without bringing heaven
crashing down on earth? Of course, these were questions for cosmic
time, rather than the season of a Party congress. But, just like the
Monkey King, Bo Xilai had wreaked havoc in heaven and now even
cosmic time was running out.

As the opinions battled back and forth, it was clear that it had
become impossible to separate the Party from its battling families.
With every opinion came a memory, and with every memory came
a flash of the Party's savage past: backs stabbed for a quick advantage, innocent children sacrificed like lambs, blacker sheep protected
with lies. Power-grabbing wrongs had been buried to keep the truth
from rising, feuds had been fuelled from generation to generation; and
almost every friendship, sooner or later, had been betrayed for somebody's gain. Everybody had a family tree of friends and foes inked deep
into their hearts. As the claims and counter-claims were hurled across
Zhongnanhai's courtyards, few could fail to notice the indelible legacy
of the bigger past: Mao's blood red betrayals, the sacrifices of the questioning intellectuals, the buried bodies of the Great Leap Forward, the
assassinations of the Cultural Revolution, the betrayal of Tiananmen
and the bonfire of state-ownership that had been followed by the phoe-
nix-like rise of the Party leaders' wealth. As each troubling trough of
the Party's past was once again revealed to be just a matter of someone's private store of family secrets, Hu Jintao and the other Party
members who had risen through the ranks outside the Zhongnanhai
family ring could only watch as bystanders. They had plenty of time to
reflect upon the fact that Deng Xiaoping had warned everyone to keep

the princelings in a box. Jiang Zemin had disobeyed him. And now they were all paying the price.

Time turned. High summer dimmed and autumn began to whisper in the wind. Within the portals of Zhongnanhai, the battles continued to blaze. Outside, the lights of the internet struggled to keep up. By the end of September, though, a fragile truce seemed to have broken out and Zhongnanhai opened its gates to make an announcement: Bo Xilai had been expelled from the Party. Returning to battle out the finer details of the families' fires, the internet was left to its own devices, and the restaurants kept on chattering. Few days passed without some rumour or other of a lost temper – and when Xi Jinping disappeared from his vice-presidential functions for a couple of weeks, some began to fear for more than just his health. By November, however, when the Great Hall of the People opened its doors to the Eighteenth Party Congress, the heavenly battles seemed to have all been settled: well, perhaps not settled, but at least momentarily set aside. Xi Jinping was finally clapped to the clouds.

Anointed as general secretary of the Party, chairman of the Central Military Commission and president of the People's Republic of China (in that order of importance), Xi Jinping was nothing if not prepared. Head of the Central Party School for the past five years, it had long been clear to him that there was a backlog of heavenly questions about every kind of order to be addressed – from the order of the people, to the order of nature, to the disorder of the rest of the world. At the same time, it was clear to others that, after such a long time at the head of the Party School, Xi was in a strong position to address the questions, although what he would be able to do with the feuding Party family was still anybody's guess.

Successor to a Communist School that had been created as a substitute for the Moscow original, the Central Party School was an institution that had been forged in the caves of Yan'an. Ding Ling had been one of its many early students, taught by Liu Shaoqi, the then-rising star whose 1930s thoughts on the importance of Communist self-cultivation (*How to be a Good Communist*) had become one of the Party's classical texts. While the idea of a Party school might have come from the Russian big brother, however, the idea of a Party bureaucracy that prided itself on scholarly credentials had been grounded in the Chinese lands since the time of the Duke of Zhou and his Hall of Light. As Confucius himself had once observed: 'Thinking without studying is a dangerous occupation'. Education was everything. How could anyone be Chinese without it?

As revolution had turned to power, the Central Party School, with its rapidly expanding branches and members, had become the pivot of the Party's future – training millions of new recruits for a Communist Party which had come to rule from nowhere. With every single position of power, central and local, under their command, Party membership had leapt by millions in the first ten years of its rule. By the time Deng Xiaoping had taken the helm, it had reached sixty million. And although enthusiasm had waned a little across the 1980s and 1990s, when the Party had opened itself up to privately enterprising members in 2001, the number had leapt forward again: more than eighty million members by the time Xi Jinping arrived at the Party School in 2008 – all needing to be trained.

With branches spread across the country, the Party School had a formidable reach. And with every branch not only teaching the essential theories of Communism with Chinese characteristics but also giving lessons in both the practical skills and the knowledge of current affairs required for rule, it had a formidable understanding of what its members needed to learn. For the very highest Party members, and faithful to its scholarly tradition, the Central Party School in Beijing gathered together the greatest minds from home and abroad to stretch everyone's ideas. Refreshing courses were offered on the latest developments in Marxism-Leninism and Mao Zedong Thought, together with updating programs on current world affairs, and a constant exploration of both the essential challenges facing the Party itself, and the comparative qualities of political parties around the world – particularly those which kept the most successful parties in power. Compulsory courses included investigations into how to make sure that the Party was always the greatest interpreter of the classical Communist texts, including the newer classics of Deng Xiaoping Theory, Jiang Zemin's Three Represents and Hu Jintao's Scientific Development. But the most important course of all, a course that was not only compulsory but one that no Party power would ever want to miss, was the one which explored the questions that had occupied the minds of every ruler since the beginning of China's imperial time: how does a Son of Heaven maintain the order of heaven and earth? And while the Son of Heaven is working out the answer to that cosmic question, how can he keep the foreign barbarians at bay?

When the wealth of the Western capitalist world had gone up in smoke in the late summer of 2008 (just as the Olympic fireworks exploded above Beijing), the first of these two questions had been at the forefront of leading Party minds – with suggested answers splashed across almost all of the Party school's curricula. The Olympic applause of visiting Western titans (soon to be paupers) had been reassuring music to Zhongnanhai's ears – a long-awaited recognition of the value of the Party's wisdom. But as 2008 had turned into 2009, it had also become clear to everyone in the Party School (and pretty much everyone else in China) that the rapid rise in Chinese fortunes had become a rollercoaster of a ride, with everyone rattling in their seats. As He Qinglian (the historian-economist now in the US) had pointed out, those in the lowest classes were having the toughest time – so tough that some of them had been thrown off the train. And while there were certainly more people now sitting on the softer seats and in first class, the problem was that most of them were either members of the Party or people who, whether as relatives or friends, had managed to find their way into a Party pocket or two. Meanwhile, the natural landscape through which the train was passing seemed to be rebelling, even as everyone was losing their tempers; not to mention the selfish separatists at the edges of order who were insisting on their bombs. Of course, the Party had realized that unless and until the minds of the people reached the necessary *gao suzhi*, high quality, thinking, protests were to be expected, with any resolution of the problems certainly taking all of the hundred additional years of revolution that Deng had explained would be required. In the interim, however, the problems would have to be managed – and managed in a twenty-first century state, where the control of communications had been undermined by the availability of the internet to anyone with a mobile phone. Fortunately, the Patriotic Education Campaign was now well underway: explaining to everyone that without the Party there would not only not be any *Xinhua*, New China, but there would also not have been any 'China' at all. But there were always those stubborn low quality spirits who just refused to learn. Maintaining the order of China was not getting any easier.

The heart of the problem was really the old question of whether heaven was a single-top down ordering mind or some muddled up idea of reflecting the people. The latter had been most recently expressed in that Fifth Modernisation (the voices of the people) that the electrician Wei Jingsheng had plastered on the 1978 Democracy Wall. Not content with advanced industry, science and technology, agriculture and national defence, everyone had to be able to have their say as well – all 1.4 billion of them. Of course, Wei Jingsheng was long gone: eighteen years in jail, then off to America, far out of anyone's Chinese sight and increasingly out of their minds. But as the Party had produced economic miracle after miracle, other inconvenient voices seemed to have leapt, one after another, into Wei Jingsheng's stead. Waving the most simplistic interpretations of Marx like magic talismans, these voices were not only protesting but suggesting that even a hundred years of Party-driven socialism would not lead the people to a Taiping world of a great and comforting peace. Some had even taken to twittering that it was time for the Communist Party to open up its mandate of heaven to the chaos of a competition for all. After everything the Party had done for everyone, the ingratitude beggared belief.

Looking at the scale and complexity of the challenge, Xi Jinping turned the Central Party School into a glittering Hall of Light. Gathering his scholars together, they were instructed to scour heaven and earth for any and every idea that might help. Digging deep into the past, they investigated everything. Advancing through the history books, they found themselves in the reassuring presence of ancient minds which had argued with astonishing perspicacity both that the legitimacy of a ruler's power depended on everybody's satisfaction but that the people themselves were very unlikely to be the best judges of how they might be satisfied. That things are unequal had been acknowledged as a matter of fact for the last two thousand years – as had the sad fact that, while the highest quality minds can understand the complexities, one cannot do much about the level of understanding of those below. For this, there was no alternative but for a ruler to accept that his responsibility was to *rule*.

Wading on through the history books, the apocalyptic nightmare of the decline of the Zhou into the battles of the warring states leapt out at them – a tale, if ever there was one, for a world where the bright star of America was dimming fast. Fortunately, that terrible time had been followed by the triumph of the First Qin Emperor who had unified everything. Helpfully, the scholars who had shaped his thinking had also left behind their precepts, from which everyone could learn. 'Loving mothers are the ruin of their children', was the most obvious one. 'Swords are sharpened on whetstones', was another. There was also the one that helpfully explained that 'wood is straightened with a tight rope, and turned into a wheel by aligning it with a compass'. And then there was the wise observation that 'a household with clear rules and punishments runs as smoothly as water'. Contemplating the clockwork efficiency of the Qin realm, it was clear why Mao had been so devoted to the memory of the First Qin Emperor: castigated by lily-livered scholars across the ages, he was a man who had been much misunderstood. 'Those who rule are supported by those who are ruled; all that matters is that the ruler is fit for the task.' Such an obvious and simple proposition – but one those lower quality minds had always found so difficult to understand. The task of a ruler is hard indeed.

Turning then to the second question of 'how to keep the foreign barbarians at bay' Xi Jinping and his Party School scholars found some surprising wisdom in the Western world of thought – although being barbarians, it seemed that the foreigners were incapable of under-standing and acting upon their own good ideas. There was the Greek idea that only qualified men should have a voice: clearly a world that had understood the importance of high quality people. Then there was that nineteenth-century perception – so familiar to everyone in China – that the world was engaged in a bitter struggle for the survival of the fittest. But, having failed to follow Confucius' model of *zhi* knowl-edge, and being infants in the art of order, the foreigners had not only been unable to learn from their own past but incapable of even remem-bering it. They had also, as Liang Qichao had so astutely observed after the First World War, seized on science with such alacrity that they had ended up abandoning philosophy and morality for wholesale materialism.

The problem for China was that in their ignorance, the foreigners were getting the people in the heavenly lands confused as well. Instead of concentrating on the *qualities* of the ruler, they had tangled them-selves, and everyone else, up in questions about *who got to choose* the ruler. And with more than their own fair share of low quality minds (what do you expect if you don't give education a truly Confucian respect?) they had clucked around like a bunch of women in skirts, fussing about the importance of 'one man, one vote'. No consideration at all had been given to either the quality of the individual voting or to the fact that unless everyone is equal to start off with, the poorest voices inevitably get bought up by the rich. What had they ended up with? A gaggle of rulers currying favour with claptrap, and democracies of voters who could not tell chalk from cheese. No wonder the West had got itself, and so much of the rest of the world, into such a mess.

Investigating everything, Xi Jinping then directed Party School attention to the question of Russia's Soviet Union and the lessons that Deng had urged everyone to learn. Lenin had given his comrades a model of ordering discipline, complete with the necessary understanding of the critical importance of unity, on which all order rests. With the chaos of imperial capitalism all around, it was Lenin who had hit upon the idea of an advanced guard of Party members to get the revolutionary show on the road. And it was Lenin who had understood that democracy was a treacherous shoal, with more than one false meaning. There was only one democracy which would save the world, and that was the Democratic Dictatorship of the People: 'democratic centralism', for short. Once a revolution had been carried out and a new order battled into power (the democratic part), decisions should be made by whoever had won the revolution (the centralism). Let the people's voices sing as much as they liked, but one had to put them in a hierarchy of order, and make sure that they were guided at every step of the way. Those at the bottom could elect local representatives to sing for them at a higher level – as long as those local representatives had been properly pre-qualified by the ruler. Those so pre-qualified and (s)elected could go on to elect representatives to sing for them at the next level up – as long as they were only choosing from those who had also already been pre qualified and (s)elected. Proceeding on up the hierarchy, by the time one got to the central top, there would be a manageably small number of representatives who would also be sufficiently well-educated to see that only a Son of Heaven who has carefully studied everything can be in any position to rule. As Lenin himself put it: 'You can have as much voice as you like, as long as you don't disturb the unity required for definite action'.

Russia, of course, had collapsed. Or rather, the Soviet Union had collapsed, and in letting that happen the Russians had also lost their Communist Party. It was as clear to Xi as it had been to Deng that the reasons for, and consequences of, the Russian Party's failures were probably the most helpful of all the lessons for China to learn. Without a deeply rooted appreciation of the importance of investigating things, once Lenin had gone it had probably just been a matter of time before the Russian brothers tripped and fell. If they had just kept the faith with Lenin's architecture of order, and listened to their more educated Chinese brothers, they might have been able to keep their Party going. But that amateur Gorbachev had been seduced by the bright lights of America and its cacophony of opinionated voices. In 1991, when the Soviet Union and its Communist Party had both been cancelled, and before anyone could say *glasnost*, the Soviet satellite states – as many of them in China's backyard as in that of the Russian West – had rushed off to an impatient independence, leaving China to deal with a host of rebellious Central Asian dreams in the neighbouring province of Xinjiang.

With the vast territories of the Soviet Union floating away like clouds, up in Moscow, Russia's waiting-in-the-wings capitalists, the oligarchs, had then not only occupied the state's assets but stuffed them into their own private banks. Meanwhile, the dreaming Gorbachev had been replaced with the drunkard Yeltsin who, predictably, had soon begun to fall off his drunken stage. Presenting Putin as a puppet had been a rather astute step by the oligarchs: with his KGB discipline, he had certainly had the best chance of digging in his heels and stemming the rot. But it had all been far too late. Even Putin couldn't conjure up the towering majesty of a Leninist Party on his own: it would take another revolution for that. Russia had found itself in the same position as China in the time before the Zhuanxu Emperor, over four thousand years ago, with the people allowed to think whatever they wanted, and to shout it even louder. Talk about cutting yourself off at the knees. Vodka at the ready, a twentieth-century nuclear power and master of one of the world's biggest piles of arms, the country had been reduced to a drunken fighting spirit (no doubt the influence of the Mongols who had occupied them for so long). The nuclear weapons and the arms were a worry: admittedly increasingly rusty but far too close to Xinjiang and Mongolia to be of any comfort. And, with such cracks in the stately order, there was clearly going to be a need for some careful Chinese footwork in Central Asia and neighbouring India, not to mention some careful management of the tricky Japanese whose islands flanked the Siberian coast of the Russian Far East.

But the truly salutary tale for the Party School to teach was that, with no understanding of the need for learning, the Russians had managed to lose both their Party and their empire – and in so doing, they had put any *suzhi*, quality, of their people into reverse as well.

As Xi Jinping and the Party School looked back across the stories, the lessons were clear. That order and unity were everything had been proven as much from the recent collapse of Russia as from the ancient triumph of the Qin state. 'Democracy', as 'one man, one vote', was simply the irresponsible hallmark of the uneducated and uncivilised barbarian. But, how to get the stubborn internet voices that the Westerners had unleashed, to understand?

On these thorny questions, though, the Western barbarians seemed, once again, to have come up with some useful ideas. Digging deep into the American past, Party School's scholars came across the observations of Thomas Jefferson and his later successor Andrew Jackson. Jefferson had noted that any democracy would need a reasonably intelligent public that could keep itself informed. Jackson had then followed up with a warning that, in a world of rising corporations, everyone would end up a slave unless someone found a way to keep minds free – to which end, America had decided to give its investigating journalists the power to ask any questions they liked. By the 1920s, with the journalists' reckless questions wreaking havoc in all directions, stronger American spirits had realised that the public mind was going to have to be managed if their 'civilisation' was going to survive. Attention had then shifted to the importance of protecting the people and the state from the irresponsibility of untamed opinions. Soon after that, the European barbarians had, once again, tangled themselves up in a world of war – and, in the process, stumbled upon the useful lessons that propaganda could be as powerful as a military weapon, and that advertising might be one of the most powerful tools of all.

Looking deeper into the history, Xi and the Party School found that it had been the German Nazis who had first grasped the possibilities of propaganda. But the British and their American allies had not been slow to catch up. Realising that difficult times required backbone, they had recognised the need to help low quality human minds come to grips with facts that they might not otherwise understand. Fear had been grasped as the most powerful tool: whenever an important point of principle seemed to be at risk of getting lost, pure animal anxiety was spread among the people. And wherever there were individuals or countries who were obviously enemies but the people had not yet understood their threat, rabid names had been launched at them like rockets to emphasise the risk. At the end of the war, being well ahead in their science, and with advertising cheaper than violence or bribery, the American government and its corporations then raised an armoury of technological tools designed to make sure that the minds of the public stayed in order. To which, the wisdom of a new science of psychology was added, offering new opportunities to get deep inside the people's heads. As the science of the mind advanced, the electronic pulses of television and radio were switched on to amplify the effect. It turned out that even the internet had not been a problem – or if it had, the West had quickly overcome it. At the turn of the twenty-first century, with Britain lagging in so many other scientific ways, its Prime Minister Blair had worked out how to apply the sum of the new scientific know-how to propel a New Labour party to power; keen like all foreigners to crow about his discoveries, he had been more than happy to share the knowledge with the Central Party School. Invited to listen, the Party's Propaganda Department had been very keen to learn.

Charged with teaching the highest leaders in the land, Xi Jinping had gathered plenty of knowledge about the present and the past. With China's star now shining so brightly, he had also had the opportunity to explore various ideas with some very powerful minds. The all-important first question of 'how to maintain the order of heaven and earth' had been particularly carefully looked at (behind closed doors of course) in terms of how to keep the Party in power. Studies of almost every success and failure – across time and around the world – had been delivered, and then pushed and prodded until every ounce of learning had been extracted. All of it had been tested with the help of visiting Westerners whose lecturing ideas could ensure that China remained the fittest survivor of them all. Which had, of course, provided the key to the second question, of 'how to keep the foreign barbarians at bay'. With every study of the Western ideas done, and every lecture learnt, the fundamental wisdom of Deng Xiaoping had been proven, not only on how to maintain the order of heaven and earth through the principle of a highly disciplined Party power through order and unity, but also on dealing with the barbarians.

Ai guo, love the country, was what it was all about. Or rather, as Deng Xiaoping had understood so well, it was really *ai dang*, love the Party, first. After sixty years of the Party having built a Xinhua, New China, and thirty years of a Patriotic Education Campaign, the two were, quite rightly, becoming impossible to tell apart. Of course, that was not always obvious to everyone, particularly with those pesky Westerners constantly banging on about freedom and independence: as if such recklessness could ever be truly real, or even possible. It had not been easy. After the Tiananmen 'incident', the Party's Propaganda Department had had to work hard to get the people to understand that, without the Party, everyone would have been back in the opium dens of imperial Hankou. But with Deng firmly at the helm, the minds of the Party's members had been swept root and branch for even the smallest sign of a failing heart; interrogations had been conducted and, naturally, the Party School had stepped forward with a training programme for all.

It had been the mantras of the Patriotic Education Campaign (the triumph of the Party over the humiliations of the past) that had slowly guided the people to an understanding of the fact that it was the pillar of Party patriotism that really defined what it meant to 'be Chinese'. Plastered in every possible place of learning and knowledge, stories and images of the Party's sacrifices had also been splashed across every possible site: from schools and universities, to museums and parks, not to mention television and radio stations, newspapers, public broadcasts, billboards and even films. History books had been rewritten to tell the tale more clearly, and new museums had been raised to make sure that the widest possible public could see and understand.

Some thought the campaign had gone into overdrive, but given the challenges of the last few years, it was becoming clear that it had not gone far enough. 'A hundred years of humiliation' at the hands of barbarians had been overturned in fifty years of Communist Party rule – what an astonishing achievement. But after thirty years of rising fortunes, there were a number of selfish people who had taken the sacrifices of the Party's revolutionary heroes for granted, or worse. Without the Party there would have been no new China: it could not be repeated enough. 'Get it into their heads, get it into their ears, get it into their hearts', the leader of the Propaganda Department had pounded. And he had been quite right. Anyone could come up with bad news; and with a Party of eighty million official adherents, any fool could come up with a member who looked like a monkey. But the real challenge, as every Great Man ruler across the past five thousand years of Chinese history had shown, was to live up to the responsibilities which heaven had sent. Rule; and in your ruling, concentrate everyone's minds on the positive possibilities of everything.

Which brought one back to the question of the foreigners: a problem which, as China's fortunes had risen so far and so fast, had only got worse. Of course, as the New China had risen, the Western barbarians had intensified their war of Peaceful Evolution – that conspiracy of words with which a 1950s America had imagined that China could be seduced out of her revolutionary conviction. After 2008, with the once-glittering palaces of the West dimming, it had become a little more difficult for the barbarians to persuade the Chinese people that the West was a better world. But, never content to keep to their own channels, the Westerners had crept ever closer to the East, encouraging every state in the Asian neighbourhood to forget the lessons of the past hundred years. Not, of course, that the tricky Japanese had needed much persuading.

Deng Xiaoping had been right that China and the Party should bide their time: let China first quietly rise. But as Xi Jinping looked at the landscape, it was clear that the facts had changed. China's light had been hidden for so long that the Westerners had not only forgotten their barbarian nature – they had also forgotten their proper place. It was time for the West. and the rest of the world, to get an education. And if they were not capable of educating themselves, it was obviously going to have to be the next Party Son of Heaven who would have to do it for them. Geography and history would be good places to start. After hundreds of years of sailing around the planet, armed only with their own misguided maps and without a history book of the real world to rub between them, the Western adventurers had completely failed to understand not just the facts on the ground but

the very principles of heaven on which everything was based. Poor old
Lin Zexu, that nineteenth-century Confucian who had tried so hard to
get the opium peddlers to see the errors of their ways. He had certainly
tried to explain the principles of heaven to the barbarians, but, to quote
Confucius, he might as well have been 'playing the zither to an ox'. One
spreading sky, ruled by a single Son of Heaven, and guided by the pole
star idea of *ren* benevolence and humanity (putting oneself in other
people's shoes): how hard was that to understand?

But the foreigners had insisted on their idea of sovereign states –
and stuffed it in their steamboats, gunning up the eastern coast fuelled
by their own self-righteous rage. As, indeed, they had insisted on the
old chestnuts of sovereign self-interest and invisible hands – shot
straight from the barrel of Adam Smith's British mouth. Once they
had dumped their ideas on Chinese lands, it had not been long before
the foreign rot had set in. Treaty ports had been snatched up and down
the nineteeth-century coast, as if heaven had never existed; Hong
Kong and Macau had been pocketed; and the edges of Qing-protected
Tibet had been snatched away, as if they were nothing but clouds. The
northern lands had been traded under the far-off tables of early twentieth-century Versailles. And then, after the Second World War the map
of Asia had been redrawn with far-off America becoming everyone's
patron state. Of course, when one understood what Charles Darwin
and Herbert Spencer had written, it was all crystal clear: the 'sovereign state' and the 'invisible hand' were not principles but weapons in
a battle for the survival of the fittest people on earth. Mao had seen
them for what they were – barbarian imperialist ideas – and packed
them off, back to their own borders. But when Deng had opened the
door to their science and technology, the West had simply relaunched
them, whispering Peaceful Evolution as if the celestial kingdom were
just a historical aberration in need of a change.

And then, of course, one had to remember the Japanese. After a
hundred and fifty years of imperial dreaming, it was about time they
too began to read a few more history books – and take a closer look
at the geography as well. The history was certainly clear: a heavenly
navy wiped out in 1895; Taiwan pocketed like a stone in a game of
weiqi; a battle with Russia, in northern China, over who was going
to own which bits of the northern heartlands; a dastardly deal with
a two-timing Republican politician to appropriate Germany's stolen

Chinese lands; the raising of a puppet state of Manchuria; and then a full-scale assault launched across the country, north and south. (True, Mao had thanked them for distracting Chiang Kai-shek in the 1930s and clearing the northern fields for the eventual Communist victory; but everyone knew that Mao had always had his Monkeyish side.) Even after a Second World War in which they had been proven to be patently wrong, they had continued to look at the islands of the South and East China Seas as if they were their own. Looking at the geographic facts, Japan was nothing but an upstart archipelago which, two thousand years ago, the Qin emperor had mistakenly imagined to be the Penglai home of the immortals (well, we all make our mistakes). In reality, they were nothing more than a bunch of orphans – a flotsam and jetsam of a people who had probably first been born in the Yellow Emperor's lands and then, floating off on the waves, had not only forgotten their history, but their manners as well.

Deng Xiaoping had, indeed, been wise to counsel the Party to hide its martial light under a bushel and bide its time. It was just the kind of advice that the Crouching Dragon, Zhuge Liang, would have given – a man whose instinct for the less visible tracks of the *dao* had been faultless. But China's rise had been faster than Deng could have predicted, and the foreigners' fall had been faster and more spectacular than anyone could ever have dreamt. The facts had changed, and the foreigners had got trickier. That war of Peaceful Evolution had been carried on as if butter wouldn't melt in their mouths: the internet and its so-called 'freedoms'; free speech, as if anything ever came without a price; 'non-governmental' organisations, as if anything could exist without the will of the state; all flooded with reckless voices, complete with piles of free Western cash. Irresponsibly carping Chinese intellectuals had been welcomed to their foreign capitals for feasts; the Dalai Lama – the greatest traitor of them all – had even been invited to express his opinions on Tibetan lands that were not only clearly part of China's unity, but essential to the security of all. Even the obvious terrorist Rebiyah Kadeer had been offered safe harbour in America. From Fang Lizhi, the Big Bang physicist, to Wei Jingsheng and his Fifth Modernisation, not to mention countless other subversive enemies of the state, America had welcomed them all. Did these barbarians have no shame? Deng Xiaoping's wisdom had been right for the conditions of his day, but now it was time for everyone to face facts and name names. Near or far, the barbarians needed to decide where they stood in the world – on the side of a heavenly order, or against? It was a pretty simple question: no room for sitting on the fence.

After five years at the helm of the Central Party's School, and decades of his own diligent observations on the ground, when Xi Jinping finally reached the top of the Party, his thoughts on affairs at home and abroad, were as clear as crystal to those who read the Party texts. With the quiet confidence of a prince who had trained himself to be both a guerrilla and a sage, he had planned every step of his new power with care. And having studied the past and consulted the present, he was clear, like every Great Man ruler before him since the Duke of Zhou, that the best way for the people to learn was to watch, or better still, take part in, a choreographed performance of words and movements, a ritual, that everyone could follow, and remember.

Flanked by his six highest Politburo peers, in November 2012, Xi Jinping demonstrated the principles of unity and *ai guo* patriotism in an appearance at the country's National Museum. Illustrating the points for even the lowest quality minds, colourful images showed him inspecting an exhibition which traced the ups and downs of the more turbulent recent past – from the floating boxes of opium in the 1840s, through the revolutionary sacrifices of the Party's heroes, to the triumphs of the present day.

At the end of the visit, and rather unusually for Chinese leaders accustomed to a more invisible pursuit of the *dao* way, he paused to share a dream. 'With so much already achieved by the Party', observed Xi, 'it is now time for the Chinese nation to stand tall.' The dream declared, in the first week of December, he went on to Shenzhen, to stand before a statue of Deng Xiaoping that celebrated the aged warrior's southern vacation – the vacation which had set off a revolution all of its own. By the end of the year, Xi had stood up and declared his dream in the army strongholds of all seven of China's military regions to an audience of the two million soldiers of the People's Liberation Army, the PLA, who were also part of the choreographed cast.

Message clear to those at home – and as clear as he could possibly make it to those abroad – by the start of the 2013 new year, Xi Jinping was beginning to light a few necessary fires, starting with a campaign against the tigers and flies of corruption. Bearing in mind the acrobatics of Bo Xilai, it seemed appropriate to conduct himself in the popular homespun image of Mao. At the front of the house, flowers were stood down and bottles of *mou tai*, every official's favourite white spirit, were dismissed. Behind the scenes, the Party's Central Commission for Discipline Inspection was set off on a silent hunt for piles of hidden cash. Having sharply observed that corruption was the greatest threat to the survival of the Party and the state, it was reasonable to think that the hunted would include every tiger and fly that could be found. But with so many tigers and flies at large, few were surprised when Xi seemed to concentrate on the monkeys who were causing the greatest havoc in the Party family's heaven.

The liberal values of the West, however, still had the power to confuse. Keen to emphasise the democratic credentials of the Party, in the spring of 2013 Xi pointed to the paramount importance of the People's Constitution, and to its rule of law. His words picked up by a gaggle of tricky intellectuals, he found them twisted into rumours that the freedom to ask and answer questions was now to be permitted, with a flurry of ordinary individuals also taking it upon themselves to blow whistles on errant Party officials across the land.

Clearly, the people still had a lot to learn. While any truly red heart would understand the meaning of the Party's constitutional text and its rule of law, as ever, the intellectuals were always the last to grasp any important point – just as they were always the first to shout about whatever it was they mistakenly thought they had learnt. When mentioning the constitution, one should also point, plainly, to the finer print: to the single operative sentence under which its pages were obviously to be interpreted; the one in the preamble which put everything under the unifying leadership of the Party and its mind. And when mentioning the rule of law, one should be clear that this is the 'socialist' rule of law – the one where the harmony of Party wisdom is far more important than any black and white rules. Realising that there was a lot more work to be done if the intellectuals in particular were to understand the true meaning of order, Xi decided to spell it all out with a clarifying statement of 'seven not-to-be-mentioned things': things not to be mentioned by anyone in the public eye. Obvious to anyone who had read the Party classics, or China's history, the seven things included most of the armoury of the West's Peaceful Evolution campaign: so-called 'universal' values, freedom of speech, civil rights, judicial independence – and, naturally, any historical mistakes which the Party might accidentally have made.

In August 2013, with the script now surely plain enough for the people to follow, Bo Xilai was presented to a Shandong court, flanked by the people's guards. Accused of bribery, corruption and abuse of power, he was obviously Number One of the tigers that Xi Jinping's corruption campaign had in mind. As Bo stood in court, the Party's Propaganda Department, in no doubt about its critical role in choreographing the Party's celestial constellation, furnished the covering journalists with sufficient tales of jets and lavish lifestyles to kill any rising Maoist sun. Some, reading the stories, were as shocked as the Party wanted them to be. But while the Propaganda Department had done its best, it had not been quite enough: many of the readers saw the stories as confirmation that everyone in the Party was awash with the ill-gotten riches of power.

Out on the wider streets, however, there was an even bigger challenge. Devoted to the Monkey King who had lit up their lives with the promise of some truly revolutionary change, those who had sung Bo's revolutionary chorus so faithfully when he had been in the seat of Chongqing power were now taking up their song sheets and singing again. On that point, though, the Propaganda Department was better prepared. Laptops at the ready, and with the handy tool of fear to hand, the Party's papers spread a host of editorials asking the people if they *really* wanted the ravages of the Cultural Revolution to return? At the end of it all, after five days of listening to a pack of Bo Xilai's lies, the socialist court of law discharged its duty, and (as instructed) declared Bo Xilai to be guilty of the bribery, corruption and abuse of power with which had been charged. Sentenced to life imprisonment in Beijing's elite Qincheng jail, if Xi Jinping had anything to do with it, it was unlikely that he would ever appear in public again.

With Bo Xilai despatched from the public stage, Xi could breathe a little more easily – although there were still a lot of Bo's friends and relations to deal with. If the unity of the Party was to be truly maintained, that pack of tigers would have to be painstakingly hunted to the end – with any surrounding flies firmly swatted, and probably quite a few monkeys too.

As the Party's Central Commission for Discipline Inspection spread the exercise of its terrifying powers across the land, though, it seemed that the People's Armed Police had been a little less well schooled in their own responsibility for maintaining order. At the end of October 2013, just days before the grand meeting of the Party's annual plenum in Beijing, a four by four following an everyday route of traffic across Tiananmen Square suddenly wheeled off its course; gunning its engine for the portrait of Mao Zedong, it had exploded into a ball of flames. Clear about his history and geography, from behind the vermillion walls of nearby Zhongnanhai, Xi saw the desert prints of Xinjiang's Uighurs stamped across the shocking scene.

Remembering the words of his hero Deng Xiaoping, Xi Jinping observed the situation all around him, coolly held his ground, and, sending the security forces off for better training, calmly moved on. Thinking about the struggle to improve the *suzhi* quality of the people, and the on-going battle for the survival of the fittest state, he returned his own attention to the heavenly Party and the mechanics of its power.

And then, reminding everyone of the critical importance of a heavenly order, he repeated his dream: a great Chinese nation, united at home and abroad.

CHAPTER 2
EARTH BELOW

In the book of history, it is said: heaven having produced the people in the lower earth, it appointed for them rulers and teachers.

Mencius (372 – 289 BCE)

IT WAS EARLY IN December 2011 when the coastal village of Wukan found itself cut off from heaven. Waking up one morning, the villagers looked out to see their roads to everywhere blocked by walls of bullet-resistant shields, held in place by men clad in rubber-black. Visors down, it was impossible to tell whether the faces had come from near or far: but there were so many of them that it seemed unlikely they had been mustered from the minor stables of the local Lufeng county alone.

When the villagers had first decided to fight for the land which had been stolen by a Party secretary, no one had thought much beyond some brave petitioning trips to the seats of higher government, and perhaps a banner or two. Just along the coast from the Haifeng where Peng Pai had raised his Peasant Union, they had thought that once the early memories of his band of landless peasant brothers had been revived, the superior spirits of the Party would soon stand along their side. But when the villagers had sent their representatives to Lufeng's county-town, its officials had become as scarce as snow. Warned by their county cousins, higher-up officials in the superior prefectural city of Shanwei had similarly melted away. Even petitioning letters, sent to the governing heights of Guangdong province, had failed to find an audience. And when the villagers had decided to deliver their petition by hand – printed in large letters on a six-foot board of card – Lufeng had sent its county cats to lie in wait at the entrance to the provincial government's buildings, determined to keep the mice of Wukan at bay.

After two years of playing Stability Maintenance some of the villagers had exploded in anger. But wiser heads had asked an older villager – one who had survived the pitched battles of the Cultural Revolution – for advice. Reflecting on those past years of anger and bitterness, the once-cultural-revolutionary had offered up three lessons: don't hurt anyone, don't destroy anything, and make sure you have black and white evidence to support your cause. The villagers had found their evidence: papers showing that it was not only their own Party secretary and Village Committee who had profited from the sale of the land, but renegade Party powers in Lufeng as well.

Armed with nothing but the truth, four thousand of Wukan's villagers had peacefully marched to Lufeng's county town, asking for the return of their land. The mayor had made a promise, hearts had rejoiced and the villagers had marched back home. But like the land rights that the villagers had once owned, the mayor's promise had quickly turned to dust. Resisting the temptations of violence, Wukan had followed up with a strike: fishing boats stayed in their harbour, and the market stood down for a rest. Shocked at the interruption of local productivity, the superior Shanwei prefecture had retaliated with a warning force of police, beating up every villager who could be caught and issuing a 'most wanted' list for all of the ringleading state-subverters the police had been unable to catch.

As the villagers were plastering pictures of wounded brothers on their walls, one of the arrested heroes reappeared – offered up on the slab of Lufeng county's mortuary. Bruised from head to foot, a ring of black around his neck, the county claimed he was the victim of an 'it-could-happen-to-anyone' heart attack. By the time the rubber-black battalions had cut the village off, the younger inhabitants of the village had bonded together in a Wukan Blood Youth League with which to provide a security of their own: twenty-four hour walkie-talkie protection for every villager on the 'most wanted' list, bamboo poles and steel pipes for every able-bodied resident and, most importantly of all, a secret motorbike shuttle for journalists to come and write Wukan's side of the story.

Laptops set up in a makeshift news centre, stories began to flow: of how Wukan's Village Committee had shared in the spoils of stolen land with the Party secretary; of how the Party powers of Lufeng had been part of the game; and of how not even the memories of Peng Pai and his peasant union, had been able to make a dent in the Party wall.

The internet plugged in, the plight of Wukan began to fly across the country and around the world. Days passed, food began to run low and the remaining grains of rice were counted out and passed to the poor. More days passed, and with red flags of defiance still flying, the villagers prepared to make a last stand: a desperate dash to bring back the body of their fallen hero, so that he might be allowed to float in peace to another world.

Hours before the break out, a message arrived: Guangdong's heavenly Party secretary had finally read their letters. If Wukan promised to go back to work, the villagers could set about electing their own honest men as leaders, and start on the job of getting back their land. Heaven seemed to have heard their prayers. Hope could rise again.

The dream of a more popular voice for the countryside had first revived during those 'thinking again' years in the early 1980s – the time when Deng Xiaoping had made it clear that the five winds of the communes, particularly the winds of commandism, chaotic directives and cadre privilege – needed to yield to something more productive. With peasants permitted to pursue individual incomes on farming patches of household responsibility, it had seemed only sensible to recognise that, however the city chose to see the facts, most of China lived in one of its now nine hundred thousand villages.

With a sharp eye to government order, Beijing had looked at its maps and consulted the geometry of rule: one heavenly centre, thirty-one provinces reporting to the centre, three thousand counties reporting to the provinces, and all of the villages under the official care of a county. Looking at the gap between the counties and the villages, it had been decided that a new layer of 'townships' would be inserted: designed to absorb the energies of the now-redundant commune leaders, redirecting them away from mass production and more towards a general management of everything, with a regular report up to the counties above. The villages themselves would also be re-organised: no longer the messy hamlets of 'natural' villages which had sprouted like tumbleweed over the millennia, but 'administrative' villages which could gather the hamlets of the older villages into something a bit bigger and easier to order.

With the map of order a little clearer, attention had then turned to the knottier roots of decision-making and action on the ground. Under the old communes and production brigades, questions about which crops should be planted, and where and when, had been decided by the Party, on behalf of the people. The peasants, of course, had had a say, of sorts, in keeping with the pyramid principles of the Democratic Dictatorship of the People. Like everyone else at the productive bottom, they had been allowed to elect representatives for their production brigades, who had then elected representatives for the commune, and so on up the chain until a manageable number of representatives had been chosen to represent the people at large in the National People's Congress. Of course, given the importance of unity under the Party, even this pyramid of elections had had to be carefully managed, with only Party-qualified candidates standing. Up and down the country, obeying orders from the centre, Party Secretaries at every level (from production brigades and communes to counties and provinces) had appointed election committees to manage the process, with each committee choosing the local Party members who would be qualified to stand.

It had not been easy. The first and most important task had been to decide who the candidates were going to be. Meetings had then been convened where everyone could express whatever views they wanted – as long as they observed the all-important principle of unity (which, under the highly changeable conditions of the Great Leap Forward and the years which had followed it, obviously meant agreeing with whoever was in power at the top). With everything clarified in advance, when elections had been held, they had been models of heavenly order. And if ever, for some unaccountable local reason, they were not so orderly, Party people from higher levels had always been ready to come and fix the problem on the ground. True, things had taken a bit of a battering under the Cultural Revolution – when everyone had been fighting for the all-important seals of authority with which heaven stamped its decisions. But such unruly changes had obviously been undesirable. In fact, the one good thing one could say about the Cultural Revolution was that it had provided an excellent lesson to everyone in the dangers of unbridled democracy: too many voices, and no one in charge.

When the new peasant world of household responsibility had been launched, some had argued that the old Democratic Dictatorship of the People also needed a change. Up in the cities, in 1978, Wei Jingsheng had argued for his Fifth Modernisation, with democracy as a voice of the people themselves rather than that of the Party on the people's behalf. Although Wei had been swept off to jail, and a following campaign of spiritual civilisation had been launched to make sure that everyone else's minds stayed pure, many of the peasants thought he had a point. When Deng Xiaoping had then announced that individual households could decide how to farm their own patches of earth, a number of peasants had begun to argue that perhaps it was indeed time for the Democratic Dictatorship of the People to be modernised as well. How could fields be individually farmed if decision-making was always subject to Party-driven unity? It had all been very well when the Party had been an army of donkey drivers and snow really had fallen in summer. But as Party member- ship had mushroomed in the decades after 1949, it had been hijacked by a pack of rats who had progressively hollowed out the people's prosperity. If Deng truly wanted to boost production, he would need to change the way in which decisions were made – and the people who made them.

Deng had been advised of the peasants' arguments, and had even seen their logic. But it seemed to him to be wholly unfeasible. If the principles of the Democratic Dictatorship of the People were ever dislodged, how on earth could the Party conduct the orchestra of the country at large? Things had been left as they were, and the villages had remained under the charge of the townships, albeit with commit- tees of their own which, headed by village leaders appointed by the Party, were really there just to save the townships' time by making sure the villagers were kept as quiet as mice.

By the time the people of Wukan had discovered that their land had been written off the village books, things had moved on a little. From 1999, villages across China had been allowed to 'elect' their village committees. The kind of elections the villages got depended on the location of the soil, and the patterns of the past. In areas where the spreading promise of socialist wealth was unlikely to be much more than a pipe dream – and where taxes were accordingly not likely to amount to much either – most people were too busy struggling to survive to worry much about the details of elections. Conversely, in places where accidents of fate meant that there were some brave local individuals who still insisted on asking questions, there was a chance that the peasants might be able to make their own choices, and cast their votes accordingly. Everywhere else, however, individual Party powers had dug themselves in so deeply that few peasants dared to question their suggestions as to who to vote for. As a general rule, the closer one got to the fringes of any fortunes to be made, the more likely it was that the villagers' votes would be bent to the superior order of the township's Party minds: those quickest to see the possibilities of profit, and with the sharpest understanding of how to work the levers of power.

As in the communal past, election committees organised by the township told the villagers who their candidates could be, with the election committees headed by the Party's appointed secretary for the village, and manned by men who he could trust. Anyone attending an election committee meeting was advised to remember that unity was everything. If anyone seemed tempted to forget their place in the orchestra and try to ask a question, a helpful reminder could easily be delivered by 'a friend'. If anyone seemed to have gone tone deaf, stronger voices, and rougher hands, could always be found.

Heaven forbid that anyone should think of standing for election without an invitation; but if they did, there were plenty of persuasive means available to change their mind. Rules were an obvious place to start: young candidates were told that they did not meet the qualifications of experience; more experienced ones were told that they were too old. Whenever any independent candidates asked to see the rules for themselves, there was always a local lock-up, where they could be given time to reconsider their request. Of course, some stubborn candidates would keep on asking, but the local Party war-chest was full of clever ideas: an independent candidate inviting villagers for a conversation over a bowl of noodles was a clear case of vote rigging; insisting on standing for election even when patient Party minds had set out the facts was an obvious indication that the candidate was a criminal in disguise, responsible for a recent spate of unsolved thefts. As for anyone who wanted to make electioneering claims that peasants still owned land that had already been sold, that was plainly a subversion of the power of the state.

As the glittering train sped up across the 1990s, the peasants' anger had risen almost as fast as the speed of the train. Farmland was being sold from under their noses and then concreted over to reappear as a local government-blessed factory; taxes were collected and then buried under someone's Party garden. By the year 2000, it seemed to the population of the countryside that the 'elected' village chiefs and local Party secretaries (very often one and the same), had turned into rich and powerful *tu di*, local emperors. So rich and powerful were they that even their chickens and dogs were living in heaven, with their wealth stored so wisely that the *tu baozi*, country bumpkins, who lived alongside them could scarcely find a wholesome meal, let alone afford a waterproof roof to put above their heads. In some cases, the local emperors were new brooms – nominated by someone above, whether for the value of their money or their willingness to do what they were told. In others, they were old hands who had navigated the raging tides of the Cultural Revolution and managed to come sailing out on top. Either way, the faster the train travelled, the tighter the Party's local officials closed their grip on the profitable village worlds – and the faster those worlds began to crumble. Land won by the revolutionary sacrifices of parents and grandparents had been sold beneath the peasants' feet, fields had turned black with soot, rivers had taken to running red and a lot of children had been born blue.

The countryside possibilities of the glittering train were not limited to the land, though. From the 1990s onwards, local Party secretaries and government officials plumbed every imaginable depth in their eagerness to find a profit. Deng Xiaoping's one-child policy had been one opportunity – providing an excellent stick with which to force stubborn village minds with too many children to cough up the heavenly fines. In Henan province, local officials found an even better idea. With peasants living on pennies, the officials offered them the chance to make a few bucks in return for letting them milk their blood for onward sale to hospitals. Ever keen to boost productivity, the blood was pooled in blood banks, stripped of its red cells and then reinjected back into the peasants so they could be quickly milked again; but while the red cells had been removed, in many cases, a dose of HIV had inconveniently found its way into the blood banks, and AIDS swept across the fields. Of course, those villages most infected soon lost their value and had to be buried in silence. But there were always other ideas. A popular one in many provinces was children: snatched up by snakehead brothers who smuggled them in to brick kilns, the profits of their labour were shared with the local Party secretaries and officials who had turned the necessary blind eyes.

Nor were the possibilities limited to immediate profit Careers, with their potential for longer-term gain, were important too. So essential to the natural ordering of things, they were all dependent upon keeping in the good books of any superior supervision: particularly in terms of the measurable indicators of productivity created, wealth generated and births avoided, by which every local Party career was judged. Up and down the country, village lands were transformed into job-creating factories or, better still, hopeful cities-in-progress. Whenever the central government inconveniently asked to check the numbers of births, local officials rounded up any women who might have slipped the educating net, and pushed them into steel-rimmed surgeries to cut the cord of life. If anyone threatened to raise an alarm to a higher-level authority, it was easy to shut them up in jail – just put it down to Stability Maintenance. And if a spell in jail didn't do it, it might just be worth an official's while to have the inconvenient would-be whistleblower extinguished.

For a long time, many villagers continued to believe that the Party's heaven was still up there: it was just that a few bad clouds had got in the way. Disregarding those who insisted that, after thousands of years of communications having been cut between heaven and earth, one shouldn't have any expectations of change, these more trusting spirits argued that the Party had started out as a heroic band of brothers – and that leopards did not change their spots. The problem, they insisted, must just be in the lower ranks who had obviously lost their way or, come to think of it, should not have been in the Party at all. All they had to do, the loyal peasants argued, was to find a way to get their messages past the local snakes, and up to the heavenly skies. Willing to give anything a try, and aware that the Party's government, like all imperial dynasties before it, had set up 'letters and petitions' offices precisely for this purpose, petitions had been prepared by the bucket-load, inked in the best hands that the villagers could muster.

Writing petitions was one thing. Getting them through the guarded portals of the letters and petitions offices, however, was quite another. Charged with Stability Maintenance, lower level officials became masters of the art of keeping uncomfortable messages from getting anywhere close to the higher echelons of power. Once alerted to the fact that a village was thinking about writing anything on paper (there were always spying eyes and ears happy to pass on such news for a favour or a fee), the misguided letter-writers would be invited to 'have a cup of tea' at the welcoming offices of the local Public Security Bureau. If that didn't work, the same spying eyes and ears could usually be relied upon to give the township or the county an advance warning on what the villagers were planning next. Any village mice thinking of making a personal visit to the provincial government could usually be headed off at the local bus or train station. But, just to be sure, guarding cats could also be sent to keep watch over the higher gates of power themselves. And if any mice looked as if they might jump all the way up to Beijing, all available stability-maintaining energy would be deployed to head them off. Hired hands in plain clothing would stake out the railway stations and every possible train. If that failed, the same hands would be sent to the intended petitioning destination, and told to use every crafting wit they could muster to hunt the devilish mice down. The most obvious destinations, other than the letters and petitions offices, were the television stations. With both placed under a 24-hour cat surveillance, the face of any mouse which appeared to match any 'wanted' images would be whisked off the streets and into one of the special 'black jails', which every province kept in the capital, ready for a bumpy ride home.

By 2008, though, so many people were falling off the glittering train that it was getting hard to find villagers who still believed in the dream of a Party heaven. Driven to desperation by the deception of the Democratic Dictatorship of the People, many villagers forgot the trains and simply went on local rampages. White-tiled pavilions of township and county power started to explode in flames; sleeping police cars shot up like fireworks. With villagers now convinced that there was no difference between local Party officials and the gangster criminals who served them, the heavenly Party's representatives increasingly found themselves at the pointed end of pitchforks and hoes. Fear of Party power now trumped by the loss of almost everything, villagers began to argue that if one wanted to talk about patriotism, the 'people', who had fought and won the revolution, had not been an abstract collective, but their very own ancestral fathers and grandfathers. Whatever 'heaven' the thieving official thugs might claim to be representing, the land that the peasants stood on was theirs.

With the thousand year-old tale of Song Jiang and his fellow marsh outlaws carried deep in their hearts, many peasants vowed, like their forefathers, to stand together, or die. Fortified with the memory of the hero Guan Yu, the god of war who always protected the weak, they then stood up in their hundreds of thousands to protect their earth. Just as inspired by the stories of the Monkey King as Mao Zedong (not to mention Bo Xilai), they refused to be dazzled by any of the claptrap references to the 'socialist rule of law'. Masters of the adventures of the *Outlaws of the Marsh*, they began to occupy even the land that had already been snatched away.

Although China's villages had been carefully corralled into isolation by the Party's Leninist principles of administrative organization (every village under an administrative order of its own), and although each was a tiny pocket, scattered across the vast expanse of the country, all of them had drawn on the same common store of stories, strategies and courage which had served their ancestors across thousands of years. Threats raining down upon their heads from the townships and the counties above, the villagers simply wrapped themselves more closely together – and shut their ears. Of course, the villagers were not the only ones to have read the story of the *Outlaws of the Marsh*: local government-hired hands in plain clothes, having also grown up with the familiar tale, had smuggled themselves into the villages and picked off the weakest villagers, throwing them into jail. Sworn to the brotherhoods, however, the families of the fallen had been clutched to the hearts of surviving brothers; protective timbers had then been cut from trees and rolled across village roads to keep the evil interlopers out.

With so many parts of Hu Jintao's New Socialist Countryside struggling, and with Beijing getting more and more anxious about unity, more of the local governments began to hit back in greater force. Equipping themselves with great new armies of bulldozers, rubber batons and shields, village by village, they beat the villagers down. Blood and tears washed the streets; jails filled to overflowing. Within their midst, though, a new generation of men were becoming local heroes, with some of them well on their way to the local pantheons of the gods.

———

As the peasants watched the tragedy of the countryside unfold, some sharp eyes observed that the socialist market economy was issuing an increasing number of laws to supports its new ideas of order. Indeed, from the end of the 1990s, a few peasant minds had begun to wonder if salvation might not in fact lie in the law. Not the *socialist* law, which put the Party above everything: that had obviously not been designed to help. But with the crafting of so many new laws to support the glittering train and its markets, there were a few which seemed to be giving the peasants a bit of a chance against the local rats who ruled their world. One of them even granted a right to sue local government officials. Of course, that right did not extend to suing local Party secretaries; in the socialist legal system, anyone in the fold of the Party would always be above the law. But it was a beginning. Certainly, given the desperate state of affairs, anything was worth a try.

Where to start? Full of peasants, few villages had ever seen a lawyer, let alone raised one in their midst. For most of China's peasant children, schooled on rough benches, the very idea of mastering the endless strokes of black rules inked on white would have been dizzying enough, without the discouraging observations of teachers who knew that their pupils would struggle to find a job in a factory, let alone anything more. But with every peasant's child trained in the art of 'eating bitterness', as some got older and left school they decided that they would just apply that art to swallowing textbooks on law. The most dedicated were those who had found themselves tested by local government and Party forces far more frightening than any ink that might jump off a page.

Almost all of the would-be lawyers were stubborn minds chasing a stolen justice. Prepared to apply themselves to endless homework at the end of their daily labours, they buried their eyes in the pages of government regulations that might be able to save the day. The most difficult job was getting hold of the relevant texts. Most of the basic regulations that governed the rights and duties of the country-side could be bought for pennies on an open market. Covering a host of issues – from land use rights, tax collections and local elections, to procedures for imprisonment, administrative actions against government officials and appeals – they were a treasure-trove of information. But in the socialist world of law, any local court would read the regulations in the context of Party principles of unity, and firmly beneath the many 'local notices' issued for guidance in applying central government regulations to conditions on the ground. Which, of course, was another problem: the most important of the local notices – the inconvenient ones most likely to help a peasant, or those which were themselves a flagrant breach of higher laws – were often kept under lock and key, lest anyone should ever try to send a copy up to Beijing.

It seemed that the skills required for studying the law were not much different to the guerilla tactics of cunning and stealth that the villagers had learnt from the *Outlaws of the Marsh* and the Cultural Revolution. Thanks to Mao, though, if one bought the basic regulations at a market stall – and one was able to liberate the relevant pages of the local notices from their official filing cabinets (usually only a matter of greasing someone's palm, or calling in a favour), mastering the basic rules was surprisingly easy. Converted early on to the First Qin Emperor's school of law, Mao's view of the law was that it was only a matter of stating rules plainly – and ensuring that the punishments were clear. Deng had agreed, so that even when the socialist market economy demanded more laws with more details, the bureaucrats had been told to write them in simple words that anyone could understand.

With such an earthy approach to the law, one would have thought that even the least educated of the officials would have been able to keep their local notices broadly in line with the rules at the top. But as more and more of the peasant lawyers managed to liberate more and more of the notices, they noticed that not only were the grubby characters of the texts often at obvious odds with central regulations issued by Beijing, but many of them were also at odds with themselves. Notices purporting to give official approval to the expulsion of families from their fields were found to be nothing but local lies. Other notices approving peasant arrests were found to have no more legal authority than an inkpot. It was not long before the peasant lawyers were turning the tables and waving the fine print of the local notices before the very noses that had written them.

Consoling themselves with tea and cigarettes, the local officials cast their thoughts back to the socialist basics. No wonder Mao had beaten the intellectual lawyers to within an inch of their lives: if spiritually polluted rightists like these self-taught peasants were allowed to poke their opinions into everyone's business, it would not be long before heaven collapsed. Skip the rules, they concluded; go straight to the punishments; and, given the ease with which these peasants communicate with their brothers, make sure you capture their mobile phones before you carry them off to jail.

Many peasant lawyers disappeared: some into jail, some shut up for an educational spell of house arrest, some never to be seen again. Despite this, few gave up. Doors open to anyone with a problem, willing to work for nothing in order to defend a fellow man, they did whatever they could to steel themselves against the inevitable storms of official fury. Clear that the key to survival was less about the letter of the law and more about the number of brothers who could be mustered, they looked for, and gave each other, plenty of *hu zhu*, mutual assistance. Sweeping the internet, they were quick to spot their fellow travellers: a journalist here, a blogger there, other peasants-at-law in nearby villages and counties; even academic law professors in far-off cities, whose sympathetic city pockets would, from time to time, also send supporting cash when the peasants' own meagre resources ran dry. And whenever there was a case to lodge, others with similar claims were invited to join their applications.

Learning quickly, the wisdom of every lesson was shared, posted up or printed off for others to see. And if ever the peasants thought that one of their number was about to be 'disappeared', they made sure that their defences were strengthened – notifying brothers in law who could be relied upon to try and come to their rescue, particularly, the city bloggers and law professors who would be ready to splash the black text of truth across the four quarters of the internet.

It was not always enough to keep a peasant lawyer out of jail, but the knowledge that no one would be forgotten enabled everyone to cling on in hope.

———

While peasant lawyers were going into battle for the people of the lower earth, many of the peasants were calling the countryside quits. It was hard enough to make the price of a meal in the middle of nowhere, let alone battle against forces of heaven that had clearly got out of control. Some peasants packed their bags and took their chances, counting on finding a job in one the factories that had now spread like new-generation forests around the southern coast. Others paid a fee to the snakeheads to fix them up with a position in advance. Floating or pre-paid, squashed into crowded trains heading east and south, the warmth of fellow companions, all travelling in the same direction, gave their hearts a lift. The green-eyed demons of the village officials left behind, the peasant migrants shared their stories with the black humour that only a bleeding human heart can understand. Windows open to softer winds, hopes began to rise.

Unfortunately, once through the factory gates, most of their hearts had fallen. Assembly lines and systems scientifically primed for social-ist efficiency, the migrants found that the days were long, the rules were longer and the cost of disobedience was more than most could afford. The basic day was thirteen hours; the basic week forgot about week-ends. Talking on the job was punishable with a five yuan fine; packets of pay were docked for every minute wasted; and the first two months of everyone's wages were held as a deposit against reliable time-keep-ing. Pleading tales of children left behind who needed the money for food and school were ignored, with those responsible for docking their pay informing them that they themselves were only doing their jobs, and if anyone didn't want to work like a machine, they should not have turned up in the first place. After a while, though, the peasant workers found that the hours and the pay were the least of their worries: with profits to make and fees to pay to local government and Party officials, factory owners were cutting every safety corner in sight. Accidents were a fact of life; compensation was a dream.

At night, packed into dormitories like sacks of rice, young hearts would remember their hopes of freedom and whisper to each other in the dark. Some would suggest that they band together and walk off the factory floor. Older heads, who had already been on the job for a while, would explain that the last time they had tried that, the factory bosses had cut the lights, and then unleashed their thugs to drag them out and beat them up, docking their pay to boot. Refusing to give up, some of the younger ones would suggest that they follow their peasant lawyer brothers in the countryside and look at the law: surely even the social-ist legal system didn't allow factory owners to treat their workers like beasts. At which point, one or two eager voices would pipe up, saying that they had heard about lawyers in nearby cities who might be willing to help. Hopes rising, communication with the lawyers would then be made on someone's mobile phone.

Whenever the lawyers were contacted, the answer would always come as a shock. First, the rules would be outlined: always painful for trusting hearts looking for threads of red justice in a world where everything was so black. Apparently anyone could join a union, as long as it was a branch of the Party's mass labour organisation – that All China Federation of Trade Unions, ACFTU, into which every union had been bundled up just after the 1949 revolution. But although ACFTU was grounded on the Democratic Dictatorship of the People, this did not quite mean what it said. The democratic part was limited to having chosen the Party in the first place. And, with the Party having become the revolutionary representative of 'the people', it was the Party that exercised the 'dictatorship', rather than any upstart workers. As ever, explained the lawyers, in the Party's legal system, unity was all. To which, they would add wistfully that the constitution used to have a right to strike – not that many had dared to use it. But once the glittering train of the socialist market economy had left the station, the drafters had had a change of heart, and struck it out of sight.

Hope sinking in the ears of the listeners, the lawyers would note that it did not necessarily mean that one had to give up: there was still a labour law, with rules that any employee could use. The only problem with relying on the labour rules was that it would probably cost the petitioner his job: that and any held-over pay that had not yet made it into his hands. To which one had to add the fact that the socialist judges of justice were also charged with applying the principle of heavenly unity, so that in any case involving labour, the local officials would need to be consulted. And given that the local officials were likely to be on the payroll of the factory bosses (just to make sure that they were always in the productive loop), the ultimate decision would probably lie with the factory head.

After so much bad news, a number of hearts would falter. Many, particularly those with children in schools, or parents expensively sick at home, would go off to find the snakeheads who were always prowling the factories, looking to profit from a migrant's pile of debt. But, others, desperate to find a way out of their nightmare, would decide to brave a strike in the hope that some good Party official in heaven could, somehow, be touched: you never know, it had happened before; maybe snow could fall again in summer. The lawyers would then be asked to do whatever they could to help; although neither lawyer nor client had any idea of whether, when or how, the cost of their services was ever going to be met.

Having heard the stories of the factory floors, not all of the villagers who left the countryside went to the production lines of the coast. Many decided to try their luck in the cities instead, eyes caught by the sparkle of a Beijing or Shanghai. Apart from the price of the train fare, though, there was that difficult question of storming the city's *hukou* passes in order to get in. Born in a village, the essential household registration papers of every peasant were stamped with the name of the village from which they came, and in which they were expected to spend their lives. When Deng Xiaoping had called for a faster socialist market economy, millions had been given the special red chop which opened the gates to one or other of the new factory towns: free to stand at the assembly lines for as long as they wanted. For a fee, smaller cities could even be persuaded to overlook the dirty question of birth, and change the chop. Getting a chop to go to a real city, however, was quite another matter. Of course, there was not a building site or a restaurant in the country that did not want the cheap souls of the countryside to come and lend a temporary hand. But living wages were another matter, and storming the big city passes without paying a king's ransom was the hardest trick in the land. Steeped in a history of brave adventurers, many peasants decided to try. The price of their efforts, however, would be high.

With city officials under orders to limit the size of their own populations, and equipped with the powers to check everyone's *hukou* papers day or night, any migrant who smuggled themselves into the bright city lights either needed to keep in the dark or find the money to persuade the *chengguan*, urban enforcement agents, to turn a blind eye. Most of the migrants found it easier and cheaper to keep to the dark. Making their way to the rough-and-tumble edges of the city world, they did everything they could to avoid the searching lights of detection, whatever the price. Squeezing into surviving 'urban villages' around the cities, whose land had not yet been sold to a high rise – the migrants paid through the nose for every inch of electricity, and for every drop of water too. Try as hard as they might to hide, only a few succeeded. Most found themselves stung for a honeyed bribe to keep someone's lips sweet. Those unable to afford the bribe were packed off on a slow train back to the countryside, with any wages they were owed lost as a lesson in order. Those who succeeded soon realised that, however many lips they sweetened, life in the city could only ever be a temporary arrangement: once their limbs hit thirty, they would be replaced with younger models. Meanwhile, for as long as they were in the city, no hospital would open an affordable door to their illnesses and injuries; and no school would contemplate taking on the clutter of their children's muddy feet.

Some of the more confident would-be migrants tried to persuade the forces of order that they were really city people just waiting for a chance. It was an argument for which they had been well prepared. Schooled in the struggling countryside, they and their parents had always been clear that getting into a city would be the greatest 'survival of the fittest' battle of their lives. Digging deep into threadbare pockets, parents put every possible penny into the education of the single child who, given the current state of the glittering train, would one day have to be their pension. Mindful of the hurdles ahead, rural schools tried to even out the odds by extending the hours at school. By the end of the 1990s, most were opening seven days a week, with lessons of up to fifteen hours a day. Given the hours and the distances – many children would walk hours to get to school and back – dormitories were usually made available. Aware that peasant children would be unable to compete with the textbooks of the city, let alone the computers, they were taught to swallow every possible bitterness – with a stiff dose of physical training added, to give them an extra edge. Hard wooden desks doubled up as beds to toughen up the body; blackboards kept a constant rallying tally of which children were ahead. The *shuda-izi*, bookworms, of the city might have their libraries and laptops, but the children of the countryside would have their age-old power to eat the bitterness of hardship, taught from the youngest age. Those who managed to stay the course would then battle with each other and everyone else in China to pass the exams which could win the dream of a place in a city university – and the promise of a job which would be something other than the '3D' dangerous, dirty and demanding labour that was the usual peasant's lot.

These, of course, were not the only hurdles. In the world of the survival of the fittest, with so many students looking for results, and with peasant children so obviously lacking the *gao suzhi* higher qualities of the mind, just getting to a university did not guarantee a degree. Those who failed to secure the life-changing certificates then found themselves back in the pool of all the other would-be-migrants and its general luck of the draw. Chasing whatever paper certificates might be on offer – English lessons, computer training, hospitality – every possibly affordable course was swallowed like the sky. Then they would put their best feet forward, bravely presenting themselves for the formal approval of city officials who had the gift of a limited number of urban places for candidates with the appropriate skilled qualifications. Either that, or find the money required to help an official tick the right box. Even then, while their parents' labour might squeeze them through or around the extra years of study, no certificate could disguise their low quality earthy accents, just as no amount of peasant savings could cover up their clumsy clothes. For most, the best hope was a job at the bottom of someone's city dump, or in the back rooms of something better: somewhere they could not sully with their low quality country ways.

———

While the peasants were fixing their eyes on the possibilities of the bright city lights, those born with a city *hukou* were struggling to keep up with the demands of the high quality life. With television sets now broadcasting the virtues of consumption, some in the smaller cities imagined that the greatest demonstration of high quality was to have enough money to buy a foothold in the sparkling metropolises of Beijing or Shanghai. And with billboards in Beijing and Shanghai smiling most brightly on the *gao suzhi*, high quality, consumer, the residents of these cities were clear that only a sweeping apartment at the height of a newly rising tower, or a spreading villa in a gated and guarded suburban compound, would do. At the end of the day, wherever one came from, everyone knew that high quality was a question of money, and that unless one had a Party official on tap, money was a matter of finding or creating the most rewarding kind of position.

Crystal clear about the calculus, those born to the cities climbed their careers with the dedication of mountaineers. By the early years of the twenty-first century, ordinary hours in the office were simply badges of honour, with any failure to stay late considered a matter of personal shame. As everyone battled their way up the same narrow paths, with the same sparkling credentials, it was obvious that what really made the difference was the quality of one's relationships. Given the all-important powers of the Party over everything, the best quality relationships would naturally be with Party people who could either provide a promoting approval themselves, or offer an introduction to another Party power who would be able to help. And as relationships always needed delicate nurturing, restaurants became essential institutions for the promotion of one's career. Indeed, as the years passed, and as the glittering train got faster, the line between the office and the restaurant got thinner and thinner, until few could tell the difference. Not that dining out in restaurants offered any kind of rest for the career-builders. Given the number of favours on which every relationship depended, time spent at the table usually created an ocean of extra work. And however high anyone climbed, with prices rising and everyone else climbing up as well, it was not only clear that one could never be high enough, but that any heights reached just made it frighteningly further to fall.

As the first decade of the new millennium advanced, insomnia became a ticking time-bomb, depression stalked the streets, and every now and again, and more than in the two decades before, the peace of another world would be found at the end of a rope. The city was just like every-where else in the heavenly lands: a tooth and claw struggle for survival.

No one understood the nature of the struggle better than city parents. Sights fixed on the education that would determine the quality of their children, tiger mothers scoured every inch of the school curric-ulum looking for space to squeeze in yet another lesson, while reading every quality raising self-help book available. Many decided to use the pre-birth months for extra advantage: Tang dynasty poetry was popu-larly intoned for the womb; and with Confucius having made an official comeback, flocks of parents turned to the now rediscovered classics for the early years. *The Great Learning* was the most popular text: the one with which Confucius (possibly with the help of someone in the later

Han dynasty) had set everyone off on a two and a half thousand year journey of cultivating themselves, even as they strengthened the family and the state beyond. Another popular light from the past was the *Yi Jing, The Book of Changes*, from the time of the Duke of Zhou.

Fretting about the limited number of hours in a day, city schools found themselves transformed into places where everyone could test themselves, with the real front-line of advantage moving to after-school tuition and self-cultivating activities. Exams were set like races, races were timed like the Olympics and evenings and weekends were requisitioned for yet more reading and writing, with punctuating lessons in tennis and swimming taught as master classes. If the ancestors had been able to eat the bitterness necessary to pass the imperial exams, there was no reason why their descendants should not be able to match up. At home as well as at school, children were taught to keep self-evaluating records, charting both how well they completed a given task, and the quality of the thoughts with which they worked. Meanwhile, everyone was exhorted to emulate the physical prowess that had kept the Long Marchers on their road to victory-against-the-odds.

Being children, many tried to launch rebellions. Although, as the years passed, as exams piled upon exams and as the stories of their parents' and their grandparents' sacrifices were constantly heaped upon their heads, most eventually accepted their lessons. But as the time drew nearer for the exams that would decide which children would go to a university, and which university they would go to, some turned to the windows of their high-rise, homework-filled, bedrooms and saw the promise of another world.

Counting the increasing number of suicides, many teachers and onlookers said that it just confirmed what they had been saying all along: the children of today were just not tough enough to win the battle for the survival of the fittest. Others looked up at the skies and wondered why such young lives had to die.

By 2005, looking at the more human quality of their citadels, many of the city people were beginning to wonder if the price they were paying for a high quality life had not become a little too expensive. Forests of chimneys had spread in all directions; city roads had become mobile car parks. Taps were pouring out water tinged with the chemical waste of over-enthusiastic production; and more and more food was being packaged with poison for somebody's profitable gain. In Beijing, *hutong* lanes of houses were demolished under the feet of their occupants, while spreading pavilions that had survived the past were falling ever faster to the demolitions of a runaway present. And in every older city, inconvenient residents were redirected to new homes outside the city limits, whether or not there was a bus. New and old, city neighbourhoods found themselves exposed to polluting power plants. The dust of destruction for construction was in everyone's eyes, even as the pursuit of profit prowled across everybody's lives. Sparkling malls offered compensating fountains of consumption for those who could afford them, but the ticking minutes of every waking day had become nothing more than a race whose only end was not to fall behind.

Spirits already exhausted by a lack of sleep, many began to lose their tempers. Angry voices rose on overcrowded buses, in the streets of neighbourhood communities and even in the clubhouses of the gated compounds and the towering apartments.

Thinking on the stresses that were driving the rage, those who lived along the streets turned to the neighbourhood committees whose job was supposed to be looking after the local households. Turning up at the meetings, however, most found that the committees were governed by the same Democratic Dictatorship of the People that ruled everything else. They also found that the local powers were repeating the same heavenly mantra of unity that everyone could read, whether in the daily papers or in solicitous government messages now regularly sent directly to mobile phones: 'build a harmonious society'.

Things were not much easier in the gated compounds. True, the more privileged, higher quality, people who owned such homes were able to describe their meetings as 'residents committees'. But it was not long before they learned that the same Party powers which plagued the countryside and the city's neighbourhood committees had found their way into the richer city compounds as well. As owners with a paper title to their property and contracts with developer-managers, they might have expected their voices to carry the day. But any well-organised management would have local officials on a payroll of some sort. And with most of those who could afford the gated compounds working every available hour of the day, few had the time or energy to do battle. Many resorted to crossing their fingers – hoping that heaven would eventually get around to solving their problems one day.

Exasperated by the deceptions of the Democratic Dictatorship of the People, some, with the same idea as the peasants in the countryside, decided that the only way a harmonious society was going to be built was if they created the harmony themselves. Having read the same books as the peasants, and far more of them, up and down the country, a number of city-dwellers began to organise themselves into their own bands of brothers, determined to fix what was going wrong. A chemical factory to be built in a southern city? Residents collectively pulled out their mobile phones and organised a million-strong 'stroll'. *Hutong* lanes to be swept away, along with the last memories of Beijing's past? City spirits launched themselves across the internet and bombarded the district mayors' headquarters with copies of rules and regulations, accompanied by logical arguments which tore any local notices to shreds.

Seeing strength in their own numbers and abilities, many of the city-dwellers proceeded to create their own mutual self-help societies. Digging deeper into problems than any official ever had, and reaching out across the crowds, the organisations not only came up with smart solutions that took the officials by surprise – but also offered to muster whatever manpower might be required to make the solution happen. As fixed as ever on unity, the Party and its government insisted that every one of these 'non-governmental' organisations should register itself under the tutelage of a superior government institution. Many thought this might not be such a bad idea – it was always easier to win a war with an official at your side.

For a while, it seemed as if the self-helping societies were making progress, and that even the Party might begin to appreciate some of the helping hands from below. Journalists began to float supportive stories; and while technically bound to the Party, editors began to print them – turning a blind eye to the idea that the principle of unity meant that the Party had to do, and to be seen to be doing, everything that the people could ever want or need. But as time turned, and as it seemed that everyone wanted to have their own 'conversation with heaven', the Party began to tighten the lines. Many of the organisations found that government institutions that had once offered tutelage suddenly withdrew their support. Others woke up to find that someone had manufactured a charge against their leaders – droppable after a clarifying 'cup of tea' and an agreement that the organization would give up whatever solution it thought it was providing, with the alternative being a socialist court of law and a sentence in jail. As the people's self-help was forced into retreat, editors of newspapers also found themselves under pressure to call in their journalists and remind them to 'harmonise' their words.

Unwilling to give up, some tried to work within the stricter rules – faithfully believing that heaven would *eventually* come to its senses. Others were less sure. Believers or not, almost everyone began to look to the internet for assistance. The *hu zhu* self-help groups began to recreate themselves in the virtual world: assembling together in whatever numbers they wanted, and communicating with anyone and everyone they wanted to, at any time of the night or day. True, there were 'firewalls'. Installed before the internet had ever been allowed to enter China, and significantly strengthened with the benefit of experience since then, these virtual fortresses had created a 'Chinese internet garden', in which every site and user in the country was subject to the harmonies of the state, and where inconvenient words triggered alarms. There was even a special internet police to guard the electronic borders.

Given the pedestrian nature of so many of the issues which the people were dealing with, in the early days, few of the alarms which the Party had put into the system rang – and many of the organisations flourished. Quick to learn, though, as the online organisations flourished, the Party and its state responded with a more revolutionary zeal: the number of words, and names, which triggered the alarms was substantially expanded – ambitiously attempting to include anything which might conceivably be interpreted as threatening the principle of unity, or as somehow suggesting that the state was failing to meet its heavenly obligation to delivery harmony for all. More eyes were also added to the force of the internet police, to find more words; and more technology was added, to automatically shut down the sites which threatened everyone's unity. A *wu mao dang*, fifty-cent party, was also raised, deploying hundreds of thousands of cyber-surfers, each apparently paid in units of fifty cents to scan the internet for 'inharmonious' sites and posts, and redirect the online chat with more appropriate views. To these resources were added new, Western, technologies that could freeze a disobedient computer, and issue an electronic warning of worse to come.

But the Party had underestimated its people, and the power of the past. The old stories of the *Outlaws of the Marsh*, not to mention the legends of the Crouching Dragon, Zhuge Liang, were all as fresh today as they had been in the times when the stories were first told; and all as applicable to the corrupted power of the Party as they had been to that of imperial officials of old. VPNs were used to leap across electronic borders, and the expanded lexicon of alarm-triggering words was quickly learnt and shared, so that everyone could simply type around them. Of course, the Party ordered a crackdown: widen the lexicon (again), strengthen the internet police, lock up offending computers. But the online spirits just jumped higher, and learnt more words. In the end, the Party resorted to the socialist rule of law. Deciding to kill a few monkeys to scare the chickens, it began to cart the most annoying offenders off to jail.

It was not long before the internet became yet another game of Party cat and people's mouse. And as the stakes of jail grew higher, some of the internet users decided to follow the peasants, and turn their attention to the law. With cities being close to universities, and with a number of university professors being not just the high quality city residents which the modernising Party wanted to embrace, but accomplished internet users as well, many assumed that the prospects of success would be much brighter. Like their peasant peers, many lawyer-professors were willing to take up cases for the values of truth and justice alone. Laws were read, documents were prepared, applications for hearings to adjudicate government actions were made.

In the beginning, a number of measured judgements seemed to offer hope. But as the number of petitions rose, the lawyers found themselves bumping up against the model of a socialist judge. Unveiled by the Party in the same revolutionary spirit with which it had once conjured up the diaries of Lei Feng, one of the model judges was named Chen Yanping. Suddenly appearing online in 2010, Judge Chen reminded everyone about the judicial principles of a harmonious society. With her judgements directed to setting any wavering courts straight – and to redirecting any misguided litigants – the model judge reminded all courtroom adventurers that the fine print beloved of Western lawyers was only fit for barbarians. The black and white texts and the mechanical procedures of the West were nothing but the desperate refuge of bourgeois states who had lost the hearts of their people. In any and every case, the facts of a matter should always be explored in the softer light of harmony – ideally, out of the glare of a court, and over a cup of tea.

The lawyers did not give up, but some of them began to disappear. And over time, others, seeing the dark judicial winds blowing across the internet, packed their bags and left the country, continuing to offer their help, but henceforward from afar.

———

By 2010, it was not only the internet and the courts that were getting darker. Overwhelmed with chimneys and cars, city skies had got a lot darker too, particularly in Beijing. Blue had been on the retreat for a number of years, with its appearances now limited to an exceptionally strong breeze, or a Party-convened meeting which had the power to close down production. True, a number of power plants and factories had been moved to other less visible places (smaller cities, or better still, the countryside) in an attempt to clear the air. But with the glittering train speeding ahead, not everything could move: and whatever stayed behind just had to work harder, belching out galaxies of smoke.

Meanwhile, the city's roads had become so congested that they were more like car-parks, with fuel tanks overflowing into fuming clouds. What had once been an imperially bright ether had not only been transformed into a productive grey, but was also getting worryingly clogged up with dust: *xi-ke-li-wu*, fine particulate matter, as it was called by the scientists who understood these things; 'gdp particles' to the coughing people on the ground. Across the, now very mobile, internet – and particularly on the twittering *Weixin*, Wechat, microblogs with features of Facebook, that were becoming increasingly popular among Beijing's twenty-odd million residents – the people loaded up images of a city that was racing out of control. To which, they added scores of the blackly humorous jokes which Beijingers had always conjured up whenever heaven had lost the plot: 'Want a cigarette?' they asked each other. 'Just open a window and take a smoke.'

Then, in the late summer of 2012, at the height of the squabbling months before Xi Jinping rose to the head of the Party, the city itself was washed into a flood – swept by rains which had tried to fall on a once-soft land, only to find hard concrete instead. Motorists caught on the streets turned their mobile phones to the radio stations of the People's Republic for news and guidance, but found themselves serenaded by nothing more than the music of uninterrupted harmony broadcast across the waves. Before long, cars were cut off by lakes that had once been intersections, and engines were drowning in rivers that had once been roads. Desperate drivers looking for news had then turned to the microblogging Wechat world that held the twittering chatter of their friends. And news there was. Where the broadcasting stations of the Party-state had been silent, the people had rolled up their sleeves and got down to the job of serving themselves. Posting up maps and bulletins to guide their fellow travellers through the washed-away land, they had even proceeded to organise 'the people's' cars to pick up anyone in need of a ride.

Seventy-nine Beijingers died in the days of the flood, many of them drowned. For a short while, Beijing shed its sparkle, looking more like Bangladesh. In the days and weeks that followed, even more of Beijing's people poured into the Wechat world, trying to make sense of a city that had sunk. Immersing themselves in a wild virtual society where questions could not only be asked but would almost certainly be answered, they posted not just questions, but opinions, images, and jokes. Most of the posts raised the obvious simple queries: 'How could a city that had spent so much on the Olympics forget about its drains?' and 'How could a Party so proud of its propaganda fail to master the practical news that could have saved lives?' One of the jokes even thanked the Party for giving everyone a wash.

In the months that followed, and as the Party carried on with its pre-Congress squabbling, things seemed to go from bad to worse, not only in Beijing but across the country at large. Hardly an hour passed without an image of some chaos or other appearing on the internet. Pictures of buildings and roads collapsing under the weight of the socialist market economy were two-a-penny. Just as common were pictures of people exploding with rage. Many were the victims of Stability Maintenance, and of a 'harmonious society' that had left them with nowhere to turn. A number were peasants who had been pushed beyond the limits of endurance in villages that had once been invisible pockets of countryside and were now beginning to appear online. Beyond despair, peasants were now turning the tables on local officials, killing them with knives, pipes and hoes. Others were the raging casualties of city dreams that had vanished in the puffs of other people's profit: parents who had lost their children to poisoned food; husbands and wives who had lost each other to hospitals that had taken large deposits and then failed to deliver a cure. Yet others were the simple explosions of the ticking timebombs of people who could not keep up: one was a Party official who, delayed at an airport, had smashed his rage on terminals of computers – with the help of a nearby chair.

When Xi Jinping was clapped to the clouds in November 2012, the people certainly watched with interest. If nothing else, the twisting tales of Bo Xilai's adventures, and of Xi Jinping's mysterious disappearance, offered a whole new novel to the classics of the time. With things so clearly out of the harmonious order that the Party liked to insist upon, it seemed obvious that any new ruler was going to have to introduce some kind of change. The only questions seemed to be what, how, and when? Some thought that Xi Jinping's dream offered interesting possibilities. But it had not been long before the microbloggers replied with dreams and observations of their own: 'Fresh air, clean water and vegetables that are safe to eat', was a popular one. 'If I were an official, I wouldn't need to dream', was another.

Meanwhile, life in the People's Republic continued: local officials raked in their profits, roads collapsed, trains crashed and more and more of the people decided to pursue a rough justice of their own. The internet was flooded with more images, and more posts piled up on Wechat, as did the blackly humourous comments of a people who had come to the conclusion that China's history was doomed to repeat itself. 'Anyone in government arrested for siphoning off a million or less should be lauded as a clean official, and released immediately', cracked one microblogger. 'After chemical hotpots and poisonous rice, the Chinese people are now fit to survive any biological warfare', joked another. When ten thousand pigs floated up Shanghai's Huangpu river, lighter hearts suggested that everyone should just turn on their taps, add a bit of sesame oil and enjoy a heaven-sent bowl of soup. And when Xi Jinping announced a crackdown on corruption, the internet had been flooded with pure derision: 'tigers will make their reports, foxes will clap with laughter, flies will hum along happily, and only the mice will run scared in the streets'.

As the cities wrapped themselves up in clouds of humour, Xi Jinping and the Party family became less and less amused. And when battalions of high quality city-dwellers started blowing Wechat whistles on corrupt officials, the Party's propaganda troops were put on full alert. Anyone who stepped across the boundaries of harmony found their Wechat accounts cancelled. Those who had more than a handful of followers were reminded that the crime of counter-revolution had been replaced with the new, but equally treacherous, offence of 'subversion of the state' – and that subversion of the state took place every time the unwelcome opinions of a reckless twitterer were re-posted by five hundred people or more. Meanwhile, journalists who tried to jump on the bandwagon of telling the truth, were instructed to remember that their revolutionary duty was to deliver positive news.

In the early months of Xi Jinping's general secretaryship, as 2012 turned to 2013, a Guangzhou based newspaper, inspired by the idea of a dream, decided to prepare a front page story to explore the possibilities. 'What exactly is the dream of the Chinese people?' the story asked, following up with 'How did China come to have this dream?' and 'If this is really a dream of the Chinese people, how can everyone help to make it come true?' Presented to the local spirits of the Propaganda Commission for editorial review, the story was swiftly spiked. Telling the journalists to work overnight to prepare a more acceptable alternative, the official in charge of the harmonies of the printed page suggested that they try a more appropriately worded tribute to the Party's unifying powers.

Shocked that even the dream of a dream was going to be hijacked by the Party, the paper's pens argued back. No one could possibly be a journalist, they pointed out, if every word was unified from the top. Encountering a familiar silence, they then crafted an open letter to the Party asking what they had done wrong – and went on strike. The presses of the paper fell silent; flowers and banners of popular sympathy piled up outside the newspaper's doors. But it was not long before the superior forces of harmony put the paper quietly and obediently back on the stands.

Meanwhile, as a cool winter wind blew across the Guangdong south, a little up the coast – not far from the old Haifeng home of the long dead local hero Peng Pai – Wukan's villagers were still looking out to sea. After two years of chasing the tigers and flies who had stolen their land, they had been outfoxed at almost every turn. Once made, heaven's promises had, yet again, been snatched away by a local wind. Who on earth could tell whether and when they would ever come true?

CHAPTER 3

BEING CHINESE

You cannot write my poems; just as I cannot dream your
dreams.

Dreams and Poetry, Hu Shi (1921)

U P ON THE EDGE of Beijing's city, the black of winter had hardened the concrete of a cold confinement; ice had chilled its steel.
Outside, warmer bodies would be chasing the pleasures of the glittering
train. Inside, evening drawing to a close, time turned like the seconds
of a century, or a millennium: an endless night. Clouds passing across a
small window above, the solitary heart of a man who had told his truth
too often and too loud looked out and floated up towards the moon. The
walls of the prison might be thick but the freedom to fly depended only
on the mind, even as a mind depended wholly on being able to tell the
truths that really connect heaven and earth through man.

The raw coughs of fellow prisoners a distant echo, the spirits of the
ancient past swept across the captive's thoughts with the full force of
the present. That old poet-prince Qu Yuan, dismayed by the treach-
eries of Qin and asking heaven's porter to open the gates to another
world, was one such spirit. The brave Song dynasty brush that had
insisted on painting the miseries of the 'floating people' to an emper-
or-in-denial, was another. But for the man behind the bars of steel,
the loudest of the voices were the young ghosts of a summer-spring
in the not-so-distant past: a summer which had turned to the death of
autumn; a spring which had changed every life that it had touched –
including his own.

Some of the ghosts appeared as struggling screams, smashed bones
and blood-soaked bodies; many wrapped with fallen bicycles in a dying
embrace. Others surfaced like the surge of a great river that had washed
into and across the heavenly city over weeks of softening days. Youthful
spirits rising like sap, banners floating on high, they had picked up the

rocking chords of a popular Taiwanese voice and sung themselves as children of a dragon whose fate had become intertwined with their own. 'In the ancient East there is a people', they had choroused: 'They are all the heirs of the dragon'. Hope flushing through their veins, the heirs of the dragon had then looked at Zhongnanhai and asked a question: why is it that the heavenly dynasties have never thought that the people were worth the candle of a conversation? Standing before its vermilion walls, the dragon's heirs had then begun to sway to the beat of a Beijing guitar, singing the words of another star whose song everyone knew by heart: 'I want to give you my dreams, but you always laugh at me; me with nothing to my name; just get it together, and come with me'. As the young voices had rounded on the 'nothing to my name' refrain, they had not been alone. Beijing had poured out to join them: workers and street vendors, imagining that the people might have a part in the future; old men and women, crying at the possibility that a three thousand-year-old dream might finally come true. Even the police had whistled along to a tune that warmed the hearts of every Chinese.

Behind the vermilion walls, a world away from the floating people across the land, and after months of a messy chaos gathering on the streets of Beijing, the stubborn East Winds had whipped themselves up into such a fury that even heaven could not make itself heard. When, on 3 June, a group of four older spirits, *junzi* gentlemen, had joined a group of students in their hunger strike, the sun had carried on shining, but tanks had begun to gather, growling like dark clouds across the far-flung street. Loudspeakers announced that a storm of troops was coming. No one in their wildest dreams thought that they would fire, although some imagined that a rubber bullet or two – the price of a voice, they reasoned – might come their way. As the heat of that early June evening turned to dusk, many Beijing spirits, young and old, ran onto the streets asking the tanks and their following trucks of soldiers to think again. Subjectively remembering the art of being human, some of the troops stopped in their tracks. Others, obeying the commands of the last five thousand years, paused, blindly loaded their guns with live ammunition, and shot to kill. A boy here, a mother there, a father, a daughter, a husband, a wife; by midnight, all across the streets surrounding the square, they had fallen in their hundreds or more.

By the earliest hours of the morning of June 4 1989, Tiananmen Square was encircled by soldiers and tanks crawling in for the kill. The small band of older hunger-striking friends had looked at the thousands of students marooned within and decided that someone needed to ask heaven's troops to give them a safe passage home. One of the friends who volunteered was the 'Taiwanese voice' who had written *Heirs of a Dragon* from his home in Taipei; his name was Hou Dejian. Jumping the Taiwan Straits, Hou had defied the enmity of a divided nation to come to Beijing in search of what it meant to be Chinese. By 1989 he was not only famous, indeed infamous, in Taiwan, he was a rare and shining musical star in the still-grey mainland Chinese world. Looking across the vast expanse of the now-black square, Hou hitched a lift to the frontline in an ambulance full of doctors, and stunned a troop of battle-ready soldiers when they saw their idol appear like a dream in the midst of a nightmare. Begging a colonel for the crack of a corridor through which to march the students free, he was offered the last ticking minutes of the moon: just until dawn. Snatching a loudspeaker, Hou and his band of hunger-striking brothers implored the students to leave. With comrades fallen in the streets all around, many wanted to make a stand and die where they stood. One hand at a time, the small band of friends pulled them to their feet, persuading them to live for their future, rather than die for a dream. As the first rays of the sun appeared, the impatient troops began to step forward, tanks advancing into the early twitches of light, warning bullets shot to the sky. Just in time, the last straggling souls were swept from the square, and shepherded to safety.

Protected by the hunger-striking friends, no one died that night in Tiananmen Square. But as the spirits of the dead of the streets around had flown to another world, the earth-bound ghosts of the departed had swirled with the questions which now haunted the heart imprisoned in a Beijing jail, just as they had haunted every human heart from the beginning of China's time: *'What is heaven?' 'Who are the people?' and 'How, on earth, are they ever going to be able to talk to each other?'*

It had all begun with the cutting off of communications by the Yellow Emperor's grandson, Zhuanxu. Beside himself with worry about the flooding waters, he had become convinced that everything would work much better if heaven had only one earthly voice to listen to. Time had passed, and while many of the surviving shamans had tried to explain that the idea of order was as ephemeral as Zhuangzi's later dream of a butterfly, successive emperors had found themselves unable to change course.

The ancient Zhou had tried to adjust a little, influenced by the text of an even older history that told of a heaven that 'hears as the people hear and sees as the people see'. But what was it that the people heard and saw? Without being able to ask them, no ruler could possibly know. Meanwhile, fixed on the importance of order, the strongest men had raised city-states of glittering splendour. And while Confucius had urged them to moderate their greed and ambition with a *ren* humanity, an *yi* integrity, a *li* ritual to prompt forgetful minds and a *zhi* regard for the pursuit of knowledge, it had not worked. Before long, the stately cities had been at war with themselves, a war which had been resolved by a state which, following the logic of Zhuanxu, had gripped the people together in a single heart, and then proceeded to forge the warring city states into the unity of one – Qin – world.

Of course, it had not lasted. As Laozi had explained, any iron will that tries to grasp the world in its hands will ultimately fail. But the dynasties that had followed Qin had found it impossible to set the dream of unity aside. The learning of the past having been burnt to a cinder by the First Qin Emperor, the following Han dynasty had raised a new library of books, with a special place for a train of Confucian thought which seemed to embrace the *ren* humanity, the *yi* integrity, the *li* ritual and the *zhi* knowledge, but in fact placed all of those virtues under the unity of an iron fist. Unity had then been pursued beyond the edges of the Chinese world, bringing chaos down on Chinese heads – not only from barbarians outside, but from the human portents of Chinese peasants pushed beyond endurance. New emperors had risen; and raising schools of well-trained scholars, they had repeated their insistence on the single order of a Son of Heaven, underpinned with scholarly interpretations of Confucian texts that insisted on unity above all. From time to time (whenever an emperor had failed), packs of wolves had descended from the steppes above the Chinese lands. Eventually, the Manju Qing had appeared, wrapping up the Confucian ideas in the discipline of a barbarian hunt. Which only seemed to prove the point: unity was all. In 1850, Taiping rebels had then risen up against the Manju Qing, only to be put down by a new, self-strengthening, Confucian army. And then, different, Western, barbarians had arrived from the sea, insisting on ideas of sovereign states, and demanding a right to occupy Chinese ports and land.

At that point, some of the modern scholars had stepped outside their training and questioned the very foundations of everything. Kang Youwei, the late nineteenth-century scholar whose ideas had inspired the hundred day reforms, had smashed the idea of an imperial heaven, while retrieving an ancient dream of Da Tong unity: not unity under the single iron-fisted rule of an emperor, but unity under a heaven of self-cultivated people at large. As foreign imperial powers snatched away at more of the weakening empire of the Qing, the young Tan Sitong, the Hunanese who had been so inspired by the *Treasures of Chu* and the story of the poet-prince Qu Yuan, had argued that the only truly independent state was one whose people had the freedom to have independent minds as well. Abraham Lincoln's promise of a 'government of the people, by the people, and for the people' had struck a particular chord, as had Darwinian theories of a tooth and claw nature in which only the fittest survive. Young hearts had then turned to the dream of a new people whose independent minds at home would make them fit enough to ensure the survival of the Chinese nation, even if it would take a revolution to achieve.

For a brief moment, from 1911, a dream of a Republic seemed to be within the people's grasp, with a promise of science and democracy as guarantors against the blind imperialism of old. And while Yuan Shikai's hijacking of the National Assembly had given way to corruption and warlords, within the corridors of Peking University, more dreams rose: of finally wiping away not just the emperors of the past, but the imperial deceptions; and of raising a people who could think for themselves, not only in the cities but in the countryside as well. In the turmoil of wars between self-strengtheners and a young Communist Party, and between China and Japan, the dreamers had scattered. Many went to other cities across China, some to the caves of the new Communist city state in Yan'an. Eventually, Mao had proclaimed a new truth for a new age, and in 1949, declared the country to be a People's Republic of China, under the Democratic Dictatorship of its People. Not everyone had been convinced: families had divided, and many left the mainland to find a way of being Chinese in other parts of the world. By 1957, those who had stayed realised that the Democratic Dictatorship of the People was about the same kind of iron-fisted single mind with which the Qin emperor had once unified everything. Over the next fifteen years, as the Communist Party subjected both science and human voices to the greater truth of a perpetual revolution, China's very human beings found their dreams transformed into a nightmare of lies, in which tens of millions died.

By 1978, a calmer Deng Xiaoping had taken the helm, raising a banner of Four Modernisations, but dismissing any question of China's people having a voice to the silence of a prison cell. Party members who had been despatched to *laogai* labour camps, whether in the countryside or at the brutal edges of empire, were quietly returned. But while many had been happy to join Deng's glittering train, some had raised their voices. Ai Qing, a favourite Party poet, had dreamt of the possibility that 'a time will come when we, this ancient nation ... will accept Light's invitation to knock at gates now firmly closed'. When Tiananmen Square had been lit with human songs and opinions, the Party had made it clear that that time was not yet. 'On economic matters, relaxed controls; for political matters, tight controls' had been swiftly adopted as the appropriate slogan for the Party – with a shorter version of 'stability must crush all else', for the benefit of the wider public.

Within hours of the sun's rise on 4 June 1989, television signals had broadcast the names of the 'most wanted' individuals, in a bid to keep them from smuggling themselves underground. Some six thousand people were swept up in the grid of steel that was flung across the land; thirty or more were executed as counter-revolutionary enemies of the state. With the lesson of the 1911 revolution still ringing in its revolutionary ears (the lesson that even the army of a heavenly empire could be riddled with invisible rebels) the Party began a spring-clean. A needle-fine investigation was launched across five million of its own members; every imaginable organisation of anything put under the careful eye of a watchful Party cell; and 'intellectuals' – anyone who had read a book and dared to express a contrarian opinion – were hounded into the ground. When the rock musician Cui Jian (the star whose guitar had called out to the Party to join the people) emerged from temporary cover, the Party told him to cut the offending track along with any others likely to pollute the spiritual civilisation of the people. When Cui's strings kept strumming, the stages were removed. Within a year, Hou Dejian, the Taiwan-born voice, had been rounded up from a sound studio and smuggled on to a fishing boat: pushed across the Taiwan Straits in the dead of night, he had been sent back to the renegade island from which he had sprung.

Concerned to ensure that the people understood how much the top was doing for the bottom, the Party's Propaganda Department and its Patriotic Education Campaign had then advanced to the front line of thought. Exhibitions were raised to make sure that everyone could see the true face of the counter-revolutionary rebellion, and understand that it was only through the sacrifices of the Party that the land had been cleansed of its humiliations of the past. Re-educated minds had then been redirected to the single patriotic idea of the Party's order.

Time had continued to turn, Deng's modernising train set off for the south, and the intellectuals divided. After the shock of Tiananmen, many of the intellectuals had buried themselves deep in whatever and wherever it was they were studying, trying as hard as possible not to come out. But as the train began to gather speed, they divided: some choosing to remain in the silent protests of their studies, others deciding to contribute their hard-won knowledge to Deng's new idea. When it became clear that the collapse of the Russian big brother had ushered in a decade of such economic disaster that the Russian people had struggled to eat, more had joined those flocking to Deng's dream. Others, however, not least the outspoken economist-historian He Qinglian, had refused to give up the ghost of being human – even for a temporary hundred years. Investigating the roots of everything with their own hearts and minds, the intellectuals had stubbornly insisted that the relationship between heaven, earth and man was a question for everyone – and that the enquiring descendants of the shamans had a five thousand-year-old duty to question the idea that a single mind knew everything: a duty to ensure that the Party heaven heard as the people heard, and saw as the people saw.

The price had been high: many of the questioning intellectuals found themselves out of jobs; some found themselves in and out of jail. More than a few, including He Qinglian, took themselves into a self-imposed exile so that they could continue to tell the Chinese truth. One of them set up a Democracy Party for China in the other world of America, which a number of followers joined. Others decided that the best way to be Chinese was to stay where they were and to dedicate themselves, as best they could under the circumstances, to being not just the ears and eyes of the people, but also their voice.

Those who stayed behind to keep up the questions were united in their belief that heaven was not a single mind but the art of being human. Whether from the city or the countryside, the brush became an increasingly valued tool: in a country where only twenty years before, the educated youth of the city had been despatched to the country-side in their millions, and where rural rebels had always been among China's most popular heroes, intellectuals were not only to be found in the cities. Some, like the artists of the past, chose to make their points in carefully calculated novels and paintings: portraying the misery of the present in coded terms of art. Others dared to write the truth for all to see. With the Patriotic Education Campaign rising, and with younger minds being directed towards a Party history that disguised the facts, many begged the people to open their eyes and look again at the coun-try's calendars, not least at 4 May. Not an anniversary of Communist Party sacrifice (the Party had not even been founded in 1919 – and its founding had had more to do with Moscow than Beijing), but a monu-ment to a Chinese youth whose greatest dream had been of an order grounded in a people who could think for themselves.

One man, a wandering soul rather than a battling intellectual, had been so shocked by what had happened at Tiananmen that he wrote a poem about a Party which had 'smashed the skulls of its own people', and 'blasted a hole in the stars'. Sent to prison for his art, Liao Yiwu then spent his time in jail gathering together the stories of his fellow *leifan*, jailbirds, into a book which he titled: *Interviews with People from the Bottom of Society*. Many of those who managed to read it called it a true history of the people, written from the raw stuff of life which any history should take as its source: beggars, human traffickers, murder-ers, grave robbers, migrant workers, teachers, *Falun Gong* spirits, and all of the other 'mad men and women' who made up both the brutal cruelties and the heart-breaking kindnesses of life in the People's Republic. Published in renegade Taiwan, the Party had not considered it suitably harmonious reading for the Chinese people at large. After more time in jail, Liao Yiwu, like so many others, would eventually find that the only way that he could keep the idea of being Chinese in his heart was to leave the country and the Party behind.

It was not only the hungry ghosts of Tiananmen that haunted the minds of the stubborn intellectuals. For older men and women, it was also the memories of the great Party campaigns of the past. From the Anti-Rightist purges of 1957, through the Great Leap Forward and the Cultural Revolution, lesson after brutal lesson had been learnt about the dangers of a top-down order executed in the silence of a heavenly night. Or rather, the lessons had been taught, but it was not at all clear that the Party had learnt them.

One man whose mind was haunted by the lost lessons of the past was Yang Jisheng. Like so many others, Yang was the son of a father whose life had been shrunk to the skin and bones of a Great Leap Forward death. Loyally writing off his parent as a casualty of socialist progress, the young Yang had become a journalist with the Party's Xinhua News Agency. But when living Chinese bodies had been smashed on the streets around Tiananmen, his mind had returned to the memory of his father's sunken eyes, and he found that his head had been cleared of a mist. Having become one of Xinhua's most senior journalists, in 1990, he decided to use his rank to reveal the human story of what had happened in the Great Leap Forward – and in so doing, raise a tombstone to the memory of his father.

Travelling up and down the country, Yang used his senior cover to scour the caves of local archives, looking for the traces of deaths that, whether for fear or shame or both, everyone – Party members, government officials and the people at large – had buried. As clear as everyone else that the Party had declared the Great Leap Forward a lesson that was never to be named, Yang was aware that, in the process, he might well be digging not only his own grave but those of any who helped him. Across the country's county towns, though, secretly sympathetic men and women quietly directed him to where the answers were buried: in the dusty records of population statistics, and in the reports of weather and grain production with which the Party's bureaucracy had recorded the acceptable past. Line by buried line, over the next ten years, Yang painstakingly pieced together the fragments of local facts across each of China's thousands of counties. As he did so, he began to see a monumental historical truth: not one or two million dead, but thirty-six million Chinese people starved to an excruciating extinction by a single top-down mind. And the voices of their surviving family and friends silenced with a rule.

In 2008, Yang published his work – entitled '*Tombstone*' – across a thousand pages, all, necessarily, printed in Hong Kong. As he did so, he respectfully suggested that it was time for the Party to come to terms with heaven, the people and the past. A 'truth and reconciliation commission' seemed to him to be the answer. Not one of those clumsy commissions of the West which seemed to make nothing but a mess – and certainly not an 'investigation of things' which limited any questions to a set of approved textbooks – but the kind of investigation of things which Confucius must surely have originally had in mind, and for which, two thousand years later, that senior Ming dynasty minister, Wang Yangming, had argued: an actual enquiry into the real world, guided by the human conscience. Yang also suggested that it was time for the Party to step aside from the heavenly illusion that a single Great Man at the top could ever be relied upon to know the everything on which the security of human beings relied. 'Scattered across a people', he declared, 'human memories might seem messy, but they are our only ladders to the future.' Or, to put it another way: it was not bad people who had caused the deaths, although plenty of those could be found, but a top-down way of heavenly thinking which had been haunting the lands of the Yellow Emperor for far too long.

Yang was not alone. Others had also been digging into the past: from the children of parents who had been terrorised to death in the Cultural Revolution, to the mothers of children who had died or disappeared more recently in the streets around Tiananmen. Many went a step further, arguing that it was time for the Party to live up to the promises of the constitution which it had written itself: promises which included the right of everyone on earth to speak to heaven, including all of those whose pasts had been consigned to hell.

It was not, however, just the terrors of the Great Leap Forward, or any of the other individual campaigns, that were on the stubborn intellectuals' minds. There was also the bigger question of the whole of China's story. When Deng Xiaoping had introduced the Patriotic Education Campaign to replace any memory of Tiananmen with the greater story of the sacrifices of the Party and its triumphal successes, the Propaganda Department had embarked on its own long march – this one for the rewriting of history. Raising a new revolutionary banner of *wu wang guo chi*, never forget the national humiliation, immediate attention was centred on the 'hundred years of humiliation' inflicted by the foreign barbarians. From the opium spat in 1839, with its following British gunboats, across the division of China's northern lands by the wider imperial powers, to Japan's invasions: a string of national humiliations which had nearly lost not only China the state but China the people as well.

Setting aside the inconvenient details of the homegrown poppy fields – and not mentioning the Taiping rebellion and the following decades of self-strengthening feudalism which had followed – the Party had directed popular attention to the opium which the foreigners had dumped on the docks of Guangdong, and to the Western gunboats which had then sailed up and down the coast, forcing open 'treaty ports' at every profitable point of call. The burning of the *Yuanming Yuan*, Summer Palace (the Manju Qing's Jesuit-designed fantasy that, raised for a conquering emperor and never open to the Chinese people, had been selected by the British for retaliation after a murder of some of their negotiators during the 'opium wars') was claimed as a particular affront.

Rather improbably, to anyone who *did* remember their history, Zeng Guofan, the nineteenth-century capitalist self-strengthener and defeater of the Taiping peasant rebels, reappeared as a national hero. And the Boxer rebels, who had so terrified the Dowager Empress that she turned them on the foreigners, were resurrected as patriots. The battles that the Guomindang and their Chinese soldiers fought against the Japanese were also swept under the carpet. As were the young voices of the Communist Party who had been silenced by Mao, not to mention the factional fighting between Mao and other Communist leaders that had led to so many deaths. As was the leading role of Moscow in the 1949 revolution's success. And the fact that many of the lands which the new Republic had claimed in 1912, and which the Party had insisted upon at the point of its 1949 victory, were the conquests of the 'barbarian' empire of the Manju Qing, was a detail of the past best forgotten. The Tiananmen 'incident' was recast as a dream (or a nightmare) that had happened in someone else's land.

By 2005, as the Party's Propaganda Department was congratulating itself on the fact that anyone under twenty-five was now patriotically clear that stories of a June Fourth massacre in Beijing were either a foreign lie or a Western conspiracy, older heads began to worry about the truth. Alarmed at the risks the Party was taking with lessons from the past which were essential to everyone's future security, a professor of philosophy, Yuan Weishi, put pen to paper and tore into the textbooks that schools and universities were being told to teach. 'China's children', he railed, 'are being fed on a wolf's milk of whipped up patriotism liberated from the truth.' Turning to the past, Yuan pointed to the Anti-Rightist campaign of 1957, when the Party had attacked every expert opinion other than its own, claiming that their truths were lies. 'Look where that got everyone', urged Yuan: 'A nation of people too timid to tell the truth, and with black universally accepted as white'. Then he had turned to the manufactured anger of the Cultural Revolution that had produced a generation of people so badly damaged that they no longer believed in anything or anyone: 'Is the next generation to be transformed into blind nationalists and bitter xenophobes – the kind of 'human portents' who would almost inevitably (and, remembering the rebellions of the past, not for the first time), bring heaven down on everybody's heads?'

Within two weeks, the Party magazine that had published Yuan Weishi's 'opinion' was suspended. Noting that his stinging words had 'gravely violated historical facts' and 'hurt the feelings of the Chinese nation', any future reference to the article in which Yuan had expressed his opinions was promptly banned. Privately, the Party repeated its position to itself: Mao had been thirty per cent mistaken and seventy per cent right; the Great Leap Forward and the Cultural Revolution had been regrettable errors but, as Mao had always said, truth was always discovered from facts. Guided by history, the Party was crossing a river by feeling for the stones; and without the learning, the new China could never have found its feet.

Officially out of bounds for the public at large, Yuan's article and the Party's private views then circulated in the depths of the underground. As they circulated, the public added questions of their own: 'If the lessons are so important', many whispered, 'why isn't everyone allowed to learn them?' and 'Given that the deaths were those of the people at large, why is it always the sacrifices of the Party that are celebrated, rather than those of the tens of millions of Chinese who paid for the lessons with their lives?' Others went on to wonder whether the Chinese people would ever be anything more than stones to support the river-crossing steps of whichever imperial dynasty had most recently hijacked heaven.

As Yang Jisheng and Yuan Weishi were battling for the truths of the past, another intellectual was looking at the landscape of the natural world, and wondering how heaven had ever allowed the emperors to insist on a unity that struck at the security of all.

Wang Lixiong started out as a truck mechanic who had once posted an idea – for a slow and carefully considered drive towards elections – on the Democracy Wall of 1978 Beijing. In 1984, as Deng Xiaoping was battling against the treacherous Fifth (voice of the people) Modernisation, Wang decided to launch himself into the heart of China's natural world to listen to the stories it might tell. Lashing a raft of tires together, he had hurled himself down eight hundred miles of the upper reaches of the Yellow River. Observing crystal clear waters running at the old Tibetan top of the Qinghai plateau, as he journeyed downstream, he noticed that the closer the river flowed to the Chinese east, the muddier, and yellower, it became. Floating through a northern landscape that had been so deeply inter-twined with China's dreams of order, Wang's heart had been tugged by a haunting and disappearing beauty. It was a tug that would only get stronger when the Party fired on Beijing five years later, and again when Deng's glittering train took off.

Returning, over the years to the haunting plains of Tibet, and even venturing into the neighbouring lands of Xinjiang, Wang Lixiong eventually came to the same conclusions as Tan Sitong and the earliest revolutionaries. 'Heaven', in his intellectual opinion, was indeed composed of the eyes and ears of the people, rather than the self-strengthening plans of rulers at the top. And the guiding princi-ples of earth were nothing less than the *ren* art of being human, the *yi* responsibility that everyone had for their own integrity and the *zhi* need for everyone to absorb knowledge in order to understand. If, reasoned Wang Lixiong, all of that was too difficult to imagine across a land that had grown to the great size of China, then maybe one should start with individual counties and communities, and help them to find their feet first. Given the great differences between the many very different people of China, if one were to do that, then one would also need to reconsider the towering importance which the Party, and every previous imperial dynasty, attached to the idea of forcing unity across the very different races of the Chinese lands.

Thinking on the matter of unity, Wang asked himself why Mao had raised up the illusory idea of autonomous regions in the first place: had he really wanted to create a cauldron of rage? Consulting the records of the Long March and the promises that had been made, Wang found it hard to find an answer – other than the fact that Lenin had thought that a common program of socialist nation building for minorities was a good way of avoiding the problems of independence, and Stalin had set off to force Central Asia into a world of socialist republics under the Russian wing.

As to why the Party had raised up hundreds of individual *minzu* dreams only to rework them into fifty-six artificially manufactured compounds of a very complicated past – who could tell? Pondering the mysteries of the Party's minds, Wang wondered whether it was just because they like the imperial picture-books; or was it just the fact that 'big brother' Stalin had created a colourful cast of nationalities?

But things were as they were: Xinjiang and Tibet had been forcibly wrapped into China's borders, with a once-hesitating Inner Mongolia gathered up as well. Meanwhile, the other *minzu*, once part of a woven fabric, had been pulled out and put into artificial parks of their own. The question now was how to manage the future.

Trying to imagine solutions, Wang Lixiong began to sketch a set of ideas with which a mutual respect might be coaxed, rather than a unity forced from the barrel of a gun. His ideas had a lot in common with those which he and others considered that the Han Chinese would need themselves if they were ever to be free: the power of different people in different places to think for themselves; local elections with which the people could protect themselves from official wolves; and a rule of law that would guarantee both independence and a voice. With these fundamentals, surely the many different people could be woven together into a wider tapestry which, given a fair competition of qual-ified hearts and minds, could elect a nationally governing party. And if such a wider tapestry could be woven, surely it would be able to raise the necessary security required to protect everyone from any hungry foreign wolves outside.

As far as Wang Lixiong could see, with every year that passed, however, the obstacles to unity were only getting greater – particularly in the lands of Xinjiang and Tibet, where the anger of the people was now getting out of control. The military trucks of Han settlement (the *Bingtuan* Production and Construction Corps of the PLA) had already spread across the oases of Xinjiang. And as Wang was writing, the glittering train was already sweeping carriages of Han Chinese up to Lhasa, and setting them down to work their productive magic in the city-sanctuary of the gods. It would not be long before Tibetans followed the Inner Mongols into being a rare species in their own lands. Not that they would go quietly into that silent night: after sixty years of violent occupation, the monks were clearly going to continue to chant 'Free Tibet!' to the end. Just as the angry Uighurs were going to carry on reciting the truth of their Quran until their last dying breath – not to mention building every possible bridge with those outside spirits (Islamic, Russian or anything else) who might offer a helping hand.

After more than two thousand years of pursuing unity, Wang, like so many others before him, wondered whether anything at all had been learned from the past. The Patriotic Education Campaign had unleashed a generation of young Chinese whose only idea of history was a sense of being a trampled-upon people, betrayed not only by the West but by the Xinjiang and Tibetan edges of their own order. When, in March 2008, blood and flames had swept out of Lhasa to haunt the Chinese torch of Olympic harmony as it made its way around the world – and as the Party's patriotically educated populace had exploded with rage at an ungrateful Tibet – Wang Lixiong bravely tapped out an open letter with *Twelve Suggestions* for resolving Tibet's questions. Asking his friends to join him, three hundred and seventy dared to sign their names.

One of the intellectuals who Wang Lixiong approached was in no doubt about the risks that he was taking. As a university lecturer who specialised in human freedom – and as one of the four hunger-striking friends who had urged the students to leave Tiananmen Square in the early hours of June Fourth – he had long ago decided that he had a duty to serve the people. His name was Liu Xiaobo. Originally going to the square to talk to the students about the art of being Chinese (and the importance of not getting carried away by the anger of the day), Liu had shouted his words for all to hear: 'There is no enemy other than hatred and violence'. It was Liu Xiaobo who had realised that someone needed to talk to heaven's troops on the square. And as Hou Dejian, the 'Taiwanese voice' and a close friend, had raced to the front line, it was Liu Xiaobo who had stayed in the students' midst, persuading them to let go of the guns that they had 'liberated' from soldiers in the surrounding streets. Bullets exploding, sirens blaring, messengers arriving with reports of the injured and dead from the streets around, it was also Liu and his friends who had urged the desperate students to set aside their anger. Eventually, having walked the students safely out of the square, while others had scrambled underground, Liu Xiaobo had chosen to walk home in the bright light of the dawn. Two days later, he was snatched from a street, bundled into a van and despatched to Qincheng jail – three dark years of being haunted by the searing memories of the dead.

Released in 1991, detained again in 1995, and again in 1996, in the years that he was free to be at home Liu Xiaobo used his time to write. He was as shocked as the historian economist He Qinglian at the speed with which the Party was throwing the peasants off the glittering train even as their labour was being used to fuel it. He was also incredulous at the seemingly eternal silence of so many Chinese intellectuals across thousands of years of a hijacked heaven. Why had so many of the country's scholars always limited their battles to their private inkpots? Why had it not been until after the end of the Manju Qing that they had thought about rolling up their silken sleeves and fighting alongside the people on the ground? And why had so many of them allowed themselves to be corralled back into their libraries again after 1989? Whether it had been studying in their own pavilions or jumping onto Deng's glittering train to find fortunes of their own, so many minds seemed to have left the true search for heaven to rough bands of peasants – men who had not hesitated to stand up for their brothers.

Returning home in 1999, from a three-year spell of *laogai* labour, Liu Xiaobo had found the gift of a computer waiting for him. Taking to its keys like a mind to a book, he had flown off into the clouds of the web, revelling in the power of the internet to give virtual substance to the idea that heaven was a people rather than a single top-down mind. Recalling the silenced voices of the ancient past, remembering the First Qin Emperor's burning of the books and burials of scholars alive, Liu watched the internet light up China as if it were a magic engine sent directly from heaven above. And as he watched, stars of other minds began to join him, exploding new light into the darkness: peasant brothers banding together to find and tell the truth; migrant workers organising for a strike; and brave lawyers advancing to the front line in an attempt to defeat the false logic of the Democratic Dictatorship of the People.

As the internet ignited, however, so did the Party powers charged with maintaining a harmonious order. Liu found that the Party had provided a personal online guard to keep an eye on his conversations. And in 2004, when his tapping keys tripped over a forbidden word, the computer and all of his files found themselves under arrest. Another computer was acquired. As the censoring eyes carried on reading and blocking, Liu's fingers kept on typing. With true believers in Communism now as rare as unicorns, and with those in the front carriages of the glittering train seemingly oblivious to the dangers of its speed, Liu pounded out a steady stream of posts and articles to try and wake everybody up. 'The people are not a bunch of precious animals to be raised like prey for a hunt', he argued: 'A single hijacked heaven has not only corrupted itself, but eroded the power of millions of China's most educated minds to think for themselves'. To which he added that everyone's security lay in the ability of 1.4 billion Chinese to work out not only how to talk to heaven, but also how to talk to each other without a black cloud of officials getting in their way.

When Wang Lixiong asked Liu Xiaobo if he would add his name to the *Twelve Suggestions for Tibet*, Liu had agreed. Both knew that nothing could come of any call for resolving Tibet's problems unless and until the Chinese people had a voice of their own. And for that voice to be found, the very meaning of 'being Chinese' would have to be constantly repeated, again and again: the *ren* humanity of putting yourself in other people's shoes, the *yi* integrity of telling the truth, the *zhi* knowledge that included investigating things with your own heart and mind. The dangers of not doing so were getting clearer by the year. If someone did not start listening to Tibet and Xinjiang soon, any dream of unity would be swept away in the kind of nightmare which had brought heaven down on the adventuring heads of the Han and successive dynasties ever since.

Conscious that every journey of ten thousand miles starts with a single step, Liu signed. A few months later, he was asked by another band of internet brothers to sign another open letter; he agreed again. This one, a Charter known by its year, 2008, got closer to the main point. Setting out an argument for a change in the relationship between heaven and earth, it included some practical suggestions on how China could start a responsibly slow but steady march towards a heaven that would be based on the voices of China's many people, rather than on a single top-down idea. Liu Xiaobo not only agreed to sign but helped the drafters make sure that their ideas were carefully and calmly presented as an invitation extended to the Party for a conversation – rather than a threat.

Casting minds back over the same hundred years covered by the Party's Patriotic Education Campaign, the final draft of Charter 08 set out its own version of the milestones of China's history that had created the disasters of the past. The devils, explained the text, were not foreign gunboats and opium, but homemade self-strengtheners who had sold the people up their own treacherous rivers of fortune. There were certainly heroes – but they began with Kang Youwei, the originator of the hundred day reforms, and Liang Qichao, the man who had set such store on 'imagining a people', and whose ideas had spread across the decades to the lawns of Peking University, to the dreams of a Mr *Sai* Science and a Mr *De* Democracy; and they included Li Dazhao and the rural reconstructionists, whose practical expeditions of city minds to find the peasants in the countryside had tried to bridge the gap between the city and the village worlds. To this, the draft added a note on the guns of Chinese warlords who had split the country, and the squabbles between the Guomindang and the Communist Party that had opened the country's doors to a waiting Japan.

Also described in the text of the Charter, was the rise of a Communist Party that had promised the treasured dream of a People's Republic, and delivered the nightmare of a Democratic Dictatorship of the People. Intelligent men and women had been attacked and buried for questioning facts; a Great Leap Forward, the Cultural Revolution, a Tiananmen massacre and the glittering train had carried off countless lives – not to mention dreams, and let alone nature – and dumped them all in a ditch. The miracle of the 'New China', noted the text, was only a miracle if one didn't count the cost.

And as for those who wanted to pin their hopes on a benevolent celestial emperor at the top, the Charter noted, no one should imagine that that would fix the problem: China's true problems were not the result of messy conversations on the ground, they were the trouble that naturally arises when a single mind insists on doing everything. Some might argue that the Chinese people were still nothing but a loose tray of sand; they might even point to the failures of the 1911 revolution and the National Assembly, and to the brutality of the Cultural Revolution, as evidence that this was a people who would never be able to govern themselves, a people for whom democracy would always be a danger. But, urged the Charter, just look at the peasants trying, against extraordinary odds, to teach the lower levels of the Party how a simple human being should behave. And while the foreigners were not always clear about its meaning or possibilities, democracy was not an all or nothing idea: what might be a reckless cacophony in some wild places, could, in others, be a natural harmony of many different human voices, underpinned by a principle that a self-cultivated reason should govern all. What mattered was the quality of the relationship between heaven and the people: and after thousands of years of thinking about order, the Chinese people had surely learned more than enough lessons to be able to make it work.

Clearly, patiently and in simple words of black and white, the drafters of the Charter set out a pattern under which heaven and earth could come together, safely conducted by the *ren*, human being. A constitution that meant what it actually said – not only in a few words buried in a preamble which slyly put everything under the unity of the Party, but across every following 'right'. Constitutional freedoms that went beyond a splash of black on white to genuinely protect the right of the people to be human: a judiciary that reached its judgements independently of a Party phone call; and an elected government, and a military, that was independent of this or any other political party; officials accountable to the people. For all of which, China would need cities that did not see themselves as protected palaces, and a people – in both the city *and* the countryside – who accepted the responsibilities of knowledge but were also free to speak their minds.

Caught within the garden of the Chinese internet as much as any beast corralled in the grounds of a hunt, the draft text of the Charter was read by censoring eyes before it was even finished. On December 8,

2008, two days before it was published online, Liu Xiaobo was detained on suspicion of rumour-mongering, slander, subversion of the state and plotting to overthrow the socialist system. One year later he stood in a Beijing Court, charged with inciting state subversion. Knowing that his guilt had already been determined by the fact of his arrest, and aware that any defence would only inflate his sentence, he stood up to make a statement for the benefit of future generations: 'Criticism is not rumour-mongering. Opposition is not slander. Changes in the relationship between the Party and the people should be gradual, peaceful and orderly – precisely for the purpose of avoiding the sudden leaps which have caused such chaos across China's past.' And, quoting from a Chinese text passed down by questioning minds across hundreds of years, he reminded everyone that, in a land where people can think for themselves, there is no danger in speaking the truth: 'Say all you know in every detail: a speaker is blameless because listeners can think. If the words are true, make your corrections; if they are not, just take note.'

Cutting Liu Xiaobo's speech short, the judges of the Democratic Dictatorship of the People noted that a Defendant was allowed no more time to make a statement than that taken by a Prosecutor to make his case. Moving swiftly through their judgement (guilty), they announced the sentence: eleven years in the dark and silent prison of the single top-down mind. Liu Xiaobo was returned, once again, to the cold confinement of a jail, with the souls of the dead still echoing in his ears.

On 12 May 2008, when a dragon of an earthquake struck at the dreaming hills and valleys of remoter Sichuan, questions of life and death had again crashed into every Chinese mind. The first hundred dead had quickly become tens of thousands. China quivered with shock and anyone who could, rushed to the scene. Visiting the wreckage of lives lost, the then premier, Wen Jiabao, declared the sorrow of a nation – but suggested that the rescue and recovery should be left to the single mind of the state.

Watching Chinese soldiers bravely pulling children from the wreckage of nature's wrath, many agreed. But as the days passed, and as the toll of the dead rose and bodies were buried in a collective mass, an official mist seemed to descend on the land. Surviving villagers began to look at the landscape and ask some questions of their own: 'Why is it that some buildings stood their ground while others crashed to the ground?' and 'Why did the worst of the crashes attack the classrooms of the schools?' Reminding people of the unpredictable changes of nature, officials offered devastated parents a handful of money and the chance to have a second child. Rocked with grief, the villagers rubbed their eyes in disbelief: surely after the highest heavenly hearts had expressed such sympathy, the story of what had caused so many deaths was not going to be buried as well? It was not long before local spirits were digging into the rubble and asking stubborn questions; and it was not much longer before policing officials were reminding the questioners that rumour-mongering and defaming the state were serious offences, and that inconvenient enquirers would find themselves disqualified from receiving any cash.

It was not long after that a Beijing artist with a reputation, decided to do some digging of his own. The son of Ai Qing (the Party's favourite poet who, like so many truth-telling revolutionaries had once been despatched by his closest comrades to the bitterest wastelands at the edges of the empire), Ai Weiwei had grown up in brutal camps of labour. Returning to Beijing in the rehabilitating 1970s, he had encountered a bickering chorus of Zhongnanhai 'aunts and uncles', each blaming the other for the collective shame of the Cultural Revolution. They had seemed like a family from hell, and Ai Weiwei had given them as wide a berth as he could. Time passed, Ai Weiwei dabbled in ink and sculpture. He even added artistic touches to a Bird's Nest stadium for the Olympics, before sensing that the games had become a grand stage for the Patriotic Education Campaign. Noting that, as the Bird's Nest had risen, much of old Beijing had been bulldozed to the ground, Ai Weiwei stood aside from his work, and declared that, mesmerized by the glittering train, the choreographers of the games had forgotten the art of being human.

The Party's shock was palpable. Being part (albeit an eccentric part) of the Party family, Ai Weiwei's words were initially brushed under the red carpet. The artist himself was left to the madness of his studio, with a hope that he would stay there in that cloud of 'art' that, as Mao had always said so clearly, was nothing to do with the people. For Ai Weiwei, however, art was at the forefront of any revolution: no artist was worth anyone's salt if he did not speak for the people at large.

And so it was, that when Sichuan's people fell into the nightmare of both the earthquake and the concealing official mist, Ai Weiwei gathered together some volunteering energies, and took it upon himself to make a few enquiries of his own. Dialling directly into the offices of the local officials responsible for the hundreds of grieving villages and towns, he framed his questions with the experience of a man who knew his way around the Party, with the confidence of an artistic voice that was used to being heard and with the plain-speaking bluntness of a revolutionary spirit. 'What sort of condition was your local school in when it fell through the floor?' he enquired; 'And while you are checking your reports, perhaps you could give me a list of the children who are dead and missing as well.' Across every line, the answers were short, and astonishingly uniform: 'Any question about the condition of the buildings is a matter for the government alone. And, as every true Chinese ought to know, the lists of the missing and the dead are secrets of the state'.

Determined that the people should be served with the art of being human, Ai Weiwei and his team of volunteers spread out across the settlements struck by the earthquake and, together with a number of brave and equally stubborn people on the ground, pieced together the fragments of a disaster that had been anything but natural. They found that the answer to the question of the condition of the buildings was relatively simple. When, in 2006, Hu Jintao had tried to replace the nightmare of SARS with the dream of a New Socialist Countryside, counties and towns across the country had been commanded to roll out the schools necessary for a promised nine years of compulsory education, while cutting the burden of taxes on peasant heads – all to be achieved within two years. Pinching and pocketing pennies by the billions, the services of surveyors and architects had been dispensed with. Concrete had been mixed with sand; steel had been set aside as an unnecessary expense. Hu Jintao's heavenly deadline had been met. But the youngest and smallest of the people's voices had been set to study in the least safe of all places: classes of rooms that had been made from little more than the *doufu* curd of beans.

The answer to the question of the names of the dead and missing took a little more time, and a lot more work. Over the course of the next twelve months, patiently and painstakingly, the investigating volunteers covered the heart-breaking ground of the villages and towns shaken by the earthquake, and patched together a list of the names of those children who had disappeared or died. Forty-five names here, ninety-four names there: village by village, town by town, the numbers mounted up. In the end, they found 5,385 small souls enrolled in ninety-six shattered schools. All of the shattered schools had been built with sand.

Determined to keep the memories of the children alive, when the list of the dead and the missing was complete, Ai Weiwei and his team invited 5,385 living voices each to speak a single name out loud – and then spread them across the internet for the ears of the wider world to hear. As the voices were reading out the names, Ai Weiwei went to open an exhibition in Munich. While he was there, he raised a 'remembering' wall of bright blue children's backpacks. Across the backpacks, he painted the text of one of the thousands of messages that his investigating volunteers had received from Sichuan: 'She lived happily on this earth for seven years'. They were the words of a mother who had wanted only one thing for the death of her daughter – that her memory should survive.

While Ai Weiwei had been preparing the lists and the backpacks, however, an inconvenient questioner on the ground had been bundled away to a prison in the Chengdu capital of Sichuan. His name was Tan Zuoren. A local writer and lover of nature, he had started an investigation of his own into who was dead and missing, and why. Tan was not the only one to be arrested: there had been a steady stream of parents and teachers who, insisting on rumour-mongering, were obviously begging to be carried away. In Tan's case, a charge of 'subverting the state' had been added as a twist. Early on in his investigations, and as aware as everyone else of the risks he was taking, Tan had wrapped a white scarf of truth around his neck, and spoken to a camera before he could be swept out of sight. 'Better to spend years in another world', he had declared, 'than to live among a people who have lost the power of speech – years which one could pass in the hope that, at some time in the future, China's people will have reflected on what has happened and on what has been learnt about how to be Chinese.'

Hearing of Tan's arrest and impending trial, Ai Weiwei decided that he would attend the Chengdu hearing, and give his own evidence of the truth. No one was in any doubt that Tan would go to jail, but if the Party was going to imprison him for subverting a state which was supposed to be a 'People's' Republic, Ai Weiwei could testify to the fact that Tan had not only been working *for* the people, but *with* them as well. As Tan's lawyers confirmed: while it certainly would not help Tan to secure an easier sentence, when the judges passed their judgement, it would be clear to every independent mind, and to the judges themselves, that any sentence passed could not be truthfully said to be in the name of the people. It was not much. But with a journey of ten thousand miles stretching out before everyone who believed in the art of being human, it was one of those important first steps.

The Party, however, was equally decided that Ai Weiwei should keep his peace. The night before the trial, hired thugs (or plainclothes policemen: it had never in all of China's history been easy to tell the difference) exploded into his hotel room. Beating him heavily about the head for his stubborn questions, they then kept him under the wrap of a blanket until the court had delivered Tan's sentence. Ai Weiwei responded with an under-the-blanket recording of the hotel proceedings – for later launch as a made-for-the-internet movie, with the thugs appearing as themselves. The following morning in the courtroom, Tan's lawyer gathered a courage of his own, and rose to defend his client in the face of what Tan, and all the families who had lost their children, believed to be a lie. Quoting from a command engraved above the gate to one of Chengdu's oldest and best loved temples, he read the following words aloud: 'It is those who understand the people's hearts who are fit to rule; all you who come to govern these lands of Sichuan, think on this.' The temple in question was not just any temple, and the words were not just any words. Raised to the memory of the Crouching Dragon, Zhuge Liang, the temple had been standing for almost two thousand years. The words had stood above it as an enduring testament to the very essence of what it meant to be Chinese. With judicial eyes aware of the meaning but reading from the Party's script, the adjudicators of the socialist rule of law sentenced Tan Zuoren to five years in the prison of the single top-down mind.

Within two years Ai Weiwei found himself in a prison of his own. Although, being part of the Party's extended family, the events of his imprisonment were not only touched with strokes of heavenly opera, but also shot with the mind-leaping logic of the Monkey King.

It had probably all begun with the rather clumsy surveillance that the Party had arranged since Ai Weiwei had begun a personal investigation of things – starting with the succession of undercover thugs who pretended to be on holiday outside his Beijing home. Insisting that everyone practise the art of being human, Ai Weiwei had consistently made a point of politely asking the suburban tourists to assume responsibility for their own *yi* integrity, and give him their names. When the names were refused, Ai Weiwei took photographs for the people's 'family album', and posted them on the internet.

Later, returning to China after his 'backpack memorial', and recovering from an operation for a brain haemorrhage brought on by the hotel beating in Chengdu, Ai Weiwei had decided to demonstrate his own *yi* integrity, and make an official complaint: the Chengdu police force was respectfully requested to acknowledge the unjustified violence of their actions. Long months of idle inquisition made it clear that Ai's case was unlikely to get very far. On one of his many visits to the police station, though, Ai Weiwei accidentally happened upon one of the hotel thugs – comfortably installed behind a supervising desk. The official 'thug' refused to give his name. Ai Weiwei, the artist insisting on the truth, removed the man's dark glasses and took his photograph instead. The colour of the photograph was not enough to make a difference to the legal process; and no one, least of all Ai Weiwei, was surprised when his case was summarily dismissed. But up and down the country, the people saw the image of the thug-official shining across the internet; and many felt that at least a certain kind of justice had been done.

Time turned to 2010. Ai Weiwei had continued his 'art of being human' campaign; the Party continued its insistence on Stability Maintenance at all costs. A battle of wills was clearly underway. Pressing his point a little further, Ai Weiwei gathered up a hundred million hand-painted sunflower seeds, and took them to London to show the Western world what it meant to be an individual in a Chinese crowd. Meanwhile, raising the banner of a *hexie*, harmonious society, at home, Hu Jintao's forces of Stability Maintenance demolished Ai Weiwei's studio in Shanghai. Ai Weiwei responded with a lesson in literature. With the pronunciation of the two written characters for *he* and *xie* (*hexie*, harmony) sounding like the two written characters for the 'river crab' which the Shanghainese love to eat, he announced a Shanghai crab banquet to which everyone was invited to come and eat the President's 'hexie', harmonious, words.

As 2010 turned to 2011, and as spring began to foment in the deserts of the Arab world, the Party became ever-more anxious about unity. The Democratic Dictatorship of the People launched an attack on harmony-disrupting bloggers and put a number of them in jail. Long expelled from the walls of China's internet garden, Ai Weiwei carried on tweeting as freely as a bird. Worried friends tried to warn him that there was a time and a place for being human, and that the time and place was not now, and not in Beijing. The artist did not stop. 'To be human or not to be human? It's a simple question', tweeted Ai Weiwei, 'and in case you haven't noticed, you get the chance to answer it a million times a day.'

And then, in April 2011, Party patience finally snapped and Ai Weiwei was snatched from sight under the bright lights of Beijing's airport. Bundled into a van, he was carried off to a shady hotel for a 'chat' about the Party's policies on art. In the Zhongnanhai garden, the Party family squabbled about what to do with the Monkey in their midst.

Confined to yet another hotel room, as the Party family squabbled, the artist found himself under the constant guard of a pair of uniformed teenagers, with regular interrogating visits from older minds who were struggling to understand their instructions from above. Interrogating an artist was not a problem – but what exactly had this particular one done wrong? With heaven in confusion, the young guards ended up telling Ai Weiwei the story of their own imprisoned lives: peasants who had joined up for the uniforms, only to find their days spent inside airless rooms, they longed to be free. The older interrogators – at a loss to know what to talk about in the absence of any clear instructions – first found themselves engaged in a little light conversation about Marx and Engels' dialectical materialism, and then in a rather exhausting exchange of quotes from Mao's *Little Red Book* (everyone present knew the quotes by heart). Added time was strung out on a debate about the comparative virtues of Beijing noodles: with spring onions or without? After eighty-one days in which everyone had ended up banging their heads against the brick walls of the prison, Ai Weiwei was released to a pinching pair of propaganda shoes, and an un-free kind of freedom.

On the airwaves of the outside world, broadcasts scripted by the Propaganda Department denounced him as a bigamist, a pornographer and a tax dodger. On the ground, he was told in no uncertain terms that his liberty depended on shutting up, not only about the circumstances of his arrest but about any other matter on which he might have an artistic opinion. Some months later, a bill for a fifteen million renminbi fine (two million US dollars) was delivered to his studio, payable in fifteen days. As the Propaganda Department published the opinion of the Democratic Dictatorship of the People that no artist on earth had the right to tell the people what the difference was between right and wrong, tens of thousands of hundred renminbi notes began to flutter over the wall of Ai Weiwei's studio and into the garden of his truth beyond. With the image of Mao Zedong beaming out from the face of each and every one of them, they seemed to carry the words of voices who had fought for the earlier, 1911, revolution, not to mention the banners of May Fourth: 'not in my name'.

While Ai Weiwei was pushing the boundaries of the art of being human, an advancing Arab Spring was putting the Party and its police onto an ever-higher state of alert. Troublemaking questioners – journalists, documentary film makers, actors, writers and professors – were whisked away. Arrested? It was hard to say; most of them simply dropped out of sight.

By the end of 2011, increasing numbers of city lawyers were bravely stepping into court. Not many dreamt that they could get their clients out of jail, but they were beginning to believe that, with heaven changing its son in 2012, the time had come to stand up not only for the Chinese ideal of *ren* humanity, but for the ideals of *yi* integrity and *zhi* knowledge as well. Pointing to the Constitution of the People's Republic of China, as promulgated by the Party itself, the lawyers noted that, apart from helpfully describing heaven as a Democratic Dictatorship of the People, it also clearly guaranteed all of the necessary freedoms – of speech, the press, assembly – which enabled individual beings to act as humans as well. But as the Party so often pointed out, every freedom in the constitution was hostage to that single phrase in the preamble that put everything and everyone under the unified leadership of the Chinese Communist Party, and its guns. With every one of the people as much a prisoner of the Leninist Party as any defendant in a dock, the lawyers harboured no illusions: judges had no choice but to apply Party instructions, just as the police had no alternative but to make up whatever twists and turns would keep Stability Maintenance on the ground. But each time a lawyer advanced into the courtroom – and each time a defendant dared to question his sentence – they were making a statement that the people had been trying to make for thousands of years: heaven is heaven when it listens to the people, not when it conducts itself like a single top-down mind. The Party might have used the power of the gun to paint itself the façade of a courtroom but, like the peasants in the countryside and the secret supporters of Ai Weiwei, the lawyers in the cities were increasingly saying: 'not in my name'.

As 2011 moved towards 2012, and as more and more of the high quality population began to ask themselves what was going on, even the forward carriages of the glittering train began to blaze with questions. Some of them had heard the arguments of the city lawyers, and thought they had an obvious point. Others had been shocked into their questions by a book that had spread from Hong Kong.

Published in 2009, set in the near future of 2013, and entitled *The Fat Years*, the book was a fictional fantasy about the miracle of the glittering train. Painting a picture of a future golden age of China's ascendancy where (almost) everyone is happy, the author, Chan Koonchung, told the story of a handful of misfit friends who find themselves mysteriously unable to share in the universal joy of the People's Republic. Where once their microblogging friends and acquaintances had joined them in lambasting the Party for being a single top-down mind which stopped the people from being human, they now seemed to be marvelling at the fact that the Party's hard work and wisdom had not only spared China from the scourge of a global economic recession, but had saved the rest of the world as well. The microblogging friends and acquaintances were even arguing that the Party had been right all along: it was indeed only a Democratic Dictatorship of the People, under the leadership of the Party, which could deliver the kind of prosperity and satisfaction that the Chinese people now enjoyed. If anyone ever mentioned the Cultural Revolution, it was only to remark on what fun those years in the countryside had been. And if any of the misfit friends made a reference to Tiananmen, almost everybody else's faces just went blank; unless the friends or acquaintances were under thirty, in which case they insisted that it was all a Western imperial lie.

Even more worryingly for the novel's misfit friends was the fact no one seemed to be aware that the month of February 2011 had gone missing, nor did they seem to remember the events which had led up to it. The terrifying unravelling of the global economy that had spread fear in every direction and pushed rumour into overdrive; a Party crackdown that had sent even the monkeys running scared; the return of the PLA to the streets of Beijing; and an all-China bird flu vaccination which everyone was supposed to have had. The Party insisted that February 11 had been a calendar day, just like any other. And with everyone else bathing so blissfully in the harmony of everything, when the misfits try to share their concerns about the missing month, nobody else seems to care.

The misfits become convinced of a link between their inability to join in the general joy and the fact that February had been forgotten. They agree that the only way they will ever be able to get to the bottom of what had happened would be to ask a senior Party member. Given, of course, that no senior Party member would ever talk to the likes of them, they realise that the only way to have such a conversation would be to kidnap one of them, and squeeze him until he talked. Through a friend of a friend, they manage to catch a member of the Politburo and tie him up for a night of frank questions and answers.

Eventually, the Politburo member admits that the month of February 2011 had indeed been disappeared. But he insists that there had been no other way. 'You think it's easy to look after 1.4 billion people?' he snaps: 'We had to do it'. And with that, he proceeds to describe what had actually happened. With the rest of the world in the grip of its economic crisis and spiralling out of control, China had been on a knife-edge. Western demand flattened, the factories were slowing down and the Chinese people were up in arms about everything; the Party family was squabbling; and Tibet and Xinjiang were poised like tinderboxes, waiting to explode. The Politburo had wracked its brains to find a solution. Finally, it realised that the only way to avoid the end of everything was to create an opportunity out of the crisis. It had not been easy, but eventually they had come up with an 'Action Plan for Ruling the Nation and Pacifying the World'.

The idea behind the 'Action Plan' had been to let the people work themselves up into such a frenzy of rioting chaos and fear that they would rejoice at the comforting sounds of the steps of the PLA. With the army firmly on the streets, the Party could then set about changing facts on the ground. *Bian!* they had turned a quarter of the people's savings into vouchers which could only buy things made in China, and had to be spent within six months. *Flash!* they had ripped away the red tape which tangled up production, and let the factories produce like pistons to satisfy the waves of demand. *Swoosh!* and the land of the peasants had been privatised so they could turn their attention to making some money for themselves. Another quick *flash!* and the Chinese internet had been commandeered to create an automated system of price controls to keep everyone happy. After which, a string of *cloud-somersaults* had been undertaken to wrap up the messy corners of the rest of the world. With China rising, and everywhere else collapsing, it had not been very difficult. Japan was embraced as a most-favoured-forever partner – which meant that the interfering Americans could be sent back to their barbarian corner of the world. At the same time, the PLA rattled its rockets and made it clear to everyone, especially the Americans, that if anyone started muttering about an over-confident China, China itself would be the first to attack. Those feats achieved, the Party had been left with the question of the people themselves and their inconvenient memories. For that, they had just added a mild 'ecstasy-like' substance to everything the people drank, and *bian!* everyone had forgotten everything. As a final touch, they had then added a jab of a bird flu vaccination, and a quick clean of the Chinese internet, and, with the Great Man mission accomplished, everyone in the Party and the population had been able to get on with the harmonies of their lives.

At the end of the Politburo member's account of events, the misfit friends blast him with anger. 'What sort of a Party do you think you are? Hijacking heaven and the people just like the emperors of old, but this time with the added twist of technology to turn truth into lies'. To which, the Politburo member suggests that they just look at the harmony spreading all round them, and at the peace which has settled across the world. Could they really, he asks, believe that truth is better than lies? And while they were thinking, he suggests that they also look at the mess which the foreigners have created with all of their crashing around the world as if they owned everything, not to mention their total disregard for history, geography and anything else that didn't fit into the simple fixes of their tiny, irresponsible worlds. 'If you have any better ideas', he concludes, 'the Party would be delighted to hear them. But you might just want to give us some credit for swooshing a paradise up out of nowhere, while the rest of the world has been scrabbling around in the dark.'

The friends look at the Politburo member in disbelief, and remember the question, familiar to all Chinese, posed by the works of the towering, and Party-favoured, early twentieth-century writer, Lu Xun: 'Which would you prefer: a counterfeit paradise or a good hell?' It was obviously not a pleasant choice, but now it seemed that it was not even theirs to make. A single top-down mind had decided the matter for one and all, and done it in such a way that no one would ever again be able to tell the difference between black and white. True, the boundaries between the real and the not real had been a question since the time of Zhuangzi's butterfly dream, if not long before. And true, history could be a bit painful and the world is a complicated place. But to lose the power of your own mind and memory, and to be turned into a character in someone else's dream: it was a hell of a leap of faith.

Circulating under intellectual tables – banned in China, but smuggled in from small bookshops in Hong Kong – Chan's book might not have lit the kind of prairie fire that brought everything down in its wake, but it was certainly a significant spark. Many in the Party read it in the privacy of their studies, and thought that it pretty much summed up something they had been trying to say for years: 'We may not be perfect, but this is a difficult world'. A few were pleasantly surprised that an intellectual could have come up with such a clear understanding of how hard the Party had to work. Some outside the Party sighed with regret, but wondered what one could do: 'It was all a bit sad, but the world had changed, and if one could manage to make it as painless as the author had imagined, perhaps it would be all for the best.' Piling on to China's glittering train as fast as their feet could carry them, even the foreigners seemed to be agreeing that a counterfeit paradise was preferable to a good hell. Who needed to tell the difference between black and white, as long as you could keep on shopping?

Many others, however, reeling in shock at how close the future had become, began to think again. As Zhongnanhai squabbled its way to a new Son of Heaven, some of those others began to play a game of 'what if'. 'What if' being Chinese meant that you actually saw heaven as the voice of real human beings, rather than the choreographed broadcasts of a Leninist symphony? It might seem fantastical but, frankly speaking, Chan Koonchung's book seemed a bit fantastical too. Yet everyone knew, in their heart of hearts, that so much of the spirit of what it described was already true: 'Could China ever be a country where the people themselves could be trusted with a voice?'

Thinking again, many reflected on the fact that in another, admittedly much smaller, Chinese world, a group of Chinese people had been given a voice only fifteen years before. From 1949, schooled in the same ancient ideas of order, the Guomindang had ruled the renegade island of Taiwan as a single top-down mind, supported by the barrel of the gun. But then, in the 1980s, Chiang Kai-shek's son and heir had experienced a sudden and surprising *snow-in-summer* change of heart. Defying the rockets of rage that the Party flung across the Taiwan straits in 1996, heaven, at least in Taiwan, had been liberated, and communications, including elections of both a president and a legislature, had been handed over to the people without a single muzzle of a gun. Could the next leader of the Chinese Communist Party possibly be another snow-in-summer ruler who would finally open communications between heaven and earth for the mainland of the country as well? It was hard to believe, but given that every Son of Heaven since the beginning of time had been taught to keep his counsel silent, could anyone really tell?

As 2012 began to change into 2013, Xi Jinping – the new general secretary of the Party, had stood up and repeated the traditional announcement of the Party's historic sacrifices and successes. He had then, in something of a departure from the usual practice, gone on to declare a dream, imagining China as 'a strong and prosperous nation', and the Chinese people as 'happy and free'. While the idea of a dream was new – and a lot more interesting than 'One centre, Two points', 'the Three Represents' or 'Scientific Development' – with peasants manning the barricades in the countryside, cities spluttering in smoke and the Party continuing to insist on unity at the expense of human lives, the words had seemed to be a little hard to reconcile with the facts. Within days, the twittering Wechat was awash with humour. Some suggested that the Party state was working way too hard. All of that building and demolishing, surveilling and policing; and all of that exhausting worrying about the state of everyone's hearts and minds: grateful though the people were for its attentiveness, the Party was clearly well overdue for a long-earned break. Others noted that if only the internet police could swap places with the government's food administration, everyone's dream of being able to eat safe food would be realised, with the added advantage that they would also be able to talk to anyone they liked.

Sensing a danger to the Democratic Dictatorship of the People, the Party's Propaganda Department quickly came to the defence of Xi Jinping's dream, and rafts of twittering Wechat users were thrown off their accounts. Familiar with the game of cat and mouse, the users simply assumed the names of ancient heroes – characters from the *Outlaws of the Marsh* were particularly popular – and reincarnated themselves with new accounts. Almost as adept at the game as the users, the Propaganda Department hit back with a rule that anyone who reposted a 'rumour' more than five hundred times would be committing a serious crime. Up and down the country, the internet police, supported by the *wu mao dang* fifty cent party of cleansing cybersurfers, flew into overtime. The most irreverent, and popular, bloggers had been invited for a cup of tea and a chat at their local police station. Those who were slow to get the point had been invited to stay the night.

Some of the bloggers fell by the wayside, but others just kept blogging. Where inconvenient posts were harmonised with a deletion, the deleted posts were quickly reposted. As more and more inconvenient words and names were banned, the blogosphere searched through dictionaries to find harmless alternatives of characters which looked completely different when written down, but when pronounced sounded exactly the same. As it had always been, in the battle between the single top down mind and being human, the Chinese language had been requisitioned for the war of words. One writer suggested that it would save a lot of time – and a lot of 'character' crimes – if the Party could just publish a glossary of 'sensitive strokes'. Others noted that, at the rate at which words were hitting the dust, it might be hard for any glossary to keep up. Some just wanted to announce to whoever was reading their private email, that they were not class enemies, troublemakers or overthrowers of governments: they were, just like Xi Jinping, dreaming of a better world. But unlike Xi Jinping, they could see what was going on in their very local corners of the Chinese world, and they wanted to report some seriously corrupted Party officials in the hope that everyone's dreams might come true. The Party struck back with a call for ever-greater harmony with a dose of *zheng nengliang*, positive energy, as well. It also polished the campaign against corruption with a crackdown on the whistle-blowers.

Across 2013, peasant protests carried on rising, and arrests of city intellectuals were becoming harder for anyone to ignore. For many, dreams of freedom and happiness seemed to be in recession. A number of the intellectuals who had once trustingly offered their mind-emancipating services to the Party began to worry that the glittering train might come off its tracks. Xi Jinping moved swiftly to reassure. With many eminently qualified minds to hand, policy after policy flew over the walls of Zhongnanhai and the wider government, all designed to steady the rails. Consummately skilled in the art of investigating everything, the Party also floated policies to address some of the knottier questions of the time: peasant land, single children, *hukou* passes, and the *laogai* labour camps in which oceans of stubborn minds were still being held. Soon it was announced that peasant land would be reformed (once again), more people would be able to have two children instead of one, more migrants would be able to get a *hukou* passport to live in a city, and the *laogai* labour camps would disappear.

Meanwhile the anti-corruption campaign rolled on with such thunder that even the doubters began to wonder if this time it might be real. Across the restaurants of the capital, and every other city, concerned minds tried to fathom the direction of Xi Jinping's new order. Was he possibly drawing the reins of power closer to himself so that he could first defeat the Party's factions, and then give the people a voice? Or was he just another Party man, dressing up the Leninist-imperial order with a propaganda trick?

Some hopeful chopsticks pointed not only to the new policies but to a host of lower Party officials who were having to give up their Swiss watches as well as some of their numerous homes. Others pointed back to the past: corruption campaigns had always thundered in their early stages, before gradually dying out; and they were always a cover for targeting some inconvenient senior spirit or other, rather than the mass of corruption at large. And as far as Party policies were concerned, they added, one should always read the fine print. Land reform without giving the peasants a voice was, as the whole of history could testify, tantamount to handing any newly acquired gains straight into the waiting arms of Party wolves on the ground: any land given to the peasants would soon be consumed in taxes and fees, with the land itself eventually being picked up by a local power for a song. As for child births and *hukou* passes, the Party state was not proposing to give up its controls, only to adjust the settings. While the loss of the *laogai* labour camps was to be welcomed, what about the black jails, the hotels and the psychiatric asylums that were always ready to accommodate the subjectively subversive mind? Back and forth the chopsticks went, until someone would eventually sigh and remind everyone at the table that the members of the Party's family were a law unto themselves: hidden behind their screens, who could ever really know what they thought. And even if Xi Jinping wanted to change the heavenly order, one 'good official' on his own would never be able to make a black system white.

Some, however, looked at Xi Jinping and wondered. Maybe he was not intending to fundamentally change the relationship between heaven and earth, but perhaps with a bit of popular encouragement, he might come around.

Going back to their Wechat microblogs, believers and doubters alike began to exchange some thoughts on what would really be required to make 'the dream' come true. As their suggestions were noted by the Party's Propaganda Department, more Wechat accounts were closed, and heaven began to look for a few monkeys with which to scare the rest of the chickens on earth. A highly respected busi-nessman who had become a popular blogger was arrested. Having suggested that business would struggle to thrive if the Party wasn't put under some kind of law, he was given even tighter shoes than Ai Weiwei: accused of prostitution, he appeared on television to make his self-criticism in chains. Another popular blogger, the founder of a company that had designed and built much of new Beijing, was invited to denounce the rumour-mongering blogosphere on prime-time television, explaining to the people at large, and with obvious discomfort, that harmony was everything, and blogs were nothing but troublemaking chat.

Those who continued to openly and publicly argue that it was time for communications between heaven and earth to be improved soon found themselves picked up and deposited in the single-minded top-down jail. Some used the time to reflect on the truth of an observation made by Confucius two and a half milllenia ago: 'Whenever heaven invests a person with great responsibility, it tests his resolve, exhausts his body, starves his person, leaves him destitute and confounds his every endeavour: thus are patience and endurance developed and weaknesses overcome.' Others decided that it was time to take themselves off to other worlds: to quiet studies where they could dream of misty mountains, or to real lands abroad. Yet others decided that there was no alternative to staying at home and being the best Chinese they could. One of these was another lawyer, by the name of Xu Zhiyong. Like the drafters of Charter 08, he had raised a banner arguing for a constitution whose rules would govern the Party as well as everyone else. And, like the late nineteenth-century Liang Qichao so long before him, he had gone on to create a *Xinmin*, New Citizens, movement of people who would gather together peacefully, perhaps over dinner, to find the myriad local and practical ways through which the idea of heaven as a people could come true on the ground.

After an initial spell of house arrest, in August 2013, Xu Zhiyong was formally arrested and charged with disrupting public order by gathering a crowd. At his trial, in the first wintery month of 2014, Xu stood up and made a statement of his own. 'Being human is about more than having a full stomach', he observed. 'And any investigation of things can only work if the people can apply their own judgement to what they see and hear – and if the people themselves can be heard'. Guided by a Party telephone, and applying the socialist rule of law, the judges sentenced him to four years in the jail of the single top-down mind.

As Xu Zhiyong departed, other wilful hearts thought on a world where anyone could talk to heaven and say whatever they wanted to say. Some thought that it was just a foolish dream. A world without a single top-down order, how could that be real? Others cast their minds back across everything that had happened in the Chinese lands since the beginning of time: on the dynasties that had risen and fallen; on the brave men who had stood together as bands of blood brothers; on the irrepressible spirits who had dared to tell the truth as they saw it; and on the memory of an ancient time when anyone had been able to talk to heaven whenever they wanted, and say whatever they wanted to say. Remembering, they whispered: 'You may be a Party. But we are all Chinese'.

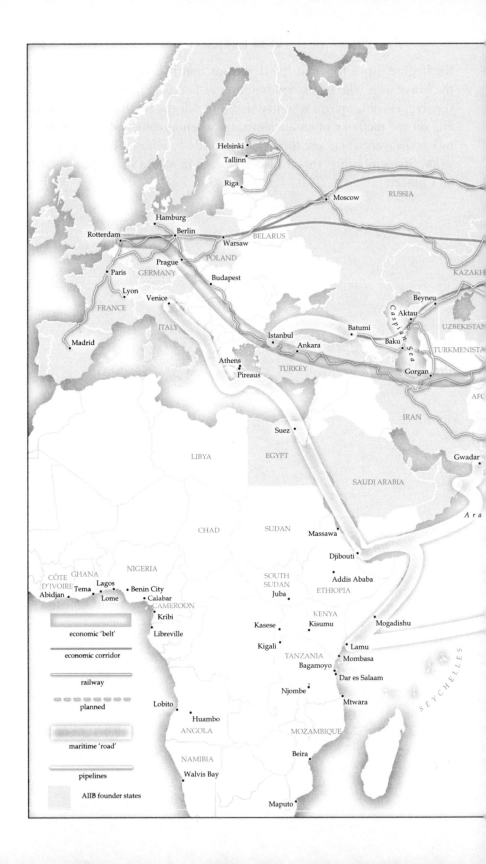

Helsinki
Tallinn
Riga
Moscow
RUSSIA
Hamburg
Rotterdam
Berlin
BELARUS
Warsaw
Prague
POLAND
Paris
GERMANY
Budapest
Lyon
Venice
FRANCE
ITALY
KAZAKH
Beyneu
Aktau
Caspian Sea
Baku
UZBEKISTAN
Batumi
TURKMENISTAN
Madrid
Istanbul
Ankara
Athens
Pireaus
TURKEY
Gorgan
AF
IRAN
Suez
Gwadar
LIBYA
EGYPT
SAUDI ARABIA
Ara
CHAD
SUDAN
Massawa
Djibouti
NIGERIA
SOUTH
SUDAN
Addis Ababa
CÔTE
GHANA
D'IVOIRE
Tema
Lagos
Juba
ETHIOPIA
Abidjan
Lome
Benin City
Calabar
CAMEROON
KENYA
Kribi
Kasese
Kisumu
Mogadishu
Libreville
Kigali
Lamu
TANZANIA
Mombasa
Bagamoyo
Dar es Salaam
Njombe
Mtwara
Lobito
Huambo
ANGOLA
MOZAMBIQUE
NAMIBIA
Beira
Walvis Bay
Maputo

SEYCHELLES

economic 'belt'

economic corridor

railway

planned

maritime 'road'

pipelines

AIIB founder states

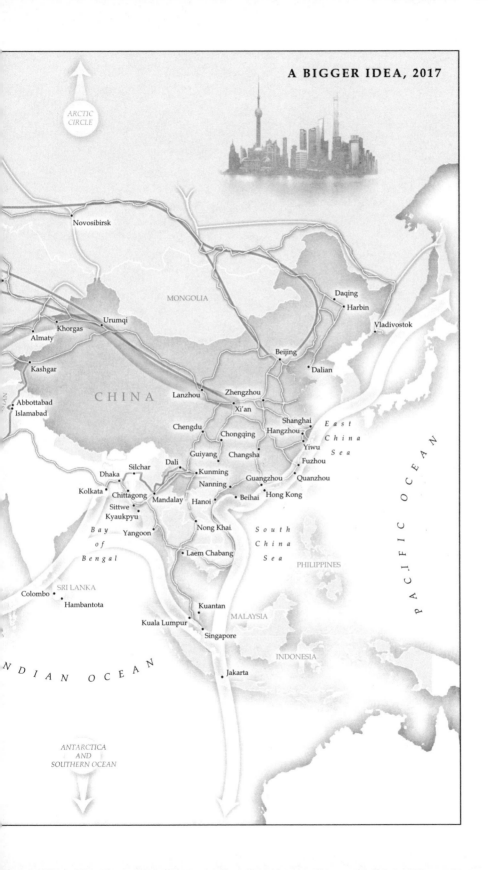

A BIGGER IDEA, 2017

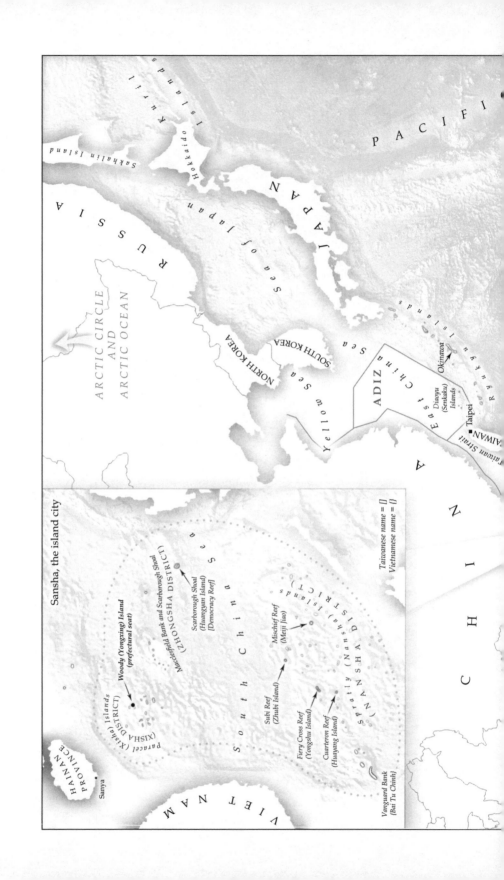

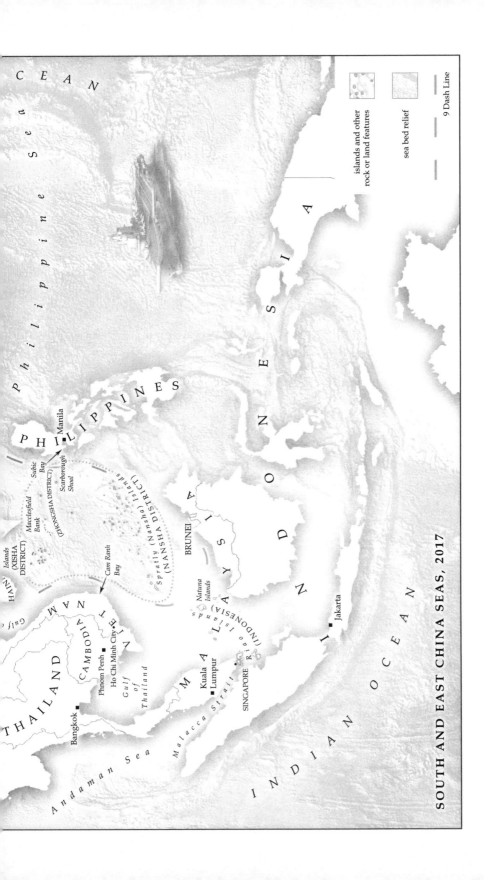

islands and other rock or land features

sea bed relief

9 Dash Line

SOUTH AND EAST CHINA SEAS, 2017

CONCLUSION
BECOMING CHINA

From the Son of Heaven down to the mass of the people, all must consider the cultivation of the person as the root of everything.

The Great Learning, Confucius (551 – 479 BCE)

'*G*E WEI GUANZHONG, *wanshang hao*', intoned the familiar grey-suited anchor, 'respected viewers, good evening'. Thus welcoming over a hundred million households to the Party's evening news, China Central Television, CCTV, turned its cameras to the left, and an equally familiar anchor, dressed in a more feminine red suit, announced the headline, and indeed the substance, of the news of the day: '*The Sixth Plenum of the Eighteenth Congress of the Central Committee of the People's Republic of China's Communist Party has come to its four-day end.*' Prepared footage loaded, viewers were then taken to the sky above Tiananmen Square, and an aerial view of the Great Hall of the People, before being swept down to earth and into an auditorium. Gathered together along serried ranks were the 248 (s)elected members of the Central Committee of the eighty seven million strong Party as well as a large number of equally ordered expert guests. Attentive viewers would have immediately spotted the fact that this was not one of the many auditoriums in the Great Hall of the People but a more convenient hall, used by long convention, in a closely guarded Beijing hotel.

In normal years, CCTV's viewers saw the Central Committee's plenum meetings as something of a Party ritual whose script could be summed up in three simple phrases: 'The leaders are busy, the motherland is developing rapidly, other countries are in chaos'. Of the six plenums held within each congress, the sixth was usually the most interesting: the point at which those who read the Party's tealeaves could get a sense of the changes of Party personnel, and thus Party policy, that might be likely to appear in the following year's new Congress. If it marked the end of the first of a leader's two five-year terms, they would also be looking for a hint as to who was in the running to become the next General Secretary, leader of all. But the last four years had been anything but normal – unless one counted the 'new normal' that had initially seemed to be about economics but now seemed to be about

639

everything. This 2017 year, the tealeaf readers were looking less for the likely next new leader and more at the bigger, revolutionary, question of whether there would be any new leader at all.

Trained to tell the Party's stories through the angles of their lenses, CCTV's camera focused first on the man who seemed to have taken a sword of faith to both Party and state: the man who, if the rumours were to be believed, had already survived a number of attempted assassinations as well as a coup, Comrade Xi Jinping. Travelling on, it featured the serious countenances of each of the six other members of the Politburo's Standing Committee, in strict order of rank. These included Comrade Li Keqiang, the premier: technically second in rank but with a voice that seemed to have declined during his years in office; and Comrade Wang Qishan, technically sixth in rank, but as secretary of the Party's Central Commission for Discipline Inspection and in charge of the greatest anti-corruption campaign in living memory, more like number two.

Across the next half hour, CCTV carried selected footage from the four day event: images of the twenty-five Politburo members turning the pages of their officially approved documents; images of the pens of the wider ranks of committee members diligently taking notes; images of Xi Jinping delivering his annual work report to the full assembly; and images of arms raised in unison as the words of the leader were approved with a vote. They also featured more relaxed moments, carrying viewers into the sessions of smaller working groups, many led by a patient and gently smiling Xi Jinping. As the scenes played on everyone's screens, the critical content was highlighted by a voice-over: the special Chinese characteristics of China's pursuit of socialism; the *si ge qianmian*, Four Comprehensives, with which Xi Jinping was leading the Party and the people to the realisation of the China dream; brief summaries of the galaxy of initiatives being undertaken to get to the dream; and a note on the affirmations of future best behavior, which was what usually gave the best clue as to what had gone wrong in the past. This year, after scandals of vote rigging, the sale and purchase of Party positions, and yet more Central Committee members expelled for abuse of their positions, some of the strongest affirmations were those of the democratic rights and duties of Party members, and of the discipline, sacrifice and unity required for success.

And then, buried in the rather boring summary of the Party's closing communiqué, came a carefully crafted statement anticipated by those who prided themselves on reading the future from the tealeaves of the present: while the collective leadership that underpinned the democracy of the Party should always be followed, Party members would now closely unite around the Central Committee, with Comrade Xi Jinping as the *hexin*, core, leader of all.

It had taken four years, if not forty. Four years of riding not one tiger but many, and of flogging not only one sun but all of the other nine mythical suns that an ancient archer Yi had once shot down. Four years of taking the Party by its tail and turning it inside out to make the new normal clear: a *comprehensive* rebuilding of society with Party cadres getting back among the people for the moderate prosperity of all; a *comprehensive* deepening of reform to address not just economics but the very foundations of the Party and its state; a *comprehensive* government of the nation through unambiguous rules of law; and a *comprehensive* governance of the Party itself to ensure that it was fit both to rule and lead the country to the ultimate revolutionary victory: a truly socialist state.

Carried by satellite, the signals of the breaking prime-time news were broadcast across all twenty-three provinces, including the renegade Taiwan, four municipalities, five autonomous regions and the two still-special administrative regions of Hong Kong and Macau, that make up the People's Republic of China. Rebroadcast across the networks of all of China's local television stations, they appeared on the dinnertime screens of almost every Chinese household: including those watching from the new ocean city islands of Sansha – but excluding the stubborn spirits in Taiwan, who refused to pick them up. Extracts were even carried by the local networks of the Central Asian states who were keen to join the belt and road that would bring them into the orbit of the China dream, as well as states who were not quite clear what the belt and road was but understood that it was important.

As the news spread across the world, reaching those who dreamed of becoming part of China's journey, those who didn't, and those who feared the direction that the journey might take, almost everyone asked themselves the same questions: did the idea of a core leader mean that the Party was going to find its dream of a future in the story of its past; and if so, how far back was the Party likely to go?

It was Confucius, or someone pretending to be Confucius, who had summed up the essence of the Chinese idea, and in so doing set the rulers and their people on a journey to utopia on earth. Not the false prophets of the West, with their ideas of a material world for earthly matters and a spiritual world that was responsible for something better, but a rational understanding that life on earth was composed of the material and the metaphysical, and that if one could not work out how to manage things in this world, what on earth was the point of trying to think about things in the next one? Kangxi had tried to address this point with the Jesuits in the seventeenth century but while some of them had clearly understood, their man in 'Rum' had never quite managed it. Burying themselves in the *Yi Jing*, the *Dao De Jing* and Confucius' *Analects*, the Jesuits had sent translations back to Europe, with readers found in Leibniz (the early eighteenth century mathematician who was fascinated by the idea of yin and yang but saw it more in terms of the binary options with which he would create the calculator), Jean-Jacques Rousseau (the later eighteenth century philosopher whose *Social Contract* paved the way for the French Revolution) and Voltaire (who saw God as a moral necessity rather than a truth, and the ritual arrogance of the Catholic church as a risk for all). But the followers of the Western Enlightenment quickly forgot the Chinese inspiration for many of their ideas, and when the natural philosophers who emerged from the Enlightenment battled against their own rulers, the result had been a standoff: a division of church and state, and with it the separation of morality from an increasingly scientific world.

Western ideas of separating material matters from those of an other worldly 'religion', had never had much traction in the Chinese lands. Whatever gods they might call on, for China's intellectuals and most of its people, the cosmos had always been church, state and home; and the greatest faith had been the determined belief in man's ability to unlock the secrets of the cosmos for a better, or longer, life on Earth. For a long time, the official texts had been the Confucian classics; with the unofficial texts including, the *Yi Jing* and the *Dao De Jing*, and even the rebellious principles of the heavenly kingdoms, the text of the *Taiping Jing*. And then Kang Youwei, who had understand it all so clearly, had declared the Confucian classics to be the deception of a Han dynasty ruler, and Marx, Engels and Lenin had appeared to fill the utopian gap. Deception or not, the principles of the Confucian classics had already worked their way into everyone's ideas about being Chinese, and once the Party had got over its initial revolutionary exuberance, its leaders, from Jiang Zemin onwards, had increasingly returned to Confucius' aphorisms to make important political points.

That was the beauty of China's *wenming*, civilisation: ideas about what it meant to be human in the society of others had become so bound up in the history that gave rise to them, that the two, the ideas and the history, ran together like the blood coursing through the veins of the people themselves. With the biggest question of the cosmos always that of man and the quality of his relationship to others, it was no surprise that thinkers through the ages had battled over the fundamental question of whether man was good or bad; nor was it a surprise that the nature of a dynasty and its order had depended heavily on the founder's ideas of morality. Inspired by the Duke of Zhou, Confucius (or whoever it was who had written for him) had argued that man was fundamentally good, but needed the ritual help of songs and dance to keep ordinary forgetful people on the straight and narrow track. Accordingly, the Confucian view was that the achievement of a golden age of peace and security on Earth depended on a ruler who nurtured the moral qualities of the people for the benefit of all. Conversely, the First Qin Emperor had believed man to be bad and had accordingly put the people into an iron grid of order, bound by mutual surveillance and underpinned by brutal laws and punishments. Liu Bang, the rebel who became the first Han emperor, had decided that the best solution was to hedge one's bets: stiff laws of the state for obedience but wrapped within a Confucian idea of morality that would appeal to hearts as well. The result had been a *wenming* (*wen* for writing, *ming* for bright) belief in the enlightening power of moral texts for the achievement of harmony on earth: a civilisational idea.

As successive rulers and their scholars, seeking to distinguish themselves with ever-more elaborate interpretations of Confucius, had got progressively more ensnared in the detail and less clear on the bigger picture, generals on their battlefields and scholars in their private studies had looked to other worlds. The *Yi Jing* and the *Dao De Jing*, whether in their original texts or translated into folk wisdom, had been obvious guides. Also important, not only for the generals, had been Sunzi's *Bingfa* and a set of thirty-six aphoristic stratagems that everyone knew by heart. Sunzi's *Bingfa* should technically have been

translated as the 'rules of war', but so esoteric was it in its understanding of the yin and yang changes, that the French Jesuit who first
converted it into a European language, recast the 'rules' as 'art'. With
almost everyone, big and small, fighting either the battle between
earthly good and evil or the battle of which belief should guide the
order of the day, the aphorisms of the *Thirty-Six Stratagems*, had become
as much a part of the lexicon of daily life as the threads of Buddhism
and Daoism. In the fourteenth century writers had told the tales of
the big battles of the past and their stratagems – battles between peasant rebels and their imperial oppressors, and battles between rulers
competing to be the single Son of Heaven – through the books that had
travelled as the stories of the *Outlaws of the Marsh* and the *Romance of
the Three Kingdoms.*

And then, in the eighteenth century, a writer whose family had
lost its wealth in an imperial succession wrote a semi-autobiographi-
cal epic of life in a world where the confusion of morality and power
made it hard for anyone to tell the difference between what is real
and what is not. Drawing on the Daoist and Buddhist ideas equally
woven through the Chinese story, *A Dream of Red Mansions* buried
Chinese readers in the detailed machinations of life within a grand
family whose great fortune depends on tying itself to the favours of an
all-powerful emperor, with the fortune being lost when the emperor
is succeeded by a son with a different idea (set in the Qing dynasty,
every reader understood the two rulers to have been the glorious
Kangxi and Yongzheng, his corruption-beating son). In what would
become an iconic phrase, the book describes the dilemma at the heart
of the battle to deliver utopia on Earth: *jia zuo zhen shi zhen yi jia*,
truth becomes fiction when the fiction is true, *wu wei you chu you huan
wu*, real becomes not real where the unreal is real. Confucius had his
place, but everyone knew that it was this fundamental contradiction,
between the real and the not real, that was really the hallmark of the
wenming civilisation.

It was Mao who brought the texts together for the dream of building a revolutionary state: a state dedicated to defeating the forces that
stand between the people and utopia, and then allowing itself – an
obstacle to the ultimate freedom of utopia – to wither away once the
people have developed the ability to live together in peace and security without anyone else having to tell them what to do. Mao, with

his love of the Crouching Tiger, Zhuge Liang, whose tale appeared in the *Romance of the Three Kingdoms*, of Song Jiang, the Robin Hood bandit immortalised in the *Outlaws of the Marsh*, and of Sun Wukong, the Monkey King whose Daoist-Buddhist *Journey to the West* forced everyone to face up to the fact that in the search for utopia on earth, truth is less of an absolute and more of a question. Indeed, Mao even saw a lesson in the bourgeois *Dream of Red Mansions*: in the battle between morality and power, truth can only be a contradiction; but in the hands of a ruler dedicated to delivering utopia on earth, truth can change its fate and become the driving force of the will of the people to make a different world.

The first General Secretary to have been raised in the Party, the first to have headed the Party School, Xi Jinping brought an element of revolutionary preparedness unmatched since Deng Xiaoping. Long thinking about how the order of heaven and earth could be maintained while also keeping the foreign barbarians at bay, he had read everything that Mao had read, and probably more. Xi had also read every word spoken or written by Mao Zedong, and every one of the texts that made up the Marxism-Leninism canon. As his career had progressed; he had also read the works and speeches of Deng Xiaoping, Jiang Zemin and even Hu Jintao. Among the many Western texts he had consulted was *The Old Regime and the Revolution*: Alexis De Tocqueville's mid-nineteenth century observation that the greatest time of danger for a state is when it reforms, thus raising expectations of a change that will take longer to realise than human patience is usually prepared to wait, with the risk that the state and the people divide.

When he had been clapped to the Party clouds in November 2012, Xi had been clear that most of China's troubles were grounded in an economic opening-up that had outpaced political reform, together with a false, Western-inspired, intellectual expectation that political reform would take the shape of a constitutional democracy. What was required, in Xi's opinion, was a fulfilment by the Party of its founding promise: the promise of the Democratic Dictatorship of the People that, with the Party as their vanguard, the people would be led to a socialism of economic equality and social justice, predicated on a learned understanding that socialism can only work if everyone puts society first.

Drawing on the learning of the past to serve the needs of the present, Xi Jinping took the advice of both Confucius and Mao. Confucius' contribution was a comprehensive set of sequenced steps with which any state could recover itself and its morals. Contained in the sacred text of *The Great Learning*, arguably the most important of China's *wenming*, civilisational texts, Confucius began with the observation that 'things have their roots and branches; affairs have their beginnings and ends; to know what comes first and after is to be near the Dao'. He then set out, line by line, the steps through which a ruler, starting with a thorough 'investigation of things' would nurture the sincerity with which the people would cultivate themselves and their families and, with which, the state would naturally be rightly governed and the world would be at peace.

Mao's contribution was twofold. First was the idea that the truth of the future was created from the facts of the present, that the facts of the present were always contradictory and that, rather than seeking to eliminate the contradictions, one had to try to understand their underlying causes through a persistent process of trial and error. 'Correct knowledge can be arrived at only after many repetitions', Mao had observed, 'leading from practice to knowledge and back to practice'. Second was Mao's conviction that the art of war should be applied to everything.

With the Party being held in ridicule by the end of Hu Jintao's term, Xi Jinping had quickly made it clear that winning or losing public opinion was a matter of Party survival or extinction, and that unless the battle for public opinion was won, the Party would be unable to lead the people to socialism and thus the nation, divided, would be lost. Turning to Mao for the tactics that could help him put his insight into practice, he naturally began where Mao had begun: with the 'mass line'. 'From the masses to the masses, Mao had insisted. 'Go to the masses and learn from them', 'act in accordance with their needs and wishes'. Being 'modest and prudent, guarding against arrogance and rashness', the Party should serve the people by gathering up their ideas, reorganising them, propagating them back among the people, testing them, and repeating the process 'over and over again in an endless spiral, with the ideas becoming more correct, more vital, and richer, each time.' 'Every word, every act and every policy must conform to the people's interests'.

Launching his Mass Line campaign in June 2013, Xi Jinping told the Party's officials that over the course of the next year, they would need to get close to the people, and in so doing, they would need to demonstrate frugality, work on their own self-purification, and painstakingly and humbly gather the knowledge on which an effective Action Plan for a better future performance could be developed. Ideology and faith, Xi noted, would be key to strengthening the Party; humility and service would be the hallmarks of success.

Over the following months, CCTV's cameras followed Xi Jinping, and every one of the other six members of the Politburo's Standing Committee, on visits to the poorest parts of the country. Under the directions of a special purpose 'Leading Group', supported by forty-five central supervisory teams as well as seventy-nine cadres at key ministerial and provincial levels, all lower level officials had been required to follow suit. 'Go out and do a survey' they were told, 'put on a hard hat, roll up your sleeves, shake a villager's hand, or better still, put a brotherly arm around a villager's shoulder.'

By December 2013, the Mass Line campaign had resulted in detailed policies to regulate spending and adjust the personal behaviours and morality of Party officials. Within eighteen months, seventy-four thousand cadres had been punished for their bad work style, and sixty-three thousand had been given their marching orders. Propaganda officers had been placed in Party cells across the nation: in every institution of Party and state at all levels, and many in the private sector as well. Within each cell, and under the innovation of new 'Democratic Life' meetings, criticisms and self-criticisms had been conducted. Some officials came through relatively unscathed, others succumbed to early retirement or suicide; many whispered that they would not have tried so hard to join the Party if they had realised it would end in a rectification campaign. With 'four dishes, one soup' as the Party's frugal mantra of the day, Xi Jinping himself celebrated the end of the year with a casual call at roadside café, ordering a pork b*aozi*, bun, with some simple vegetables. Images of Xi eating with some of the country's simplest people spread on social media; within hours, the café was inundated by people looking for the 'President's platter' and the banquets of the recent past vanished under a wave of simple fare.

Calling an end to the Mass Line campaign nearly nine months later, in mid September 2014, Xi Jinping then reincarnated it as an 'everlasting mission'. Guided by twelve virtues, including integrity, kindness and dedication, Party members were instructed to take what they had learned and spread it everywhere; they were also told that there were too many weeds among them and that the Party could do with thinning its ranks. A book of Xi Jinping's speeches and reports, *The Governance of China*, flew off the shelves; it was accompanied by a mobile phone app whose name '*Xue Xi*, *Study Xi*, played on the fact that the '*xi*' of Xi Jinping's surname was the second of the two characters that made up the *xuexi* word for learning. Students were exhorted to 'go to the tough places in the grass roots and deliver extraordinary performances in ordinary situations'. As the Party turned to virtue, the *tu hao*, conspicuous consumers of any stripe, were put firmly in its sights. In the summer of 2014, a twenty-three year-old material girl celebrity, Guo Meimei, appeared on television, without make up, in orange prison attire and facing a long sentence in jail. Formally she had been charged with running a casino. But everyone knew that it was the Maserati, the Hermes handbags and the Shenzhen mansions that had done for her.

As the Mass Line rolled into its everlasting mission, Xi Jinping's corruption campaign was getting into its stride. The task was enormous. Everyone knew that its web had been woven under Deng Xiaoping's third-choice successor, Jiang Zemin: the man who had tried to bolster his limited leadership credentials by exchanging political favours for support. Since then, it had crept into almost every part of the Party and the state. Senior central officials collaborated with provincial Party secretaries, and mayors; all of them collaborated with the SOEs, with the security services, and even the secret societies; and at some level or other – usually when an SOE was being laundered through the restructuring that led to a listing on a stock market, most of them collaborated with private businesses as well. In some parts of the country, the web of corruption was so sophisticated that it might be described as a parallel faith, if not a parallel state. Almost as distorting as the corruption, however, were the tactics employed to undermine the corruption campaigns. Hu Jintao had tried everything: centralisation to squeeze the life out of local power, decentralisation to cut the limbs from the head, but neither had worked. The central state could never control enough to be effective, and the local powers had always turned every inch into a thousand steps – or resorted to the ancient tactic of going slow whenever the centre wanted something that disagreed with their plans, thus putting the country's entire economy at risk. 'The centre has its measures, and the local officials have their countermeasures' was a familiar phrase to everyone, high and low. With the Party-state and the parallel faith of corruption entwined in such a close dance, few believed real change would be possible without a revolution.

There was also the sensitive matter of the family. With no aristocratically red lineage, Jiang Zemin had traded favours with the princelings to give him a *pai banzi*, do the deal, hand in dealing with the Party. Hu Jintao, also with no red family, had tried to counteract Jiang's tentacles with the talents of the Party's Youth League, the technocratic base of his own power and the route through which he had made it to the top. Xi Jinping, a Party princeling *and* a member of the Youth League, had tried to work his way to the top without upsetting either faction while stepping neatly to avoid the threads of Jiang Zemin's dark web. As he had moved closer to the heart of power, however, members of his own family had not only begun to accumulate the riches that naturally followed power but also the inextricably linked obligations-for-favours that the nature of the system required. Then Bo Xilai had smashed everything. Gambling on the hope that Jiang Zemin would fix the odds behind the scenes and *swoosh* him to the top, he had unleashed a 'sing red' campaign among the people of Chongqing, while stuffing everyone's pockets, including the secret societies, the military and any other Jiang Zemin pets, with gold. Hu Jintao had had him arrested; Xi Jinping had put him through the court. But after the risks and expectations that Bo had raised, the challenge of managing the treacherous shoals of his own family's wealth while also battling corruption and getting on top of Jiang Zemin's formidable factions had been a challenge indeed. In 2012, the New York Times and Bloomberg had led with stories on the Party families' billions, with fingers also pointing to Xi's backyard. Under the Party's circumstances, the only option had been to ban them.

Appreciating the contradiction – that his own power to change the destinies of 1.4 billion people rested upon the same Party base that facilitated the corruption – Xi had put the anti-corruption campaign into the hands of a trusted friend, Wang Qishan. A historian who had married into the Party family, with the added advantage of a successful career in finance and as mayor of Beijing, highly regarded at home and abroad, it was with Wang that Xi had shared the deprivations of the countryside during his Cultural Revolution youth. Both were clear about the possibilities of the Central Commission for Discipline Inspection, the CCDI. With powers almost as terrifying as those of the Ming dynasty's imperial censorate (a *qilin*, unicorn, that could smell good and bad from a thousand paces) and its Eastern Depot (the eunuch terror that had destroyed the scholars of the Donglin Academy), the CCDI could move across the chessboard of power like a knight. And while most expected it to concentrate on rooting out graft and factions, given that almost everyone was corrupt to some degree, there was no reason why, in intelligent hands, its inspections could not be directed to the advancement of wider policy as well.

Armed with the *Thirty-Six Stratagems*, Xi and Wang set out to 'cross the sea without the emperor's knowledge' (one of the earliest stratagems) with Jiang Zemin as the 'emperor', and the emperor's faction including senior spirits in the military and security services. Given that their prey were also masters of the *Thirty-Six Stratagems*, however, they would need every lever of power, artifice and secrecy to disable Jiang's faction before it could neutralize, compromise or evade them. And they would need to 'shut the door to catch the thief': taking the time necessary to cut off any and all routes of escape before moving in for the final kill. Preparing their ground carefully, they equipped the best intelligence officers they could find with the technology – cameras, microphones, facial recognition tools, big data and, of course, passports – that would enable them to access the secret lives of their prey at home, and to hunt them down wherever they were, including abroad.

The first step was to 'besiege Wei by rescuing Zhao', finding the weaker points in Jiang Zemin's relationships through which they could work their way into his dark web. Given that the web reached across almost all of the Party's institutions, and across the country, there were a large number of possibilities to consider. And given the size and complexity of the web, there was also a risk that many of the possibilities would be rabbits leading them into a hole. Not to mention the fact that the web included a number of tigers with individual webs of their own. Wang Qishan decided to start with the web around the biggest of Jiang Zemin's supporting tigers, a man called Zhou Yongkang. One of the most powerful men in the country, Zhou's career had given him access to the Party's greatest *fuqiang* wealth and power: once Party Secretary of Sichuan, before that Party Secretary of the China National Petroleum Corporation, CNPC, that would become one of the biggest and most powerful of the SOEs, Zhou had risen to become Minister of Public Security. From 2007 until his recent retirement at the age of sixty-nine, he had gone on to become Secretary of the *Zhengfawei*, the Central Political and Legal Affairs Commission that controlled all enforcement bodies, from the police to the courts, including a paramilitary whose budget had been inflated by Zhou to become even bigger than that of the PLA.

Looking for 'borrowed swords', Wang Qishan sent CCDI investigation teams off to find the individual officials and family members whose own corruption could be used to turn them into weapons for the final attack. Arriving without notice, unchecked by any higher powers or laws, they occupied desks, searched files and pulled in anyone and everyone – associates, subordinates, and lowly clerks – who could show the way. Some disappeared and reappeared within a matter of days; others reappeared a year or more later, after they and their families had been broken by interrogations and expelled from the Party: filmed as penitents in courts now answering directly to Xi Jinping. In September, Wang's teams pulled the first of Zhou Yongkang's tiger teeth, snatching a man who had previously been head of the CNPC, had acted as a 'white glove' for many of the senior leadership's more embarrassing dealings, and had been rewarded with the directorship of the SASAC body that controlled all of the SOEs. In December, they pulled the second of the tiger teeth: detaining a son who had created an empire out of his father's energy connections, Zhou Bin. By the end of the year, Zhou Yongkang was beginning to look more like a sick cat than a tiger.

As Wang moved across the chessboard, he took every opportunity to 'pilfer a goat', taking particular satisfaction when the goats turned out to be linchpins of other factions as well. One, Ling Jihua, was the father of a young man who had smashed a Ferrari on a Beijing ring road, killing himself, and one of the two naked girls on his lap, in one of the junior-princeling races that had become a popular form of late night entertainment in the capital. Head of the Party's General Office under Hu Jintao, Ling had also been a significant member of a Shanxi provincial faction known as the '*Xishan* society', its name cleverly playing on an inversion of *Shanxi*, the province, while also referring to Beijing's '*Xishan*', Western Hills, where the faction was said to hold its secret meetings. Another goat was a man called Liu Han. A timber trader who had moved into commodity markets, his friendship with Zhou Bin had led him to an empire of energy, real estate, and finance; but a gang shooting at a teahouse had then taken him to jail. Protected from execution by his Zhou family connections, it was, in the end, those connections that sealed his fate: as the CCDI searched for routes into Zhou Yongkang's dark web, Liu Han came to their attention and was sent back to the courts for a death sentence.

By the beginning of 2014, it was rumoured that Zhou Yongkang had been removed to a heavily guarded military base in Inner Mongolia. In July, he was declared guilty of 'serious violations of Party discipline' and expelled from the Party, the first member of the Politburo Standing Committee to be expelled from the Party since the fall of the Gang of Four. To pull in their quarry, the CCDI had detained or arrested over three hundred relatives, political allies, business associates, underlings and staff. Once snared, the depths of his depravity were colourfully displayed on everyone's televisions, with a parade of treasure jubilantly removed from his home.

Aware, however, that as virtue rises one foot, vice rises ten, Wang Qishan continued to clean the stables, with Jiang Zemin still firmly in his sights. Meanwhile, Xi Jinping used the eternal mission of the Mass Line campaign to 'stomp the grass to scare the snake'. Launching searching sessions of criticism and self-criticism to shine a light on other usefully weak links, teams of cadres were sent across the Party and into the provinces to conduct more of the new two-day sessions for the investigation of ideological orientation and behaviour: the ones that Xi had named 'Democratic Life'.

Still thinking about snakes, in November 2013, Xi Jinping opened
the third plenum of the Eighteenth Party Congress. Having declared
a dream of rejuvenating the great Chinese nation, and with third
plenums typically used to set out key policies for the five-year term
of the Congress, most assumed that he would focus on the practicalities of the economy. Given the received, Western liberal, wisdom that
accompanying political reforms would be required to unleash positive
change, most were also looking for the kind of reforms that would
provide a more even playing field against Party power – one that
would release a burst of growth and innovation. Key to the nature
of the playing field were the SOEs. A Party power unto themselves,
they were employers of over thirty million people, whose excesses of
production were flooding markets with overcapacity. Built on debt,
their excess capacity was not only eating away at their own foundations but at those who had been ordered to fund their non-performing
loans: the state-owned banks, and the state-owned investment vehicles
that had subsequently been raised to try to save the banks. Clear that
he was battling Party factions addicted to the creation of wealth, Xi
Jinping used a market-reassuring *383 Plan* developed by Li Keqiang,
the Premier, to 'openly repair the gallery roads', while presenting
his own *60-point Decision on Several Major Questions about Deepening
Reform*, 'to sneak through the passage of Chencang'.

The *383 Plan* was a product of the special purpose Party Leading
Group responsible for Finance and Economics, originally established
by Deng to co-ordinate the early process of 'reform and opening up'
and traditionally headed by the Premier. Its name was a clear description of its functions: a blueprint of *three* reform concepts, covering
eight key areas and focusing on *three* major breakthroughs. The three
concepts were more opening of the market, transforming the relationship between government and market and putting innovation
into enterprise. The eight key areas were directed to achieving more
market and less government, including less red tape and some sort of
reform of the SOEs. The breakthroughs included a market for land
that would pave the way for industrial-scale farming and thus looked
as if it would finally fix the question of who owned what land.

Opening with the usual preambular references to Marxism-
Leninism, Mao Zedong Thought and wider Party theory, and replete
with standard revolutionary references, Xi Jinping's *60-point Decision*

was even more ambitious. Setting out probably the most comprehensive plan for reform ever put forward at a single point in China's
time, its targets were not only economic, but political, legal, military,
social, cultural and ecological as well. Headline goals included the
setting of a 'double hundred': a '*xiaokang*, moderately well off, society'
by the hundredth anniversary of the founding of the Party in 2021;
and a 'strong, democratic, civilised, harmonious and modern socialist country' by the hundredth anniversary of the Party's founding
of the People's Republic of China, in 2049. Partly on grounds of the
boring revolutionary language, partly because matters of politics and
law were not within their skill-set, and partly because they thought
they had heard it all before, Western markets, and thus most Western
media, ignored it, preferring to concentrate the world's minds on the
snappier and simpler *383 Plan*. Skimming the headlines of the *60-point
Decision*, some did note, however, that vowing to 'unswervingly …
give full play to the leading role of the state-owned sector', while also
'unwaveringly encouraging the development of the non-public sector'
was a bit of a contradiction. But not understanding dialectical materialism, they assumed the contradiction was a failure of logic, rather
than understanding that the contradiction was the point.

With the West happily focused on a dream of open markets, Xi Jinping
quietly established a new Party Leading Group for Comprehensively
Deepening Reform. Some Westerners noticed that there was a bit of an
overlap between the Premier's Finance and Economics Leading Group
and the General-Secretary-President's new group, but most assumed
it was just a sign of Xi Jinping's enthusiasm for achieving the dream.

Within China, and for those both inside the Party *and* up to date on
Marx' articles of faith (by no means everybody), the situation seemed a
little less simple. Trained to read the revolutionary lines of text with a
toothcomb, not only did they see the obvious traces of Confucius' dream
of a rightly governed state as a moral economy grounded in a cultivated
people, but many detected a much closer attention to Marxist ideology.
Marx – who had shared the ancient Chinese idea that utopia was to be
pursued in this world rather than in any life after death – had insisted
that the economy was key to any revolution that would create a new
society. He had also been clear that it was only when a state reached
the capitalist stage of development, with all of its tensions between
the workers and the bourgeoisie, that any ultimate revolution could

be realised. Inheriting Mao's economic mess, and being an expert on Marx, Deng Xiaopiong had diagnosed the problems of the Great Leap Forward and the Cultural Revolution as the consequences of an over-enthusiastic rush from feudalism to socialism. The solution, Deng had explained, was to take the country 'backwards' to the capitalist stage so that it could sort out the sequencing and get to the revolutionary future with a little less pain. Given his armed response to Tiananmen, Deng had clearly not been looking for a revolution that would throw the Party out of power. But as wealth had divided the people, the Party had forgotten the snow-in-summer mechanics of a soft and gradual change, and had come to rely too much on the rubber-black forces of Stability Maintenance. Some suspected that Xi Jinping had decided to redirect the redirection: capitalism having reminded everyone of what the tooth and claw struggle for survival looked like, if blood were to be avoided, Xi would force the Party to change its own nature before the Party was changed by events.

When, in late 2013, Xi announced a National Security Commission that would be looking at how to create the conditions of security rather than just maintain it, the suspicions seemed confirmed: this was not the kind of reform that everyone had been used to for the last few decades. It was not even the kind of revolutionary reform that Deng had launched with his 1992 train journey to the south. Rather, it seemed to be a make or break march that would either get everyone to the ancient dream of a golden utopian age, or end up with another Cultural Revolution. As most carried on looking out of the windows of the train, reassuring themselves that Xi Jinping's novel slogan of a 'new normal' was just a matter of economic prudence required to pave the way for future greater economic gain, others began to buckle their seats.

Exploring the resources with which China could realise its dream of a rejuvenated nation, Xi Jinping was already turning his mind to the wider world. Drawing on the mapping talents of Yu the Great at home, and on the excursionary ideas of the martial emperor, Han Wudi, abroad, as 2013 had advanced, Xi Jinping had begun to refer to a 'Belt and Road' of opportunity, with additional references to a rising theme of a 'community of common destiny'. Struggling to catch up with what the President might mean by a belt and a road, Party and state officials eventually concluded that the Belt was a highway that followed the ancient silk road, and the Route was a maritime equivalent. By the end of 2014, appreciating the economic possibilities, if not necessarily the wider social, cultural, political and geopolitical ones, another new Leading Group was established, this time under the State Council rather than the Party. Led by a Vice-Premier, the Leading Group for Advancing the Development of the Belt and Road began to add a host of earlier initiatives across the relevant geographies, including pre-existing silk route projects, a China-Pakistan corridor, an Asian Infrastructure Investment Bank and a Silk Route Fund. Maps began to appear for both the belt and the road. The Belt showed a number of threads through Central and West Asia, to the Middle East and on to Europe; the Road seemed to retrace the routes of the Ming admiral Zheng He, through South East Asia and the Indian ocean, to the Mediterranean and Africa, adding updates that reached into the Pacific ocean, through the Malay archipelago to the tropical islands of Oceania, and on to Australia as well. For a State Council responsible for delivering another economic miracle, the possibility that the SOE's overcapacity and debt might be rescued by the prospect of bigger markets, was tantalizing.

Appealing as the possibilities of the Belt and Road were, though, it was probably the promise of a 'Ring' of maritime and polar power that most captured Xi's attention. With seventy per cent of the world's mass composed of oceans, seas and ice, and with the blue waters of the world carrying ninety per cent of the world's trade, this was not just a cornucopia of food, minerals and energy that the Western world had failed to tap, it was also the space within which China could begin to command military and political respect – in the world at large, and particularly along the vast and open eastern coast of the country so vulnerable to interference from the West. The foundations had already been laid by Hu Jintao: investments in the science and technology required to plumb the depths of the oceans and the poles; a 'string of pearl' ports around the Indian ocean from South East Asia across to Africa; a nurturing of naval power; a rising foreign policy emphasis on the 'protection of China's rights and interests abroad'; and a continuation of Deng Xiaoping's patient raising of islands from the rocks and reefs of the South China Sea, leading to the launch of an ocean city of South China Sea islands, Sansha, in 2012. In July 2013, though, declaring that the world 'has entered an era of large scale development and usage of oceans and poles', Xi Jinping dedicated a Politburo Collective Study Session to the question of 'Constructing a Maritime Power'. As the politburo's deliberations led to a leap in maritime and polar initiative, the population at large was invited to think of itself as a maritime and polar people. Maritime tourism was promoted in the South China Sea, expeditions to the Antarctic were introduced, aquatic and polar theme parks were raised across the nation; all were showcased on everyone's television screens, complete with exhibitions and documentaries on China's maritime and polar expeditions and research, not to mention images of polar bears and penguins.

Predictably enough, however, the foreign barbarians soon sailed into the picture and started to muddy the waters, not only in the wider world but close to home as well.

The trouble had started in September 2012, with the Japanese government's purchase from a private Japanese owner of a disputed archipelago of islands in the East China Sea: the Diaoyu islands to China, the Senkaku to Japan. Held by Japan since 1879 as reparations for an earlier spat on Taiwan that had killed fifty-four shipwrecked Japanese sailors, at the end of the Second World War, the then 'Senkaku' had been bundled up with another archipelago of Japanese islands, the Ryuku, and earmarked for American trusteeship. Preoccupied with their own affairs, however, the Western powers had never finalised the details of the end of the Asian theatre of the Second World War. In 1972, with China caught up in its Cultural Revolution, and Japan tied to America by a Treaty of Mutual Co-operation and Security, Washington had agreed that the Ryuku should be formally returned to Tokyo; control of the Senkaku islands, whose status had remained in limbo, had passed to an unclear Japanese ownership. Part of the empire of the Manju Qing before 1879, and with China having been a victim of Japanese atrocities in the early decades of the twentieth century, Beijing objected in the strongest of terms to the idea that the islands should become part of the Japanese state.

It had not been long before other nautical neighbours tried their hands. In January 2013, the government of the Philippines petitioned the Permanent Court of Justice in the Hague for a ruling on a reef called 'Mischief' in the South China Sea. Exposed only at low tide, the Philippines argued that the reef fell within Filipino waters set by international law, and that it could not possibly have the greater status of an island that might enable another state to claim it as their own. China, for whom Mischief Reef was surely its very own *Meiji Jiao*, replied that questions about the hundreds of islands and reefs in the crowded South China Sea were matters for neighbours to sort out, taking due regard of the size and responsibility of the neighbours involved, rather than a matter that fell within the jurisdiction of the Hague. Typically for the interfering Western powers, while the Hague Court of Justice acknowledged that it could not assume jurisdiction in a case in which one state refused to accept it, the matter was passed to the related Permanent Court of Arbitration who had no qualms in taking it on. Long forgotten were the days when China's neighbours had been proud to pay it tribute, grateful to receive the treasures of its protection in return and Confucianly clear that the best order of the world was one where big countries, like big brothers, were responsible for everyone's common destiny.

Unsurprisingly, every small country with a coastline on the South and East China Seas then began to pitch in. On 19 May 2013, North Korea snatched a Chinese fishing vessel from the East China Sea and demanded a ransom for its return. Less than ten days later, Vietnam accused China of sinking one of its fishing boats, following up with a volley of mobile video footage showing a flotilla of Chinese fishing boats surrounding the vessel before one of them rammed it till it sank.

In October 2013, at a Party Conference on Diplomatic Work with Neighbouring Countries, Xi Jinping stood up to say that it was time for a *mingyun gongtongti*, community of common destiny, to take root. But over the course of the next year, as Japan refused to give up the Diaoyu-Senkaku, or at least return the situation to a little more ambiguity, as other neighbours carried on harassing and complaining about Chinese fishing vessels, and as America declined to acknowledge the wisdom of China's position, Xi Jinping took the advice of an admiral and launched a 'battle for recognition'. The foundations for the community of common destiny would now be more carefully prepared with a heightened command of respect. On 23 November, the People's Republic of China declared an Air Defence Identification Zone, ADIZ. Presenting an old map with a 'nine dash line' around a block of hundreds of square kilometres of East China Sea – a space that included the Senkaku islands as well as wider waters also claimed by both Koreas, Taiwan and Japan – China then notified all aircraft of any state wishing to fly within the zone that unless they registered their flight paths in advance, the Chinese air force would adopt 'defensive positions'. Some called it a Great Wall in the sky, and while the Chinese Ministry of Foreign Affairs declared that it was not directed against any particular territory, Japan and America saw it as a clear message to themselves, while other states saw themselves as collateral.

Within days, America flew in B-52 fighter jets without making the required advance notification and, jointly with Japan, added a naval drill near the zone for additional effect. Over the coming months, hundreds of jets would be scrambled on all sides, with frigates steaming in. Over time it would come to seem that such a level of air and sea activity was a 'new normal' as well.

And then, in March 2014 the renegade province of Taiwan chimed in with a sunflower protest that had begun in a tale of wild lilies. The heart of the matter was a cross-straits agreement on trade with the mainland that the Guomindang Nationalist Party had agreed. Although the Guomindang was at that point in power, the nature of its rule had been dramatically changed since the early 1990s when, after decades of rising calls for a constitutional democracy, the 1989 image of a single man defying a tank on the road to Tiananmen had unleashed memories of the similar spirit of Wang Shiwei, the young journalist-author who, in 1942, had dared to suggest that wild lilies, although bitter to the taste, were of great medicinal value. The Guomindang had eventually agreed to the introduction of competitive political parties – an act of such recklessness that, when the first elections had been held in 1996, the mainland Party had threatened a return to the height of seventeenth century hostilities between the renegade Zheng family and the Manju Qing, with a missile crisis that Xi Jinping had observed from the decks of Fujian. Time had passed, though, and as the mainland rose in *fuqiang*, wealth and power, wiser spirits seemed to have prevailed: the Guomindang had been voted back into power and, in power, it had taken the Party's preferred idea of a stronger relationship with the island very seriously, particularly in trade and television. In 2010, angry at a growing cross-straits co-operation that was beginning to pool print and television news, students in Taiwan had exploded in protest. When the Guomindang had announced a formal cross-straits agreement with the mainland that no one, other than the Guomindang themselves, had agreed to, the island exploded. In the same spirit of Beijing in 1919 and 1989, while students provided the energy, the protestors included people of all ages and from almost all backgrounds. Raising sunflowers to shed light on the 'black box' of the Guomindang's dealings with the dark forces of the mainland's Communist Party, Taiwan's people insisted that Taiwan and the mainland were not one and the same, waving posters which declared that Taiwan was 'not for sale'.

As if that was not enough, in September 2014 a rally of students in Hong Kong rocked the boat as well. As Confucius had said, things have their roots and their branches. This particular branch had its root in 2011, when the idea of a 'Moral, Civic and National Education' had been floated. Described as an 'essential element of whole-person education which aims at fostering students' positive values and attitudes through the school curriculum', students, parents and teachers had all objected. Including respect for others, responsibility, perseverance, national identity and commitment, the positive values and attitudes in question had seemed both unnecessary for what had hitherto been a remarkably orderly city-state, and suspiciously like the kind of socialist morality that the Communist Party was so concerned to instil on the mainland. With the further publication of a *China Model National Conditions Teaching Manual* referring to the Communist Party as an 'advanced, selfless and united ruling group' and to the American political system as one of 'fierce inter-party rivalry that makes the people suffer', everyone's suspicions had been confirmed. Convinced that Hong Kong minds were better for Hong Kong people, secondary school students had raised an alliance against moral and national education. Naming their alliance 'Scholarism', in the late summer of 2012, the teenage student leaders had called upon the Hong Kong people to bring their tents and occupy the Government headquarters on Civic Square. With the students making themselves hoarse with cries of "No' to the brainwashing of the Hong Kong people', Hong Kong's Beijing-approved Chief Executive followed what Chinese generals had always said was the most important of the *Thirty-Six Stratagems*: 'when all else fails, retreat'.

Things had quietened down for a bit but then a disagreement about the terms of the Basic Law, negotiated by Britain and China as the constitutional foundation of the 'one country, two systems' arrangement, put a spanner in the works. One article of the Basic Law stated that the 'ultimate aim' was the 'selection of the Chief Executive by universal suffrage upon nomination by a broadly representative nominating committee in accordance with democratic procedures'. British influenced Hong Kong had chosen to assume that, with two systems, the 'relevant democratic procedures' would be British in nature, rather than those of the Communist Party. Representing the 'one country', in August, the National People's Congress in Beijing declared that only candidates whom it had pre-qualified would be able to stand in any election. Returning to Civic Square in September 2014, the students found that it had already been barricaded off by police forces; their now eighteen year-old leader, Joshua Wong, asked everyone to bombard the headquarters. As the police responded with pepper spray and batons, and as more student forces arrived, the resulting battle acquired the name of 'Occupy Central with Love and Peace', with universal suffrage the battled-for prize.

Surviving on donations, working around the clock to organise their own free-of-charge everything from water, food, rubbish and recycling, to medical care, internet and security, the students created a world of their own. A study area was equipped with lamps, wifi and mobile charging stations, powered by generators and wind turbines; student marshals were appointed to manage the combined threats of tear gas and malware. Umbrellas being one of the most useful agents in protecting against tear gas, the movement soon acquired a nickname: 'The Umbrella Revolution'. Mobile phone images of yellow umbrellas were shared with all the usual hotspots of Peaceful Evolution: from outside the White House in Washington DC and in front of the Chinese Embassy in London, to Taipei's Liberty Square. Meanwhile, back in Hong Kong, whenever the state looked as if it would overwhelm them, the students followed the same stratagem as the Chief Executive: retreat. For the students, however, 'retreat' was simply code for relocation to another part of the city and the next new camp.

In the autumn of 2014, Hong Kong divided. The Chief Executive described what had come to be known as the 'Occupy' movement as an assault on the rule of law. One page advertisements taken out by global and local businesses in the local press indicated that they shared the Chief Executive's view that the rule of law meant rule by law, rather than the law being above the power of a ruler, as well as the view that the primary duty of the law was to protect the economy. The chairman of the Hong Kong Bar Association, however, expressed concern about 'an increasing tendency on the part of the executive … to emphasise the 'obey the law' aspect of the Rule of Law'; he had then added an observation that the Occupy movement, joined by a wide spectrum of Hong Kong's population, had actually demonstrated the very respect for the rule of law that made Hong Kong so special.

Unlike Taiwan though, under directions from the top, the police dug in, reinforced both by the foot soldiers of the secret societies whose interests ran like blood between the mainland and Hong Kong, and by a tremendous cyber force dedicated to smashing the 'Firechat' wall with which the students were trying to protect their communications. By the middle of December, a combination of attacks, arrests and threats, including official applications for Care and Protection Orders for younger protesters, finally wiped the students out, just like a monsoon rain.

Back in Beijing the propaganda and paramilitary forces of the Party jumped on almost everything that looked likely to express an irresponsible opinion, whether about Taiwan, Hong Kong or any other part of China and its wider world. And while the greatest energies were expended on the mainland, the Party's United Front Work Department, responsible for building bridges between the Party and other people at home and abroad, was mobilised to step up its work in spreading positive energy everywhere. At the same time the Cyber Administration was exhorted to strengthen its management of the internet anywhere in the world where an opinion about China might appear. Facebook, having been blocked in 2009 on grounds of use by Uighur separatists in Xinjiang, Twitter blocked in 2012 for telling tales about the riches of the Party families, Gmail and Instagram now joined the list of Peaceful Evolutionary platforms to be kept out. Also banned for as long as anyone could remember were the online voices of contrarian overseas Chinese, now with a reinforcement of the firewall to guard against the surreptitious use of VPNs.

When the fourth plenum of the Eighteenth Congress opened in late October, the focus of attention was the rule of law. Declaring that morality and law were two sides of a single coin, and that the country and the people would be 'comprehensively' governed according to the law,

Xi Jinping reminded everyone of the words of one of the early warring state advisors to the young state of Qin: 'No country is permanently strong. Nor is any country permanently weak. If conformers to law are strong, the country is strong; if conformers to law are weak, the country is weak.' The People's Daily then declared that a new epoch had been opened in which the rule of law with Chinese characteristics would be 'comprehensively implemented'. The people should henceforth understand that strict rules would be applied to everyone (except the Party which had its own rules); the courts should make sure that there was no discrimination in their application; and the foreigners should realise that China's rule of law included an increasing focus on Chinese rights and interests, underpinned by a comprehensive study of the laws and rules of the global order. Mice across the country feared that the cats of Stability Maintenance were to be given fangs. The foreigners took a while to catch up.

A few weeks later, Xi Jinping addressed a Beijing Forum on Literature and Art. Urging writers and artists to embrace the Marxist view of creativity, Xi explained that art and culture were critical to the positive energy required to reach the China dream. Art, Xi reminded an audience that had not been born when Mao had addressed the original Yan'an forum on Literature and Art in 1942, was neither about the entertainment of the senses, nor about getting rich; it was about training the people to take their responsible place in society. Urging the artists to retain a sense of morality when expressing themselves, Xi also stressed the importance of a good tale: 'China is not short of extraordinary stories; what we need is the ambition to make them into epic works.'

Sure enough, it wasn't long before another Ding Ling appeared, demonstrating, yet again, just how little the intellectuals understood about morality. On 28 February 2015, China's equivalent of YouTube streamed a documentary that captured everyone's attention. Taking its name from the artificial atmospheres of air-filtered shopping malls and housing to which China's more affluent people were retreating, it was called *Under the Dome*. The producer, a one-time CCTV journalist named Chai Jing, had conducted interviews with government officials, environmentalists and business executives and spliced them together with footage of factories, graphic displays of data and her own personal story of environmental trauma, to argue that the state was failing to protect the people from the ravages of pollution. Through the film, Chai also argued that China's energy SOEs were responsible for the worst of the damage. Within three days, the film had been viewed over 150 million times, a new environmental protection minister had applauded its courage and research and Chai Jing had been interviewed by the Party's newspaper, The People's Daily. Within five days, the premier had opened the annual National People's Congress with the observation that 'environmental pollution is a blight on people's quality of life …we must fight it with all our might.' Within a week, with three hundred million views, the documentary disappeared from sight. Some suggested that it owed its brief airtime to Wang Qishan's interest in shaming the energy SOEs. Others were astonished that the Party's Propaganda Department had failed to note the similarity between Chai Jing's thoughts and those of the May Fourth students who had raised their banners of Mr Science and Mr Democracy in 1919: 'One day', Chai's voice had carried over the footage, 'tens of thousands of ordinary people will say no. They will say they are not satisfied, they do not want to wait and they do not want to evade their own responsibility. I have to stand up and do something, and I will do it right now, right here, in the very moment where I am. I am the change.' Chai Jing was not arrested for her colourful opinions, but within a year, the internet was populated with images of her in America; added comments called her a hypocrite and a traitor.

In April, though, there was a far more positive victory to report: Zhou Yongkang finally appeared in one of the cold People's courts that used to belong to him. Accused and convicted of bribery, abuse of power, and the disclosure of state secrets, while his trial having been conducted behind closed doors, television viewers were invited to observe the judgement and its sentence. Black hair turned to white, head bowed, Zhou appeared as an exemplary penitent, accepting life in jail for corruption, with concurrent sentences for abuse of power and leaking state secrets. 'The host and the guest' were exchanging roles: Wang Qishan had opened up the path to Jiang Zemin.

On the first day of July 2015, the Standing Committee of the NPC announced the passing of a National Security Law. Xi Jinping having stated that 'China now faces the most complicated internal and external factors in its history', the law promised 'comprehensive security'. The text of the law covered everything from the security of the Chinese people, the defence of China's territorial borders and international interests and unity within its borders, to the security of socialist values, the environment, energy, food, information, innovation and culture. It also covered the security of the socialist system with Chinese characteristics, the Party and the revival of the great Chinese nation. Every individual and every organisation, whether Party, state, military or civilian was charged with the safeguarding of everything. Xi Jinping described it as a 'national security path with Chinese characteristics'. Others suggested that it looked as if the moral pursuit of utopia was to be achieved at all costs. Given the nature of the challenge, a National Security Education Day would soon be introduced, accompanied by textbooks and a media campaign to alert the public, young and old, to the threats of foreign spies within their midst.

Just over a week later, on the ninth day of the seventh month of 2015, the Party followed up with a '709' crackdown on lawyers who had failed to understand the socialist rule of law. Within a month, almost two hundred lawyers and activists had disappeared from sight. As other lawyers tried to help, they also vanished. Some were released within days or months, others appeared in the People's Courts charged with 'picking quarrels and provoking troubles'. Yet others, not detained, found themselves pulled aside at airports and refused exit on grounds that they would 'endanger the security of the state'. A following chorus of Party paper columns explained that the arrested lawyers were part of a secret criminal gang that had been conspiring to undermine the social order since 2012. Some of those disappeared would eventually reappear, either in court or back at home; some would still have the minds they had left with; others would be left with nerves so frayed that the real and the unreal were hard to tell apart.

Accompanying the crackdown was a continuation of the wider battle for public opinion. One strand of the campaign focused on opinion leaders, beginning with crackdowns on the so-called 'Big V' bloggers – the 'big' referring to their large number of followers, and the 'V' referring to the fact that their accounts had been officially verified to ensure that they were writing under their own names – and expanding to bans on academics who had ignored the rules against teaching universal values. Another strand worked on disappearing hundreds of thousands of websites (some were truly disappeared; others, less easy to tamper with, were hidden in new search engine settings) and regularly reminding the broadcast media of their duty to support the Party with a greater spread of 'positive energy'. Yet another strand offered advice to the *wu mao dang*, with online manuals on cybersurfing skills, such as 'hogging seats on the internet sofa' and 'diluting negative attitudes online'. On university campuses outside the country, associations of Chinese students with Party affiliations also began to take a little more interest in the thoughts of their brothers and sisters as well.

While the Party was battling to attach its ideas of the rule of law to the morality of thought and conversation, in early summer some inconvenient economic data burst the bubble of the country's stock markets. By mid-July, a large number of fortunes, big and small, had collapsed, and the Party, pointing to rumour-mongering analysts, warned of 'black hands' stirring up trouble. In late August, after an even greater stock market shock, CCTV and every other network in the country, was directed to 'rationally lead market expectations to prevent inappropriate reports from causing the market to spike or crash.' Accused of 'fabricating and spreading false information about securities and futures trading', a reporter for a highly respected financial journal was arrested. Shortly afterwards, he appeared on CCTV to confess his crimes and apologise to the public for 'causing panic and disorder'. Ignoring the morality of the matter, the markets stubbornly insisted on spiking and crashing for a number of months to come. As the markets rumbled, Wang Qishan took the opportunity to pilfer a few more goats in the form of a string of Chinese businessmen and women – disappearing them and reappearing them over the coming months. Some, like Guo Guangchang – chairman of a group that had made a fortune through partnering with SOEs – were said to be 'assisting in an investigation'; others reappeared declaring that they had taken time out to meditate. Watching the ups and downs of the market, some saw traces of Wang Qishan, the knight whose moves were not just battling corruption and factions but were also taking the opportunity to concentrate the energies of everyone's businesses on the importance of a moral market.

On a late evening in August, as Confucius' *Great Learning* and Sunzi's *Art of War* were being practiced on the stock markets, the country was rocked by yet another explosion. Beginning with a sudden fire in one of the vast number of warehouses in the port of Tianjin, when firefighters attempted to douse the flames with water, a secret armoury of prohibited chemicals set off a chain reaction. Registering on the Richter scale, the subsequent explosions sent shockwaves kilometres away. By the end of a weekend, some eight hundred people had been injured, and nearly two hundred died. Many of the injured, and thousands of others who lost their homes, had been residents of new property developments built within a kilometre of the warehouses. Many of the dead were firemen. As the internet flashed with mobile phone images of what looked like a warzone, early messages wondered whether it was an act of Xinjiang terror. It wasn't long, however, before *Wechat* erupted with speculation about whose Party families had been related to the warehouses. The CCDI sent an investigation team, and within a week a man who had once been mayor of Tianjin and then become director of the State Administration of Work Safety was detained; other detentions followed. The one-time mayor was sentenced to fifteen years in prison for accepting bribes; the chairman of the company that had stored the explosive chemicals was sentenced to death, with a two-year possibility of conversion to life. Once the dust had settled, the *Wechat* spirits picked up again, pointing out that explosions were happening all over the country, and wondering what it was that made China such a risky society. Some suggested that it might have something to do with the rule of law with Chinese characteristics.

Fortunately, high summer turned to autumn, with an opportunity for a Victory Day Parade. Tiananmen dressed up for a crowd, twelve thousand troops of the PLA were joined by a thousand troops of smaller, largely Central and South East Asian, neighbours to celebrate China's Second World War defeat of Japan. As tanks and guided missiles stormed down the Avenue of Eternal Peace, Taiwan objected to the Communist Party taking credit for the victory, but not many people listened. Standing by Xi Jinping's side as the proud guest of honour, Vladimir Putin, the Russian leader who most closely shared the faith of the Party's principles, even though Russia's Communist Party had long ago been lost. Putin also had the distinction of being the only head of a state that had clashed with Japan on China's own territory. Indeed, Russia was still technically at war with Tokyo – the consequence of the Great Powers' failure to settle the sovereignty of yet another archipelago of East China Sea islands, the Kuril, at the end of the Second World War.

Never forgetting Sunzi's wise advice about the art of war, even in the company of friends, one had to admit that Putin had so far proved himself to be a valuable neighbour. From an original Shanghai Five of China, Russia, Kazakhstan, Kyrgyzstan and Tajikistan, established in 1996 to explore the political, economic and military possibilities of Eurasia, China and Russia had gone on to create the Shanghai Co-operation Organisation, with Uzbekistan as an additional member, and India and Pakistan approved for membership and waiting to join. Others, registered as observers, also queuing up to join now included Mongolia, Iran, Afghanistan and Belarus, with more expressing interest. To which was added an expanding number of dialogue partners including Armenia, Azerbaijan, Cambodia, Turkey, Nepal and Sri Lanka. In the early years, reduced to 'manual control' in the absence of a Leninist party, Putin could only look on as China snatched at the old Soviet order: the loyalties of central Asian states were turned, tempted with glittering pipelines, highways and trade; and the Russian Far East, a vast vacuum of ice and cold that touched the shores of the Arctic to the north and the Pacific to the east, became home to an increasing number of land- and market-hungry Chinese. Meanwhile, the vast grasslands of Mongolia, seen by early twentieth century Japanese militarists as the pivot of the world, also the point at which Russian and Chinese missiles had been meeting since the 1960s, became a silent tug of war.

As always, though, the changes had surprised everyone. Putin had raised a new economy on the back of oligarchs and oil and when that had floundered in the wake of the 2008 global crisis, he had rattled Russia's world-class arsenal with a touch of *sistema*, the Russian way of getting things done. Looking for a little respect, Putin had then rustled up a Eurasian Economic Union, an EEU. A reminder to Europe that it did not control the world, the EEU was also a gentle nod to Chinese historians who might like to note that the people of the Central Asian world not only shared the same blood of the Mongol empire that had infused the lands of Rus before they became Russia (including the blood of the Cossacks who had built the tsars an empire while chasing the Mongols back to the East), but they also shared the blood of the old Turkic tribes, including Xinjiang's Uighurs. Looking for even more respect, in 2014, Putin annexed the Ukrainian territory of the

Crimea, reminding all Ukrainians that Kiev was the common capital of two people who were really brothers. As the respect rose, China offered lifelines of oil, gas and capital for a new economy. And as the maps of Xi Jinping's Belt and Road began to touch on the trade agreements of the EEU, an idea of combining the two under the Shanghai Co-operation Organisation began to take root. As the tanks and the missiles streamed through Tiananmen Square, few would disagree that Putin had earned his place of honour.

Nearly two weeks after the victorious war parade, a more peaceful anniversary closer to home was overlooked: the hundredth anniversary of the 15 September day, 1915, when the first edition of *Xin Qingnian*, New Youth, had appeared; the magazine that had carried the voices of an earlier revolutionary generation, and whose calls for a Mr Science, a Mr Democracy and a new idea of what it meant to be Chinese, had gone on to rock the capital on 4 May 1919.

Soon it was October again, and the Party gathered for the fifth plenum of the Eighteenth Congress. The subject was the *shi san wu jihua*, the Thirteenth Five Year Plan. Like every five year plan, it had been four years and 12 months in the making. This one's central focus was on the scientific development and innovation that would enable China to *feiyue*, leapfrog forward, taking every possible opportunity to *wandao chaoche*, do some corner-overtaking, as well. With innovation an important theme, it was accompanied by a psychedelic musical cartoon for the benefit of foreigners who always prefer the simpler explanations, and usually get their facts from YouTube. In three minutes, the Road to Rejuvenation Studios took a viewer through a song and dance routine that started with the news that Xi Jinping 'has a new style' and then told everyone how the country's five year plans were developed: from high to low, at the centre and across the provinces, cities and counties, with research conducted and reports reviewed across tens of thousands of participants from government ministers and think tanks, to business people, professionals and engineers, over and over again, until the government's understanding gets as good as it can. Noting that the state has to get it right because over a billion lives are at stake, a jaunty chorus reminded forgetful western minds that 'if you want to know what China's gonna do, best pay attention to the *shi san wu'*.

Within the vast text of the *shi san wu*, and across each of the local plans that sat below it, more diligent readers would see the combined influence of Confucius and Mao. Confucius' exhortation to investigate things in an 'extension of knowledge to its utmost'; Mao's insistence that truth is *developed*, through an almost endless spiral of testing ideas over and over again. Comprehensive in its coverage, impressive in its co-ordination of a myriad of themes and agencies, the Plan set out a blueprint for the deeper reform of the economy and society that Xi Jinping had in mind.

Among the many programs wrapped up in the Plan was a *feiyue* Internet Plus idea for leapfrogging what were already some of the most technologically wired cities on the globe into a fully altered state of internet-everywhere: smart homes, smart transports, smart objects, and machine-to-machine communications. Alongside it, sat a *wandao chaoche* Made in China 2025 project with which China's information technology industries would change lanes and overtake the global competition. Beneficiary of some of the most advanced manufacturing facilities in the world, with the most developed of global supply chains, the project looked to information technology and robotics to transform the process of production into something much smarter, faster, cheaper and more reliable than anything a factory operated by humans could achieve. Together, the two programs would unleash an even greater innovation: a remaking of the productive relationships between state and industry, between the centre and the provinces, between China and the production and consumption possibilities that lay waiting in the Belt and Road beyond and, of course, between man and machine. As Xi Jinping noted, China's biggest advantage was that, as a socialist country, it could 'pool resources in a major mission'. Mao's socialism was certainly a factor, but Confucius' *Great Learning* was playing a role as well.

Sceptical about the state's investment in anything, many sniffed. Foreigners declared that China would never be able to pull off the necessary technical without the free and independent thinking that true science required. Few of those at home, however, were worried about mastering the technology: China's leading urban areas were already smarter than anything in the West, with big data adding advantages by the day. The generation, capture and consumption of data was already among the highest in the world, and city data clouds were beginning to add whole new dimensions of virtual and augmented reality to the management and experience of urban life. The real and the not-real were coming together in ways that the ancient Zhuangzi's dream of a butterfly could never have imagined. In terms of opportunities, with the People's streets stopped with traffic and the skies stuffed with even more of the *xi-ke-li-wu* particles that clogged up everyone's lungs, China's urbanites were also far more sophisticated in their use of mobile technology than any others in the world. With a population wired to their phones, Wechat had taken its users beyond a twittering microblog, to a combination of social networking, instant messaging, media streaming, entertainment and online payments that was the most sophisticated virtual mobile experience on the planet. True, the Democratic Dictatorship of the People had its risks, but as so often, the risks were also opportunities. And in the world of technology it was important to remember that not every corner of the people's economy was tied to an SOE. China's biggest internet and technology businesses, Baidu, Alibaba, Tencent, had been raised by individuals who had come of age long after the SOEs had been founded, and while each had had to make their peace with the Party, their models owed as much to the West as to China. More importantly, founded by individuals with a burning desire to make being Chinese a mark of distinction, like the late Qing dynasty Zeng Guofan and Yong Wing, they had combined the lingua franca of Western structures with the quintessentially Chinese talent, inherited from the Crouching Tiger Zhuge Liang, for changing the nature of the thing rather than its wallpaper – that and the ability to *chi ku*, eat bitterness. As Facebook spent its time trying to work out how to twist itself to fit within the Great Firewall of China, those who had founded Baidu, Alibaba and Tencent had been born with the understanding that in a world of constant changes and fundamental contradictions, the answer to anything was never a binary yes or no but an ongoing deployment of the *Dao*, way, with the future being simply a set of facts to be found.

What did worry those at home was the possibility that the Party's politics and policies might amplify the technical risks. 'What if mistakes are programmed into robots that can't be controlled?' and 'What if the country unleashes an overcapacity of robots?' Others worried that the technology would amplify the risks of the Party's politics – tying up the game of *weiqi*, Go, so that even the blood brotherhoods and the Monkey Kings wouldn't have any space left. Most, though, noted that these were problems that everyone in the world was facing, and that while the risks might be clearer in China, for once this could be an advantage. After thousands of years of dealing with emperors who fiddled with communications and re-engineered the rivers and the land, with a language primed for code, and with ancient ideas of Stability Maintenance meaning that everyone was always ready for a battle, the Chinese people were probably a lot better equipped to deal with the risks of technology than those of the West. Look at the *Fat Years*, they remarked. Published as science fiction, Chinese readers had been quick to see the present in its future. Read in the West as a moral tale about China's Dictatorship of the People, it had taken the shock of Edward Snowden's revelations for the Westerners to wake up to the fact that, confronted with a crisis, their world might not be so different.

But the Thirteenth Five Year Plan was not only about production and consumption. Running through it like a river was the vision of China as a *shengtai wenming*, ecological civilisation that, having lost its environment to economic growth would now use an advanced 'investigation of things' in the form of science and technology, to rejuvenate itself. Mapped within the pages of the Plan was a spatial imagination of both challenges and solutions that would have made Yu the Great proud: how China's urban world would be realigned to sit with nature, how the relationship between the city and the countryside would be regenerated, and how the Plan would be deployed, on land and on water, at home and abroad, including across the Belt and Road, on the high seas, in the polar regions and even outer space.

Timed for perfection, just over a month later, in November, Xi Jinping and Barack Obama sat down in Zhongnanhai for a fireside chat about the state of the earth. By the end of the evening they had agreed a US-China Joint Announcement on Climate Change that included robust targets for the reduction of carbon emissions. The long road to that agreement had included a careful study of the work of an American physicist-environmentalist, Amory Lovins, whose *Reinventing Fire*, written for a climate-changing America, had also been avidly read by senior Chinese officials. Lovins had been invited to think about how fire could be reinvented under Chinese conditions as well. In December, the two greatest powers and polluters in the world would meet again in Paris and lay the foundations for a UN climate conference that would make a *feiyue*, leap forward, in the battle to keep the rise in average world temperatures below the critical two degrees.

As the Party had long been telling the people, however, pollution comes in many guises. Progress had been made on the environmental front but spiritual pollution was proving harder to control, not only within mainland China but from the increasingly difficult wider Chinese world as well. In April 2015, the Party had been forced to come up with a Guangdong Action Plan, authorising plain clothes excursions into Hong Kong to enforce the new normal rules on what could and couldn't be said in the People's Republic against a stubborn crew of Causeway Bay booksellers who seemed to think that the mainland was another country. By the end of the year, a succession of five publishers-cum-booksellers had disappeared, most either from Hong Kong or on visits to Shenzhen. One, seemingly captured through the global fugitive searches of the CCDI, had disappeared from Thailand. Initial family requests for Hong Kong authority help had been quickly withdrawn as phone calls and faxes from the booksellers themselves insisted they had voluntarily smuggled themselves across borders in order to co-operate with judicial investigations in the mainland. One appeared on CCTV confessing to a serious crime; others appeared on local channels with mainland connections, confessing to illegal sales of books that had 'brought a bad influence', with supplementary news commentary noting that they might be allowed home if they showed a good attitude. And then one had been recklessly sent back to Hong Kong to retrieve a hard drive with a list of the bookshop's customers, on condition that he came back within a week. After a few days of reflection, he jumped ship and appeared in the press, giving a shameless description of CCDI interrogations. As Hong Kongers demanded that their Chief Executive remind Beijing of the One Country Two Systems arrangement, with its guarantee of 50 years of free speech and independent jurisdiction over crimes, others remembered an observation made by Xi Jinping in 2014: 'In the best of Chinese traditions, generations of overseas Chinese never forget their home country, their origins, or the blood of the Chinese nation flowing in their veins.'

Important though books were, the Party was clear that in the battle for public opinion, it was the internet that was both the major source of spiritual pollution and the major theatre of battle. In mid-December, a small town in Zhejiang province by the name of Wuzhen hosted the second of the Cyber Administration's now annual World Internet Conference. Entitled 'Building a Cyberspace Community of Common Destiny', the conference opened with an address by Xi Jinping on the critical importance of cyberspace in shaping humanity's common destiny, and on the related need for innovation. Respect for cyber-sovereignty would be essential to the maintenance of peace and security; the cultivation of good order would be critical to the guarantee of responsible freedom; openness and co-operation between sovereign cyber-nations would be key. 'Where there is mutual care', Xi quoted from an ancient text, 'the world will be at peace; where there is mutual hatred, the world will be in chaos.' With these foundations, he presented what the Peaceful Evolutioneers in the West would see as a contradiction: more internet, more internet innovation and more platforms for mutual online learning, but also more attention paid to the quality of the human beings online. For those in China, though, the promotion of science and technology had long gone hand in hand with the objectivity of obedient opinions; for Xi Jinping, it was the frontline of the battle for a better world.

The Russian Premier, Dmitry Medvedev, attended the Wuzhen conference, as well as leading Chinese tech entrepreneurs. China being home to more online users than any other country in the world, the conference was also widely attended by the senior leadership of America's leading tech and internet businesses. Indeed, with Facebook diligently working on the geographic filtering features that would give it a pass through the Great Firewall of China, and WeChat having already launched a 'One App, Two Systems' model to help it navigate the challenge of satisfying mainland censors while Chinese users travelled around the world, the technical features necessary to underpin the cyber-dimensions of the common community of destiny were already falling into place.

Stubbornly plugging their ears against the common destiny mantra, in mid-January 2016, a little before the Chinese new year, the Taiwanese people took themselves to their presidential polls. With the Sunflower dream of an independent Taiwan, the winner was not the head of the Guomindang with which the Party had forged such a close relationship, but the leader of the opposing Democratic Progressive Party, DPP – Tsai Ying-wen. Online, mainland nationalists declared a 'sacred war': one and only one China, with its capital on the mainland. After nearly seventy years of playing games, in their opinion, it was time for the renegade province to come home.

In February, with the 'internal and external factors' becoming more complicated by the month, Xi Jinping advanced into the headquarters of the Party's media. On message that 'all news media run by the Party bears the surname of the Party', and mindful of the fact that one of their own, a star anchor, had been swept up by the CCDI in 2014 and not yet reappeared, CCTV welcomed Xi with a banner declaring: 'The Party is our family name'. Urging the Party's pens to join the guns in securing the revolution, Xi referred to the Long March, whose hundredth anniversary was now being celebrated. Recalling the brave journey across snow-capped mountains, reminding everyone of the ongoing battle to protect the Party with unity, love and commitment, he highlighted the importance of positive energy and objective science as the flag-and-sword articles of faith. Unperturbed by the uncomfortable experiences of earlier business bloggers commenting on Party politics, Ren Zhiqiang, a successful property developer and Party member with thirty-seven million Wechat followers, asked a question: 'When did the People's Government turn into the Party's Government?' Naturally, the reckless question was purged, along with the blog account that launched it. Officials of the Cyber Administration then launched a campaign declaiming Ren as a treacherous advocate for capitalism. A financial magazine published an interview with an academic on the matter who called for the state to listen to the views of the people. The Cyber Administration classified the content as 'illegal' and told the magazine to take it down. Re-interviewed, the stubborn academic said he couldn't see anything illegal in his text; that content was declared illegal as well.

In March, just as the nation prepared for the annual spring meeting of the National People's Congress, the NPC, an anonymous letter appeared on a little known website, accusing Xi Jinping of concentrating too much power in his personal hands. Comparing the silencing of 'improper discussion of the centre' to the Cultural Revolution, the letter called for Xi's resignation 'for the future of the country and the people'. A hunt was launched for the state-subverting authors. Undeterred, another journalist for the same magazine addressed a letter to the NPC, the Supreme People's Court and the CCDI, requesting the authorities to investigate the Cyber Administration's attacks on Ren Zhiqiang as an infringement of the people's constitutional right to free speech that had triggered public fear and outrage. As the opera continued, a dean of communications studies asked if the media's reporting on the NPC could skip the boring descriptions of who sat where and how the food was prepared, and just explain to everybody who was directing the show.

Challenging though the people's voices were, Wang Qishan and Xi Jinping had been making progress in the military threads of Jiang Zemin's dark web. Equipped with the powers of the CCDI, Wang Qishan had managed to purge the higher levels of the armed forces. Meanwhile, as chairman of the Central Military Commission, Xi Jinping had set about the most ambitious restructuring of the military in its history, including the removal of the senior pillars of the PLA infiltrated by Jiang, an absorption of the paramilitary People's Armed Police whose powers Zhou Yongkang had so treacherously abused, and a dramatic realignment of the respective strengths of the land, air, sea, cyber and outer space forces, with a particular focus on the electronic and electro magnetic field capabilities where China's asymmetrical talents could shine. The reform also included a redesign of the old geography of the guns. Henceforth, the country would have one unified Joint Battle Command with five new combat zones: a North, a South, an East, a West and a Central. The northern zone concentrated on tackling the threats of both Koreas as well as the Russian Far East and Mongolia. The western zone was reinforced to deal with the threats of separatism and terror coming from Tibet and Xinjiang at home and the Belt and Road territories of Pakistan and Afghanistan abroad. The eastern and southern zones were focussed on the choppy waters of the East and South China Seas. And the centre was responsible for protecting Beijing.

On 21 April, armed with a title chosen to emphasise the importance of unity, Xi Jinping appeared at his new military headquarters as Commander in Chief of the Joint Battle Command of the Central Military Commission. Within a year, he would also be Chairman of a newly created Central Commission for Integrated Military and

Civilian Development. As Sunzi had once so wisely advised: 'The greatest victory is that which requires no battle', but if you have to fight, 'know yourself and know the enemy, and you can win a hundred battles without disaster'.

With the guns under lock and key, Xi Jinping returned his attention to the contradictions that were slowing the economy. Given that the Western political system was not for China, any valuable lessons from abroad would be around the better technical management of the bird in the cage, rather than in the exhortations of marketeers to scrap the cage, free the bird and end up losing the very revolution that the China dream was all about. Long a leader of Party study sessions on dialectical materialism, Xi reminded everyone that economic reform was part of a comprehensive deepening of reform overall, rather than handing over decision-making to the short-term thinking of those who made a living on market trades. He also reminded them that, as Mao Zedong had explained, it would all take time: 'correct knowledge can be arrived at only after many repetitions ... leading from practice to knowledge and back to practice'. The SOEs were indeed in a mess, and the CCDI was working on the corruption and factions that had made them so. Costs had risen, debt was high, and competition with the rest of the world was cutthroat. With hundreds of millions of Chinese still below the *xiaokang*, moderate prosperity, goal at one end of the equation, and with a world-class number of billionaires and millionaires at the other, there was no easy solution. The fact that those at the bottom had little education, those at the top had a lot of everything, and the country was awash with mobile phones and loudspeakers, just made things even more complicated.

The technocrats responsible for the economy understood the logic of a moral economy but worried that, even if it were correct, the country was running out of the time required to avoid a crisis. At an international summit in Shanghai in February, the Minister of Finance, Lou Jiwei, took the liberty of sending a coded communication to Xi Jinping, disguised as a gentle word of warning to the masters of the global economy: 'A person may fall off a cliff, but a country can't. If that happens, what is left is just endless suffering. It is best to anticipate crises when one is a kilometre away rather than waiting until the last metre and falling off.' Given that China did not have a monopoly on economic problems, many in the West acknowledged the wisdom of his words. For the man to whom they were directed, though, they were an illustration of just how difficult it was going to be to get to grips with the kind of deep reform required. Socialism certainly did not mean being poor. But for socialism to be successful, the Party could not be seen to be leaving the poor behind; and if the poor were not to be seen to be left behind, deeper reforms were required. They would not be easy, they would take time, but as the author of *The Fat Years* had so clearly understood, the Party would do whatever it took. Meanwhile, Xi Jinping redoubled his efforts to overcome the 'countermeasures' with which obstinate local officials were holding up the dream. In November, Lou Jiwei would be replaced.

Wishing to illustrate the industrial possibilities of the Thirteenth Five Year Plan, in late April, Xi Jinping appeared in Hefei, at the old University of Science and Technology, where the physicist Fang Lizhi had once argued that no science should be above the test of subjective human eyes. Fang had since departed, first to America and then to the ancestors. An Institute of Advanced Technology had recently been established and its engineering scientists had come up with part of the solution to the problem of managing heaven and earth: robots. Greeting his president with a *ni hao*, hello, the first, rather industrial looking, robot introduced himself and said how glad he was to be participating in the great process of rejuvenating China. A second robot, with long black hair and a plastic finish that made her seem far more human, greeted the President with a *ni hao*, hello, and then asked the assembled cameras to step back when taking pictures so that her face wouldn't look too fat. With most eyes attracted to her beautiful features, her makers explained that she would be slower to enter mass production, but the next stage was to get her to laugh and cry.

Meanwhile, the forces of Stability Maintenance had been directed to pay closer attention to some worrying gatherings that had been taking place around the country, particularly in the ancient Luoyang, now capital of Henan. Once a capital to the Zhou and the Han dynasties, briefly captured by the rebellious Yellow Turbans for their Taiping Kingdom, Mao had entrusted it with the Number One Tractor Factory that produced the *Dongfanghong*, East is Red, tractors that had once represented the industrial dreams of the nation. An icon, the front of the factory had been enhanced with a giant statue of Mao. Many of the Luoyang gatherings had been convened in secret, but some had taken place under the grey skies and red banners that surrounded the statue, attended by the old, the young and the in-between casualties of an increasing economic slowdown and the rising preference for robotic production lines. In early April, a brave man in a threadbare suit grasped an echoing loudhailer and took a stand in front of Mao. Reading his words from a scrap of paper, he recalled the revolutionary courage of the Party and the tragedy of the Party's subsequent revisions that had lost everyone the socialist prize. Noting that the battle drums had now sounded, he acknowledged the gesture of Xi Jinping's mass line and offered him the support of a proletariat that would, in any event, be advancing, once again and for all time, to smash the bourgeoisie so that future generations would never have to suffer again. '*Mao Zedong sixiang wansui!*', he shouted in conclusion, 'Mao Zedong Thought forever!' No one dared to confront the broken promises of the past by closing down the gathering on the day but over the coming weeks, as with other gatherings, the most obvious protagonists would disappear. Fought at the other end of the economy, the battle against the new Maoists was easily as big as Wang Qishan's battle against corruption, albeit directed against a diametrically opposing faith – not the one that was trying to strengthen the sinews of capitalism but the one that was, according to its secretly circulated manifesto, dedicated to overthrowing the 'bureaucrat monopolist capitalists and their bourgeois fascist dictatorship'. Over the following months wildcat strikes, mobilised on Wechat, hit at factories up and down the country. With each strike, the leaders were detained or disappeared. And with each man gone, the surviving brothers vowed to carry on.

Technology, of course, was the key to managing the contradictions, and had been for quite a while. Offering the opportunity of a grid more seamless than that of the First Qin Emperor, the scientists of the state had worked with a trio of 'S' technologies originally, and highly successfully, pioneered for London: GIS, geographic information systems, and the satellite-powered GPS and GS, global positioning and remote sensing systems respectively. The idea of a technology-guided grid had been pioneered in Beijing's Dongcheng district, from 2004. Naturally,

Chinese characteristics had been added. The district had been divided into one hundred square metre 'cells', with individual *chengguan*, urban enforcers, responsible for twelve cells each, and equipped with *chengguan tong*, mobile devices, to gather and share on-site data. Over the years, more and more authorities with an interest in enforcing official orders (the courts, the People's Armed Police – now under the Joint Battle Command – and various other bodies of Party and state) had been invited to join the system: adding to, and sharing in, the information gathered. With every year that passed, the system became bigger and better. Higher capacity computers, faster internet, bigger databases, remote sensors, surveillance cameras and wireless routers, all came together to provide a seamless circuit of real-time geographic information, including coverage of polluting local opinions, protests and any other criminal acts. By 2007, the Dongcheng experiment had been expanded to include the rest of a Beijing preparing itself for the Olympic Games; it had then been expanded to other cities. Protesting troubles in Tibet and Xinjiang in 2008 and 2009 made their capitals of Lhasa and Urumqi obvious early choices. By 2010, Urumqi had forty thousand surveillance cameras covering four thousand four hundred streets and alleyways, two hundred and seventy schools and one hundred large shopping malls and supermarkets. After the spate of colour revolutions that sprang up in the Arab and Central Asian world from 2011, the Dongcheng experiment was then expanded across the country, with upgrades as the technology evolved and extensions to the wider world, where the plotters of terror as well as any fugitives from charges of corruption and spiritual pollution might roam.

By 2012, the technology was also offering the possibility that the people would be able to start to serve themselves. Again, the West provided interesting models: credit scoring and travel forums like TripAdvisor that enabled everyone to keep an eye on everyone else. As the big data got bigger, engineers began to work on algorithms to rate as much as possible to scale. In Shanghai, a pilot project compiled digital records of the social and financial behaviour that made for the highest quality citizens. Those losing their temper on airplanes, anyone not looking after their parents, people not paying their debts or fines, troublemakers accused of picking quarrels: all useful data for the black marks that could be viewed by anyone thinking of working with them. The highest levels of scrutiny were reserved for those aspiring to be lawyers, teachers or journalists. Tech start-ups then added more positive features, enabling advanced individuals to opt into scores for education levels and general performance in order to earn more positive points that could be spent on perks like travel upgrades. 'Building up their online profiles, people will become more aware of what they need to do to behave themselves better', observed one enthusiastic social-rating entrepreneur.

Remembering Confucius' *Great Learning* observation that 'knowledge being complete, the thoughts of the people would be sincere; and that, thoughts being sincere, hearts would be rectified, persons would be cultivated, families would be regulated, states would be rightly governed, and the world would be at peace', Xi Jinping noted that the technology presented the possibility of building sincerity into the fabric of economics and society. Noting its potential to heighten the capacity to anticipate and prevent all manner of risks, and thus to *feiyue*, leap forward, the civilisation of cities and their people, he added that 'The trustworthy will be able to roam everywhere under heaven, while the discredited will find it difficult to take even a single step.'

As the cities raced towards the future, the land of the countryside also began to get its promised upgrade. Too many small plots for too many small people, not enough food produced to meet demand, and far too much space to be covered efficiently by one hundred square metre cells, the Party-state declared that the future of the land would be in industrial scale corporate plots. Side-stepping the question of who would control the corporations, the protests of the past could now be swept away. Meanwhile, back in Wukan, with villagers still refusing to give up on the promise of the return of their land, the local cultural revolutionary, since elected as village leader, Lin Zuolan, disappeared, only to reappear on television confessing to bribery and corruption. Clear that the confession had more to do with his unrelenting battles with the Lufeng county powers and the arrest of a grandson rather than any trumped up government contracts, Wukan's villagers rose up again in protest, and once again found themselves cut off from heaven – this time outnumbered by battalions of surveillance cameras.

On 1 July 2016, Xi Jinping opened the celebrations of the ninety-fifth anniversary of the officially recognised founding of the Party with a speech. The world's poorest country had become its second biggest economy, and miraculous though that may seem, it was an achievement grounded in the advanced theories of a Party that understood both the trends of history and the historical responsibility of a vanguard to pursue the people's destiny with sacrifice and faith. 'The whole Party', Xi declared, 'should remember that what we are building is socialism with Chinese characteristics, not some other kind of 'ism''. The earliest milestone would be the long-promised achievement of a *xiaokang*, moderate prosperity, by 2020; the greatest milestone would be the achievement of the 'strong, democratic, civilised, harmonious and modern socialist country' promised for 2049. Having encouraged Party members to test their knowledge of Party theory in quizzes, and to copy out the fifteen thousand characters of its constitution by hand, Xi was reasonably confident that the troops in the aisles were clear about the bigger picture. Just to be sure, though, he reminded them of the headlines: revolutionary ideals were purer spiritual convictions than any superstitious studies of heaven; truth from practice was the only way that anyone on earth would ever get to the socialist utopia; the selflessness of objectivity was the highest calling; and demanding though the painstaking repetitions were, the wavering of faith was the greatest danger. As Marx had predicted, new productive forces emerge, social relations change; but the duty of every Party member was to hold firm in their conviction that only a People's Democratic Dictatorship could get the Chinese people to their dream. Advancing on all of the five-in-one civilisational fronts of economics, politics, society, culture, and ecological civilisation, the Party would not only lead China to its future but would also work with the institutions of the wider world to achieve greater clarity and order everywhere. To help in the task, a China Program of global governance would be offered for the benefit of all.

Yet again, it wasn't long before the foreigners chimed in. On 12 July, the Hague Court of Arbitration delivered its ruling on Mischief Reef. Disregarding the natural hierarchy of big states over small states and oblivious to the importance of neighbours forging their own community of common destiny, the judgement concluded that Mischief Reef belonged to the Philippines and not to China. Ignoring its judgement,

Xi Jinping directed the Party to open some evening chats with the new President of the Philippines, Rodrigo Duterte, a man whose even stronger emphasis on law and morality promised much more hope of a common sense solution than anything out of the West. Seeing reason, after three years of wasted argument, Duterte agreed to work with China for the greater benefit of the South China Sea.

The South China Sea, however, had now become a problem. Encouraged by the idea of a Hague ruling, every inch of its waters had come under the pixelated attention of high tech Western eyes and pictures of a quiet island-building project, begun over thirty years ago by a patriotic admiral had been flashed around the world. Passionate about returning China to its rightful place in the world, with Deng Xiaoping's support, the admiral had started with surveys of the most important island chains, and then sent his ships to the Fiery Cross Reef (the Spratly islands to the West) with a few tonnes of concrete to explore the possibility of building blocks. Across the South China Sea, with time and technology, reefs that had once appeared only at a low tide had been raised first into platforms and then into floating camps. On Eternal Prosperity (Woody island to the West), the largest of the Xisha archipelago of reefs, banks and rocks (called the Paracels by the West and Hoang Sa by Vietnam), the groundwork of a garrison had eventually raised a floating conurbation. Described as an urban innovation, equipped with a port and airport, a city hall, museums and shops, Woody Island was now the seat of an ocean city whose districts included both the Spratlys and the Paracels as well as the also-disputed Macclesfield and Scarborough shoals. The name of the ocean city was Sansha.

Meanwhile, across the South China Sea, fortified by the Hague ruling, the West was continuing to insist on frequent freedom of navigation operations, and other neighbours, including Vietnam and Indonesia, were arguing that bits and pieces of what China held for the security and benefit of everyone, were actually theirs. Given the level of tension, Mischief Reef and other outcrops were armed with anti-aircraft weapons and a new 'sea-whiz' missile defence system to keep them safe from other people's fire. Soon, similar reefs would be considered for environmental monitoring stations.

Fortunately, Russia was helping to hold the line. Joint exercises in the East and South China Seas had added weight to China's argument that Japan should retreat from islands that were clearly Chinese, and that America should keep its Pacific distance. A united stand on the Wuzhen idea of an internet of individual cyber-sovereign states had added substance to the claim that a new online order was required. And a common interest in reminding Europe that its fading power could no longer support the luxury of bourgeois liberal opinions, and in reminding the West in general that non-government organisations were unqualified to interfere in any countries' business, was matched by the greater goal of getting America to keep to its own backyard.

In the East China sea, Russia then set an example of a kind of community of common destiny solution with a suggestion to Japan that the question of who owns the Kuril archipelago of islands (presently occupied by Russia but with an unresolved status since the end of the Second World War) be set aside and the two countries simply get on with a joint economic development. Indeed, Russian and Chinese ideas of regional order seemed to be dovetailing well. When South Korea had agreed to host America's new anti-ballistic missile system (the THAAD, terminal high altitude area defence) aimed at a trigger-happy North Korea, both had immediately seen the possibility that the system could easily be redirected to the Chinese lands above the Korean peninsula and the Russian lands behind them (of course, Xi Jinping had also seen the risk that China might once again find itself caught in the middle of a Russian war with America). To the Central Asian west, the two countries were aligning in a battle against the terror that threatened everything that the now related projects of the Belt and Road and the Eurasian Economic Union hoped to achieve. Of particular importance were the black mountains of Waziristan which, sitting between Pakistan and Afghanistan, had become training grounds for extreme minds fighting wars from Syria to Xinjiang.

Xinjiang: gunning for Mao Zedong in a 4 x4 in 2013, its separatists had raised yet another competing faith. Beijing had spread the grid management system across the province and tightened it, but still the infidels were striking at Han Chinese with knife attacks and explosions. Nor was the Uighur separatists' violence limited to Xinjiang: attacks were being launched in other Islamic areas of the edges of order, not least the old sultanate in the south-west province of Yunnan. With its mineral wealth and its corridor to a pearl of a port in Pakistan's Gwadar, Xinjiang was not only a source of risk to the Chinese state but was becoming a critical risk for the Belt and Road.

Reminding everyone that the long-term stability of Xinjiang was vital to national unity, prosperity, security and ethnic harmony, the wider Han Chinese population and the SOEs had been invited to put their capital resources and human talent into the desert oases. With an eye to the longer term, prizes had even been offered for mixed marriages.

Mass military and paramilitary rallies thundered in Xinjiang's cities; beards and burkhas were banned in difficult districts; prayer meetings were subjected to official approval and limited to conduct under officially approved imams. Sweeping arrests had long picked up even modest sympathisers, including an academic Uighur in Beijing, by the name of Ilham Toti, a man who had insisted on setting up a website for greater Uighur-Han understanding; in 2014 Toti had been given a life sentence for separatism. Still the knives and explosions came. Looking back to the ancient past some picked up the chorus of the old Han generals – arguing that the iron embrace was exacerbating risk rather than calming things down. But this time the generals were safely under Xi Jinping's new Joint Battle Command and its new Western Combat Zone with a hint that the latter might move its headquarters from the peace of Sichuan to the heart of Xinjiang. Meanwhile, taking advantage of America's ebbing energies in the Central Asian theatre of terror, Russia and China joined hands to strengthen their relationships with Pakistan and Afghanistan and, through the Shanghai Co-operation Organisation, they decided to build a common economic destiny that would reach as far as Iran. In June 2015, the two countries had celebrated a twenty-year strategic partnership. At the end of August 2016, a truckload of explosives was driven into the compound of China's embassy in the Bishkek capital of Kyrgyzstan: to Xi Jinping and Putin, the wisdom of the partnership seemed to be confirmed.

And then, in early September 2016, Hong Kong took itself to the polls for a new Legco (Legislative Council). Ignoring the wisdom of Beijing, voters elected some of the very 'Occupy Central with Love and Peace' troublemakers that the NPC had been trying to keep out. When would they learn?

Once again what felt like the heat of high summer soon turned to autumn, and with it came the sixth and last plenum of the Eighteenth Party Congress, the point at which Xi Jinping would deliver the final details of his first five-year term. Normally, it would also be the point at

which the incumbent General Secretary would hint at his likely successor and give a steer about openings in other key positions. But by now
everyone knew that there was a new normal for almost everything. With
so many comrades lost to corruption, there were quite a few positions to
fill, and with the country once again on a revolutionary footing everyone was anxious to know who the next generation of the leadership
might be. If Xi Jinping had any idea who would succeed him in the 2022
Twentieth Party Congress, he kept his counsel. Some suggested he was
still working on building his own supporting faction; others speculated
that he had probably acquired so many titles that no one else could possibly fill his shoes. Yet others argued that he was following Deng's advice
and biding his time; to which others replied that if one were working
on the cosmic time of dialectical materialism, even a twenty-year term
might not be enough. For Xi Jinping, the speculation was not only a
distraction but also a clear illustration of how much the Party's senior
members needed to experience the cleansing benefits of reform.

Rising to the Party podium, Xi revealed a set of 'Guidelines on
Inner Party Life in the New Situation'. Cutting to the chase, he then
delivered some long-needed home truths to his audience: populated
by victims of infirm ideals and beliefs of disloyalty and laziness, the
Party had been undermined by threads of individualism, decentral-
ism, and liberalism, not to mention factionalism, mountain-stronghold
mentalities and a craven worship of money. Buying and selling official
positions, and generally abusing their power, members had polluted it
with bribery, corruption, cronyism and violations of law and discipline.
Within these unclean waters, an extremely small number of people had
developed swollen political ambitions, engaging in political conspiracies while pretending to obey – banding together for their own selfish
interests and forming gangs and cliques to secure power and positions.
The damage had been great. Ideologically and morally, everyone had a
lot to learn. Newly anointed 'core' of the Party, Xi Jinping announced
a root and branch campaign to comprehensively improve Party discipline. Before the end of the year, the two-day Democratic Life sessions,
with their self-critical purging of inner thoughts, would be extended
to the twenty-five select members of the Politburo. Everyone was on
notice that they should get ready to cleanse their hearts and minds.

As a number of Party members squirmed in their seats, Hong Kong
delivered an illustration of just what could go wrong without the

foundations of faith. Having allowed troublemakers to be elected into the legislature, no one should have been surprised when the trouble-makers made trouble. Standing to take their oaths of allegiance, one of the Occupy candidates brandished a yellow umbrella, while two others carried blue flags proclaiming 'Hong Kong is not China' and replaced the oath of allegiance to the one country of the People's Republic with inflammatory separatist words. When the oath-taking became yet another battle, Hong Kong's Chief Executive asked the NPC for another clarification of the Basic Law. The NPC confirmed that the oath was to the motherland and not the local outpost, and the Chief Executive insisted that the courts disqualify the offending candidates. In the interim, two thousand lawyers and others, dressed in black and ignorant of the principles of the Democratic Dictatorship of the People, paraded through Hong Kong's Central district in silence.

Back in the Great Hall of the People in late November, Xi Jinping rose to the occasion of the 150th anniversary of the birth of Sun Yatsen with a speech reminding everyone of the principles that the great man had stood for: patriotism, putting the people first, and most impor-tantly of all, unity. 'All activities designed to divide the country will be firmly opposed by the Chinese people', said Xi. 'We will never allow anyone, any organisation, any party, to split off any tract of territory from China anytime, or in any way.'

On 20 December, however, a princeling general with a reputation for speaking his mind, threw a scud missile into the fray. Observing that 'great critics are often great patriots', he lamented the missing medicine of truth. 'Our situation today', he observed, 'is that the common people don't believe anything, the experts don't understand anything, the media doesn't say anything and political education is useless.' Referring to Lu Xun, the great revolutionary writer who never trusted any politi-cal party, the general noted that it was a combination of love and hatred that had inspired the revered author to pick up his pen and write such great and powerful truths – not least the truth about the choice that the people faced between a counterfeit paradise and a good hell.

At the end of 2016, Xi Jinping and Vladimir Putin exchanged seasonal greetings. From a strategic partnership that had begun with mutual mistrust in 1996 to a twentieth anniversary celebrated in June, when the leaders of the world's twenty biggest economies had met in Hangzhou in September, theirs had been the dialogue that had stolen the show. As Putin himself had noted, on matters from the rule of law to the internet, from the South China Sea to the Mediterranean, 'our views are either similar, or coincide'.

With the all-important Nineteenth Congress scheduled for the latter part of 2017, Xi Jinping prepared for what everyone expected to be a final lap to something but nobody was quite clear what. As Wechat and the world wondered whether the leader with more titles than anyone since the Qianlong emperor would continue with the conventions of a succession set down by Deng Xiaoping, Xi focused his attention on the critical matter of unified hearts and minds. Clear as to his Party responsibilities, the Chief Justice of the People's Supreme Court declared that the rules of law and virtue should be seen as one and the same by the judiciary. He also declared that judicial independence was an ideological error, that the courts should stand up against anyone who challenged the socialist rule of law with Chinese characteristics, and that declarations of absolute political loyalty were to be given by everyone involved with the law. When a veteran Party economist posted a challenge to the Chief Justice on the website of his own outspoken think tank, the Cyber Administration called for a crackdown on online news services operating without a licence. Moving on, similar declarations of faith and loyalty were required of those whose work was of special ideological importance, particularly those in media and education. Prohibitions on textbooks preaching Western values were repeated, and university campuses were asked to introduce more, and more interesting, classes on ideology and politics, deepen their theoretical research on Marx, and generally clean up their pollution. For younger learners, textbooks would be introduced to ensure a 'perfect personality education' – they would sit alongside other textbooks focusing on national security education in general and, in particular, on how to report spies. Across the country, in all institutions and at all levels, a new wave of traditional culture was to be launched to remind students that morality and law were one and the same. Just as *The Great Learning* had observed: 'from the Son of Heaven down to the mass of the people, all must consider the cultivation of the person to be the root of everything'.

Meanwhile, the forces of order made it clear that the duty of self-cultivation applied to every person born Chinese, wherever they might have gone. In Hong Kong, a Chinese billionaire businessman close to the Party was escorted from his Four Seasons home to assist with a CCDI investigation in the mainland. In the mainland, overseas Chinese carrying awkward ideas to Chinese cities found that being Chinese was a matter of birth rather than choice, and the acquisition of a foreign passport couldn't change one's nationality.

It was also clear to everyone that, whatever was going on in the Chinese world, the wider world was also changing. The liberalism of the West was losing its lustre, not just to Western rulers but to a number of their people. Walls were rising in popularity, management of problem populations was becoming more important, and electoral democracy seemed to have become the risk that the Party had insisted it was, not just for those who practiced it, but for the outside world as well. With America now led by a property mogul with no sense of history or civilisation, Europe unable to even recognise a common future and Britain having traded leadership for periodic 'ask the people' referenda, there was some comfort in having a Chinese ruler who understood the past, took responsibility for the present and was prepared to work like Yao and Shun to find a way to balance heaven and earth in this most complicated of times. Following in the early twentieth century footsteps of Liang Qichao and his worries about America, Wang Lixiong, the author of *Twelve Suggestions for Tibet* asked the question that could be found on almost everyone's Wechat: 'If the United States, a model for democracy, can elect a Trump, why wouldn't such a result be even more likely in China, where popular education in civic values and in the nation's history is much weaker?' Remembering *The Great Learning* that Xi Jinping had been reading, others nodded: 'it cannot be, when the root is neglected, that what should spring from it will be well ordered'.

Still winter, a chill crept across the capital. But the roads, the cinemas and the restaurants were still full; the stories that made up China were still the best in the world; and Wechat, still chattering, was far more interesting than Twitter, Facebook and all the rest of the world's social media combined. And while Xi Jinping was still worrying about the authors' ability to write about the present, he was clearly missing the fact that in terms of science fiction futures, China's authors were on track to lead the world.

In early spring, Beijing moved towards its annual season of spring meetings, including the *liang hui*, two meetings, of the NPC and of the Chinese People's Political Consultative Conference (CPPCC). With the NPC responsible for approving policy and laws, the responsibilities of the CPPCC – whose membership was composed not only of senior Party officials but celebrity entrepreneurs, economists, intellectuals and artists as well – included building a 'united front' between Party and non-Party spirits within China and around the world. With Xi Jinping's dream of a community of common destiny to be guaranteed by technology, and with the West adrift, the country's greatest tech entrepreneurs gathered in Beijing to suggest that the Party-state should create a plan to lead the world in artificial intelligence; those with seats in the CPPCC tabled a series of motions for action. 'Artificial intelligence has reached a tipping point', they argued, 'whichever country makes a breakthrough will lead the world'.

Educated in Deng Xiaoping's China, with further studies in the US, China's intellectual-entrepreneurs were united by a belief in the importance of giving something back to the country in which they had been raised. Too busy building platforms to compete with Silicon Valley to have been touched by the Party's web of corruption, they were, in many ways, like the original group of nineteenth century self-strengtheners: Zeng Guofan, the imperial official who raised a personal army for the love of his country, and Yong Wing who had helped Zeng build a navy out of nothing. *Ai guo*, 'patriots', like Zeng and Yong, their devotion was not particularly to a flag or a nation state, but to the much bigger belief in China as a *wenming* civilisation. United by a story that went back thousands of years, their heroes were everyone's heroes: from the Crouching Tiger, Zhuge Liang, who had tamed impossible situations with the *dao*, to the Monkey King who had added the magic forces of a Daoism-Buddhism combined; from Guan Yu, the god of war who loved the people, to Song Jiang, the outlaw who mixed his blood with his brothers to fight for a better world; not to mention a hundred, if not a thousand, other heroes in between. Sharing a common language with codes that went far deeper than simple words, having read the same texts of the *Book of Changes*, the *Art of War* and the *Journey to the West*, like all of those who had gone before them, they had inherited the power to communicate the meaning of a cosmos with a character.

In their great love of China, the entrepreneurs who took their ideas to the Party were in some ways like the students who had flooded the streets in May, 1919. Almost, but not quite. They had been highly educated among a billion people in a land exposed to the best and worst that man could do. Born of parents who had seen at first hand the battles between the ideas of man as good and man as bad, and who had experienced the battle between science as an objective fact and science as a subjective experience, they had been raised in a land and among a people who carried the scars of its twentieth century past. Coming of age in a China that still believed that the world was a tooth and claw battle for survival of both the individual and the state, they understood that truth is a faith to be used for the building of future facts. Running businesses that had become part of the fabric of society, they found themselves in a time when the Party and many of the people believed that the road to utopia depended not only on the state but on a state- and Party-driven cultivation of the people themselves. They also found themselves in a time when the West clearly had no better ideas to offer. With the stories of five thousand years of heroic leaps, epic battles and an endless struggle between the individual and the collective, they understood the compromises required for survival, even as they understood the hidden meaning of a nature that, epitomised by thirteenth century paintings of rocks, bamboo, and plum blossom, survives through endurance.

Most of all they understood that, in a cosmos of constant change, nothing is more enduring than the battle to create the best truth and reality in the time in which one lives, with the best truth and reality often to be found in the virtual world. In the words of the eighteenth century author who wrote *A Dream of Red Mansions*: '*jia zuo zhen shi zhen yi jia*', truth becomes fiction when the fiction is true, '*wu wei you chu you huan wu*', the real becomes not real where the unreal is real.

Becoming China? I suspect we have only just begun.

We have created and composed these writings ... as a means to
knot the net of the Way and its Potency,
and weave the web of humankind and its affairs,
above, investigating them in heaven,
below, examining them on earth,
and in the middle, comprehending them through patterns.

Thus, numerous are the words we have composed
And extensive are the illustrations we have provided,
Yet we still fear that people will depart from the root and follow the branches.

The Huainanzi (second century BCE)

KEY SOURCES AND FURTHER READING:
A SHORT BIBLIOGRAPHIC NOTE

The story of China's dreams of order is told through a vast and varied literature. I have highlighted a very small selection of the many works that were consulted in the research on which *Becoming China* is based. Each has been chosen either because it illustrates an important point made, or because it offers a deeper perspective into times and issues described which may be of interest to the general reader. Some of the later works are novels: more than in many other parts of the world, much of China's truth is coded in its fiction. Most of the historical works are by academics, distilling decades of scholarship (and usually published by university presses, 'UP's); *Becoming China* would not have been possible without their work, and while I appreciate that this is a very different kind of book, I hope that it will bring many new readers to their extraordinary research.

The very last part of the book, the period from 1989 to 2017, draws on my own experience of the time, including much professional research and many conversations, as well as on published works.

GENERAL REFERENCE

There are a number of histories of China: the greatest in size and scholarly insight is the 15 volume *Cambridge History of China* – with an additional volume on the ancient history of China (Cambridge UP, from 1978 onwards). Chronologically ordered, each of these volumes contains a series of essays addressing detailed aspects of life and thought across each period of China's history. Far shorter, and highly readable, is Patricia Ebrey's *Cambridge Illustrated History of China* (Cambridge UP, 1986).

The best detailed and readable history is Jonathan Spence's authoritative work which covers China from 1644 to the end of the twentieth century: *The Search for Modern China* (1990; 2nd ed., Norton, 1999).

Translations of the ancient texts can be found in the work of the Scottish missionary-scholar James Legge: The Chinese Classics (1861 – 1872; reprinted by Cosimo 2006), and in selected chapters of Max Muller's monumental *Sacred Books of the East* (which include works beyond China and are accessible at The Internet Sacred Text Archive, www.sacred-texts.com).

For a good geography with maps, see Caroline Blunden and Mark Elvins' *Cultural Atlas of China* (Equinox, 1983). For an excellent environmental history, see Mark Elvin's *Retreat of the Elephants* (Yale UP, 2006)

On mythology, see Anne Birrell's *Chinese Mythology: An Introduction* (John Hopkins UP, 1999) and her translation of the *Classic of Mountains and Seas* (Penguin Classics, 2000). On cosmology, see Wolfram Eberhard's *A Dictionary of Chinese Symbols* (Routledge and Kegan Paul, 1986). On beliefs, see *The Religion of the Chinese People*, Marcel Granet (Basil Blackwell Oxford, 1975).

On philosophy and political thought, see Benjamin Schwarz' *The World of Thought in Ancient China* (Harvard UP, 1985), and the much shorter *Political Philosophy of the Middle Kingdom* by Tongdong Bai (Zed Books, 2012). For a sense of China's political philosophy in the context of the wider world, see Francis Fukuyama's *The Origins of Political Order, From Prehuman Times to the French Revolution* (Profile Books, 2011). See also *An Intellectual History of Modern China*, Merle Goldman and Leo Ou-fan Lee (Cambridge UP, 2002).

On cities and walls at various points in China's history see Paul Wheatley's *The Pivot of the Four Quarters, A Preliminary Enquiry into the Origins and Character of the Ancient Chinese City* (Edinburgh UP, 1971), Mark Edward Lewis' *The Construction of Space in Early China* (State University of New York Press, 1999), and Arthur Cotterell's *Imperial Capitals of China, an Inside View* (Pimlico, 2008). On Beijing, see Jasper Becker's *City of Heavenly Tranquility: Beijing in the History of China* (Oxford UP, 2006). See also Geremie Barmé's *The Forbidden City* (Harvard UP, 2012). On the 'Long Wall', see Julia Lovell's *The Great Wall: China Against the World, 1000 bc – ad 2000* (Grove Press, 2007).

On modern China, Graham Hutchings' *Modern China, A Guide to a Century of Change* (Harvard UP, 2001) is a wonderful reference work. *The China Leadership Monitor* is an excellent source of contemporary insight on politics and policy. *Chinasmack* offers uncensored coverage of some of the stranger sides of life on the ground. Mao's works can be found online at the Marxist Internet Archive (www.marxists.org).

BOOK I – FROM THE BEGINNING

PART 1   A HEAVENLY EMPIRE

CHAPTER 1   THE MISTS OF TIME

The story of China's earliest ancient past is well told by archeologists, led by K. C. Chang (1931 – 2001). It is K C Chang who confirms what I had guessed, namely that China's ideas of order emerged from a world of shamans; see, for example, *The Archeology of Ancient China* (4th ed, Yale UP, 1987). See also K.C.

Wu's *The Chinese Heritage, A New and Provocative View of the Origins of Chinese Society* (Crown Publishers, 1982). For a sense of the shamans' world, see the poet-prince Qu Yuan's Heavenly Questions (in *Songs of the South: An Ancient Chinese Anthology of Poems by Qu Yuan and other Poets*, transl. David Hawkes, Oxford: Clarendon Press, 1985).

The story of the Hall of Light is told by the long-time China resident and scholar William Edward Soothill (1861 – 1935) in his now-rare work *The Hall of Light: A Study of Early Chinese Kingship* (Philosophical Library, New York, 1952).

For descriptions of the early migrations and settlements and of life, see the works of K. C. Chang, particularly, *The Archeology of Ancient China* and *The formation of Chinese Civilisation* (4th ed. Yale UP 1999, and 2005; also *Art, Myth and Ritual: the Path to Political Authority in China* (Harvard UP 1988).

For a description of the DNA links between the early Chinese & the earliest humans (those who walked out of Africa roughly 70,000 years ago), see Spencer Wells *The Journey of Man: A Genetic Odyssey* (Random House, 2004).

CHAPTER 2   A HEAVENLY PEOPLE

The opening account of life in the fields of ancient China is drawn from the descriptions of Marcel Granet in *Chinese Civilisation* (Routledge, 1997).

For a sense of the mythological past (including a debate about whether the Shang were preceded by an earlier dynasty, known as the Xia), see Sarah Allan *The Shape of the Turtle: myth, art, and cosmos in early China* (SUNY Press, 1981) and *The Myth of the Xia Dynasty* (Journal of the Royal Asiatic Society, 1984). Roland Stoerckx's *The Animal and the Daemon in Early China* (SUNY Press, 2002) provides a wonderful account of how nature provided the pattern for China's ideas of order.

K. C. Chang's *Shang Civilisation* (Yale UP, 1980) describes life under the Shang (including the flight of the black-haired people, a phenomenon seen from questions regularly engraved on the oracle bones). On the oracle bones and their meaning, see David Keightley's *Sources of Shang History: The Oracle Bone Inscriptions of Bronze Age China* (California UP, 1978). On Shang cities, Mark Elvin's *Retreat of the Elephants* (Yale UP, 2006) suggests that the Shang ruled over a population of 4 – 4.5 million people divided between those who lived within walled cities and those who tilled the fields without). Elvin also describes the garrison-like nature of Shang cities, noting that it would have taken 3,500 men, working 200 days a year, over 10 years to build the early Shang capital of 'Aodu'. The story of the construction and mechanics of Shang cities (including the cosmological principles on which they were modelled (designed to reflect heaven on Earth) is told by Paul Wheatley's *Pivot of the Four Quarters* (Edinburgh UP, 1971).

The story of Zhuanxu's cutting of communications with heaven is told by K C Chang in Art Myth and Ritual (Harvard UP, 1988)

CHAPTER 3   HEAVEN ON EARTH?

The 'Martial' opera described in the opening paragraph of this chapter draws on Edward Shaughnessy's contribution to *Before Confucius*, in *From Liturgy to Literature: the Ritual Contexts of the Earliest Poems in the Book of Poetry* (SUNY Press, 1997). For an account of the importance of music in harmonising hearts and minds, see Lothar von Falkenhausen Suspended Music: Chime Bells in the Culture of Bronze Age China (University of California Press), 1994.

The idea of the Mandate of Heaven first appears in The Great Declaration, 1047 ('The iniquity of Shang is full, Heaven gives command to destroy it'). Seven hundred years later, during the time of the warring states, one of Confucius' followers (Mencius) would observe that '(i)t was by humanity that the three dynasties gained the throne, and by not being human that they lost it.'

On Zhou cities, see Mark Lewis' chapter *The City State in Spring and Autumn China*, in Mogens Hansen's *A Comparative Study of Thirty City-State Cultures* (Royal Danish Academy of Sciences, 2000). For an illustration of the cities' detailed attention to correspondences between heaven and earth, see *The Annals of Lu Buwei* (transl. John Knoblock and Jeffrey Riegel, Stanford UP, 2000), which also describes the idea of yin and yang as a constant revolution. In *Retreat of the Elephants*, Mark Elvin notes that the climate of northern China changed considerably during the time of the Zhou – which may account for the extreme meticulousness. The Duke of Zhou's thoughts on meditation are set out in *The Zhou Li* (the Rites of Zhou, attributed to the Duke of Zhou). There are many versions of the *I Ching*. One of the most highly regarded is Richard Wilhelm's translation (with a foreward by Carl Jung) (Princeton UP, 1967).

What Confucius really thought is still being argued about. Key texts attributed to him are *The Analects, The Great Learning,* and *The Cultivation of the Mean* (Penguin Classics). The clearest and most detailed descriptions of what he is thought to have said are found in the text of Mencius. The clearest insights into what he probably said and how that has been interpreted over the millennia can be found in Benjamin Schwarz' *The World of Thought in Ancient China* (see above). For a fascinating account of the story of writing and ideas (including the intellectual descendants of the shamans who became the Duke of Zhou's scholarly bureaucrats) see Mark Lewis' *Writing and Authority in Early China* (SUNY Press, 1999).

There are many translations of the *Dao De Jing*; my favourite is Martin Palmer's *The Illustrated Tao Te Ching* (Vega, 2003). For translations of the works of Zhuangzi, Mozi and the works of the most important 'legalists' (Xunzi, and Han Feizi), see Burton Watson's translations (Columbia UP, 2003). The competing ideas of the Confucians, the pursuers of the Dao and the legalists, are beautifully described by the early twentieth century English sinologist Arthur Waley in *Three Ways of Thought in Ancient China* (Stanford UP, 1939). For a deeper look at the intellectual battles that began at this time and have continued ever since, see A. C. *Graham Disputers of the Tao* (Open Court, 1989).

CHAPTER 4   A SINGLE HEART

The battle for Shangdang is known as the Battle of Changping (after the area to the south in which it was fought). The loss of Shangdang marked a crucial turning point in the warring states. For an idea of what a Qin attack might have felt like, see Zhang Yimou's film, *Hero* (2002).

The Qin dynasty is excellently described by Timothy Brook in *The Early Chinese Empires: Qin and Han* (Harvard UP, 2010). The ideas of Qin are powerfully illustrated by *The Book of Lord Shang* (transl. J.L.L. Duyvendak, The Lawbook Exchange, 2011), and well described by Derk Bodde in his now-rare work, *China's First Unifier: A Study of the Qin Dynasty as Seen in the Life of Li Si* (E. J. Brill, 1938). On the violence of the Qin (and earlier dynasties), see Mark Edward Lewis' *Sanctioned Violence in Early China* (SUNY Press, 1989). Arthur Cotterell provides a very readable account of the life of the First Qin Emperor (with illustrations), in *The First Emperor of China* (Macmillan, London, 1981).

For an account of the *chang cheng*, Long Wall, (from the earliest times to the present day, including its American-inspired recasting as the 'Great Wall') see Julia Lovell's *The Great Wall, China Against The World, 1000 bc – ad 2000* (Atlantic Books, 2006).

PART 2   DREAMS

CHAPTER 1   ONE HEAVEN, ONE EARTH?

For a wonderful description of life in the Tang dynasty, see Edward Schafer's *The Golden Peaches of Samarkand* (California UP, 1963); see also Charles Benn, *Daily Life in Traditional China: The Tang Dynasty* (Greenwood Press, 2002).

China's battles against nomadic tribes are well described by Nicola di Cosmo in *Ancient China and its Enemies: The Rise of Nomadic Power in East Asian History* (Cambridge UP, 2004). For a description of the Xiongnu, see David Christian, *A History of Russia, Central Asia and Mongolia, Volume 1, Inner*

Eurasia from pre-history to the Mongol Empire (Wiley-Blackwell, 1998). The story of Zhang Qian is told by Sima Qian in *The Records of the Grand Historian, Han Dynasty II* (transl. Burton Watson, Columbia UP, 1995).

For an idea of the arguments made in the 'conquest debates', see Mark Edward Lewis' *The Construction of Space in early China.* The arguments are not dissimilar to the present debates about Chinese foreign policy and militarisation. The supremacy of Confucianism over legalism was finally secured by the triumph of the Confucians in the debates known as the White Tiger Discussions (*bohu luntang*) which took place in 79 BCE.

There are many competing theories about the origin of the Mongols (who were not the only 'northern barbarians'). They first came to the attention of the Chinese as a tribe under the Shiwei clan of the Xianbei; some say that they were remnants of the old Xiongnu; others that they emerged from the Xianbei; given that both were confederations of tribes in an area that was constantly swirling with nomads, both or neither may be true.

Mark Edward Lewis tells the story of the Han Dynasty in *The Early Chinese Empires: Qin and Han* (Harvard UP, 2010); he goes on to cover the period from the Three Kingdoms to the end of the Sui in *China Between Empires: the Northern and Southern Dynasties* (Harvard UP 2011), and then to tell the story of the Tang Dynasty in *China's Cosmopolitan Empire* (Harvard UP, 2009).

For a sense of the time of the Three Kingdoms in general, and Zhuge Liang in particular, see John Woo's film *Red Cliff* (2008).

For a discussion of the complications of race at this time, see Marc Abramson, *Ethnic Identity in Tang China* (Pennsylvania UP, 2011).

The ideas of Zhu Xi (Chu Hsi in Wade-Giles) can be seen in *Learning to be a Sage: Selections from the Conversations of Master Chu* (transl. Daniel K Gardner, University of California Press, 1990). For a fascinating account of dissent among Song dynasty intellectuals, see Alfreda Merck, *Poetry and Painting in Song China: The Subtle Art of Dissent* (Harvard University Asia Centre, 2000). For a highly readable story of Chinngis Khan, see Jack Weatherford's *Genghis Khan and the Making of the Modern World* (Crown, 2004).

For thoughts on how the Chinese of the various times saw themselves and their land, see Richard Smith, Chinese maps (Oxford UP, 1996).

CHAPTER 2   A BRIGHT IDEA

Geremie Barmé's *Forbidden City* (Harvard UP, 2012) is a succinct masterpiece. May Holdsworth & Caroline Courtauld offer a wonderfully visual account in *The Forbidden City: The Great Within* (Odyssey Publications, 1998). For those able to travel, there is little to compare with a combined visit to the Forbidden City in Beijing and the Palace Museum in Taibei (where many of the objects that once adorned the Forbidden City are displayed).

The story of the Ming dynasty (including the story of how a changing climate terrorised the Ming rulers, as well as the battle about the meaning of 'investigating things') is well told by Timothy Brook *in The Troubled Empire: China in the Yuan and Ming Dynasties* (Harvard UP, 2010). (The more detailed story of the weather and order is well told by Mark Elvin in *Who was Responsible for the Weather? Moral Meteorology in Late Imperial China* in *Beyond Joseph Needham* (University of Chicago Press, 1998)). Brook goes on to provide a wonderful description of wealth and its costs in daily life in *The Confusions of Pleasure, Commerce and Culture in Ming China* (University of California Press, 1998). See also Jonathan Spence's *Return to Dragon Mountain: Memories of a Late Ming man* (Norton, 2008). Craig Clunas' *Empire of Great Brightness: Visual and Material Cultures of Ming China, 1368 – 1644* (University of Hawai'i Press, 2007) is a visual delight as well as an interesting source on state intelligence and violence. For a fascinating account of the imperial examination system see Ichisada Miyazaki's *China's Examination Hell: Civil Service Examinations of Imperial China* (Yale UP, 1981).

For more detail on policy, economics and eunuchs, see Albert Chan's *The Glory and Fall of the Ming Dynasty* (University of Oaklahoma Press, 1982) and Ray Huang's 1587 *A Year of No Significance: the Ming Dynasty in Decline* (Yale UP, 1981). For a deeper account of the emperors, see John W Dardess' *Ming China, 1368 – 1644: A Concise History of a Resilient Empire* (Rowman & Littlefield, 2011). The story of Zheng He is well told by Timothy Brook in *The Troubled Empire* (see above); a more detailed account can be found in Ma Huan's fascinating *Overall Survey of the Ocean's Shores, 1433* (transl. J. V. G. Mills, Cambridge University Press for the Hakluyt Society).

The story of Asian trade (interwoven with the story of silver) is important in understanding the latter fortunes and misfortunes of the Ming. Timothy Brook provides a wonderful perspective in *Mr. Selden's Map of China: The Spice Trade, a Lost Chart and the South China Sea* (Rotterdam 2014); a shorter version of the story is told by the journalist Bill Hayton in his recent work *The South China Sea: The Struggle for Power in Asia* (Yale UP, 2014).

CHAPTER 3   THIS WORLD AND BEYOND

The opening of this chapter was inspired by an eighth century (Tang dynasty) poem, by Wang Wei, called *Passing Xiangji Temple*; it can be accessed at Jean Ward's Wang Wei Remembered (Lulu.com).

Derk Bodde describes Chinese ideas of retreat in *The World of Nature*, in *China's Cultural Tradition, What and Whither? Source Problems in World Civilisations* (Holt Reinart and Winston, Inc.,1957). The earliest recorded account of a flight from the world is by Qu Yuan in his epic poem *Li Sao* (*Encountering Trouble*, in *Songs of the South*, Penguin Classics, 1985). Early accounts of hermits are also given in the *Book of the Later Han* (6 – 189 AD); Laozi's *Daodejing* captures the appeal of retreat. More rational arguments for becoming a hermit are made by Zhuangzi. Bill Porter's *Road to Heaven: Encounters with Chinese Hermits* provides a wonderful contemporary account of China's hermits (Counterpoint Press, 1993).

The story of the arrival Buddhism in China is told in two short but beautiful books: Daisaku Ikeda's *The Flower of Chinese Buddhism* (transl. Burton Watson, Middleway Press, 2009) and Arthur Wright's *Buddhism in Chinese History* (Stanford UP, 1959). On the battle between Buddhism, Daoism and Confucianism during the first millennium, see Mark Edward Lewis, *China Between the Empires*, and *China's Cosmopolitan Empire* (see above). Meir Shahar gives a fascinating account of the Shaolin monastery in *The Shaolin Monastery: History, Religion, and the Chinese Martial Arts*, (University of Hawai'i Press, 2008). For a wonderful account of Buddhism from the personal perspective on a 20th century life, see Sun Shuyun's *Ten Thousand Miles without a Cloud* (Harper Collins, 2003).

The story of Daoism is told by Holmes Welch in *Taoism: The Parting of the Way* (Beacon Press, 1971; Holmes Welch and Anna Seidel gather an interesting set of essays in *Facets of Taoism* (Yale UP, 1979) as do Livia Kohn and Harold D. Roth in *Daoist Identity: History, Lineage and Ritual* (University of Hawai'I Press, 2002). The influence of Daoism on the Tang Dynasty is told by Stephen R Bokenkampf in *Time After Time: Taoist Apocalyptic History and the Founding of the Tang Dynasty* (Academica Sinica, 1994).

Henri Maspero's *The Mythology of Modern China* in Asiatic Mythology (George G. Harrap & Co., 1932) provides a wonderful description of all beliefs, including the most popular. For an account of the battling fabric of Chinese beliefs, see *Unruly Gods: Divinity and Society in China*, ed. Meir Shahar and Robert P Weller (University of Hawai'i Press, 1996).

The most accessible (and shortest) version of the story of the Monkey King is the abridged 'Monkey' by Arthur Waley (Pengin Classics, 1942). By far and away the best translation of the story of the Monkey King is *The Journey to the West* by Anthony C. Yu (4 magical volumes; University of Chicago Press, 1977 – 1983).

PART 3   WHOSE HEAVEN?

CHAPTER 1   SOMEONE ELSE'S SKY

The events at Shanhai Guan are described in the wonderful work of Gertraude Roth Li, *State Building Before 1644* (Vol. 9, Part 1, Cambridge History of China (Cambridge UP, 2002).

For excellent descriptions of the Manju see Pamela Kyle Crossley's *The Manchus* (Wiley-Blackwell, 2002) and Mark Elliot's *The Manchu Way: The Eight Banners and Ethnic Identity in Late Imperial China* (Stanford UP, 2001). The Manju Qing's hunting grounds are beautifully described by Philippe Forêt's *Mapping Chengde* (University of Hawai'i Press, 2000).

The story of the Qing empire is very well told by William T. Rowe in *China's Last Empire: The Great Qing* (Harvard UP, 2009). The story of the Qing conquests is wonderfully told by Peter C Perdue's *China Marches West: The Qing Conquest of Central Eurasia* (Harvard UP, 2010). On the question of the Manju and their identity as the Qing dynasty, see Pamela Kyle Crossley's important *A Translucent Mirror* (California UP, 2002).

For excellent accounts of the reigns of Kangxi and Qianlong, see Jonathan Spence's *The K'ang-hsi Reign* and Alexander Woodside's *The Ch'ien-Lung Reign* (Vol. 9, Part 1, Cambridge History of China); see also Jonathan Spence's *Emperor of China: Self Portrait of Kang-hsi* (Knopf, 1974). The Hall of Mental Cultivation and of its Qing dynasty occupants is well described by Geremie Barmé's *Forbidden City* (see above).

The economics of the early Qing are told by Ramon H Myers and Yeh-chien Wang in *Economic Developments* (Vol. 9, Part 1, Cambridge History of China); see also Ramon Myers' wider *The Chinese Economy: Past and Present* (Wadsworth 1980).

The story of the Jesuits (and of the battle between Kangxi's ideas of an effective temporal order and the Pope's dream of an empire of souls that would come to be known as the 'Chinese Rites Controversy') is told by Jonathan Spence in *The Memory Palace of Matteo Ricci* (Viking Penguin, 1984). See also Spence's wonderful tale, *The Question of Hu* (Vintage, 1989), the thought-provoking story of a man who found himself caught between the two.

CHAPTER 2   RIVERS OF FORTUNE

This chapter owes much to Wiilliam T. Rowe's masterful account of late Qing dynasty Hankou, including its inhabitants and guilds: *Hankow: Commerce and Society in a Chinese City, 1796 – 1889* (Stanford UP, 1984); see also Rowe's parallel work, *Hankow: Conflict and Community in a Chinese City, 1796 – 1895* (Stanford UP, 1985).

For a wonderful description of life in Qing China during the 18th century, see Susan Naquin and Evelyn Rawski's *Chinese Society in the Eighteenth Century* (Yale UP, 1989). See also Benjamin Elman's *The Class of 1761: Examinations, State and Elite in Eighteenth Century China* (Stanford UP, 2004). For a rich description of the rise and fall of a Chinese family whose fortunes depended upon imperial favour, see Cao Xueqin's classic Qing dynasty novel *A Dream of Red Mansions* (transl. David Hawkes as *The Story of the Stone*, Penguin Classics, 1973). Cao's own family fortunes were made as Han loyalists to the Manju Qing with Cao's grandfather becoming a childhood friend of the Kangxi Emperor; they collapsed with the death of the Kangxi Emperor and the confiscation of their properties, the imprisonment of the family patriarch and the impoverishment of the family members, including a then very young Cao Xueqin. For a sense of the wealth created by China's rivers of fortunes and the challenges faced by their descendants, see Zhang Yimou's film *Raise the Red Lantern* (1991), set in the 1920s, and based on the true story of the Qiao family (scions of a Shanxi banker).

The world of rural China is masterfully described and analysed, region by region, by George W. Skinner in his classic work *Marketing and Social Structure in Rural China* (Journal of Asian Studies, 1964 – 1965). Skinner also provides an excellent account of the evolution of Chinese cities in his edition of essays *The City in Late Imperial China* (Stanford UP, 1977). The story of Shanghai is told by Linda Cooke Johnson in *Shanghai: From Market Town to Treaty Port*, 1074 – 1858 (Stanford UP, 1995).

Arthur Waley provides a magnificent and succinct account of the opium wars (including a wonderful account of Lin Zexu and his letters to Queen Victoria) in *The Opium War Through Chinese Eyes* (Stanford UP, 1958). Peter Perdue's online course materials on *The First Opium War – The Anglo-Chinese War of 1839 – 1842* are a wonderful example of a fascinating and accessible academic work (ocw.mit.edu).

Stephen Platt provides an excellent account of the Taiping rebellion (including the way in which the Western 'opium warriors' got tangled up in the story) in *Autumn in the Heavenly Kingdom: China, The West and the Epic Story of the Taiping Civil War* (Atlantic Books, 2012). Jonathan Spence tells the story of Hong Xiuquan in *God's Chinese Son: The Taiping Heavenly Kingdom of Hong Xiuquan* (Norton, 1996).

Mary Clabaugh Wright's *The Last Stand of Chinese Conservatism* (Stanford UP, 1962) provides a fascinating account of the rise and ideas of the self-strengtheners.

CHAPTER 3   IMAGINE A PEOPLE

The inspiration for the title of this chapter, and a source of many thought-provoking insights, is a collection of essays: *Imagining the People: Chinese Intellectuals and the Concept of Citizenship, 1890 – 1920* (ed. Joshua Fogel and Peter Zarrow; East Gate, 1997). The story of the Hunanese is magnificently told by Stephen Platt in his *Provincial Patriots: The Hunanese and Modern China* (Harvard UP, 2007). The revolutionaries and their ideas are beautifully described by Jonathan Spence in *The Gate of Heavenly Peace: The Chinese and Their Revolution, 1895 – 1980* (Viking Press, 1982).

The story of the Battle of Weihaiwei was pieced together from many different historical sources.

The geopolitics of the Great Game are importantly described by Halford Mackinder in *The Geographical Pivot of History* (The Geographical Journal, 1904).

Joseph Esherick's *The Origins of the Boxer Uprising* (University of California Press, 1987) is an excellent account of the causes of the Boxer rebellion, which are far more important than the more popular stories of the Boxers' defeat.

On the impact of the ideas of West (many of which were brought to China through the tranlsations of Yan Fu), on the rise of the self-strengtheners, and on the pursuit of *fu qiang* wealth and power, see Benjamin Schwarz *In Search of Wealth and Power: Yen Fu and the West* (Harvard UP, 1964). More recently, see Orville Schell and John Delury's *Wealth and Power, China's Long March to the Twenty-First Century* (Random House, 2013).

The ideas of Kang Youwei are set out in Kung-ch'uan Hsiao's *A Modern China and a New World: K'ang Yu-wei, Reformer and Utopian* (Washington UP, 1975). A more readable account is given by Young-Tsu Wong in *The Search for Material Civilisation: Kang Youwei's Journey to the West* (Taiwan Journal of East Asian Studies, Vol.5, No.1, 2008). Liang Qichao's story is told by Hao Chang in *Liang Ch'I-ch'ao and Intellectual Transition in China* (Harvard UP, 1971) and, more recently, by Pankaj Mishra in *From the Ruins of Empire* (Farrar, Strauss & Giroux, 2012). Liang Qichao set out his thoughts on America in *The Power and Threat of America* (1903; which can be found in *Land Without Ghosts: Chinese Impressions of America from the Mid-Nineteenth Century to the Present*, eds. R David Arkush, Leo O. Lee; University of California Press, 1993).

The story of Sun Yatsen is told by Orville Schell and John Delury in chapter 6 of *Wealth and Power* (see above). The story of Sun's kidnapping is told in *Kidnapped in London: being the story of my capture by, detention at and release from the Chinese Legation, London* (1897; reprinted by the Foreign Language Teaching and Research Press, 2012).

The story of the Dowager Empress Cixi is told by Orville Schell and John Delury in chapter 4 of *Wealth and Power* (see above). A more controversial account is given by Jung Chang in *The Concubine Who Launched Modern China: Empress Dowager Cixi* (Anchor, 2014).

By the mid nineteenth century, photographic images of the Qing dynasty begin to appear: see Liu Heung Shing's *China in Revolution* (Hong Kong UP, 2011).

BOOK II – TWENTIETH CENTURY IDEAS

The divergence between traditionally accepted China history and more recent 'revisionist' works is extreme in these two parts, with the Party's view of history directly challenged by many relatively recent authors. As highlighted in the Author's Note, where the stories are highly divergent, key revisionist works are referenced. The fact that such divergent views can exist, and that the past works of highly regarded China scholars accepted many 'facts' which are now contested, is an indication of the challenge of an order which places harmony above truth.

PART 4   UP IN THE CITY

CHAPTER 1   MIDNIGHT

Xu Zhimo's poems can be found in *Xu Zhimo, Selected Poems* (Oleander Press, 2012).

The opening to this chapter draws on the works of Chinese novels of the time.

For a beautiful description of the story of Republican Beijing, see Madeleine Yue Dong's book, *Republican Beijing, The City and Its Histories* (University of California Press, 2003). See also David Strand's *Rickshaw Beijing: City People and Politics in the 1920s* (University of California Press, 1989) and Stephen Haw's *Beijing, A Concise History* (Routledge, 2008). For a sense of the old and the new, see Jasper Becker's *City of Heavenly Tranquility: Beijing in the History of China* (Oxford UP, 2006). For a book on present-day Beijing that includes a perspective on the past, see *Beijing Time* by Michael Dutton, Hsiu-ju Stacy Lo and Dong Dong Wu (Harvard UP, 2010).

The story of the last emperor (including contemporary remarks on the last years of the Qing and the early Republic) is told by Reginald Fleming Johnston (the Scottish academic and British diplomat who became Puyi's tutor) in *Twilight in the Forbidden City* (Cambridge UP, 1934). It can also be seen in Bertolucci's film *The Last Emperor* (1987).

On the economics of Republican China, see Albert Feuerwerker's *Economic Trends in the Republic of China 1912 – 1949* (Center for Chinese Studies, University of Michigan, 1977).

The Republican era saw a flourishing of literature, as China's new generation of intellectuals turned their attention to describing the real life of the people. Of the many wonderful authors, see the works of the novelist and playwright, Lao She (1899 – 1966), whose *Camel Xiangzi* describes the life of a rickshaw driver (various translations, including *Rickshaw Boy* transl.

Howard Goldblatt, Harper Perennial, 2010) and whose play, *Teahouse*, covers fifty years of change in the conversations of a teahouse, from 1898 – 1949 (transl. John Howard-Gibbon, China Books, 2013). See also Lu Xun's *Diary of a Madman* (transl. Julia Lovell, in *The Complete Fiction of Lu Xun*, Penguin Classics, 2009).

For a fascinating view of 1920s Beijing, see Sidney Gamble's *Peking, a Social Survey* (H. Milford, 1921), and the magical archive of his photographs available at Duke University's online library (www.library.duke.edu/ digitalcollections/gamble).

For an account of the events of May 4, 1919, see Rana Mitter's *A Bitter Revolution: China's Struggle with the Modern World* (Oxford UP, 2005). See also Vera Schwarz' *The Chinese Enlightenment: Intellectuals and the Legacy of the May Fourth Movement* (University of California Press, 1986).

The story of Peking University and Cai Yuanpei was drawn together from many different sources, Chinese and Western. The original *honglou* red brick building of Peking University is now a museum and can be visited (29 Wusi Street, Dongcheng, Beijing).

The story of Liang Shuming is told by Guy S. Alitto in *The Last Confucian: Liang Shu-ming and the Chinese Dilemma of Modernity* (University of California Press, 1979). For an account of the impact of some of the foreign ideas that China was exploring, see David Kelly's *The Highest Chinadom: Nietzsche and the Chinese Mind, 1907 – 1989* in *Nietzsche in Asia* (ed. G. Parkes, University of Chicago Press, 1991), and Tagore in China (eds. Tan Chung and Amiya Dev, SAGE Publications, 2011).

The story of the 'science debates' is told by Zuoye Wang in *Saving China through Science: The Science Society of China, Scientific Nationalism, and Civil Society in Republican China* (Osiris, second Series, Vol. 17, Science and Civil Society (2002)), and by Wang Hui in *Scientific Worldview, Culture Debates, and the Reclassification of Knowledge in Twentieth-century China*, (Boundary 2, (2008)). China's science debates anticipated a later debate in 1930's Britain – described as a battle of 'cultures' (science versus humanism). The British battle was reprised 30 years later (in 1959) when it came to be known as the 'science wars', led by a battle between C P Snow and a Cambridge Literary Critic F R Leavis, with Snow arguing for the superiority of science (see C P Snow, *The Two Cultures*, Rede Lecture, Cambridge May 7, 1959), and with Leavis arguing for the superiority of human values (and the study of the humanities).

For an account of the impact of the Japanese war on the civil war within China, see Rana Mitter's *China's War with Japan, 1937 – 1945: The Struggle for Survival* (Allen Lane, 2013).

CHAPTER 2   A BRAVE NEW WORLD

The story of the Front Service Corp's 1938 journey (and the story of Ding Ling and the first part of her life) is told by Charles J. Alber in *Enduring the Revolution: Ding Ling and the Politics of Literature*, (Praeger, 2001). Ding Ling's fictional account of He Yepin's execution was called *A Certain Night (Mouye)*; her loyal account of Communist reforms in 1930s China is set out in her novel, *The Sun Shines over the Sanggan River* (1948; Foreign Languages Press, 1984). For the story of the second part of Ding Ling's life, see Charles J. Alber, *Embracing the Lie: Ding Ling and the Politics of Literature in the Peoples Republic of China* (Praeger, 2004).

The story of Mao is told through many, now dramatically different, accounts. The classic work is Edgar Snow's still fascinating but now highly challenged *Red Star over China* (Penguin Books, 1972). The most dramatic of the revisionist works is Jung Chang and Jon Halliday's *Mao, the Unknown Story* (Vintage, 2007) which, based on the accounts of hundreds of those who were close to Mao, offers a compelling revision of the traditional story, albeit one which is challenged by many leading academics. Part of the controversy around the book results from the very different approaches taken by academics and non-academics, raising important and difficult questions about 'truth'. Jonathan Spence provides a very short and wonderfully readable account of Mao in *Mao Zedong: A Life* (Penguin Books, 1999).

The story of the evolution of the relationship between the Republican state and the secret societies (and of the road to the 1927 massacre of the Communists) is told by Joseph Fewsmith in *Party, State and Local Elites in Republican China: Merchant Organisations and Politics in Shanghai, 1890 – 1930* (University of Hawai'i Press, 1986). The role of China's secret societies, then and now, is important (and often overlooked).

The story of the Long March is heavily contested, with new works relying on first hand accounts and greater access to archives. The traditional account of the Long March is told by Harrison Salisbury in *The Long March: The Untold Story* (McGraw Hill, 1987). A far more credible account (drawing on first hand interviews and materials only recently made available) is given by Sun Shuyun in *The Long March* (Harper Perennial, 2007) who describes the Long March as the founding myth of the Party; see also Ed Jocelyn & Andrew McEwan's *The Long March Remembered* (2006), and the accounts of the Long March in Jung Chang's *Mao, The Unknown Story*.

For an interesting account of the Russian choreography of the war between the Guomindang and the Communists, see Jung Chang's *Mao: The Unknown Story* (see above). For a fascinating account of China on the eve of the 1949 revolution, see A. Doak Barnett's *China on the Eve of Communist Takevoer* (Praeger, 1961).

For a first hand description of Yan'an, see Sidney Rittenberg's *The Man Who Stayed Behind* (with Amanda Bennett; Duke University Press, 2001). Rittenberg (born 1921) was an American journalist who went to China in 1944 and found his way to Yan'an; an occasional conduit for communications and an obvious target for suspicions of the West, he was imprisoned twice, once in 1949, for six years, and again, in 1968, for nearly 10 years.

For a description of Mao's art and literature campaign, see *Wild Lily, Prairie Fire: China's Road to Democracy, Yan'an to Tiananmen, 1942 – 1989* (ed. Gregor Benton & Alan Hunter; Princeton University Press, 1995). For a description of the techniques applied in thought reform, see Robert Lifton's *Thought Reform of Chinese Intellectuals: A Psychiatric Evaluation* (The Journal of Asian Studies, Vol. 16, 1956). Lifton's work was based on seventeen months of interviews with Chinese intellectuals who had managed to find their way to Hong Kong. For an understanding of the Party's idea of 'revolutionary' man and the impact of thought reform, see Theodore Hsi-En Chen, *The New Socialist Man* (Comparative Education Review, Vol. 13, No. 1, 1969).

On the ideas of those who wanted to build a bridge between the countryside and the cities, see Margherita Zanasi, *Far from the Treaty Ports: Fang Xianting and the Idea of Rural Modernity in 1930s China* (Modern China, Vol. 30, No. 1, 2004).

For a fascinating first-hand description of 1949 Beijing (including the search for books that would explain the new revolutionary order), see Derk Bodde's *Peking Diary – A Year of Revolution* (Henry Schuman Inc, New York, 1950).

Stuart Schram gives a wonderful account of Mao's ideas in *The Thought of Mao Tse-tung* (Cambridge UP, 1989). See also Roderick MacFarquhar, Timothy Cheek, Eugene Wu eds *The Secret Speeches of Chairman Mao: From the Hundred Flowers to the Great Leap Forward* (Council on East Asian Studies, Harvard U, 1989). Mao's works (and speeches) can be found online at the Marxists Internet Archive (www.marxists.org/reference/archive/mao). On the 'withering away' of the state, see Solomon Bloom's *The 'Withering Away' of the State* (Journal of the History of Ideas, Vol. 7, 1946).

On the Hundred Flowers campaign, see Roderick MacFarquhar's edition of essays *The Hundred Flowers Campaign and the Chinese Intellectuals* (Octagon Books, 1974). See also Merle Goldman's *Literary Dissent in Communist China* (Harvard UP, 1967) and *China's Intellectuals and the State: In Search of a New Relationship* (ed. Merle Goldman and Timothy Cheek, Harvard UP, 1987).

For an account of trade unions (and strikes) in the 1950s, see *Urban Spaces in Contemporary China: the potential for autonomy and community in post-Mao*

China, (ed. Deborah S Davis, Cambridge University Press, 1995). For an account of life in a labour camp, written by an intellectual who spent 22 years – from 1957 to 1979 – in a camp in Ningxia, see Zhang Xianliang's novel Half of Man is Woman (transl. Martha Avery, Norton, 1986).

For a description of Liang Sicheng's architectural life, see Wilma Fairbank's *Liang and Lin: Partners in Exploring China's Architectural Past* (University of Pennsylvania Press, 2008); for a vision of the architecture that he loved, see Liang Ssu-ch'eng and Fairbank, *Chinese Architecture: A Pictorial History* (Dover, 2005). For a description of the 1959 National Day, see Sang Ye and Geremie R Barmé, Thirteen National Days, a Retrospective (China Heritage Quarterly, No. 17, 2009).

For contemporary descriptions of the revolutionary role and significance of the urban communes, see D. E. T. Luard, *The Urban Communes* (China Quarterly, No. 29, 1960), and Janet Saleff, *The Urban Communes and Anti-City Experiment in Communist China,* (China Quarterly, No. 29, 1967).

The story of Deng Tuo is told by Timothy Cheek in *Deng Tuo: Culture, Leninism and Alternative Marxism in the Chinese Communist Party* (Clarendon Press, 1997). The story of the Cultural Revolution is magisterially told by Roderick Macfarquhar in *Mao's Last Revolution* (Harvard University Press, 2008).

CHAPTER 3   THINKING AGAIN

The poem describing the game of Go can be found in an article by Zu-yan Chen, *Great Chant on Observing Weiqi: An Archetype of Neo-Confucian Poetry* (Journal of the American Oriental Society, 2006). In the summer, it is still played in the street.

For a view of working life in 1970's China, see Michelangelo Antonioni's film *Chung Kuo Cina* (1972).

For an account of Fang Lizhi's work and life (including his 1972 article and the denunciations which followed), see James H Williams' *Fang Lizhi's Expanding Universe* (China Quarterly, 1990). See also Fang Lizhi's own words in the article *China's Despair and China's Hope* (transl. Perry Link, The New York Review of Books, 1989). For an account of the relationship between revolutionary China and Albert Einstein, see Danian Hu's *China and Albert Einstein: The Reception of the Physicist and His Theory in China, 1917 – 1979* (Harvard UP, 2005).

Life in post-Mao Beijing is well described by Martin King Whyte and William L Parish, *Urban Life in Contemporary China* (University of Chicago Press, 1984).

Life in post-Deng Beijing is well described in *Urban Spaces in Contemporary China: the potential for autonomy and community in post-Mao China* (ed. Deborah Davis, Cambridge UP, 1995).

The voices of the intellectuals are powerfully described in *Mao's Harvest: Voices from China's New Generation* (eds. Helen Siu and Zelda Stern, Oxford UP, 1983). The political battles are described in *Sowing the Seeds of Democracy in China: Political Reform in the Deng Xiaopng Era* (ed. Merle Goodman, Harvard UP, 1994). The text of Wei Jinghsheng's 'Fifth Modernisation' can be found at www.weijingsheng.org. The changing role of Tiananmen is described by Wu Hung in *Remaking Beijing: Tiananmen Square and the Creation of a Political Space* (Reaktion Books, 2005).

Heshang, the documentary, can be accessed on YouTube. The series had such a powerful impact, and was so full of cultural references, that two exiled intellectuals, Su Xiaokang and Wang Luxiang, wrote *Deathsong of the River: a Readers' Guide to the Chinese TV Series Heshang* (transl. Richard Bodman and Pin Pin Wan, Cornell University East Asia Series, 1999).

The complex of economic and political challenges are described by Ken Lieberthal in *Governing China – From Revolution through Reform* (Norton, 1995). See also Maurice Meisner's *Mao's China and After, a History of the People's Republic* (The Free Press, 1999). Ezra Vogel's *Deng Xiaoping and the Transformation of China* (Harvard UP, 2013) offers important perspectives.

A first hand account of events from 1979 to 1989 can be found in Zhao Ziyang's personal recollections, published as *Prisoner of the State: The Secret Journal of Premier Zhao Ziyang* (ed. and transl. Bao Pu and Adi Ignatius, Simon & Schuster, 2010). The account was recorded by Zhao Ziyang in his courtyard prison, and hidden among his grandchildren's toys before being smuggled out of the country; banned in mainland China, it was published in Hong Kong, where it became a bestseller (with sales to visiting mainlanders as well as Hong Kong Chinese).

PART 5　　DOWN IN THE COUNTRYSIDE

Many of the general works referred to in Part 4, including those on Mao, are also sources for Part 5.

CHAPTER 1　　SNOW IN SUMMER

The story of the market was inspired by Sigrid Schmalzer's wonderful article *Breeding a Better China: Pigs, Practices and Place in a Chinese County, 1929 – 1937* (Geographical Review, Vol. 92, 2002).

The story of Ding Xian is told by Charles Hayford in *To The People, James Yen and Village China* (Columbia University Press, 1990). See also Pearl Buck's interview with James Yen: *Tell the People, Talks with James Yen about the Mass Education Movement* (John Day & Co., 1945). Pearl Buck wrote *The Good Earth* (John Day & Co, 1931) a book about China's peasants which was a classic in its time but in the light of the new history, has become controversial. The story of medicine in the 'rural reconstruction' is told by Chen Zhiquan in *Medicine in Rural China: A Personal Account* (University of California Press, 1989).

The engagement of the intellectuals with the countryside is wonderfully described by Xiaorong Han in *Chinese Discourses on the Peasant, 1900 – 1949* (SUNY, 2005). See also Lu Xun's short story *Hometown* (1921). Chang-tai Hung's *Going to the People, Chinese Intellectuals and Folk Literature, 1918 – 1937* offers a fascinating insight into how the early students' journeys to the countryside shaped China's post-revolutionary culture. Sidney Gamble's photographs illuminate the countryside as well as the city (see above).

Fei Xiaotong's early works provide wonderful insights into the fabric of China's rural world, from *Peasant Life in China: A Field Study of Country Life in the Yangze Valley* (Routledge, 1939) to *Earthbound China* (University of Chicago Press, 1945) and *China's Gentry, Essays on Rural-Urban Relations* (rev. and ed. Margaret Park Redfield; University of Chicago Press, 1953). Morton Fried's *Fabric of Chinese Society* (Octagon, 1969) is a wonderful companion to the time. Liang Shuming's rural work is described by Guy Alitto in *The Last Confucian* (see above); it is also considered by Wu Shugang and Tong Binchang in *Liang Shuming's Rural Reconstruction Experiment and its Relevance for Building the New Socialist Countryside* (Contemporary Chinese Thought, Vol. 40, 2009). On the economics of the countryside, see William Skinner's thee-part work, *Marketing and Social Structure in Rural China* (see above).

Peng Pai's own story can be found in *Seeds of a Peasant Revolution: Report on the Haifeng Peasant Movement* (transl. Donald Holoch, Cornell University East Asia Papers, 1973). A very different story of Peng Pai is told by Jung Chang in *Mao, The Unknown Story* (see above) and by Fernando Galbiati in *Peng Pai and the Hailufeng Soviet* (Stanford UP, 1985). The contrasts are a reminder of how difficult it is to point to a historical 'truth'.

CHAPTER 2　　LEAPING AHEAD

The account of Liu Lin village is based on Jan Myrdal's *Report from a Chinese Village* (Pantheon Books, 1965); Myrdal referred to it as 'Liu Ling' in his book. Like Edgar Snow's *Red Star Over China*, and Harrison Salisbury's *The Long March*, Myrdal's account is now seen more as an example of successful Party propaganda: the same propaganda heard and read by the Chinese of the time.

William Parish and Martin King Whyte provide a thorough account of the countryside under Mao in *Village and Family in Contemporary China* (University of Chicago Press, 1980). See also William Hinton's personal account of village life during this time in *Fanshen – A Documentary of Revolution in a Chinese Village* (1966; University of California Press, 1997). Hinton was an American farmer who was sent to China as a technician in 1948, and stayed on after the revolution, attaching himself to a land reform work team in Long Bow.

The story of the famine and the Party's reactions to it is best told by Yang Jisheng in *Tombstone: The Untold Story of Mao's Great Famine* (transl. Stacy Mosher and Guo Jian, Allen Lane, 2012); it is Yang who describes the 'five winds'. Sulamith Heins Potter and Jack Potter tell the post-Mao story of the peasants in *China's Peasants, The Anthropology of a Revolution*, (University of California, 1990).

CHAPTER 3   WINDS, AND MORE WINDS

The account of Long Bow Village's power seizure is based on William Hinton's Shenfan (Random House, 1983).

William Hinton continues the story of the countryside with Shenfan. Having returned to the US in 1953 for a visit, he was swept up in the McCarthy investigations, and accused of anti-American behaviour; his passport confiscated, he remained in the US for fifteen years. Returning to China (and Long Bow Village), Hinton tells the story of the unravelling of the revolution. Hinton was a farmer and a revolutionary in his own right. Although I did not know that I would write *Becoming China*, Bill was one of the first people I met when I arrived in Beijing in 1989, and, when he wanted to use the early Joint Venture laws to help Long Bow Village find its feet in the new world, he became one of my first pro bono clients; his story was fascinating and he was one of the most straightforward people I have ever worked with.

The story of reform in the countryside is well told by Susan Whiting in *Power and Wealth in Rural China: The Political Economy of Institutional Change* (Cambridge UP, 2006).

The story of the sent-down students is well told by Thomas P Bernstein in *Up to the Mountains and Down to the Villages: The Transfer of Youth from Urban to Rural China* (Yale UP, 1977). For a description of the twists and turns of the Cultural Revolution (including the rise of the Red Guards and the counter-rise of the Rebel Red Guards), see Jonathan Unger's *Education Under Mao: Class and Competition in Canton Schools, 1960 – 1980* (Columbia UP, 1982). For the truth of a novel, see Dai Sijie's *Balzac and the Little Chinese Seamstress* (Vintage, 2001; also a film, written and directed by Dai Sijie). Dai spent four years in rural Sichuan in the early 1970s. The views of the students are captured in their own, very powerful, voices in *Mao's Harvest: Voices from China's New Generation* (see above).

The story of the transformation of the countryside from Mao through Deng is well told by Jonathan Unger's *The Transformation of Rural China* (M.E. Sharpe, 2002). The story of Wenzhou is wonderfully told both by Yia-Ling Liu in *The Private Economy and Local Politics in the Rural Industralisation of Wenzhou* (China Quarterly, 1992), and by Anita Chan and Jonathan Unger in *Grey and Black: The Hidden Economy of Rural China* (Pacific Affairs, Vol. 85, 1982). The continuing post-Mao story of the peasants is well told by Sulamith Heins Potter and Jack Potter in *China's Peasants, The Anthropology of a Revolution* (see above). For a very human and thought-provoking account of what it was like to grow up in a small provincial town in the Cultural Revolution – and a wonderful insight into being Chinese, see Yu Hua's *Ten Words* (Gerald Duckworth & Co., 2012).

PART 6   GREAT MAN

CHAPTER 1   FULL SPEED AHEAD

The opening description of Deng Xiaoping's journey to the south is based on details gathered from various books and articles.

Ezra Vogel's *Deng Xiaoping and the Transformation of China* and Zhao Ziyang's *Prisoner of the State: The Secret Journal of Premier Zhao Ziyang* (see above) are important sources.

The story of the special economic zones and of China's wider urbanisation is covered by many. Having spent years observing and analysing it for myself, I most enjoyed Thomas Campanella's *The Concrete Dragon: China's Urban Revolution and What It Means for the World* (Princeton Architectural Press, 2011).

The best description of the transformations of a village in southern China during this period is in the wonderful *Chen Village – Revolution to Globalisation*, by Anita Chan, Richard Madsen, and Jonathan Unger (University of California Press, 2009). The story of the transformation of rural China is well told by Ezra Vogel in his biography of Deng Xiaoping. The work of the PLA is widely recorded; additional insights come from my own dialogues with Chinese property developers who had built their fortunes in Shenzhen (and become dedicated Buddhists). During my early years in China, I also spent a lot of time working with early Chinese financial institutions, and international development agencies, on projects spread across the country; I visited many towns and villages which were being swept up in the change, both exploring, in professional detail, the mechanisms of that change, and listening to many stories not only of the present but the past. I experienced, first hand through many conversations, the dream that snow might fall in summer.

He Qinglian's *The Pitfalls of Modernisation* was first published in Hong Kong (Mirror Books, 1997; China Today Publishing House, 1998) and then (in a revised text) in China, where it sold over 100,000 copies. The preface to *China's Descent into a Quagmire: The Political Economy of the Transition Era in China* has been translated into English (transl. Nancy Yang Liu and Lawrence R Sullivan, Chinese Economy, Vol. 34, 2001). Translations of some of He's articles can be found at www.hqlenglish.blogspot.com. The New York based Epoch Times (avowedly 'anti-Communist') also carries English language articles by He Qinglian (www.theepochtimes.com/n3/author/he-qinglian).

There is a vast literature about the economics of China's change. The best works are written by those who understand that the economics are inseparable from the politics on which everything is based. Important works include Barry Naughton's *The Chinese Economy: Transitions and Growth* (MIT Press, 2007), Minxin Pei's *China's Trapped Transition: The Limits of Developmental Autocracy* (Harvard UP, 2006), and Cheng Li's *China's Emerging Middle Class, Beyond Economic Transformation* (Brookings Institute, 2010). The book that I found most helpful in retracing the chronology of events and ideas of this period was Joe Fewsmith's *China Since Tiananmen: From Deng Xiaoping to Hu Jintao* (Cambridge UP, 2008). On the complexity of the human issues, see the excellent essays in *One China, Many Paths* (ed. Chaohua Wang; Verso, 2003).

The idea of *gao suzhi* is rooted in Confucius' belief in the importance of self-cultivation and in the importance of calling things by their proper name (known as the 'rectification of names'). It acquired a 20th century importance with questions of *minzu* minorities, and with the introduction of the one-child policy and a rising concern that attention should be given not just to the number of the people but their quality. There are many wonderful academic articles on gao suzhi; see, for example, Ann Anagnost's *The Corporeal Politics of Quality (Suzhi)* (Public Culture, Vol. 16, 2004) and Andrew Kipnis' Suzhi: A Keyword Approach (China Quarterly, 2006). Yinghong Cheng's *Creating the 'New Man', From Enlightenment Ideals to Socialist Realities* (University of Hawai'i Press, 2009) provides a powerful perspective.

The story and significance of the Patriotic Education Campaign is well described by Zheng Wang in *Never Forget National Humiliation, Historical Memory in Chinese Politics and Foreign Relations* (Columbia UP, 2012).

The story of the Falun Gong is told by David Ownby in *Falun Gong and the Future of China* (Oxford UP, 2008).

The first years of Hu Jintao's rule (including the Party's management of SARS) are described by Willy Wo-Lap Lam in *Chinese Politics in the Hu Jintao Era: New Leaders, New Challenges* (M. E. Sharpe, 2006). Hu Jintao's reference to people at the root of any power is a reference to the writings of Mencius (329 – 289 BCE) in *Mencius* (transl. D C Lau, Penguin Classics, 2004).

Li Changping's letter to Zhu Rongji was first published by the brave Chinese newspaper Southern Weekend in 2000 (August 24); it then became the inspiration for his book *I Spoke the Truth to the Premier* (Chinese language, Guangming Daily Publishing House, 2002). *The Investigation into the Lives of Chinese Peasants* (the work of Chen Guidi and Wu Chuntao) was published in English as *Will the Boat Sink the Water? The Life of China's Peasants* (transl. Zhu Hong, Public Affairs, 2006).

There are many academic accounts of the technical changes to the cities. See, for example, the essays contained in *China's Emerging Cities* (ed. Wu Fulong, Routledge, 2007). For a fast paced account of the changes across city and countryside alike, see Jonathan Fenby's *Tiger Head, Snake Tails: China Today, How it Got There and Where It Is Heading* (Overlook, 2013). See also *Chinese Politics, State, Society and the Market* (eds. Gries and Rosen; Routledge, 2010).

CHAPTER 2   NATURE'S TRAILS

Many different sources were consulted for the story of Banqiao's flood, including Dai Qing's Yangzi, Yangzi (see below).

The ancient story of China's environment is best told by Mark Elvin's Retreat of the Elephants (Yale UP, 2006).

Mao's battles are wonderfully described by Judith Shapiro in *Mao's War Against Nature, Politics and the Environment in Revolutionary China* (Cambridge UP, 2001).

On the Cold War story of the US, the USSR and China see Gordon Chang's *Friends and Enemies: The United States, China, and the Soviet Union, 1948 – 1972* (Stanford UP, 1990). An account of the Third Front is given by Barry Naughton in *The Third Front: Defence Industrialisation in the Chinese Interior* (China Quarterly, 1988).

The story of the one child policy is well told in Susan Greenhalgh's *Planned Births, Unplanned Persons* (American Ethnologist, Vo. 30, 2003). An important account of the combination of population and environmental stress is provided by Qu Geping and Li Jinchang in *Population & the Environment in China* (ed. Robert Boardman, transl. Jiang Baozhong and Gu Ran, Lynne Rienner Publishers, 1994).

Early and important accounts of China's environmental crisis can be found in Vaclav Smil's *The Bad Earth: Environmental Degradation in China* (M.E. Sharpe, 1984) and Elizabeth Economy's *The River Runs Black: The Environmental Challenge to China's Future* (Cornell UP, 2004). The story of the industrial destruction of the countryside is very well told by Bryan Tilt in *The Struggle for Sustainability in Rural China: Environmental Values and Civil*

Society (Columbia UP, 2010). It is also described by Bill Hinton in The Great Reversal: The Privatisation of China, 1978 – 1989 (Monthly Review Press, 1990).

The human perspective is probably best recounted by China's novelists. For a sense of the extremes to which officials pushed their villages in efforts to keep up with the modernising winds from Beijing, see the fictional account of Liven village, in Yan Liangke's *Lenin's Kisses* (Grove Press, 2013). For an account of the human costs of the environmental devastation, see Yan Liangke's *Dream of Ding Village* (Grove Press, 2011). For an academic account based on field work, see Anna Lora-Wainwright's *Fighting for Breath: Living Morally and Dying of Cancer in a Chinese Village* (University of Hawai'i Press, 2013).

Dai Qing's 'homework' for the National People's Congress was initially bound and published in China; it was then banned in the mainland and subsequently published in Hong Kong and Taiwan with an English language edition entitled *Yangtze! Yangtze! Debate Over the Three Gorges Project* (transl. Nancy Liu et al, ed. Patricia Adams and John Thibodeau, Earthscan, 1994). The subsequent story of the Three Gorges Dam, including a description of its risks, is told by Dai Qing in *The River Dragon Has Come!* (eds. John Thibodeau and Philip Williams, transl. Ming Yi, M.E. Sharpe, 1998). For the story of a village that was resettled, see Jun Jing's excellent work, *The Temple of Memories, History, Power and Morality in a Chinese Village* (Stanford UP, 1996). See also Jia Zhangke's film *Still Life* (2006).

For a perspective on China's cities and the consumption of resources, see John Fernandez' *Resource Consumption of New Urban Construction in China* (Journal of Industrial Economy, Vol. 11, 2007). For a perspective on Beijing's present-day pollution, see Chai Jing's *Under the Dome* (February 28 2015, watched over 150 million times in the first 3 days, then banned in China; it can still be found on YouTube through individual posts).

Overall, perhaps the most comprehensive and readable account of China's environmental devastation is Jonathan Watts' *When a Billion Chinese Jump* (Faber & Faber, 2010). For a picture book of China's natural world, see *Wild China, Natural Wonders of the World's Most Enigmatic Lands* (Yale UP, 2008).

CHAPTER 3   THE EDGES OF ORDER

The protests described at the end of the opening paragraphs are those of March, 2008.

The ideas of the civilised and the wild are well described in Roland Stoerckx's *The Animal and the Daemon in Early China* (see above).

The story of the Qing's expansion of China, and of their encounters with the tribes are well described by Pamela Crossley in *A Translucent Mirror: History and Identity in Qing Imperial Ideology* (University of California Press, 1999). See also *Empire at the Margins, Culture, Ethnicity, and Frontier in Early Modern China* (eds. Pamela Crossley, Helen Siu, Donald Sutton; University of California Press, 2006). On the Manju embrace of the tribes, see Laura Hostetler's *Qing Colonial Enterprise, Ethnography and Cartography in Early Modern China* (University of Chicago Press, 2001). The story of earlier imperial encounters is told in *Cultural Encounters on China's Ethnic Frontiers* (ed. Stevan Harrell; University of Washington Press, 1995). The ancient and enduring impact of the northern nomads on China's worldview is well covered in Nicola Di Cosmo's *Ancient China and Its Enemies, The Rise of Nomadic Power in East Asian History* (Cambridge UP, 2002).

The very important story of how the Manju Qing forged an empire which became present-day China is told by Joseph Esherick in *How the Qing Became China* (eds. Esherick, Kayali and Young; Rowman & Littlefield, 2006). For a description of the ancient unification of the Shu, the Ba and the Chu, whose lands became present-day Sichuan, see Steven F. Sage, *Ancient Sichuan and the Unification of China* (SUNY, 1992).

The racial complications of independence are fascinatingly described by Steven Platt in *Provincial Patriots: The Hunanese and Modern China* (see above). The most important work on the subject of race is Frank Dikotter's *The Discourse of Race in Modern China* (Hurst & Company, 1992).

The story of the Long March and its encounters with the wilder Chinese world is well told by Sun Shuyun *The Long March* and is included in Jung Chang's *Mao, The Unknown Story* (for both, see above).

The Party's attempts to sort out the question of the *minzu* minorities is well told by Thomas Mullaney in *Coming to Terms with the Nation: Ethnic Classification in Modern China* (University of California Press, 2011). For an example of an imperial picture book, see *The Art of Ethnography, A Chinese 'Miao Album'* (transl. David Deal, Laura Hostetler and Charles McKhann, University of Washington Press, 2006). Colin Mackerras offers a good overview of the challenges (past and present) in *China's Ethinic Minorities and Globalisation* (RoutledgeCurzon, 2003).

The story of the Mongols' pursuit of independence (and its impact on Inner Mongolia) is told by Liu Xiaoyuan in *Reins of Liberation: An Entangled History of Mongolian Independence, Chinese Territoriality, and Great Power Hegemony, 1911 – 1950* (Stanford UP, 2006)

Every aspect of the story of Tibet (including Francis Younghusband's maxim guns) is masterfully recounted by Sam Shaik in *Tibet, A History* (Yale UP, 2013). Charles Bell's early 20th century account of Tibet is a classic

(Oxford Clarendon Press, 1928). Xinran's moving novel, *Sky Burial: An Epic Love Story of Tibet* (Vintage, 2005) is an attempt to find a path to peace.

The story of China's Muslim World is wonderfully described (and illustrated) by M.A. Aldrich and Lukas Nikol in *The Perfumed Palace, Islam's Journey from Mecca to Peking*, Garnet Publishing, 2010). The late 20th century story of the lands to the west is well told by A. Doak Barnett in *China's Far West: Four Decades of Change* (Westview Press, 1993). See also Jonathan Lipman's *Familiar Strangers: A History of Muslims in Northwest China* (University of Washington Press, 1998). The story of the Muslims' battle for independence is told by Dru Gladney in *Muslim Chinese, Ethnic Nationalism in the People's Republic* (Harvard UP, 1991).

The story of Inner Mongolia is told by Uradyn Bulag in *The Mongols at China's Edge: History and the Politics of National Unity* (Rowman and Littlefield, 2002). The story of Inner Mongolia's Cultural Revolution is told by Kerry Brown in *The Purge of the Inner Mongolian People's Party in the Chinese Cultural Revolution, 1967 – 69, A Function of Language, Power and Violence* (Global Oriental, 2006). The story of the grasslands is best told by Jiang Rong in the novel *Wolf Totem* (the pen-name of Lu Jiamin, who based the novel on his own personal experience; first published in China in 2004 where it became a best-seller; transl. Howard Goldblatt, Penguin, 2009).

On the Dalai Lama's idea of Tibet as a Zone of Peace (part of a Five Point Peace Plan presented in an address to the US Congressional Human Rights Caucus, September 21, 1987), see www.dalailama.com/messages/tibet/five-point-peace-plan.

There are a number of specialist books which tell the stories of the many southern minorities. See Erik Mueggler's *The Age of Wild Ghosts: Memory, Violence, and Place in Southwest China* (University of California Press, 2001), *Perspectives on the Yi of Southwest China* (ed. Stevan Harrell; University of California Press, 2001) and Nicholas Tapp's *The Hmong of China: Context, Agency, and the Imaginary* (Brill, 2002). It is Tapp who tells the story of etchings on the Sichuan cliffs, and of the two brothers and their book. See also Louisa Schein's *Minority Rules: The Miao and the Feminine in China's Cultural Policies* (Duke University Press, 2000); it is Schein who tells the story of the Chinese Miao scholar who unearthed the origins of the Miao.

Rebiya Kadeer tells her story in *Dragon Fighter: One Woman's Epic Struggle for Peace with China* (with Alexandra Cavelius; Kales Press, 2009)

For an account of a journey through China and to the edges of its order, see Ma Jian's *Red Dust, A Path Through China* (transl. Flora Drew, Vintage Books, 2002).

For a powerful exploration of the relationship between China and Tibet, see the conversation between Wang Lixiong and Tsering Shakya in *The*

Struggle for Tibet (Verso, 2009). Ian Johnson's interview with Wang Lixiong and his wife, the Tibetan poetess Woeser, can be found in The New York Review of Books, August 7 and 8, 2014).

BOOK III – WHAT CAME NEXT

The chapters in this book draw as much on my personal experience (both professional and human) as on published works.

PART 7   HOW MANY SUNS?

CHAPTER 1   THE HEAVENLY PARTY

The opening account of the journey to the Great Hall of the People is based on whispers circulating in Beijing at the time, including an inner architectural insight shared by Richard Spencer.

The full text of the *Great Chant on Observing Weiqi* can be found in Zu-yan Chen's article (see above).

The stories of Bo Xilai and Xi Jinping draw heavily on John Garnaut's *The Rise and Fall of the House of Bo* (Penguin, 2012) and the work of the South China Morning Post brought together in *The China Renaissance, The Rise of Xi Jinping and the 18th Communist Party Congress* (ed. Jonathan Sharp, South China Morning Post, 2013). More recently, see Evan Osnos' excellent *Born Red: How Xi Jinping, an unremarkable provincial administrator, became China's most authoritarian leader since Mao* (The New Yorker, April 6, 2015).

For an insight into Party scandals, see Chen Fang's novel *Wrath of Heaven: Scandal at the Top in China* (in Chinese, subtitled *The Anticorruption Bureau in Action*; Edko Publishing, 2000); the novel is based on the scandal which brought down Chen Xitong, one-time mayor of Beijing and head of a 'Beijing clique' who fell foul of Jiang Zemin and his 'Shanghai Clique'.

The Party is very well described in Richard McGregor's *The Party: The Secret World of China's Communist Rulers.* Frank Pieke provides excellent detail both generally and on the Party school in *The Good Communist: Elite Training and State Building in Today's China* (Cambridge UP, 2009). David Shambaugh follows the challenges and rise of the Party in *China's Communist Party, Atrophy and Adaptation* (University of California Press, 2008).

The lead-up to the change of power in 2012 had a huge impact on life in Beijing, highly visible in the restaurants of the city and the frenzied schedules of those expecting promotions (or expected to support the bids for promotion). The speculation about the left or right outcome was the intense subject of everyone's conversations, and Wechat, for over a year. Wen Jiabao's observations on the risks facing the Party were publicly made, and publicly reported by the world's press (see for example Tania Branigan's *China needs political reform to avert 'historical tragedy, says Wen Jiabao*, The Guardian, March 14, 2012; and Jamil Anderlini's *Wen attacks party conservatives*, March 14, 2012, The Financial Times).

On the philosophy of the past as it influences the Party, see Tongdong Bai's wonderfully succinct *Political Philosophy of the Middle Kingdom* (see above).

The work of the Party's Propaganda Department (and the influence of Western ideas and technology) is well described by Anne-Marie Brady in *Marketing Dictatorship, Propaganda and Thought Work in Contemporary China* (Rowman & Littlefield, 2008). Yinghong Cheng's *Creating the 'New Man'* (see above) is worth referring to again in this context. On *gao suzhi* high quality people, see the articles referred to above.

China's increasing attention to foreign policy and its rising nationalism are addressed in Zheng Wang's *Never Forget National Humiliation* (Columbia University Press, 2012) and William Callahan's *China, The Pessoptimist Nation* (Oxford UP, 2010). China's strategic choices are interestingly explored by Edward Luttwak in *The Rise of China vs. the Logic of Strategy* (Harvard UP, 2012). *Chinese Nationalism* (eds. Jonathan Unger and Geremie Barmé; M.E. Sharpe, 1996) brings together a collection of essays which provide important context.

CHAPTER 2 EARTH BELOW

Many sources were consulted for the account of the events in Wukan. These included contemporary news reports and documentary films; see *Wukan: After the Uprising* (AlJazeera, 2013).

On land disputes, see Eva Pils' excellent *Land Disputes, Rights Assertion, And Social Unrest in China: A Case from Sichuan* (Columbia Journal of Asian Law, 2006). For more on Stability Maintenance, see He Qinglian's *Stability Maintenance and China* www.hqlenglish.blogspot.com/2013/07/stability-maintenance-and-china. On village elections, see Kerry Brown's wonderful *Ballot Box China, Grassroots Democracy in the Final Major One-Party State* (Zed Books, 2011). The issue of a voice for the peasants goes back to the earliest days of the Party.

On the train journeys of peasant-migrants, see Lixin Fan's documentary, *Last Train Home* (2009).The challenges of China's labourers are explored in *China's Peasants and Workers: Changing Class Identities* (ed. Beatriz Carrillo and David S.G. Goodman (Edward Elgar Publishing, 2012). Conditions in China's factories are described by many: see Leslie Chang's *Factory Girls: Voices from the Heart of Modern China* (Picador, 2008); also see *Factory Towns of South China: An Illustrated Guidebook* (Hong Kong UP, 2012). For an insight into China's great transformation, see Jia Zhangke's documentaries: *The Hometown Trilogy* (1997 – 2002).

There are many excellent academic articles about China's protest leaders, peasant lawyers and their battles for justice. These include Benjamin Liebman's *Class Action Litigation in China* (Harvard Law Review, Vol. 111, 1998), Ethan Michelson *Climbing the Dispute Pagoda: Grievances and Appeals to the Official Justice System in Rural China* (American Sociological Review, Vol. 72, 2007), Liangjiang Li and Kevin O'Brian's *Protest Leadership in Rural China* (China Quarterly, Vol. 193, 2008), and Carl Minzner's *Riots and Cover-ups: Counterproductive Control of Local Agents in China* (University of Pennsylvania Journal of International Law, 2009).

The challenges facing 'low quality peasants' are well described by Rachel Murphy in *Turning Peasants into Modern Chinese Citizens: 'Population Quality' Discourse, Demographic Transition and Primary Education* (China Quarterly, 2004). For an excellent account of the challenges facing China's rural migrants, see Hsiao-Hung Pai's *Scattered Sand: The Story of China's Rural Migrants* (Verso, 2012). For the daily extraordinary in rural (and urban) China, see ChinaSmack (www.chinasmack.com). On the question of *hukou* see Fei-ling Wang's *Conflict, resistance and the transformation of the hukou system* in *Chinese Society: change, conflict and resistance* (ed. Elizabeth Perry and Mark Selden; Routledge 2010)

On city education and *gao suzhi*, see Carolyn Hsu's *The city in the school and the school in the city: ideology, imagery, and institutions in Maoist and market socialist China* (Visual Studies, Vol. 23, 2008). Also see Amy Chua's *Battle Hymn of the Tiger Mother* (Bloomsbury, 2012) which offers a sense of the power of the best-selling Chinese language *Harvard Girl Liu Yiting: A Character in Training* (Writers Publishing House, 2000) a book that sold 1.5 m copies in its first 16 months). See also Gary Sigley's *Suzhi, the Body and the Fortunes of Technoscientific Reasoning in Contemporary China*, Luigi Tomba's *Of Quality, Harmony and Community: Civilisation and the Middle Class in Urban China*, and T. E. Woronov Governing *China's Children: Governmentality and 'Education for Quality'* (all: Positions, Vol. 17, 2009) and Andrew Kipnis' *Subjectification and Education for Quality* (China, Economy and Society Vol. 40, 2011).

On life in the city, see Li Zhang's *Strangers in the City: Reconfigurations of Space, Power and Social Networks within China's Floating Population* (Stanford UP, 2001), also see *In and Beyond the Headlines* (ed Timothy West and Lionel Jensen; Rowman & Littlefield, 2012). On change, see John Gittings' *The Changing Face of China: From Mao to Market* (Penguin, 2006) and *Chinese Characters: Profiles of Fast-Changing Lives in a Fast Changing Land* (eds. Angilee Shah and Jeffrey Wasserstrom; University of California Press, 2012). For a novel's perspective, see Xiaolu Guo's *Village of Stone* (Vintage, 2005). On the stresses of life in the city, see Emily Ng's *Heartache of the State, Enemy of the Self: Bipolar Disorder and Cultural Change in Urban China* (Culture Medicine and Psychiatry, Vol. 33, 2009) and note the reports of the China Sleep Research Society, which puts Beijing at the top of its sleeplessness ranking.

On urban civil society, see David Kelly's *Citizens' Movements and China's Public Intellectuals in the Hu-Wen Era* (Pacific Affairs, Vol. 79, 2006). On urban heroes, see Philip Pan's *Out of Mao's Shadow: The Struggle for the Soul of a New China* (Simon & Schuster, 2008).

On the idea of the global city, see Saskia Sassen's *The Global City: New York, London, Tokyo* (Princeton UP, 1991); see also Ian Cook's *Beijing as an internationalized metropolis* in *Globalisation and the Chinese City* (ed. Wu Fulong, Routledge, 2006).

My description of residents committees and village committees is based on personal experience as a resident of both a gated compound and a village, and on the experiences of friends, including friends who I have, as a lawyer, advised. Similarly, while many of the strolling (and other) protests were reported either in the media or over Wechat, a number of those in Beijing involved friends and colleagues, including friends who are also lawyers and journalists (as did the problems of the ngos). The cat and mouse game of the internet is familiar to almost everyone who lives in Beijing. Many articles have been written about it: see Rebecca Mackinnon's *Flatter World and Thicker Walls? Blogs, censorship and Civil Discourse in China* (Public Discourse, Vol. 134, 2008). One friend had the pleasure of living on the floor below an office of official cyber-surfers, where the lift offered interesting insights into another world.

There are many important works on the role of lawyers; see for example Jerome Cohen's *The Struggle for Autonomy of Beijing's Public Interest Lawyers*, in *Human Rights in China* (www.hrichina.org/en/content/3692). For an excellent description of China's legal system, including the socialist rule of law and model judges, see Carl Minzner's *China's Turn Against the Law* (American Journal of Comparative Law, 2011). On the challenges of being a journalist under Hu Jintao, see David Bandurski's *Jousting with Monsters: Journalists in a Rapidly Changing China* in *China In and Beyond the Headllines* (above). Being a journalist has become a lot more difficult since then. The rages of the people can be found at ChinaSmack (see above).

On the wider importance of Wukan's protests, the loss of trust and the rise of shadow brotherhoods, see John Lagerkvist, *The Wukan Uprising and Chinese State-Society Relations: Toward 'Shadow Civil Society'?* (International Journal of China Studies, Vol. 3, 2012) and Kevin Hand's *Constitutionalising Wukan: The Value of the Constitution Outside the Courtroom* (China Brief, Vol. XII, 2012). See also Minxin Pei's *Trapped Transition* (see above).

KEY SOURCES AND FURTHER READING

CHAPTER 3   BEING CHINESE

An account of life in a Chinese prison can be found in Jiang Qisheng's *My Life in Prison, Memoirs of a Chinese Political Dissident* (transl. James Dew, Rowman & Littlefield, 2012) and Liao Yiwu's *For a Song and a Hundred Songs, A Poet's Journey Through A Chinese Prison* (transl. Wenguang Huang, Houghton Mifflin Harcourt, 2013). At the time of writing, Liu Xiaobo is in Jinzhou Prison, Liaoning.

There are many descriptions of the events of June Fourth. My account is based on discussions with journalists and diplomats who were there at the time and subsequently 'investigated things' on the ground. For a poet's truth (and a first hand recollection), see Liu Xiaobo's *June Fourth Elegies* (Jonathan Cape, 2012). For the declaration of the hunger striking friends, see *Tiananmen Square Hunger Strike Declaration* (World Affairs, Vol. 152, 1989-1990). On Hou Dejian's story, see Linda Jaivin's *The Monkey and the Dragon: A True Story About Friendship, Music, Politics and Life on the Edge* (Text Publishing, 2001). On the impact of Tiananmen, see Louisa Lim's *The People's Republic of Amnesia* (Oxford UP, 2014).

For a thorough description of the Datong Great Unity ideal, see Albert Chen's *The Concept of 'Datong' in Chinese Philosophy as an Expression of the Idea of the Common Good* (Hong Kong University Faculty of Law Research Paper No. 2011/020; accessible at www.ssrn.com/link/U-Hong-Kong-LEG).

Liao Yiwu's *Interviews with People from the Bottom of Society* can be found in an abridged form in *The Corpse Walker: Real Life Stories, China from the Bottom Up* (Anchor Books, 2009). On the challenges of being an author in China, see the acceptance speech of one of China's most widely read authors, Murong Xuecun (pen name) for the 2010 People's Literature Prize (11 November 2011; reported in the New York Times, 29 March 2012).

Yang Jisheng's *Tombstone* is available in English (see above). Heavily researched, it is the abridgement of an original 2 volume (1,208) page account. The most vocal of the parents looking for truth are the members of the group Tiananmen Mothers. Yuan Weishi's article was entitled *Modernisation and History Textbooks* (published by *Bingdian*, Freezing Point, January 11, 2006). On the world of China's intellectuals of the time, see Geremie Barmé's *In The Red: On the Contemporary Chinese Culture*, Columbia University Press, 1999.

Wang Lixiong founded China's first environmental ngo, Friends of Nature, with Liang Qichao's grandson (Liang Sicheng's son) Liang Congjie. His thoughts on Tibet (including the *Twelve Suggestions*) are set out in *The Struggle for Tibet* (see above); his thoughts on elections are set out in *Dissolving Power: A Successive Multi-Level Electoral System* (published in China in 1994);

his thoughts on Xinjiang were set out in *My West China, Your East Turkestan* (published in China, 2007).

For Liu Xiaobo's own voice, see the selection of essays and poems compiled by Perry Link and others in *No Enemies, No Hatred: Selected Essays and Poems* (Harvard UP, 2012). For an important biography of Liu Xiaobo, see Yu Jie's *Steel Gate to Freedom: The Life of Liu Xiaobo* (Rowman & Littlefield, September 1, 2015); Yu Jie is a Chengdu-born writer and activist who emigrated to the US in 2012 after a years of threats, torture and a year of house arrest – he is well known for his 1998 essays *Fire and Ice*, which pointed to the calendars that celebrate May Fourth (1919) and asked people to look again at the banners of the day. On Charter 08, see Jean-Philippe Beja, Fu Hualing and Eva Pils' *Charter 08 and the Challenges of Political Reform in China* (Hong Kong UP, 2012) – and on the crime of state subversion, see Chapter 13 (*The Political Meaning of the Crime of 'Subverting State Power'*) written by Teng Biao, one of China's most respected *'weiquan'* ('rights protection') lawyers, a term used to describe lawyers committed to defending the civil rights of the people. At the time of writing, Teng Biao is in the US, a visiting fellow at the Harvard Law School.

On Ai Weiwei, see the documentary *Never Sorry* (Alison Klayman, 2012) and his own video clips. On Ai Weiwei's journey to Tan's hearing, including the under-the-blanket recording of the hotel beating, see Ai Weiwei, *Lao Ma Ti Hua* (www.youtube.com/watch?v=TUizD8WDDFI). The temple referred to by Tan Zuoren's lawyers is Wuhou Temple (Chengdu).

For Ai Weiwei's crab banquet, see Ai Weiwei / River Crab Feast @ Shanghai Studio on Vimeo (2010). On his internment, see Barnaby Martin's *Hanging Man: The Arrest of Ai Weiwei* (Faber & Faber, 2013) and Howard Brenton's play of the same name.

On censorship in China, see Perry Link's *The Anaconda in the Chandelier* (The New York Review of Books, April 11, 2002). On the rising arrests of China's intellectuals, see Evan Osnos' *Born Red* (see above). On the impact of the Party's controls, see Perry Link's *China After Tiananmen: Money, Yes; Ideas, No* (The New York Review of Books, March 31, 2014 On the Party's idea of 'the intellectual', see Eddy U's *Rectification of the Chinese Intellectual: On the Origins of the CCP Concept of Zhishifenzi* (Modern China, Vol. 35, 2009). On China's exiles, see Rowena Xiaoqing He's *Tiananmen Exiles, Voices of the Struggle for Democracy in China* (Palgrave Macmillan, 2014).

Chan Koonchung's *The Fat Years* (first published by Oxford UP Hong Kong and the Rye Field Publishing Company, both 2009; transl. Michael Duke and with an excellent preface by Julia Lovell, Doublebday, 2011). Chan describes his book in *Chinese Author: 'My Book Was Banned in My Home Country'*, www.huffingtonpost.com/chan-koonchung/book-banned-china).

On the importance of the rule of law, see Carl Minzners' *How China's Leaders Will Rule on the Law* (Chinafile, October 15, 2014) and the subsequent conversation of some of the most experienced foreign China lawyers: *Rule of Law – Why Now?* Ira Belkin, Don Clarke, Jerry Cohen et al (Chinafile October 17, 2014). For thoughtful reflections on why China continues to battle over the idea of order, see Wang Hui's *The End of the Revolution: China and the Limits of Modernity* (Verso 2011) and Joseph Fewsmith *The Logic and Limits of Political Reform in China* (Cambridge UP, 2013). On the problems of crossing the river by feeling for stones (also known as 'gradualism'), see Minxin Pei, China's Trapped Transition: the limits of developmental autocracy (see above). For an insight into the many different voices in China, see Evan Osnos' *Age of Ambition: Chasing Fortune, Truth and Faith in the New China* (Farrar, Strauss and Giroux, 2014).

CONCLUSION – BECOMING CHINA

Almost everything described in this chapter can be found in online newspapers, film and video although not necessarily all in English. For those reading in the English language and looking for easily accessible reporting, see The South China Morning Post (published in Hong Kong, now owned by Jack Ma). Various official organisations now produce websites and video footage in English or with English sub-titles reporting on key policy matters and Party initiatives; these include the State Council (english.gov.cn), Xinhua (xinhuanet.com/english) and CCTV (english.cctv.com). Alternative perspectives in the English language are provided by overseas Chinese news platforms and websites, including China Digital Times (chinadigitaltimes.net) and The Epoch Times (theepochtimes.com), based in Berkeley and New York, respectively.

Contemporary commentary on most of the events can be found within the spectrum of the major press (the New York Times, the Washington Post, the Financial Times, the Guardian). Many of the events described, including CCTV's reports on the sixth plenum of the Eighteen Congress can also be found on YouTube.

The Great Learning can be found in a variety of translations, published in print and online.

The texts of key articles and speeches (whether those of Mao or Xi Jinping) can largely be found online. Mao's major works can be found at the Marxists Internet Archive (marxists.org). Mao's thoughts on seeking truth from facts can be found in 'Where Do Correct Ideas Come From?' Other key works of Mao (all from 1937) include 'On Guerilla Warfare' (1937),'On Contradiction' (1937) and 'On Practice' (all available online at www.Marxists.org/reference/archive/Mao/selected

For Xi's thoughts on order, see *Revolutionary Ideals are Higher than Heaven-Studying, Comrade Xi Jinping's Important Elaboration concerning Strengthening Ideals and Convictions*, updated 22 December 2013, Autumn Stone, available on China Copyright and Media (www.chinacopyrightandmedia.wordpress.com)

For a Chinese description of Xi Jinping's Mass Line campaign, see *CPC Launches Mass Line Campaign* english.cntv.cn/special/cpcmassline/homepage

For a thorough history of China's battle with corruption see Jon S.T. Quah, *Minimising Corruption in China: Is this an Impossible Dream?* (Maryland Series in Contemporary Asian Studies: Vol.2013: No.4, Article 1); for a sense of the corruption campaign, see CCTV's public education documentary *To Forge Iron One Must be Strong*, 2017, available on YouTube (Chinese language only; www.youtube.com/watch?v=ReyRGcCvtHg

There are a large number of Western reports on the Belt and Road – and a wide variety of maps; for the State Council's evolving description see *The Belt and Road Initiative* at www.english.gov.cn/beltandroad

On the South China Sea, including the story of Sansha, see Bill Hayton's *The South China Sea: The Struggle for Power in Asia* (Yale University Press, 2014)

For an early commentary on Xi Jinping's thoughts on diplomacy, see *Xi Jinping's Address to the Central Conference on Work Relating to Foreign Affairs*, Michael Swaine (China Leadership Monitor no. 46, 2014)

On Taiwan's Sunflower movement see www.youtube.com/watch?v=X9A8eWeGy7U.

On Scholarism, see 'Interview with Joshua Wong and Adam Ng', YouTube www.youtube.com/watch?v=D6W102yKIvI

For a sense of the Occupy Central protests, see 'Hong Kong Protest 2014: The Evolution of Joshua Wong', The New York Times, YouTube www.youtube.com/watch?v=r2nSFBaN2NM

For the speech of the chairman of the Hong Kong Bar Association (12 January 2015) see www.HKBA/org/sites/default/files/OLY%20Speech%202015%28E%29%20web.pdf

On the LegCo oathtaking, see *Three Hong Kong lawmakers have oaths rejected*, South China Morning Post October 12, 2016

Under the Dome can be found on YouTube (www.youtube.com/watch?v=fk4YqPtvJao)

The text of the National Security Law, and other laws, can be found at China Law Translate (www/chinalawtranslate.com)

On the early story of Russia and Central Asia, see David Christian, A History of Russia, Central Asia and Mongolia, Volume I: Inner Eurasia from Prehistory to the Mongol Empire (Wiley, 1998)

On the idea of a pivot of the world, see Halford Mackinder, *The Geographical Pivot of History*, (The Geographical Journal, Vol. 23, No.4, (April 1904), 421-437)

On Russia's Sistema, see Alena V Ledeneva 'Can Russia Modernise?: Sistema, Power Networks and Informal Governance' (Cambridge University Press, 2013

Xinhua's cartoon introduction to the Thirteenth Five Year Plan can be found on Youtube ('The 13 What')

Internet Plus and Made in China 2025 can both be found on the State Council's website (english.gov.cn)

For a very thorough description of the Party's thinking on ecological civilisation, see Sam Geall's three-part series 'Interpreting Ecological Civilisation' (www.China Dialogue.net)

Wuzhen's own report on its 2016 conference can be found at www.wuzhenwic.org

On Lou Jiwei's speech, see He Qinglian 'China's Economy is Just 'One Kilometer' Away From a Cliff (February 27, 2016; www.theepochtimes.com/n3/author/he-qinglian)

For an example of a neo-Maoist rally, see 'An anti-revisionist people's rally in Luoyang, Henan, China' at Serve The People (mike-servethepeople.blogspot.co.uk)

See China Labour Bulletin for a map of 2016 strikes maps.clb.org.hk)

For an overview of the evolution of the grid management system see Wu Qiang's 'Urban Grid Management and Police State in China: A Brief Overview (ChinaChange, August 12, 2014)

On what is increasingly being described as China's 'racial sovereignty' see *The Empire Strikes Back*, Ruben Gonzaelz-Vicente, Political Geography (2016)

On Xi Jinping's reorganisation of the military, see Kenneth Allen et al, *The PLA's New Organisational Structure: What is Known, Unknown and Speculation*, China Brief Volume: 16 Issue: 3 (For a thoughtful perspective on China's defence industry by one of its most experienced commentators, see Tai Ming Cheung's 'Fortifying China: The Struggle to Build a Modern Defense Economy' (Cornell University Press, 2013)).

INDEX

A NOTE ON THE TYPE

The text of this book is set in Bell. Originally cut for John Bell in 1788, this typeface was used in Bell's newspaper, *The Oracle*. It was regarded as the first English Modern typeface. This version was designed by Monotype in 1932.